Europe in the Seventeenth Century

DAVID OGG

EUROPE
SEVENTEENTH

IN THE
CENTURY

COLLIER BOOKS
NEW YORK, N.Y.

This Collier Books edition is published by arrangement with The Macmillan Company

Collier Books is a division of The Crowell-Collier Publishing Company

First Collier Books Edition 1962

Preface to the Eighth Edition

THE TITLE OF THIS BOOK may seem ambitious, but at least the author's approach has been modest, for he has always regarded this exposition of a comparatively short period of European history as no more than an interpretation, within the limits of his personality and experience. That this interpretation should provoke challenge is not necessarily a bad thing; it may even be a sign of life. It is now thirty-five years since the book first appeared, and in that time the author has had this advantage that he has been able to incorporate some of the lessons of experience in successive revisions of the book. In this latest revision many minor changes have been made, and the last chapter has been almost entirely rewritten.

Contents

MAPS

Europe in the Seventeenth Century

Chapter 1

Seventeeth-Century Society and Institutions

THE PERIOD DEALT with in this volume, though terminating in 1715, may for practical purposes be regarded as the seventeenth century. Division of historical eras into centuries is often arbitrary and may sacrifice perspective to convenience of treatment, but the claim of the seventeenth century to be studied as a distinct epoch having its characteristic problems and institutions has usually been admitted by historians. In this century the Empire and Papacy were definitely relegated to positions of little more than academic interest, the religious motive was overshadowed by the economic, the first practical proposals for religious toleration and international arbitration were formulated, and the main conceptions of the system known as the Ancien Régime were defined and applied. A period of increasing absolutism in the theory and practice of government, and of revolutionary progress in philosophic and scientific thought, this epoch illustrates a divergence between speculative idealism and political materialism, a divergence becoming more marked as the seventeenth century fades into the eighteenth, and resulting eventually in those fierce antagonisms of principle which joined battle in the age of Revolution. The main interest of seventeenth-century continental history lies in this, that as politics became stereotyped abstract thought became more original. Stability was preserved only because the thinkers challenged everything but the sanctions of the governments under which they lived, for the age of Descartes and Leibnitz held sacred the prejudices and conventions which aroused the scepticism of Voltaire and Rousseau. The gradual disillusionment of the eighteenth century was preceded by the confidence and conviction of the seventeenth.

The purpose of this chapter is to describe briefly some of the objective characteristics of the period: its territorial changes, its ruling families, its administrative principles, and the institutions for the expression of public opinion. In the last chapter an attempt will be made to estimate the subjective achievements of the century and its contribution to European civilization.

In seventeenth-century Europe there was no problem of population[1] as it is understood to-day, and in consequence it was not a period of great colonial expansion or mechanical invention. In the apportionment of states the populace were regarded as little better than chattels, even the humanitarian Grotius regarding subject populations in this light. The most important territorial changes were those effected by the treaties of Westphalia (1648) and Utrecht (1713). The chief additions to French territory were Navarre (north of the Pyrenees) in 1598, Alsace in 1648 and 1681, Roussillon and Artois in 1660, Franche Comté in 1678, additions which helped to eliminate certain obvious geographical anomalies,

---

[1] Reliable estimates of population in this period are difficult to obtain and generally conflict with each other. By 1700 France had more than eighteen million inhabitants, Italy five or six millions, the Empire between sixteen and twenty-five millions, the United Provinces about two millions. Owing to the expulsion of about 400,000 Moriscos in 1609 and the voluntary emigration of many Spaniards to the South American colonies, the population of Spain sank from about eight millions at the beginning of the century to about five millions at the end. The casualties in the Thirty Years' War were about 350,000, but the loss of civilian population directly due to this war was considerably greater. It is estimated that nearly half a million Huguenots were lost to France by the intolerance of Louis XIV. In *The Economic Writings of Sir William Petty* (ed. Hull) will be found some contemporary estimates of population: in 1688 the population of England and Wales was said to be five and a half millions. For an estimate of casualties in the wars of the seventeenth century see G. Bodart, *Losses of Life in Modern Wars*.

since on the south-west the Pyrenees became the natural frontier, while on the east the ranges of Vosges and Jura were reached by acquisition of Spanish and Imperial territory. The treaty of Utrecht left the French north-eastern frontier very little different from what it is to-day. By the treaty of Westphalia the Empire practically lost Germany, but in the course of the century the Hapsburg emperors absorbed Bohemia, Hungary and Transylvania into their territories, and so the Empire became Austrian rather than European. By the terms of the treaty of Utrecht, Austrian was substituted for Spanish rule in Italy and Belgium.

The countries showing the most striking territorial changes are Sweden, Poland, Russia, Turkey and Brandenburg. Before 1648 Sweden possessed Ingria, Esthonia, Karelia, and a claim to Livonia; the treaty of Westphalia gave her Western Pomerania, with Bremen and Verden, thus making her an important German as well as Baltic power. The wars of Charles X. wrested Halland, Bleking and Schönen from Denmark; the treaty of Oliva (1660) confirmed the claim of Sweden to control practically the whole coast of the Baltic. But in the wars of Charles XII. most of the gains made by Gustavus Adolphus and Charles X. were dissipated; by the treaty of Nystadt (1721) Sweden surrendered her possessions on the eastern shore of the Baltic. She had lost nearly all of her German possessions, and thus a small Baltic empire was created and lost with dramatic suddenness. The diminution of Polish territory in the second half of the seventeenth century is equally striking. Poland, at the beginnng of this period, formed a great confederation of territories, undefined by clear frontiers and at the mercy of ambitious neighbours on every side. The three main divisions were Great Poland, which then included Pomerelia, Kulm and Marienburg;[2] Little Poland, composed of Galicia, Red Russia, Podolia, Bukowina, Volhynia and Western Ukraine; and Lithuanian Poland, including Litvania, Courland, White and Black Russia. Only by a glance at the map can the extent of these lands be real-

---

[2] These constituted Western as distinct from Eastern or Ducal Prussia. The latter was acquired in full sovereignty by Brandenburg in 1657, the former was added to the Prussian monarchy by the first Partition of Poland (1772). By the acquisition of Dantzig and Thorn in 1793 Prussia was completely detached from Poland.

ized. In the Swedish and Russian wars Poland steadily lost territory. Eastern or Ducal Prussia was surrendered to Brandenburg in 1657; Livonia was definitely ceded to Sweden in 1660; the Ukraine east of the Dnieper was given up to Russia by the treaty of Andrussovo (1667), and further concessions to Russia included Smolensk in 1667, with Kiev and Podolia in 1686. The great War of the North (1700-1721) completed the distintegration of the territories still remaining and prepared Poland for the era of partitions.

These changes benefited chiefly Russia and Brandenburg. By the successive losses of Polish territory the western frontier of Russia approximated more closely to the courses of the Dnieper and the western Dwina, while with Sweden's withdrawal from the eastern Baltic the Tsars obtained an uninterrupted coast line stretching from Ingria to Riga. It was on one of these conquered territories that the city of St. Petersburg was built. The progress of Brandenburg was as steady as that of Russia. At the beginning of the century the Hohenzollern territories formed a loose chain across northern Germany; Cleve and Mark were added in 1614; East Prussia was acquired in 1657; Eastern Pomerania, with several secularized bishoprics, had been obtained in 1648. Profiting by the anarchy of Poland and the wars of Sweden, the Electors of Brandenburg extended their claims over nearly all of Pomerania and Prussia, thus building up a kingdom from a series of duchies, and in 1700 the Elector Frederick III. became king of Prussia as Frederick I.

The military decline of Turkey in Europe dates from the battle of Lepanto (1571), but, until the date of the Truce of Vasvar (1664), Turkey continued to make conquests at the expense of the Hapsburgs, and, as late as 1669, the Ottomans captured Candia from Venice. During the greater part of the seventeenth century, moreover, Transylvania and a part of Hungary were under Turkish suzerainty; against Russia, the Turks fought for control of the Ukraine, and in 1683 a great invasion of Europe was foiled when the Turks were driven from Vienna. This was the chief Ottoman disaster in a war waged against the Empire, Russia, Poland and Venice, a war ended by the treaty of Karlowitz (1699), when the Porte surrendered Transylvania, Hungary, Croatia, the Morea and Azov. Thenceforth the Turks retained, outside the Balkan peninsula, only Moldavia and Wallachia, with a strip of territory to the north of the Danube, intersected by that river at Karlowitz and stretching west to the Croatian frontier.

Directly connected with these territorial changes was the alteration in the relative status of several European cities. Prague, Pressburg, Strasburg and Kiev all became provincial towns, the first two in consequence of the extension of Hapsburg domination, the third because of Louis XIV.'s acquisition in 1681, the fourth by absorption into Russia. Four new capitals came into being—St. Petersburg, Turin, the Hague and Berlin. Antwerp remained in the ruined state to which Spanish rule in the sixteenth century had reduced it. Amsterdam became a world money-market after 1648.

These territorial changes are the concrete results of the dynastic struggles which play such an important part in the history of the seventeenth century. It was in this period that the great European reigning families became sacrosanct, that their private quarrels were accepted as perfectly legitimate causes for national war, and that even the existence of these dynasties was considered not only as necessary but as part of the divine order of things. At this point it may be well to consider some of the personal characteristics of the ruling families whose feuds left a heritage of racial hatred and revenge. The most important were the Bourbons, the Hapsburgs, the Vasas and the Romanoffs. Of the Hapsburgs some had ability, many had virtue, and all, without exception, had religion; but impecuniousness and mental eccentricity had been hereditary characteristics ever since the days of Maximilian *pochi danari*[3] and Juana *the Mad*.[4] They were intimately connected by war and marriage with the Bourbons whose rule may be said to date from 1593. Louis XIII. and his sister Elisabeth were married respectively to a daughter (Anne of Austria) and a son (Philip IV.) of Philip III. of Spain. The son by the first marriage (Louis XIV.) married the eldest daughter by the second (Maria Theresa). The Emperor Ferdinand III. married another daughter of Philip III., and so the heads (Louis XIV., Leopold I. and Charles II. of Spain) of the three dynasties whose conflicts threatened

[3] 1459–1519.

[4] Daughter of Ferdinand and Isabella. She married Philip of Burgundy and was the mother of the Emperor Charles V. (1500–1558). Ferdinand and Isabella, the rulers of Spain, were cousins.

to extinguish European civilization altogether were first cousins. Philip IV.'s second marriage was with his niece, and the result of this marriage was Charles II., regarded by contemporaries as a medical curiosity, suffering throughout life from at least half-a-dozen serious defects. His mother (who was thus his first cousin) wished him to marry one of his Austrian first cousins, but he married a more distant relative, and all the prayers, drugs and incantations of Spain were then exhausted in the attempt to procure a child by this union, until eventually the queen succumbed to the poisonous mixtures forced upon her. This policy of intermarriage brought its physiological retribution, extinguishing the Spanish Hapsburgs in 1700 and producing marked degeneration in several members of the Bourbon and Imperial Hapsburg families. The Dauphin (who died in 1711) was of stunted intelligence, although the most elaborate pains were taken with his education, and Louis XIV. was predeceased by nearly two whole generations of his descendants.[5] The only plea for santity in these matters came from the madman Campanella,[6] and had not natural predilections sometimes overruled diplomatic considerations, some of the dynasties of western Europe might have been extinguished by physical causes.

Similar characteristics are seen in other ruling houses of the seventeenth century. The Turkish Empire continued to be governed by a race of men born of female slaves, brought up among effeminate and enervating surroundings, and encouraged by the institution of the harem to develop symptoms characteristic of general paralysis of the insane. The Swedish Vasas, who in the sixteenth century included a king of homicidal tendency (Eric XIV.), produced a great man and a great king in Gustavus Adolphus, but his daughter Christina was erratic and unstable, while to at least one of his male descendants war became a physiological necessity to be appeased only by continual sacrifice of human life. Charles XII. of Sweden would have been considered a lunatic but for his spectacular career: his complete insensibility to pain in himself and in others is a symptom of considerable significance to the alienist, and, though he is rightly regarded as a great

[5] There are some interesting facts on this subject in A. Corlieu, *La Mort des rois de France*, 109-122.
[6] *De Monarchia Hispanica*, cap. ix.

hero-king, his death was the salvation of his country. It was in Russia, however, that the most extraordinary monarch of the period was born. The Romanoffs, pious and conscientious in rulers like Michael and Alexis, gave birth to Peter the Great, who combined intellectual curiosity with a capacity for swift executive action. He had all the naïveté and primitive forcefulness of "natural man" as understood by the eighteenth-century philosophers, and he left the imprint of his personality on the most vast and unwieldy of European states. Less spectacular were the houses of Orange and Hohenzollern. The grim tenacity of the first was exemplified in the career of William III, who led European opposition to Louis XIV; the traditional pietism of the second, not unmingled with perfidy, was illustrated in the life of the Great Elector, who laid the foundations of Prussia.

But while it is easily shown that monarchs shared the imperfections of ordinary humanity (a view not always endorsed even to-day), it should not be forgotten that kings were themselves sometimes as much the victims of the system as were their subjects, and that the only possible alternative to monarchy was the rule of the nobility. Moreover, while there were infinite opportunities at hand for a vicious or evilly-disposed monarch, so there were countless ways in which a wise king could act in the interests of his country. In the sixteenth century attention had been directed to the secular bases of sovereignty, and the revived Roman Law had stereotyped, in the tradition of the Lex Regia,[7] a formula of absolutism which traced the monarchical principle to an irrevocable surrender of authority by the people, such as was supposed to have taken place at the inauguration of the empire of Augustus Caesar. In the seventeenth century there were two occasions on which a Lex Regia was enacted: in Denmark (1661) and in Sweden (1682). Both of these were to a certain extent revolutionary; they were carried out, however, not by bloodshed but by skilful management, and were made possible by the support of the bourgeoisie. By the first, an "instrument"

---

[7] This is generally known to English readers from its opening words, but for an understanding of its meaning the whole maxim, as enunciated by Ulpian, may be given: "Quod principi placuit legis habet vigorem: utpote cum Lege Regia, quae de imperio eius lata est, populus ei et in eum omne suum imperium et potestatem conferat."

was drawn up by the lower Estates, offering the realm to the monarch Frederick III. and his line, an offer in which the nobility and Senate were, by a show of force, induced to concur; by the second, the Senate and Estates of Sweden were coaxed into a surrender of their privileges to Charles XI., with the proviso, however, that on important matters they should be consulted. The Danish instrument is the more noteworthy of the two, because it was a real surrender of powers previously exercised by representative assemblies, and the document setting forth the terms of this surrender was called the *Kongelov,* or Royal Law. For both countries these silent revolutions were necessary in order to keep the nobility in check, and were, on the whole, of most benefit to the bourgeoisie and peasants who always suffer more from anarchy than from despotism. The idea of sovereignty originating in a voluntary abdication by the constituted representatives of the people is quite foreign to English political thinking, but it did not seem strange on the continent, where so many countries had already undergone a "reception" of Roman Law, and where this system of jurisprudence was not a mere academic study, but a body of fundamental principles, some of them incorporated in legal and constitutional practice.

It was, however, in the period of the Renaissance that Roman Law wielded the greatest influence on theories of government; in the seventeenth century the basis of sovereignty had broadened so as to include a sanction far more potent than any provided by secular jurisprudence. The temporal basis of authority came to be completely displaced by the spiritual sanction which influenced almost every European government, including England, in the theory of Divine Hereditary Right. In France this theory received its fullest exposition in the reign of Louis XIV., and it has this to be said for it that, instead of invoking a contract, supposed to have been signed at some remote period, or a surrender of authority, supposed to have been made by the Senate of Ancient Rome, it appealed to a sentiment existing in all races and at all times, namely, devotion to a single and hereditary personality, and to a book, the Bible, which Christendom venerated as the sacred repository of divine injunctions for the conduct of every department of human life. By insisting on the Divine Right theory, monarchy changed from an institution into a religion; its ministers became hierophants and its critics blasphemers. It remained only for Hobbes[8] and Spinoza[9] to prove the limitless authority of the sovereign not from the Old Testament but from expediency, and monarchy was elevated to a transcendent and impregnable position, secure from all possibility of attack, because churchman, lawyer, soldier and thinker had combined to place it there.

After the monarchy came the nobility, an institution which could also claim to be a result of divine forethought, for God only can make an heir. In most European countries nobility was regarded as a status possessing privileges without duties, and, especially in France, there was the assumption that even the most turbulent members of the noble caste must be patiently borne, because their existence was inevitable as floods or earthquakes. Of these La Fontaine wrote: "The universe is grateful for the evils they *omit* to do." The French nobility claimed particularly valuable privileges, including all surviving feudal rights, such as those connected with local justice; they formed after the clergy, the second estate of the realm. They monopolized honorary offices at Court as well as most of the army commands: military academies were open only to aspirants of approved pedigree, and the higher ranks in the Church were recruited almost solely from their number. At the Universities they could secure dispensation from the more irksome duties required from students of common mould, and, if a noble had to undergo compulsory exit from this world, he could do so in a more dignified way than his social inferiors, for while these were hanged, he was executed. The writers of the period were unanimous in the opinion that the noble caste must be maintained at all costs, and that good family must be the first requisite in a candidate for exalted state employment. It was the opinion of Richelieu,[10] himself a man of noble birth, that men of low extraction rarely have the qualities necessary for a magistrate, and that the virtues of a man of good birth are higher than those found in the lower orders. The doctrine was expounded thus in a *Guide for Courtiers*[11] published in 1634: "Those whose

[8] *Leviathan*, Pt. II., xviii.

[9] *Tractatus Theologico-Politicus*, ch. xvi.

[10] *Testament politique* (ed. 1764), 205.

[11] Le Sieur Faret, *L'honneste homme, ou l'art de plaire à la Court.*

ancestors distinguished themselves by memorable exploits find themselves constrained, in a sense, to follow their example: those who are born of the common people do not consider themselves obliged to rise above their lowly origin." Men of quality did not even have to undergo the drudgery of learning: "Les gens de qualité savent tout sans avoir jamais rien appris."[12] Equally, courage was the monopoly of the well-born. Sir William Temple believed that courage and good feeding went together: any man might be made a coward by six weeks' fasting; hence, it was argued, the well-fed upper classes are braver than the half-famished peasants.[13]

At a time when nobles and landlords were still numbered among the wealthiest members of the community, it was held, with whatever justification, that private fortune and the independence generally expected of good birth were the two best guarantees against corruption among ministers and high officials: poor men, or those unendowed with the special qualities which pedigree alone can bestow, were, on this view, likely to be shameless in their pursuit of private gain at public expense. The truth may have been that what, in a noble, seemed merely the exaction of a perquisite inseparably connected with his rank, might be considered robbery when done by a commoner. But in France, at least, the nobility were confined to honorary functions, and Richelieu contradicted his own theory by commencing the tradition which excluded nobles from all the important administrative posts, though the best interests of the French monarchy suffered from the fact that the provincial governorships remained in the hands of the aristocracy, many of whom, before the coming of Louis XIV., were ready to betray their country for bribes.

This caste system might have been harmless had it not engendered the idea that all manual work is degrading; it might even have been consistent, and to a certain extent justifiable, had not the ranks of the nobility by birth been swollen by the nobility of bought titles. In western Europe wealth increased considerably in the seventeenth century; in addition, money moved more rapidly as fortunes changed hands; consequently there were many alliances between impoverished aristocrats and wealthy plebeians, and governments soon real-

[12] Molière, *Les Précieuses ridicules*, Act. I. Scene x.

[13] Sir William Temple, *Observations upon the United Provinces of the Netherlands* (ed. 1673), 156.

ized that a considerable amount of revenue could be obtained from those whose sudden wealth conjured up visions of coronets and all the paraphernalia of noble birth. It has been asserted[14] that in the period between Louis XIII.'s reign and the Revolution practically every rich man in France became ennobled, consequently many people of ancient family found themselves under the suzerainty, nominal or effective, of ex-serfs. In one year alone Louis XIV. ennobled 500 persons at 6000 livres[15] each: moreover, the exigencies of the Spanish Succession War compelled Louis to make such creations a normal source of revenue. Even in Spain, where nobility by birth was accorded more respect than anywhere else in Europe except Ireland, the needs of the Spanish monarchy compelled the adoption of the same expedient for raising money, and it is recorded that a Portuguese Jew purchased the right of wearing his hat in the presence of the king.[16] This had originally been the special prerogative of the twenty-five Grandes de España, but by this time their number was considerably increased. The Spanish hidalgo class was filled with *nouveaux riches,* and everywhere in the peninsula there was a craze for heraldry and pedigrees. The whole province of Guipuzcoa claimed to be hidalgo,[17] and Sancho Panza complained that there were more Dons than stones on his island of Barataria.[18] Spanish rule in dependent Italy was made possible only by periodical showers of high-sounding titles,[19] and in the course of the seventeenth century a new nobility of plutocrats and officials gradually displaced the old nobility of the sword.[20]

[14] D'Avenel, *Richelieu et la monarchie absolue* (ed. 1895), ii. 110.

[15] In 1689 the livre was worth about 1 fr. 89 centimes in pre-1914 French money. Thereafter it fell to 1 fr. 24 in 1706. See article "Monnaie" in Marion, *Dictionnaire des institutions de la France.*

[16] Legrelle, *La Diplomatie française et la succession d'Espagne,* ii. 42.

[17] Altamira y Crevea, *Historia de España y de la civilizacion espanola* (ed. 1913), iii. 192-194.

[18] *Don Quixote,* Pt. II. ch. xlv.

[19] *La vita italiana nel seicento,* lectures 1-3.

[20] In 1791 Burke wrote of Spain: "it does not possess the use, it only suffers the abuse of a nobility" (*Thoughts on French Affairs*).

The Scandinavian countries exemplified clearly the dangers inseparable from the existence of an over-powerful aristocracy. In Sweden the greater part of the royal domain was given away to importunate courtiers, thus making necessary Charles XI.'s strict "reduction" policy in the later part of the century. It was Christina of Sweden who was most active in this respect, for in her short reign she created no fewer than 17 counts, 46 barons and 428 lesser nobles.[21] Nor was this all, for these persons, mostly worthless, had to be provided with revenues and lands in order to maintain their dignity; accordingly crown property was recklessly squandered and mortgaged. This went so far that all donations of royal land had to be made subject to the proviso that the land had not already been conferred on some one else; hence even the Swedes came to think that the proposed abdication of Christina might not be such a national calamity as it had at first seemed. Fortunately for Sweden, her nobility were given frequent employment in war abroad, otherwise they might, between them, have destroyed their country. Denmark, until 1661, was threatened by danger from the same quarter, and there the menace was even more serious, for the peasants were serfs, and so the private property of the nobility. The career of the Danish noble Corfits Uhlfeldt may be taken as an example. In 1637 this man, by marrying a daughter of Christian IV., acquired a seat in the Senate, and for several years was able to combine the offices of Mayor of the Palace and Lord High Admiral. In 1648, with three other nobles, he sat in the Council of Regency, compelling the young Frederick III. to divide power with the Senators; when, in 1651, he was criticized for concluding on his own authority a disadvantageous peace with the United Provinces, he entered into negotiations with the Vatican[22] for the overthrow of the monarchy and the restoration of Catholicism in Denmark. Failing to obtain money for this scheme he went over to Swedish service, and thereafter waged war against his native country. He betrayed his Swedish employer Charles X. in 1659 and was sentenced to death, but—a subtle stroke— was reprieved and sent back to Denmark, where he was promptly imprisoned. Released in 1661 he went to Bruges and

[21] Nisbet Bain, *Scandinavia*, 225.
[22] For details of this plot see the documents cited in the Appendix to Ignazio Ciampi, *Innocenzo X. Pamfilio e la sua corte.*

in revenge tried to induce the Elector of Brandenburg to ally with him in a plot to dethrone the Danish monarch. Frederick William communicated this plot to the Danish government, so Uhlfeldt was again sentenced to death, this time *in absentia*. For some years the Danish court remained in terror of this man, and his death in 1664 was an event almost worthy of national rejoicing. France, again was very nearly destroyed by the second Fronde, led by the greater French nobles; and it may be said that, though seventeenth-century monarchy was often irresponsible and despotic, it saved Europe from something far worse.

After the monarchy and the nobility the most important secular institution of the period was the army. The modern conception of military service as a duty of citizenship did not exist in the seventeenth century, and though such men as Cervantes, Descartes and Calderon served as private soldiers, armies were professional as well as cosmopolitan. A soldier was defined, not as a man who has taken up arms to defend home and country, but as "one who, being neither criminal nor philosopher, slays and exposes himself freely to death."[23] The ownership of land had not yet lost its connection with military service, consequently the nobility still assumed leadership in the field as an inalienable right, though by the end of the century Vauban and Catinat were proving that military genius is not the monopoly of one class. Twice in Louis XIV.'s reign was the feudal *arrière ban* convoked— in 1674 and in 1689—on which occasions the holders of fiefs were summoned to serve in person, while women, ecclesiastics and minors were required to provide substitutes. Otherwise there existed no compulsory military service, though fraud and violence were often used by the professional agents who scoured the slums, and sometimes even the prisons, for recruits. Captains having royal commissions to raise a company generally made their own bargains with recruits, and, as military service was thus a private affair between officer and soldier, it could not be expected that the state had any interest in the fate of the latter. Moreover, as soldiering was considered a distinct profession, so seventeenth-century opinion would have been shocked by the spectacle of priests or law-

[23] *Catéchisme des courtisans,* quoted by d'Avenel, *op cit.* iii. 6.

yers, or members of any other profession, taking service in the ranks. In addition, there was complete indifference to nationality. In the Thirty Years' War the condottiere Mansfeld had an army of English, French and Germans; Sweden raised troops in Scotland and England; the Duke of Parma was authorised to raise men in Dauphiné; Holland recruited from Normandy, and even Venice quailed in the presence of her Dutch mercenaries.[24] Troops were hired like workmen for the year or even for the month, and in practice the army provided the only solution of the unemployment question. Pillage was often the main incentive, for when a city was captured, the soldiers could claim everything except arms and church bells; but even churches were not spared, for lead coffins were dug up and sold, while ecclesiastical vestments were sometimes used to make harness for stolen cattle. A friendly army quartered in a district was only one degree better than a hostile one. In the later stages of the Thirty Years' War soldiers were accompanied by their wives and families, for whom a subsistence was obtained chiefly by brigandage or begging, and for a time the movements of such rabbles made cholera and bubonic plague endemic in central Europe.[25] "There are more days in the year than sausages" was a maxim current among Spanish soldiers; readers of *Don Quixote* will recall the graphic description of soldiering given by one who had much practical experience.[26] Descartes recollected his army experiences with disgust. "I have difficulty," he wrote,[27] "in placing Arms among the honourable professions, considering that idleness and debauchery are the chief motives inducng men to become soldiers."

Ample evidence in support of this view may be found in a remarkable volume of Memoirs[28] written early in the seventeenth century by a Spanish soldier named Alonso de Con-

[24] D'Avenel, *Richelieu et la monarchie absolue,* iii. 20.

[25] For this see *Epidemics resulting from Wars* (ed. Westergaard), 77 ff.

[26] *Don Quixote,* Pt. I. ch. xxxix. See also Miguel de Castro, *Vida del soldado español* (1593–1611).

[27] Quoted in Charvériat, *Histoire de la Guerre de Trente Ans,* i. 205.

[28] *Vida del capitan Alonso de Contreras,* ed. Sarrano y Sanz (1900). There is a French translation by Lamet and Rouannet (1911).

treras, a book noticed here not as a mere literary curiosity, but as giving authentic evidence of the innumerable possibilities which at that time lay before the soldier of fortune, and interesting because of the contrast it provides with the more disciplined and limited career open to the soldier of to-day. The Memoirs of Contreras have the same importance for the early seventeenth century as those of Benvenuto Cellini have for the early sixteenth century; like Cellini, Contreras was an artist, but of a different kind, and the fact that his book is practically unknown may excuse a fairly full reference to its contents. Contreras, according to his story, had to leave school at an early age as he accidentally killed a schoolmate; after a brief but unsatisfactory apprenticeship to a goldsmith he became a soldier. For some time he served on the Spanish galleys in the Mediterranean, a life which gave full scope for his love of adventure and change. Robbery, abduction and piracy appear to have been his daily pursuits while employed in what he calls "the galleys of the Religion." He noted many curious phenomena that came to his notice, such as that the bodies of dead Turks always float face downwards while those of Christians float face upwards, and in Lampedusa he found a magic cave containing food offerings left by mariners for the sustenance of escaped slaves, whether Christian or Turkish.[29] Any one not in want who touched this food found, on returning to his ship, that it could not leave its moorings. The exploits of Contreras in this service acquired for him such notoriety that one potentate, who had suffered by his depredations, offered rewards for his capture, specifying at the same time the nature of the tortures he proposed to inflict on him before death,[30] and the soldier-biographer noted with pardonable pride that portraits of himself were to be found exhibited at almost every Mediterranean port.

Tiring of this at last he transferred himself ashore, and incurred serious trouble by attempting to murder his captain —an offence, he notes, which Spanish military etiquette regarded in the same light as want of respect to a superior officer.[31] His fortunes were not improved when the rumour became current that he was the king of the Moriscos in dis-

[29] *Ibid.* ch. iii.
[30] Ch. v.
[31] Ch. vii.

guise.[32] For him life was now one continuous succession of
quarrels, fights, escapes, intrigues and murders, in which he
always endangered his life but never his prospects of promotion in the Spanish army. As any moment might be his last,
he enjoyed every hour with complete zest, but, like Cellini,
he had his moments of repentance, and it was during one of
these moods that he decided to become a hermit.[33] Packing
into a bag the chief necessities of a hermit's existence, such
as a hair shirt and a skull and cross bones, he went to a
mountainous solitude—not without considerable difficulty at
the hands of the local customs officials, who considered his
looks and bearing out of keeping with the contents of his bag;
but, once established in his retreat, he subjected himself to
the most elaborate austerities, living mainly on herbs and oil.
Seven months of this vegetative life were ended when he was
arrested by emissaries of the Holy Brotherhood, or police
force; he was accused of having concealed Morisco arms and
conveyed to prison. There he found the diet so rich that he
became ill and had to have medical attention; once recovered
he was put on the rack, but declined to commit himself.[34]
Eventually he was able to prove his innocence, and on release
he reassumed the military profession.

His adventures now assumed an even more lurid hue; he
killed on the slightest provocation, and found a full measure
of excitement in keeping out of the clutches of the Holy
Brotherhood and away from relatives of deceased acquaint-
ances and abandoned wives. He saw considerable service in
Flanders and Italy, and while in the latter country noted that
poison played the same part as the dagger in Spain, indeed
attempts to poison him were so numerous that he acquired
a degree of immunity, even against arsenic.[35] He was nearly
killed during an eruption of Vesuvius; he was excommunicated, and became Governor of Aquila. Returning to Malta
he was again given a ship, and, sailing to the West Indies,
engaged in fierce combat with Sir Walter Raleigh;[36] after his
return to the Mediterranean he was appointed Governor of

[32] Ch. ix.
[33] Ch. ix.
[34] Ch. x.
[35] Ch. xi.
[36] Ch. xiii.

Pantellaria.[37] He had already been elected a "Brother Servant of Arms" of the Order of St. John of Malta—the Chapter General electing him was composed of over two hundred persons, and the election was unanimous.[38] Contreras had, by that time, been married several times, but when he obtained this semi-ecclesiastical dignity he was celibate. Throughout his Memoirs he insists, with pride, on the fact that neither he nor his ancestors had ever incurred the slightest suspicion of heresy, and he bequeathed considerable property in Pantellaria in order to pay the cost of masses for his soul. Appropriately enough his Memoirs break off in the middle of a line—doubtless his end was in keeping with his career.

In recent years attempts have been made to prove that certain nations have, in the past, been specially notorious for atrocities committed in war. Such theories ignore the experience of the seventeenth century, when armies were not national, and every military race was guilty of atrocities too appalling for record. The truth is that so long as war and human nature remain the same, even the most brilliant campaigns may be marred by inhuman conduct, for the psychology of the mob differs completely from that of the individual. In this respect it may be noted that the word "Hun" was extensively used of the French by the Germans after the second invasion of the Palatinate[39] in 1688, and, throughout the whole century, some propagandist use was made of records of barbarities committed by enemies or invaders, whether they were French, Swedes, Spaniards, Germans or Lorrainers; but for calculated and systematic atrocity the Turk had the most unimpeachable reputation. In spite, however, of the mixed armies, and the impossibility of arraigning any particular nation for specially immoral conduct in war, contemporaries entertained certain traditional opinions regarding the military prowess of each country. Thus the Italians were considered good in attack, the Germans best fitted for a prolonged campaign, and the Spaniards for a long siege.[40] The Spaniards lost their military reputation in this period—a Venetian ambas-

[37] Ch. xv.
[38] Ch. xi.
[39] See *infra*, p. 304.
[40] *Relazioni degli ambasciatori veneti*, ed. Barozzi e Berchet, 1st series (Spain), i. 231.

sador noted[41] that few Spaniards were willing to serve except as generals. That Spanish cavalry was weak their defeat at Rocroi proved, but even then their artillery was good, and the battle of Nördlingen was won by Spanish infantry. Undoubtedly the most military race of the seventeenth century was the French; the French king was said to have the greatest number of troops at his command, because all his subjects were soldiers.[42] The Swedish armies were noteworthy for their good training and discipline.[43]

Before the use of the bayonet became general, the infantry was normally composed of an equal number of pikemen and musketeers.[44] The muzzle-loading muskets could not easily be fired unless supported, consequently the musketeer marched with his five-foot musket on one shoulder and a wooden fork or trestle on the other. After the complicated process of loading, a lighted taper was applied, but when the ground was frozen, as at the battle of the White Hill (1620), the supports could not be stuck into the ground, and so the muskets became practically useless. The Swiss practised an infantry formation in squares, like the Macedonian phalanx, a practice which became general in Europe, though the development of artillery made it a dangerous one. It was usual for the musketeers to advance in front of the pikemen, fire, and then retire behind the pikemen in order to reload. An infantry regiment was nominally composed of about 3000 men, really of about 1500. Heavy cavalry at the time of the Thirty Years' War consisted of cuirassiers, in heavy armour, using sword

[41] *Ibid.* 127. See also, for a modern account of Spain's military decline in this period, Canovas del Castillo, *Estudios del reinado de Felipe IV*, ii. 375 ff.

[42] *Relazioni degli ambasciatori veneti*, 2nd series (France), iii. 45.

[43] A contemporary wrote of the Swedish troops at the battle of Leipzig (1631): "I do not think that any of them ever fled or can fly, and all his [Gustavus Adolphus'] army are more desirous to fight than to rob or play as we and all the Imperialists have always done" (Coke MSS. i. 441 in *Hist. MSS. Commission Reports*). In the Polish campaign of 1654 one Swedish general hanged 470 of his soldiers for looting (*Tagebuch des Generals P. Gordon* (ed. 1849), i. 18).

[44] For this see Charvériat, *Histoire de la Guerre de Trente Ans*, I. ch. viii.

and pistol, who, when they fell, had to be picked up or left behind. The carabineers had a three-foot carbine and two pistols. Until they could join contact with pike and sword, the cavalry advanced in double rows, one to fire while the other was reloading. Cavalry regiments consisted usually of about 600 men. In the course of the century the size of armies increased and made necessary some kind of government system to replace the old private bargaining of captain and recruit, but it was not till the time of Louvois that the first really national armies took the field. It was Vauban who made the science of fortification an exact one. Other developments occurring in the seventeenth century are the perfectioning of such arms as the bayonet, the greater importance attached to the infantry at the expense of the cavalry, and the new cooperation with the artillery, a branch hitherto regarded as completely independent and often under civilian control.

The class of the community which suffered most from the activities of these armies was the peasants.[45] Europe was still mainly agricultural, but agriculture was a very precarious industry so long as the ravages of armed bands were left unchecked, and, in war, the plight of the peasant was unenviable whether the army in his neighbourhood was supposed to be friendly or not. Much of his time—and that of his village—might have to be spent in performing the innumerable corvées demanded by the lord, and as these corvées included such serious enterprises as road building, the time which the serf could devote to his own holding was a very variable commodity. In the average French village of the Ancien Régime the manorial lord had most, if not all, of the following rights: he had the right of toll on goods passing through the village; he could levy a tax on wines sold within his jurisdiction; he had the perquisite of the tongues of animals slaughtered for food; he could require the villagers to have their corn ground exclusively at his mill, and, in some villages, could insist that no baking be done other than in the seignorial bakehouse; he exacted fines on all transferences of land; he might require the villagers to take their turn at his plough teams; if his villagers bred stock, he claimed some of the increase under the right of champart, and, in addition, he was in regular receipt

---

[45] See Babeau, *Le Village sous l'Ancien Régime.*

of rents whether in money or in kind, as well as having claims to feudal aids from lands held of him by a noble tenure. Such a lord might have the hunting rights of the demesne, in which case his peasants could never be sure that their lands would not continually be overrun, and he generally had in addition a pigeon loft as well as a rabbit warren, both maintained at the expense of the peasants' crops. On the principle that the noble fought for him and the priest prayed for him, the peasant had to bear the brunt of practically all the direct taxation, and thus the obligation to pay the *taille* was inseparably associated with the servile status. The harshest feature in the social life of the seventeenth and eighteenth centuries was the disgrace and degradation attached to the oldest and most honourable of all occupations.

For the man who was not a peasant, and wished to be neither priest nor soldier, there were a great number of municipal and government offices for which he might qualify. These offices were attractive not only for their social benefits, but because they conferred the much-valued immunity from direct taxation. The avenue leading to such posts was a knowledge of Latin, and statesmen of western Europe were agreed that infinite harm was done to the State by the indiscriminate teaching of Latin to the children of the poor. "Once a man gets his nose into text-books he is rendered useless for any honest occupation. When a villager has learned three words of Latin, he at once stops paying the *taille*; he becomes a procurator, a syndic or a sergeant, and proceeds to ruin his neighbors."[46] Richelieu and Colbert voiced similar complaints; in Spain the numerous Jesuit schools were accused of turning out boys whose knowledge of Latin divorced them from the soil or manual labour. The anonymous author of *Le Paysan français* suspected that a certain amount of guile was a useful adjunct to an acquaintance with Latin in the hunt for lucrative offices: "When a peasant, more cute and unprincipled than his neighbours, becomes tired of work and prefers to cross his legs in the village tavern, his idea is to become a procurator or sergeant, and if he is sufficiently unscrupulous he rises to the judicial bench. Our lives and

[46] *Avis donné à MM. de l'assemblée du clergé, 1627*, quoted in Hanotaux, *Histoire du Cardinal de Richelieu,* i. 460.

property are in the hands of such people."[47] It has been calculated that in proportion to population three times as many boys were taught Latin in the seventeenth century as are taught to-day.[48] But these outspoken opinions err in attaching particular blame to the peasant, because in order to obtain an office (as distinct from a temporary commission in government service) some capital, as well as an elementary knowledge of Latin, was required. At a time when there was no regular Civil Service, an office was regarded from the point of view of the candidate as an investment yielding a regular income, certain perquisites, a social position, immunity from capitation taxes, and a heritage for his descendants; while, from the point of view of the government, it was a means of obtaining funds (the purchase price), and provided a system of caution money for the good behaviour of the official class. This is particularly true of France; similar conceptions, however, prevailed throughout western Europe. The great State offices were subject to royal nomination, but the innumerable administrative and judicial posts were as vendible as were votes and seats in eighteenth-century England. It may be added that in France, with the steady increase of wealth, the smaller bourgeoisie was the class to which this method of investment made the strongest appeal,[49] and it is literally true to say that the nearer a government approached bankruptcy the more offices it created.

In the sixteenth century the French jurist Hotman[50] had made the interesting suggestion that the plague of multiplicity of offices had visited those countries where the Roman Law of Justinian had been "received": this he attributed to the influence of the Byzantine administrative system, with its innumerable hierarchies of officials.[51] A comparison between France and England in the sixteenth and seventeenth centuries supports this contention. Early in the former century Claude

[47] *Le Paysan français* (1609), 28.

[48] Hanotaux, *op. cit.* 462. Excluding the Jesuit schools, there were in Spain (1619) over 4000 schools in which Latin was taught (Altamira y Crevea, *Historia de España*, iii. 544).

[49] A full account of this will be found in C. Normand, *La Bourgeoisie française au XVIIe siècle.*

[50] *Anti-Tribonianus* (ed. 1681), 128-9.

[51] On this subject see M. Göhring, *Die Ämterkäuflickeit im Ancien Régime*, 1938.

Seyssel[52] complained of the disproportionate number of officials in France. In the average French town of about 3000 inhabitants there were the bailli, the prévôt, the lieutenant, the procureur-fiscal, six notaries, twelve procureurs, four greffiers and a host of clerks.[53] To remain in the roturier class implied ignorance or lack of initiative. From the reign of Henri III. onwards municipal, judicial and financial offices were reduplicated; in Henri IV.'s reign they became hereditary on payment of the *paulette*; and soon there was no law court without its swarm of satellites, no corporation without its numerous and imposing functionaries, no commodity without its army of government inspectors and controllers. Loyseau estimated that in the first half of the seventeenth century about 50,000 such offices had been created. "To-day half the inhabitants of the towns are officials: since our forefathers discovered this method of raising money from the ambition and folly of the idle, it provides a manna that never fails."[54] As well as creating new offices, the government would sometimes introduce subdivisions into those already existing, the sub-lessees exercising their rights every second, third, or even fourth year. Between 1689 and 1715 the port and markets of Paris were burdened with more than 2000 additional officials, not because they were needed, but because the wars of Louis XIV. made ready money more than ever necessary. Controllers of perruques were first appointed in 1706. So long as the annual salaries of government offices were paid there was no trouble, but while the English Parliament fought to maintain certain fundamental constitutional principles, the Parlement of Paris rebelled because, among other actions, Mazarin interfered with the payment of government *rentes* and official salaries. Therein lies a fundamental contrast between England and France of the seventeenth century.

Further light is thrown on the conceptions dominating the public life of the seventeenth century by a reference to some of the main systems of taxation. For this purpose France and Spain may be chosen: France, because her civilization was more intricate and more fully developed than that of any other

[52] Seyssel, *La Grant Monarchie de la France,* vii b.
[53] Hanotaux, i. 459.
[54] Quoted in article "Offices" in Marcel Marion, *Dictionnaire des institutions de la France aux XVII⁰ et XVIII⁰ siècles,* 405.

continental country; Spain, because her possessions in Europe were so extensive. The chief direct tax in France was the *taille*, which played the same part in seventeenth-century budgets as is played by the income-tax of to-day; it was, however, assessed without regard to either justice or political economy. In the Pays d'Etats,[55] forming about a third part of the area of France, the *taille* fell on real property and was not a harsh tax, because it spared the landless man. The local Estates of each Pays d'Etats agreed with the government on a composite sum, which was then apportioned among all owners of real property within the province. In the Pays d'Elections, on the other hand, the *taille* was a most inequitable levy, for it was a capitation tax, falling almost entirely on the peasants, the privilege of exemption being zealously guarded by the nobility, the clergy, and all holders of municipal or government offices. There were, in the Pays d'Elections, no local Estates to intervene between the Treasury and the taxpayer; in their place was an array of district tribunals (*Elections*), each with a hierarchy of officials who had bought their offices and were responsible only to the crown. Direct contact with the taxpayer was through the *élus*, a hated class, whose name has often given rise to confusion,[56] because it seems to imply that they were elective functionaries. The name is one of the many euphemisms to be found in the nomenclature of the Ancien Régime, for, since the sixteenth century, the *élus* were mostly ambitious and calculating men who had bought their offices and were determined not to lose by the investment. In Colbert's time they were displaced by the intendants, who represented a much better class, but in the greater part of France the *taille* still remained a most unjust tax, and, indirectly, it

[55] The Pays d'Etats were those provinces which had more recently been incorporated with the French monarchy and still retained their Estates. They included Brittany, Burgundy, Dauphiné, Provence and Languedoc. Most of the central provinces were Pays d'Elections. For the French financial system in the seventeenth century see d'Avenel, *op. cit*. ii. 139-371.

[56] The *élus* must not be confused with the *asséeurs*. The latter were elected in the rural parishes to collect the *taille;* for this they received no recompense, and if they failed to make up the quota they had to pay the deficiency or go to prison. Consequently there was no competition for the elective and honorary office of *asséeur;* in some villages a good proportion of the peasants were in gaol through failure to collect the *taille* (d'Avenel, *op. cit*. ii. 193 ff.).

helped to ruin Henry IV.'s schemes for introducing new industries into France; moreover, it kept the French peasantry in a state of poverty and degradation.

It is, however, in the administration of the *gabelle* or salt-tax that the unplumbed depths of seventeenth-century officialdom are revealed. Like the *taille*, it was not uniformly assessed, for some provinces[57] were exempt altogether; of the others, some were Pays de Petite Gabelle[58] and others Pays de Grande Gabelle.[59] In days when it was unusual to keep cattle through the winter, salted foods were far more widely used than now, and, in Catholic countries, pickled fish was the staple diet on Fridays and Fast Days; moreover, salt was commonly used as a fertilizer and in several tanning processes. At least one sixteenth-century war had been caused by disputed claims over salt-pits;[60] and the economic importance of salt in the succeeding century was still very great. Like tobacco in modern France, salt could be sold only by licensed retailers or *regratteurs*, and the purchase of a definite minimum was compulsory. The *regratteurs* bought their supplies in coinage of Tours and sold only for money of Paris, making 25 per cent profit on the exchange alone; and as they sold only in small quantities at a time, much hardship was imposed on those living in remote districts, since they were obliged to travel considerable distances at frequent intervals in order to complete their quota. On the coast the temptation to produce salt from brine was a great one, the article thus obtained being of much better quality than that sold by the State, but harsh measures were imposed in order to maintain the government monopoly. The government sold several different grades of salt, enforcing strict injunctions against any attempts to economize by using the coarser kinds for domestic purposes; elaborate registers were kept, and a host of officials was employed to see that the requisite purchases were made, that they were used for the specified objects, and that no salt was used which had not been

[57] The exempted provinces were Artois, Hainault, Béarn, Navarre and Brittany, but none of these was thoroughly French.

[58] Lyonnais, Beaujolais, Mâconnais, Bresse, Languedoc, Provence, Roussillon, Velez and Forez.

[59] Il-de-France, Orléannais, Berry, Bourbonnais, Maine, Anjou and Touraine.

[60] Notably in disputes involving the salt-pits of Ferrara, *e.g.* the war waged against Ferrara by Pope Julius II. in 1511.

bought from official vendors. The expedient of poisoning the coarser salt required for tanning processes in order to prevent its use in the kitchen was adopted, but sometimes several varieties were inadvertently mixed by careless officials, followed by casualties among the consumers. Where a district was suspected of making its own salt, such deaths from salt poisoning would provide conclusive evidence that government salt was being used. The salt intended for cattle was mixed with gravel, and many a peasant lost all his stock through disease directly due to this adulteration. Great differences in the price of salt throughout the various provinces led to smuggling, and there was a considerable trade in this "faux saunage," which provided cheap salt to supplement the minimum "sel de devoir." Dogs were trained to carry the smuggled salt; when these were captured by the customs officials they invariably, in accordance with the ruthless logic of officialdom, suffered the death penalty. Villages were sometimes left completely deserted through peasants migrating from a province where the *gabelle* was heavy to one where it was not so harsh; the prisons and galleys were full of men who had contravened the *gabelle* regulations, and the gibbets, always a familiar feature on the landscape of seventeenth-century France, supported the bodies of those who had offended too often.

The taxes in Spain[61] were more humane and were intended in the interests of the consumers, but they had the incidental disadvantage of ruining the commerce of the country. Among the methods whereby money was raised in the chief bullion-importing country in Europe were the following: the alienation of royal rights and rents, sale of titles of nobility, legitimation of natural sons and the sons of the clergy, forced loans from nobles and ecclesiastics, eleemosynary gifts—Philip III.'s major-domos and priests went from door to door begging money, and lastly, debasing the coinage. When these extraordinary measures failed, the number of taxed articles was increased: salt, stamped paper, playing-cards, tobacco, and even ice used for culinary purposes being all utilized for purposes of taxation. In order to prevent scarcity at home there were prohibitions and restrictions on exports, resulting in a balance of trade permanently against Spain, and what bullion reached the country was speedily exported. Very heavy postal charges reduced literary communication to a minimum; wool was heavily taxed and therefore universally smuggled; a tax of six months' salary on promoted officials did not encourage industry or efficiency among men constitutionally inclined to indolence, and a tax on the upper stories of dwelling-houses, instead of raising revenue, merely served to stereotype the domestic architecture of Spain.

The two indirect taxes were the *alcabala* and the *millones*, the former a tax of 10 per cent on all sales, even of necessities, and the latter a levy on oil, wine and vinegar. Money was also raised by the Bulls of Crusade, a tax dating from the early years of the sixteenth century, when Pope Julius II. had authorized the king of Spain to sell Bulls of Indulgence for such things as drinking milk on fast days and eating meat during Lent, the prices varying according to the province and social position of the recipient. But, with all these devices, seventeenth-century Spain drifted nearer and nearer to bankruptcy. In the reigns of Philip IV. and Charles II. "juntas de medios" were frequently convened in order to suggest practical schemes for raising funds. In Naples it was seriously proposed[62] that money might be saved if every one would undergo a day's fast in each month. In 1693 a royal commission, sitting in Madrid, after prolonged deliberation, could suggest no more brilliant plan for replenishing the Exchequer than that the royal plate should be coined and the queen's jewels pawned.[63]

Of the most characteristic conceptions dominating the public life of the seventeenth century there remains to be noted the tremendous importance attached to questions of ceremony and precedence: a sentiment associated with the great respect always shown to the external evidences of wealth and power. No French gentleman of any standing could dispense with a *maître d'hôtel*, even if it meant that meals had to be curtailed: Richelieu, when only Bishop of Luçon and very poor, did not dare to dispense with this necessity,[64] nor was it unknown for

[62] Callegari, *Preponderanze straniere* (in Vallardi, *Storia politica d'Italia*), 148.

[63] Altamira y Crevea, *op. cit.* iii. 289.

[64] D'Avenel, *op. cit.* ii. 16.

two impoverished gentlemen to take turns as serving-man to the other. In Poland, for an equipage to be respectable, at least twenty-five horses had to be used, and when Louis XIV. went forth to meet his bride the equipage was several miles in length. No seigneur of the Ancien Régime was complete without his own culinary staff, his chaplain, his choir, his doctor or barber, his confessor, his gentleman secretary and master of ceremonies, not to mention a small army of stable menials. In Spain these things went to an unheard-of length, where they were rendered ludicrous by the extreme poverty with which they were often associated. Decline in material wealth only served to accentuate this characteristic, and the classic instance of determination to keep up appearances in adversity was the Spaniard who, having only one finger of a glove, shrouded himself in his cloak from which one (gloved) finger protruded.

The seventeenth century can hardly be understood unless it is realized how much importance was attached to such matters. At Münster and Osnabrück the proceedings of Europe's first peace congress were constantly being delayed and thwarted by petty questions of precedence and ceremonial.[65] Negotiations between France and Spain were made possible in 1659 by the fortunate fact that in the stream (the Bidassoa) dividing the two countries there was a small island on which the French and Spanish agents could meet without any prejudice to the precedence claimed by either country.[66] At Karlowitz in 1699 the peace negotiations were jeopardized on more than one occasion by the most absurd and quibbling points of etiquette and precedence. These matters were given an enhanced importance by the great increase in the diplomatic personnel of Europe. At the beginning of the century every independent European state, except Turkey,[67] had a diplomatic corps, and it was the duty of the members of this comparatively new profession to insist on the punctilious observation of international etiquette as well as to maintain, in

[65] For this subject generally, see H. Brocher, *Le rang et l'etiquette sous l'ancien régime* (1934).

[66] See *infra*, p. 221.

[67] But, by the treaty of Sitva-Torok (1606), the Porte undertook to maintain an agent in Vienna. An ambassador representing the Emperor was stationed in Constantinople (Dumont, *Corps diplomatique*, v. pt. ii. 78).

their own persons, the status which they claimed for the country they represented. By granting the right of direct representation to the separate states of Germany, the treaty of Westphalia greatly increased the diplomatic personnel of Europe, and diplomacy soon came to be a distinct profession, drawn from an exclusive class, distinguished by exceptional privileges, and having an elaborate code of ceremonial and conduct. There is nothing in the historical literature of the seventeenth century to show that diplomatic agents were intended to help the cause of European peace; rather there is evidence that ambassadors were often regarded as spies,[68] and Wootton's definition implies that they were also liars. Even more, it might be claimed that the extreme punctiliousness with which these men insisted on the precise degree of respect due to themselves and their principals helped to create a feeling of tension between the greater states, an atmosphere which was always generating "incidents," and sometimes leading directly to war. It is no exaggeration to say that the question of peace might depend on the arranging of a public procession: in 1661 the brawl between the servants of the French and Spanish ambassadors in London involved several casualties, and war was averted only because Spain was so weak that she had to apologize. In 1679, when Marie Louise of Orléans was sent to Spain as the bride of Charles II., a pontoon was constructed on the Bidassoa, equidistant from the Spanish and French banks, so that there would be no dispute regarding boundaries when the French escort handed her over to the Spanish.[69]

These bickerings over formalities would be merely ludicrous were it not that they often had important historical consequences. Thus it frequently happened that two princes or diplomats, each claiming precedence over the other, and entrusted with the duty of negotiating with the other, would be quite unable to communicate so long as neither yielded. The only solution was for one to go to bed, making it possible for the other to call on the "invalid" without any surrender of

---

[68] "Les agens, nonces, ambassadeurs et légats sont envoyez et pour épier les actions des princes étrangers, et pour dissimuler, couvrir et déguiser celles de leurs maîtres" (Gabriel Naudé, *Considérations politiques sur les coups d'État*, ed. 1667, 55).

[69] *Instructions données aux ambassadeurs de France depuis le traité de Westphalie* (Spain), i. 297.

dignity. When a French agent at Constantinople was igno-
miniously treated by a newly appointed Grand Vizier known
to be hostile to foreigners, and was refused the dignity of the
"soffah," the agent of the English Levant Company, knowing
that his turn would come next, immediately took to bed, and
so avoided an insult to his nation by a margin of minutes.[70]
Among private persons there was the same insistence on the
point of honour. The hagglings over precedence at the court
of Louis XIV. are sometimes too ludicrous for belief and too
trivial for record, except by writers of the inordinate industry
of Saint Simon, and the prominence attached to this topic in
the literature of the period sometimes tempts one to think that
common sense is a modern virtue. In Spain and its dependencies the question of precedence came second only to religion.
In Naples, on one occasion, the Viceroy left the Cathedral
because the Archbishop was given two cushions when entitled
to only one, and in the same city the burial of a princess was
delayed for weeks because her coffin bore arms to which, it
was held, she had not in life been entitled. The cities of
Cremona and Padua contested precedence for over eighty
years until the Senate of Milan decreed that the question was
insoluble.[71] The rigid etiquette and ceremony of the Spanish
court produced an atmosphere which foreign observers described as suffocating.[72]

In the political history of the seventeenth century the two
most important subjects are the dynastic struggle of Bourbon
and Hapsburg and the racial struggle of Ottoman and Slav.
Of these the first dates from the accession of the Bourbons,
whose anti-Hapsburg ambitions were merged with the Thirty
Years' War by Richelieu; it was the inspiration of Louis
XIV.'s foreign policy; it was fought out in the Spanish Succession War, and ended only by the treaty of Utrecht, when
a Bourbon was established on the throne of Spain. This struggle involved practically the whole of western and central

[70] There is a good account of this incident in G. F. Abbot,
Under the Turk in Constantinople, ch. xiii. The Grand Vizier was
Kara Mustafa; the English agent, Sir John Finch.
[71] Nencioni, "Barocchismo," in *La vita italiana nel seicento*, 282.
[72] See the Report of M. de Rebenac (1688–89) in *Instructions
données aux ambassadeurs de France* (Spain), i. 424, and the
Report of M. de Marcin (1701–2), *ibid*. ii. 12.

Europe, for the Austrian Hapsburgs controlled the Empire, their Spanish cousins ruled Spain, with its European dependencies Italy and Flanders, while the Bourbons governed France. Its consequences are to be seen in the histories of every other European country: it affected the fortunes of Sweden and Brandenburg in the Wars of the North; it made monarchical rule (in the crisis of 1672) essential for the Dutch, and it encouraged the Turks to embark on a great scheme of European conquest, of which the siege of Vienna in the year 1683 was intended to be only the preliminary. In eastern Europe, Poland provided a battle-ground for the perpetual feuds of Ottoman and Slav, a contest from which Russia emerged as a great power. In order that these political and racial struggles may be properly understood, it is necessary that something should be known of the material resources of the combatants, and how far their states possessed any institutions for the expression of class interest. The countries concerned are: the Empire, France, Spain, Italy, Poland, Russia and Turkey.

THE EMPIRE—The mediaeval Holy Roman Empire was nominally a great federation of Christian states under an elective head, but long before the seventeenth century this institution had been replaced by the conception of nationality, of which, on the Continent, France was the first and the most vigorous embodiment. Strictly speaking, Germany was all that remained of the old Imperial dominions, the Austrian lands being the family possessions of the Hapsburgs. When in 1648 the German feudatories were given the right of contracting treaties and alliances, provided these were not against the Empire, the last of the Imperial lands was tacitly withdrawn from Hapsburg control. Nevertheless the Emperor still continued to take precedence over every other Christian monarch; he could confer titles of nobility and could raise certain taxes, including the "Roman Months," so called from the fact that they were originally granted for a period of months, in order to defray the expenses of the imperial coronation in Rome. The Golden Bull of 1356 had fixed the number of electors at the mystic number seven—the three ecclesiastical electors, namely, the Archbishops of Mainz, Cologne and Trier, and the four lay electors, the Margraves of Saxony and Brandenburg, the Elector Palatine of the Rhine and the King of Bohemia.

The deliberative body was the Diet (*Reichstag*) which generally met at Ratisbon, and contained representatives of Electors, Princes and Towns, the deputies being mostly lawyers or the *gens togata*, who were usually financially interested in prolonging proceedings. The three Estates deliberated separately, and only those decisions in which each concurred became general laws of the Empire; but while contests among the Estates were rare, there was endless delay and indecision. "The Estate of Germany," wrote a contemporary, "is this day much perverted, so as if the Emperor doth call a diet or parliament, the princes will not come in person but send their agents, to whom they give no authority to resolve or conclude anything . . . and for this reason they despatch little."[73] The treaty of Westphalia introduced the "jus eundi in partes" or right of separating into two bodies when religious questions affecting Catholic and Protestant had to be discussed, and this was a further cause of delay, besides intensifying the antagonisms from which Germany suffered so much.[74] The Diet was accused by contemporaries of wasting time in quibbles and refinements: "It is like drinking up the sea to describe all their ceremonies"; "they drank Spanish wine in the morning and Rhenish wine at night," and their other activities were defined by Leibnitz as *contradiciren, litigiren, schulmeisteriren*.[75] Subterfuge and procrastination were considered the main characteristics of this body which might, however, claim to be one of the very few active representative institutions left in seventeenth-century Europe.

The Thirty Years' War changed the Emperor from head of the Empire to secular head of the Catholic party, and very few seventeenth-century publicists claimed that his power was absolute. The first serious criticism of the Imperial constitution was the sixteenth-century "book of Sleidan."[76] In 1640 a German writer, Philip Chemnitz, writing under the name of

[73] E. Grimstone, *The Estates, Empires and Principalities of the World*, translated from the French (of Davity), 1615, 546.

[74] For good accounts of the Germanic constitution in the seventeenth century see *Instructions données aux ambassadeurs de France* (Germanic Diet), lv. ff., and C. V. Wedgwood, *The Thirty Years' War*, 32-41.

[75] Quoted in Auerbach, *La France et le Saint Empire Romain depuis le traité de Westphalie*, ch. i.

[76] *Comment. de statu religionis et reipublicae . . .* (1572).

Hippolithus a Lapide, declared[77] that the Imperial powers were merely honorary, and that real sovereignty lay with the separate German states. This book attracted considerable attention because of its bitter attack on the House of Hapsburg, to which it attributed the misfortunes of Germany. Chemnitz suggested than an Emperor should be chosen from another family with powers modelled on those of the Doge of Venice, and the book acquired additional importance from the fact of its being burned in Vienna. Later in the century Seckendorf[78] and Conring[79] developed these arguments, contrasting the practical and territorial sovereignty exercised by the princes with the nominal and obsolete claims of the Emperor. Leibnitz[80] believed, however, that the house of Austria must be retained if only as a counterpoise to the Turks, and in order to withstand France and Sweden. But though their prerogatives were diminished, and though they had to reckon on the hostility of many theorists, the Hapsburgs retained their hold on the Empire, and, with only one exception,[81] the Electors continued to elect members of that House until the abolition of the institution in 1806. One of the Venetian ambassadors[82] suggested an interesting, if cynical, reason for this tradition. The Emperor Rudolph (1576-1611), ruined by his researches in alchemy and astrology, was obliged to pawn the valuable river dues of Germany to the Electors at a price little more than the amount of their annual revenue, and the Electors knew that if a wealthy prince (such as the Duke of Bavaria) were elected, he would be able to redeem these mortgaged revenues, and so the Electors would lose a source of revenue. But for whatever reason, the empire became more and more nominal, a development leading to an increasing distinction between the Emperor and the institutions of the Empire. The treaty of Nymegen was signed by the Emperor without the participation of the Diet; in 1727 France declared war on the Emperor while insisting on the neutrality of the

[77] *Dissertatio de ratione status in imperio nostro Germanico.*
[78] *Teutscher Fürstenstaat* (1656).
[79] *De finibus Imperii* (1654).
[80] *Quanti sit momenti Imperium esse apud domum Austriacum,* in *Œuvres de Leibnitz,* ed. Klopp, i. 170.
[81] Charles VII. (Wittelsbach), 1744–45.
[82] Giustiniani (1654) in *Fontes rerum Austriacarum* (ed. Fiedler, 2nd part, xxvi. 403.

Empire.[83] But until 1806 the Empire remained a great Germanic confederation, giving birth in the seventeenth century to the interesting but short-lived pacific experiment, known as the League of the Rhine,[84] and providing in the eighteenth century a deadweight in central Europe, supposed by many writers to be essential for maintaining the equilibrium of the Continent.[85]

For administrative purposes the Empire had been divided in the sixteenth century into circles as follows:

1. Bavaria.
2. Swabia, including Würtemberg, Baden, the bishopric of Augsburg and many Imperial cities.
3. Franconia, Würtzburg, Bamberg, Ansbach and Baireuth.
4. The Upper Rhine—Zweibrücken, Lorraine and part of Alsace.
5. Westphalia—Jülich, Cleve, Berg, and Mark.
6. Lower Saxony—Brunswick, Mecklenburg, Holstein, Bremen and Magdeburg.
7. The Lower Rhine—the four Rhenish Electorates of Cologne, Mainz, Trier and the Palatinate.
8. Upper Saxony—the Electorates of Saxony and Brandenburg, with Pomerania.
9. Burgundy—the Netherlands, Luxemburg and Franche-Comté.
10. Austria—the hereditary lands such as Austria, Styria, Carinthia and Carniola, with the bishoprics of Trent and Brixen.

The Burgundian circle is included in this list because, although in the seventeenth century it was composed almost entirely of Spanish territory, the Peace of Westphalia definitely included it in the Imperial lands. Bohemia and Hungary were outside the scope of this arrangement: the former was nominally an elective kingship until 1617, and was incorpo-

[83] Auerbach, op. cit. xv. and ch. iv.
[84] See infra, p. 218.
[85] The general eighteenth-century view was that a federation of small states is more likely to seek and maintain peace than a single large state. For this see Montesquieu, De l'esprit des lois, ix.; Rousseau, Projet de paix perpétuelle, and Volney, Considérations sur la guerre actuelle des Turcs.

rated in the Hapsburg hereditary dominions by the Constitution of 1627; Hungary was also in name an elective monarchy, but, after a chequered history, its crown was declared hereditary in the Hapsburg line in 1687, though it was not till 1711 that the country was completely subdued. Both countries remained faithful to the Hapsburgs until 1848. Lands formerly part of the Empire, such as the United Provinces and Switzerland, were recognized as independent states in 1648; Brandenburg became the kingdom of Prussia in 1700.

The excessive provincialism which Imperial administration thus encouraged in Germany was intensified by religious differences and by the application of the principle *cujus regio, ejus religio*. In 1610 the chief Roman Catholic states were Bavaria, Berg, Jülich, Hesse-Darmstadt and the ecclesiastical states of Mainz, Trier, Cologne, Würzburg, Bamberg, Münster, Osnabrück, Paderborn, Bremen, Verden, Minden, Hildesheim, Passau, Ratisbon, Salzburg, Speier, Strassburg and Constance. The chief Lutheran states were Saxony, Brunswick-Lüneburg, Brunswick-Wolfenbüttel, East Friesland, Holstein, Mecklenburg, Würtemberg, Neuburg, Baden and Saxe-Lauenburg. The Calvinist states were Brandenburg, Baireuth, Ansbach, the Palatinate, Zweibrücken, Hesse-Cassel, Nassau, Anhalt and Pomerania. Cleve and Mark became Calvinist on passing to a Calvinist master, and there were frequent changes in the official religion of the other states, until gradually the greater part of North Germany became uniformly Protestant while the southern part remained Catholic. Of the secular rulers in Germany the most important were the Lutheran Electors of Saxony, who owed their fortunes to the Emperor's dispossession of the elder or Ernestine branch after the battle of Mühlberg (1543), and therefore, in spite of their religion, always tended to the Imperialist side; the Calvinist Electors of Brandenburg, who profited by the disputes of Sweden and Poland to aggrandize their territories and, apart from their Dutch connections, showed no principles in their alliances; the Catholic Dukes of Bavaria, who were the first of the German princes to possess a permanent army and a well-filled treasury, which they devoted to the cause of Catholicism in Germany. In the Thirty Years' War the Elector Palatine Frederick V. and Christian of Anhalt are of special prominence as the leaders of militant Calvinism. An eighth electorate was created for the family of the dispossessed Elector Palatine in

1648, the Palatine electorate having been granted to Bavaria in 1623, and in 1692 a ninth electorate was added by the elevation of Ernest Augustus of Brunswick-Lüneburg to the dignity of Elector of Hanover.

Thus Germany in the seventeenth century could hardly be called a nation, and, though it had a vernacular, did not possess a literary language. In the reign of Louis XIV. many German princes were merely the pensionaries of France, nor until their lands were devastated by French troops did the German peoples became conscious of any national feeling, voiced most clearly by the great patriot and philosopher Leibnitz.[86] The seventeenth century was thus for Germany as for Italy a period of disunion and degradation.

FRANCE—For a time, the constitutions of mediaeval France and England had developed on parallel lines; in both, the Curia Regis was the embryo from which administrative and judicial functions were differentiated, and there was much in common, as regards structure and policy, between the England of Edward I (1272-1307) and the France of Philip the Fair (1285-1314). But England, unlike the Continent and Scotland, never had true "Estates," and her House of Commons, in which, from the first, there were Knights of the Shire as well as Burgesses, gradually assumed an exceptional role in legislation; moreover, the Wars of the Roses and the despotism of the Tudors destroyed the old feudal nobility. The principles of public order and executive responsibility were fostered by the English Common Law, which survived even the Reformation, and provided parliamentarians with arguments, whether justifiable or not, for the rights of the subject. There remained plenty of "feudal" survivals, but these were mostly innocuous or even graceful. In other words, for a study of continental institutions we must take England not as the normal, but as the exceptional.

This can be illustrated by contrast with seventeenth-century France where mediaeval survivals, often ludicrous, and usually

---

[86] Cf. *Mars Christianissimus* (1685), *Manifeste concernant les droits de Charles III* (1702) and *Justice encouragée contre les chicanes et les menaces d'un partisan* (1702). These have been reprinted by Foucher de Careil and O. Klopp in *Œuvres de Leibnitz,* iv. See also Auerbach, *op. cit.* ch. iii.

vexatious were not extinguished until the Revolution. By far the most serious of these was the French nobility, a large and powerful caste, which was steadily increased by bought peerages. Another survival was law. There was no national jurisprudence, the main distinction being that Languedoc was the *pays de droit écrit*, based on Roman Law, while in the North and East was the *pays de droit coutumier*, consisting of numerous local systems of customary law. To the seventeenth-century Frenchman, law symbolised heterogeneity, inconsistency, privilege, exemption and oppression. As for representative institutions, the States General, composed of clergy, nobility and burgesses, had old traditions of free enquiry into matters of national moment, but the two upper estates often combined against the third, and moreover independent burgesses could be bullied or bribed. Its dissociation from land made the third estate almost impotent. As for the Parlement of Paris,[87] it was a remnant of the old Curia Regis, and provided an illustration of what, but for exceptional circumstances, might have become of our own mediaeval parliament which was, as it still is, a supreme royal council and judicial tribunal, on which other important functions have been grafted. The Parlement of Paris, unlike that at Westminster, never grew up. It remained the highest royal council and law court in the realm, but it represented no more than the sovereign and the legal profession, for therein the king could order the registration of his edicts by a body of presidents and councillors who had mostly bought their offices. Early in the reign of Louis XIV it lost even its right of protest, and was ordered to confine itself to judicial functions, a measure intended to reduce it to the status of the provincial Parlements, but nevertheless it continued to represent the strongest and most enlightened element in the bourgeoisie of seventeenth-century France.

The States-General met for the last time before the Revolution in 1614. In its abeyance there were occasional meetings of the semi-feudal Assembly of Notables, but these were always called for a specific purpose, and so it would be practically true to say that in seventeenth-century France there was no regularly constituted body to come between the monarch and subject. The rule of French kings was abso-

---

[87] The best account of the Paris Parlement is by Glasson, *Le Parlement de Paris et son rôle politique*.

lute, and Henry IV. succeeded in tempering absolutism with discretion and geniality; but the opinion of the century favoured autocracy disguised by councils, and monarchs like Louis XIV. found ample encouragement in the political philosophy of their day. In the later half of the century, when the system reached its full development, the French king exercised a personal rule[88] assisted by four councils—the Conseil d'Etat, the Conseil des Dépêches, the Conseil des Finances and the Conseil Privé. Of these, the first discussed foreign policy, questions of peace and war, and other supreme matters of state. It met twice or thrice a week, and was composed of the few persons, seldom more than four in number, definitely summoned as "ministres d'Etat." This title was an official one, implying simply membership of the Conseil d'Etat, a council containing no *ex officio* members; moreover none of the four secretaries of state was necessarily summoned. Louis hesitated before admitting his own son, and refused to admit his brother. But though a supreme deliberative council, it sometimes interfered with matters of justice and administration, thus providing an instance of that absence of clear distribution of powers which made the personal rule of the French monarchs seem so natural and reasonable.

The Conseil des Dépêches was established in 1630 to deal with all matters of interior administration, and generally included one secretary of state. If an English parallel may be allowed, this council combined the functions of Home Office, Office of Works and the old Local Government Board, but, in addition, it exercised judicial functions, in this respect often coming into collision with the Parlement. The edicts of this council, even on the most unimportant matters, always bore the royal signature, and the mere signing of such multifarious documents must have consumed no inconsiderable part of the monarch's time.

The Conseil des Finances was reconstituted in 1661 after the disgrace of Fouquet and the suppression of the office of *Surintendant des Finances*. It generally consisted of the Chancellor and three Intendants of Finance. Its decrees are not

---

[88] See Lavisse, *Histoire de France*, VII. i. bks. 2 and 4; Chéruel, *Histoire de l'administration monarchique en France*, ii. chs. 4 and 5; and Marion, *Dictionnaire des institutions de la France*, under "Conseil."

always easy to distinguish from those of the Conseil des Dépêches; the two often met on the same day and may have sat in the same chamber. This council provided the medium through which the Controller-General of Finance, in consultation with the king, promulgated his decrees on the levy of the *taille* and the regulation of the national revenues. As the Controller-General of Finance did not have the same wide prerogatives as the old Superintendent of Finance, fortunes were made out of the revenues, not by state dignitaries, but by the tax-farmers who in the eighteenth century had to seek safety in anonymity.[89]

The Conseil Privé or des Parties was a privy council, composed of *conseillers d'état* and *maîtres des requêtes*, exercising the king's justice as distinct from the public justice administered by the Parlement—a very significant distinction. It was a High Court of Appeal as well as a Court of Equity, and it supervised the conduct of the judicial bench; it adjudicated also on disputed questions of jurisdiction and on conflicts between the different departments of state. It exercised a *droit administratif* as distinct from the *droit civil*, and could suspend a case already begun, or withdraw a case from the jurisdiction of Parlement to have it tried elsewhere or not at all, in this way making it possible to provide for the servants of the executive a special protection that practically sheltered them from the consequences of their official acts, and thus exemplifying the converse of the English principle of equality of all before the law. The office, or rather commission, of *conseiller d'état* was much sought after, and was a recognized avenue to higher appointments. The Conseil Privé was presided over by the Chancellor.

The great officers of state included the Chancellor, the Controller-General of Finance and the four secretaries of state. The Chancellor was Keeper of the Seals, head of the whole judicial system, and superintended the censorship of the press. Also, he exercised jurisdiction over universities and academies and, as if to symbolize the eternity of justice, he did not wear mourning at the king's funeral. After 1665 the Controller-General of Finance added to his financial functions duties connected with the regulation of agriculture, industry

---

[89] For the malversations of French financiers see De Janzé, *Les Financiers d'autrefois, Fermiers généraux.*

and communications. It was Colbert who made this office approximate, by its great scope, to the position of a modern prime minister, with the difference, however, that he was responsible to the king, not the nation. The Controller-General was almost always a minister of state, and he might also be a secretary of state, as was Colbert, in which case his activities covered a very wide field indeed. The secretaries of state were divided between the four departments of War, Foreign Affairs, Marine and Royal Establishment (Maison du Roi). Originally subordinate clerks or notaries, the secretaries had become important officials by the beginning of the seventeenth century. Their functions were complicated by the fact that different provinces of France were assigned to each. Thus in 1626 the secretary of state for the Maison du Roi had also a certain responsibility for the Ile de France, Berry and the Orléanais; Languedoc and Guienne were allotted to the secretary for Foreign Affairs; the Bourbonnais, Champagne, Burgundy and Normandy were the domain of the secretary for Marine; while War and the Fleets of the East were linked, in this extraordinary way, with the administration of Poitou, the Limousin, Angoumois, Dauphiné and Provence. Not only did the four secretaries divide the country between them, but they also divided the year, each one having a period of three months in which he dealt with general correspondence. To make confusion more confounded, Foreign Affairs included pensions, War entailed control of frontier provinces, Marine included colonies, commerce and consulates, while Maison du Roi involved, in addition to control of royal buildings and staffs, presentation to livings, the affairs of the Huguenots, and supervision over the administration of Paris. Between 1669 and 1693 Colbert was Controller-General of Finance and secretary of state for both Marine and Maison du Roi; the mere enumeration of his functions would therefore be tedious.

As the century progressed there was increasing contrast between the economy of France and that of the maritime states, England and Holland. With her comparatively large population, her natural resources, which were rich in all but minerals, her highly centralised bureaucracy, France was exploiting to the full the advantages of a civilisation more static and self-contained than that of her rivals, because less dependent on shipping and overseas markets. In consequence

French industry and commerce did not benefit to the same extent from the new opportunities in the eastern and western hemispheres which brought such advantage to English and Dutch, a fact which helps to account for at least two distinctive things in the later history of France. One is that the fiscal system became more rigid and stereotyped, because, as it could not utilise new sources, it had to tighten the pressure on old ones; as there was little increase from the Customs, more had to be extracted from capitation taxes and the sale of offices. The other consequence followed, namely, that as the French seigneur had less opportunity for making money, he was obliged to retain and even intensify those feudal dues and exactions which were falling into desuetude in England, where so many better sources of income were available. While the English landlord was making a fortune from corn, or wool or minerals, the French landlord was squeezing the last *sou* from his mills and manorial dues. In this way there was produced a certain hardening, or even ossification in the structure of French society, contrasted with the more free interplay of classes in England, and with the gradualness whereby many privileges were mitigated or tacitly surrendered.

SPAIN—Seventeenth-century Spain illustrates two characteristics of Spanish history—the strength of traditionalism, and the sustained antagonisms of both national interests and old kingdoms. Neither Renaissance nor Reformation had left an enduring mark on the peninsula; and, as in no other country, mediaevalism still survived, with its Christian literalism, its dislike of innovation and experiment, and its willing tolerance of poverty. The two main industries—sheep-farming and agriculture—were kept in antagonism, as nowhere else in Europe, by the royal support given to the Mesta,[90] or national gild of sheep farmers, which still represented the older nomadic and pastoral economy, contrasted with enclosures for arable or afforestation for timber. But the Mesta, though still rich, was now deriving much of its wealth from sources other than sheep farming; and enclosures, whether for cattle or agriculture, were impeding the annual migra-

[90] For this see J. Klein, *The Mesta* (1920).

tions, so that by the end of the century a good proportion of the sheep industry had passed from the control of the Mesta into the hands of the stationary grazier. Even thus, however, agriculture did not prosper under the Spanish Hapsburgs, mainly because there was little national aptitude for the routine labour and personal organization requisite for successful farming. Another economic factor was the decline in the bullion imports from the New World.[91] Many mines were already used up; the treasure fleets had often to run the gauntlet of English and Dutch freebooters, and moreover, the Spanish colonists, as they began to trade directly with Asia, became more independent of the mother country. The immediate result had been that Philip II. was obliged to debase the coinage, and this was carried to such lengths by his successors that gold and silver were practically driven out of circulation. Moreover repudiation of public debt still further weakened national credit. Hence the seventeenth-century rulers of Spain had at their disposal economic resources inadequate for the world-wide commitments inherited from their predecessors.

Spain was by no means a homogeneous nation, and in the seventeenth century there still survived much separatist feeling in the provinces. Six Spanish kingdoms preserved their Cortès or representative estates—Castille, Aragon, Catalonia, Valencia, Majorca and Navarre. These assemblies, consisting of representatives of clergy, nobility and towns, acknowledged the heir to the throne, registered the king's coronation oath and, when called upon, voted subsidies. But they had no initiative; they were not regularly summoned, nor had they any public support behind them, for the towns regarded representation as a burden. Gradually they ceased to interest themselves even in taxation, and in 1624 Philip claimed the right to levy taxes without reference to the Cortès, while in 1665 an edict[92] transferred the right of granting taxes to the municipal councils. The Cortès of Castille were not once summoned between 1665 and 1700; though Aragon, Catalonia, Valencia and Navarre still held assemblies, their

[91] E. J. Hamilton, *American Treasure and the Price Revolution in Spain.*

[92] Altamira y Crevea, *Historia de España*, iii. 258.

meetings were infrequent, as they insisted on the presence of the king. Like France, therefore, Spain, in the course of the seventeenth century, lost her representative institutions.

A Venetian ambassador[93] declared in 1605 that the government of Spain savoured more of a republic than a monarchy. This is accounted for by the fact that Spanish kings were little better than titular presidents of the councils to which was entrusted the practical work of administration. These councils were: the Council of State, the Council of the Inquisition, the Council of Finance, the Council of Crusade and the Council of War. There were also two Senates, one sitting at Burgos or Valladolid, the other at Granada. The Councils of State, Inquisition and War were absolute: the first received ambassadors and decided questions of foreign policy; the Council of the Inquisition, in addition to its ecclesiastical control, regulated sequestrated estates and questions connected with usury, intervening also between the Papacy and the Church of Spain; the Council of War had control over the entire military resources of the country. It was remarked[94] that if Henry VIII. of England had been assisted by such councils he would have been able to obtain his divorce without breaking with the Papacy. Valencia, Catalonia and Aragon, with the islands of Majorca, Minorca and Sardinia, were united with Spain in the crown of Aragon, but each province had a viceroy and retained its own laws. The power of the councils was, however, steadily diminished in the seventeenth century by the increasing prerogatives of the three secretaries representing the Cabinet (*Despacho*), the North and Castille, and Italy, these permanent officials forming, with the first minister and the confessor, an informal and secret council (*consulta*). In this way the kings of Spain proved easy victims for greedy favourites, and so government in seventeenth-century Spain was personal and capricious; it was also corrupt, for no other country could offer so many sinecures.[95] Nearly a fifth part of the population was composed of state servants; and as a considerable proportion of the remainder were priests, it may

[93] Simon Contarini, in *Relazioni degli ambasciatori veneti* (Spain), i. 293.

[94] Simon Contarini, in *Relazioni degli ambasciatori veneti* (Spain), ii. 278.

[95] Altamira y Crevea, *op. cit.* iii. 336 ff.

be said that Spain in this period lived mainly by prayers and pensions. In 1627 it was declared that the monasteries were the only places where people were not dying of starvation.[96]

It was sometimes wondered how Spain managed to employ troops in so many parts of the world: it was done by keeping the pay of the army in permanent arrears.[97] The national revenues were pledged to the bankers of Genoa for several years in advance, and the interest exacted was a high one. Not till Spain lost her European dependencies did she become solvent—an illustration of the truth that territorial conquest does not necessarily bring wealth. It was a country of vast natural resources and the most grinding poverty, of minute legislation and incompetent officialdom; combining innumerable schools and universities[98] with a high percentage of national illiteracy; where, in the absence of a strong middle class, there was a sharp antithesis between, on the one hand, the grandee, whether lay or ecclesiastical, and, on the other, a population of shepherds, vine-dressers and wool-workers.[99] As perhaps the only country in Europe where family pride was always placed before wealth, Spain interested a few observers, because this quality was becoming rare in the seventeenth century, and there are signs that foreigners[100] were sometimes charmed by the harmonious combination of glaring inconsistencies which formerly impressed travellers in this the least commercialized and most enigmatic of European countries. One characteristic expression of this family pride is seen in the practice of entailing estates, a practice very common in the seventeenth century. Poor people who had saved a little were tempted to invest their money in land and devise their estates in such a way as to provide the best security that at least one of the family would always be idle. These *Mayorazgos*,[101] as such entailed estates were called, provided an incentive to limitation of the population, and, where there

[96] Picatoste, *La Grandeza ye decadencia de España,* iii. 36.

[97] *Relazioni degli ambasciatori veneti* (Spain), i. 333.

[98] Altamira, iii. 540 ff.

[99] "Restano con la lor gonfiezza pieni di crassa ignoranza" (Soranzo, 1602, in *Relazioni . . .,* Spain, i. 127).

[100] *E.g.* the French ambassador Rebenac in *Instructions données aux ambassadeurs de France* (Spain), 424 ff.

[101] Altamira, *op. cit.* iii. 423 ff.

were younger sons, emigration was often the only alternative to destitution. At least one contemporary regarded this as a cause of Spain's decline.

ITALY—Inheritor of the legacy of ancient Rome, Italy had already produced, in St. Thomas Aquinas and Dante, the greatest of the mediaeval scholastics and poets; she had provided the inspiration for at least two "renaissances," that of the twelfth century and that of the fifteenth, and she still afforded a contrast of extreme intellectualism and intolerant obscurantism. But long before the expedition of Charles VIII of France (1494) Italy had been invaded or exploited by a succession of foreigners, notably Angevin, Spanish, French and German, and in this period was apportioned, in accordance with the treaty of Cateau Cambrésis (1559), as follows: the whole of the Milanese (including Pavia and Cremona), with Naples, Sicily, Sardinia and the Tuscan defended ports[102] (*presidi*), all became Spanish territory, ruled by viceroys, leaving as independent states—Savoy (which then included Piedmont, most of the modern French departments of Savoy, and a large area of the modern Hautes-Alpes); the republic of Venice (stretching from the Adda to the Adriatic and including Dalmatia up to Ragusa); the republic of Genoa (possessing Corsica); the republic of Lucca; the marquisate of Montferrat and the duchy of Mantua (both under the Gonzagas); the duchies of Parma and Piacenza, under the Farnese; Modena and Ferrara,[103] under the Este; Tuscany, under the Medici; Urbino, under the Della Rovere; and Rome, under the Papacy. The internal frontiers underwent little change, but the control of Mantua and Montferrat was fiercely disputed between France and Spain; moreover, Richelieu's acquisition of Pinerolo was a source of constant disquiet. The hold acquired by the French, first on Pinerolo (1631), then on Mantua (1631), finally on Casale (1681), prevented Spain maintaining uncontested control over northern Italy, especially as the policy of Venice was consistently pro-French and anti-Hapsburg, while that of Savoy, in spite of vacillation, was

[102] Porto Ercole, Porto San Stephano, Orbitello, Piombino, Telamone and Porto Longone in Elba.
[103] Ferrara was acquired by the Papacy in 1597 on the extinction of the line of Este.

mainly anti-Spanish. It should be noted that Mantua and Casale were then among the most important fortresses in Europe. Savoy, the most vigorous of the independent Italian states, was governed by a line of able and ambitious dukes; in the seventeenth century the duchy became more distinctively Italian and Piedmontese, Turin becoming the capital in place of Chambéry.

Of the dependent states Milan and Naples were, politically, the most important. In Milan the power of the governor was tempered to a certain extent by the existence of the Estates of clergy and nobility. Early in the sixteenth century Louis XII. had established a Senate on the model of the Paris Parlement. The Senate could interpose its veto three times, after which it had to yield. The *Ufficio Camerale Giudiziario-Finanziario* controlled finance and was generally at variance with the Senate. The *Consiglio Segreto*, of which about half were Spaniards, dealt with all matters requiring secrecy and despatch, and, after the death of Philip II., this council displaced the Senate in importance. The viceroy nominated all state officials.[104] Sicily was in worse plight, because it was saddled with a permanent Spanish garrison, its judicial administration was controlled from Spain, and it was under the Inquisition. The three Estates of Sicily—ecclesiastical, baronial or military, and popular or demesne—still met and voted subsidies, but they were subordinate and had to vote without discussion. Naples was governed by a viceroy, and until 1642 there existed Estates whose powers were nominal. Thus it is true to say that in the Italian dependencies Spanish rule was for the most part absolute, and rode roughshod over such representative institutions as still survived.

But in more subtle ways Spain contrived to ruin Italian character and independence. Thus in the preceding century Sicily had been a great grain-exporting province. Spain now made a monopoly of grain,[105] storing the surplus in government granaries and imposing a prohibitive tax on export. In this way merchants from Venice and Lucca were obliged to send to Egypt for supplies. The universal craze for rank and elaborate armorial bearings was cleverly utilized to create a large clientèle of sycophants, while the mob was kept quiet by

[104] Callegari, *Preponderanze straniere*, 136 ff.
[105] *Ibid*. 142.

innumerable spectacles and processions.[106] As direct taxes fell almost entirely on the poor, and indirect taxes almost exclusively on necessities, the greater part of the subject population was kept just on the level of subsistence, a sudden rise in the price of bread or fruit being frequently followed by revolution. "They will pay," said a Spanish official, on hearing that a new tax would involve great hardship on the poor, "even if they have to sell the honour of their wives and daughters." In addition, Italy suffered from the usual inflictions of tax-farming, debased coinage, repudiation of government contracts and openly venal justice. Coronations, marriages and wars all provided pretexts for further demands on the exhausted sources of Italian revenue, and honest Spanish administrators were generally recalled, as it was believed in Madrid that personal interests could best be combined with the interests of the state.[107] A fragment of a manuscript diary of 1670 describes Neapolitan life late in the seventeenth century in the following terms: the religious orders were at strife as to which should most exalt its patron; the nobility, who should excel in pomp and zeal in defending his honour; the lower classes, who should show greatest skill in cheating or should be most easily provoked to kill, and all this in a mass of saints' days, processions, masquerades, tumults, challenges and duels.[108] Well might Charles Emanuel of Savoy declare in the Memoirs intended for his heir: "Of all servitudes, the most harsh and insupportable is that of Spain."[109] It is noteworthy that the Philippics[110] against Spain, written by Tassoni, were inspired by this Duke of Savoy, who alone among Italian princes resented the onerous yoke of Spain, and in whose descendants Italy was one day to find her kings.

POLAND—The one exception to the general rule of political evolution in the seventeenth century is provided by Poland,[111] an exception so striking that it must have served as an object lesson to both statesmen and theorists. While in other coun-

---

[106] Ibid. 155, and La vita italiana nel seicento, 80.

[107] Callegari, op. cit. 147.

[108] Ibid. 155.

[109] Ibid. 157.

[110] See V. Biagi, Le Filippiche in Miscellanea Tassoniana.

[111] A good account of Poland in 1664 will be found in the Instructions to Bonsy in Instructions données . . . (Poland), 52 ff.

tries kings were shaking off the last remaining shackles of popular control and bulding up absolutist and militarist states, the Republic[112] of Poland was restricting more and more the power of its kings and illustrating vividly the lengths to which disunion might go. A loosely joined federation of predominantly Slavonic states, Poland had been united with Lithuania by the Jagellon kings, a line of able monarchs who waged a successful war against their rivals the Teutonic knights and in the fifteenth and sixteenth centuries made the Republic a great power. With the accession of the Vasa kings in 1587 (the crown having become elective), centrifugal forces again asserted themselves and the period of degeneration begins. Elsewhere feudal institutions had helped to create powerful burgher communities and a great middle class in which kings had found their best support against a powerful nobility, while throughout western Europe the Church, as the sole repository of culture and recruited from all ranks, had provided valuable servants for the state and had identified itself with national aspirations.[113] But in Poland there was no middle class, and in the seventeenth century the Church was controlled by an international order—the Jesuits. The *Szlachta* or great landowners monopolized both landed property and political power,[114] disguising their sovereignty behind a puppet king (whose hands were tied by the *Pacta Conventa* limiting his prerogative), and administering their vast domains by the help of Jewish intendants who created a monopoly that included the fundamental rites of religion. The Jesuits proved to be the only educative political force, and, despite their allegiance to a foreign power, they provided the only institution capable of rousing any national sentiment in a country where patriotism itself was often a mere pretext for disorder. Long before the era of partitions Poland presented a mass of contradictions and inconsistencies—a country of immense extent but no frontiers, of intense national feeling and constant dismemberment, of perpetual war but no conquests, insisting on equality

---

[112] *Respublica* in the Roman sense.

[113] See N. A. de Salvandy, *Histoire du roi Jean Sobieski et du royaume de Pologne* (ed. 1876), i. 24 ff.

[114] The Polish nobility might lose their status by "abuse of liberty" or by "state crimes." In 1633 the former was defined as "exercising a vulgar occupation, taking up commerce or owning a cabaret" (*Instructions données* . . ., Poland, Introduction).

and everywhere submitting to the most iniquitous oppression, devoted to the cause of liberty and admitting the worst forms of serfdom, having a constitution that provided for innumerable checks and balances but not for effective government, with obedience as the chief kingly virtue and anarchy the permanent national characteristic. No state can function unless minorities can at any time be ignored or crushed: the British House of Lords is unique in allowing to minorities the privilege of recording their dissent. But by the *liberum veto* the Polish Diet insisted on absolute unanimity, the dissent of one member being sufficient to nullify proceedings; it is not remarkable, therefore, that meetings of the Diet were sometimes enlivened by casualties, and where the exerciser of the *liberum veto* had found safety in flight, he generally made his next public appearance at the head of an armed following. The history of Poland proves that idealism and practical politics are not always compatible, and that peoples too quixotic to rule themselves are eventually ruled by others.

RUSSIA—Russia had been diverted from the main stream of European development by two things—conversion to the Orthodox Greek Church at the end of the tenth century, and the invasion of the Tartars in the thirteenth, followed by their domination for more than two centuries. Like Poland, the Muscovite state had been immune from most of those mediaeval conceptions and institutions which in western Europe constituted the system loosely designated Feudalism, for the Grand Duchy of Moscow had no classes of knights and burgesses, and the Church, divided sharply between cloistered monks and village priests had no opportunity for providing the statesmen and administrators who had played such a decisive part in the West. Moreover Russia was uninfluenced by either Renaissance or Reformation. Other characteristics can be accounted for by her geography and her precarious frontiers. Apart from the Arctic regions and the Caspian area, there was always a vital distinction between the forest lands of the North and the steppes of the South, the first under the semi-oriental autocracy of Moscow, the second under the more flexible rule of Kiev.[115] From the West, there was the continual pressure of Swedes, Lithuanians and Poles, and of

[115] P. Milioukov, *Histoire de Russie*, i. 58-9.

Tartars from the South and East. It was due mainly to her central position that Moscow was not continually over-run by these hordes, and so the Grand Duchy survived into the seventeenth century, and was enlarged into an effective suzerainty by the Romanoffs. But though some degree of unity was achieved, it was the unity of an armed camp.[116]

The main interest of seventeenth-century Russia is that events forced on the Tsars a development of the state which outstripped the national economy.[117] In this process foreign models were bound to have influence. Nearest to hand was the Greek or Byzantine model, with its minutely-regulated bureaucracies, its elaborate ceremonial and its obscurantism; alternatively, there was the German or western model, with its greater freedom from tradition, its co-operation with the towns and burgesses, and its more highly developed sense of the amenities of life. It was the latter which finally prevailed in the reign of Peter the Great, and for long Russians contrasted Greek with German, the first a symbol of reaction, the second of progress. In the nineteenth century a number of radicals substituted "Tartar" for "Greek" as the origin of the reactionary forces in Russian society, but a more recent school[118] has rejected altogether these estimates of the part played by external influences, and has claimed to find in the Tartar or Mongolian element an explanation both of the tenacity of the Russian character and of its freedom from those symptoms of race degeneration which writers like Spengler have purported to find in the West. These theories merely serve to illustrate the variety of forces which have gone to the making of modern Russia.

Defence against the invader was the primary duty of the seventeenth-century Tsars, and the administration of the state developed as a series of rapid improvisations, some of them followed by chaos, until late in the life of Peter the Great, when a measure of stability was achieved. This evolution is reflected by the changes in landholding. In the preceding cen-

[116] A. Miller, *Histoire des institutions agraires de la Russie centrale du XVIᵉ au XVIIIᵉ siècle*, 34-44.

[117] P. Milioukov, *op. cit.* 178.

[118] *Ibid.* 30-31. This school, composed mainly of young refugees, has taken the name of Eurasian, and finds its starting point in the empire of Genghis Khan. See G. Vernadskij, *History of Russia*, 1929.

tury the unit was the *Pomestia*, of which the use—it might be only the life use—was granted to the *Pomestchik*, usually a civil or military functionary,[119] who provided some definite service to the state, and cultivated his holding, occasionally with the help of serfs (who were few in number) but more usually with the help of free peasants. But in the course of the seventeenth century, with the beginnings of foreign trade, a monetary system was introduced, and the agrarian economy began to lose in importance. The wars helped to discredit the Russian territorial cavalry, and more regular battalions of infantry and cavalry, and even of mercenaries had to be employed.[120] In this way the *Pomestia* lost its connection with state service; the *Pomestchik* became a hereditary landowner, and as his new ownership extended to the peasant cultivators, many of them already in his debt, these were everywhere becoming serfs. It is true that Peter the Great restored the old connection between land and state service, but meantime serfdom had become an established institution in Russia. This was the most important social consequence of those changes in military organisation which alone made possible the achievement of national unity, and it may be said that much of Russian history in this period can be explained as the result not of development from within, but of pressure from without.

TURKEY—In the fifteenth century the constitution of Turkey in Europe had been promulgated and defined by Mohammed II. in his Kanoun Namé of fundamental law, and seventeenth-century Turkey was still regulated mainly in terms of this edict.[121] Four was the mystic number, and the principal dignitaries were the *Grand Vizier*; the *Kazi-Asker*, or Judge Advocate; the *Defterdar*, or Minister of Finance, and the *Nichandji*, or Secretary of State. The Grand Vizier had custody of the Seals and corresponded to the Chancellor in western European countries. The Kiuprili dynasty provided, in the seventeenth century, a line of able and energetic Grand Viziers. Characteristic of the union of theology and jurispru-

---

[119] Miller, *op. cit.* 47-8.

[120] *Ibid.* 72-3.

[121] La Jonquière, *Histoire de l'Empire Ottoman*, ch. ix., and Zinkeisen, *Geschichte des osmanischen Reiches*, III. ch. i.

dence to be found in many Oriental countries is the semi-religious office of *Grand Mufti* and the corps of the *Ulemas*. The *Grand Mufti* was not only the chief religious dignitary, but also "the oracle of all doubtful questions in the law";[122] from the *Ulemas* were recruited civil servants, magistrates and teachers, so that this body provided a great hierarchy of the professional classes, promotion being regulated by study and examination. There was no system of appeal in the Turkish judicial system, on the ground that once a case had been decided it could not again be considered.

"If a man seriously consider," wrote Rycaut,[123] "the whole composition of the Turkish Court, he will find it to be a prison and banniard of slaves, differing from that where the galley slaves are immured only by the ornaments and glittering out-side. If a man considers the contexture of the whole Turkish government, he will find it such a fabrick of slavery, that it is a wonder if any amongst them should be born of a free, ingenious spirit. The Grand Seignior is born of a slave." The same writer regarded frequent changes among officials as a measure conducing to the welfare of the Turkish state; hence the importance of the executioner in the constitutional history of Turkey. There were said to be seventy-two religious sects in Turkey,[124] but the one common creed was a belief in predestination, for it was held that every man's destiny is written on his forehead. Owing to the uncertainty of life the arts were not cultivated, the Turk seldom making any plans for more than ten years ahead.

The Kanoun Namé had sanctioned the murder of the Sultan's brothers, but in the sixteenth century this practice was modified; in the seventeenth, each Sultan could exercise his own discretion. The power of the Sultan was absolute except in so far as he was expected to consult the *Ulemas*, who, as the repositories of law and religion, had the prerogative of giving advice on any proposed enterprise. Strong personalities like Murad IV. acted independently, but some of the seventeenth-century Sultans were constitutionally inca-pable of thinking for themselves and so deferred to the opinion

[122] Rycaut, *The Maxims of Turkish Policy* (4th ed., 1675), 190.
[123] *Ibid.* p. 16.
[124] *Ibid.* p. 210.

of the *Ulemas*, or, as more often happened, practically transferred their powers to the Grand Viziers.

The conquerors never assimilated themselves with the subject races of the Balkans, leaving them to retain many of the worst features of Byzantine administration, and always emphasizing a social and religious superiority. In Sophia, for instance, Jews and Christians alike were obliged to construct their doors three feet from the ground so that their houses could not conveniently be used as stables by Turkish horsemen.[125] Only in vice was there any real community between European and Turk. Nevertheless the Ottomans trained up the sons of Christian captives to form the famous corps of Janissaries, the mainstay of the Turkish army, and many descendants of Christians attained high rank in the Turkish civil service.

It should be remembered that the resources of European Turkey were frittered away in the defence of the Persian frontier, which played the same part in Turkish destinies as the Flemish frontier played in Spanish. An exclusively theocratic and military state, Turkey declined as soon as one of these elements weakened, and it was held together only by the energy and military capacity of such Grand Viziers as the Kiuprilis. After the defeat of Lepanto and the passing of Suleiman the Magnificent, Turkish prestige diminished. An interesting comment on this decline is provided by the *Rissala*[126] or Report which Khodji-Beg, the so-called Montesquieu of Turkey, presented to Sultan Murad IV. Among the causes of decadence noted by this thoughtful and observant Turk were, first, the custom whereby the Sultan had withdrawn himself from public gaze and confined himself to effeminate and luxurious pursuits; second, the appointment of favourites to the highest posts in the Empire; third, the increased influence of the harem on public life; fourth, the acquiring of military fiefs by minors and women who could not perform military service; and, fifth, the admission of Turks and Jews into the corps of the Janissaries for the social advantages which mem-

---

[125] *Travels of Peter Mundy* (ed. Temple, Hakluyt Society), i. 152.

[126] Khodji-Beg's *Rissala* is a description of the evidences rather than the causes of Turkey's degeneration.

bership conferred. Lastly, the conservative mind of Khodji-Beg was shocked by the almost complete abandonment of the long-tried Turkish institution whereby the Sultan's younger brothers were killed off as early as possible; they were now frequently allowed to live and so become centres of intrigue.

But even thus, the military resources of the Ottoman Empire were not to be despised, and Turkey "in decline" has long survived to upset the calculations of Western diplomats by abundant proofs of a vigorous old age.

Chapter 2

Restoration of the French Monarchy, 1598–1610

ON THE 17th of September 1595 Henry of Navarre's two emissaries, Du Perron and D'Ossat, received formal absolution on behalf of their master from Pope Clement VIII. Kneeling before the pontiff in the presence of the Curia, the two supplicants recited the *Miserere* to the accompaniment of taps on their persons from the papal rod, and, but that Henry himself was not present, the wars of the League might thus seem to have ended in a new Canossa. "It felt like a mouse going over my shoulders," was the recorded impression[1] of one of the royal agents. Though preachers like Boucher proclaimed that even God could not absolve the renegade Henry, yet the ceremony of papal absolution eased the consciences of many who could not think that the Bourbon's conversion was sincere. Thus was completed what Arques and Ivry had begun, and with the help of the *Satire Ménippée* the surviving Leaguers were completely discredited by the most potent weapon in the public life of France— ridicule. There were misgivings that a Huguenot who turned Catholic for the sake of a kingdom might still be a Huguenot at heart, and it was significantly remarked that "the pocket still retains the smell of the herring," but for the moment

[1] Quoted in *Instructions données aux ambassadeurs de France* (Rome), xc.

Frenchmen were prepared to sink their religious differences and welcome a ruler who had already given such signal proofs of valour and resource.

In the stormy years when he was fighting for a throne, the first of the royal Bourbons had shown himself possessed of unusual qualities. Now in his forty-third year, of middle height, his body disciplined by long campaigns and his mind broadened by contact with men who were colleagues before they were courtiers, Henry exacted unswerving obedience from his servants, and could disarm even enemies by an engaging simplicity. Frankly sensual, he did not make his failings worse by hypocrisy. His thoughts flowed in single and direct channels, so that in speech he was straightforward and clear; and his letters[2] still charm by their candour and naïveté. Vivacity, imagination, intelligence and common sense are the qualities which made him the best ruler of his age and the most beloved of all French kings. Add to these his romantic career and tragic death, his bourgeois tastes and his European pre-eminence, his bad example as a husband and good qualities as a father, his intensely serious task and unfailing sense of humour, and one acclaims in Henry IV. a king who was great enough to be human. "Je suis gris au dehors, mais tout doré au dedans,"[3] was his characteristic method of proclaiming that, though by profession a king, he had the understanding and sympathies of a man.

With the conclusion of peace between France and Spain at Vervins (2nd May 1598), and the withdrawal of Spanish troops from Picardy, the settled rule of Henry IV. may be said to commence. The Edict of Nantes had been signed a few days before (13th April), and this marked the culminating point of a long series of concessions to the Huguenots. During the later part of the sixteenth century the French Protestants had gradually built up a state within the state, having their own troops, their own organization and assemblies, and endowed with the privilege of securing uniformity within their walled towns by expelling minorities. Civil war had only strengthened this formidable body; accordingly one of Henry's first acts was to come to terms with an armed

[2] There is a good selection in Nouillac, *Henri IV, Raconté par lui-même.*

[3] Pierre l'Estoile, *Mémoires Journaux*, vii. 138.

organization of which he had himself once been leader. The Edict of Nantes granted liberty of conscience to Huguenots in every part of the kingdom, allowing public exercise of their cult in all places where it had become established in the two preceding years, with the exception of the area within five leagues of Paris. Ministers of state, courtiers and officers could, even when in attendance at court, celebrate the reformed faith in their lodgings, provided the doors were closed and the psalm-singing not loud enough to attract attention. Protestants were accorded all the civil rights enjoyed by Catholics; *chambres-mi-parties* or composite committees were created for adjudicating suits in which Huguenots were involved, and these served as adjuncts to the Parlements of Paris, Bordeaux and Grenoble. All administrative and official posts were in future to be open to Protestants, their separate organization, with its synods and representative assemblies, was legalized, and, even more, they were allowed to retain for five years about a hundred walled towns which they could organize for defence, including the important fortresses of La Rochelle, Montauban and Montpellier.[4] The garrisons of these towns were to be maintained at the expense of the state. Finally, the Edict was declared irrevocable and perpetual. Until 1629, the Huguenots formed an armed, independent minority, and until 1685, a peaceable and industrious religious community.

As a comprehensive measure of religious freedom accorded at a time when toleration was practically unknown, the Edict of Nantes has probably no parallel in history. It seems almost to err on the side of generosity, for it granted the Huguenots political as well as religious independence. But it must be remembered that there was an ulterior object. The idea that a state must be absolutely homogeneous in religion was so generally accepted by statesmen and political theorists as scarcely to require enunciation: force had failed to convert the Huguenots, might not clemency succeed? The hope was always entertained that the exponents of the "Religion Prétendue Réformée" would eventually see the error of their ways and gratefully return to the fold. When this expectation proved futile, and the Huguenots were seen to be more con-

4 Lavisse, *Histoire de France,* VI. i. ch. ix.

firmed than ever in their faith, legal chicanery was put to work and the Edict subjected to pettifogging interpretations which, long before its revocation, robbed it of its value. But for a time the Protestants of France were safe; the civil wars were over, and after more than thirty years of strife and anarchy Henry IV. commenced his rule over a pacified but exhausted France.

In his work of restoration and revival Henry showed by his choice of ministers that, while ready to reward old friends, he was prepared to forget past enmities. Of his ministers, Villeroy, Jeannin and Villars were former Leaguers; they collaborated with the Huguenots, Sully, Lesdiguières and Olivier de Serres, while even the unyielding Duplessis-Mornay, who had opposed Henry's abjuration, retained his governorship of Saumur. The executive consisted of the king in council, a council not yet clearly differentiated but appearing in three forms—the *Conseil Privé*, the *Conseil d'Etat et des Finances*, and the *Conseil pour la direction des Finances*, of which the third merely prepared statistics for the guidance of the second. The council was nominally open to all the greater nobles and upper clergy, but in practice Henry reduced the number of effective councillors to about a dozen, including Bellièvre, Sillery (who became Chancellor in 1607), Sully, the great finance minister, Châteauneuf, and the President Jeannin. An informal and executive Council of Affairs considered reports from the four secretaries of state in order to advise the king on matters of general policy. Henry's rule was absolute, but it was an intelligent and unostentatious absolutism,[5] and its details were carried out by men who were not merely personal favourites. There were no *lits de justice*, but the Parlement was nevertheless required to register his edicts, and though the great nobles were excluded from all but honorary functions, the king reserved the right to summon those members of the nobility whom he desired to consult. The States-General did not once meet

---

[5] "He" (Henry IV.) "used soft language with determined conduct. He asserted and maintained his authority in the gross, and distributed his acts of concession only in the detail. He spent the income of his prerogative nobly: but he took care not to break in upon the capital" (Burke, *Reflections on the Revolution in France*).

in his reign and there was only one Assembly of Notables,[6] but, on the other hand, the provincial Estates were frequently convened. Ominous for the future is the fact that the distinction between Pays d'Etats and Pays d'Elections was not always respected, while Henry's attempt to lessen municipal privileges and to model the constitutions of the towns on that of Amiens (whose mayor was a royal nominee) must be numbered among his more arbitrary acts.

Henry had ceased to live with his queen, Marguerite of Valois, and was under the sway of Gabrielle d'Estrées, whose two sons he wished to legitimate, probably in order that one of them might succeed to the throne. Gabrielle died suddenly[7] on the 10th of April 1599, and contemporaries coupled this event with the activities of those who, in the interests of the monarchy, wished to save Henry from himself. Late in the following year he married Marie de Medici, by whom he had a son, the Dauphin, born in September 1601. This unfortunately did not free him from an ex-favourite, Henriette d'Entragues, and her turbulent relatives, since he now had a son by Henriette and was said to have given her his promise that he would marry her if she gave him a male heir. The hope of seeing the legitimate son ousted by the illegitimate led to an extensive plot which involved the Constable Montmorency, and later developed into a dangerous conspiracy headed by Biron, Governor of Burgundy, and the Duc de Bouillon, the most powerful and discontented Huguenot in France. The plot included also Charles Emanuel of Savoy, its avowed object being the subversion of Henry's government and the complete independence of the provincial governors. It is to the credit of the Huguenots that, though offered the control of the south-west and Dauphiné, they refused as a body to take part in what was clearly an attempt to restore feudal anarchy in France. By the month of March 1602 Henry was in possession of all the facts.[8] Arrested in June of the same year Biron was handed over to the Parlement for trial, and was executed in July. The Count of Auvergne, an illegitimate son of Charles IX. by Henriette's

[6] At Rouen in 1596. For this see Sully, *Mémoires et sages œconomies d'estat* (ed. 1664), I. lxvii.

[7] For details see Pierre l'Estoile, *Mémoires Journaux*, vii. 352. One of her sons was the Duc de Vendôme.

[8] Lavisse, *Histoire de France*, vi. pt. 2, ch. ii.

mother, was spared, thereby estranging public opinion, which contrasted this leniency with the swift justice meted out to Biron.[9] Bouillon fled, and thereafter posed among the German Protestants as a religious martyr.

The restoration of France in this reign was mainly economic, and the briefest survey of events in the last two decades of the sixteenth century will reveal how essential was this reconstruction if the country was ever again to play a leading part in the politics of Europe. A great economist and administrator might have attempted to clear out the augean stable known as the financial system of the Ancien Régime, but such an attempt would certainly have ended in failure or revolution. Originality or brilliance might have been equally fatal. Fortunately none of these qualities was to be found in Maximilien de Béthune, Marquis of Rosny, known to posterity as the Duke of Sully, on whom now devolved the task of saving his country from bankruptcy. An austere Protestant, he had been distinguished from youth by qualities of caution and economy—virtues that commended themselves to Henry, who, like his great Tudor namesake, could appreciate in others qualities that he himself did not possess. Sully's private fortune had been considerably augmented by perquisites acquired during the troublous times of the League, but as Superintendent of Finance he could claim, for perhaps the first time in French history, that his budgets were honest. Six years younger than Henry, he was nevertheless able at times to assume an air of guardianship and even tutorship,[10] sternly refusing money when he suspected that it was required for personal pleasures. Sully combined the office of Superintendent of Finance with the offices of Grand Master of Artillery, Minister of Public Buildings (*Surintendant des Bâtiments*) and Director of Communications (*Grand Voyer*). These diverse duties had this in common, that each contributed to the work of restoring commerce, industry and finance in order that the military defences of the country might be secure. Under this multifarious administration, roads were mended and new ones constructed, flanked with

9 L'Estoile, viii. 41.
10 For instance, see Sully's harangue in his *Mémoires* (ed. 1664), ii. 572, and *ibid.* iii. 276, where Henry promises Sully that he will restrict his gambling operations.

trees nicknamed by the peasants Birons or Rosnys, according as they were cut down or left standing. These improved communications, besides encouraging internal commerce, made possible a better postal service. The army became more national, though strengthened by Swiss and German mercenaries; the number of effectives was increased to nearly 100,000 men; officers ceased to be recruited solely from the nobility; a system of pensions was introduced and a military hospital was established in Paris. By the Briare Canal the Seine and Loire were connected; a beginning was made with a canal joining the Loire to the Saône, and in this way it was intended to link the Channel with the Mediterranean; while the projected Bordeaux-Narbonne canal would have opened up access to the Atlantic. These various schemes, though not completed in this reign, were part of the new administration introduced by Sully.

This administration may be considered in two aspects, according as it aimed at conserving already existing sources of wealth or at devising new ones. It is in keeping with Sully's limitations that the former is the more important category. He conserved national wealth and resources by intervening between the monarch and the large band of greedy and influential harpies who otherwise would have battened on Henry's generosity and weaknesses: to the importunities of such persons his cold glance and ready sarcasm were generally sufficient answers. How much was saved in this way may be conjectured by recalling the enormous sums lavished on favourites at the courts of James I. and Philip III. In Sully's household budgets the royal mistresses had to be provided for, but the line was drawn at their relatives. As well as this, he bought back many valuable sources of revenue which had been pawned during the civil wars in return for sums representing little more, and sometimes even less, than their annual incomes. These creditors included powerful and potentially dangerous foreigners, such as Queen Elizabeth, the Elector Palatine, the Grand Duke of Tuscany, and the republics of Switzerland and Venice. The same policy was applied to those feudal and inalienable rights of the crown that had been lightly sacrificed, and in this way many local officials, such as registrars and governors of prisons, had to repurchase their offices at an enhanced price. An attempt was also made to gain back for the king all those rights pertaining to the royal demesne that had been surrendered, but this failed because of the enormous number of subordinate officials who would have had to be bought out.

Sully could not dispense with the system by which the taxes were farmed out,[11] but he tried to simplify it in order to reduce the number of middle-men. In 1604 all the revenues coming under the category of feudal aids were put up to auction as a consolidated grant (bail général), and were acquired by one man for a period of ten years. Hoping to make the best of a bad system, Sully tried to uproot the most notoriously extortionate and dishonest of the tax-farmers.[12] A judicial commission was established as early as 1597 to inquire into the misdeeds of the more prominent malversators, who promptly warded off the menace by inducing Henry to accept a large "loan," in return for which the commission was cancelled. Thereupon they exacted ransom from their subordinates in the financial hierarchy, and did this so successfully that they made a profit on the whole transaction. But Sully continued his onslaughts on the parasites who were draining the life-blood of the country, so that by the end of the reign their number was considerably diminished. With equally limited success he tried to reform the institution of national life annuities (rentes).[13] Here there was no regular system; the rate of interest was not uniform, and, while the Hôtel de Ville, which issued a portion of this stock, conducted its rente business cheaply, the private bankers insisted on a substantial commission. The project of a general reduction of interest and cancellation of doubtful holdings caused such commotion among the numerous fund-holders in Paris that the proposal had to be abandoned. Nevertheless he was able to effect some economies by redeeming, as cheaply as possible, a considerable part of the stock. Dividends on this national security remained in permanent arrears.

Connected with this first category of Sully's reforms is the order and routine which he introduced into the conduct of his own office. He was not above "wielding the quill" himself, and he was the terror of his clerks. He studied carefully the details of the whole financial system, a system for which the word "complicated" is too generous. In the days before

---

[11] The chief exception was the taille which was not farmed.

[12] Sully, iii. 94.

[13] Sully, II. § xxxvii. and III. § xxv.

regular ministerial salaries he managed to combine his labours with the accumulation of a large private fortune, but this he himself attributed to royal gifts, and by the standards of his day he was scrupulously honest. On entering office he found that expenditure exceeded revenue by more than 50 per cent, and that the national debt amounted to more than 300 million livres. Such figures appear trivial when compared with twentieth-century budgets, but they must have seemed terrifying at a time when French national resources were undeveloped and the mysteries of high finance not understood. It is to Sully's credit that, while initiating no consistent scheme for debt reduction, he did not over-estimate his assets, but aimed at balancing each year's expenditure with receipts. He was even able to reduce the *taille* in 1598, and again in 1600 and 1602, but though these concessions could not be maintained[14] they are specially noteworthy, because many of Sully's schemes of reform required the expenditure of capital in order that important sources of revenue might be redeemed and that the national finances might ultimately benefit. An attempt to extend the *taille* to those who, by acquiring nominal offices were evading it, had only, however, a temporary success. Above all, Sully stopped the peculations of his subordinates, introducing a system of strict bookkeeping to replace the vague generalizations behind which fraud was so easy. Thus he saved the country from bankruptcy, and when in 1609 Henry was about to embark on a European war, there was a treasure of about twelve million livres stored up in the Bastille.

Turning to the second category of Sully's reforms[15]—measures for increasing the national revenues by exploiting new sources—his inventiveness seems disappointing, and the opinion is confirmed that, in comparison with Colbert, Sully was little better than a painstaking clerk. He revived the *don gratuit* or benevolence of the clergy which had fallen into desuetude since 1585, thus providing an additional fund for the payment of the *rentes*. He increased the iniquitous *gabelle*, raising the price of government salt in the Pays de Grande Gabelle by as much as 30 per cent, and, as this tax provided about a fifth part of the total annual revenues, the

14 *Ibid.* III. § xxvi.
15 Lavisse, *Histoire de France*, VI. ii. ch. 3.

measure brought a considerable sum to the Treasury. Moreover, as commerce expanded, the customs gave a larger yield. Offices were subdivided so that they were shared by several persons, and their cost was increased; moreover, when they were transferred, an annual tax of a sixtieth of their net value was imposed. This new tax, instituted in 1604, was named the *paulette*, from the circumstance of its having been farmed for six years to one Charles Paulet; by its payment judicial and administrative offices became practically hereditary. With the steady increase of wealth among the bourgeoisie there was greater competition for these offices, and the state, benefiting by the higher prices, was not anxious to disinherit an incompetent heir, as this would involve a refund of the purchase price.[16]

The meagreness of the constructive side of Sully's work is accentuated, when it is added that many of the most feasible and enterprising projects of the day[17] were hampered or ruined by his open aversion or niggardly support. In this respect Henry showed himself much more enlightened than his minister. The frontispiece to *Le Paysan français*[18] shows a peasant kneeling, beside his harrow and spade, in the presence of Henry and a royal hawking party, and in the text[19] the suppliant announces that "we are just beginning to taste some of the sweet fruits of peace and a restoration of several things that were destroyed by the armed bands." From the first, Henry showed an intelligent appreciation of the importance of agriculture. He forbade the nobles to ride over ripening corn-fields or vineyards, and he applied an elastic policy in export regulations, forbidding the export of wheat only in times of scarcity. He suppressed the ravages of irregular troops; forbade the carrying of arms by private persons; allowed the nobility to claim exemption from the *taille réelle*

[16] The effect of the *paulette* was to make offices hereditary in the sense that the heir would succeed if he had the minimum qualifications. Where there was no heir having any qualifications, the state, in theory, would purchase the office by paying back its original price. In practice, the office would generally be sold to some one having the minimum qualifications.

[17] There is a full account in Fagniez, *L'Economie sociale de la France sous Henri IV*.

[18] 1609.

[19] p. 11.

on lands cultivated by their dependants, and in this way hoped that the peasantry would enjoy greater security and that the nobility would take more interest in the cultivation of their lands. Even more important was Henry's interest in the schemes associated with two Huguenots, Olivier de Serres and Barthélemy Laffemas, for reviving the French silk industry. Experiments in the cultivation of the mulberry tree and the silkworm were made in some of the central and southern provinces, the material, together with an official text-book, being supplied by the government, and practical help was also provided by a corps of experienced silk growers who visited the villages. Unfortunately the expenses of the scheme had to be paid by the peasants themselves, in the form of an increased *taille*, and this discouraged enterprise in a class constantly hovering on the subsistence line and easily tempted to adopt an attitude of fatalism towards any enterprise intended for its benefit. Sully might well have forgone the extra *taille*, but he was prejudiced and regarded silk as an insidious luxury. Nevertheless, although there was little immediate return in this reign, a beginning had been made, and Colbert's subsequent development of this important industry was made possible by the plantations of mulberry trees started at this time.

It is too early to speak of scientific agriculture in the seventeenth century. Implements were primitive and mostly of wood; the properties of the soil were not known, and in the almost universal absence of root crops, such as the turnip, cattle were generally killed in the autumn and salted down for the winter. Not till the turnip became an agricultural crop,[20] as it did in eighteenth-century England, could cattle easily be kept through the winter, and only then did improvement of the breed become possible. But for the scientific improvement of agriculture on a national scale, an enlightened and public-spirited land-holding class is the first essential, and this France did not possess. So long as the fields were at the mercy of armed bands and predatory nobles, no improvement was possible. "A Grand Seigneur," wrote Arthur Young[21] in 1787, "will at any time and in any country explain the reason

---

[20] For the use of the turnip in seventeenth-century Flanders see Prothero, *English Farming Past and Present*, 107.
[21] *Travels in France* (ed. Betham-Edwards), 64.

of improvable land being left waste." Olivier de Serres' book, *Théâtre d'agriculture et mesnage des champs* (1600), was one of the first attempts to interest the French nobility in the peaceful pursuits of country life and was circulated with Henry's cordial approval, but it found little response. Had seventeenth-century France been blessed with a few keen and wealthy agriculturists as England was in the eighteenth, her history might have been very different, and her nobility, from being both idle and dangerous, might have found diversion, profitable for themselves and their dependants, in occupations which, more than any others, help to neutralize human passions by contact with the great and permanent forces of nature.[22] The French landowning classes were interested in the fields merely because they provided sport, in which the peasant was sometimes as legitimate a quarry as the hare. The later schemes of Colbert received no assistance from the nobility, and titled landholders who were too poor to live at Versailles had their revenge by imposing their presence on their estates. The great inquest known as "Les Grands Jours d'Auvergne"[23] (1664) revealed a "tyranny of the country-side" more terrible than any in the annals of English history.

There is a different reason for the only partial success attending Henry's schemes for creating new industries: here not a class of the community, but current economic theories were at fault. It was part of the general opinion of Europe that economic forces could be controlled by edicts and reports of commissions, and that all industries which did not, in some direct way, minister to the military strength of the country were indefensible. A Chamber of Commerce, established in 1601, in which Laffemas was a leading spirit, drafted proposals for regulation of hours of labour, conditions of apprenticeship, supervision of quality and workmanship, and also evolved schemes for new manufactures such as those of glass, gold thread, steel, linen and carpets. These schemes

[22] There were even proposals to grow rice in France at this time. See *Recueil de ce qui se passa en l'assemblée de commerce de Paris*, 1604 (by Laffemas) in *Archives curieuses de l'histoire de France*, xiv. 242.

[23] There is a good account of the abuses revealed by the "Grand Jours" in Feillet, *La Misère au temps de la Fronde*, 490 ff. The best contemporary account is in the *Mémoires* of Fléchier (1665).

were considered by the council, but, while there was plently of legislation, there was little practical encouragement, and in consequence they languished. Moreover, the spirit of initiative was discouraged by Sully, who regarded commercial prosperity as necessarily at the expense of agriculture, and so a menace to national safety. He could not see that even luxury trades may be economically defensible, whether the products are exported or not, but in this respect he voiced the general opinion of his time. It is here that Sully, as compared with Colbert, reveals his limitations. In its economic history Henry's reign, therefore, is one of tentative beginnings rather than completed results.

In other respects the policy of Henry IV. was distinguished by moderation and foresight. Thus, while sharing in the Counter Reformation, the Catholicism of his reign was vigorous without being reactionary. Henry never admitted the disciplinary decrees of the Council of Trent, which, though formally accepted by the French clergy in 1615, were never officially promulgated in France. On the other hand, he recalled the Jesuits in 1603 and, in spite of opposition from Parlement and University, founded their college of La Flèche. The favour which he showed to Coton, Superior of the Jesuits in France, led to the remark that "he had cotton in his ears." It was only by tact and a certain amount of compliance that Coton and his Society avoided strife, for contemporary Catholic opinion was divided on this subject. Henry was quite aware of the doctrines of tyrannicide taught by some of the Spanish Jesuits, but he argued that if the king of Spain could utilize the services of the Jesuits, why should not he? On the whole, the Society did good work in this reign, avoiding as far as possible political entanglements, surviving wide-spread accusations of complicity in Ravaillac's deed, and afterwards becoming strongly entrenched in France until their explusion in 1762. The history of their manifold activities in that period has yet to be written.[24] It is characteristic of Henry's broadmindedness that he patronized literature in the person of Malherbe, learning in Pasquier, Loyseau and De Thou, and invited the Protestant scholar Casaubon to reside in France. Pierre Pithou's *Code of Gallican Liberties*[25] was published in

[24] It has been done (to 1645) by P. H. Fouqueray.
[25] See *infra*, p. 287.

this reign. No other monarch of the century could have associated himself with intellectual activities so spontaneous and divergent.

For the historical student, one of the most important of these writers is the jurist, Charles Loyseau (1566-1627), who is best known for his *Des Seigneuries* (1608) and *Du Droit des offices* (1610). In the *Des Seigneuries* a distinction is made between public and private seigniory, the latter being a matter of private property, while the former—the public seigniory exercised by the state—can be exercised only as consistent with the principles of justice and so is removed from the sphere of personal caprice. In connecting sovereignty with the rights of property Loyseau was following in the footsteps of Bodin, but it was a dangerous path, for nothing was easier than to dispense with reservations which these lawyers made. For Loyseau these reservations consist of certain laws —the laws of God, the natural and positive laws of justice, and the fundamental laws of the state. It was agreed even in Louis XIV.'s time that there were certain fundamental laws, but these were never clearly defined, and in practice were sometimes broken.[26] Bounded by such restrictions, the monarch of Loyseau's theory can make laws, appoint ministers, conclude peace or make war, and coin money. As delegates of royal authority, ministers and magistrates are worthy of special honour, even if they are themselves ignoble persons, for insult to them is insult to the state. Loyseau protests against the venality and heredity of offices, condemning the *paulette* because its institution removes from the king his control over the personnel in his service. The French craze for offices he condemns in unmeasured terms.

Loyseau's theories, while not without liberal elements, show a certain amount of indecision, because they do not make clear the precise limits of the royal power; they tend to make the royal officials sacrosanct, and by equating sovereignty with rights of property they provide a short cut to the completely irresponsible absolutism of Louis XIV. He denies to the Estates any participation in sovereignty and, though he requires that royal edicts shall be registered in Parlement, he admits that the latter can neither reject nor modify such edicts. Loyseau is therefore a good exponent of the theories

[26] There was no official statement of these fundamental laws.

underlying Henry IV.'s practice, but, in common with his contemporaries, he did not realize to what these theories might lead in the hands of a king completely lacking in Henry's sense of humour and proportion. This writer has a further claim to notice in the history of this period, because he is one of the very few in the whole course of the Ancien Régime who protested against the indignity, and even shame, associated with the vocation of agricultural labourer, for he was heretic enough to declare that such labour is in itself dignified, and that the labourer should be accorded a higher social status. But, on the other hand, he believed that the artisans were the most vile in the social order, and only one stage better than able-bodied beggars.

Thus, though Henry's reign was destined to be of comparatively short duration, in it were laid the foundations of the great economic, military and intellectual structure which dominated Europe throughout the seventeenth century. These were years of peace, but intelligent observers had no doubt that over the whole of Europe the clouds were again gathering, and France could not hope to escape from the storm so soon to descend. The old rivalry of France and the Empire, transmuted into the conflict of Bourbon and Hapsburg, appears as a faint but sombre background, and its details come into more vivid prominence during the months immediately preceding Henry's death.

The treaty of Vervins[27] had left unsettled the claim of Charles Emanuel of Savoy to the marquisate of Saluzzo which, or its equivalent, he had undertaken to restore by the treaty of Paris (February 1600). Taking advantage of Biron's conspiracy, the Duke of Savoy delayed fulfilment of this promise, and Henry's reply was to occupy Chambéry[28] with French troops in August of the same year.[29] Fearing that this act of hostility might be followed by a French invasion of Piedmont, Pope Clement VIII., who was influenced by Spanish protests, offered his mediation, and the treaty of Lyons was signed early in 1601. As an equivalent for Saluzzo, the small terri-

[27] Signed in May 1598 between Henry IV. and Philip II. of Spain. Spain restored her captures in Picardy, while France gave up Cambrai.

[28] Chambéry was the old Savoyard capital; it was acquired by France in 1792.

[29] E. Rott, *Henry IV, les Suisses et la Haute Italie*, 78 ff.

tories of Bresse Bugey and Gex were surrendered to France, leaving to Savoy, on the eastern side of the Rhone, a small piece of territory by which Spanish troops could pass through Savoyard territory into Franche Comté. Thus France obtained a valuable addition on her south-eastern frontier, and avoided the entanglements that might have accompanied the possession of a marquisate beyond the Alps. For Italy, it was a confirmation of her subjection to Spain.

During the remaining years of his reign Henry's relations with the Duke of Savoy were friendly, and he had no reason to fear that the Duke would allow Spanish troops to pass through his territories. If he could secure the help of the Swiss cantons, Henry might hope to control the route from the Milanese through the Alpine passes into Franche Comté (then in Spanish possession), and in this way he would sever an important link in the chain between Spanish possessions in northern Italy and in the Low Countries. At the Diet of Soleure in December 1601 the Cantons renewed their alliance with France, conceding free passage for Henry's troops and those of his allies. The Grisons in 1603 accorded to Venice the same privilege in respect of their territories. Thereupon the Spanish Governor of Milan, Fuentes, erected a fort near Lake Como in order to control the Valtelline Pass and so keep Italy exclusively for Spain. Traffic was now diverted to the St. Gothard Pass, and the Grisons, failing to elicit any active support from their allies France and Venice, were left exposed to the constantly increasing threat from Spain. But the Valtelline question did not become serious until Richelieu's time, and, on the whole, Henry's policy in Italy was one of waiting on events, for he was not yet ready to take any decisive step. Venice and Florence admitted his patronage; the Papacy accepted his mediation in the dispute with Venice,[30] and obtained Henry's assistance when Ferrara was taken over on the failure of the line of Este. With Savoy his friendly relations were cemented by marriage. But, bearing in mind the short-lived Italian conquests of his predecessors Charles VIII. and Louis XII., and knowing that in Italian politics personal ambition counted for more than national aspiration, Henry wisely refrained from serious intervention south of the Alps.

[30] See *infra*, p. 376.

Among the princes of Germany, French diplomacy of the sixteenth century had often found allies; Henry developed this policy. By means of his Calvinist agent Bongars he maintained friendly relations with Maurice of Hesse, the Elector Palatine and the Elector of Brandenburg, while, but for the intrigues of the rebel and exile Bouillon, Henry might have obtained considerable support beyond the Rhine.[31] Under the usual pretext of safeguarding German "liberties" he tried to induce Maximilian of Bavaria to offer himself as a candidate for the Empire, but in vain; on the other hand, the Evangelical Union (formed in 1608 by several German princes, including the Count Palatine of Neuburg and the Duke of Würtemberg) regarded Henry as a patron whose aid might one day be invoked. So far as Henry was concerned, it required only the Cleve-Jülich question to precipitate events. The lord of these territories died in March 1609 without heirs, and, of the many claimants to the succession, the two most important were the Elector of Brandenburg and Wolfgang William, Count Palatine of Neuburg, both related to sisters of the deceased Duke. These territories, though small, were rich, and included a considerable proportion of Protestant inhabitants; even more, they were of great strategic importance, for the two fortresses of Berg and Jülich controlled the lower reaches of the Rhine. After the chief claimants had made a provisional division between themselves, the Hapsburgs intervened; Rudolph pronounced the sequestration of the duchies, requiring the parties concerned to submit their claims to his arbitration, and despatching at the same time a military expedition commanded by Leopold, brother of Ferdinand of Styria. Hostilities commenced and, on the 11th of February 1610, Henry signed an alliance with the Evangelical Union at Schwäbisch Hall. Meanwhile events were further complicated by one of Henry's many love affairs. Charlotte de Montmorency, married for convenience to Condé, resisted the advances of her royal admirer, and in November 1609 the young couple, anxious that their union should be one in fact as well as in name, fled to Brussels, where they placed themselves under the protection of the Archduke Albert. Condé was first prince of the blood; it was not impossible, therefore, that, under Spanish instigation, he might menace the throne itself. This love affair has been

[31] Anquez, *Henri IV et l'Allemagne*, 177 ff.

considered by some historians the chief reason for Henry's embarking on hostilities, but, though the French king was passionately attracted to the runaway bride, he had other and better reasons for entering into a struggle of which the Cleve-Jülich question was only the nominal cause.[32]

The Catholic princes of Germany, alarmed by the Protestant alliances, and fearing lest the Cleve-Jülich territories should fall into Protestant hands, had already grouped themselves into a Holy League. The Evangelical Union was soon divided. It had been joined by Brandenburg, but, on the other hand, the Elector of Saxony, in accordance with his traditional policy, was taking his stand with the Emperor. England refused any definite help; the Dutch, however, promised a contingent of 8000 men; Venice remained neutral, and thus Henry could depend only on the doubtful support of the Evangelical Union, the Duke of Savoy, the Duke of Mantua and the Dutch. These were feeble forces to range against the combined might of the Empire and Spain; Henry, nevertheless, pressed forward his preparations, and a large army was rapidly equipped.

The justification of these armed preparations lies in this: Henry was a patriotic Frenchman; all his life he had fought the insidious intrigues of Spain to corrupt the French nobility; his crown had been won in the teeth of Spanish opposition, and he honestly believed that the menace to the peace of Europe came from the ambitions of the Hapsburgs. Marriage he had rejected as a means of reconciling the two dynasties; the objects and policies of the two houses were so radically opposed that, in his own words, "la grandeur de l'un était la ruine de l'autre."[33] But in 1610 Henry was fifty-seven years old and, now that he was on the eve of what seemed likely to be a decisive struggle, he found that he no longer possessed the energy and confidence of youth. It was noted in the early summer of 1610 that for the first time he was solemn and preoccupied. He feared that his allies might fail him; his sleep was troubled; he sought strength in prayer, and he surprised his consort by an unusual and tender affection. A Spanish

---

[32] This is proved by the fact that Henry's preparations for war were begun four months before the flight of the prince and princess. See Anquez, op. cit. 187.

[33] Quoted in Hanotaux, Richelieu, i. 260.

almanac was said to have prophesied that a king would die in this year; Henry himself had, on at least one occasion, referred to a regency. On the afternoon of May 14, 1610, he left the Louvre in order to visit Sully at the Arsenal for a conference on the military preparations then nearing completion, and it is recorded that he bade farewell three times to his queen, who, moved perhaps by some premonition of evil, begged him not to go.[34] In the crush of the narrow Rue de la Ferronnière he was fatally stabbed by Ravaillac, the mad schoolmaster of Angoulême, who made no attempt to escape, and afterwards confessed under torture that, without accomplices, he was the instrument of divine vengeance against the Catholic monarch who was preparing to fight by the side of heretics.[35] The Jesuits had no part in the crime, though Coton considered it expedient to publish a vindication of the Society's innocence.[36] But the Spanish Jesuits had already taught that a Catholic monarch who betrays his religion is no longer a lawful king, and that assassination of such apostates is the behest of the Almighty. That was the solitary idea in Ravaillac's mind, and it is one of the ironies of fate that the most tolerant and enlightened of seventeenth-century kings should have perished at the hands of a religious maniac.

Henry IV.'s reign has an epilogue. His minister Sully lived in retirement for the remaining twenty-eight years of his life, brooding over the great events with which he had been associated, and weaving a halo of romance over the king whom he had served. He committed his recollections to paper, and gradually, after important revisions, the famous *Mémoires et sages économies* took shape, the first part being published in 1638, the second in 1662. For the years before 1598 these Memoirs have considerable historic value, though some of the figures relating to his financial administration are exaggerated. Scattered throughout the text are references to a

[34] Richelieu, *Mémoires* (ed. Société de l'Histoire de France, i. 73). No trace of the Spanish prophecy can be found.

[35] See Loiseleur, *Ravaillac et ses complices*. The opinion of Michelet (*Henri Quatre*, 127) that Henry was the victim of a Spanish Jesuit plot has long since been exploded. Ravaillac's confession is in *Mémoires de Condé*, VI. (Supplement), pt. iii. See also L'Estoile, *Mémoires Journaux*, ii. 315-323.

[36] *Lettre déclaratoire de la doctrine des PP. Jésuites* (1610).

great scheme by which Henry intended to humble the house of Hapsburg, redistribute Europe at the expense of the Empire, and inaugurate an era of perpetual peace. As the manuscript was revised this project was assigned greater importance, and the author laid some stress on the contrast between the imaginative and idealist character of the supposed author of the plan, and the sceptical criticism and even disapproval on the part of the unenthusiastic financier who, in retirement, was writing as a convert to Henry's proposals. This literary device, almost worthy of Defoe, deceived practically every reader of the original editions, and it was not till the nineteenth century that critics discovered how Sully had given greater verisimilitude to the scheme by deliberate forgeries and untruths.[37] It is still possible, by consulting the original editions of the Memoirs, to trace the growth, from comparatively small beginnings, of what has been called the Grand Design, and by omitting a few minor inconsistencies it may be described as follows:[38]

Beginning in 1598, Henry conceived the plan of building up a series of foreign alliances, with the aim of destroying Hapsburg power in Europe. The Spaniards were to be driven from Flanders and Italy, liberty of election restored to Bohemia and Hungary, the Empire wrested from the Hapsburgs, and their territories were to be divided among neighbouring states. Once the hereditary foes of France were consigned to their last remaining possessions beyond the Pyrenees, Europe was to be divided into six hereditary monarchies—France, Spain, England, Sweden, Denmark and Lombardy; six elective monarchies—Rome (with Naples), Venice, the Empire, Poland, Hungary and Bohemia; and three federal republics—the Helvetic, consisting of Switzerland, the Tyrol, Franche Comté and Alsace; the Belgic, composed of Holland and Flanders; and the Italic, containing Genoa, Lucca, Florence, Modena, Parma and Piacenza. Three religions—Catholicism, Lutheranism and Calvinism—were to be admitted, princes having the

[37] Notably in chs. xvii., xviii. and xx. of vol. ii. (1664 edition), where he describes his visits to the English court. Sully's statements regarding the movements of Elizabeth and James can easily be tested by reference to the *Calendar of State Papers* (*Domestic*).

[38] See Pfister, *Les Economies royales de Sully* in *Revue Historique*, 1894, and Ogg, *The Grand Design of Henry IV*. (Grotius Society Publications).

right to expel dissenters. Muscovy was ruled out of the scheme altogether as Asiatic and dangerous. War was to be restricted to a campaign against the Turk, and the affairs of Europe were to be regulated by seven general councils, of which six were local, and the seventh, meeting in some city of central Europe, was to decide questions of common interest. This seventh or general council was to be modelled on the Amphictyonic Council of ancient Greece, and was to include delegates from all the states participating in the scheme: it was to remain in permanent session and to consist of sixty-six persons, who would have to retire or seek re-election once every three years. Disarmament was to be general; control of a composite army, to which each state would contribute, was to be in the hands of the Supreme Council. The decrees of this council would thus have effective sanction. For participation in the project, the immediate inducement was to be a share in the dismembered Hapsburg territories, but once adhesion was obtained by such bribes it was hoped that desire for territorial gain would be eliminated as the full educative value of the scheme came to be realized. In one part of the Memoirs Henry was quoted as desiring no territorial advantage for himself, but in another place he is assigned some territorial gains. Each country was to be confirmed in that type of constitution for which it showed itself adapted by tradition and inclination.

Quite apart, therefore, from the question of authenticity,[39] the Grand Design is worthy of independent consideration as an important contribution to irenist theories and as the real starting-point of many constructive schemes of perpetual peace. It is not difficult to distinguish between its elements of permanent and temporary value. On the one hand, it might be considered as merely an ideal sketch of what Richelieu

---

[39] In his *Mémoires* (ed. Société de l'Histoire de France, i. 23) Richelieu credits Henry with the design of giving Milan to the Duke of Savoy and interesting the Italian princes in his projects. Richelieu thought that Henry might have had similar ambitions in Flanders. In his *Journal* (ed. Michaud et Poujoulat, 68) Bassompierre states that Sully and other Huguenots frequently incited Henry to attack Spain. Evidence of Henry's proposal to league with Savoy, Venice and Mantua will be found in Callegari, *Preponderanze straniere*, 397. See also L. Carnevali, *La morte di Enrico IV et la sua politica italiana secondo i documenti mantovani* in *Arch. Stor. Lombard*, XII. series ii. 449 ff.

nearly achieved and what Henry IV. may have dreamt of doing, with the added attraction of a League of Nations scheme; and on the other hand, it must be remembered that Sully enunciated an important principle, not rediscovered until the twentieth century, that in the complications of modern warfare the plight of the victor may, economically, be at least as bad as that of the vanquished.[40] In its details the Grand Design shows some historic sense. Considerable insight is shown in the classification of the participating states according to the types of constitution for which they are best adapted; room is left for the old international organizations of Empire and Papacy; and, while there is no violent breach with the past, there is a recognition of the importance of the new republicanism. Sully's attitude to toleration is no worse than that of his contemporaries; in political insight he is immeasurably ahead of them. In view of the tremendous influence which the project has exercised on European thought, he may perhaps be pardoned for the liberties he took with the truth.

The Grand Design might have continued to excite a mild interest in the minds of those who took the trouble to collate the scattered references in the early editions of the Memoirs, had not two eighteenth-century abbés directed their activities to the subject. In 1719 Charles Irenée Castel, Abbé de St. Pierre, published his *Projet de paix perpétuelle*, in which the Grand Design served as a basis for a theory of perpetual peace, the most carefully thought out and the most widely known in the eighteenth century. The encyclopaedic interests and activities of the Abbé de Saint Pierre have recently attracted the interest of historical students:[41] hitherto he has been known chiefly from Rousseau's brilliant essay on the *Projet de paix perpétuelle*. But the wonderful edifice of the Grand Design was not completed until in 1745 the Abbé de l'Ecluse des Loges published a new edition of the Memoirs, in which he carefully collected all the scattered references to the project and had them printed as a composite chapter at the end of the book. This was quite in accordance with the un-

[40] *Mémoires* (ed. 1664), iii. 436.
[41] See J. Drouet, *L'Abbé de Saint Pierre* (1912). Copies of Saint Pierre's writings are rare in British libraries, apart from the British Museum. This Abbé de Saint Pierre should not be confused with Bernardin de Saint Pierre (1737–1814).

critical standards of the period, and it served to give a new lease of life to the Grand Design, for this version of the Memoirs was printed in a great many editions; it was translated into English, and it gave to its numerous readers the impression, not only that Henry IV. was the author of the scheme, but that Sully had devoted a special chapter to its exposition. The only complete modern English version of Sully's Memoirs[42] is merely a literal reprint of the eighteenth-century version, and traces of one or both of the above two interpretations will be found in practically all the older books referring to the subject. The second supposition—that Sully himself wrote the chapter in which the scheme is described—is still a commonplace of our historical literature. Nor are these matters of merely pedantic interest, because it was by such fortuitous circumstances that the Grand Design came, in the eighteenth century, to be considered not only as a concrete scheme planned by a great king, but also as the philosophical basis of all idealist attempts to eliminate war from international relations. The pacific doctines of Rousseau, Kant and Bentham were directly influenced by the reveries of an austere seventeenth-century Huguenot and the textual liberties of an uncritical eighteenth-century editor.

[42] In Bohn's series.

Chapter 3

The Counter Reformation and the Empire

THIS CHAPTER is concerned mainly with the attempt, within the lands of the Empire, to undo the work of the sixteenth-century Reformation. It is necessary to preface the account with a brief summary of the general results of that Reformation.

At least two phases can be noted in the historical interpretation of the sixteenth-century Reformation. In the nineteenth century, when a doctrine of human progress was implicitly accepted, many historians regarded Lutheranism as a logical completion of the Renaissance, in so far as by its direct appeal to the Bible and the human conscience it emancipated men from the shackles of the mediaeval Church. On this view, Luther was both liberator and moral reformer, whose sensitive revulsion from iniquity was shared by the majority of his fellow Germans. This interpretation has of necessity been somewhat modified by experience of more recent events in Europe. More popular is the economic interpretation, which has behind it all the authority traditionally attached in England to the pronouncements of German historians.[1] On this view, the Reformation was an expression, in the guise of religious terms, of the new capitalist spirit, of the revolt

---

[1] Cf. Max Weber (English translation by T. Parsons), *The Protestant ethic and the spirit of Capitalism* (1930).

against the old canon-law prohibition of usury, of the quest for new markets, of the commercial ambitions of the rising middle classes, in fine, of that greedy, a-moral industrialism which has incurred such discredit in the twentieth century. On this hypothesis many things in the sixteenth and seventeenth centuries can be satisfactorily explained. Theological distinctions are transmuted in terms of modern class conflict, and the eternally damned fit naturally into a scheme for exploiting wage slaves. Calvin is seen to have inaugurated a "get rich quick" movement which, among other things accounted for the execution of Charles I., whose solicitude for the poor was inconvenient to Puritan profiteers. A scientific age naturally welcomes a theory which explains so much.

It is easily possible to substantiate such an interpretation of the past by playing fast and loose with words having a distinctively modern connotation, and by ingeniously fitting a selection of historical facts into the accepted categories of modern economic theory. Conveniently ignoring the fact that usury and capitalism were firmly established in many Catholic communities, it is argued that Calvinism, by setting aside the Canon Law inhibition of usury, provided its bourgeois votaries with their main incentive for the accumulation of wealth. It is sometimes forgotten also that greed is as old as humanity; that different civilisations provide characteristic outlets and restraints for the encouragement or repression of the acquisitive instinct, and that race and personal temperament, combined with opportunity, are more likely to account for success or failure in the quest for riches, which in all ages, mediaeval as well as modern, has been an accepted characteristic of humanity. Even more, the "economic" interpreters of the Reformation have assumed that parallelism in time is an expression of cause and effect. The later sixteenth and the whole of the seventeenth centuries were undoubtedly periods of economic expansion, wherein a leading part was played by countries like England and Holland which had rejected the old faith. But it by no means follows that the Reformation was therefore inspired solely or even mainly by economic motives or impulses, for the new spirit of economic exploitation could as fittingly be fathered on the fifteenth-century geographical discoveries, which were achieved by Catholics. Still more, when the generalizations of the more popular economic interpreters of history are carefully examined, it is often found that they are no more than truisms about the conflicting eco-

nomic interests of the social classes within the state. But the
platitude disguised as a profundity is always a most effective
literary device.

The age of the reformers had neither a theory of progress
nor a theory of economic self-interest. Luther's mentality was
essentially scholastic, and he won unexpected publicity by an
academic, even pedantic act—his challenge to all comers that
he could demonstrate an inconsistency between the doctrine
and the practice of the Church. He was quite right, but he
did not realize that a great Church may have to reconcile
many inconsistencies. Protests against clerical immorality were
as old as Christendom, but here was something new, for it
was a challenge to the competence of clerical professionalism,
a much more sensitive point than clerical morality. Justification by faith served to enforce the challenge, for the doctrine
eliminated the priest as intermediary between God and Man,
and imposed on the layman the necessity of devising his own
means of salvation, without recourse to a hierarchy. There
was added a national element. Why should the money be sent
to Rome when it could be spent to better advantage in Germany? In this way, the German Protestant movement was
primarily directed against the professional monopoly of the
priest and the financial monopoly of the pope; in its turn,
Lutheranism soon developed its own technique of exclusiveness. It needed only the intervention of an educated man like
Calvin, untrammelled by local prejudice or subservience to a
secular prince, and the movement became European. In all
this there was little or nothing about better morals, or progress, or economic advantage, but a great deal about the
Scriptures and the Early Fathers, whose authority was as
uncontested as the interpretation of their statements was diverse. The reformers, having discovered that the mediaeval
church was a fraud, proceeded to devise their own systems for
providing the layman with professional guidance and (if necessary) compulsion. New hierarchies came into being, and a
sole monopoly was divided among rival lessees.

Historians are at the mercy of an accepted terminology, and
divergence therefrom may savour of pedantry. Thus the general word "Protestant" is used, and indeed has to be used, of
those greater religious movements of the sixteenth century
which came into conflict with Rome. But convenience is sacrificed to truth when the terms Protestant and Reformed are
regarded as interchangeable. Contemporaries always distin-

guished between them, because while they both denoted alternatives to Catholicism, they meant very different alternatives. The description "Protestant" came from a protest[2] of German princes and towns against a decree of the Diet forbidding, among other things, the secularizing of Church lands and the confiscation of ecclesiastical revenues; in other words, the original Protestants were protesting not only against Popery, but against an attempt to deny them access to land and money that was not their's. Generally, the name came to be applied to the evangelical churches of northern Germany and Sweden, churches distinguished by compromise in theology and organization, by mediocrity and time-serving in their leaders, and by the quality of absolute submission to the state in their lay adherents. For some time there was a chance that these churches would be reunited to the fold. With the reformed churches of Calvin and Zwingli, on the other hand, there was never such a possibility, for both these men were scholars who, while unable to appreciate the spiritual appeal of the mediaeval Church, were well informed about its intellectual weaknesses. Rejecting all the accumulated paraphernalia of the middle ages, Calvin and Zwingli re-formed their churches on what they claimed to be the theory and practice of primitive Christianity. They had a sense of purpose, discipline and propaganda such as the Evangelicals or true Protestants never possessed.

Luther and Calvin had started from St. Augustine, but Calvin went much farther. The Saint (for reasons not quite clear to the inexpert) had limited the number of the Elect to that of the fallen angels, and the Elect were defined as those on whom Grace had descended. Free Will was therefore ruled out of court, and it remained only for Calvin to draw (and enforce) the logical deduction of Predestination, with the embarrassing result that Calvinism outside the Church and, later, Jansenism[3] within the Church thus owed one of their fundamental beliefs to the greatest of the early Catholic theologians, and so might with some justice claim that on this vital point they were at least as much in accord with orthodox tradition as were their opponents. This was why Calvinism on its doctrinal side was much more difficult to combat than the comparatively simple Lutheranism, which many candid

2 At the Diet of Speyer, 1529.
3 See *infra*, Ch. 8.

writers attributed to the disordered mind of an ignorant and low-born monk.

Moreover, Calvinism was a specially dangerous heresy from the Catholic point of view, because it was both revolutionary and constructive. Its founder was in many respects the antithesis of Luther. Of good family and education, the Frenchman, John Calvin, was endowed with great earnestness of character, combined with that narrow, incisive logic and total impenetrability of intellect which are characteristic of the true revolutionary. From his classical studies he derived not a humane culture, but a Stoic philosophy and a philological pedantry, the latter of which was forcibly impressed on the youth of Geneva. Though cold and reserved in manners, he won the loyalty of a devoted body of men, and, after one set-back, he succeeded in establishing at Geneva the system of theocracy outlined in his *Institute*. As a religious centre Geneva was in an ideal strategic position; by 1570 Holland, Scotland, Switzerland, the Palatine Electorate and a considerable part of France were won over to his views. Taking advantage of the old municipal laws of the city, and its freedom from any religious or territorial control, Calvin imposed a minutely regulated despotism which made men either rebels or bigots. Even outsiders were made to feel the heavy hand of the new theocracy, and the Spaniard, Michael Servetus, was burned outside the city walls, an example of intolerance from which modern Calvinists have expressly dissociated themselves by the erection of an expiatory monument on the site where this heretic[4] was murdered.

In theology, Calvinism was more conservative and also more revolutionary than Lutheranism. It pressed the Augustinian theory of Grace to its most repellent conclusions, and it modified the doctrine of the Sacraments, emphasizing their symbolic element and denying the Real Presence, which Luther had held to be present in the cup, in the sense that heat is present in hot water. For the tyranny of the old priest Calvinism substituted the rule of elders and presbyters, committees of laymen in which the government of each congregation was vested, while episcopal control was replaced by local and representative synods, the whole edifice being crowned by a central assembly of clergy and laity. In form, therefore, the Calvinist church was democratic; laymen appointed their

[4] His book, *De Trinitate*, questioned the doctrine of the Trinity.

minister and could criticize his private life and his theology; the humblest layman was eligible for membership of the central or national assembly. If religious democracy means that the most uneducated persons have a direct voice in the choice of their pastors and the government of their church, then Calvinism was a democracy. The nations with which it found most acceptance—the Dutch and the Scottish—were generally regarded as republican, and it has always been a convenient generalization that while Lutheranism was, on the political side, autocratic and Erastian, Calvinism was republican and democratic.

Like many generalizations, however, this one does not always accommodate the facts. Though in the sixteenth century Dutch opposition to Spanish rule was republican in spirit, yet the United Provinces in the seventeenth century were a burgher oligarchy,[5] not a democracy; and in spite of the republican manifestos of George Buchanan, secular life in seventeenth-century Scotland was dominated by the nobility and the royal burghs. In comparison with the English Independents, the Scottish Calvinists had a strong sense of political tradition, and after the disordered Puritan experiments of the Commonwealth, they combined with the English royalists to restore Charles II. The French Calvinists were republican only after their expulsion from France.[6] Calvin himself had always had the greatest respect for the principle of authority in the state, and his rule in Geneva could be called democratic only in a very special sense. Committee rule, such as is characteristic of the Calvinist ecclesiastical government, may sometimes be as irresponsible as the domination of the personal despot, for an executive committee decides according to an arithmetical majority; hence, taking shelter in the anonymity of the vote, a voter may evade moral responsibility for an act which, as a solely responsible person, he might hesitate to commit. It may be argued that this is characteristic of all democracies, but while it is true that Calvinism had an organization ostensibly democratic, in practice it was at least as intolerant and autocratic as any other religious body. The

[5] See *infra*, p. 391.

[6] In his *Defensio pro populo Anglicano* Milton included the French Calvinist, Bochart, in the same school as Bossuet and Hobbes. Bochart was, like many seventeenth-century Huguenots before 1685, an advocate of Divine Right. See Galland, *Quid S. Bochartus de Jure Regum disseruerit.*

Lutherans sought shelter behind absolute princes; the Calvinists, with greater assurance, visualized the state in terms of a theocracy and, like the Jesuits, subordinated the lay to the clerical power. Calvinist and Jesuit agreed that "princeps in religione nihil statuat . . . non est enim arbiter religionis sed discipulus."[7] It has never been suggested that the Jesuits were a republican or democratic body, but it was with the Society of Jesus that the Calvinists were most commonly associated by both Lutheran[8] and Catholic.[9] This was not because of any resemblance in their theological opinions, but because both agreed in the complete subordination of all secular activities to the rule of an autocratic hierarchy.

The truth is that such a vague term as democratic can be used of seventeenth-century organizations only with very careful reservations. The political heritage of the Renaissance was absolutism in the state, and the Calvinists were quite as much influenced by this conception as their opponents. Political science at this period was just sufficiently developed to provide several convenient catch-words, and the Jesuits made their own use of democratic conceptions in order to prepare the way for their ecclesiastical absolutism. The difference between the two great rebel churches was probably as much one of temperament as of organization or doctrine. At his worst, the Lutheran was a sanctimonious time-server; at his best, a conscientious and obedient citizen. But the Calvinist seemed to derive from, or perhaps carry into, his religion a fervid spirit, impatient of check or control, intolerant of criticism or dissent, united with a great tenacity of purpose and the sense of a divine intention in human life. Austerity, a conviction of personal responsibility and a desire to dominate others, a suggestion of intolerance and an attitude of exclusiveness and reserve, were typical of the true Calvinist, as they are of all "chosen peoples." At the basis of his mentality was a paradox—the combination of fatalism with intense and

[7] Adam Contzen, S.J., *Politicorum libri decem* (1620), II. ch. xvi.

[8] See *infra*, p. 124. Lutheran preachers like Hoë von Hoënegg associated the Calvinists with Jesuits and Turks.

[9] The Catholic, Etienne Pasquier, in his *Catéchisme des Jésuites* (1602) associated the Jesuits with Calvinists and Jews. See also Krebs, *Die politische Publizistik der Jesuiten und ihrer Gegner . . .*, 210.

unceasing effort. To label the Calvinist republican or democratic is to ignore altogether the complexities of his temperament and to omit the general seventeenth-century opinion of
his character and capabilities.

The Calvinists and the Jesuits are the two protagonists in
the Counter Reformation struggles, and, as in every complete
antithesis, the extremes have certain important things in common. The founder of the Jesuit order was Ignatius Loyola,[10]
a Spanish soldier, whose mentality was affected to some extent
by a wound that had never properly healed. After giving up
his military career, he packed his belongings on a mule and,
though middle-aged and uneducated, he went to study in Paris,
where Calvin was already a student. In practical ways he
encouraged the frequency of the great visions by which he
was inspired, and these methods he formulated in the *Exercitia
Spiritualia*. His life's object was achieved by the foundation
of the Society of Jesus, which was devoted to the restoration
of Catholicism under papal control and the conversion of
heathendom. As befitted its founder, the society was military
in organization; its head was called a General and it carried
to extremes the military virtue of unquestioning obedience. As
in no other religious order, the Jesuit had to surrender, not so
much his time and property as his personality and intelligence; he had to submit to his superior *perinde ac cadaver*,
and thus it was in its unity of organization[11] and tenacity of
purpose that the society was best fitted to deal with Calvinists.

The Jesuits had privileges which marked them out as the
advance guard of the Church. They could change their original statutes in order to suit circumstances; they could build
churches and institutions; they could speak in public; they
were not bound by the full monastic vows; they were given
exceptional powers of absolution; they were outside the jurisdiction of all prelates not of their own order; they were
exempt from taxes and, while they could teach in Catholic
universities, they could not be subjects of temporal princes.
The professed of the four vows formed, as it were, an inner
ring, flanked by novices and assistants who could carry on the
secular work of the order. The powers of the General were
almost boundless, but by his side was a monitor to give advice,

[10] 1491–1556.

[11] The best short account of the organization and history of the
Jesuits is that of J. Brucker, S.J. See *infra*, Bibliography.

and a council of four assistants who convened the congregation on the death of a general or for his removal. At the other end of the hierarchy were the novices, for whom the entrance test was a strict one, such things as general health and appearance being taken into consideration. Men of poor intelligence, however virtuous, were rejected, as were also descendants of Jews or Mohammedans. The novices, when they had fulfilled the probationary tests, took the three vows—obedience, poverty and chastity: full membership involved a fourth vow —to live in the order in conformity with its statutes and take part in the mission against heretics. Thus the society consisted of concentric rings, comprising novices, with lay and ecclesiastical co-adjutors on the outside; then the professed of the three vows; thirdly, the professed of the four vows; fourthly, the inner council of four with the monitor; and lastly, the General in the centre.

It was this contact with the outer world, while the duties of citizenship were evaded, that gave the society its religious and political influence in the seventeenth century. Withdrawal from the world had been the ideal of the mediaeval orders: intervention in worldly affairs for a spiritual purpose was the unconcealed object of the Jesuits. There were two ways in which this might be done—by education of the young and by monopolizing the confessional. The Jesuit schools provided the most thorough education available, and a list of their pupils would prove their success as educators. As confessors they could influence the consciences of adults, in which capacity they provided the most assiduous spiritual advisers at a time when every Catholic of high social position had a private confessor. To qualify its members for these responsible posts, the society developed an elaborate system of regulations, unparalleled except perhaps by the minute regulations of modern armies and navies. Thus the *Regulae Societatis Jesu*, published in 1607, provide, among other things, that letters shall be censored;[12] obedience paid to all,[13] even to subordinates having temporary authority; vows are to be renewed twice a year;[14] members must go out in public only in pairs, and the regulations are to be read and copied out once a month. On entering the seminary, the "tintinnabulum" at the door is to

12 p. 39.
13 p. 38.
14 p. 53.

be neither loud nor frequent but "ut par est," speech is to be in subdued tones "ut religioso decet," and no one is to have the window of his bedroom open at night.[15] In each class the rector was to have "censores secreti" who would inform him of matters that would not otherwise reach his notice.[16]

The two most serious and best-founded accusations against the seventeenth-century Jesuits are that they taught the doctrine of Tyrannicide[17] and introduced Casuistry into the confessional. The subject of casuistry will be considered in its place:[18] here it may be noted that the clearest exposition of the doctrine of tyrannicide will be found in the writings of the two Spanish Jesuits, Suarez and Mariana.[19] These writers make free use of the Contract theory which had been brought into prominence in such Huguenot writings as the *Vindiciae contra tyrannos*; ostensibly the Jesuit political theorists are democratic, basing temporal sovereignty on popular consent, in contrast with spiritual sovereignty which has divine sanction. But whereas the Huguenot writers had stopped far short of tyrannicide, at least one of the Jesuit theologians (Mariana) had no such compunction. A usurper could be killed by the first comer—that was a generally accepted maxim, but a lawful monarch could equally be slain if he became an apostate or if he did not serve the interests of his religion.[20] Contemporaries attributed the deaths of William the Silent and Henry III. of France to the direct instigation of the Jesuits, and some, though without foundation, attributed the assassination of Henry IV. to the same source.[21] The real aim of the Jesuits was to subordinate the Catholic monarchies to papal tutelage,

[15] These are rules in the *Regulae Communes* appended to the *Summarium Constitutionum*.

[16] P. Natalis, *De Studiis Soc. Jesu*, in *Monumenta Paedagogica S.J.* (ed. Rodeles and Lecina, Madrid, 1901).

[17] This is the subject of a considerable literature. For a very able and accurate defence of the Jesuit point of view see Brou, *Les Jésuites de légende*, I. ch. vi. See also Figgis, *From Gerson to Grotius*, lecture vi.

[18] *Infra*, Ch. 8.

[19] See particularly Mariana, *De Rege et Regis institutione*, **v.** and vi.

[20] It should be noted that Mariana's views were not endorsed by the society as a whole, and that Mariana had serious differences of opinion with the society.

[21] The Jesuit Keller in his *Tyranicidium* (1611) exculpated the society from share in Henry IV.s assassination, and argued that

and the argument from a democratic contract theory was an unscrupulous one. In at least one case it proved to be a boomerang. The Jesuit Parsons wrote a book attacking Queen Elizabeth as a usurper, since she was the daughter of Anne Boleyn, and the exposition of the rights of nations to expel a usurper who is endangering the religion of the state was so forcibly expressed that, in the debates over the Exclusion Bill, the Whigs had the book reprinted as an attack on the Catholic James, Duke of York.[22]

Poland was the first country to be made uniformly Catholic by the Jesuits, and although Protestantism had never gained a foothold there, the Orthodox Greek Church had to be eliminated before the country could be turned into one of the two most uniformly Catholic states in Europe. They returned to France in the reign of Henry IV.; in Spain they were powerful, though not supreme, because there was the Inquisition, managed by their rivals the Dominicans; they dominated the Italian states, though they were expelled from Venice. They established themselves in Bohemia, Bavaria and Silesia, where they enjoyed the full confidence and co-operation of Hapsburg and Wittelsbach. Even in Protestant England they managed to eke out a precarious existence, but they had to go in disguise, and the penal laws against them were very severe. Nor was their work confined to Europe, for they were zealous missionaries and pioneers, travelling to the utmost confines of the known world, exploring and converting in India, Africa and Thibet, disputing with the English in Japan, and preaching in the islands of the Pacific. From the mines of Peru to the observatories of China the representatives of this great and devoted international order were to be found strenuously engaged in the attempt to restore that unity of religion which universal opinion held to be requisite for the salvation of the soul and the safety of the state.

It is not surprising that on a small basis of fact a great deal of legend grew up concerning the society. Hasenmüller's *History of the Jesuits*[23] is the first of the "impartial" histories

---

Jesuit doctrines were directed only against usurpers, not lawful kings.

[22] *A Conference about the next Succession to the Crown of England* (1594), reprinted in 1681 "with licence," and also privately. See Sommervogel, *Bibliothèque de la Compagnie de Jésus*, vi. 303.

[23] 1593.

—a collection of scandal intended only for readers who were prepared to believe anything of the order. In 1612 was published the *Monita Secreta Societatis Jesu*, a book which attracted wide attention, as it claimed to be a revelation of the secret instructions of the order, though it was probably either a satire or written in revenge by an expelled member. Its purpose was to prove how, by a parade of poverty, the society inveigled wealthy persons, especially women, to leave them legacies. The attacks on the Jesuits in the seventeenth century alone would fill a library of considerable size, and they did not all come from the pens of Protestants. They were compared with Janissaries, Templars, the Assassins, Pharisees, disguised Friars, Moloch, the Plagues of Egypt, the Flood, and even Balaam's ass.[24] The agitation against them, in which many zealous Catholics joined, can be compared only to the great waves of anti-Semite feeling by which certain parts of Europe have at times been convulsed. Putting aside the mass of fable in which the history of the Jesuits lies smothered, it may be said that in the period of the Counter Reformation they tightened the bonds among Catholic countries, and led the campaign against the heretics with a ruthlessness that appalled even men accustomed to the worst manifestations of religious fanaticism. Though they were all highly educated and included men of great scholastic and scientific eminence, they did not hesitate to crush every movement for enlightenment if they thought that thereby the interests of the faith would be in any measure safeguarded. They were the sworn enemies of Galileo and the new scientific movement in Italy; they would have crushed Pascal had their power in France been stronger; they destroyed the soul of Bohemia with a calculating thoroughness. Believing, like their fellow Catholics, that heretics are worse than murderers, they insisted that faith need not be kept with them. But, in some interesting respects, the Jesuits differed from other Catholics, and in consequence were maligned and even persecuted by the Church. Thus, as missionaries, they believed that some temporary concessions should be made to highly civilized infidels, such as the Chinese; as men of culture, they were not opposed to the Stage; as men of intelligence, they did not believe in witchcraft, and were pioneers in the attempt to end the persecution of witches.

[24] Krebs, *Die politische Publizistik und ihrer Gegner in den letzten Jahrzehnten vor Ausbruch des dreissigjährigen Krieges* (in *Hallesche Abhandlungen zur neueren Geschichte*). 70.

It is significant that their greatest pupil—Voltaire—directed his sarcasm, not against his educators—for whom he retained some regard—but against the obscurantism and intolerance of the Church to which they owed allegiance.

It was not a Jesuit, but a Dominican, who gave clearest expression to the ideals of this revived Catholicism. In 1599 was published the first redaction of Thomas Campanella's *De Monarchia Hispanica*, and by 1620 the work was well known in Germany in at least one translation. The obscurities and vagaries of this strange visionary repel modern readers, though in France and Italy there is a revived interest in his writings, and some of his poetry is imperishable. The *De Monarchia Hispanica* was taken seriously by contemporaries and was deemed worthy of a reply: for the historian it represents a practical exposition, in relation to the politics of his time, of the theories propounded in his later and better known book, *The City of the Sun*. In his *De Monarchia* Campanella begins by declaring that the end of the world is not far off; the kings of Spain will soon succeed to the Holy Roman Empire, which is in direct line with the empires of Persia, Babylon and Macedonia; all things will thereafter fall into a state of anarchy, which will be ended only by the establishment of a true Christian empire on earth. The great conjunction of planets in Sagittarius will reveal more details of this cosmic evolution.[25] Meanwhile a start must be made: the king of Spain must obtain the Empire; the three Protestant Electors are to be anathematized by the Pope and deprived of their dignities unless they submit; the secular forces of France, Italy and Spain are to be united for this purpose and to compel the submission of heretics. The dilatoriness of thought and execution to be found in the German character suggests that speed of design and execution is the best guarantee of success.[26] German youth should be distracted from heretical activities by philosophical and mathematical studies, by the construction of ships and armaments, and by encouragement to conduct astrological observations in the New World which is eminently suited for this purpose. Eminent Teutons who might become centres of disaffection are to be exiled or segregated;[27] spies are to be set on German colleges, councils and magistrates. The Catholic world looks to Spain

[25] *De Monarchia Hispanica* (ed. 1640), 51.
[26] *Ibid.* 52.
[27] *De Monarchia Hispanica* (ed. 1640), 282.

and the Spanish king for a lead. The chief quality requisite in the Spanish monarch is sapience, which includes the virtues, and as this is influenced by ancestry, the climate and the stars, and as the Spanish monarchy is hereditary, the choice of his consort must be on strictly eugenic lines, since "the progeny of kings is the world's concern."[28] Spain is marked out as the country of the future, for though its resources are not properly exploited, yet, unlike its neighbours, it enjoys complete freedom from civil and religious strife, because its turbulent spirits are employed abroad in suppressing heresy, especially in Flanders and South America. The Spanish prince is to be trained by bishops and captains: in arms and mathematics, not in effeminate frolics; in laws rather than in grammar. If the French and German rulers had trained their minds as well as their bodies, they would not now be the slaves of Huguenots and Lutherans.

The author of this remarkable book attempted to hasten the millennium of which he dreamed by taking part in a conspiracy against Spanish rule in southern Italy, and his views were not rendered more moderate by the twenty-seven years of imprisonment that ensued.

The reply came from Gasper Scioppius,[29] who drew up an eloquent appeal to German patriotism in face of the Spanish Colossus which threatened to dominate the world. Great empires, he maintained, had had their day; only by some form of balance of power could the ambitions of princes be neutralized; only by a united effort and a keen sense of the impending danger could Germany hope to preserve its nationality in a world of enemies. Scioppius's manifesto is, however, one of many that have long lain forgotten in the tomes of Goldast. The early years of the seventeenth century witnessed an outburst of patriotic German literature which, in its fervid appeal for unity against Spain and the Jesuits, provides a counterpart to the agitation directed, nearly two centuries later, against Napoleonic exploitation. Thus a book[30] published in 1602, and dedicated to the Protestant Electors, attacked the Jesuits as the sowers of sedition among the German peoples who, if united, would be invincible. In his *Trinubium Europaeum* (1612) Berger[31] proclaimed that the

[28] *Ibid.* 67-68.
[29] Krebs, *op. cit.* 6.
[30] Goldast, *Imperialia* (1614), 682 ff.
[31] *Ibid.* 722.

only hope for the future lay in close union between Germans, Hungarians and Bohemians. This book was dedicated to all seven Electors. More remarkable is a book by Stephen Pannonius of Belgrade, published in 1608.[32] Declaring that the troubles in Hungary and the Low Countries were due to interference by the Pope and the Jesuits, he recommends the Emperor to follow the French example of using Protestant ministers. Peace is possible with the Catholic Church, but not with the Jesuits. Complete liberty of worship should be granted to Catholic, Lutheran and Calvinist; ministers should be chosen not for their religion but for their worth; all who believe in the Trinity should be left in peace. It is not the men but their measures that are dangerous: "Papismum, non papistas, doctrinam non homines fugimus." Pannonius, like Dante, thinks of a great and united empire as the fundamental requisite for European peace. On the east it would include Judaea, Greece, Hungary, Bohemia and Poland; on the west, England, Spain, the Low Countries, France and Italy; while Germany in the centre would be the core of this new civilization based on enlightenment and toleration, recognizing differences of nationality, law and language, and united in obedience to that government which still claimed direct affiliation with the Caesars. The book clearly shows how, thus early, the mediaeval empire was coming to be idealised, and how remote was that ideal in a world which, having lost a literal faith, was divided by the wranglings of proselytising substitutes.

But Germany was long past such appeals as these, and it needed the wars of the French Revolution to make German patriotism a serious political force. Otherwise the literature of post-Reformation Germany is for the most part melancholy reading and helps to prepare one for the events that were to come. In so far as it is a reflection of national life, the vernacular literature of Germany from Fischart to Grimmelshausen is likely to create in the mind of the reader a feeling of disappointment. It depicts a society which, while abounding in many sterling qualities, appears to have entered on a stage of arrested or distorted development, resulting in a miscellaneous collection of states, none of them endowed with a distinctive culture and most of them perpetuating religious antagonisms now a century old. It may be that, like the painter

[32] *Ibid.* 742.

Breughel, the popular writers of the day preferred to describe only those things that no one cares to see in life; but if the literature of a nation is any guide to its social qualities, then Germany of the early seventeenth century was a country in which obscenity was more dismal and insistent than anywhere else in Europe. There was something wrong with a country in which every popular writer aped Rabelais.[33] The spiritual forces of the Reformation had spent themselves; the Renaissance had not left in Germany a great heritage as in other lands; the forces of religious bigotry were so terrible because they were so evenly matched. The comparison between the unhealthy atmosphere of Fischart's[34] productions and the sunny gaiety and unquenchable drollery of his contemporary Cervantes[35] has more than a literary significance.

At the abdication of Charles V. (1555) the Imperial territories had been divided into two branches—the Empire, to which Charles's brother, Ferdinand I., succeeded, and Spain, with its dependencies in Europe and the New World, which became a hereditary monarchy in the line of Charles's son, Philip II. The solution of the religious question embodied in the Augsburg settlement was a recognition of the two standard creeds, Catholicism and Lutheranism, and by the *cujus regio* principle rulers could procure conformity with one or other of these religious systems by expelling dissentients. If it was hoped that by this splitting up of the great Hapsburg Empire into two branches, and the establishment of some kind of working agreement between Catholic and Lutheran, dynastic and religious strife would be lessened, these hopes were doomed to disappointment, for the Hapsburg menace still survived in the co-operation between the Spanish and Imperial branches, while, within a few years, two great religious protagonists were to be added whose importance could hardly have been foreseen by the Augsburg settlement—the Jesuits and the Calvinists. In France there ensued a long period of religious wars concluded by the Edict of Nantes, but in the Imperial lands the forces at work were more complicated and more elemental. The forces were gathering strength in the

[33] Cf. the *Affenteuerlich naupen-geheuerliche Geschicht-klitterung* of Fischart, first published in 1575. See Janssen, *History of the German People*, xi. 376 ff. and vol. xvi. *passim*.

[34] J. Fischart or Mentzer (1550–1614).

[35] 1547–1616.

second half of the sixteenth century, and the fact of the great struggle not coming earlier is partly due to this, that of the Emperors succeeding Charles V., namely, Ferdinand I. (1558-1564), Maximilian II. (1564-1576), Rudolph II. (1576-1611), Matthias (1611-1619) and Ferdinand II. (1619-1637), only the last took the initiative. Ferdinand I. had not been opposed to conciliation and was not sufficiently sure of his position to seek a decision; Maximilian II. was quite indifferent to religious extremes; Rudolph II., though surrounded by religious fanatics, exhausted his money, his prestige, and what acumen he had inherited in a vain search for the Philosopher's Stone and a means of making gold from base metals;[36] moreover, though anxious for uniformity, he was personally averse to persecution. Matthias was past middle age at his accession and could not alter the circumstances into which his changed fortunes suddenly placed him; in consequence, during this half-century of unenterprising emperors, terminating in the accession of the young and fervid Ferdinand II., the day of settlement was put off, while the initiative was gradually transferred to the Austrian archdukes and the greater German princes.

In Sixtus V. (1585-1590) the Counter Reformation had an able and enthusiastic leader who purged the Curia of many irregularities and introduced a business-like and efficient control into the administration of the now militant Church. By the beginning of the seventeenth century Protestantism in the German-speaking lands was either at a standstill or on the defensive, while the Catholics were just beginning to win back lost ground. In 1577 the affair of Gebhard Truchsess, Archbishop of Cologne,[37] had resulted in definitely winning over the ecclesiastical electorates from Protestant influence; and though Calvinism was established in Germany at this time, infusing fresh energy into the Reformation movement, it caused a fatal breach in the Protestant ranks of which the Catholics were not slow to take advantage. More than its opponents, the neo-Catholic movement realized the value of unity, organized control, propaganda and education. The

[36] Denis, *Fin de l'indépendance bohème,* ii. 411; Coxe, *House of Austria,* ii. and iii., can still be read with profit for the careers of these emperors.

[37] This arose from the Archbishop Elector of Cologne, Gebhard Truchsess, marrying a nun. He attempted to retain his ecclesiastical-electoral dignity, but was driven out by the Bavarians.

Council of Trent[38] had clearly defined Catholic dogma and discipline; with the help of the new religious orders the Papacy strove to retain a more intimate contact with the now restricted area of Europe recognizing its suzerainty; the religious life of Catholicism was restored and reinvigorated by great religious personalities like Saint Theresa in Spain, Saint Charles Borromeo in Italy, and Saint Ignatius Loyola in every country admitting Catholics; while by their reorganized universities and schools the advocates of the old religion aimed at drilling the laity and educating the clergy in doctrinal principles that rested mainly on historical tradition and the interpretation of a great mass of theological literature. This is in marked contrast with the disorder and disunion among the Protestants, who had not yet had time to assimilate their gains. The steady decline of the Protestant University of Wittenberg in the sixteenth century, and the equally steady rise of the Catholic University of Ingoldstadt in the same period, provide the most ominous comment on the relative equipment of the two combatants.

The secular leaders of the Counter Reformation in Germany had both been trained at Ingoldstadt—Ferdinand of Styria,[39] the future Emperor, and Maximilian of Wittelsbach,[40] Duke of Bavaria. They were almost exactly contemporary, both succeeding to their hereditary dominions in the last years of the sixteenth century, Maximilian to rule his duchy for fifty-four years and survive Ferdinand by seventeen years. Maximilian proceeded with youthful enthusiasm to restore order into the finances of his duchy, to create with Tilly's help a permanent army, and to lay low the heretics of his own and (if possible) surrounding states. Without the idealism and fervour of Ferdinand, he was endowed with practical and political qualities which enabled him to rise from a position of comparative obscurity to a dictatorship in both German and Imperial politics. There were not enough Protestants left in Bavaria to form a serious minority— Maximilian's grandfather, Albert V., had seen to that—so the new ruler signalized his accession by attempting to con-

[38] 1545–1553.

[39] The best account of Ferdinand is that by his confessor Lamormain. Unfortunately it is in neither the British Museum nor Bodleian.

[40] 1581–1651. For Maximilian's reorganization of his duchy see Schreiber, *Maximilian*, i. 57 ff.

vert one of his Protestant neighbours, the Count Palatine Philip of Neuburg, with whom he exchanged pamphlets for refutations. A conference at Ratisbon (1602) to settle their differences was attended with considerable public interest, but with each session the discussions became more heated and personalities more frequent. After this failure Maximilian confined himself to more effective means of propagating his views.[41]

His first public employment was in the affair of Donau-worth.[42] There was a Protestant majority in this town, but on April 11, 1606, the Abbot led a religious procession through the streets in spite of the Town Council's objection. The procession was disbanded by the Protestants; there was some violence on both sides and, after a hasty inquiry, Rudolph put Donauworth under the Ban of Empire, entrusting to Maximilian the task of humiliating the town. Feeling in Donauworth was strong and practically unanimous; the town offered a brave resistance before superior forces, but in December 1607 it had to yield. The terms of surrender were the harshest possible. Donauworth ceased to be an Imperial city and, though Protestant, was forced to admit into its council a majority of Catholics: still worse, it was consigned to Bavarian rule. To the Protestant inhabitants the punishment must have seemed a personal one; they specially resented the Emperor's having imposed the Ban without reference to the Diet, and the fact of his entrusting its execution to the director of the Bavarian circle instead of to the director of the Swabian circle, the Duke of Würtemberg, as he ought to have done. Insignificant in itself, this affair proved that the religious peace of Augsburg was no longer valid and that German Protestantism would have to fight for existence.[43]

[41] See Huber, *Geschichte Österreichs,* bk. ix. ch. i.

[42] There is a good account of this in Droysen, *Zeitalter des Dreissigjährigen Krieges* (Oncken's Series), 442 ff. The best general studies of Maximilian's policy are in *Die Politik Maximilian von Bayern,* ed. W. Götz, and *Die Politik Bayerns* (in *Briefe und Acten zur Geschichte des Dreissigjährigen Krieges in Zeiten d. vorwaltenden Einfluss der Wittelsbacher).*

[43] It also affected Maximilian's chances of succeeding to the Empire, as it united the Protestants against him. See Baudrillart, *La Politique de Henri IV en Allemagne (Revue des Questions historiques,* xxxvii. 418). For the Catholic literature directed

The incident caused some anxiety, and this was deepened in 1608 when Rudolph sent as his representative to the Diet of Ratisbon, not his conciliatory brother Matthias, but his bigoted cousin Ferdinand. The Protestant element in the Diet refused a grant for the war against the Turk until the Augsburg settlement had been reaffirmed and extended; whereupon the Catholics asserted that the Peace of Augsburg had been nullified by the Council of Trent. The Protestants had no alternative but to organize for defence. The Calvinists were already grouping themselves round the Elector Palatine Frederick, and in May 1608 there was an important conclave at Ahausen, attended by Count Wolfgang William of Neuburg, Margrave Frederick of Baden-Dürlach, the Duke of Würtemberg, the Margrave Joachim Ernest of Brandenburg and Christian of Anhalt. The chief aim of the alliance was to obtain the comprehension of the Calvinists in the religious peace, to maintain what ecclesiastical possessions they already held, to organize for defence of the Protestant cause, to act as one party in the Diet, and to insist on a Protestant succession in Cleve-Jülich. This Evangelical Union found a patron in Henry IV. of France and a leader in the Elector Palatine; it had the sympathies but not the active assistance of the Elector of Brandenburg; it received no support from the Elector of Saxony, and it is important as one of the few alliances in which Lutheran and Calvinist worked together. It was an illegal union, since the Empire did not permit such alliances among its subjects, and it might be considered treasonable since it looked for help to France. But these accusations would apply only on the assumption that seventeenth-century Germany was a nation. The Catholic alliances were equally illegal and were even more dependent on foreign support.

One of the aims of the Evangelical Union recalls the fact that religious and territorial questions were at this time inextricably mingled. The Religious Peace of Augsburg had left untouched all lands secularized by Lutherans before the year 1552, but nothing was said about lands which might be secularized after the date (1555) of the Religious Peace itself. Where the Protestants were in a majority, lands con-

---

(1608–1617) against the Augsburg settlement see Krebs, *Die politische Publizistik der Jesuiten und ihrer Gegner . . . (Hallesche Abhandlungen,* xxv. 207 ff.).

tinued to become secularized, though the moral deduced from the case of Gebhard Truchsess was that when a bishop, elected by a Catholic chapter, became Protestant, his episcopal lands reverted to the Church. The Ecclesiastical Reservation was the name given to the ruling of the Emperor that all ecclesiastical princes abandoning Catholicism should surrender their ecclesiastical lands; but, though this was often applied, the Protestants had never really accepted the principle, and successfully maintained their contention that it did not extend to those cases where a Protestant chapter had elected a Protestant bishop. Small concessions on both sides made possible a working settlement, but neither side abandoned its principles. On the one hand, it had been conceded by the Emperor Ferdinand that, in return for Lutheran acceptance of the Ecclesiastical Reservation, Protestant townsmen and nobles in Catholic states should not be obliged to emigrate, and, on the other hand, where lands were secularized by a Protestant chapter electing a bishop or incumbent of their own faith, the Protestants admitted that in such cases papal confirmaion was necessary, but evaded this difficulty by obtaining an indult from the Emperor on the pretext that papal approval would be too expensive. Thus the Emperor was a party to the arrangement by which most of the North German bishoprics became secularized, though the obvious result of the process was that a considerable number of elective Catholic states were fast becoming hereditary Protestant territories, for a Protestant bishop could marry. But while the Emperors tacitly consented to the existence of Protestant bishops or administrators in certain parts of Germany, they could hardly be expected to approve of the application of the hereditary principle, and by the time that the bishoprics of Magdeburg, Bremen, Lübeck, Verden, Minden and Halberstadt had come under the control of the Protestants, the Imperial and Catholic party in Germany felt that matters had gone too far, and that a dangerous process should be checked by all means in their power. Equally the Protestant princes were anxious to retain these possessions, for, in virtue of the *cujus regio* principle, territory involved a right of religious domination just as in the Middle Ages it had included a right of jurisdiction. The whole position was anomalous and obscure: no one was satisfied, and when action was taken it was generally in a spirit of irritation or defiance.

The Evangelical Union of 1608 was soon faced with a formidable Catholic alliance. Under the leadership of Maximilian of Bavaria, a number of Catholic princes, including the three archi-episcopal Electors, signed on the 10th of July 1609 a defensive League.[44] Its objects were to resist additional encroachments on episcopal lands and to maintain the Catholic religion. Maximilian was appointed Colonel of the League, and Spain promised a subsidy on condition that the objects of the League were approved by the Emperor. Meanwhile the territorial difficulty was brought to a crisis by the question of succession to the Cleve-Jülich territories. The two Protestant claimants—the Elector of Brandenburg and Philip Louis, Count of Neuburg—established themselves in the disputed territories, and this Protestant intrusion into the valley of the Lower Rhine seemed to contemporaries a direct menace to the ecclesiastical electorates, for it completed a process whereby *nearly all* of northern Germany became Protestant, and it seriously imperilled the integrity of the Spanish Low Countries. It came to be considered almost a test case in religious politics; the crisis was passed only when one of the Protestant intruders became a Catholic. But for this unexpected circumstance the Cleve-Jülich question would have been sufficient to precipitate war, as neither party would have allowed all the heritage to go to the other.

Thus by the year 1609 there were two opposed and armed organizations within the Empire, both illegal, both counting on foreign help, and neither having the full support of its co-religionaries. Both had internal difficulties, for the Calvinist Elector Palatine found his Lutheran allies embarrassing, and Maximilian was equally perplexed by solicitations from two different quarters: from Henry IV. that he should become an official candidate for the Empire, and from the ecclesiastical electors that he would use the forces of the League to expel the Protestants from the Cleve-Jülich lands. The sequestration of the Cleve-Jülich territories by the Emperor Rudolph caused the Evangelical Union to ally with Henry IV. in February 1610. In the same month the Catholic League was joined by several bishops and by Ferdinand of Styria, but it failed to obtain from Rudolph any expression of approval.

[44] The idea had first been suggested in 1607. Its initiation was due mainly to Zuñiga (Spanish Ambassador at the Imperial Court) and Maximilian. Zuñiga practically guaranteed Spanish help (C. A. Cornelius, *Die Grundung der deutschen Liga*, 29-30).

This prevented Spain giving public help; in order to remove this obstacle Maximilian resigned in favour of his brother-in-law Ferdinand, a step which served to afford the League just enough Hapsburg complexion to qualify it for the Spanish subsidy. Philip III. was thereupon declared Protector of the League, with Ferdinand as his lieutenant, and Maximilian was induced to accept the directorship of the League's military forces. In May 1610 by the treaty of Prague Spain promised subsidies for three years, and papal approval was also obtained. Both parties were thus prepared for war when the unexpected death of Henry IV. in May 1610 again postponed a decision. The Protestants, realizing that without French help they could do little, decided to temporize,[45] and the opposing forces were left free to harbour their strength for the crisis that was bound to come.

Not till four years later was the Cleve-Jülich question settled. The Count Palatine of Neuburg entrusted his son Wolfgang William with the duty of taking over these territories in conjunction with the Elector of Brandenburg. The two soon quarrelled and then sought for allies. Wolfgang William married the youngest daughter of Maximilian of Bavaria and turned Catholic; with Dutch help, Brandenburg seized Jülich and with equal facility turned Calvinist. With Bavarian money and Spanish troops the Imperialist General, Spinola, expelled the Dutch, and the combatants then agreed on another division of the spoils. By the treaty of Xanten, October 6, 1614, Neuburg obtained Jülich[46] and Berg, while Cleve with Ravensberg was assigned to Brandenburg. There were fresh partitions[47] later in the century, and the dispute always provided a convenient pretext for war, but the House of Brandenburg eventually secured the whole heritage.[48]

The year 1614 is noteworthy also as the year in which

[45] In October 1610 there was an attempt to unite Catholic Germany (represented by Bavaria, Mainz and Cologne) with Lutheran Germany (represented by Saxony, Coburg and Brunswick) in an Association for Constitutional Defence (*Bund für Vertheidigung der Reichsverfassung*). The project failed because of irresolution on the part of the Emperor and Elector of Saxony. For this see K. Lorenz, *Die Entwicklung der kirchlisch-politischen Verhältnisse in Deutschland*, 13.

[46] Jülich remained in the house of Neuburg until 1794, when it was captured by the French. Given to Brandenburg in 1814.

[47] Notably in 1624 and 1666.

[48] In 1814.

was published the only plea for unity between the two opposing sections of the Protestant faith.[49] In his *Irenicum*, Pareus, Professor of Theology at the Calvinist University of Heidelberg, advocated the summoning of a general Protestant Synod to discuss Calvinist and Lutheran differences and heal a schism from which the Catholics were deriving tremendous advantage. This proposed "Syncretism," as it was styled, excited little interest among the Protestants, but it called forth several attacks from the Catholics, and the Jesuit, Adam Contzen of Mainz, was so alarmed at the prospect of unity among the enemies of his faith, that he directed two manifestos[50] against Pareus, in one of which he attacked Syncretism or "false peace," proclaiming that the Irenicon[51] or "true peace" is possible only when there is complete unity of religion. Heretics must return to the fold before there could be any question of peace. The Protestant cause, he announced, was a losing one, and within a few years would be only a memory. Already three princes—the Elector Palatine, the Landgrave of Hesse and the Elector of Brandenburg—had changed from Lutheranism to Calvinism: what was there to prevent them from completing the circle and returning to the Catholic fold? "Facile est Europae fidem reddere." A general council would settle all doctrinal differences and inaugurate a new millennium of peace and unity. These two writers—Pareus and Contzen—clearly reflect the temper of their times. The one voices a solitary plea for unity within the Protestant ranks; the other insists, with all the weight of orthodox authority behind him, that, whether united or divided, the Protestants must yield unconditionally to the Church from which they have strayed. In such an atmosphere there could be no compromise; the sword must decide because the theologians could not agree.

It was in German lands that this great religious struggle was to be decided, and the united front which the Catholic Church was now showing had its counterpart in a gradual concentration of forces within the Hapsburg family. These

[49] See Krebs, *Politische Publizistik . . .*, 93.

[50] *De Synodo Evangelicorum* and *De pace Germaniae*. See also K. Brischar, *P. Adam Contzen ein Ireniker*, 41 ff.

[51] Contzen's use of the word Irenic*on* may be a tacit criticism of Pareus's use of the word Irenic*um*.

forces had been dispersed at the abdication of the Emperor
Charles V., and Ferdinand I. had carried this further by
bequeathing Tyrol, Breisgau, Styria, Carinthia, Carniola and
Alsace to cadet members of the family. The result of such
family settlements was that when Rudolph succeeded to the
Empire, he possessed, as hereditary lands, only Austria,
Bohemia and Hungary, of which the last two had strong
nationalist aspirations and were already in a state of incipient revolt. Under the leadership of Bocksay, Hungary rebelled, and with Turkish reinforcements Austria was invaded
(1605). Upper Austria and Transylvania were then overrun
by Bocksay, while the Turks took Pesth and Gran. In face of
this joint Turkish and national menace it seemed likely that
most of the Hapsburg lands in eastern Europe would be
lost and thereby the family hold on the Empire endangered
—a fear which caused Rudolph's brothers, Matthias and
Maximilian, and his cousins, Ferdinand and Maximilian
Ernest, to combine, in order to force the incompetent
Rudolph to resign some part of his power. Their proposal
was that Matthias should be declared Emperor-designate and
Vicegerent, but Rudolph refused to accept any such suggestion; moreover, open hostility to his younger brother caused
considerable anxiety among the Archdukes.[52] At Vienna in
April 1606 they forced Rudolph to admit Matthias as his
successor, and the latter then negotiated, later in the same
year, the treaty of Sitva-Torok by which the Turks retained
the fortresses of Gran and Canischa, but gave up their claim
to an annual tribute, while Bocksay was established in
Transylvania under Hapsburg suzerainty.[53] At the same time,
making a bid for popular support, Matthias granted religious
toleration in Hungary,[54] and Rudolph, irritated by this, refused to ratify the treaty of Sitva-Torok. Two years later,
however, Rudolph yielded, conceding Hungary, Austria and
Moravia to Matthias, and retaining for himself only Bohemia
and Silesia. The career of the Emperor at this period is

[52] The Papacy made strenuous efforts to heal the breach. Cf.
the *Instructions* to Cardinal Millino, legate to Rudolph, from
Paul V. (1608), printed from the Vatican Archives in Ehses,
Festschrift des deutschen Campo Santo in Rom., 1897, 267 ff. The
Papacy believed it essential that Matthias should be appointed
king of the Romans.

[53] Dumont, *Corps diplomatique*, v. pt. 2, 78.

[54] *Ibid.* 68.

obscure. He had for some time been liable to fits of insanity, and by 1606 his prerogative had passed to the Archdukes, headed by Matthias and inspired by his minister Khlesl. Rudolph's conduct seems hesitating and inconsistent,[55] but, although his archives were destroyed, and he is known mainly from the reports of his enemies, he may well have been inspired by two main motives—horror of heresy and a certain sense of duty as ruler. He believed that control of Hungary was absolutely essential for the safety of the Empire, and he strongly resented Matthias' recognition of the rebel Bocksay; equally he was an ardent Catholic, but averse from persecution. By the year 1608 the only important territory left to him was Bohemia, and thus for some years Prague—once the favourite residence of a greater Emperor[56]—became the nominal capital of the Empire.

This concentration of territories in the hands of the Emperor-designate had not been obtained without some sacrifice. Protestantism had taken root in eastern Europe, and under the leadership of such men as Illeshazy in Hungary, Zierotyn in Moravia and Tschernembl in Austria,[57] it had become a formidable movement. Matthias had strengthened his position by concessions, but these were not everywhere the same—thus in Hungary religious liberty was given to towns, villages and the nobility, while in Austria and Moravia this privilege was given to the nobility only. In Bohemia Rudolph had found it expedient to make concessions, and in July 1609, against the advice of his ministers, Lobkowitz, Martinitz and Slavata, he signed the *Letter of Majesty* by which the nobility and royal towns of Bohemia, Silesia and Lusatia were accorded the right of building temples and practising the Bohemian form of Lutheranism. These rights were extended also to Moravia, and thus it may have seemed to contemporaries that a *modus vivendi* had been reached.

The peace that now descended on Europe was only the calm before the storm. The Hapsburgs were waiting for the death of Rudolph in order to embark on their reactionary policy, and in Bohemia there already existed all the materials

[55] Denis, *Fin de l'indépendance bohème*, ii. 346.

[56] Charles IV. (1316–1378).

[57] For this subject see Gindely, *Die Gegenreformation und der Aufstand in Oberösterreich im Jahre 1626*, in *Sitzungsberichte der kaiserlichen Akademie der Wissenschaften*, Band cxviii.

for a great conflagration. In no other country were the traditions of religious dissent so deeply engrained; nowhere else was there such a conscious and assertive nationalism. A form of Protestantism had existed in Bohemia long before the Reformation: the martyrdom of John Hus and the strenuous campaigns of Ziska[58] were but incidents in an old story. The Luxemburg Emperor Charles IV.—although himself a Teuton—had already in the fourteenth century developed the latent aspirations of the Tcheques by encouraging native language, literature and commerce, and making Prague a European capital. By the seventeenth century, of the Bohemian towns only two—Pilsen and Budweis—were Catholic, and of the population only about one in ten was German.[59] It was thus predominantly Slav and non-Catholic, but, by its extraordinary mixture of Catholicism, Utraquism, Lutheranism, Calvinism and the doctrines of the Bohemian Brethren, it seemed more like a change-house for all the creeds of western Europe, old as well as new. Bohemia was the storm centre of the Counter Reformation, and of no other country can it be so truly said that Christianity brought not peace but a sword.

Utraquism had long ceased to be a heresy in Bohemia, and as an almost official religion had lost a good deal of its force. Its main difference from Catholicism was its insistence on giving the cup to the laity as well as to the priest, and, although it had derived some additional elements from the sixteenth-century Reformation, it was not a dynamic force in the seventeenth. What prevented the formation of a united Lutheran party in the country was the Bohemian Brotherhood, founded in the fifteenth century, a movement which met with an enthusiastic response from many whom the old Utraquist tenets had ceased to satisfy. The Brotherhood, although no revolutionaries like the Taborites,[60] were helped by the moral decadence of Utraquism. Their aim was, by a literal interpretation of the Gospels, to live as they thought Christ would have them live, and their ethics were those of the Sermon on the Mount. Guided by pious men like Kounvald and Loukatch, they became evangelists and demo-

[58] Leader of the Hussites, 1360–1424.
[59] Denis, op. cit. ii. 324.
[60] The followers of Ziska. They denied the real presence and rejected the doctrines of the sacraments and of purgatory.

crats but never rebels, incarnating in their lives the virtues of poverty, humility and submission. On the principle that "every man is a priest" they admitted laymen into the government of their organization, but they had none of the positive, constructive elements which made Calvinism a warring and conquering creed. Their outlook was one of other-worldliness, which they combined with many practical activities; they were devoted educators, and in Comenius they produced the greatest exponent of the science of teaching since the time of Plato. But they tended to be unsocial and to abstract themselves from the conventions of society, believing that agriculture is the only absolutely justifiable occupation, that town life is necessarily wicked, and that Christ and the World cannot exist together. They came into contact with the state in 1602, when they were banned and their churches handed over to Catholics and Utraquists: thereafter they lived a precarious existence, retaining their hold by secret conventicles and by the leadership of a wealthy landowner named Boudovets, who had been converted to their doctrines.[61] But these doctrines were, for the seventeenth century, worse than impracticable: they were fatal, because they automatically deprived their adherents of all initiative and left them defenceless in a world of scheming enemies. They helped to intensify those elements of mysticism and spiritual idealism which made Bohemia such an easy prey for Hapsburg ambitions, qualities which have interfered with the political destinies of the Slav race. The movement had an important share in the great tragedy through which the ill-fated country was so soon to pass.

While most of the peasants were nominally Utraquist or Catholic, many were secretly influenced by the Bohemian Brethren. The Lutherans had a large majority among the middle classes; the nobility included some Calvinists as well as Lutherans. The mediocrity of the Lutherans and Utraquists was in marked contrast with the fervour and devotion of the Calvinists, the Jesuits[62] and the Bohemian Brethren. The Bohemian nobility was one of the chief curses of the country.[63] In many cases their conversions had been effected for

[61] Denis, *op. cit.* ii. 340.

[62] There were about two hundred Jesuits in Bohemia in the early years of the seventeenth century.

[63] Denis, *op. cit.* ii. 325.

sordid objects, their aim being a state religion which could be enforced on their dependants without involving any adherence on their part to its doctrines. They had no patriotism; they regarded the bourgeoisie and the peasantry as their natural enemies, and they were generally ready to betray their country for the lowest personal motives. It was recorded by Slavata,[64] who was not likely to be prejudiced against his own caste, that in the time of Rudolph and Matthias it was very rare for proceedings to be taken against them even if convicted of capital crimes. They paid no taxes, and as there was no army they had no outlet for their passions. One of the few beneficent results of the Hapsburg conquest of Bohemia was that by the Constitution of 1627 their enormous powers were considerably curtailed. In addition to the forces of disunion created by the war of sects and the intrigues of the nobility, there was the old race hatred of Slav and Teuton; and in this connection it should be recalled that though the Germanic element in seventeenth-century Bohemia was very much less than it is to-day, the small alien minority often irritated national feeling by an ostentatious and arrogant superiority. Tcheque patriots protested vehemently against the steady increase of the Teutonic element in the governing classes and the tendency to make German the language of the Government. It is a remarkable fact that of the leaders responsible for the defenestration of Prague very few could speak the national language,[65] and one of the most bitter indictments of the German character came from a Bohemian patriot at this time: "Like a caterpillar in a cabbage, a serpent in the breast, a rat in the granary, a goat in the garden, so in Bohemia the German steals, cheats and deceives."[66]

The *Letter of Majesty* was followed by an attempt to reconcile the Lutherans with the Bohemian Brethren and unite the two sects in the general cause of toleration. It was intended to do for Bohemia what the Augsburg settlement had done for the Empire, and it achieved that object, for, by its grant of partial toleration, it raised wild hopes and encouraged other sects, such as the Calvinists, to demand inclu-

[64] *Ibid.* 368.
[65] Charvériat, *Histoire de la guerre de trente ans,* i. ch. 3.
[66] Denis, *op. cit.* 423.

sion. The turbulent Calvinist, Christian of Anhalt, came from the Palatinate to Prague in order to make this demand, in return for the support of the Evangelical Union, whereupon there ensued a conflict in the policy of Rudolph between his natural instincts, which were in favour of peace and toleration, and his convictions as a ruler, which demanded religious uniformity. He was not unpopular in Bohemia, where some allowance was made for his mental affliction by a nation quick to condone faults or misfortunes in a ruler who showed some sympathy with the national temper; moreover, it was known that he was anxious for peace, that he was opposed to extremes, that his retirement to Bohemia was dictated by his personal preference, and that his most incautious acts were prompted by the reactionary half-Spanish camarilla around him. His last years were clouded by continued estrangement from his relatives, by anxiety at the increasing demands of the Protestants, and disgust at the evidences of intrigue and rancour in the city where he had chosen his residence. In 1611 he was induced to give up even the crown of Bohemia and consent to the election of his brother Matthias in his place, so that for the last months of his life Rudolph was little more than a private person. He died on the 20th of January 1612, and it is recorded that one night shortly before his death he opened a window of the Hradschany Palace overlooking the city and solemnly cursed Prague and Bohemia.[67]

The accession of Matthias made little difference in the atmosphere of tense expectation which hung over the greater part of central Europe. Like his brother, Matthias was incapable, impractical, dilettante, and liable to be dominated by stronger personalities. His evil genius was Khlesl. The Government and the Archives were transferred from Prague to Vienna, and Bohemia became a province administered by foreigners. The executive was usurped by Khlesl, who attempted to introduce absolutist methods into a country which prized liberty above all things. Moreover, difficulties were soon found in the working of the *Letter of Majesty*. The landowners and municipal councils had power to veto any proposed building of churches within their jurisdiction, and this led to constant disputes, while the Lutherans soon became alienated from their strange and unworldly allies, the

[67] Coxe, *House of Austria*, ii. 425.

Bohemian Brethren. In 1617 an edict was issued requiring the surrender of all religious foundations to the purposes intended by their founders, and this created turmoil and resentment. Under Lohelius, Archbishop of Prague, Catholic priests were disseminated throughout the country districts, where many Protestants were too poor or too widely scattered to afford a pastor. The royal towns were compelled to give burgess rights to Catholics, and a beginning was made in the process of removing Protestants from the municipal councils. In every way the slender concessions of the *Letter of Majesty* were whittled down,[68] and the reactionary party was testing how far it could go before definitely cancelling the little that had been conceded. It is significant that, in the hour of need, Bohemia had no national leader. The head of the anti-Hapsburg movement in Bohemia was the Calvinist, Henry Matthias of Thurn, descended from the Milanese Della Torre family, his chief lieutenants being Wenceslas Ruppa and Colonna de Fels. Boudovets and Zierotyn were too punctilious and conscientious to inspire a following, and the doctrines of the Bohemian Brethren had induced a quietist temper which practically submitted to oppression without condoning it.

Meanwhile the question of Matthias's successor continued to agitate the Archdukes. The Emperor was childless, and the choice lay among his relatives. Spain favoured the candidature of Don Carlos, son of Philip III. and great-nephew of Matthias, but this claim was never pressed, and in 1617 was abandoned in order that the way should be free for Archduke Ferdinand of Styria. In return for this, Ferdinand undertook to give Alsace to Spain if he were elected—a concession of very doubtful value since Hapsburg rights in Alsace were not clearly defined. Matthias was then induced to designate Ferdinand as his successor, and this fact was announced at a meeting of the Bohemian Diet in June 1617. Matthias himself had been elected king of Bohemia, but there were precedents the other way; the Diet now accepted Ferdinand as king, and so in a measure confirmed the view that the crown was hereditary in the Hapsburg family. At the same meeting of the Bohemian Diet it was demanded that the *Letter of Majesty* should be maintained, and this Ferdinand promised to do, provided his spiritual advisers

[68] Denis, *op. cit.* ii. 492 ff.

approved. On the 19th of July 1617 Ferdinand was crowned king of Bohemia.

The next step was to make certain of Hungary. There were more precedents for elective right in Hungary than in Bohemia, and so special precautions were taken not to raise this important constitutional question.[69] The Hungarian Diet met at Pressburg in May 1618 to consider a letter from Matthias requesting that Ferdinand should be proclaimed king, the word election being carefully avoided. The lower nobility made some resistance, but at length a compromise was reached by declaring that, though the crown was elective, it could not go out of the Hapsburg family. The Spanish agent tried to persuade Ferdinand not to accept this, but the Emperor-designate was conciliatory and yielded. On the 16th of May Ferdinand was declared "unanimously elected according to the ancient customs." It remained only for the new king of Bohemia and Hungary to obtain the Empire and this dynastic concentration of Hapsburg lands would be complete.

Contemporaries could not have failed to note the ominous fact that at the meeting of the Bohemian Diet which proclaimed Ferdinand king, two nobles, Martinits and Slavata, had opposed the demand for the maintenance of the *Letter of Majesty*. Late in 1617 Matthias left Prague, leaving the government in the hands of eleven lieutenants, of whom seven were Catholics and four Protestants, and of this council Lobkowitz, Martinitz and Slavata were leading members. As the forces of reaction gained strength, the Protestant faith was still more imperilled by attacks on church property, and in December 1617 the destruction of the Protestant temple at Klostergrab caused a profound sensation throughout Bohemia. At the same time one of the Regents, Michna, made no secret of his ambition to restore Catholicism through the intermediate step of Utraquism.[70] Moreover, the year 1617 was an important one in the Protestant annals, for it was the first centenary of Luther's fixing his ninety-five theses to the church door of Wittenberg—an anniversary marked by a renewed outburst of theological literature, in which one cannot fail to detect the suggestion that Protestantism, having

[69] Coxe, *op. cit.* ii. 433-440.
[70] See Gindely, *The Thirty Years' War* (English Translation), i. 53.

been tried for a century and found wanting, was now about to yield before the onslaught of the purified and re-invigorated Church. The great war about to commence was preceded by a battle of the books in which opinion was hardened and embittered by the brutal personalities then in vogue.

An Imperial letter of March 1618 forbidding meetings of Protestants was the spark which set aflame the combustible material that had long been accumulating in Bohemia. On the 21st of May a Protestant Diet met at the Carolinum, and Thurn declared that only force would bring to reason the reactionary members of the Regency. An act of defenestration was decided upon by Thurn, Ruppa and Colonna de Fels. Two days later they met in the old palace in the presence of four Catholic lieutenants—Sternberg, Martinitz, Slavata and Lobkowitz, with Fabricius as secretary in place of Michna, and these were asked to declare whether they had taken any part in the edict forbidding their meetings. A tumult ensued, when Martinitz and Slavata were accused of alliance with the Jesuits. In a scene of confusion Martinits and Slavata were thrown from the window, followed by the protesting Fabricius. The drop was a considerable one, but only Slavata was injured. Catholic witnesses saw the falling Regents supported by angels, but Protestant writers attributed their escape from death to the heap of paper and rubbish in the basement into which they fell.

Chapter 4

The Thirty Years' War

THE REBELLION in Bohemia, punished two years later by the hanging of twenty-six rebels in Prague, led to a European war unique in its length, its constant shifting of scene and motive, its dreariness and ferocity. The narrative is relieved by few stirring episodes: there were few great personalities involved; the generation ending it had long since outlived the quarrels and hatreds that began it. Gathering momentum as it proceeded, considered interminable by those who suffered from its ravages, it was ended only by the exhaustion of the combatants and the perpetuation of injustices and resentments breeding future wars; for this melancholy struggle gave birth to the first of modern peace congresses which, in attempting to stabilize the frontiers of Europe, brought into prominence a great cause of unrest in modern times—the Rhine frontier. The Thirty Years' War retarded the civilization of Germany by more than a century, and the destinies of Europe have been profoundly influenced by that fact.

So complicated was the Thirty Years' War that it may assist the reader if some important facts are first of all emphasized. The causes of religious ferment in Germany and rebellion in Bohemia have been considered in the preceding chapter. None of the greater German Protestant states (except the Palatinate) was directly involved in the war until the issue of the Edict of Restitution and the intervention of Gustavus Adolphus (1629). Saxony and Brandenburg had to

take up arms against the Hapsburgs after the sack of Magdeburg (1631), but they made their peace with the Emperor in
1635 (treaty of Prague). Spain and Lorraine were the active
allies of the Empire; the Papacy (under Urban VIII.) gave
no support, and the Catholics were divided into the League
party on the one hand, headed by Maximilian of Bavaria, intent on preserving Catholic lands as well as recovering secularized bishoprics, and the Imperial party on the other, led
by Ferdinand and Wallenstein, anxious to transform the Holy
Roman Empire into an Austrian despotism. Territorial and
religious ambitions were thus mingled in the minds of the
protagonists. In the early stages of the war England gave unofficial and ineffective support to the dispossessed Elector
Palatine; the war between the Vasas of Poland and Sweden
did not leave the latter free for the contest in Germany until
1629; with the termination in 1621 of the Twelve Years'
Truce between Spain and the United Provinces, the Dutch
may be considered as combatants in the struggle. The nationalist ambitions of Hungary were also involved, and, under
Bethlen Gabor and Rakockzy, the Magyars threatened the
Hapsburgs from the east. France was an eager spectator
after 1626, a combatant after 1635; her ally Bavaria, at first
the leader of conservative Catholicism in Germany, was
forced, by Swedish invasion, to join forces with the Emperor,
but the Peace of Westphalia saw her again on the side of
France. Sweden played the most distinguished part in the war,
but difficulty was caused by the divergence between the
policy of Richelieu and that of Gustavus Adolphus. French
ambitions transformed the Thirty Years' War from a terri-
torial-religious struggle into a dynastic war.

Directly connected with the war were the questions of the
Valtelline and the Mantuan succession. The Valtelline controlled the route[1] from the Milanese into Germany and
Austria; the duchy of Mantua included the two important
fortresses of Mantua and Casale. By the treaty of Monzon
(1626) France deserted her Protestant allies in the Valtelline,
while by the treaty of Cherasco (1631) a French nominee
acquired Mantua, and so the French were enabled to contest
Spanish control of northern Italy.

Finally, it should be noted that although warfare was

[1] By the Splügen and Stelvio passes.

chronic throughout the whole of this period, there were five battles directly influencing the course of the struggle. These were the battle of the White Hill (1620), by which the Bohemian rebellion was ended and the conquest of the Palatinate made possible; Lütter (1626), which compelled the withdrawal of Denmark; Breitenfeld or Leipzig (1631), which restored the fortunes of Protestantism and proved the turning-point of the war; Lützen (1632), resulting directly in the death of Gustavus Adolphus and indirectly in the assassination of Wallenstein; Nördlingen (1634), which undid the work of Sweden. After 1634 the war became one of exhaustion waged by France and Sweden against Bavaria and the Imperialists, a war spreading disease and starvation throughout Germany, in which no important German question was involved, and in which hundreds of thousands of the civilian population perished. Of this period, five years (1643–1648) were spent in peace negotiations.

For the purposes of study the war is generally divided into four parts according to the nationality dominating each period—the Bohemian or Palatine, the Danish, the Swedish and the French, these in the order of their succession, and this arrangement is useful if attention is to be directed solely to the campaigns, many of which are of little military or historical interest. An alternative method, however, is to consider three main stages—I. The loss of the Palatinate and the collapse of German Protestantism, complete by 1629; II. The restoration of Protestantism by Sweden, 1630–1635; and III. The intervention of France, 1635–1648. The advantage of this division is that it keeps clear motives as much as campaigns, and in this chapter it will be adhered to. This third and final section will deal also with the Peace of Westphalia.

I. The loss of the Palatinate and the collapse of German Protestantism, 1618–1629.

At the time of the defenestration Ferdinand was in Pressburg and Matthias in Vienna. The Emperor was not anxious for war; with Khlesl he did his best to localize the issue and treat the rebellion as a temporary effervescence. Ferdinand, on the other hand, supported by the Archdukes and by

Spanish promises, resolved that the hour had come. His first step was to remove the forces favourable to peace. Khlesl dominated Matthias and was not a party to the designs of the Archdukes; his removal was therefore necessary. Poison and papal excommunication were considered as alternative means of dealing with him, but the Emperor-designate was chary of using either method and had him arrested instead. The five years of imprisonment that followed removed the Imperial minister from the scene of action. On all sides the militant Catholic party could count on support, or at least neutrality. Sigismund of Poland and the Archduke Albert of the Low Countries promised active help; Cosimo of Tuscany, Ferdinand's brother-in-law, sent troops; James I. of England was still seeking a Spanish alliance. At the French court the discredited Bouillon[2] was the only advocate for intervention, and, though Pope Paul V. refused to make a grant on the ground that he already contributed to the Catholic League, his successor, Gregory XV., gave an annual subsidy of 200,000 florins. Through the Spanish ambassador Oñate constant communication was maintained with Madrid, and in Germany itself, though Hungary, Moravia and Silesia were tempted to join the Bohemians, John George of Saxony was hostile to the insurgents by temperament and conviction, while Brandenburg was neutral. The *Flugschriften*[3] or pamphlet literature of 1618-1619 shows that the Bohemians themselves regarded the matter as a local and personal one between them and the Emperor, and thus the revolt could easily have been isolated and settled without endangering European peace.

Immediately after the defenestration the rebels appointed a Directory of thirty deputies under the presidency of Wenceslas Ruppa, and it was publicly announced that the movement was directed not against the person of the Emperor but against the violators of the *Letter of Majesty*. Supported by all the Bohemian towns except Pilsen and Budweis, this provi-

[2] See Hanotaux, *Richelieu*, ii. pt. 2, for Bouillon's intrigues at the French court. See *Mercure français* (1619), vi. 342-370, for a Memoir sent to the French court in order to counter Bouillon's intrigues. It was argued in this Memoir that the revolt was of republican origin.

[3] About 1800 pamphlets appeared in the year 1618 alone; cf. Gebauer, *Die Publicistik über den böhmischen Aufstand von 1618.*

sional government, after expelling the Jesuits, proceeded to arm the enthusiastic town bands. What made the breach irreparable, however, was the sudden intervention of Frederick V., the Elector Palatine, who in 1612 had married Elizabeth, daughter of James I. His declared willingness to accept the Bohemian crown was not received with unanimous enthusiasm by the Directory, as his incapacity was notorious, and though it was assumed that Frederick would have the full support of the Protestant Union behind him, a vain effort was made to enlist the help of Saxony instead. Of the Bohemian Protestants only a Calvinist minority, headed by Ruppa and Thurn, were favourable to Frederick; the Lutheran majority naturally turned to the Elector of Saxony as the official head of German Protestantism and the German prince most likely by his status and resources to make the movement legitimate and successful. But the elector John George preferred to keep peace with the Emperor, and even if he had not been influenced by instincts of self-preservation, he would never have bargained with any organization that included active Calvinists.[4] It was the emphatically expressed opinion of many Lutherans that the triumph of the Calvinist Frederick would be more dangerous than that of the Catholic Ferdinand, for the Calvinists, they said, were as bad as Mohammedans, and their confession of faith no better than the Koran. There was therefore little hope of a united Protestantism at this crisis in their fortunes.

A new turn was given to events by the interference of the Catholic Emanuel of Savoy, who, anxious to press his candidature for the Empire in the turmoil that seemed likely to ensue, sent the condottiere Albert of Mansfeld with troops to the help of the insurgents, nominally in the name of the Elector Palatine. Mansfeld captured Pilsen in November 1618, forcing many of the Catholic population to emigrate. This was the most important military enterprise in the first year of the war. In the summer of 1619 Thurn and his troops advanced to the gates of Vienna, but the sudden firmness of Ferdinand and the arrival of reinforcements in the capital caused the Calvinist general to abandon the idea of a siege and fall back on Bohemia.

Matthias' death in March 1619 removed the only person

[4] The judicial murder of Barneveldt by a Calvinist tribunal in 1619 may have helped to increase Lutheran dislike of Calvinists.

who even yet might have secured peace. The date of the election was fixed for July 20, 1619, and, with three non-Catholic Electors in a college of seven, it was clear that the Bohemian vote would be the deciding factor in the event of the Protestant Electors agreeing on a candidate outside the Hapsburg family. To some it seemed that now was the unique chance for a Protestant and non-Catholic Empire, while to others it appeared that the Empire might very well terminate at this point. Hence the suddenly enhanced importance of the Bohemian crown. To Frederick, delay was essential in order that he might consolidate his position in Bohemia: once in secure possession of the Bohemian crown, his election to the Empire was probable. Of the other likely candidates, Charles Emanuel of Savoy was keen but had little chance, while the Duke of Bavaria had a good chance but was not keen; the king of Denmark might also have been a candidate. Although Ferdinand had been crowned king of Bohemia, the Bohemian Diet claimed that he had not yet been invested with his prerogatives, and that, in accordance with the provisions of the Golden Bull, the Bohemian vote was therefore vested in the Diet. But in spite of such efforts to influence the election, Ferdinand was unanimously elected Emperor in the cathedral of Frankfort on the 28th of August 1619. The deputy of the Elector Palatine at first gave his vote for Maximilian of Bavaria as the only serious rival candidate, but afterwards rallied to the side of the majority. Eleven days earlier the Bohemian Diet had deposed Ferdinand, and on the 26th of August had elected Frederick king of Bohemia.

Frederick's act in accepting a crown offered by rebels was looked at askance by all the Protestant rulers, as it was directly opposed to the accepted political morality of the time.[5] His father-in-law strongly disapproved and contemporaries were unanimous in the opinion (possibly erroneous) that he was being urged on by his wife, who, it was said, "would rather eat sauerkraut with a king than baked meats with a prince." Matters were made worse by the conduct of the Bohemian Directorate. They exercised a meticulous tyranny, such as is often found during revolutions, when self-constituted bodies become conscious of their isolation and of

[5] The responsibility of Frederick and his wife for the Thirty Years' War is discussed in C. V. Wedgwood, *The Thirty Years' War*, 148-9.

an irreparable breach with the past. The death-penalty was decreed for all who opposed the revolution; subsidies for the ill-organized town bands were obtained by confiscation, in which the Imperial art treasures suffered, and acts of vandalism occurred which intensified the hatred of the Bohemian Lutherans for the Calvinists. Frederick abandoned the direction of policy to the violent Calvinist preacher Scultetus, while military affairs were entrusted to the fiery Christian of Anhalt. Disillusionment soon followed when Frederick showed that he was unfit to be a national leader, and soon the open profligacy of himself and his court deeply shocked a nation distinguished by its conviction that religion necessarily includes morality.

These events had a faint echo in Hungary, where the crown was now accepted by a man as little competent as the Elector Palatine to lead a nation. Bethlen Gabor was one of those sudden apparitions from the fringes of civilization that sometimes startle Europe by a meteoric flight. Having disposed of his predecessor and benefactor,[6] he had himself recognized in 1613 as Prince of Transylvania, and, though half civilized, he showed that he had some education and a good taste in art. An assiduous reader of the Bible, he claimed to be a Calvinist, and not even a life of daily dissipation could lessen the activity of his mind and body. Chafing under Turkish and Hapsburg suzerainty, he aimed at founding an independent state. The war gave him an opportunity of selling his services to the highest bidder and exercising his chief political quality—perfidy. With such allies it is not surprising that the Bohemian revolution was so short-lived. Having been elected king of Hungary in October 1619 Bethlen joined forces with Thurn and the Bohemians; the two armies invaded Austria, and for the second time in five months Vienna was besieged. But at the critical moment the ill-disciplined troops showed that numbers can never compensate for organization and control. On the first show of resistance Bethlen and Thurn retired from the walls, and thus by their incompetence betrayed the party which they had undertaken to lead.[7]

The rebels were never again to have such an opportunity.

[6] Bethlen Gabor became virtual ruler of Transylvania after he had removed his predecessor, Gabriel Bathori, with the help of assassins (1613).

[7] Huber, *Geschichte Österreichs*, X. iii.

In the same month as Vienna was being besieged Ferdinand signed the secret treaty of Munich with Maximilian of Bavaria by which the latter, in return for military help, was promised the Palatine Electorate. This was quite as illegal as Frederick's acceptance of the Bohemian crown, for Frederick had not yet been deposed from his Electorate, and it was not for the Emperor, without the concurrence of the Estates, to make such a promise. The only semblance of legality that could be invoked was the fact that the Bavarian Wittelsbachs had once been Electors, but, in accordance with a long recognized division, the electoral vote had been confirmed in the Palatine branch. Frederick's acceptance and Ferdinand's disposal of dignities to which neither had any legal right were the two things that changed the Bohemian revolt into the Thirty Years' War.

The military incompetence of the Bohemian and Hungarian rebels, together with the unity and strength of the Catholic forces, helped to lessen what inclination the German Protestants may have felt to take part in the struggle. Indeed, several members of the Protestant Union showed a disposition to recede from the position they had already taken up. In April 1620, French mediators[8] conducted negotiations with the Union and, early in July, a treaty was signed at Ulm whereby the Union definitely abandoned its leader, the Elector Palatine, while, on its part, the League promised not to attack the lands of members of the Union. The Elector of Saxony and Louis of Hesse-Darmstadt were now won over to the Imperial cause, the former undertaking to supply a contingent of troops in return for the promise of Lusatia. At the same time the Duke of Savoy, abandoning the Union, offered his services to the Emperor, thereby making public his conviction that more was to be gained from alliance with the Hapsburgs than from hostility to them. These things constituted the first real Hapsburg success; they were soon to be followed by victory in the field. Between them, the forces of the League, the Imperialists and the Saxons numbered about 60,000 men, commanded by Maximilian of Bavaria. Having

[8] There were Austro-Spanish influences at work in the entourage of Marie de Medici; and the Council, headed by Jeannin, acted mainly in the interests of the Hapsburgs. French mediation was concerned with reconciling the Protestant Union and the Catholic League. Cf. Jeannin, *Mémoires*, ed. Petitot, xvi. 63 ff.

reduced rebellious Upper Austria to submission, the Duke of
Bavaria marched on Prague, and on the 8th of November
1620 was fought, a few miles outside the city, the battle of
the White Hill. Though holding a good position on the slopes,
the Bohemians were completely outnumbered. They were
undisciplined; they did not use their artillery, and eventually
the sight of fugitives from his army made Frederick follow
their example, so precipitating a crushing defeat. Maximilian
was hailed as the saviour of the Empire; Te Deums and fireworks in Rome celebrated the victory as if it were a deliver-
ance from the Infidel, and the German Lutheran princes
hastened to congratulate the Emperor on the extermination
of the dragon of "Turco-Calvinismus." They could not have
foreseen that their turn was yet to come, and that the war
which might very well have ended here was to last another
twenty-eight years.

On the general European situation and on the fortunes of
Bohemia the battle of the White Hill exercised a considerable
influence. On his own authority Ferdinand proclaimed the
Ban of Empire on Frederick and Christian of Anhalt (January 1621), and soon afterwards these two Calvinists were
further discredited by the publication of papers seized in the
sack of Prague just after the battle of the White Hill. These
papers purporting to emanate from the Anhalt Chancery, appeared in public as the *Anhaltische Kanzlei*, edited by William Jocher,[9] one of Maximilian's councillors, and in this
form they provide an interesting specimen of war propaganda.
The purpose of the compilation was to show, by extracts from
Christian of Anhalt's correspondence, that the principles of
Calvinism were necessarily subversive of all law and order as
understood in western Europe, and that the aim of the Protestant Union, in the hands of unscrupulous Calvinists, was to
introduce a Turkish domination. Jocher cleverly separated
German Protestantism from the activities of Christian of
Anhalt and the Elector Palatine, arguing that the unscrupulous
machinations of these two were adequate justification for the
Ban of Empire. But this literary weapon could be used by
the other party as well. In the spring of 1621 the Capuchin
monk Hyacinth was sent on a secret mission to Madrid in
order to win over the Spanish court to the proposed transfer-

[9] Koser, *Der Kamzleienstreit*, 15.

ence of the electoral dignity from Frederick to Maximilian. Considerable importance was attached by the Curia to the project of replacing one of the Protestant votes by a Catholic vote, since by this means the Catholic majority in the Electoral College would be rendered absolutely safe, and Carafa, the Papal Nuncio in Vienna, wrote a letter on this subject to the Nuncio in Brussels, but the courier carrying the letter fell into the hands of Mansfeld's troops on the Upper Rhine. This letter, with other correspondence, was published in 1622 as the *Cancellaria Hispanica*.[10] Compiled probably by Camerarius, one of Frederick's secretaries,[11] the book purported to be the first of a series of publications intended to show the double dealing in Catholic policy, emphasizing the growing cleavage between the Imperialist and the League designs; it attributed responsibility for the war to the Catholics, citing Hyacinth's mission to Madrid as an instance of how the reactionary element was soliciting foreign help in order to continue the war, and it maintained that, by his Imperial Ban on Frederick, the Emperor was using an important Imperial institution for the purpose of fulfilling his obligations to Bavaria. "Spain pipes while Germany dances" is the theme of the *Cancellaria Hispanica*. The controversy raised by these two publications lasted until 1626.

But in this war of pamphlets the Imperialist party had the first blow, and there can be no doubt that the success of the *Anhaltische Kantzlei* helped to bring about the dissolution of the Protestant Union (April 1621). German Protestantism was thenceforth divided into the responsible, conventional, time-serving element, headed by the Elector of Saxony, and the discredited, but still warring and ambitious party, represented by such leaders as Frederick and Christian of Anhalt. The first result of the collapse of the Protestant Union was the invasion[12] of the Lower Palatinate by the troops of Spinola and Tilly, forcing the "Winter King" to take ignominious refuge in Holland, where the Twelve Years'

[10] The title-page of the first edition gives the place of publication as Freistad.

[11] Koser, *op. cit.* 32.

[12] There is a contemporary account of the campaigns in the Palatinate by a Spanish soldier (Fr. de Ybarra), reprinted by Morel Fatio in *L'Espagne au XVIIème et au XVIIIème siècles*, 328-480. This account is of interest only for military history.

Truce with Spain, concluded in 1609, had now come to an end. Mansfeld withdrew his motley troops to Alsace and the Rhineland, where they lived entirely by pillage, thus inaugurating one of the characteristic phases of the Thirty Years' War. The effects of the battle of the White Hill extended to Hungary, where, after months of negotiation, Bethlen Gabor renounced his title, accepting as compensation several territories and the dignity of Prince of the Empire.

But it was in Bohemia that the battle of the White Hill led to the most important results. The victory was followed by the public execution[13] of twenty-six persons suspected of complicity in the rebellion, but these scapegoats, who included at least one octogenarian and several men of noted piety and learning, were of a very different type from the military leaders who had drawn Bohemia into this struggle and had already made good their escape. The resources of the country in men and money were now to be ruined in a concerted policy of bigotry and confiscation. A syndicate, headed by the notorious Liechtenstein, was formed to sell the forfeited estates; the entire coinage of the country was expropriated and replaced by money having only half the intrinsic value of the old.[14] Even Catholics were not spared in this persecution. Municipal property of great value was impounded; large estates were sold at a ridiculously low price to those in league with the syndicate, and from this period date the fortunes of such Bohemian families as the Bucquoys, the Trautmannsdorfs, the Metternichs and the Marradas. Worse still was the systematic repression of Protestantism by a host of Jesuit missionaries who carried their campaigns into the remotest part of the country with all the resources of the secular power behind them. In such circumstances it it not surprising that "conversions" were numerous. One Jesuit is said to have boasted six thousand converts. Suspected books were destroyed, and children were taught to take part in religious plays, acted in public, in which was depicted the triumph of orthodoxy over heresy. The old Tcheque hymn-tunes were used for a new Catholic hymnal, and the more credulous were exploited by frequent "miracles"—chief among which was the miraculous virgin of Mikoulof, a great auxiliary in the reli-

[13] An English account of these executions will be found in *Harleian Miscellany*, iii. 409.

[14] Denis, *La Bohème depuis la Montagne Blanche*, i. 19 ff.

gious propaganda of Cardinal Dietrichstein. Many emigrated, but the great majority of the nation had to assist sullenly in this process whereby the spirit of Bohemia was systematically broken.[15]

By the year 1632 the Catholic triumph in Bohemia was complete; Protestantism had been extirpated, and the persecutions then ceased. In that period the country passed through a humiliation almost insupportable, because intellectual as well as material. The memoirs of the time show that it was accompanied by frequent manifestations of religious hysteria. Visions, charms and incantations became the order of the day, and a more sinister sign of national collapse is seen in the great increase of prosecutions for sorcery.[16] Learning and education necessarily decayed in such a stifling atmosphere, and at the University of Prague, once famous for its scholarship, classics and history ceased to be taught at all, while science was reduced to the study of approved mediaeval compilations. From their fortress on the Clementinum the Jesuits controlled the whole intellectual life of the country, everywhere suppressing originality or independence of thought, and maintaining that dead uniformity of opinion which is the negation of thinking itself. The religious life of Bohemia, once so rich in its vigour and variety, became a narrow freemasonry centring in the numerous *Sodalitates Marianae,* and only in the lives and writings of the *émigrés* did anything of the old Bohemia survive. The patriot Paul Stransky (1583-1657) outlined in his *Respublica Bojema* the aspirations of the Tcheque bourgeoisie and the native feelings of resentment against the Teutonic domination. Of greater importance was Comenius,[17] who incarnated all that was best and most practical in the aims of the Bohemian Brotherhood, and in whose life scientific, religious and educational motives were harmoniously combined. His strongest belief was in the natural goodness of humanity and the power of education to elucidate it. Driven from place to place by the dragoons of Liechtenstein, he never ceased his activities as an educator,[18] winning numerous con-

---

[15] *Ibid.* i. 95 ff.

[16] Denis, *op. cit.* i. 348. It should be noticed, however, that several Jesuits attacked the craze for witch-hunting, *e.g.* the *Cautio Criminalis* of Frederic Spee, S.J. (1631).

[17] 1592–1671.

[18] See Keatinge, *The Great Didactic of John Amos Comenius.*

verts to his enlightened methods in Bohemia, Moravia, Poland and Transylvania, and eventually terminating a career of devotion and self-sacrifice at Amsterdam in 1671. His studies included history, theology, philosophy and philology; he was the true predecessor of the eighteenth-century encyclopaedists in spite of the fact that his science was outmoded, for he continued to assume the truth of the Ptolemaic system. But, apart from such men, Bohemia intellectually ceased to exist in the campaign of greed and bigotry to which she was subjected in these years.

The terms of the Bohemian subjection were defined in the Constitution of 1627,[19] by which the country was assimilated with the other Hapsburg possessions, a constitution which remained in force until 1848. The monarchy was declared hereditary in the male line of the Hapsburgs, and the Diet was empowered to elect only if that line failed. The Chancellor had to follow the king—that is, take up his residence in Vienna—and national custom was displaced by the amalgam of Germanic law and Roman jurisprudence which did service elsewhere in the Hapsburg dominions. In consequence, the status of the free peasant was debased, for it was now influenced by the typical Roman Law conceptions of slavery. It was enacted that the lord had a right of property in his serfs and that the serf had no right of prescription against his master; serfdom thus became a legal institution in Bohemia, and organized man-hunts brought back many peasants who had tried to take refuge in flight. The serf was thenceforth subjected to a harsher moral code than that applied to his superiors: adultery, for instance, was punished by death; the amusements of dancing and gaming were forbidden him; he could not change his master, and the gilds were forbidden to receive fugitives. Only against excessive cruelty on the part of his lord had the Bohemian peasant any right of redress. Finally, it may be said of the Constitution of 1627 that it created Teutonic predominance in Bohemia; it suppressed, so far as human laws could do so, the language and nationality of the Bohemians, and it laid up a great store of bitterness and resentment which found some outlet in the revolutions of 1848.

Not till the time of Wallenstein did Bohemia again enter

19 Huber, *op. cit.* X. vii.

the Thirty Years' War. The battle of the White Hill had thus been followed by the elimination of the country where the first incidents of the war had been enacted. As usual, differences soon appeared among the conquerors. Ferdinand showed some unwillingness to fulfil the conditions of the treaty of Munich, by which the Palatine Electorate had been promised to Maximilian of Bavaria,[20] who, as security for his expenses in crushing the Bohemians, held valuable rights in Upper Austria. Maximilian was now exhorted to use his army and resources for the conquest of the Upper Palatinate, which he was to keep in exchange for the Austrian pledges. This he at last consented to do, thinking possibly that by this step he would terminate the war, but it was with great difficulty that he managed to obtain from the League an agreement to supply a contingent of 15,000 men. This induced Mansfeld, then established in the Upper Palatinate, to come to terms with Bavaria, and in October 1621 an amnesty was signed by which the Protestant condottiere, in return for a sum of money, agreed to withdraw or disband his army of 20,000 men. Maximilian then completed the conquest of the Upper Palatinate. But Mansfeld had no intention of keeping faith. Transferring himself to the Rhine valley, he proceeded to overrun the Lower Palatinate as if he were the enemy rather than the ally of the Elector Palatine.[21] Entering Mannheim on the 23rd of October 1621 he was joined by an English contingent under Sir Horace Vere, and soon Heidelberg, Wimpfen and Heilbronn were occupied. It was difficult to distinguish this "protection" of the Lower Palatinate from its devastation. In December of the same year Mansfeld took Haguenau in Alsace, acting in all respects not as a paid soldier but as an independent leader. By the beginning of the year 1622 he commanded 35,000 men, and in April of that year he was joined by Frederick himself, who had meanwhile secured two allies in Christian of Brunswick and the Marquis of Baden-Dürlach. Of these, the first was the administrator of the Halberstadt bishopric, an enthusiastic young Calvinist, fired by a chivalrous passion for his cousin Elisabeth, the

[20] Charveriat, *op. cit.* I. ch. x.

[21] Gardiner, *op. cit.* IV. ch. xl., and Gindely, *op. cit.* I. vii. This second devastation by Mansfeld, an ally of the Elector Palatine, may seem inconsistent, but the subject populations of Germany in the Thirty Years' War had to accustom themselves to such inconsistencies.

Electress Palatine, whose glove he wore on his helmet; while the other, whose chief object was booty, was of a more practical turn of mind, having invented a chariot with spiked wheels intended for use in breaking up cavalry charges. This contrivance did not prevent his being completely defeated by Tilly at Wimpfen (May 6, 1622), and in the following month Christian of Halberstadt and his Brunswick troops met with a similar defeat at Hoechst. These defeats and a realization of the true objects of his military allies caused Frederick to make his second flight, this time to Sedan, while Mansfeld and Halberstadt crossed over into the Low Countries, where they helped Maurice of Nassau to raise the siege of Breda. It remained only for Tilly to complete the conquest of the Lower Palatinate, a province which had already been overrun twice in two years. Heidelberg was taken by assault (10th September 1622), and by April 1623 the Winter King retained as assets only his relatives and personal belongings. His lands were given in trust to Maximilian of Bavaria; his library was removed to Rome; the Bishop of Spires was appointed administrator, and a contingent of Jesuits was despatched to Calvinist Heidelberg. Thus by 1623 the Rhenish Palatinate shared the fate of Bohemia.

It was easy to dispose of Frederick's lands, but it was more difficult to deal with his electoral prerogative. A Diet was summoned to Ratisbon in January 1623, where all three colleges expressed disapproval of the Emperor's arbitrary act in imposing, by his personal authority, the Ban of Empire on Frederick. Ferdinand was under secret pledge to give the Electorate to Maximilian, but it was clear that if he persisted in so doing, an entirely new complexion would be given to the war. In 1294 the Wittelsbach family had been divided into two branches, the Palatine and the Bavarian, the one holding the Lower, the other the Upper Palatinate, each to exercise the electoral vote alternately. The Golden Bull had modified this by conferring the Electorate exclusively on the elder or Palatine branch, but in later years the Dukes of Bavaria had refused to recognize this on the ground that the Golden Bull had never received papal approval. So far, therefore, as public law was concerned, there were arguments on both sides. But Frederick, though discredited and in exile, refused to hear of any surrender of his dignity, while the Electors of Saxony and Brandenburg saw a serious danger in a change which would reduce the Protestant vote to two. Spain was opposed to the transference, because at that moment she was anxious to retain the friendship of Frederick's father-in-law, James I. In spite of the lawlessness of the period, there still remained some respect for established rights, many holding that at least the claim of Frederick's heirs to the Electorate should not be prejudiced. On the other hand, the candidature of Bavaria was supported by France, anxious to set a Wittelsbach against a Hapsburg, and by Pope Gregory XV., in order to weaken German Protestantism. After some deliberation the Diet recommended that the Electorate should be retained in Frederick's family, and that the Protestants in Bohemia should be dealt with leniently. Maximilian offered to surrender his claim provided his military expenses were paid— a condition which, as he knew, Ferdinand could not fulfil. Eventually a compromise was effected whereby Maximilian was to have the Electorate for his liftetime, and the question of its ultimate destination was to be decided by a diet of Electors; accordingly on the 23rd of February 1623 this translation was performed against the opposition of Spain, the Lutherans and the Calvinists.[22]

In consequence of these events, the Imperialists were now at the high-water mark of their fortunes, and everywhere in Germany the situation became more menacing for the Protestants. Mansfeld emerged from his Dutch winter quarters to ravage Frisia and Oldenburg, hoping to set himself up as an independent prince. Tilly, anxious to pursue the war into Holland, defeated Christian of Halberstadt at Stadlohn, and in December of the same year routed Mansfeld at Freisoythe. This destroyed the little of Mansfeld's reputation that was left. There was no native leader willing or ready to take the field, and Germany seemed about to succumb before the triumphant forces of the Counter Reformation.

Meanwhile in the years 1624-1625 there appeared on the scene three new actors in what was becoming a European drama. The first of these was Richelieu, who had risen to power in France in 1624. Though it was not till 1635 that he definitely intervened, yet the Valtelline[23] question gave him

[22] Gindely, op. cit. I. vii.
[23] For the Valtelline question see Horatio Brown in Cambridge Modern History, IV. ch. ii.

the first opportunity of testing his strength. For Spain the strategic importance of the Valtelline was even greater than that of Franche Comté, because, while the latter provided a route from Italy to the Netherlands, Savoy lay in the path, and at this period Savoy was a very indeterminate factor, whereas the Valtelline could be entered directly from Milanese territory and access thus obtained into Bavaria and the Tyrol. Tilly's conquest of the Lower[24] Palatinate accentuated this advantage by linking up the Rhenish territories with Alsace and Lorraine. The Valtelline, that is, the valley of the Adda stretching east and west (northwards of Lake Como), was dominated by the Protestant Grisons communities which found natural allies in France and Venice, while the Catholic natives of the valley looked to Spain. Accordingly the policy of successive Spanish Governors of Milan was aimed at ousting the Grisons from their overlordship, for which purpose they built forts in the valley. By such measures the Grisons were, in 1622, compelled to renounce their rule over the dependent Catholic population and seek the friendship of France in the hope of restoring this domination. The French Government thereupon allied with Savoy and Venice, with the object of re-asserting Protestant control; Urban VIII. began his pontificate by intervening and filling the Valtelline with papal troops.[25] Richelieu came into power at this time (August 1624) and expelled the papal garrisons, taking care to disavow the act of the officer to whom this duty was entrusted; in 1626, however, he was obliged to yield, mainly because his tenure of office was precarious and the Huguenots were arming. By the treaty of Monzon (1626), without consulting either Savoy or Venice, he undertook, with Spain, to guarantee the independence of the Valtelline Catholics and the maintenance of their religion, a measure which deprived the Grisons of their predominance and, in effect, left the passes in the hands of Spain. In his Memoirs[26] Richelieu congratulated himself on having won a success for French diplomacy by this treaty, but in reality he was not at that time (1626) strongly enough established to assert himself in Europe, nor had he yet secured himself against the menace of

[24] The student should distinguish the Upper from the Lower Palatinate by a reference to the map.

[25] Fagniez, *Le Père Joseph et Richelieu*, i. 194.

[26] *Mémoires* (ed. Société de l'histoire de France), v. 203 ff.

the Huguenots. The treaty contains no reference to the passes, but there is ample evidence to show that the Grisons regarded themselves as robbed of their independent status by the terms of the treaty and left to the mercy of the Valtelliners and Spain. It would be harsh to condemn the French minister for this withdrawal, but that it was a withdrawal must be insisted on, for the laudatory statements in the Memoirs are merely the euphemisms of the cardinal's scribes and are not to be accepted as unimpeachable historical evidence. Richelieu, therefore, began his diplomatic career by throwing over his allies (Savoy and Venice) and betraying the community (the Grisons) which he had undertaken to support.

The importance of the treaty of Monzon in the military history of the war is obvious, for Spain was left free to send troops from the Milanese into Germany and Austria: moreover, by controlling the passes, she made it very difficult for Savoy or Venice to co-operate with France. The important Catholic victory of Nördlingen (1634) would not have been won had Spain not possessed this advantage. In the years after 1626, therefore, Richelieu had to content himself with a watching brief, while he looked round[27] for allies who might be subsidized with French gold to fight against the Hapsburgs.

The second personage to enter the fray at this time was Christian IV. of Denmark, brother-in-law of James I. The English monarch was not fortunate in his relatives by marriage, because they involved him in foreign entanglements and sometimes expected him to do more than his share. The two main motives inspiring the conduct of the Danish king were intense jealousy of Sweden and a desire to obtain the mouths of the Elbe and Oder. His son Frederick was administrator of the bishopric of Verden and wished to add Minden to his possessions. He purchased the bishopric of Halberstadt from Christian of Brunswick, but the chapter refused to recognize this transaction, and Frederick, encouraged by French promises, resolved to occupy Halberstadt by force. In the spring of 1625 Christian was busy with his plans for armed intervention. He took into his service Ernest of Saxe-Weimar, and, in his capacity of Duke of Holstein, allied with such German princes of the Lower Saxon circle (e.g. the

---

[27] For Richelieu's intrigues with Catholic and Protestant German princes at this time see a posthumous article by Gindely in *Archiv für österreichische Geschichte*, lxxxix. 40 ff.

Duke of Mecklenburg) as wished to retain the already secularized bishoprics. The subjects of these princes had no desire to fight for such an object, and though some contemporaries saw in the secularized bishoprics the best guarantee for Protestantism in North Germany, others regarded the motive of the Lower Saxon princes as simply territorial greed. Denmark's intervention was therefore prompted by motives than can be defended but not lauded. By the end of the year 1625 Christian was counting on support from England, France and Holland, and by the spring of 1626 he commanded an army of 30,000 men.

The third member of the trio augmenting, at this time, the personnel of the Thirty Years' War has been the subject of more than sixteen hundred books and monographs.[28] Albert Wenceslas of Waldstein, or Wallenstein as he has been traditionally called, was born of a noble Bohemian family in 1583. In his earliest years he had been brought up by Lutherans and later by the Bohemian Brethren; when he became a pupil of the Jesuits his mind was no longer pliable, and the conflicting religious influences on his early years seem to have produced indifference to everything supernatural except astrology. Nominally a Catholic, he had no religious convictions. Contemporaries were impressed by his ambition, his audacity, his insolence and his eccentricities. He had first distinguished himself by his bravery against the Turks in the Hungarian campaigns, and since 1618 had won the favour of Ferdinand by his military exploits in the Imperialist cause, becoming Prince of Friedland in 1620. He combined the functions of condottiere with war profiteer—what sustenance his troops could not obtain by pillage was sold to them from the produce of his extensive estates;[29] he was also a very successful land speculator. A firm belief in his horoscope gave him a fortitude and determination above that of his fellow-men, while frequent attacks of gout caused fits of intense irritation in which he could not endure the slightest sound. His career has an element of melodrama to which posterity has done ample justice, for some of his biographers have compared him with Napoleon, others have seen in him the predecessor of Bis-

---

[28] See Veit Valentin, in *Slavonic Review*, xiv. 1935. A good biography is that of F. Watson, *Wallenstein*, 1938. Cf. also C. V. Wedgwood, *The Thirty Years' War*, 170 ff.

[29] Denis, *La Bohème depuis la Montagne Blanche*, I. ch. ii.

marck, while many Tcheque historians have regarded him as one of the most heroic figures of their history. *Distringit librorum multitudo*: it is difficult to arrive at any balanced estimate of Wallenstein's aims and achievements because there are so many books about him.

The years 1624 and 1625 may fairly be regarded as a breathing space, and the armies facing each other in the spring of 1626 were much larger and better equipped than those of the early years of the war. In this interval the cleavage within the Catholic ranks became acute and led to a division of forces. On the one hand, Vienna was weary of the domination of Munich and the League; on the other, a dynastic element was being introduced by the intrigues of France to win over Maximilian (together with Protestant allies) in order to unite them against the Hapsburgs. Tilly,[30] the general of the League, had fought well and successfully; his armies were not discredited by the iniquities which stained the honour of Mansfeld and his troops, while he himself united the experience of a veteran soldier with the ardour of a monk. But nevertheless, if the Empire was to free itself from the continual attacks of Bethlen Gabor on the east, and assert itself in Germany against the tutelage of the League and the menace of the rapidly increasing Protestant armies, then it must have two things—an army of its own and a general. Both suddenly appeared as if from the clouds, and when in 1624 Wallenstein offered his services and an army to be raised at his own expense, there entered into vivid prominence the most romantic and least understood character of the Thirty Years' War. Wallenstein attracted recruits of all faiths into his cosmopolitan army; he gave a higher pay than any one else, and his personality helped to keep his men together as nothing else could.[31] His agreement with Ferdinand stipulated that captured artillery and munitions should go to the Emperor, but booty was to be used for the pay of the troops.[32] Wallenstein regarded war simply as a business proposition;

[30] For the career of Tilly see Klopp, *Tilly im dreissigjährigen Kriege*.
[31] For details of the organization of his armies see Gindely, *Wallenstein*, I. ch. vii.
[32] See the "Instructions" printed by Gindely as an appendix, *Wallenstein*, ii 387.

and it is evidence of Ferdinand's destitution that he decided to accept the services of a man so little influenced by religious motives.

When the Protestants assumed the offensive in the spring of 1626 Christian of Denmark undertook to engage Tilly in western Germany, while Mansfeld was to pass through Silesia and join forces with Bethlen Gabor. On reaching the Elbe, Mansfeld was defeated by Wallenstein at Dessau (April 25, 1626), but though he lost about 7000 men, he pushed through into Hungary, only to find that the perfidious Bethlen Gabor was again negotiating with the Emperor. On his way back he died of phthisis in an obscure Bosnian village.[33] The turn of the king of Denmark came next. Abandoning a strong position, he was defeated by Tilly at Lütter in Thuringia on the 27th of August. By these battles the territories between the lower reaches of the Elbe and Weser were seriously menaced by both League and Imperialist armies, a menace from which important results ensued.[34] The king of Denmark's allies suddenly manifested lukewarmness in the cause; Mecklenburg showed a desire for reconciliation, and Charles I. of England, so far from being able to subsidize Christian as he had promised, found himself unable, owing to his war with France, to repay a loan which his father had received from Denmark. The United Provinces failed to give the promised support; Christian's subjects were unwilling to continue any further; his troops were anxious to suspend hostilities, and only the French subsidy could be depended on. His own territories of Schleswig and Holstein were invaded by the combined forces of Tilly and Wallenstein, and the triumph of the Catholic cause in North Germany now seemed assured.

In the next few years the main interest centres in Wallenstein[35] and the depredations of his armies, which are said to have numbered about 100,000 men. In 1626 his principality of Friedland was made a hereditary duchy; in the following year he acquired the principality of Sagan, and in 1628 he was given the confiscated duchy of Mecklenburg as security for

[33] November 29, 1626. He awaited death standing up and fully armed.

[34] Gindely, op. cit. I. viii.

[35] There is an interesting posthumous article on this subject by Gindely in Archiv für österreichische Geschichte, Band 89, 154-241.

money spent in the Imperialist cause. He made no secret of his intention to avoid pitched battles and sieges, and by carrying out a guerilla warfare to obtain a decision by exhaustion. The German princes, Catholic and Protestant, or rather their subjects, soon found that they were to share in this exhaustion, and when the armies of the League were treated practically as hostile troops by Wallenstein's captains, all parties in Germany began to inquire what the intended decision could be. When the great condottiere confided to the Imperial Chancellor Eggenberg that, by such methods, the hereditary lands of the Emperor would be given a chance to recuperate, in order that ultimately the Emperor might be able to reconstruct his power in Europe, it seemed clear that the war was being diverted into an enterprise for making the Hapsburgs absolute in Germany. For a time the weak Ferdinand was infatuated by such projects and, in spite of protests from all quarters, the counsels of Wallenstein reigned supreme in Vienna.[36] In order to voice these complaints, the League summoned a diet of the Electors at Mülhausen in October 1627, where the Electors inveighed against the ravages of Wallenstein's troops and censured both the Imperialist disregard for the rights of neutrals and the Emperor's omission to consult the Electors before embarking on the war with Denmark. Maximilian at the same time showed himself more willing to listen to French advances; thenceforth the League may be regarded as definitely out of sympathy with the Emperor's policy. But Ferdinand refused to listen to the representations of the Diet that peace should be concluded with Denmark, and for the latter the struggle became critical.

At this period of the war (1626-1628) the motives of the leading combatants are indescribably confused. There was no united Protestant front, the war having accentuated the antipathy between Lutheran and Calvinist; equally there was division among the Catholics, for while the League was anxious to safeguard its territories and maintain the Imperial constitution in Germany, the Emperor, aided by Wallenstein, had embarked on a course which would make the Empire a great military power independent of the Electors, Protestant and Catholic alike. Of the foreign states interested in the struggle. France was then engaged with the Huguenots, and its policy was directed by a statesman (Richelieu) who knew how to

[36] Huber, *op. cit.* XI. iv., and Gindely, *Waldstein*, I. x.

subordinate religion to political expediency. His interests were dynastic rather than religious, and every one knew that when he intervened, it would be against the Hapsburgs, though it was not clear who were to be his German allies, or even whether these would be Protestant like Saxony, or Catholic like Bavaria. Spain, then engaged in the war with the United Provinces, regarded the war as one for the forcible restoration of Catholicism in Germany, but received little support from the Pope (Urban VIII.), who, though an enemy of heretics, was a friend of neither Spaniard nor Hapsburg, and leaned by personal inclination to the French interest. The domestic affairs of England prevented any possibility of armed intervention, though the populace was against the idea of a Spanish alliance. Denmark had entered the fray in order to obtain territorial possessions, but defeat in the field had now made her anxious for peace at any price. Neither Saxony nor Brandenburg was at war with the Emperor, but their lands were continually being overrun by Protestant and Catholic troops. There remained only Sweden, then engaged in a war with Poland. It was no secret that, when the Polish-Swedish hostilities were over,[37] the Swedish king, Gustavus Adolphus, intended to come to the rescue of Protestantism in Germany, but none of the German princes regarded this proposed intervention with enthusiasm, because they knew that Swedish military success would be followed by demands for territorial compensation in Germany. At this point of the war, therefore, every one was at cross purposes, and no one could prophesy what would happen when Swedish or French troops entered the arena.

The knowledge that Gustavus Adolphus would soon be free to take part in the struggle caused Wallenstein to turn his attention to the Baltic, because only by controlling the southern coast of the Baltic could he hope to hamper Swedish operations. The ports of Stralsund and Dantzig must be preserved for Poland—the most consistent ally of the Austrian Hapsburgs. Accordingly in his rôle of Admiral of the Baltic, Wallenstein laid siege to Stralsund[38] in May 1628. In this departure from his principles of warfare Wallenstein made his greatest

[37] See *infra*, p. 452.

[38] As a Pomeranian town, Stralsund was nominally under the Polish allegiance; as a Hanse town, it was practically independent. For the maritime ambitions of the Hapsburgs see Reinhard, *Die maritime Politik der Hapsbürger*.

mistake. Gustavus had been following events closely, and the siege of an important Baltic port convinced him that he must intervene. He sent supplies into the city, and in August, after passing a wet summer in the trenches, Wallenstein was obliged to give up the siege and withdraw his 20,000 troops.[39]

This failure, together with the capture of La Rochelle by Richelieu's troops in October 1628 and the preparations for defence made by the cities of Lübeck and Hamburg, all helped to make Ferdinand more willing to listen to the advice of the League. Accordingly in March 1629 he met their demands by issuing the Edict of Restitution. In terms of this enactment, the Catholics were to be reinstated in the lands held by them directly of the Empire in 1555, and in those held indirectly at the date of the Peace of Passau (1552). The result of this was that the Protestants would have to surrender two archbishoprics, Magdeburg and Bremen, with the bishoprics of Minden, Halberstadt, Verden, Lübeck and Brandenburg; in other words, they were faced with the necessity of resigning their territorial supremacy in North Germany. Nor was the Edict of Restitution altogether acceptable to the Catholics, because to oust the Protestants from these possessions would necessitate a new war; moreover, Wallenstein[40] was against it, because it had been drawn up at the instigation of the four Catholic electors. Owing, however, to quarrels and jealousy among the Catholics themselves, the Edict was never fully carried out.

Magdeburg was the richest of the Saxon bishoprics, and if the Hapsburgs acquired control over it they would have the key to North Germany, as they already had the key to western Germany, by the possession of Swabia and Alsace. But there were other candidates in the field. For nearly a century the archbishopric had been administered by a member of the Brandenburg family, and its latest administrator, Charles William of Brandenburg, had been deposed by the Chapter for taking part in the Danish war. The Elector of Saxony had long regarded it with covetous eyes, and on the deposition of the Brandenburg administrator he had induced the Chapter to elect his second son, Augustus, aged eleven. The Edict of Restitution annulled this election, and Urban

[39] Gindely, *Wallenstein*, II. ch. iii.
[40] *Ibid.* II. ch. viii. Wallenstein was now being accused of filling the higher ranks in his army with Protestants.

VIII. nominated Ferdinand's second son, Leopold William, who already possessed Halberstadt, and so the result of the Edict was to establish the Hapsburgs securely in North Germany. Having thus obtained Magdeburg, and having made over Mecklenburg in perpetuity to Wallenstein, the Emperor did not press the Edict further; eventually both Brandenburg and Saxony benefited territorially by the confiscations which ensued.

Two months later (May 1629) the Peace of Lübeck was signed, mainly at the instigation of Wallenstein, who saw that a far more serious danger threatened from Sweden. By this treaty the king of Denmark withdrew from the war and gave up his claim to the Saxon bishoprics. Schleswig-Holstein was restored to him, and no indemnity was demanded. Thus the first decade of the Thirty Years' War witnessed the disappearance of Bohemia from European nationalities, and of the Palatinate from the German Protestant states; the futile intervention of Denmark; the Catholic resumption of secularized bishoprics; and, most important of all, the ascendancy of the Emperor at the expense of Protestant Germany, culminating in the menace of a powerful and reactionary Empire with Wallenstein as its generalissimo and the Jesuits as its councillors. It was the desire to maintain the constitution of the Empire that provided an important link between the Protestants of the north and the Catholics of the south and west. Foreign aid must redress the balance which native forces could not control, and there were at hand two great powers waiting a favourable opportunity for taking part. It was a disaster for Germany and Europe that they intervened not simultaneously but consecutively. The fortunes of the Protestants were restored for a time by the intervention of Sweden, backed up by French subsidies, and the most spectacular period of the Thirty Years' War now begins.

II. The Restoration of Protestantism by Sweden, 1630–1635.

The Diet of Ratisbon (July 1630) and the Treaty of Prague (May 1635) may be taken as the limits of this period.

The Diet of Ratisbon was really a conference between the Emperor and the representatives of Catholic Germany, for the Electors of Brandenburg and Saxony refused to attend. The main subjects for discussion were the question of the Mantuan succession, the complaints against Wallenstein, and the election of a king of the Romans. These were public matters; in addition, there were secret negotiations, the full extent of which has been revealed only in recent years. It will be necessary to consider each of these subjects in turn.

In 1627 died the last of the Gonzague Dukes of Mantua and Montferrat. The nearest heir was Charles of Gonzague, Duke of Nevers, a prominent figure at the French court, and it was important for France that the succession should fall to a family under French influence, since the territories in question included the important fortresses of Mantua and Casale, the latter on the confines of Milan and Savoy. Spain backed the candidature of Francis of Nevers, Duke of Guastalla, and, in alliance with Savoy, besieged Casale. Richelieu in person crossed the Alps in March 1629 by the pass now known as the Mont Cenis route and broke up the siege. Meanwhile the French troops had to retire in order to deal with a fresh Huguenot insurrection, and the Spanish-Imperialist troops occupied Montferrat. Early in 1630 French troops again crossed the Alps and this time captured the important fortress of Pinerolo (Pignerol). The audacity of this act startled Europe, for Pinerolo was in Savoyard, not Spanish-Italian territory, and, while its capture was a punishment for Savoy's desertion of the French alliance, it marked the beginning of the French campaign against the Hapsburg control of Italy. But meanwhile the Duke of Nevers was deprived of an inheritance to which he had the best claim, and in this was a definite reason for war between France and the Empire.

France sent an ambassador, Brulart, to the Diet of Ratisbon in order to press for a solution of this question, and he was accompanied, in the capacity of "theological adviser," by Father Joseph de Tremblay, a Capuchin monk and confidant of Richelieu. The character of the theological advice was to be revealed later. The Diet refused to support any Imperial enterprise in Italy on the ground that the Emperor's claims there were obsolete, so, with Gustavus Adolphus now on German soil and Wallenstein opposed to any Italian commitments,[41]

---

[41] Wallenstein was a friend of the Duke of Nevers and so was not anxious to fight against him. Moreover, Wallenstein feared that his armies would be devastated by plague if they campaigned in Italy.

the Emperor gave way on the Mantuan question, assigning both Mantua and Montferrat to the Duke of Nevers. The treaty of Cherasco (July 1631) regulated this on the express condition that France surrendered Pinerolo. In September 1631 the fortress was solemnly given back to Savoy in presence of commissioners representing the Emperor and the Governor of Milan. These representatives had no suspicion that the straw in a neighbouring barn[42] concealed a company of French troops, who, on the completion of the ceremony and the departure of the commissioners, quietly took possession of the citadel. The Duke of Savoy was, however, in the secret, for by a treaty with Richelieu earlier in the year[43] he had sold Pinerolo to France. The fortress was not restored to Savoy until 1696.[44]

The second point to be discussed by the Diet of Ratisbon was the question of the size of the Imperial army and the conduct of Wallenstein.[45] The League was anxious to re-assume control and to free its lands from the ravages of Imperialist troops; in this it was backed up by the French agents, who had no doubts whatever regarding the ambitions[46] of the prince of Friedland. Maximilian and the League may have taken at less than their face value French expressions of concern for the integrity of German "liberty"; it was owing, however, to the threat of a combination of forces against him that the Emperor was obliged, much against his will, to consent to the dismissal of Wallenstein. The entire credit for this decision has sometimes been erroneously attributed to Father Joseph, but the public work of the French embassy consisted mainly in pressing for a settlement of the Mantuan succession question, and in the domestic problems of the Empire the French could not have had much say. The Diet refused to elect Ferdinand's son king of the Romans; it granted an amnesty to Frederick, the Elector Palatine, if he renounced Bohemia, the electoral

[42] Souvigny, *Mémoires*, i. 262. Quoted in Leman, *Urban VIII et la rivalité de la maison de la France et de la maison d'Autriche*, 27.

[43] March 31, 1631; Leman, *op. cit.* 22.

[44] By the treaty of Turin.

[45] For this see Gindely, *Waldstein*, II. x.

[46] These were supposed to include (*a*) the capture of Constantinople, (*b*) to make the Emperor absolute in Germany, (*c*) to detach France from the enemies of the Hapsburgs, and (*d*) to make himself an independent sovereign.

dignity and all his alliances—which, naturally, he refused to do; it promised to help the Empire against the Swedish armies, but it disagreed on the vexed question of the Edict of Restitution. As a result of this disagreement Saxony and Brandenburg were forced to consider the expediency of allying with Gustavus Adolphus and embarking on hostilities.

The net result of the Diet of Ratisbon was that the Emperor had been forced to yield on three points: the supremacy in German affairs was restored to Maximilian and the League; the Emperor's son was not accorded the dignity of king of the Romans, and the Mantuan succession question was settled in favour of the French as against the Spanish candidate. Ostensibly Richelieu had not obtained what he wanted, since he publicly disavowed the acts of the French embassy on the ground that more favourable news from the Italian front warranted better terms than those agreed upon by the Diet and afterwards (July 1631) embodied in the treaty of Cherasco.

But it was characteristic of Richelieu to conceal his satisfaction with a noteworthy achievement by repudiating the authors of it. It is certain that he had ambitions in Italy, and that these were delayed for the time by the French ambassador's acceptance of the Mantuan succession settlement, yet, on the other hand, it is clear that France achieved an important diplomatic success at the Diet of Ratisbon. When sent to the Diet of Ratisbon, Father Joseph had secret orders to obtain for France an alliance with Bavaria, secret orders of which not even the French ambassador was aware. The negotiations were successful and led to a defensive alliance.[47] In March 1630 the terms were settled: the Duke of Bavaria agreed for himself and the League not to assist the enemies of France, not to break his neutrality with the Dutch (who were then within the zone of French influence), and not to oppose the claims of previous holders of the duchy of Mecklenburg,[48] who, having been dispossessed by Wallenstein, might willingly become allies of France. The contingency that Gustavus Adolphus might invade Catholic lands or attack the forces of the League was not

[47] Fagniez, *op. cit.* i. 540.

[48] The two Dukes who divided the ducal lands between them had been among the allies of the Elector Palatine in 1619. They steadily adhered to the Lutheran cause and were expelled from their lands by Wallenstein in 1628. In this year (1630) Wallenstein was in possession of the Mecklenburg territories.

provided for. Nevertheless Maximilian and the League had thus deserted the Emperor, while France obtained for a time the benevolent neutrality of the most important military power in Germany. It remained only for Richelieu to secure in his interests the most powerful of the Protestant military states, and the whole character of the war would be completely changed. From a local and religious struggle it would become a European and dynastic war, with France and Austria as the protagonists.

The unfortunate Danish episode had only served to mask the preparations of Sweden. The Swedish plan was, by making Prussia the basis of operations, to seek a decision in central Europe, while the Danish policy had been to obtain territory in Saxony and restore the Palatinate by operations on the Rhine. Intense jealousy between the two prevented any co-operation,[49] for the ultimate Swedish aim was to obtain control of the Baltic (an ambition naturally opposed by Denmark), for which purpose the first requisite was control of the German rivers flowing into the Baltic. France was fully aware of these ambitions, and Richelieu despatched Charnacé to Stockholm, where the results of his negotiations was the treaty of Bärwalde[50] signed on the 23rd of January 1631, by which Gustavus Adolphus, in return for a subsidy of 400,000 thalers, undertook to lead an army of 30,000 infantry and 6000 cavalry into Germany in order to restore that country to the position of 1618. The alliance was to last for five years, and Gustavus promised not to interfere with the exercise of the Catholic religion. At the same time Brandenburg and Savoy were assured that the desire of France was to guarantee the "liberty" of Germany, with the further assurance that this might be assisted by an *entente* with the Catholic Electors.[51] The envoys of Saxony and Brandenburg met at Leipzig in March 1631, but showed some distrust of the French proposals, and so at the very moment when there might have been possible a union between the Protestant

[49] There was an interview between the kings of Sweden and Denmark at Ulfsbeck in Smaland on February 20, 1629, but Denmark refused to co-operate (Gfrörer, *Gustav Adolf,* 532 ff.).

[50] In Dumont, *Corps Diplomatique,* VI. i. 1. It was described as a "foedus . . . pro defensione suorum respective communium amicorum, securitate etiam Maris Balthici et Oceani . . . nec non restitutione oppressorum Imperii Romani Ordinum. . . ." Notice the intentional vagueness of these words.

[51] Fagniez, *op. cit.* i. 569.

German princes and Sweden on the one hand, with France and Bavaria on the other, the timidity and suspicion of the leaders of German Protestantism revealed itself. Such a union would have realized Richelieu's ambition and would probably have brought the war to a speedy conclusion. But this policy depended for its success on maintaining a delicate balance between Protestant and Catholic allies and on keeping them strictly apart; moreover, Richelieu had been attracted to the plan mainly by his belief that in Germany he was dealing with mediocrities. If Richelieu himself could have dominated the great personality whose intervention he had invited; if he had been able to combine the German Protestants under the leadership of Gustavus Adolphus and prevent them invading German Catholic lands, then his scheme might have succeeded. But, shrewd as was his knowledge of human character, he never quite understood the subtleties of German politics, and he failed to perceive that the Swedish king was more than a mere condottiere. In attempting to use Protestant Sweden and Catholic Bavaria as tools against reactionary Austria he overreached himself; indeed his foreign policy at this time was too subtle for human conditions, and its inevitable failure considerably lengthened the war.

Gustavus Adolphus is one of the greatest kings of modern history. Like Henry IV. he had qualities of character that would have marked him out as a remarkable personage in whatever sphere of life he had been born. As a leader of men he was a genius, and he had sufficient imagination and judgement to make him revolutionize the whole art of warfare. He perceived the importance of infantry at a time when the mounted soldier was the unit of military calculation, and, in an age which believed in dense phalanxes of heavily accoutred troops, he realized how essential is mobility.[52] His troops used a musket that was a great improvement on that used by his enemies; his artillery was light but effective; his men could distinguish one another from the enemy because they were dressed in a distinctive garb of blue and yellow. The parallel between warfare and chess is seldom satisfactory, but it may not be inapt to say of Gustavus that he was the first in modern times to realize that the humble pawns, so far from being an

[52] For an appreciation of Gustavus as strategist and commander see the *Œuvres* of Napoleon III. (1856), iv. 372.

obstruction to one's pieces, are the soul of the game, and that logical development in order to secure the maximum mobility is the necessary preliminary to successful attack. He was the only real strategist of the Thirty Years' War. If it be greatness to put soldiers for the first time into uniform and change mediaeval warfare into modern, then Gustavus Adolphus was great. But he has other and possibly sounder claims on the remembrance of posterity. He was a patriot and did much for the economic development of his country.[53] He was not incapable of intellectual pursuits.[54] He inspired confidence, respect, and sometimes fear in those who knew him. He was an intelligent hero-king in an age when kingship needed both intelligence and courage. Above all, his personal motives were influenced by imagination, and so were on a different plane from the short-sighted selfishness of his contemporaries; as a fervent Lutheran he saw that the cause of Protestantism in Germany was lost if the Hapsburgs triumphed. It is because of this rare combination of qualities that he has been considered the greatest figure in Swedish annals and a unique personality in history.

The character of Gustavus Adolphus has never been in question, but there has been considerable difference of opinion regarding his motives. His declared purpose was to defend the "liberty" of Germany and restore the territories of dispossessed Protestants, such as the Dukes of Mecklenburg. His grievances against the Emperor were that he was attempting to make Stralsund a nest of Baltic pirates, and that he had oppressed the Protestant princes of Germany.[55] His contemporaries knew that Gustavus wished to make the Baltic a Swedish lake, and were suspicious of him because they realized that the essential preliminary to control of the Baltic was the possession of territory on its southern shore.[56] This is why the Swedish king was never really welcomed in Germany—Saxony was

[53] For this see J. Kretzschmar, *Schwedische Handelskompanien und Kolonisationsversuche im XVIen und XVIIen Jahrhundert* (in *Hansische Geschichtsblätter*, xvii. 227 ff.).

[54] He was an enthusiastic reader of Grotius.

[55] Charveriat, *op. cit.* ii. 39.

[56] Gustavus wrote: "Pomerania and the Baltic coast are the outworks of Sweden—they are our guarantee against the Emperor" (quoted in Odhner, *Die Politik Schwedens im Westfälischen Friedencongress*, 5). Notice that Brandenburg had serious claims on Pomerania.

distrustful of everything Swedish, Brandenburg regarded him as a rival competitor for Pomerania, and Bavaria, relying on French assurances, was soon disillusioned when Swedish troops entered the territories of the League. The rulers of Germany distrusted Gustavus because he was a foreigner and attributed to him the same motives as inspired their own conduct.

This question is further complicated by the terms of the Franco-Swedish alliance. The treaty of Bärwalde, an extremely brief document drawn up in Latin that seems intentionally vague, left untouched the vital problems in this strange partnership: thus, while France was anxious to retain the Electorate for Bavaria, Sweden was pledged to restore it to Frederick; while France wanted a brief and vigorous war, Sweden was prepared for a war of exhaustion and was not influenced by the dynastic ambitions of France; finally, and most important, while Gustavus was pledged not to attack the territories of the League, he was not required to wage the war in the Hapsburg hereditary lands. Gustavus Adolphus was influenced by two motives—anxiety for Protestantism, which seemed about to succumb before the onslaughts of the Hapsburgs; and desire for territorial recompense in Germany, by which the impoverished Swedish exchequer would benefit. Modern opinion would dissociate such motives: to Gustavus and seventeenth-century opinion they were inseparable, for religious security could be maintained only by landed possessions. The futility of arguing whether Gustavus' motives were or were not absolutely disinterested is further illustrated when it is remembered that Gustavus himself was unable to make his position clear. As the paid soldier of a Catholic country he found it expedient to keep the religious motive in the background, while, as an ardent Lutheran, he directed his greatest attack on the strongholds of the Rhine and Bavaria, thus completely upsetting the calculations of his French paymaster. The ambiguous position in which the Swedes were placed is well illustrated by the conduct recorded of Pope Urban VIII. on the news of Gustavus' death. As head of the Catholic Church he ordered Te Deums to be sung in the churches of Rome, but as an opponent of the Hapsburgs he is reported to have said a private mass for the soul of the deceased king.[57]

Gustavus' correspondence with the German princes has

[57] Droysen, *Gutaf Adolf*, ii. 665.

thrown additional light on this question.[58] On the one hand it is shown that, though in many ways an idealist, he had no faith in "scraps of paper" so far as politics were concerned, believing that in Germany only territorial and military strength would be taken seriously. On the other hand the fact emerges that in his comparatively short life-time, Gustavus' opinions developed so that he could himself distinguish[59] between territorial aggrandisement as a necessary preliminary to the settlement of Germany's religious and political troubles, and the establishment of continental Protestantism on a basis sufficiently secure to resist the ambitions of the Hapsburgs. The first he termed "satisfactio," meaning the possession of Pomerania; the second "assecuratio" or the creation of a Germanic federation, which became more important after the battle of Breitenfeld. In the *Norma Futurarum Actionum,* drawn up by him in April 1631, he declared that his ultimate aim was the creation of a new evangelical headship in Germany, and in June 1632 he wrote to the councillors of Nuremberg that there could be no security for German peace until such a "corpus" was formed as "would be able to hold its own against the united forces of Austria, Spain and the Papacy." He distinguished as follows the six different types of state that might co-operate in this "corpus bellicum et politicum."[60]

(1) States previously confiscated and restored by Gustavus, *e.g.* Mecklenburg.
(2) States existing now in name only, *e.g.* Pomerania.
(3) States opposed to the Hapsburgs, *e.g.* Brandenburg.
(4) States under some obligation to Gustavus for help rendered, *e.g.* Saxony and Hesse-Cassel.
(5) Protestant states which had assisted the Hapsburgs, *e.g.* Hesse-Darmstadt.
(6) Enemy and Catholic states to be conquered and claimed "jure belli," *e.g.* Bavaria.

[58] See the appendix to J. Kretzschmar's *Gustav Adolfs Pläne und Ziele in Deutschland* (1904).

[59] For a critical appreciation of Gustavus' aims, see C. V. Wedgwood, *The Thirty Years' War,* 331.

[60] Gustavus proposed that Sweden and Brandenburg should compromise on the question of Pomerania and that Frederick William should marry Gustavus' daughter Christina (Odhner, *op. cit.* 19).

It is clear, therefore, that Gustavus aimed at uniting the whole of Germany into a confederation, predominantly Protestant, able to resist the Emperor and the forces of the Counter Reformation. Of this confederation he himself would be the leader. The magnitude of the scheme at once distinguishes it from the merely mercenary ambitions of the majority of his contemporaries. But the idea was utterly impracticable, for Gustavus was a foreigner on German soil, and the one consistent thing in German politics was that, while external intervention was always being invited, foreign influence was the only thing against which all the heterogeneous forces of German politics could combine. While there were as many states in Germany as days in the year, foreign diplomacy was tempted to consider German politics a series of transparencies through which the external observer could always see, whereas they proved to be a bewildering kaleidoscope that eventually baffled and disgusted the most ingenious diplomacy of Europe. But Gustavus Adolphus was mercifully spared disillusionment, and his death at Lützen closed a career in which epic and idealist elements were fittingly combined.

The siege of Stralsund in the summer of 1628 was the prelude to Sweden's entry into the war. On the 26th of September 1629 Gustavus terminated the war with Poland by a six years' truce, and in the summer of the following year commenced his campaign in North Germany. He first occupied Pomerania, compelling the Duke Bogislas to guarantee him the succession, and then expelled the Imperialist troops from Mecklenburg territory. In April 1631 he took Frankfort. One of the ex-administrators of Magdeburg, Charles William of Brandenburg, now solicited Swedish aid on behalf of the city which the Imperialist general Pappenheim had been besieging since late in the preceding year: accordingly a small body of Swedish troops under Falkenberg was dispatched to the assistance of the city. Magdeburg—an important Hanse town, the most obvious strategic point for control of the Elbe—was the bulwark of Lutheranism, the headquarters of the richest and most fiercely contested of the North German bishoprics, the "fundament und centrum des Krieges,"[61] as Pappenheim called it. The fate of the city was of such moment that in the spring of 1631 Tilly joined the besiegers, and soon the inhabitants,

[61] Quoted in Wittich, *Magdeburg, Gustaf Adolf und Tilly*, v.

under the leadership of Falkenberg, were undergoing the horrors of a close siege. Gustavus had promised to come to the help of the city, but he was delayed by negotiations with the Electors of Saxony and Brandenburg for permission to pass through their lands. On the 20th of May the Imperialists took the city by assault, and their entry was followed by a massacre which horrified even contemporaries. An orgy of rape, murder and robbery was ended only when the city was in flames and more than 20,000 persons had perished.[62]

The sack of Magdeburg was the most terrible incident of the Thirty Years' War. On the wave of horror which swept over Germany and Europe, Gustavus Adolphus pushed aside the selfish German neutrality which had hitherto impeded his movements. Marching into Brandenburg he forced the Elector to yield him his fortresses and promise a subsidy; at the same time, the invasion of his territories by Tilly caused the Elector of Saxony to make up his mind, and soon Gustavus received help from Saxony, Hesse-Cassel and Saxe-Weimar. The troops supplied in the Saxon contingent were valueless, as they deserted by whole companies as soon as they were put into action, but at least Gustavus was no longer hampered by the hostility of co-religionaries, and soon the Swedes obtained the military decision they had so anxiously awaited. On the 17th of September 1631 there took place in Saxon territory the first real contest between the Swedish and Imperialist armies when, at Breitenfeld (near Leipzig), Tilly and Pappenheim,

[62] The sack of Magdeburg has given rise to a fierce battle of books. Gustavus Adolphus has incurred almost unanimous censure for not proceeding to the help of the city; Protestant writers have blamed Tilly and his troops for the massacre and destruction; Ultramontanes have tried to fix the blame on the inhabitants themselves, who are accused of having set their city on fire. Droysen's opinion (*Studien über die Belagerund und Zerstörung Magdeburgs* in *Forschungen zur deutschen Geschichte*, Band iii.) was that it is impossible to determine on whom blame rests, but a more recent writer (Wittich, *Magdeburg, Gustav Adolf und Tilly*) claimed to have discovered evidence in the Hague archives proving that the entire responsibility rests with the Swedish commander, Falkenberg. In 1885 the City Librarian of Magdeburg (Dittmar, *Beiträge zur Geschichte der Stadt Magdeburg in den ersten Jahren nach ihrer Zerstörung* in *Hallesche Abhandlungen zur neueren Geschichte*, ed. Droysen, xv.) came to the conclusion that the Imperialist troops were solely responsible.

using the old Spanish tactics, suffered disastrous defeat at the hands of Gustavus. This victory marks the turn in the tide of the Counter Reformation. The whole Empire now lay at the feet of the Swedish king, and he had to decide whether he would invade the Austrian lands to terminate the war in Vienna, or whether he would turn to Franconia and the Rhine lands to settle the religious difficulties of Germany in the rich *Pfaffengasse* (Priests' Walk). The motive of Gustavus at this point provides one of the most difficult problems of the whole war, because it is complicated with an obscure phase of Wallenstein's career. Thus it has been held that Gustavus was prompted to turn to the south-west because he was informed that Wallenstein, then suspected of intrigues with Bohemian *émigrés*, would lead an army against Austria,[63] but this explanation is improbable; on the other hand it should be noted that even the capture of Vienna would not have been fatal to the Hapsburgs, and so Gustavus may have chosen to seek a decision in Germany, and in that part of Germany where the forces of Catholicism were most strongly entrenched.[64] Leaving the Elector of Saxony to invade Bohemia, Gustavus, after having restored the Dukes of Mecklenburg to their possessions, marched on the Rhenish episcopal states. The Lower Palatinate was then overrun and the march to the Rhine was a triumphal procession. The ecclesiastical Electors had to implore the help of France against an ally whom Richelieu could no longer control. Thus in one comparatively short campaign the Swedish king had practically achieved the objects of his intervention, and in the winter of 1631-1632 his brilliant courts at Frankfort and Mainz did justice to his achievements as conqueror and liberator.

Maximilian and the League were now disillusioned and not even the skill of the French agent Charnacé could induce

[63] For this see Droysen, *Gustaf Adolf*, ii. 422 ff., and Gaedeke, *Wallensteins Verhandlungen mit den Schweden*, 17 ff.

[64] This, of course, at once upset Richelieu's plan. In January 1631 he had written as follows: "il faut porter le roi de Suède, autant qu'on pourra, à aller attaquer promptement la maison d'Autriche en Bohème, Autriche et autres pays héréditaires" (Avenel, *Lettres et papiers d'État*, iv. 251). Late in 1631 Gustavus urged Richelieu to give him permission to lead an army into the Valtelline in order to capture the passes from Spain, but this was refused on the ground that Spanish occupation of the Valtelline was less dangerous than Swedish (Fagniez, *op. cit.* ii. 131 ff.).

Maximilian to give an undertaking that he would continue to observe neutrality in regard to Sweden. There was no arresting the progress of the torrent, and the campaign of 1632 began by the defeat and death of Tilly when attempting to prevent the Swedes crossing the Lech. The death of Tilly was as disastrous for the League and the Catholic party as the loss of a pitched battle, for it was at once followed by the invasion of Bavaria. This success of his Protestant confederate cost Richelieu the support of his Catholic ally. The Protestant cause was now in the full tide of success, and so serious was the outlook for the Imperialists, that Ferdinand had to beg Wallenstein to return to his post. Although he had been in retirement, and even in negotiation with Sweden, Wallenstein accepted the invitation, but it is not known on what terms.[65] He acted as mediator between the Emperor and Saxony, and at the same time brought together a large army with which he suppressed a nascent rebellion in Bohemia organized by expelled Protestants. Joining with the troops of the League, he faced Gustavus for the first time at Nuremberg. The two leaders waited a favourable opportunity for attack, but when Gustavus took the initiative he was repulsed, and this was his first defeat on German soil. From this point his conduct of the campaign seems to lack decision; he marched into southern Germany and then back into Saxony, and just as his victory at Breitenfeld might well have been followed by an invasion of Austria, so his defeat at Nuremberg might have tempted him to retrieve the situation by taking advantage of a rebellion in Upper Austria. Meanwhile Wallenstein was joined by Pappenheim and together they commanded about 25,000 men. Hearing that they were going into winter quarters Gustavus resolved to attack, and on the 16th of November 1632 the battle of Lützen was fought. The arrival of Pappenheim rallied the Imperialists just as they were giving way before an impetuous onslaught, but his death produced consternation, and the Swedes renewed their advantage. The day was misty; Gustavus was unable to wear his cuirass owing to a wound received in Prussia, and amid scattered troops he was struck down and

[65] Gindely, *Thirty Years' War*, ii. 125. Unauthenticated conditions between Ferdinand and Wallenstein were published in some of the *Flugschriften* of 1632 and in Khevenhüller, *Annales Ferdinandei*, but the authentic treaty between them has not been preserved. See also C. V. Wedgwood, *The Thirty Years' War*, 315.

killed. Though the Swedes again rallied, the result was indecisive; of the three leaders who had joined battle Wallenstein alone escaped with his life.

The death of Gustavus led to an important reaction. Charles IV. of Lorraine declared for the Emperor; he was already associated with France's enemies, for his sister had married the fugitive Gaston of Orléans. Richelieu took advantage of this to send troops into Lorraine, which expelled the Duke from his territories, an act which indicates that Richelieu's design of extending France's eastern frontier was now maturing, and that he was awaiting a favourable opportunity for active participation. The subsidy was still paid to Sweden, but Oxenstierna's refusal to surrender Colmar and Philippsburg to the French showed that Swedish independence had not been abated by the death of Gustavus. But meanwhile Sweden, with the able diplomatic direction of Oxenstierna and the skilful military leadership of Bernard of Saxe-Weimar, kept in being a strong Protestant resistance in Germany, and Richelieu could afford to wait.

The battle of Lützen was to have another consequence. Open enmity between Maximilian and Wallenstein was the chief weakness in the Catholic cause at this time, and soon the Chancery at Vienna re-echoed with complaints against the inscrutable Duke of Friedland. It only required failure in the field, such as he had suffered at Lützen, to complete the distrust entertained by all parties of a man credited with no religious convictions, whose immense wealth and luxurious tastes seemed, moreover, to indicate monarchist ambitions. What Wallenstein's real aims were at this time it is difficult to determine. He was known to be in negotiation with Sweden, Saxony and France[66]—perhaps in order to establish a dictatorship in Germany; he listened to the proposals of Bohemian émigrés,[67] perhaps with thoughts of the Bohemian crown; his hatred of Maximilian might tempt him to seize the Palatinate, if only for revenge; his dislike of Spain might induce him to encourage French ambitions in the Low Countries.[68] For a

[66] Gaedeke, *Wallensteins Verhandlungen mit den Schweden und Sachsen.* A considerable amount of correspondence is reprinted *in extenso* in this volume.

[67] Bilek, *Beiträge zur Geschichte Wallensteins.*

[68] For Wallenstein's hostility to Spain see an article in the *Preussische Jahrbücher,* 1868, xxi. 416.

man endowed with such vast potentialities action was the only safeguard, since inactivity would necessarily be regarded as the cloak covering deep-laid schemes. To Vienna it now seemed that he had survived his usefulness and that his power was a menace. These suspicions were speedily acted upon by the enemies of the Imperial generalissimo. In January 1634 he was relieved of his command; a month later he was declared guilty of high treason and thenceforth only his chief officers remained faithful to him. Taking refuge at Eger on the Bohemian frontier he asked for Swedish protection, and it was ostensibly in order to prevent the town falling into Swedish hands that his death was resolved upon by the Governor, who was in communication with Vienna. On the 27th of February 1634 several hired assassins murdered Wallenstein's generals as they were at a banquet, after which they proceeded to Wallenstein's lodging, where they killed him as he stood defenceless in his bedroom. Just as the death of Gustavus Adolphus had been a relief to his chief ally France, so the death of Wallenstein was greeted with acclamation by the Catholics. He had risen to great heights by accidents of genius and circumstance. He fell because no man could divine his motives. He was put to death, not for doing anything wrong, but for doing nothing at all. His successor Gallas could be relied on because he was seldom sober, was intent only on plunder, and had not sufficient imagination to be dangerous.

One of Gallas' first acts as Imperial generalissimo was to lay siege to Nördlingen, and it was in order to save that place that Bernard of Saxe-Weimar offered battle. The battle of Nördlingen (September 6, 1634) ended in the utter rout of the numerically inferior Swedish forces, and at one stroke practically all the conquests of Sweden were lost. The Lower Palatinate was at once re-occupied by Imperialist troops, and the Elector of Saxony, with the agility of a weathercock, turned round and made his peace with the Emperor. By the treaty of Prague (May 1635) both Protestants and Catholics were restored to the lands they had possessed in 1627, and were to retain these lands for a period of forty years, during which the question of ownership was to be amicably settled. Lusatia was given to John George of Saxony, and his son received the administratorship of Magdeburg for his lifetime. The Augsburg Confession was to be recognized in Lusatia and in certain specified Imperial towns. This reconciliation of Saxony with the Emperor was stigmatized by contemporaries as treason,[69] but undoubtedly the Elector had made a very good bargain for himself, and his example was followed by the Elector of Brandenburg, the Dukes of Mecklenburg, Lüneburg, Brunswick, Pomerania and the Prince of Anhalt. Of the German princes only Bernard of Saxe-Weimar refused to submit. It was a humiliation for Germany, and it proved how transient were the results obtained by the brilliant achievements of Swedish arms.

Here the religious war ends. Its net result was the confirmation of Hapsburg supremacy and the practical abdication of all autonomy by the territorial princes of Germany. Sweden alone had successfully contested Catholic and Hapsburg invincibility, but she needed help to continue the fight. Otherwise, after seventeen years of intermittent warfare, no tangible results had been achieved, except that starvation, misery and sudden death had become matters of routine among the peasants of Germany. Brilliant exploits of arms will always find their narrators; the anonymous sufferings of these years will never find an adequate chronicler. This is true of all wars but specially so of the Thirty Years' War. The religious motive had, by 1635, been exhausted; the lands of the martyred peasants was nevertheless to suffer from a fresh invasion of foreign combatants. German Protestantism had shown itself unable to counter the ambitions of the Hapsburgs; neither Denmark nor Sweden had been able to effect a decision; it remained for France to cast her weight into the scale. With this intervention begins the most dreary period of the war.

III. The Intervention of France and the Peace of Westphalia, 1635–1648.

On the 19th of May 1635 a French herald was sent to Brussels in order to declare war on the king of Spain. While thus conforming to an antiquarian punctilio before embarking on hostilities, Richelieu had made preparations of a very modern character. For some years the two countries had been

[69] For the contemporary attacks on the Elector's policy see Hitzigrath, *Die Publizistik des Prager Friedens*. John George was specially blamed for signing the treaty without consulting his fellow-Protestants.

on the point of war.[70] Just before the battle of Nördlingen Philip IV. had raised troops to maintain the Palatinate for Bavaria: he had attempted by diplomatic means to embroil Poland and Denmark with Sweden and dissuade England from all further interest in the Palatinate. The Spanish ambassador in Vienna was instructed to make an effort to win over the Electors and the Protestant princes even if the Edict of Restitution had to be abandoned. At the same time Spanish support was given to the Duke of Orléans and Marie de Medici in their intrigues against Richelieu, while the resources of Spanish diplomacy were everywhere utilized in order to convince Europe that the war was now political and not religious. Late in 1631 French troops captured Moyenvic, a preliminary step to the acquisition of Lorraine, and Gustavus Adolphus invited Richelieu to invade Alsace, but the papal envoy, Bichi, urged Richelieu[71] not to invade Hapsburg territory. Richelieu held his hand, hoping after the battle of Breitenfeld that Gustavus would enter Bohemia or Austria, but the Swedish king's march to the Rhine spoilt Richelieu's plan. In January 1632 the relations between France and Spain were so strained that in a royal council held in Madrid war was actually decided on and would have been declared if the Emperor had not refused to follow suit.

Meanwhile the Papal Nuncios did all in their power to reconcile Richelieu with Olivarez; their task, however, was made difficult by the ambiguous attitude of Urban VIII. Urban was anxious to see the triumph of Catholicism in Germany; on the other hand he distrusted the Hapsburgs; he had a personal leaning to France, and his dislike of Spain led to at least one scene in the Curia. Matters came to a crisis on the 8th of March 1632, when the Spanish Cardinal Borgia, taking upon himself the rôle of an ambassador, publicly reproached Urban for his suspected partiality, in language that could only be construed as an insult.[72] Equally Ferdinand failed to obtain any papal assistance, though Cardinal Pazmany, the "Richelieu of

---

[70] Hostilities had been going on for twelve days (Valfrey, *Hugues de Lyonne*, ii. Introduction).

[71] Leman, *Urban VIII et la revalité de la France et de la maison d'Autriche*, 90. Leman's book has been extensively used in the above paragraph because of its valuable extracts from the Simancas Archives.

[72] Leman, *op. cit.* 133 ff.

Hungary," was sent from Vienna to Rome in order to win over Urban, but the wily Pope refused to be drawn, and declined to give any financial support to his co-religionaries. The result of this was that the pious and conscientious Ferdinand was placed in a dilemma—should he ally with Catholic France (which had just destroyed the political power of the French Huguenots) and crush heresy in Germany, or should he ally with German heretics in order to resist Richelieu? The Confessors and Papal Nuncia advised the first solution: secular opinion in Vienna the second. These doubts in the mind of Ferdinand and the lukewarmness of the Pope in the Hapsburg cause well depict the confused issues in this war.

But there was no confusion or hesitation in the conduct of Richelieu. On the 25th of September 1633, five days after expelling the Hapsburg protégé, Charles IV. of Lorraine, from his duchy, French troops entered Nancy[73] and when Urban proposed that the Catholic powers should discuss their differences at a congress in Rome, France at once replied by a refusal. Even after his victory at Nördlingen the Emperor was willing to consider peace proposals, but as this victory was won mainly by Spanish troops, opinion at Madrid hardened in favour of war.[74] Meanwhile France continued her preparations and extended her acquisitions on the eastern frontier. She dominated the Moselle by her alliance with the Elector of Trier; she obliged Sweden to surrender Philippsburg and fortresses in Upper Alsace; she was firmly established on the middle Rhine by her alliance with the Bishop of Basle; her troops were on the confines of Franche Comté, and in Lorraine she had an admirable base for future operations. In February 1635 Richelieu concluded an offensive and defensive alliance with the United Provinces for the purpose of effecting the independence or partition of the Spanish Netherlands. The treaty of Campiègne was dictated in April of the same year to the now suppliant Sweden, a compact by which Swedish military assistance was renewed with fresh safeguards against independence. By the treaty of Rivoli, signed in July, Savoy was added to the active allies of France.

No one was surprised, therefore, when France declared war

[73] By the treaty of Charmes, September 20, 1633, Nancy had been ceded to France by Charles of Lorraine.

[74] Leman, *op. cit.* 429.

on Spain.[75] It was the logical result of Richelieu's failure to combine Germany and Sweden against the Hapsburgs. The French statesman grafted on to the moribund stock of religious strife the vigorous bud of dynastic war. The device saved time; no one disputed the legitimacy of a process which perpetuated an organism already seventeen years old. Practically all the petty wars and disputes of continental Europe were thus united into one grand holocaust, and this is the reason why the war which ended in 1648 can be designated only by the number of years it lasted.

Despite such preparations, however, French arms were not at first successful in the field. Not since the sixteenth century had France been engaged in warfare on a large scale, and military science had developed since then. Moreover, France had no completely equipped and organized army. In 1636 the French troops had to be withdrawn from the Moselle, giving up Trier and other outposts; and in the same year Spanish troops invaded Picardy. When Paris itself was threatened, the war took on a more national aspect and Richelieu had less difficulty in finding soldiers. The death of Ferdinand II. in February 1637 and the succession of his son Ferdinand III. made no difference in the course of the struggle, except that it confirmed the change whereby the war was robbed of its religious element, for Ferdinand III. was not so much the pupil of the Jesuits as the agent of Spain.[76] With Ferdinand II. also disappeared the last of the generation that had begun the war.

The invasion of Bohemia by the Swedish general Baner in 1639 did little good to the Protestant cause, for Bohemia had long before been stripped bare, and the Swedish troops, unable to gratify their lust for plunder, murdered the defenceless inhabitants in revenge. For Bohemia, Moravia and Silesia these were years of crucifixion: many villages were entirely denuded of inhabitants and thousands of peasants died of starvation in the mountains and forests. Of those who survived, many became neurotic or unbalanced, and on such favourable soil the forces of superstition obtained a tentacle grip.[77] The exploits

[75] War was not declared on the Empire until 1638.

[76] "Ferdinand III si regola alla Spagnuolo" (Giustiniani to Venice in *Fontes rerum Austriacarum*, ed. Fiedler, second series, xxvi. 391.)

[77] For this see Denis, *La Bohème depuis la Montagne Blanche*, i. 348 ff.

of Baner's fellow-general, Bernard of Saxe-Weimar, were of a more honourable character. Confining his operations to the Rhine valley, he laid siege to Breisach and forced the surrender of the city in December 1638. Bernard refused to surrender his capture to France, but his death in the following year again relieved Richelieu of an ally who was becoming too independent. By the end of 1639 France had gained her first permanent foothold in Alsace, and next year the conquest of the province was practically completed by troops in the pay of France. At the same time the capture of Arras threatened the Spanish Low Countries, and when (in 1640) the new Elector of Brandenburg, Frederick William, the Great Elector, signed a treaty of neutrality with Sweden, the process of undermining Hapsburg power in Germany was definitely commenced. Richelieu died on the 4th of December 1642, but not before he had seen the first results of his anti-Hapsburg campaign.

The exploits of the French generals, Condé and Turenne, now revived some of the military glories of Gustavus Adolphus, in whose school they had been trained. Situated at the western extremity of the Ardennes and within twenty miles of Sedan was the fortress of Rocroi, the strategic importance of which had been recognized since 1537 when it had first been fortified. A Spanish siege of the stronghold provided opportunity for one of the few spectacular victories of the war. The French victory of Rocroi (19th May 1643) was important not only because it averted the threat to French territory, but because it destroyed what remained of Spanish military prestige. The old legend of Spanish invincibility was convincingly disproved by French dash and leadership. The victory created the military reputation of the young Duke of Enghien, afterwards the great and turbulent Condé. Following up this success, Enghien retook Philippsburg, while Turenne seized Mainz and Worms, thus restoring the French hold on the Rhine. The desperate plight of the Imperialist cause is shown by the fact that in this year, 1643, Ferdinand had to consider the possibility of accepting the help of Denmark in return for the cession to Christian IV. of Bremen and Hamburg, while even Maximilian had to think seriously of a separate peace. Meanwhile the Swedish general, Torstensson, was accomplishing in the north feats comparable with those of the French generals in the south. After invading Schleswig-Holstein he compelled Christian of Denmark by the treaty of Brömsebro (Sept. 1645) to desert the imperial cause. Oxenstierna's promises had induced

Rakockzy, Prince of Transylvania, to invade Hungary, and Swedish troops now marched triumphantly through Bohemia in order to join hands with Rakockzy, but, though eventually abandoned by this ally—as Mansfeld had been by Bethlen Gabor—Torstensson continued to maintain the war in Hapsburg states and even threaten Vienna. By 1645 the Emperor was denuded of all his allies except Spain. The Elector of Saxony opened up his states to Swedish troops; Bavaria rallied again to the French cause, and thus by the intervention of France and the military revival of Sweden the cause of Protestantism in Germany was saved. Three years earlier peace negotiations had begun.

During the protracted peace negotiations[78] at Münster and Osnabrück the war continued in a sporadic, chronic fashion, without any very important engagements or change in the fortunes of the combatants. The aged Torstensson was replaced in 1645 by Wrangel as leader of the Swedes, and in 1646 the latter was enabled to combine forces with Turenne. The result was a join invasion of Bavaria which forced Maximilian again to desert the Emperor. Having signed the truce of Ulm with France and Sweden in March 1647 he immediately played false with his allies, and attempted to expel the Swedes from his territories. But this movement was ill-timed; it depended for success on the help of Spain, and throughout the greater part of the year 1647 Spanish troops were urgently required in Naples.[79] In consequence disaster soon followed, and Bavaria was now to experience the calamity of an army of occupation. Turenne and Wrangel invaded the territories of the defenceless Elector, and in May 1648 they inflicted a decisive defeat on the Imperialist and Bavarian troops at Süsmarshausen. The Franco-Swedish armies followed up this success by invading the Hapsburg lands and for the fourth time in the war Vienna was menaced. Meanwhile Condé defeated the Spaniards at the battle of Lens (20th August 1648), and at

[78] Owing to a chance remark by Turenne in 1648, the Jesuits of Germany were often accused of having helped to delay peace. This theory is examined and refuted by L. Steinberger, *Die Jesuiten und die Friedensfrage* (1635–50). The report was founded mainly on an attack on the Augsburg settlement by a Jesuit of Dillingen named Laymann (*Pacis compositio*, 1629).

[79] See *infra*, p. 369.

the same time a detachment of Swedish troops under Koenigs-marck invaded Bohemia. Prague was stormed, but the united resistance of the Catholic inhabitants kept the Swedes at bay. Within a few days the general peace was signed (24th October 1648). Thus the war ended where it had begun and Prague, once a European capital, was to survive as a provincial town.

It would be a melancholy task to describe the social effects of the Thirty Years' War.[80] The student must seek for himself in the contemporary records evidence of the sufferings of Germany at this time. Statistics of the loss of population convey little; what matters is the moral and mental degeneration which definitely deposed Germany from her place in European civilization. Every war produces its characteristic evils, but in no other instance of modern warfare did the civilian population suffer so much as in this. It mattered little whether the army over-running a province was friendly or not; whether it was Swedish, French or Spanish, it had to be supported at the expense of the inhabitants, and if a peasant had nothing to offer, the presumption was that he must have something hidden which torture alone would reveal. Reprisals provoked more bitter reprisals; human beings murdered and maimed with a ferocity to be found only in men convinced that it might be their turn next; a general fatalism and cynicism in wickedness seem to deepen as the war drags its interminable length. No peasant could sow with any hope that he would ever reap; for many the only chance of obtaining bread was to join one of the marauding bands which in the later stages of the war included a large proportion of women and children. The war reveals a spectacle of purposelessness and hopelessness; towards the end there is complete exhaustion among all the combatants except the French; there are no brilliant feats of arms to mask the universal privation and weariness; there is no great cause or ideal for which men can make sacrifice. These are cold generalizations. The facts are that hundreds of villages were left without a single inhabitant; that many towns were reduced to less than half their population; that dead men were found with grass in their mouths; that cannibalism broke out

[80] The best modern account is that in C. V. Wedgwood, *The Thirty Years' War*, 510-520. See also Freytag, *Pictures of German Life* (trans. Malcolm), ii. 1, and W. Crowne, *A true relation . . .* (1637).

in several parts of Germany; and that even in gaol—always the safest place in war—a prisoner might have reason to fear, at the hands of a famished gaoler, a death more terrible than any which the law could inflict. The engravings of the Lorraine artist Callot depict the burnings of humble homesteads, the tortures inflicted on defenceless inhabitants forced to reveal the whereabouts of real or imaginary savings, and great trees weighed down by the suspended bodies of peasants.[81] The best contemporary evidence about the Thirty Years' War is Grimmelshausen's *Simplicissimus* which illustrates two recurring *motifs* in the popular literature of central Europe, namely, limitation of the sense of humour to the practical joke, generally obscene; and the process of sophistication whereby a simple-minded man adapts himself to the absurdity and corruption of his environment.[82]

Some of the more obvious social effects of the war can be easily pointed out. The great decrease in population[83] prevented the breaking up of large estates, and so the prerogatives of the landlords were preserved intact. Feudal institutions had a longer lease of life. Peasants remained serfs while elsewhere they were being liberated; there were therefore no small tenants or yeomen farmers to dispute the autocratic rule of the great landlords. The treaty of Westphalia, by making the imperial power in Germany merely nominal, confirmed the narrow provincialism of the numerous petty states, a provincialism which produced plenty of officials, publicists and more or less enlightened despots, but made impossible the evolution of a national and distinctive culture, such as the French, or the creation of a vigorous public opinion, as in England. In the fifteenth and sixteenth centuries Germany had shared with Italy the leadership of the intellectual world; but by the end of the seventeenth century the once free and flourishing cities of Germany were in a ruinous state and, like the old village communities, they were easily brought under the control of the territorial magnates. The leadership of German civilization thus passed to the princes and Junkers. Germany continued to produce great men, but they were mostly great in their isola-

[81] For reproductions of Callot's series of engravings, *Les Misères de la Guerre*, see P. Plan, *Jacques Callot* (1911).
[82] Cf. J. Hasek, *The Good Soldier Schweik* (English translation in Penguin series).
[83] Prinzing, *Epidemics resulting from Wars*, III. vi.

tion, and pre-eminent in those things—metaphysics and classical music—which influence only a small minority. She failed to produce a national poet, accordingly her professors were obliged to borrow Shakespeare. Teutonic liking for Shakespeare has always been gratifying to Englishmen, who have tacitly assumed that German readers appreciate the wisdom and humanity of the dramatist's mature work, and ignore the rant and carnage of spurious plays like *Titus Andronicus*. This assumption has not always been justified, for many Germans have admired in Shakespeare and the Elizabethans the quality of "youth," and in their view this quality is evidenced not so much in vigour and originality, as in coarseness and violence. "German manners," it has been confessed, "have remained a little more old-fashioned."[84] The real significance of the Thirty Years' War lies not in its wastage, which was ultimately repaired, but in its indication of a stage in the evolution of this attitude of mind. The direction of history is ultimately determined by these attitudes of mind, revealed in apparently trivial matters, and in this sense Europe is still paying for the Thirty Years' War.

To conclude the Thirty Years' War, it remains to consider the achievements of Europe's first great peace congress. As early as 1635 there were suggestions of peace when Urban VIII., the Doge and Christian of Denmark each offered his mediation.[85] In 1641 it was agreed at a conference in Hamburg between representatives of France, the Empire and Sweden that two congresses should be held simultaneously at Münster and Osnabrück in Westphalia, but not till two years later did deputies begin to arrive in these two towns. The discussions lasted more than five years, the war going on concurrently, and in these negotiations there can be detected the hope that this war would end European war. As a result we have the first reshaping of the map of Europe on lines intended to be permanent. The Peace of Westphalia established the main principles of the state system of pre-Revolutionary Europe, but its interest is not merely academic, for it attempted a task which still engrosses European diplomacy, and it made acute a problem which is still a great cause of European strife. It

[84] A. Brandl, *Shakspere and Germany* (British Academy Lecture, 1913), p. 14.
[85] Vast, *Les Grands Traités du règne de Louis XIV*, i.

confirmed the sixteenth century conception of the secular state, linked commercially with its neighbours, but always potentially antagonistic to them, and it discredited two old institutions— the Empire and the Papacy, both of which had at least claimed to base authority on something more than brute force. Hitherto the Papacy had monopolised the right of deciding among combatants which side had divine sanction; henceforward it was possible for any combatant to assert exclusive partnership with the Almighty. The mediaeval Holy Roman Empire had united men of diverse race and language in a confederation claiming to be the sole repository of the imperial traditions of ancient Rome and a bulwark of Western civilization against the barbarian; the future lay in the intensification of linguistic and racial distinctions and the establishment of power not on tradition but on battalions. For the Imperial is substituted the National; mediaeval cosmopolitanism gives way to racial self-consciousness; religious bigotry is succeeded by territorial greed. A new profession is added to those of priest, soldier and lawyer—that of diplomat. The Napoleonic Wars, by introducing conscript armies, completed what the treaty of Westphalia had begun.

The mediators in the Westphalia negotiations were the Papacy, the Republic of Venice and the king of Denmark. The first two were represented respectively by Fabio Chigi (afterwards Pope Alexander VII.) and Alvise Contarini at Münster: the Danish envoy at Osnabrück soon ceased to take any active part. Contarini's very full report[86] on the negotiations is by far the best contemporary account, but the correspondence of Chigi, recently deposited in the Vatican, has not yet been explored.[87] The Papacy in the Bull *Zelo Domini* (November 1648) disavowed the whole treaty because the negotiators had adopted the *cujus regio* principle and had apportioned among themselves lands which, in the papal view, it was not theirs to give. The protest was ignored.[88]

[86] It will be found in *Fontes rerum Austriacarum* (ed. Fiedler), 2nd series, xxvi. 293 ff.

[87] For an account of it see Ciampi, *L'Epistolario inedito di Fabio Chigi* in *Atti della R. Acad. dei Lincei*, 3rd series, i. 393.

[88] Spain also protested on behalf of the Burgundian circle. For an interesting use of the Spanish protest by the French in order to incite Dutch feeling against Spain see Adam Adami, *Relatio historica de pacificatione Osnaburgo-Monasteriensi* (ed. Meiern, 1737, XXXI. x.).

The reason for conducting negotiations in two places was that the Swedes refused to give precedence to the French, being willing to yield superiority only to the Emperor. Hence the Imperial-French negotiations took place at Münster, the Imperial-Swedish at Osnabrück.[89] This involved considerable delay and necessitated the reduplication of representatives; moreover, as each plenipotentiary was accompanied by two lawyers, the legal element among the negotiators was very strong.[90] These lawyers saw to it that matters of etiquette and legal precision were not glossed over, and many months were wasted in discussing the most absurd quibbles. The finished result contained obscurities and inconsistencies that were later to provide pretexts for aggression and war. It is important also that the treaties were drawn up in Latin, because seventeenth-century Latin was little better than a loose international jargon, admirably fitted for shrouding concessions with inconsistent reservations and distinctions without differences in a cloudy vapour of verbosity, through which the negotiators themselves scarcely dared to penetrate.

France was anxious that her allies of the United Provinces should send deputies to Münster, but their arrival was long delayed, because they could not obtain a guarantee that they would be accorded the same status as the representative of the Venetian republic. The greater part of the year 1644 was taken up by wrangles between the two French agents, Servien and D'Avaux,[91] and when in 1645 there arrived the French ambassador, the Duke of Longueville, and the Spanish ambassador, the Duke of Peñaranda, neither would approach the other, lest his country's honour should be imperilled, and each avoided any place where the other was likely to be, as the all-important question of precedence might thus arise. Communication between them was at last effected through the mediators and in the third person. Mazarin did not discourage Longueville in maintaining such an attitude, because he did not wish so powerful a French noble to have the credit of arranging peace terms, and when the French Government did realize that peace was necessary, its first step was to recall the French ambassador.[92]

[89] John Yves de St. Prest, *Histoire des traitez de paix du XVIIème siècle*, ii. Appendix.

[90] Contarini in *Fontes rerum Austriacarum*, xxvi. 317.

[91] Contarini in *Fontes rerum Austriacarum*, 299.

[92] *Ibid.* 314.

There then ensued difficulties when the plenipotentiaries exchanged powers. France objected to the Spanish title of king of Portugal and Prince of Catalonia; Spain, in turn, professed inability to proceed so long as the French monarch was officially described as king of Navarre. With a surprising zeal for popular rights, the Spanish and Imperial agents claimed that the French commissions were invalid, since they said nothing of the Paris Parlement,[93] which, they argued, must give its approval during a Regency. When such subterfuges were exhausted,[94] national animosities played their part in still further delaying negotiations. It may be noted that Franco-Swedish jealousy was so strong as to necessitate the use of different towns for their negotiations, but when these began, the jealousy between French and Imperialist in Münster proved so intense that negotiations had to be conducted through a Swede resident in Münster; equally in Osnabrück a Frenchman had to act as buffer between Swede and Imperialist. All this might have provided material for a comic opera, were it not that the war was still going on and could not possibly terminate until these personal differences had been adjusted. The invasion of Danish provinces by Torstensson in the summer of 1645 was a more serious cause of delay, because, though France managed by the treaty of Brömsebro to conciliate Sweden and Denmark, the Emperor sent an army, not to help Denmark, but to keep the Swedish armies where they were. Imperialist desire for peace varied with the location of the Swedish troops; when they were outside the Hapsburg lands, the Viennese agents were full of quibbles and quiddities; no sooner did a Swedish company enter Bohemia, Silesia or Austria than the same agents loudly protested against the innumerable delays caused by mere formalities. Naturally France was equally influenced by the achievements of her armies, hence the victories of Condé and Turenne made her representatives less inclined to hurry, especially as by 1648 Mazarin had begun to realize that a successful war abroad sometimes provides the best support for a suspected ministry at home. Added to this was the fact that France successfully intrigued to have all the German princes personally represented, and so in 1645 the Congress became a full Diet of the Empire, the Electors, Princes and Imperial cities sending

93 *Ibid.* 300.
94 They occupied nine months (Contarini, 307).

representatives to Münster or Osnabrück according as they were Catholic or Protestant. This gave the Emperor an additional grudge against France; moreover, the Catholics objected to this accession of Protestant strength at Osnabrück, claiming that Sweden now aimed at making the war a religious one. Spain's separate peace with Holland, signed in January 1648, was intended primarily as a snub to France, while the latter had her revenge by keeping Spain out of the peace negotiations altogether. The problem of the Thirty Years' War is not how it began but how it came to an end.

Contarini noted with amusement[95] that, though practically every combatant had taken up arms for the "liberty" of Germany, they all demanded territorial compensation at the Peace Conference. Not till September 1646 were the main lines of agreement reached. At first France was willing to give up her claim to Breisach on the ground that the Rhine was her natural frontier, but the Duke of Bavaria, having again thrown in his lot with France, had the whiphand over the Emperor and secretly urged the French envoys to persist in their demands, knowing as he did that the Emperor would have to yield.[96] Eventually it was arranged that both Breisach and Philippsburg should be garrisoned by the French, and not even the redoubled energies of Spanish diplomacy could annul the settlement in sight between France and the Empire. At Osnabrück, negotiations still lagged, for the elder Oxenstierna was kept in his place solely by war. The young Queen Christina was intensely jealous of Oxenstierna and, in order to close his career as a war-minister, she urged the Swedish agents to conclude peace as quickly as possible. By January 1647[97] the territorial "satisfaction" of Sweden was at last agreed upon.

Two things still delayed the conclusion of peace. The

[95] Contarini, 317.

[96] The rapprochement between France and Bavaria was mainly due to the threat of an alliance between Sweden and Saxony, and because the Duke of Bavaria was anxious to expel Swedish troops from his lands. The threat used by Bavaria was that of a separate peace with France. Bougeant (*Histoire des guerres et des négociacions* . . ., iii. 492) states that the Emperor was forced to sign by the fear of alliance between Austrian Protestants and the Swedes and by the proposal of the Bavarian deputies that the German states should sign in the name of the Emperor.

[97] Contarini, 325.

Swedes urged the claims of Protestantism, and the French maintained that as terms had been settled between France and the Emperor, the latter could no longer assist Spain. The Emperor steadily refused to allow any toleration of Protestantism in his hereditary dominions and replied to the French contention that if he could not assist Spain as Emperor he could do so as king of Hungary. In face of this deadlock the two mediators suggested, quite seriously, a war of France and the Emperor against the Turk, but the Hapsburgs had had enough of their Ottoman neighbours to guarantee them against seeking any closer acquaintance.[98] Thus at the last moment the war might again have become religious,[99] because the Protestants of Bohemia, Moravia, Silesia and Austria now saw that there would be no toleration for them, and that therefore all their sacrifices had been in vain. The Swedes then prolonged discussion by advocating that a ninth electorate should be created in addition to the eighth already reserved for the family of the Elector Palatine.[100] This was defended on the principle that in a deliberative assembly an odd number is better than an even one, but in reality the Swedes wanted the electorate for themselves.

Meanwhile the negotiators were taken unawares by a most unexpected event—the sudden signing of peace between two of their number. When Spain realized that peace with France was practically impossible, she determined to carry out a plan decided on as early as 1643.[101] This was to detach the United Provinces from France at whatever cost. The commercial province of Holland was suspicious of France and anxious for peace; maritime Zealand was for alliance with France and the continuation of the war with Spain.[102] It is not difficult to detect the motives of self-interest behind the agitation dividing opinion in the United Provinces, and for some time the Hague had witnessed a fierce conflict between the exponents of these two views. The anti-French party in Holland found

[98] Contarini, 329.

[99] Chigi wished to unite the Catholic powers, Contarini wanted help for Venice against the Turks. See Odhner, *Die Politik Schwedens . . .*, 146.

[100] Contarini, 329.

[101] *Instruccion dada por Felipe IV al Secretario Galarreta para la negociacion de la paz con Holandeses*, March 1643, in *Coleccion de documentos ineditos para la historia de Espana*, lix. 207 ff. See also, Geddes, *Administration of John de Witt*, i. 74.

[102] See *infra*, p. 400.

a valuable recruit in Madame de Chevreuse, afterwards to play a prominent part in the second Fronde, while Spanish gold was not spared in the extensive propaganda among the Dutch. The Dutch agents at Münster were accompanied by their wives, and the Spanish ambassador, provided with large funds for the purpose, made it his business to be as agreeable as possible to these ladies. By conceding practically everything the Dutch demanded,[103] peace between Spain and the United Provinces was signed at Münster in January 1648, and the full independence of the Protestant Netherlands was solemnly placed on record. Thus ended a struggle which had lasted intermittently for nearly a century, during which a rebellious province had developed into a rich and powerful nation. The symbolical significance of this event was commemorated on canvas by the greatest artist of modern times.[104]

In revenge for this separate peace France, with the help of Bavaria, induced the Emperor to consent to the exclusion of Spain, Lorraine and the circle of Burgundy (including the Spanish Low Countries) from the scope of the peace negotiations. These territories would be involved in the next war; meanwhile there was little likelihood of their fate being influenced by the existing war. This involved the question of Alsace. It was debated whether Alsace should be accepted by France in full sovereignty or as an Imperial fief; the first method would be more in accordance with French dignity; the second would serve to give France a seat in the Diet and so a lever against the Hapsburgs. French hesitation on this subject caused the negotiations again to drag, but the unexpected outbreak of the first Fronde forced Mazarin to decide on peace at once,[105] and Servien, who now acted in place of the recalled Longueville, was peremptorily ordered to conclude the negotiations. The question of Alsace—the most important question yet discussed by the negotiators—was therefore decided in haste and irritation.[106] The two treaties of Münster and Osnabrück, together called the treaty of Westphalia, were signed at Münster on the 24th of October 1648 and the Thirty Years' War was at an end.

[103] Contarini, 341.
[104] Rembrandt's *De Eendracht* (*Unity*) in Boyman's Museum, Rotterdam.
[105] Contarini, 350.
[106] Auerbach, *La France et le Saint Empire Germanique*, 20.

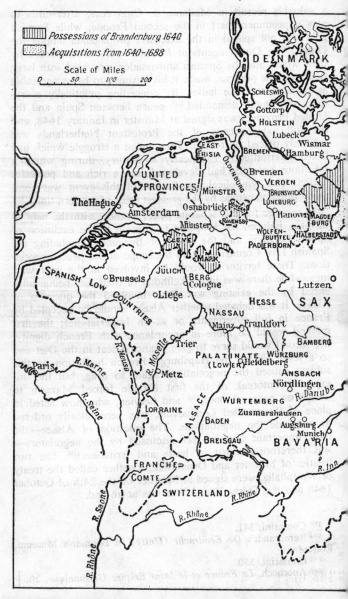

Possessions of Brandenburg 1640

Acquisitions from 1640–1688

Scale of Miles
0   50   100   200

DENMARK

SCHLESWIG
Gottorp
HOLSTEIN
Lubeck
Wismar
Hamburg
BREMEN
EAST
FRISIA
OLDENBURG
Bremen
VERDEN
BRUNSWICK
Luneburg
Hanover
MAGDE-
BURG
UNITED
PROVINCES
Münster
Osnabrück
RAVENSB
WOLFEN-
BUTTEL
HALBERSTADT
The Hague
Amsterdam
Minster
CLEVE
PADERBORN
MARK
JÜLICH
BERG
Cologne
Liege
SPANISH LOW
COUNTRIES
Brussels
Lutzen
HESSE
SAX
NASSAU
Mainz
Frankfort
Trier
R. Moselle
BAMBERG
PALATINATE
(LOWER)
WÜRZBURG
Heidelberg
ANSBACH
Nördlingen
R. Danube
Paris
R. Marne
R. Meuse
Metz
R. Seine
LORRAINE
ALSACE
WURTEMBERG
BADEN
Zusmarshausen
Augsburg
Munich
Zusmarshausen
BAVARIA
BREISGAU
R. Inn
FRANCHE-
COMTE
R. Saone
SWITZERLAND
R. Rhine
R. Rhône
R. Rhine
R. Rhône

The terms of the treaty[107] may be summarized as follows:

The Emperor retained the crown of Bohemia hereditary in his own line; he recovered without payment Upper Austria, which he had pawned to Bavaria, and he did not have to grant religious toleration in his hereditary lands. In the eyes of contemporaries the last was an important privilege, while the result of the other two was to intensify the Austrian character of the Empire.

At the behest of Bavaria it was possible to pacify the other combatants by grants of imperial fiefs in Germany. France received the three bishoprics of Metz, Verdum and Toul, with Moyenvic, Breisach, the fortress of Pinerolo and the right to garrison Philippsburg. She obtained the "landgraviate" of Upper and Lower Alsace in full sovereignty[108] (*supremum dominium*); the Suntgau, and the "provincial prefecture" (*praefectura provincialis*) of the Decapole or ten Alsatian towns, namely, Hagenau, Colmar, Schlettstadt, Weissenburg, Landau, Oberenheim, Rosheim, Münster, Kaisersberg and Turinckheim, together with all rights depending on that prefecture. These ten towns with certain specified monasteries and all the nobility of Lower Alsace were to be left in possession of those privileges which they enjoyed in relation to the Empire, provided however[109] (*ita tamen*) that nothing in this should detract from the "full sovereignty" already conceded. These are the most important provisions of the treaty, and it is not difficult to see that the drafting is, whether intentionally or not, extremely defective.[110] A concession is made: then follows an important reservation, and finally there is the declaration that nothing in the reservation is to detract from the scope of the concession. Hence obviously one party could insist on the reservation, the other on the concession, with the difference that whereas the reservation is mentioned only once, the concession of *supremum dominium* is mentioned twice. It was with such title-deeds that Alsace passed into the

---

[107] The treaties of Münster and Osnabrück will be found in Ghillany, *Diplomatisches Handbuch*, vol. i.

[108] Treaty of Münster, LXXIV. and LXXV.

[109] *Ibid.* LXXVII. See also Reuss, *Alsace*, i. 86 ff.

[110] Bougeant, *Histoire des guerres et des négociacions qui précédèrent le traité de Westfalie* (iii. 452) refers to the "ita tamen" clause as a "pious fraud' accepted by France in the hope of conciliating opinion in Alsace.

possession of France. By the guileless phrase *ita tamen* the Westphalia diplomatists provided material for future wars more deadly than all the armaments of the seventeenth century.

To Sweden were ceded as Imperial fiefs Western Pomerania, the bishoprics of Bremen and Verden, the towns of Wismar and Stettin, the island of Wollin, the territory at the mouths of the Oder and an indemnity, on condition that Swedish troops quitted all other Germany territory. Sweden thus became an important German power, with the right to be represented in the Diet, and with a secure foothold on the southern shore of the Baltic.[111]

Brandenburg, in addition to the important acquisition of Eastern Pomerania, received the bishoprics of Minden, Halberstadt and Cammin and the right of succession to the Archbishopric of Magdeburg. The Elector's territories had suffered considerably in the war,[112] but he had little claim to territorial recompense, and obtained these secularized lands mainly through the influence of France, which acted as benevolent god-mother to the infant Hohenzollern state.

The Duke of Bavaria obtained the Upper Palatinate; he retained his Electoral dignity, and an eighth Electorate was created for the son of the former Elector Palatine, Charles Louis, who was restored to the Lower Palatinate.

Among miscellaneous clauses were those declaring the full independence of Switzerland and the provision that the circle of Burgundy (which included the Spanish Low Countries) was to remain a part of the Empire until "the disputes of France and Spain shall have been terminated." The question of Lorraine was to be referred to arbitration or settled by a treaty between France and Spain. It was agreed that each of the German Imperial states should be free to make alliances with foreigners, provided such alliances were not directed against the Empire; but no questions of making or interpreting laws, declaring wars, imposing taxes, levying soldiers, raising

---

[111] The Swedes considered that their military sacrifices justified greater rewards. On the other hand, Chigi considered that they had obtained ten times more by negotiation than they could have obtained by arms (Ciampi, *Innocenzo*, x. 57).

[112] For this see Gindely, *Waldstein*, II. xii.; also Gebauer, *Kurbrandenburg in der Krisis des Jahres 1627 (Hallesche Abhandlungen, XXXIII* chs. iv. and v.).

fortifications or concluding peace were to be decided unless with "the consent of the Free Assembly of all the states of the Empire." The question of remedying defects in the Imperial administrative machinery was to be a subject of future discussion, as also the institution whereby a king of the Romans was elected in the Emperor's lifetime. The treaty of Cherasco was confirmed.

The treaty did not contain any advance on contemporary theories of toleration. The year 1624 was chosen as the normal year in reference to which the two religious parties were to hold or surrender occupied church lands—a measure favourable to the Catholics, because in 1624 the Protestant cause in Germany was at its lowest ebb. On the other hand, the administrators of secularized bishoprics were to be represented in the Diet, and, taken in conjunction with the concessions made in the treaty itself, the main effect of this clause was to confirm the Protestantism of north Germany and the Catholicism of southern Germany. Calvinism was admitted as an official religion on the same terms as Lutheranism, *i.e.* on the *cujus regio* principle, and five years were allowed in which religious dissentients could settle their affairs and leave. When the Diet had to handle religious matters involving Catholic and Protestant, it was accorded the *jus eundi in partes*, whereby it automatically divided into two sections representing each religion, and as such matters were of frequent occurrence, the division of the Diet into two unconnected parts made it more helpless than ever, but though the German princes were thus given the right to enforce conformity by the threat of expulsion, the right was not always exercised, because so sparse was German population in 1648 that rulers were anxious to see an increase rather than a diminution of their taxable subjects. Toleration entered not by the enlightenment of rulers or diplomats but by economic pressure, and both Brandenburg and Holland were soon to prove that toleration and prosperity may be combined.

It was a distinct diplomatic victory for France when her agents persuaded all the Electors, Princes and Imperial cities to send plenipotentiaries to the Congress. The treaty confirms this territorial independence of the German princes and so completes a process which had long been manifest. It amounted practically to the resignation of the Emperor from all control over German politics, for the feeble bonds which still held the German states to the Empire could easily be dissolved. As there were about three hundred and fifty separate political entities in Germany, the possibilities of diplomatic intrigue were immensely increased, and as each of these states could maintain its agent abroad and expect to have agents accredited to it, it is clear that the increase in diplomatic personnel was very great.

Finally, it should be noted that the treaty came to be considered as a great instrument of public law, standardizing the state system of Europe and providing authoritative guidance in any dispute threatening to upset the equilibrium which the treaty was supposed to have established.[113] Even such an important settlement as that of Utrecht was regarded as an adjustment of the Westphalia pacification, and throughout the Ancien Régime the treaty was considered fundamental and universal. On the pretext of maintaining its provisions France tried to justify her intrigues in Germany,[114] and not till the wars of the French Revolution was the treaty of Westphalia relegated to the limbo of antiquarian curiosities.

To be worthy of the name, a profession must sometimes see that work is left for posterity; omniscience and infallibility are the most sterile of virtues. The diplomats of Münster and Osnabrück were not wanting in this respect. When they transferred the "Landgraviate" (*Landgraviatus*) of Upper and Lower Alsace to France, what precisely did they mean? The word has been interpreted by French writers as meaning territory and by German writers as denoting simply such feudal rights, never clearly defined, as still attached to the title in the seventeenth century.[115] Unquestionably the French assumed in 1648 that the acquisition was a territorial one, for they debated whether to have it as a fief or in full sovereignty,[116] and it is of interest that one French diplomat, probably D'Avaux,[117] was opposed to the transference in full sov-

[113] As late as 1791 Burke, in his *Thoughts on French Affairs*, complained that France regarded the treaty of Westphalia as "an antiquated fable."

[114] See *infra*, p. 218 and 243.

[115] See Reuss, *Alsace*, i. 166 ff.

[116] For the discussions see *Négociacions Secrètes de Münster et d'Osnabrück*, iii. 244-5.

[117] In *Affaires étrangères* (Allemagne, 110), quoted in Vast, *Les Grands Traités*, i. 6.

ereignty because he believed that in this way Alsace would be
"a continual cause of wars." The treaty was barely ratified[118]
before France realized that the question had been settled without a full realization of its import, for within a few years it
was suggested that a better policy would have been to accept
Alsace as a fief, in the same way as Sweden accepted Pomerania, because in this way the French would have obtained
a seat in the Diet. The policy of France in Germany during
two decades after 1648 can be explained only on the assumption that a mistake had been made in regard to Alsace, and
that a remedy had to be found if French tutelage in Germany
was to be retained. On the Imperialist side the granting of
the "Landgraviate" was no great sacrifice, because in Upper
Alsace it was a composite title, designating the heterogeneous
franchises belonging to the Hapsburgs; while in Lower Alsace
it was devoid of all meaning, as suzerainty was already vested
in the Bishop of Strasburg. There was thus a complete confusion between juridical rights and territorial possessions.[119]
A man condemned to death in the town of Haguenau would
not know whether he was to be hanged in the name of the
Emperor or in that of the King of France,[120] and there remained for some time a great deal of ambiguity regarding the
French rights, many landowners and towns resenting bitterly
the change whereby they lost the practical independence, in
which the Hapsburgs had left them, for the systematic domination of a great monarchy. It was because there were old and
vigorous traditions of freedom that Alsace was perturbed by
the momentous change in its destinies. But France transformed these devastated hands into a fair and contented
province, reviving agriculture, suppressing plague and witch-
hunting, respecting existing institutions and winning the loyalty

[118] Auerbach, op. cit. 25 ff. It is noteworthy that, in Mazarin's
opinion, it would be better to hold Alsace as a fief of the Empire
(Affaires étrangères, Allemagne, 73, f. 278).

[119] Though the nobility of Alsace became French, they continued to send deputies to the Diet.

[120] The Alsatian towns claimed that the Emperor had surren-
dered his rights as Landgrave but not as Emperor. See Reuss,
Alsace, i. 170, and Mossman, La France en Alsace après la Paix
de Westphalie. For the German point of view, see Karl Jacob,
Die Erwerbung des Elsass durch Frankreich im Westfälischen
Frieden.

of a people slow to declare its friendships and ever jealous of its self-respect. The acquisition of Alsace in 1648 was a wrong, but at least the province was not regarded as something to be crushed and cowed, but rather to be won by partnership in the great civilization of France.

Chapter 5

Richelieu and Mazarin, 1610–1660

IN THE HALF-CENTURY compressed into this chapter France experienced two minorities and the reign of a characterless king. That the crown of Henry IV. was preserved intact for Louis XIV. was due to the skill and resource of the two ecclesiastical statesmen whose names are given to this chapter. Had these statesmen been laymen, their careers would probably have been cut short by assassination; both pursued a modern policy under the protection of mediaeval insignia.

Henry IV. left as heir to the throne, a child of ten years; at the request of her friends Marie de Medici assumed the title of Regent. Her frivolous, undiscerning nature was at once exploited by a cabal led by the Papal Nuncio, the Spanish ambassador, the Superior of the French Jesuits and a Florentine adventurer named Concini. The last-mentioned had secured the good graces of the Queen-Mother by marriage with Marie's foster-sister, Leonora Galligai, his chief assets being external appearances and the air of bravado which sometimes infatuate women. The aim of the cabal was simply to reverse the policy of Henry IV. The treasure amassed by Sully, intended for the purpose of making France secure against invasion, now provided funds for the horde of greedy sycophants, intriguers and traitors who swarmed in the corridors of the Louvre. This complete break with the recent past was further emphasised in 1612 by the marriage of the young Louis with Anne of Austria, daughter of Philip III. of

Spain, and the marriage of Elizabeth, daughter of Henry IV., with the heir to the Spanish throne.

The first result of this return to an older order of things was that many of the French nobility were able to renew their trade of blackmail. Headed by Bouillon,[1] Lesdiguières[2] and Mayenne,[3] they threatened the Regency cabal with exposure; the State-General, they declared, would be summoned, the disorder in the government revealed, the malversation of national funds made public. Concini, created Maréchal d'Ancre, believed in negotiation, and in terms of the treaty of Saint Menehould (May 1614) the French nobility were pacified for a time by a share in the spoils. Every one was satisfied because, so long as the royal treasure lasted, there was no necessity for increased taxation. But there was one noble, the nearest in blood to the throne, who was determined to renew the rôle of the Duke of Guise and to revive, if possible, the days of the States-General of Blois.[4] This was Henry of Bourbon, Prince of Condé, cousin-german of the king, governor of Normandy and heir-presumptive to the throne. Grouping round him the personal enemies of Concini, such as Vendôme (natural son of Henry IV.), the Prince of Conti, the Dukes of Longueville and Nevers, he aimed at asserting the prerogatives and separatism of his caste. It was in response to the demands of Condé and his following that the States-General were summoned in 1614.

This meeting has some historical interest as the last assembly of the Estates prior to 1789; it is important also as reflecting the characteristic political doctrines of the time. The debates of the three orders of the realm are on record.[5] By proposing to abolish the *paulette*, in order to prevent the bourgeoisie benefiting by the sale of offices, the nobility at-

[1] Henri de la Tour-d'Auvergne, 1555–1623. A Calvinist. Had plotted against Henry IV.

[2] François de Bonne, duc de Lesdiguières (1543–1626). He was generalissimo of Louis XIII.'s armies.

[3] Henri, duc de Mayenne, son of the famous enemy of Henry IV. Killed at the siege of Montauban (1621).

[4] In 1576 Henry, Duke of Guise, assumed the leadership of the League party, a party which (under a veneer of constitutionalism) aimed at substituting Guise for Valois. Guise used the States-General of Blois (1576) to make himself practically absolute.

[5] See Hanotaux, *op. cit.* ii. pt. 1, and Richelieu, *Mémoires* (ed. Société de l'Histoire de France, i. 317-332).

tempted to forment a class war; they argued also that military, diplomatic and household offices should be given exclusively to the nobility by birth; they objected to the conferment of noble rank on judicial functionaries and insisted that hunting should be absolutely forbidden to all but nobles. As a counter-attack, the Third Estate demanded the suppression of pensions. Its spokesman, a deputy named Savaron, eloquently expressed the feelings of the middle classes when he contrasted the enormous wealth—amounting to 5,000,000 livres,[6] spent annually on pensions, with the poverty existing everywhere in France. This was the last official protest of its kind in the history of the Ancien Régime.

In the debates that followed, the significant fact emerged that not the prerogatives of the king but the privileges of the nobility were in question; indeed, Savaron himself published[7] shortly afterwards (1615) a treatise on sovereignty to demonstrate that the royal powers should be strengthened. Another demand of the Third Estate was that there should be placed on record, as a fundamental law of the state, a declaration "that the king is sovereign in France, holds his crown from God only, and that no power, spiritual or temporal, can deprive him of the obedience of his subjects"; but the opposition of the clergy and the suspected Gallicanism lurking in the concluding words of the formula prevented its acceptance. Parlement had recently ordered to be burned the *De rege et regis institutione* of the Spanish Jesuit Mariana, but the French clergy were not prepared to admit that there was no contingency in which subjects might be absolved from their obedience to temporal sovereigns. Otherwise, the States-General of 1614 signed a blank cheque in favour of the monarchy, and the writings of publicists like Lebret soon made familiar the doctrine of the Divine Right of kings. On their reiterated demand that they should be represented on the Conseil d'Etat when matters concerning their interests were in question, the deputies were simply locked out, a method of closing the discussion which they did not even resent. Judged by these proceedings, it might be argued that France lost little by the complete abeyance of the States-General.

Apart from the States-General, the only institution that

---

[6] For the value of the livre, see *supra*, ch. 1, *n.* 11.

[7] *Traité de la souveraineté du roy à MM. les deputés de la noblesse* (1615).

could by any stretch of imagination be considered representative was the Assembly of Notables, convened at rare intervals, the composition of which resembled that of the English Magnum Concilium, summoned for the last time by Charles I. at York in September 1640. There were meetings of the Notables in 1625 and 1626; the first specially convened to grant subsidies for Richelieu's Valtelline policy; the second summoned as a prelude to Richelieu's attack on the privileges of the French nobility. This latter Assembly was asked to sanction the penalty of confiscation instead of death for rebellion which (as was hoped) it refused to do. A proposal for the abolition of the personal *taille* had only three supporters. Many of the decisions of this Assembly were afterwards embodied in the 461 articles of what has been called the Code Michaud,[8] a comprehensive series of judicial and financial measures which did not, however, apply throughout the whole of France and so was not really a code. Thus while the States-General of 1614 was summoned at the request of the nobility and was used mainly for their diversion, the rare meetings of the Assembly of Notables gave Richelieu an occasional weapon against the nobility themselves. Such was the fate of representative institutions in seventeenth-century France.

Meanwhile the minority of Louis XIII. continued to be passed in an atmosphere of treason and plotting.[9] In 1616 a new cabal was formed against Concini, and the treaty of Loudun further enriched Condé and his following, for, once again, silence had been purchased. But the career of the foreign favourite was destined to be short. A young Provençal named Luynes[10] managed to obtain Louis's consent to the murder of the Maréchal, and in 1617 Concini was fatally stabbed in the Louvre by an assassin named Vitry, who was afterwards rewarded by a patent of nobility. Luynes now succeeded to the place of the deceased favourite, and stamped something of his mentality on the receptive mind of the king,

[8] For an account of the Code Michaud, see Glasson, *Histoire du droit et des institutions de la France,* viii. 174 ff., and d'Avenel, *Richelieu et la monarchie absolue,* i. 79.

[9] See Lavisse, *Histoire de France,* vi. 11, Bk. II., and Richelieu, *Mémoires* (ed. Société de l'Histoire de France, ii.).

[10] Charles d'Albret, duc de Luynes (1578–1621). Began as a page-boy of Henry IV. Became Constable in 1621 and died in same year. His widow became Duchess of Chevreuse.

a mentality limited almost entirely to stables and kennels. Like John George of Saxony, Louis XIII. became such a fervid devotee of the chase that it not only displaced state business but gradually produced such mental torpor as to make him incapable of understanding anything else. The rise of Luynes involved the seclusion of the Queen-Mother, but in 1619 she escaped from captivity; a section of the nobility rallied to her cause, and it was only by the skill of Richelieu that civil war was avoided, and peace between mother and son was signed at Angoulême in April 1619. This earned for Richelieu a Cardinal's hat and re-entry in the Council; the death of Luynes at this time and the departure of Condé for Italy[11] made the prospect of internal peace more certain. After years of chequered fortunes and foiled ambitions Richelieu thus made his definite entry into the politics of France. In 1622 he became Cardinal, and two years later informal head of the Council.

There are probably few great characters in modern history regarding whom there is more agreement than Richelieu. He seems to incarnate all the qualities of stratagem, finesse and ruthlessness, his flexibility is that of highly tempered steel, his refined, almost feminine features conceal an iron will, he had none of the coarseness of his contemporaries whom his cruelty sometimes shocked. "He had the intention of all that he did": never before had a man risen to such political eminence by the exercise of sheer intellectual power. If he had few friends at court, he had nevertheless a fixity of purpose and a rigid consistency of intellect infinitely more terrifying than material strength. France under Richelieu had little internal history—the death-rate among the Cardinal's enemies was too high. Some men possess a fund of animal magnetism which seems to radiate strength and confidence among their associates; others, by means equally inscrutable, seem able at will to dry up all the moral and nervous force of those with whom they come into contact, leaving them helpless and impotent. Fortunately the latter is the more rare class, but it is specially powerful because almost always associated with irreproachable morals and even with a suggestion of high idealism. Richelieu was of this type. Much of his power was

---

[11] Failing to profit by civil strife, Condé went to Italy in 1622 on the pretext of a vow.

due to this subtle personal domination unsparingly exercised over men controlled more by their passions than their intellects. Like Bismarck, he achieved great personal success at the cost of incalculable wrong; such men will always be honoured so long as men respect those whom they fear. From this point of view Richelieu has no peer in history. He never descends to the swift alternations between cringing and arrogance which justify criticism of Wolsey; but he suffers in comparison with Cromwell, in whom there was a vein of idealism covered by a rough manliness which men could understand and admire. In Richelieu there was a concentration on the immediate object that cut through every opposition and generally reached its mark with unerring aim. It is characteristic that his greatest mistakes were made when he overreached himself,[12] and it is noteworthy that just as in life he had no friends, so his biographers have been mostly apologists.

As a statesman, Richelieu seems modern in his breadth of vision, his freedom from prejudice and, above all, in his devotion to statecraft as a highly specialized occupation. But despite this modernity, he inherited his political theories from the preceding century, in which it had been announced that statecraft is a "grand compromise with evil"[13]; while in his superstition and cruelty he recalls some of the worst features of a more primitive age. Although in his struggling days he had to dissimulate and act the sycophant, yet he was not a hypocrite, otherwise he would not so candidly have admitted an admiration for Machiavelli, with the fundamental principles of whose *Prince* he was in complete agreement,[14] nor would he have borrowed the sixteenth-century Italian "virtù"

[12] *E.g.* in his dealings with Venice after 1626. See Hanotaux, *Richelieu*, ii. pt. i. 185.

[13] This definition is given by Annibale Scotti. See Toffanin, *Machiavelli e il tacitismo*, 128.

[14] He was surprised that no one had undertaken the defence of Machiavelli's principles, and induced a writer named Machon to undertake an apologia (cf. Céleste, *Louis Machon, apologiste de Machiavel*). Many contemporaries complained that while it was fashionable to condemn Machiavelli, it was usual to act on his maxims, cf.: "it does to me a little relish of paradox, that wherever I come, Machiavill is verbally curs'd and damn'd, and yet practically imbrac'd and asserted: for there is no kingdom but hath a race of men that are ingenious at the peril of the public" (*Modern Policies taken from Machiavel*, 1652, dedication).

for apotheosis in the transparent French guise of "une vertue mâle."[15] Considering that Machiavelli has been attacked or disowned by so many who in practice have outdone his axioms, it is refreshing to find one statesman not ashamed to own the great Florentine as the source of his political inspiration. Richelieu believed that in state-craft hesitation and compunction are always fatal; that the morality which controls the individual need not always apply to the state, and that, for a country like seventeenth-century France, with an overpowerful and unemployed nobility, a stern and unflinching government was the only bulwark against disaster. In his eminently logical mentality there was, however, a strong vein of superstition. He begged the Carmelites of Paris not only to pray for his enterprises, but to reveal the future;[16] in return, he was promised, in the name of Mother Marguerite of the Holy Sacrament, "a defeat of the English." On pressing for a definite date, however, he was assured that "prayer was still being offered up." The fall of La Rochelle in 1628 may have helped to confirm his faith in such prophecies. Like most superstitious men he could be very cruel. "Expose his head on a lance—that will make his fiancée die" was his order for the execution of one of the La Rochelle rebels of whom it had been specially noted that he was engaged to be married;[17] and his joy on learning that a large number of Huguenots had been drowned by the accidental overturning of a raft was sincere and unconcealed. Richelieu is so great because he has so little in his character peculiar only to his age or nation; men of his type will always triumph so long as cold, calculating intellect can override passion and sentiment.

In the days of the Regency when violence often superseded negotiation, the young bishop of Luçon had found shelter in the exile of his diocese or under the wing of Marie de Medici, from which vantage-points he could survey a world just beginning to take notice of his existence. In the company of such a characterless woman as Marie de Medici, the enigmatic and valetudinarian chaplain seemed, in the eyes of robust contemporaries, a spectacle of sinister import. It was on the sins and weaknesses of rivals that Richelieu rose to power;

[15] Richelieu, *Testament politique*, Pt. II, ch. ii.
[16] Brémond, *Histoire littéraire du sentiment religieux en France*, ii. 330.
[17] D'Avenel, *Richelieu et la monarchie absolue*, iv. 77.

and when La Vieuville, the Superintendent of Finance, was convicted of gross malversation, the way was clear. In 1624 he became leader of the Council, with the title of First Minister, and once he had shaken off feminine tutelage he inaugurated his unmerciful but efficient régime.

Thereafter, until his death in 1642, the history of France is something more than a series of palace revolutions, and is too full for merely chronological narrative. But before estimating in detail Richelieu's administrative activities it may be well to refer to the few rebellions against his rule. In 1626 there was a plot to displace him from the royal councils.[18] This, generally known as the Chalais conspiracy, was led by Louis's younger brother—the troublesome Gaston of Orléans —whose accomplice, the Duchess of Chevreuse,[19] was prominent in the numerous designs for subjecting France to foreign influence. The plot was discovered in time; Gaston was too high to be touched, but the Duchess was exiled, and one of her lovers, Chalais, whose complicity was suspected but not proved, was executed. Richelieu, like most great administrators, knew how to make use of scapegoats. In 1630 it was the turn of Marie de Medici herself to rebel against the minister whose career she had made possible. As a woman, the Queen-Mother resented the quiet assurance of absolute power in the minister; she found ready allies in Anne of Austria, Marillac[20] and Bassompierre,[21] but, a few moments after obtaining from her son a promise that the minister would be dismissed, the sudden appearance of Richelieu on the scene petrified every one except the women. Louis XIII. fled, but the Cardinal sought him out at Versailles and, after a

[18] Lavisse, *op. cit.* VI. ii. Bk. III. ch. ii.
[19] For this see Cousin, *Madame de Chevreuse*, ch. i. Marie de Rohan-Montbazon, duchesse de Chevreuse (1600–1679), married Luynes in 1617 and Claude de Lorraine, duc de Chevreuse, in 1622. Her attachment to Anne of Austria led to jealousy of Richelieu.
[20] Michel de Marillac (1563–1632). In 1624 he became Keeper of the Seals and afterwards Superintendent of Finance. Was deprived of office and imprisoned by Richelieu.
[21] François de Bassompierre, maréchal de France (1579–1646). Served in the armies of Henry IV. and Louis XIII. For taking part in intrigues against Richelieu, he was consigned to the Bastille in 1631 and released only on Richelieu's death in 1643. In the Bastille he wrote his Memoirs.

personal interview, Louis again yielded to a bondage from which he had almost escaped. Confirmed once more in power, Richelieu made it indeed a "Day of Dupes"[22] for all who had allied against him, and he now inspired terror not so much by his cruelty as by his caprice. He seized on Marillac's brother and on a trumped-up charge had him sentenced to death (by a majority of one), knowing that the sacrifice of one innocent victim on the altar of his vengeance would inspire as much terror as the punishment of many guilty persons. The Queen-Mother had to take refuge in Brussels, where she was soon joined by Gaston, and there then commenced the intrigues with Spain which had such fatal results in the second Fronde. It was a relief for Richelieu that he had now one woman the less to deal with, for his spell was infallible only for his own sex.

Gaston in exile was the real cause of the third revolt—that of Montmorency.[23] Invading France in 1632 through Burgundy, the Duke of Orléans reached Languedoc, where he was joined by the Governor Montmorency at Castelnaudary. Their joint forces were defeated by government troops under Schomberg, and Montmorency was captured. Richelieu was now more assured of his position than he had been on the "Day of Dupes"; moreover, he knew that a popular governor of a large province was game worth flying at. The Parlement of Toulouse was accordingly compelled, against its will, to put Montmorency on trial, and his execution was carried out with almost oriental haste and secrecy. To contemporaries there appeared no doubt that, by rebellion, the governor of Languedoc merited death, but even to such men, accustomed to scenes of violence, there seemed something revolting in the pertinacity with which Richelieu hunted down his quarry. The conspiracy of Cinq Mars[24] in 1641 gave Richelieu a final and welcome opportunity for sealing his dominion in blood. The treasonable negotiations of Gaston

[22] November 11, 1630.

[23] Henri II., duc de Montmorency, 1595–1632. Had served the court faithfully until 1629, when he became marshal of France; efforts were made to save him in 1632, but Richelieu was adamant.

[24] Henri de Ruzé, marquis de Cinq Mars, 1620–1642. He was irritated against Richelieu by the latter's refusal to allow him to marry Marie de Gonzague, afterwards Queen of Poland.

and Madame de Chevreuse with Spain had become infectious; the youthful favourite of Louis XIII., the Marquis of Cinq Mars, signed a treaty with Spain by which he took it upon himself to promise, in return for a subsidy, the restoration of all Spanish territories captured by French troops.[25] The discovery of this document proved the death-warrant of Cinq Mars, and with him was executed his friend, De Thou, whose sole crime was that he knew of the plot but did not reveal it.

The internal history of France in the years 1624-1642 is coterminous with the manifold activities of Richelieu, who acquired, by letters patent, the title of principal minister of state—a dignity hitherto unknown in France, and practically equivalent to a dictatorship, since the Conseil d'Etat was composed of his creatures and the Parlement of Paris had to content itself with the mere registration of his decrees. The main characteristics of his rule were uniformity, silence and swift executive action. His administration may for convenience be divided into sections according as it dealt with (a) the Huguenots, (b) the Church, (c) the Nobility, (d) the Parlement and the Provincial Government, and (e) Press, Police and Public Opinion.

(a) The Huguenots. At the Assembly of Saumur (1611) the Huguenots organized themselves into "circles" on the model of the Protestant organization in Germany. In the period between 1598 and 1629 they held nine general assemblies—two of them (in 1617 and in 1620) without royal consent. The Edict of Nantes had granted extraordinary privileges to the French Protestants in the hope that clemency would eventually bring them over to the Catholic Church; Richelieu had himself believed that they might be won over by argument. He was soon disillusioned. At his accession to power he realized that the Huguenots formed a federative republic within the state, including such good Frenchmen as Turenne,[26] Duquesne[27] and Conrart[28] (the secretary of the French Academy); and also dangerous men like Bouillon,[29]

[25] Lavisse, *op. cit.* ch. xii.

[26] French general, 1611–1675.

[27] French admiral, 1610–1688.

[28] Patron of letters, 1603–1675.

[29] 1605–1652. Took part in the conspiracy of Cinq Mars and in the Fronde. Son of the duc de Bouillon (1555–1623) who had taken part in Biron's conspiracy against Henry IV.

who took part in most of the risings against Richelieu, and Rohan,[30] a soldier of great ability but no allegiance. Richelieu's suppression of the political activities of the French Protestants can be justified on modern as on contemporary standards, for their existence as an armed republic threatened the safety of the state, while in their strongholds they were quite as intolerant as the Catholics in theirs.[31] His repression of French Huguenots in alliance with England was therefore as consistent as his alliance with German Protestants in rebellion against the Emperor. In April 1621 the Assembly of La Rochelle charged nine of its most violent members to draw up a plan of campaign; in May of the same year the whole of France was divided into eight circles for purposes of armed defence. Soon, active alliance with England and suspected help from Spain made the organization a menace to the government, and in the succeeding years the Huguenots became more assertive as well as better equipped for defence. Richelieu's siege of La Rochelle, begun in November 1627, was the logical reply to Buckingham's attack on the Isle of Rhé.[32] Only when the English fleet had failed to succour the beleaguered port and when nearly 2000 inhabitants had perished of starvation did La Rochelle surrender (October 28, 1628), and the conqueror showed a moderation that did him credit. He did not see why French Protestants should not be good Frenchmen; hence, after his troops had crushed a revolt in Languedoc engineered by Rohan,[33] he granted a general amnesty to all except the leaders, permitting also freedom of worship. The Peace of Alais (1629) settled for fifty-six years the status of the Huguenots in France. They were allowed their independent cult but deprived of their separate political existence, and thereafter they proved one of the most loyal and industrious elements in French society. They were faithful to the monarchy during the Fronde and provided distinguished generals and civil-servants, while by their industry

---

[30] 1579–1638. Son-in-law of Sully. Defended La Rochelle and took part in all the revolts against Richelieu.

[31] In his *Testament politique* (ed. 1764, i. 2) Richelieu wrote that at his accession to power "the Huguenots divided the kingdom with the monarch".

[32] See Gardiner, *History of England*, VI. ch. lx., and La Roncière, *Histoire de la Marine Française*, iv. 534-557.

[33] 1628–9. Lavisse, *op. cit.* VI. ii. bk. iii. ch. iii.

and thrift they contributed largely to the wealth of France. In his treatment of religious dissentients Richelieu showed an enlightenment in strong contrast with the bigotry of his contemporaries; by his absolute rule he protected the Huguenots from their Catholic neighbours.

(b) *The Church*. The same nationalist principles can be seen in his attitude to the French Church. As a Cardinal he could hardly associate himself publicly with the Gallican theories then gaining a firm footing in France and popularized in the writings of Richer,[34] Syndic of the Sorbonne; but as a patriotic Frenchman he had no sympathy with the Ultramontanes and gladly acquiesced in the attitude taken by the Parlement of Paris to specially notorious examples of Ultramontane propaganda. He thus mediated between the two extremes, inducing Richer to moderate his demands, and, on the other hand, keeping the Jesuits in their place. He suppressed Dupuy's *Preuves des Libertez de l'Eglise Gallicane* as well as Santarelli's *De Schismate*.[35] Without committing himself to the theory, he maintained the practice of Gallican liberties in France. To him the Church was an institution for maintaining the virtues of obedience and uniformity; religion he regarded as a social cement, not a spiritual experience. Of this state church the unit was the bishop, and Richelieu insisted that the bishops should duly acknowledge their position as state servants while retaining intact their spiritual prerogatives. For this reason he was very careful in his choice of the upper clergy, preferring clerics of good birth and administrative capacity, rather than saints or men dependent solely on ability. A bishop promoted from the ranks would, in his view, be too avaricious to maintain the full dignity of his exalted position; his ideal type of primate was the muscular and high-born La Mothe Houdancourt, Bishop of Nancy, who could, with equal facility, bless a man with his episcopal cross or knock him down with the butt-end of it. A Council of Conscience was appointed in order to advise the king on the appointment of church dignitaries, and state control was guaran-

[34] Richer expounded his Gallican views in the *De ecclesiastica et politica potestate* (1611) and *Apologie de Gerson* (1616). His views were so extreme that he had to retract them. For Gallicanism see the concluding part of Chapter 8.

[35] The titles of these two books will be sufficient to indicate their purpose. See *Instructions données* (Rome), i. Introduction.

teed by the fact that the General Assemblies of the Church were under strict supervision, even their place of meeting being appointed by the government. Richelieu was suspected of having aimed, like Wolsey, at obtaining some kind of permanent legateship in France and so creating for himself a Patriarchate on the Byzantine model. He knew that the Vatican stood between him and complete control of the French clergy, and that the innumerable ramifications of the religious orders, admitting only the authority of Rome, prevented much-needed reform, since they created a dual allegiance. But it may well be doubted whether he ever seriously entertained ambitions of spiritual autonomy, for, though his triumphal entry into Montauban after the suppression of the Huguenot rising in 1628 was under an archway on which were depicted the legatine cross and the ducal crown, yet the Cardinal may have believed that the hint would do no harm and might strengthen his position with the Papacy.[36]

(c) *The Nobility.* France had never experienced a Tudor government, consequently her feudal nobility survived in the seventeenth century as exponents of an obsolete civilization. Richelieu desired that the nobles should retain their monopoly in Church and State, but was opposed to the policy of conferring on them life governorships of distant provinces—some of them not yet fully incorporated into the French monarchy; it was therefore against the provincial governors that his efforts were mainly directed. He prevented their offices from becoming hereditary and removed a considerable number by exile. In 1614 there were sixteen such local governorships including Berry (Condé), Brittany (Vendôme), Normandy (Longueville), Picardy (Luynes), Champagne (Nevers), Auvergne (Chevreuse), Dauphiné (Soissons), Provence (Guise) and Languedoc (Montmorency). On Richelieu's death only four of these governors survived.[37] Vendôme was imprisoned for sharing in the Chalais conspiracy; Guise was deposed for encouraging revolts in Provence; Montmorency was executed; Soissons was killed in 1641; Rohan was exiled and became a condottiere.[38] It remained for Louis XIV. to make the office

---

[36] *Mémoires de Montchal* (1718), i. 17.

[37] Caillet, *De l'administration en France sous le ministère du Cardinal de Richelieu,* 30.

[38] In the service of Venice. See Bühring, *Venedig, Gustav Adolf und Rohan,* 83-135.

of Provincial Governor a nominal one, limiting its duration to three years, ruining its holders by enforced attendance at Versailles and leaving them what Madame de Sévigné called "the noise, trumpets, violins and atmosphere of royalty."

By his rigidly enforced edicts against duelling Richelieu struck at one of the most cherished privileges of the nobility. An edict of 1626 imposed a term of banishment, with loss of status for a first offence and death for the second.[39] Montmorency-Bouteville and the Count of Chapelles were executed in accordance with this edict. But duelling was never really stamped out, and though Richelieu terrified the French nobility he did nothing to make them useful members of society. That task was perhaps beyond the powers of any mortal; not till the Revolution did France settle accounts with her hereditary nobility.

(d) *The Paris Parlement and the Provincial Estates.* The Paris Parlement was a sovereign court of the realm, asserting the right to control legislation by registering only such edicts as had its approval.[40] This right had never been fully admitted; sometimes, as when asked to register the Concordat of Bologna (1516), Parlement had protested in vain, but had been forced to content itself with putting its protest on record. The monarch, as an integral part of the sovereign court, could require obedience by holding a *lit de justice* therein. But the Paris Parlement was really a close legal corporation exercising judicial functions, often acting as a supreme law court, and claiming to perform many of the functions characteristic of the English Privy Council. It was the discrepancy between its claims and privileges on the one hand and its lack of any real power or national backing on the other, that prevented the Parlement offering serious opposition to Richelieu. He allowed it to pass judgement on ecclesiastical matters, for he was in sympathy with its Gallicanism, but he did not trust it to sit in judgement on important state prisoners, preferring for that purpose extraordinary judicial commissions whose composition he could control. In this way the notorious Chambre de l'Arsenal was created in

[39] See Richelieu, *Mémoires* (ed. Société de l'Histoire de France), v. 266 ff.

[40] For a full account of the composition and claims of the Parlement see, under that word, Marion, *Dictionnaire des institutions de la France*

1631 against the emphatic protests of the Parlement, protests to which Louis replied by the message: "You exist only for judging disputes between Master Peter and Master John, and if you try to exceed your commissions I will cut your nails to the quick,"[41] language which suggests the pen of the Cardinal. When Louis proclaimed guilty of treason all who fled from France in 1626 with Gaston of Orléans, Parlement protested, but was forced to register the edict by "lettres de jussion," and was informed that it had no right to meddle in affairs of state.[42] On this occasion two presidents and a councillor were exiled. The Parlement opposed the foundation of the French Academy, thinking that it might become a rival institution, and registered the edict of foundation in 1636 on condition that the Academy confined itself to matters of philology and taste. Resistance to financial edicts induced Richelieu in 1635 to devise a subtle means of weakening Parlement. The office of Councillor of Parlement was a valuable and vendible privilege; in December 1635 funds were urgently required for the war in which France had just embarked, so Richelieu created twenty-four new councillorships and put them up for sale, thus obtaining money and at the same time weakening a privilege by multiplying it. The measure was not carried through without the exile and imprisonment of several leading members; a compromise was reached by reducing the number of new councillors to eighteen. The experiment was repeated in 1637, and thereafter provided the bitterest subject of complaint against the Cardinal. In 1641 came the final blow, when Parlement was ordered to confine itself to judicial matters and give its advice on politics only when asked, an injunction which served to keep the bait of political power dangling before the eyes of Parlement and helps to account for its intervention in state affairs during the Fronde. Not till Louis XIV.'s reign was Richelieu's work definitely completed, when Parlement ceased to be a sovereign court.

Richelieu was not quite so successful with the provincial

[41] Glasson, *Le Parlement de Paris, son rôle politique*, i. 144.

[42] "Where the Parlement formerly approved royal edicts and took part in important decisions . . . they are now ordered not to interfere in political questions" (Correr, Venetian ambassador, writing in 1641, *Relazioni degli ambasciatori veneti*, ed. Berchet e Barozzi (France), ii. 341).

Estates though he had less to fear from them than from the Parlement. The Pays d'Etats were Languedoc, Brittany, Burgundy, Provence and Dauphiné; Normandy might be included, for it retained its meetings of the Estates until 1655, but on the other hand it was subject to the detested *élus* and so was really a Pays d'Elections. The provincial Etats were far from democratic; they represented the local aristocracy and bourgeoisie; they met at long intervals and, though they had some financial autonomy and could bargain with the Government for a composite sum to be paid by way of *taille*, they had practically no initiative.[43] From Montesquieu[44] onwards it has been customary to eulogise the Pays d'Etats as compared with the Pays d'Elections, but it has been forgotten that the local states were oligarchic not popular, and that in Pays d'Elections enterprising and able intendants might carry out reforms impossible in provinces subject to moribund and reactionary assemblies. But the true despot loves uniformity, and Richelieu disliked the *Etats Provinciaux* not because they gave trouble but because they were reminiscent of a period when the king of France was little more than a *primus inter pares*. In attempting to impose "elections" or government tribunals on Languedoc, Burgundy and Provence, he may also have had another motive—to obtain money in return for the abandonment of the proposal, but in 1630 there were revolts among the Dijon wine growers, when the introduction of "elections"[45] was proposed, threats which may have deterred the minister from proceeding further. The Estates of Brittany were most amenable to Richelieu's policy and the province was specially favoured by the establishment of companies[46] of commerce, such as that of the West Indies, which enhanced local prosperity. The only province to lose its local Estates was Protestant Dauphiné (1628). The Estates of Normandy came to an end in 1655 because the deputies failed to put in an appearance. Otherwise the Provincial Estates remained in existence until the Revolution, providing

[43] Caillet, *op. cit.* 204 ff.

[44] *De l'esprit des lois*, Bk. XIII. ch. xii.

[45] Caillet, 271. For the vigorous protests of Provence against Richelieu's attempts to introduce "elections" see d'Avenel, *Richelieu et la monarchie absolue*, iv. 182.

[46] For the French seventeenth-century trading companies see Bonnaissieux, *Les Grandes compagnies de commerce*, Bk. III.

political idealists with material for proving that France had once had some traces of a constitution.

(e) *Press, Police and Public Opinion.* In every consistent despotism these three things form one department. The lifetime of Richelieu coincided with the period during which, in England and France, primitive newspapers were coming into existence, and the Cardinal fully realized the immense possibilities of the printed word.[47] The *Gazette* and the *Mercure* were absolutely controlled by him, providing publicity for such official news as it might seem expedient to impart and for justifications of ministerial policy. But the pamphlet rather than the newspaper was still the most potent weapon of literary advocacy, and if Richelieu was attacked in broadsides which it was dangerous even to possess, he took care to subsidize pamphleteers who made it their business to present his actions in a favourable light. Before taking part in the Thirty Years' War he cultivated public opinion by inspiring several manifestos reciting the grievances of France against the Hapsburgs. Nor was propaganda confined to matters of foreign policy,[48] for in Lebret's *De la souveraineté du Roy* (1632) there is a complete exposition of the Divine Right theory. According to Lebret the king alone is charged with the duty of making and interpreting laws, but, for example's sake and not because obliged to, he may communicate proposed legislation to his Councils, Estates and Parlement for their formal approval. It is for the monarch to declare war and initiate peace negotiations, but it is piously added that the wars ought to be just ones and conducted with skill. The only limit to sovereignty, according to this writer, is that the king does not own his subjects' property—

[47] For this consult H. Sée, *Les Idées politiques en France au XVIIème siècle*, ch. ii. There are also interesting instances of Richelieu's use of propaganda in both volumes of Fagniez, *Le Père Joseph et Richelieu*. See also Fagniez, *L'Opinion publique et la presse sous Louis XIII.* (in *Revue d'histoire diplomatique*, 1900, 352-401).

[48] An attempt to accommodate Catholic principle to Richelieu's policy of alliance with foreign heretics is made in *Questions décidées sur la justice des armes des rois de France* (1634). French claims on Lorraine, Milan, Roussillon, Savoy and even Genoa were made in such pamphlets. For a time Fancan and Cassan were retained as official propagandists. For Fancan see Geley, *Fancan et la politique de Richelieu, 1617-1627.*

a reservation to be withdrawn in the next reign.[49] "Reason of State" figures as a justification for acts that otherwise might appear immoral; monarchs are not bound by their treaties, nor can they be required to pay the debts of their predecessors. Similar views were expounded in another semi-official production—the *Prince* of J. L. de Balzac. The title suggests Machiavelli and some passages read like a paraphrase of *Il Principe*. It is for the sovereign to apply violent remedies when the interests of the state demand it. Heavy taxation may be as beneficial for the people as the application of leeches to a swollen body. The ruler is not bound to wait until danger threatens—he can act on a simple suspicion. In these ways Richelieu and his band of obedient publicists prepared the way for the reign of Louis XIV.

The Cardinal himself wielded the pen. In addition to several theological discourses he compiled several "Maximes d'Etat";[50] he probably wrote the *Testament politique* published in his name, and if he did not write his Memoirs, they were probably drawn up under his dictation.[51] So far as the theory of the state is concerned the general views of Richelieu as expounded in these compilations might be reduced to the following axioms:

1. Absolute monarchy is the only alternative to anarchy.
2. The nobility should be excluded from important state offices but ought to devote their lives to arms in the service of the state.
3. A minister must often be prepared to act on conjecture where, as a private person, he would require absolute proof.
4. It is better that a few should suffer, even if unjustly, than that the safety of the state should be endangered.
5. Repression and heavy taxation are, within limits, good for the common people just as mules and beasts of burden must be kept fit by constant work.

[49] For the claim of Louis XIV. that the monarch is the owner of his subjects' property see his *Mémoires* (in *Œuvres de Louis XIV*, ed. Grouvelle ii. 121).

[50] These have been published by Hanotaux in *Mélanges historiques*, iii. 705 ff. (*Collection des documents inédits de l'histoire de France*).

[51] See *Revue des Questions Historiques*, Oct. 1928.

6. So long as there are more fools than wise men the majority of people cannot know their own best interests; hence the ultimate justification for the absolute rule of one person who, in virtue of his pre-eminent position is able to gauge the real interests of each element in the state.

7. The Christian religion, by its emphasis on the duties of submission and obedience, provides the ideal fund of common principle among the governed but, in order to secure this benefit, only one form of Christianity should be encouraged.[52]

When propaganda failed to effect its object the police system of Richelieu intervened. We have already noted that Richelieu was not dependent on the ordinary courts for proceedings against state prisoners; he had his own specially appointed tribunal established in 1631—the Chambre de l'Arsenal, notorious for its midnight executions. If the ordinary judicial institutions had to be utilized, the Cardinal enforced compliance by dismissing judges whose independence was suspected and, when he compelled the Parlement of Toulouse to try Montmorency in 1632, he sent a government official, Châteauneuf, Keeper of the Seals, to preside over the Parlement's conduct of the case. In addition to this, great use was made of the Intendants.[53] The Intendants were primarily instituted to protect the individual against the ignorance and prejudice of possibly biassed local jurisdictions as well as against the pressure that might be exercised by "overmighty" subjects. They were responsible to the government alone and, while at first they visited the provinces as police inspectors and sometimes as spies, in time they settled down in their provinces as busy administrators. During the Fronde, the Intendants were suppressed, but Colbert restored the system.

[52] On the whole, Richelieu was more enlightened in this respect than his contemporaries, for he was not a believer in persecution. But later French opinion favoured the use of force. Cf. "Those who believe that a prince should not use force in religious matters . . . are guilty of an impious error" (Bossuet, *Politique tirée des propres paroles* . . ., vii. 3. 10).

[53] See Hanotaux, *Origine de l'institution des intendants de provinces*.

Even in the domain of letters the characteristic centralization and uniformity of Richelieu's administration may be detected. The French Academy was founded or rather legalized by an edict of 29th January 1635, and in this way the little band of zealous philologists and critics which met at the house of Valentine Conrart acquired an official status. Encouraged by the Cardinal, the Academy proposed, by the preparation of a Dictionary, to standardize the French language. This was not achieved until 1694. The attempt to codify the laws of prose and verse composition was not so successful, but the Academy has survived as a tribunal of literary taste.

Richelieu was greatest as a war minister, and the contributions for the upkeep of French armies were exacted only at the cost of great suffering. The rising of the "Nu-Pieds" in Normandy (1639) was due to unbearable poverty, not unconnected with the harsh fiscal régime imposed by the First Minister; the revolt was suppressed with the brutality to be found in men who doubt whether the lower orders have any right to exist. Details of budgets during Richelieu's administration convey little in terms of modern currency, but it must be emphasised that the Cardinal was interested in neither commerce nor finance, and attempts to attribute definite economic motives to his policy are futile. So long as he obtained the armies and the revenues, he did not trouble whether or not he was draining the best resources of France, far less whether the means applied for raising money were or were not equitable; and so far as he ever thought at all on economic problems, his views were no worse and no better than those of his contemporaries. It is a significant fact that in the later stages of his rule many villages became deserted, and their inhabitants were forced to take up a nomadic life. While he was concentrating all his energies on the task of making France feared throughout the whole of Europe, he failed to see that England and Holland were wresting colonial supremacy from the Spanish and Portuguese, and that the future would lie, not with the largest battalions nor the most ruthlessly efficient executives, but with the control of the sea and the development of natural resources by governments in which popular opinion had some part. The creation of a great colonial empire requires qualities of enterprise and sacrifice that cannot be compensated for by administrative qualities, no matter how remarkable. Richelieu governed but could not create.

The Cardinal died on the 4th of December 1642 and Louis XIII. on the 14th of May 1643. Except where military matters were concerned, Louis had shown little interest in his duties as monarch, leaving all responsibility and initiative to his minister. Richelieu had intended Father Joseph for his successor, but the latter had died in 1639, and thereafter Jules Mazarin, already a Cardinal, was designated to carry on the functions of First Minister. Mazarin ably continued the foreign policy of Richelieu and lived to see the triumph of France on the ruins of Spain, but his internal administration was much more troubled than that of his predecessor.

Louis XIII. left the throne to a child five years of age and by his will Anne of Austria was appointed Regent with powers as limited as possible. Anne was to act only on the advice of a Council, consisting of herself, the Duke of Orléans (who acquired the title of Lieutenant-Governor of the kingdom), the Prince of Condé and Mazarin, assisted by officials such as Séguier, the Chancellor; Bouthillier, Superintendent of Finance; and Chavigny, a secretary of state. Mazarin had by this time secured the Queen's affections;[54] their interests were practically identical, and they at once combined forces in order to rid themselves of the Council of Regency. This was not a difficult task, because Orléans and Condé were intensely jealous of each other, agreeing only in dislike of Mazarin and the official members of the Council. Prompted by her able coadjutor, Anne dissimulated her real ambitions, talked of dismissing Mazarin, and, by favouring ridiculous personages such as the Duke of Beaufort (famous for his malapropisms), she contrived to set each member of the Council against the other while, with considerable cleverness, she arranged that Condé and Orléans should ask the Parlement to grant her full Regency. Anxious once more to

[54] It is still debated whether or not Mazarin was secretly married to Anne of Austria. Hanotaux (*Etudes critiques sur le XVIème et XVIIème siècles*, 227) believes that he was. Chéruel, the editor of Mazarin's correspondence, was inclined to suspend judgment; Anne's daughter-in-law, the Duchess of Orléans, declared that such a marriage took place.

play a political part, Parlement granted this request. She was no sooner Regent than she appointed the Italian First Minister, whereupon the Council realized that they had been duped. It was not the first time in French history that feminine cleverness had outmatched masculine strength; in the years that followed there were to be many opportunities for victory in this unequal contest.

Thus, like Richelieu, Mazarin had risen to eminence on a woman's shoulders. Comparisons between the two are generally to the disadvantage of the latter. Historians have been inclined to accept the verdict of contemporary French memoir writers, forgetting that many of these memoirs were written not merely by enemies of the Cardinal but by enemies of every system of law and order. Frenchmen were prepared to believe anything of the Italian. De Retz circulated the rumour that the Cardinal had been a pickpocket in his younger days, while the more serious accusation that he was low-born was accepted then as it is now. The truth is that though Mazarin had been a gambler in youth and was one with whom it might be inexpedient to take part in a game of chance, yet he had never been convicted of theft; and as for the other accusation, he had no reason to be ashamed of his ancestry, for he was descended on his mother's side from the Colonna family.[55] The Church had attracted him because of its scope for a diplomatic career; as Papal Nuncio he had learned his craft in the complicated negotiations of the Mantuan Succession, the treaty of Cherasco being largely his work.[56] Residence in France as papal representative had given further evidence of his qualities; moreover Richelieu, a keen judge of men, had no doubt of Mazarin's ability to succeed him. This choice seems curious when the contrast between the two is considered. Where the Frenchman was straightforward, adamant and always dignified, the Italian was compromising and sinuous, courteous and deceitful, vindictive and sarcastic, winning his ends not by frontal attack but by pitting his enemies against each other; able to emerge unashamed from any disgrace, and frankly enriching himself

[55] See Cousin, *La Jeunesse de Mazarin*, ch. i., and *Lettres du Cardinal Mazarin* (*Collections de documents inédits sur l'histoire de France*), i. Introduction.

[56] There is a full account of his career at this time (1629–1631) in Cousin, *op. cit.* chs. iv. v. vi.

and his relatives at the expense of his adopted country. His wealth brought out all the contemptible qualities of the miser.[57] Richelieu had built up for himself and the French monarchy the great palace originally the Palais Cardinal, now the Palais Royal; Mazarin gloated over jewels and precious stones. But there the contrast ends. Both men were absolutely unscrupulous in their pursuit of the same end—the creation of absolutism in France; both incarnated the sixteenth-century conception of the secular ruler untrammelled by any restraints or traditions; both had to contend with anarchy in the person of the French noble. The honour of making France the greatest power in seventeenth-century Europe is evenly divided between the two, and it is evidence of Richelieu's deep knowledge of human character that he entrusted the destinies of France to a man seemingly so different from himself.

The nobility never forgave Mazarin for his share in the trick by which he and Anne became supreme; thereafter they directed all their efforts at deposing the minister. The first manifestation of their intrigues was the formation in 1643 of the cabal known as the *Importants* led by Beaufort (a useful figure-head, as he was a grandson of Henry IV.)[58] and organized by the Duchess of Chevreuse, the cleverest woman spy in the service of Spain.[59] The conspirators were called "Importants," because they adopted an air of mystery and consequence; nominally they aimed at obtaining Brittany for Beaufort, but really they wished to restore those privileges of the nobility which Richelieu had destroyed, to reverse French foreign policy, and assist Charles I. against the English Parliament. Mazarin saved himself from assassination by having Beaufort arrested (September 1643), and the accomplices fled from Paris to continue their intrigues at a safe distance. At this time the brilliant conquests of French arms in the Thirty Years' War diverted attention from political questions at home and gave temporary employment to many of the nobility.

[57] La Rochefoucauld said of him: "il avait de petites vues même dans ses plus grands projets," quoted in Chéruel, *Histoire de France pendant la minorité de Louis XIV*, I. xv.

[58] Son of the duc de Vendôme, a natural son of Henry IV.

[59] The activities of Madame de Chevreuse at this period are detailed in Cousin, *Madame de Chevreuse*, 114-198.

Nothing palls so quickly as military successes that do not bring the conclusion of hostilities any nearer, and as the war dragged out its weary course attention was directed to the administrative abuses of Mazarin's rule.[60] Like his predecessor, the Cardinal had no interest in French industry or commerce, and after ten years of war budgets the French Treasury was not only exhausted but was dependent on anticipated revenue up to three years in advance. The usual expedients of selling titles of nobility, creating new offices and obtaining advances from a fresh horde of tax farmers were all adopted at the expense mainly of the peasants. These, however, were quite normal measures; what helped to irritate popular feeling was that new taxes were invented, while officials, taking their cue from Mazarin, were busy amassing large private fortunes. The iniquitous Superintendent of Finance, d'Emeri, imposed a tax on all dwelling-houses built just outside the walls of Paris, on the pretext that such buildings were illegal. In support of this decision, he revived a statute of the preceding century, which, for the purpose of more adequately defending Paris during the wars of the League, had prohibited the building of houses within a certain distance of Paris. For more than fifty years Paris had been free from the threat of invasion, and suburbs had grown up outside the walls, but by the Edit de Toisé suburban householders had now to pay a tax or see their houses demolished, a measure greeted with such opposition that it had to be considerably modified and recourse made to a forced loan. The continuous successes of French troops, however, prevented a definite break with the government, leaving Mazarin and d'Emeri free to proceed with their disastrous policy of alienating national feeling by an organized system of robbery under the name of taxation.

It needed only government interference with the *rentes* to precipitate the movement known as the Fronde. In seventeenth-century Paris there was a large class of bourgeoisie having a considerable part of its capital invested in the national *rentes*, which were issued, without payment of com-

[60] The best account of this period is in Chéruel, *Histoire de France pendant la minorité de Louis XIV*, iii. and iv. The greater part of Mazarin's voluminous correspondence during the Fronde will be found in the *Lettres du Cardinal Mazarin* (*Documents inédits sur l'histoire de France*), vols. iii. iv. and v.

mission, by the municipal Hôtel de Ville. The only equivalent of a modern gilt-edged security at a time when there were no national banks, it was a common investment on behalf of widows and children; on the other hand, it had enough speculative interest to attract the most daring gambler, for on some occasions the *rentes* yielded an interest on outlay of 50 per cent—evidence of how low government credit might sink. The system had been first introduced into French finance in 1522 and, despite Sully's repudiation of doubtful scripts and attempts to reduce the rate of interest, people nevertheless continued to purchase *rentes*; in 1643 they represented a capital equivalent to about four million pounds sterling.

Mazarin and d'Emeri interfered with the payment of the interest on this national security in order to cause depreciation; when its price fell they purchased large amounts, paid some of the arrears of interest, and sold out when the rise took place. It is possible to crush a peasantry so that it cannot rise, but systematic robbery of a prosperous and educated bourgeoisie generally ends in revolution. Interference with the *rentes* was one of the main causes of the first Fronde or Fronde of the Parlement; but it is a mistake to attach any great constitutional importance to this movement or to compare it with the great Parliamentary struggle in England, for it was led by a close and privileged corporation fighting not for abstract doctrines, but for certain tangible things, such as reduction of taxation and the maintenance of some form of elementary honesty in the administration of the national finances. The original Frondeurs resembled the English Commons in demanding freedom from arbitrary arrest, and they were no doubt inspired to a certain extent by English example, but they had neither the traditions nor the leadership which raised the English Civil War to the level of a conflict of principles. Moreover, the first Fronde was soon submerged in the second or Fronde of the Nobles, a movement which let loose all the pent-up instincts of anarchy in the French nobility.

The word Fronde means "catapult," and *Frondeur* was originally used of the Paris hooligans who took pleasure in slinging mud at people in passing coaches. The term came to designate any one prominent in opposition to the government, whether from faction or principle. In January 1648, when the Regent ordered the Parlement to register several financial edicts, the Advocate-General, Omer Talon, addressed the queen in words which showed that the menace of rebellion was a real one. On the 13th of May in the same year Parlement by the "Arrêt d'Union" decided that all four sovereign courts—the Chambre des Comptes, the Cours des Aides, the Grand Conseil and the Parlement itself—should meet in the Chambre de St. Louis for the purpose of deciding on common measures. But Anne of Austria, though clever in managing men, was too stolid to anticipate abstract impersonal danger, so the government proceeded to postpone payment of the *rentes* for a year and abolished the *paulette*. The latter was the one tax which the Parlement wished to retain, since it legalized the heredity of their offices. The opposition of the Parlement was intensified by the exile and imprisonment of several of its leaders in June 1648: from this date the Fronde takes its beginning.

Meanwhile the joint assembly of all the sovereign courts met in the Chambre de St. Louis to draw up a plan of reform. Apart from the demands that personal liberty should be guaranteed and the Intendants removed, the scheme was composed mainly of financial proposals, such as that monopolies should be abolished, imports of foreign luxuries prohibited, the *taille* lowered, malversators dealt with by a special tribunal, no taxes imposed without due and uncoerced registration by Parlement and that the *rentes* should be paid regularly. The granting of such demands might have made France a constitutional monarchy and would have undone most of the work of Richelieu. Prompted by Mazarin, Anne saved the situation for the time by yielding on practically every point. It was the only possible course, and after all Mazarin knew that premature success may easily ruin a revolution, since concessions yielded in danger can often be revoked in safety. Nothing was said of guarantees for personal liberty, and the Government undertakings extended only to taxes that might be imposed in the future.

Condé's victory at Lens (August 20, 1648) induced Mazarin to terrify opposition by a sudden thrust; accordingly he induced Anne to emulate the unfortunate example of Charles I. and arrest the most prominent leaders of the Parlement, including the popular Broussel. On the day after the arrest (August 26) barricades were erected in the streets of Paris, and the mob soon found a head in the young Paul de Gondi, afterwards Archbishop of Paris and Cardinal de Retz. Gondi, a self-appointed leader, did more than any one else to ruin the cause he espoused; he had no ability (except as a humorist), no religion and no principles. He was specially dangerous because he was the link between two gangs of desperadoes—the Paris mob, which he subsidized with his aunt's money, and the treasonable section of the French nobility, to which he belonged by choice and birth. Believing in his own maxim that "the vices of an archbishop may well be the virtues of the head of a party," he aimed at being first a Demagogue, then a Cardinal and eventually a First Minister with the powers of a Richelieu. It was by the intervention of men such as this that the Fronde was turned into a grotesque medley of tragedy and farce.

Once again the Court yielded with a sinuosity that reflected the counsels of Mazarin. Broussel and his colleagues were released and the young Enghien, the victor of Lens and now Prince of Condé by the death of his father,[61] was summoned to Paris. The Declaration of St. Germains (22nd October) embodied all the reforms demanded by the Chambre de St. Louis, and on the following day instructions were sent to Servien, the French agent at Münster, to conclude the peace negotiations at once. The triumph of the Parlement seemed complete, and Mazarin now completely effaced himself. The signing of the treaty of Westphalia two days later seemed to augur well for all who looked forward to an era of peace and good government. These hopes, however, were soon to be dashed, for nearly four years of civil war were about to ensue.

The fact that by the conclusion of the war French troops were released for service at home and that the support of both Orléans and Condé was promised, decided the Court, after a brief lull, to revoke every concession and strike at the Parlement. On the 5th of January 1649 Anne went to St. Germains and the Parlement received orders to go to Montargis. The order was accepted as a declaration of war; accordingly Paris was vigorously organized for defence against the approaching troops of Condé. By the end of January 1649 the city was closely blockaded, and while

[61] In 1646.

Condé, outside the walls, was pressing the siege, his brother Conti was engaged with his brother-in-law, Longueville, and their associates Beaufort, Bouillon and Gondi in maintaining the defence of the city. This unsought alliance with the nobility was as embarrassing as it was disastrous for the bourgeoisie, but it helped to encourage the populace, and public interest was maintained by occasional sorties from the city in which Gondi specially distinguished himself by the speed with which he fled back to the gates as soon as any danger threatened. A more sinister event was the admission of a Spanish envoy into Paris. The fever of revolt spread to the provinces. It was the dread of implicating themselves further in the treasonable negotiations of their noble associates that forced the Parlement eventually to propose a compromise. Led by Matthieu Molé—patriot and zealous advocate of the liberty of the subject—Parlement agreed to treat with the Court, and the first Fronde was ended by the treaty of Rueil signed on the 11th of March 1649, when most of the concessions already granted were confirmed and registered by the Parlement. The conclusion of the siege was celebrated with fireworks, and the populace were glad to escape from starvation.

At this point ends the constitutional interest of the Fronde. Theoretically Parlement had won a victory, but its association with the nobility put it in a false position; moreover, the privileges just gained were soon to be whittled away. Condé had no intention of giving his help to the Court without recompense, and foolishly assumed that the concessions made by Mazarin were proofs of weakness. He had no doubt that his birth and services merited adequate reward; the post of First Minister seemed the most obvious return for his support. Urged on by his sister and brother-in-law (the Duchess and Duke of Longueville), by his younger brother (Conti), and by the Coadjutor (Paul de Gondi) he assumed a personal dictatorship, proposing, as substitute for Mazarin, a nonentity named Jarzé, an insult which made Anne the bitter enemy of the arrogant general, and by the summer of 1649 it was quite clear that the real enemies of the monarchy were not the Parlement but the Princes. By nature Condé was harsh and insolent: military success had turned his head, his blind egotism alienated friend and foe alike. He took so little care to conceal either his ambitions or his military preparations that his removal became necessary in the interests of public safety; so on the 18th of January 1650 Mazarin had him arrested, with Conti and Longueville, and conveyed to Havre.[62] This was the signal for the outbreak of the second Fronde or Fronde of the Princes.

The second Fronde[63] lasted longer and was much more widespread than the first, which had amounted to little more than a few months' siege of Paris. The provincial governor-ships held by the nobility, together with their hereditary influence, enabled them to raise the provinces, while their negotiations with Spain introduced a dangerous element, es-pecially when Turenne betrayed his country by alliance with the Archduke Leopold. Throughout the earlier part of 1650 the Court, assisted by the loyal troops, perambulated the country in the hope of restoring order, a task well nigh hopeless, for the influence of the nobility reached to every corner of France and no sooner did Turenne and his Spanish troops invade Picardy than the south-west rose in revolt. The Princess of Condé established herself as an independent ruler in Bordeaux, and only the loyalty of the bourgeoisie pre-vented the city being handed over to Spain. For some time Mazarin had been quiescent, but, ever since the arrest of the Princes, he had been actively engaged in attempting to dis-solve the alliance between the bourgeoisie and the nobility. He knew that he was safe so long as he could play the one off against the other, and his knowledge of his adopted coun-try led him to believe that there were far more elements of antagonism than concord in the two parties now ranged against him.

To produce an effective alliance between the nobility and the *noblesse de robe* was the ambition of Paul de Gondi, who worked hard to bring the two together, since only by their

[62] An account of the feeling stirred by the arrest of the Princes will be found in the *Mémoires de Madame de Motteville*, iii 131-141.

[63] There was a secret treaty between the members of the two Frondes. By this, the contracting parties undertook (i.) to secure the release of the Princes, (ii.) to remove Mazarin and replace him by Châteauneuf, (iii.) to confer presidency of the council on Orléans, and (iv.) to secure certain matrimonial alliances among the nobility. See Cousin, *Madame de Longueville pendant la Fronde*, ii. 371 ff.

cohesion would the overthrow of Mazarin be possible.[64] These activities were intensified by Mazarin's refusal to give him the nomination for a Cardinalate. In his design of uniting the responsible with the irresponsible elements in the opposition, so that from the resulting anarchy a way might be opened for his absurd ambitions, the Coadjutor was assisted by some clever but notorious women, such as the Duchesse de Chevreuse, Madame de Longueville, Anne of Gonzague (Princess Palatine), and Mademoiselle de Chevreuse. Marriage alliances were included among the objects of this clique, and, when they managed to win over both Orléans and the Parlement, they presented a union of forces which Mazarin could never hope to match.[65] Their first demand was for the release of the Princes and the expulsion of the First Minister. Once again Mazarin yielded to the storm and fled from France early in February. The Princes were released on the 11th of February 1651. Entering Paris in triumphal procession, they proceeded to the Luxemburg, then the residence of Orléans, where a national convention of Parlement and Princes was held. The queen and her son were now practically prisoners and in a position of some personal danger. Among the proposals discussed by the assembly at the Luxemburg were that a meeting of the States-General should be summoned, that Anne should be deprived of the Regency and sent to a convent, and that the young Louis XIV. should be ruled by a council of twenty, representing the three estates. This was the most dangerous crisis through which the French monarchy passed prior to the Revolution of 1789, but Mazarin, who, in his exile at Cologne, was still governing France by correspondence,[66] knew that the unholy alliance of the two Frondes could not last.

The nobility and the bourgeoisie no sooner united than they flew apart. Even in the first enthusiasm of the Luxemburg Convention there were "incidents" when some of the deputies were threatened with defenestration.[67] Mazarin's

---

[64] Mazarin to Le Tellier (*Lettres*, ed. Chéruel, iii. 976).

[65] A full account of Gondi's importance in the second Fronde will be found in Chantelauze, *Le Cardinal de Retz et l'affaire du chapeau.*

[66] This correspondence (mainly with Le Tellier) will be found in the *Lettres*, vol. iv.

[67] *Mémoires d'Omer Talon* (ed. Michaud et Poujoulat), 423.

maxim "Salutem ex inimicis nostris" was soon to be amply justified. Orléans, who had a position but no personality,[68] was unable to hold his allies together; he took action as other men take a bath—"they shut their eyes and jump in." Prejudices of birth soon manifested themselves, and when Gondi talked of raising the barricades again, Condé haughtily announced that he never took part in a war of "gutters and chamber pots." Anne used her still potent charms to complete the severance of these two castes and adroitly managed to enlist the help of the Coadjutor against Condé.[69] By May 1651 the movement had been narrowed down to a rebellion against the monarchy on the part of a section of the nobility led by Condé, and thereafter Parlement and bourgeoisie remained the most loyal supporters of the Bourbon dynasty.

Throughout the summer of this year Anne retained the support of the Parlement by dismissing some of Mazarin's most hated subordinates, but she failed to pacify Condé. The situation was still full of anxiety and danger for herself and her son, whose majority was declared at this time. She could never obtain the full confidence of Paris so long as it was known that she still corresponded with the absent First Minister; the frontiers were continually menaced by Spanish troops in alliance with the French nobility; the best generals in France—Condé and Turenne—had practically declared war on her. Her brother-in-law, Orléans, was the nominal head of her enemies; her solitary adviser and friend—Mazarin—was in exile; from Normandy to Provence the country was plunged in revolution and civil war. But the very aimlessness of the whole movement eventually proved its undoing. The rebel leaders were influenced by merely personal motives and they were soon at cross purposes. In October Condé was declared by Parlement guilty of treason, and, after pacifying Gondi with the promise of a nomination to the Cardinalate, the queen and the royal troops made a tour of the provinces and restored several cities to their former allegiance. By the end of December 1651 the situation was so far improved that Mazarin was able to return to

[68] De Retz (*Mémoires,* ed. Feillet et Chantelauze, ii. 175) said of Orléans that "he had everything necessary for an honest man except courage."

[69] Condé may have had thoughts of the crown: "il n'y aurait plus qu'à le mener à Reims" (De Retz, *Mémoires,* iii. 307).

France with a mercenary army, and in January 1652 he joined the Court at Poitiers.

When the news of Mazarin's return became public, Parlement put a price on his head but did not organize any active opposition. Orléans was at last induced to take the plunge and allied definitely with Condé against the Court. Meanwhile Beaufort and Nemours led separate armies, converging on Angers, with the object of intercepting the royalist return to Paris; Mazarin, on his part, had purchased the help of Turenne, and the early months of 1652 were occupied by what in courtesy is called the campaign of the Loire, which was really little better than a series of masquerades, enjoyed by all except the peasants whose fields were pillaged alike by royalist and noble. When Turenne attempted to take the city of Orléans the enterprising Mademoiselle de Montpensier (daughter of Gaston and suitor for the hand of her cousin Louis XIV.) captured the city for the nobility and so obtained a much-desired advertisement. At the same time (March 1652) Condé in a fit of temper quitted the south-west, where his rule was unquestioned, and joining forces with Beaufort and Nemours defeated the Royalist troops at Bléneau (8th April). Instead of following up this success he foolishly went to Paris in order to stir up the embers of hatred against Mazarin, thus giving Turenne a chance of wedging his troops between Paris and the joint armies of the Princes, a manœuvre which led to the defeat of the rebels at Etampes (4th May). Throwing to the winds every consideration but his own intense egotism, Condé now summoned Spanish troops into Artois and Picardy, and Lorrainers into Champagne, thereby completely alienating opinion in Paris, and so opening a way for the restoration of Mazarin. He tried force against the Parlement but in vain, and on the 2nd of July his troops would have been completely defeated in the Faubourg St. Antoine if Mademoiselle de Montpensier had not turned the guns of the Bastille on Turenne's royalist troops. But behind all this absurd warfare of effeminate men and shameless women was the universal desire of France—peasant and bourgeois alike—for peace; it was on this craving for a restoration of order that Mazarin and the Court could rely.

On the strength of his narrowly-won street fight Condé established himself in Paris, compelling a rump of the Parlement to appoint Orléans Lieutenant-General of the kingdom and silencing dissent by massacre. Beaufort became Governor of Paris and the affairs of the city were entrusted to a committee of nobles. The advance of Spanish-Lorraine troops to within a few miles of Paris (August 1652) caused Mazarin to leave France for a second time, not from cowardice, but in order to deprive the Princes of the pretext that so long as he was in French territory there could be no peace. The Italian's well-timed departure was followed by the sending of deputations to the Court requesting its return to Paris; with the defection of his soldiers and the increased hostility of the bourgeoisie, Condé's position became every day more untenable. In October he left the capital to throw in his lot with Spain, and with this resignation of leadership the second Fronde speedily collapsed. On the 21st of October the queen and Louis XIV. entered Paris, where they were eagerly welcomed by a populace which now realized the great seventeenth-century truth, that the only alternative to absolutism was anarchy. Orléans and the remaining leaders of the rebellion had to retire to their estates; Parlement was forbidden ever again to interfere in politics; Gondi, the mainspring of the whole movement and now Cardinal de Retz was imprisoned. All the concessions recently granted were revoked. Thus the Parlement of Paris, after its brief period of political prominence, reverted to its original function of legal corporation. These four years had coincided with the most impressionable period of the young king's life. He disliked Paris ever after and made Versailles, instead of the Louvre, the permanent residence of the monarchy. The incident of the Fronde is the only justification for the absolutism of Louis XIV.

At this point it may be asked whether the movement was inspired by any consistent political or constitutional theories. Apart from the demands of the Parlement in the first Fronde, the rebellion was based on personal and irresponsible motives —Condé wished to become First Minister, possibly even king of France; Gondi wanted a Cardinal's hat, Orléans had vague feelings that he ought to assert himself, his daughter was anxious to become queen of France (by marriage), and the women were concerned mainly with matrimonial alliances. There was a strong element of burlesque and the only common feeling was hatred of Mazarin.[70] For the nobility, the rebellion was a comedy of "billets doux" and mock campaigns; for the bourgeois it was speedy disillusionment; for the peasants it was starvation and ruin. All the self-appointed leaders wished to make history; it is the characteristic of efficient rule that this kind of manufacture is reduced to a minimum. But though the whole movement is so inconsequential, we may glean from the numerous *Mazarinades* and the pamphlets of the time some attempts to formulate definite theories of government. Writers like the Cardinal de Retz[71] maintained that despotism and the rule of a First Minister were innovations dating from Richelieu, and that the traditions of the French nation were constitutional, not absolutist; other theorists held that the monarchy had not yet lost its elective character.[72] Throughout the Fronde, the nobility urged the convocation of the States-General,[73] but, remembering the experience of 1614, the Third Estate opposed this demand, knowing that such a convocation would strengthen the hands of their enemies. It may be noted that several pamphlets recommend radical reform in the financial system and the contribution of every one to the national revenues in proportion to his revenues.[74] On the other hand, it was the general opinion that the Parlement, as a part of the Third Estate, derived its position solely from the monarch,[75] and therefore had no control over legislation; it is characteristic also that, with very few exceptions, the pamphleteers agreed in the opinion that the institution of monarchy was both reasonable and necessary, and that its prerogatives should be maintained and strengthened.

These views are important because they are typical; it is not difficult to see how they could be reconciled with the principles of Louis XIV., since their only consistent element is belief in the necessity for a strong monarchy exercised by the king in person and not by a First Minister. The Fronde

[70] For the numerous attacks on Mazarin see Moreau, *Choix de Mazarinades,* and H. Séc, *Les Idées politiques en France au XVIIème siècle,* ch. iv.

[71] *Mémoires* (ed. Feillet et Chantelauze), i. 270 ff.

[72] Moreau, *Choix de Mazarinades,* ii. 458.

[73] *Ibid.* ii. 230.

[74] Moreau, *Choix de Mazarinades,* i. 428.

[75] *Ibid.* ii. 465.

prepared the way not for the French Revolution but for the absolutism of Versailles.

When Mazarin returned to Paris in February 1653 he fully realized that the Fronde had benefited only the Hapsburgs and that France had lost much of the prestige won in the closing years of the Thirty Years' War. But while these results are emphasized by historians, and while more than ample justice has been done to the spectacular elements in the Fronde (notably at the hands of Dumas), too little attention has been paid to the social and economic effects of these years of civil war. Disturbances in the normal routine of things always react first on that part of the population which is on the subsistence line, and in this the Fronde was no exception, for the harrying of the country side by armed bands caused intense though unvoiced suffering among the peasants. Even where the wretched labourer managed to preserve his unheroic and anonymous existence, war, whether external or civil, always meant for him grinding exactions and permanent insecurity. The legend of *Bonhomme Misère*,[76] current throughout the country-side in the years immediately after the Fronde, might serve as an epilogue to the most serious rebellion in seventeenth-century France. According to the legend, Saints Peter and Paul were entertained by Poverty (unaware of the identity of his guests). On their departure the apostles offered to grant any favour that their host might demand. Poverty modestly asked that any one climbing his pear tree should be obliged to stay there so long as the owner pleased. This was accorded, and thereafter Poverty was able to catch some of his dishonest neighbours in the tree, but released them after a caution. At last Death appeared in person and was captured by the stratagem of inducing him to climb the pear tree, from which he was released only on the condition that he would not call for his captor until the Day of Judgement. So Poverty will remain to the end.

After the pacification of the provinces, Mazarin was free to turn his attention to the war with Spain, which, it will be remembered, had not been ended by the treaty of Westphalia.[77] The conclusion of the Thirty Years' War had seen

[76] Quoted in Feillet, *La Misère au temps de la Fronde*, 519.
[77] France was generally considered responsible for this pro-

the isolation of the two main combatants—France and Spain, whose conflict was not terminated until the treaty of the Pyrenees (1659). In this period there were few domestic troubles, though d'Emeri's successor, Fouquet, outdid his predecessor in financial mismanagement, and brought about his own downfall by making too public a display of his ill-gotten gains. But there was no institution in France capable of organizing effective opposition, and the nation was follow-ing with unaffected devotion and interest the progress of the young Louis XIV. Mazarin now entered on the most brilliant and constructive part of his career.

While pressing the operations against the national enemy Mazarin showed, in his foreign policy, that he was shrewd and without prepossessions. Realizing that England had now become a power to be reckoned with, he allied with Crom-well, an alliance made possible by the fact that the Protector had been completely disillusioned in his hopes of building up a great Protestant Federation with the help of the Dutch. On the 3rd of November 1655 a commercial convention was signed between the two countries, Mazarin undertaking not to assist any of the Stuart house, the chief of whom was then on the continent busily plotting with Cardinal de Retz. This alliance made Spain more anxious to come to terms.

By 1656 the end of the Franco-Spanish struggle was in sight and the usual expedient of a marriage alliance was suggested. For some time Mazarin had considered the feasi-bility of ending the Bourbon-Hapsburg struggle by a carefully chosen matrimonial alliance, and in 1656 Maria Theresa, daughter of Philip IV. by his first marriage, seemed the most obvious bride for Louis XIV. As the legitimate line of the Spanish Hapsburgs was then represented by two daughters— Maria and Margaret Theresa—and as it seemed unlikely that Philip would have any more legitimate children, the chances of France eventually acquiring the whole or a large part of the Spanish succession by this marriage seemed very great. Mazarin calculated that if the alliance could be effected, even with paper stipulations and renunciations, then the work of Henry IV. and Richelieu would be consummated, a pros-

---

longation of hostilities. See *Relacion al Rey Don Felipe IV* (1650), by Peñaranda in *Colección de documentos inéditos para la historia de España*, lxxxiv. 511 ff.

pect so dazzling that the First Minister elaborated his plans with the utmost coolness and deliberation. But the Spanish minister, Don Louis de Haro, was a match for the Italian, and as soon as the wedding was suggested, the peace negotiations were broken off (September 1656). Mazarin then turned to England and on the 3rd of March 1657 France and England signed a treaty of alliance for one year, the two countries agreeing on joint operations against Dunkirk and Gravelines, towns which, when captured, were to be apportioned among the allies.

Even in face of such a diplomatic victory as the Franco-English alliance, Spain did not press for peace. There seemed little to be gained from the frontier campaigns, which, at this period, were unimportant and indecisive; consequently Mazarin was obliged to proceed further in the process of isolating the enemy. His intervention in Naples[78] had not been successful, but he had not overlooked the unique opportunities provided by the Peace of Westphalia for meddling in the politics of Germany, and for some years a succession of agents had been "educating" public opinion on the other side of the Rhine.[79] From 1653 a permanent French agent resided at Ratisbon in order to keep in touch with the deliberations of the Imperial Diet. Mazarin vainly tried to change the possession of Alsace (granted in full sovereignty by the treaty of Westphalia) into a fief, in order that thereby Louis XIV. might obtain direct representation in the Diet. The Diet was undecided how to act, but eventually settled the question, as it generally settled all important questions, by shelving it. One of Mazarin's mottoes was "Time and I against the world." The Diet acted on the same motto, but while to Mazarin time meant a few months in which he could retire and mature his plans, to the Diet it meant the Time which solves all difficulties by oblivion.

In spite, however, of Mazarin's failure to influence the Diet, and although French calculations were upset by the election of a Hapsburg (Leopold) to the Empire on the death of Ferdinand III. in 1657, an opportunity soon presented itself of which French diplomacy was not slow to

[78] See *infra*, p. 369.
[79] For this see the instructions to Vautorte, Gravel and Verjus in *Instructions donnés aux ambassadeurs de France depuis le traité de Westphalie* (Germanic Diet).

take advantage. Since 1651 the leading German princes had meditated the idea of a league or confederation in order to infuse an element of unity into the heterogeneous mass of principalities created by the Westphalia settlement. In 1656 was formed a federation of the Ecclesiastical Electors, under the leadership of the Elector of Mainz, for the purpose of averting war and maintaining the integrity of the German states, Protestant as well as Catholic. Curiously enough the leaders of this movement supposed that the best means of effecting these objects was to ally with those foreign princes, namely, the rulers of France and Sweden, whose ambitions were known to be most inimical to German peace. This confederation, known as the League of the Rhine[80] (established in 1658), was thus an immature League of Nations, because it set itself to limit warfare by substituting compact for challenge, and in its Council, which sat at Frankfort-on-the-Rhine, it possessed a deliberative assembly capable of arbitrating in the disputes of its German members. The scheme was originated by two of the most remarkable men in Germany—Philip von Schönborn, Elector of Mainz, and his secretary, Boyneburg. The latter, remembering how, in the Thirty Years' War, France had managed for a time to keep together a coalition of Catholics and Protestants, believed that France could supply the cement required to amalgamate the warring creeds and princelings of Germany. Schönborn, who had worked his way up from humble beginnings and had shown both statesmanship and patriotism in his efforts to save his country from the constant menace of foreign aggression, was not without hope that his cherished League would have an educative influence on the public opinion of Europe, believing that his system of General Guarantee would neutralize force by alliance and ultimately lead to European peace. Stripped of their idealism, his theories provided an intelligent anticipation of the eighteenth-century doctrine that the control of central Europe by a strong Germanic confederation was the best means of keeping in check the rivalries of the great military powers in East and West.[81]

[80] The fullest account of the League is that by Pribram, *Beiträge zur Geschichte des Rheinbundes von 1658*. See also Auerbach, *op. cit.* 57 ff.

[81] See *supra*, Ch. 1, n. 85.

It was natural that Mazarin should follow this scheme with great interest, though he described its pacific ideals by the French word most nearly corresponding to the English word "fooling."[82] The French agent accredited to the Diet was instructed to carry out a propagandist tour in Germany on behalf of the League, and it was suggested from Paris that the League of the Rhine might profitably combine against the Emperor, since the Hapsburgs were the real enemies of German "liberty." The failure of French diplomacy to turn to profitable account the Imperial election of 1657 caused Mazarin to treat the League more seriously; in August 1658 France became its most enthusiastic member. Its headquarters at Frankfort-on-the-Main were within the zone of French influence, and the Emperor Leopold made no secret of his opinion that since France directed its counsels, it was a potentially hostile body. So long, therefore, as France was a member of this association, Mazarin was assured of the neutrality of Germany in his designs against the Spanish and Imperial Hapsburgs. The League of the Rhine came to an end in 1668, partly from the jealousies of two of its members—France and Sweden, and partly because the German associates began to realize how unpacific were the aims of Louis XIV. But before that date the political situation in Europe had considerably changed. France had by then definitely embarked on her campaign for the Spanish Succession, causing Germany to be drawn into a series of wars extending from the Boyne to the Danube, and the idealist aspirations of the League of the Rhine were soon to be forgotten in the clash of arms.

Thus the war between France and Spain was only one element in the contest between Bourbon and Hapsburg. It was not the least part of Mazarin's work that he closed successfully one chapter in that long struggle and bequeathed to Louis XIV. a powerful and strongly established throne. Practically isolated in Europe by the diplomatic intrigues of Mazarin in England and Germany, Spain was barely able to hold her own in the Low Countries, until the campaigns of the year 1658 put an end to her resistance. Turenne captured Dunkirk after the battle of the Dunes (June 14, 1658), and,

[82] "Patelinage." Auerbach, *op. cit.* iii.

following a spectacular entry by Louis XIV., the town was handed over to the English. Most of the Flemish coast towns were then captured, and Brabant was invaded. These victories were followed by a diplomatic ruse. In October 1658 the Court went to Lyons ostensibly in order to take part in the betrothal of Louis to the daughter of the Duke of Savoy. The device succeeded. A Spanish agent was sent post-haste to Lyons with an offer of peace on the basis of a marriage alliance, and so Mazarin's carefully planned schemes were at last to be crowned with success. Marguerite of Savoy was speedily got rid of—her outraged feelings were of no diplomatic importance since Savoy was such a small state—and the negotiations with Spain commenced. But Mazarin's victory was not really so complete as might be supposed, for the situation had altered in one ominous respect. Philip was soon to have, by his second wife, a son and heir. No one, however, supposed that the weakly child would live, and every international calculation of the succeeding forty years was based on the assumption that this son (Charles) would be dead in a few months. The unfortunate being whose birth was the one unforeseen thing in Mazarin's calculations was destined to upset every medical and diplomatic prognostication by living until 1700; the question of the Spanish succession, so nearly settled in 1658, was to cost Europe over a million human lives.

The negotiations culminating in the treaty of the Pyrenees[83] were carried out with full regard to diplomatic scruple. Fortunately there is a stream—the Bidassoa—separating France from Spain; on a little island in the stream, the Ile des Faisans, the treaty of the Pyrenees was drawn up and, after prolonged discussion, signed on the 7th of November 1659. This treaty may be said to complete the Peace of Westphalia in so far as it claimed to establish permanent national frontiers. France was confirmed in her conquests, and thus acquired Roussillon and Artois with some Flemish towns such as Gravelines, Landrecies, Avesnes and Thionville, together with Montmédy in Luxemburg. The French claim to Catalonia was abandoned, and Spain renounced hers to Alsace. Lorraine and Portugal were both sacrificed, France winning Moyenvic

---

[83] See the account in Vast, *Les Grands Traités du règne de Louis XIV*, i. 79-175.

and Stenay on her eastern frontier and abandoning Portugal in her struggle for independence. Condé was pardoned and restored to his estates. Maria Theresa was to resign all claims to the Spanish succession, and in return was to receive a dowry of 500,000 crowns, payable eighteen months after her marriage. This dowry was never paid.

It remained only to carry out the main condition of the treaty. The wedding took place in the month of June 1660 with a luxury and pomp unequalled even in the seventeenth century. The treaty of Oliva (May 3, 1660), which was negotiated mainly by French diplomacy, ended the War of the North, and so, even more than in 1648, Europe in the summer of 1660 might seem to be entering on an era of peace. In England the unpopular interregnum was at an end and the monarchy restored with a wild outburst of enthusiasm; in northern Europe, Sweden, Denmark and Brandenburg had, for the time, settled their differences; in Germany there was steady recuperation from the effects of the Thirty Years' War; in France, the civil wars were now mere memories, and the struggle with Spain had terminated in the most spectacular wedding of the Ancien Régime. In 1660 Mazarin could hand over to Louis the crown which he had preserved for him through so many dangers, and could point to the prospect of an inheritance greater than any that France might hope to win by arms.

The First Minister survived his triumph by only a few months, dying on the 9th of March 1661. Shortly before his death he was induced to offer all his money to the monarch on the assurance that this would be considered a graceful act and that it would be restored to him.[84] Mazarin was induced to comply with this strange proposal; Louis at once accepted the gift and for three days did not refer to the matter. These were the most anxious days of Mazarin's life. His last hours were soothed by the return of his money, and his millions were divided among his nieces. So enormous was the fortune that a fraction of the residue sufficed for the building of the Palais de l'Institut and the Bibliothèque Mazarine, in which the Cardinal's great library is now stored.

[84] For this see *Œuvres de Louis XIV* (ed. Grouvelle), vi. 289.

Chapter 6

Bourbon and Hapsburg

IN THIS CHAPTER falls to be considered the contest for supremacy in Europe between the Bourbons of France on the one hand and the Hapsburgs of Spain and the Empire on the other. The first stage of the contest was completed by the treaty of Westphalia, the second by the Peace of the Pyrenees; a glance at the map will show how French gains by these settlements helped to enlarge her frontiers to more natural limits; and as these gains were at the expense of the over-weighty Hapsburg territories, it is possible to maintain that such readjustments of the map of Europe helped to stabilize the balance of power. From these points of view it might be possible to justify the aggressions of Henry IV., of Richelieu and of Mazarin, since all three had to consider seriously the question of safeguarding French territory from invasion, and they did a service to Europe as well as to France by preventing the Hapsburgs from wielding a domination such as that of Charles V. But it would be difficult to urge this in justification for French policy throughout the whole of the third or last stage of the struggle, because, after 1660, the French frontiers were not threatened, the military decline of Spain was well known, and the Emperor, who had practically withdrawn from German politics, was unable to hold his own in eastern Europe against the Turk. For an explanation of French policy in the years 1660-1715 we have to consider the personality of Louis XIV.

This historical reputation of Louis XIV stands very high:

> He was by far the *cleverest* ruler born in modern times. He was laborious, and devoted many hours a day to public business. He had an excellent memory, and immense fertility of resource. Few men knew how to pursue such complex political calculations, or to see so many moves ahead . . . Every European state was included in his system, and had its part in the game. His management of each was so dexterous that *blackmail* often made war superfluous, and sometimes successful.

Those who recall the events leading up to "Munich" in 1938 will remember the melancholy kind of "game" above described, with its alternatives of blackmail or war, and some may well assume that the above passage refers to the successes scored in that game by a recent figure in world history, but others will perceive that the passage is a slightly paraphrased version of Lord Acton's classic judgment, and refers not to Adolf Hitler, but to Louis XIV. It was Lord Acton, the greatest moralist of a highly moral age who, more than anyone else, insisted on the tremendous personal responsibility incurred by the historian for his judgments, and it is significant of the flexibility of the code which he, with so many others, applied to history, that his eulogy of the most famous monarch of the seventeenth century can, by only two not-unreasonable changes of phrase,[1] be passed off for description of the most detested adventurer of our own day. To such a pitch indeed can the relativity of political ethics be developed that, in commendation of those rulers whom we wish to praise, we may applaud as meritorious precisely those things which in others we censure as criminal. The process is easy because language is so flexible, and this may be why the "verdict of history" is as subject to changes of fashion as the shape of women's hats.

[1] See Lord Acton's *Lectures on Modern History*, p. 234. The two changes are shown in the italicised words—"cleverest" in place of "ablest," and "blackmail" in place of "diplomacy." As regards the first change, Acton's account of Louis shows that he, like many others, regarded cleverness and ability as identical qualities. As regards the second change, Acton himself established their identity when he showed how Louis tried to blackmail Charles II by making public the terms of the secret Treaty of Dover.

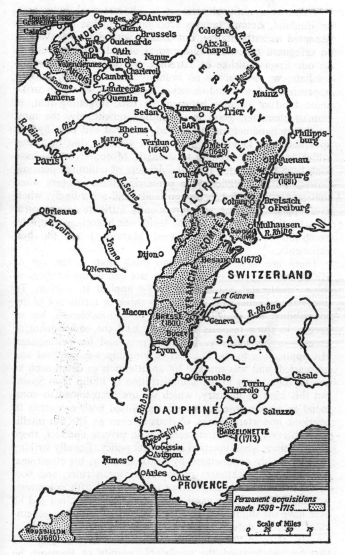

There is a national element in all historical judgments. In England, Acton's famous pronouncement has always been accepted as authoritative, but usually with slight reservations to safeguard our moral disapproval of unlimited aggression. In our English dislike of extremes, we prefer "compromise" verdicts; we disapprove of brutality and treachery, but we appreciate industry and devotion to duty, so we try to strike some kind of balance between the two, forgetting that, in human character, good is sometimes, unwittingly, the most assiduous handmaiden of the bad, and that evil may find its spearhead not in vice, which always weakens, but in virtue, which leads from strength to strength. Moreover, as we have long been safeguarded from the dangers of unlimited personal power, we have difficulty in perceiving these dangers when that power is wielded in foreign lands, and accordingly, whatever appears extreme we conveniently attribute to exaggeration. Of this preference for the tepid, our historians (with the exception of the much-maligned Macaulay) are the best exponents.

There are some however who think that, as the age of Hitler, like that of Louis XIV, was not one of moderation, so these "moderate" valuations can be applied to neither. To understand Louis XIV we have to think in terms not of responsibility, but of wilfulness, not of reasonableness, but of excess. In three respects was Louis XIV the embodiment of excess—in his industry, his cleverness and his restlessness. His application to the business of kingship was constant and unwearied, and was marked by an attention to detail such as can be found only in the administration of Philip II of Spain; but this kind of industry, which we are accustomed to commend in certain insects, sometimes caused both monarchs to overlook important things, obvious to even an idle but intelligent observer. Also, in statecraft as in private conduct, there are occasions when inaction is the best policy. Equally striking (and as highly commended by historians) was his cleverness. He knew the weaknesses of every European ruler, and how to exploit them; his huge army of spies and fifth columnists was dignified with the name of diplomatic service; nor did he ever have the slightest doubt that to cheat or corrupt a government was to defeat a nation. Thus, he cleverly detached Charles II from the potential enemies of France only to find that he had aroused the implacable enmity of England; he easily overthrew the insecure John de Witt, and in exchange had to reckon with the grim determination of William of Orange and the Dutch; he outwitted the German Princes and added their subjects to the swelling ranks of France's enemies; his policy was consistent in this that, no sooner was he engaged in war, than he applied his own and his agents' astuteness to the task of dividing his numerous enemies. Half a century of such a policy was made possible by the fact that he had behind him all the devotion and resources of the most highly civilised state in the world. Lastly, his restlessness. Like all the dictators, he never really knew what he wanted. His invasion of Holland in 1672 was prompted by neither diplomatic nor economic motives, but by hatred of the Dutch; his devastation of the Palatinate in 1688 was inspired by a sense of frustration and irritation. With his enormous superiority in arms he could, long before that date, have acquired the Rhine frontier for France had he not, to the disgust of his best general, Vauban, preferred to dissipate his energies in spectacular sieges of provincial towns and villages. His neighbours were always left "guessing." He could have peaceably acquired the Spanish Succession for his family by the Will of Charles II of Spain had he not so affronted the public conscience of Europe by menacing acts that he was obliged to fight for more than a decade in order to obtain what was already his by inheritance. In general, Louis XIV showed such disregard for his own solemn assurances enunciated in public and secret treaties; he backed his demands and threats with arguments so preposterous as to be insulting to human intelligence; he so constantly menaced the independence of his neighbours and the security of Europe by capricious use of armies, the largest and most highly organised ever known, that he must be regarded as an inaugurator of that era of European history when peace is no more than a precarious interval between great wars. These, at least, are not "moderate" things, nor do they call for "moderate" judgments. Personal opinion about Louis XIV is unimportant; it is otherwise with the standard of values which we apply to history.

The study of Louis XIV.'s wars may be divided into three periods, each terminating in a treaty. The first begins with the treaty of the Pyrenees (1659) and ends with the treaty of Nymegen (1678); the second ends with the treaty of Ryswick (1697); the third ends with the general pacification at Utrecht (1713-1715).

I. From the Treaty of the Pyrenees to the Treaty of Nymegen

The idea of reconciling the two dynasties by a marriage which would give France a portion of the Spanish inheritance was considered, from the first, not as a means of effecting conciliation, but as offering an excuse for aggression.[2] Thereafter the marriage project became an essential part of French foreign policy, and in the negotiations with Spain it was the most important question. In drafting the treaty of the Pyrenees, the French agent, Lionne, had formulated the all-important *moyennant* clause by which Maria Theresa renounced for herself, and therefore by implication for her husband, all claims to the paternal succession *provided that* a dowry of 500,000 crowns was paid within eighteen months. As the dowry was never paid, Louis, as early as the year 1662, might claim that his wife's renunciation was void.

What France wanted at this time was not the throne of Spain, nor the Indies, but the Burgundian Circle, composed of the Spanish Low Countries and Franche Comté. This was the inheritance of Charles the Bold, and had been acquired by the Hapsburgs through the marriage of Charles's heiress with the Emperor Maximilian I. So long as these territories were in the hands of the Hapsburgs, French progress to the east was barred and her eastern frontier was insecure. It was clearly realized that Paris was too near the north-eastern frontier, consequently throughout the seventeenth century France never dropped the design of strengthening that frontier by a line of forts in Flanders; in 1646 Mazarin had expressed the opinion that the "Low Countries would provide an impregnable rampart for Paris, which would then become the real heart of France."[3] Alsace and Lorraine formed links in this chain of Hapsburg states stretching from the North Sea to the Alps, and the chain had already been broken by the acquisition of Alsace. In 1662 Louis managed by bribery to obtain possession of Lorraine, leaving to its Duke, Charles IV., only the revenues for his lifetime (treaty of Montmartre); but while this arrangement gave him some strategic bases for

[2] Legrelle, *La Diplomatie française et la succession d'Espagne*, i. 6.

[3] Chéruel, *Histoire de France pendant la minorité de Louis XIV* (ii. 275-6).

further operations, it did not give him a seat in the Diet, nor did it enhance his prestige in Germany.

When Louis failed to derive any considerable advantage from his purchase of Lorraine, he turned his attention to the Burgundian Circle, where the Imperial claims were as dubious as in Alsace and Lorraine. The treaty of Münster had declared that the Circle of Burgundy was a part of the Empire (it was by possession of this fief that Spain exercised a vote in the Diet), but, on the other hand, the negotiators at Münster had expressly excluded the Circle from the general settlement on the ground that the Franco-Spanish conflict was still going on there. Hence it had been argued, on behalf of France, that Spain's occupation of the Burgundian provinces entitled France to regard them as enemy territory having only a doubtful connection with the Empire, but this contention was not seriously pressed, because acceptance of the opinion that these lands were not imperial fiefs would have prevented France claiming a seat in the Diet, should the Burgundian Circle ever come into her possession.[4] Accordingly French diplomacy had concentrated on the task of isolating the Circle from the Empire, so that its fate might depend on the result of the struggle then (1648-1659) proceeding. Realizing the danger at last, Spain had tried to obtain help for the Circle by applying for membership of the League of the Rhine, but France had circumvented this by inducing the Council of the League to adopt a resolution that no member should be admitted without the consent of all the existing members.[5] By 1660, therefore, the position was that France could treat the Burgundian Circle from two different points of view—either as hostile territory to be won from Spain by conquest, without necessarily involving the hostility of the Emperor, or as a legitimate substitute for the dowry promised by the treaty of the Pyrenees and never paid.

Eighteen months after the conclusion of the treaty of the Pyrenees, the renunciation might be considered to have lapsed. The only restraint on Louis was that his father-in-law still lived. In September 1665 Philip IV. died, his will[6] providing that in the event of his son Charles having no male heir, the Spanish inheritance was to go to his younger daughter, the

---

[4] Auerbach, *La France et le Saint Empire Romain*, 108 ff.
[5] 26th July 1663.
[6] For the will of Philip IV. see Legrelle, *op. cit.* i. 458-517.

Infante Margaret (married to the Emperor Leopold); failing her, to his sister the ex-Empress Maria (widow of the late Ferdinand III.); and, failing her, to the descendants of his aunt, the Duchess of Savoy. According to the terms of this will, therefore, neither Louis nor Maria Theresa could make any claim. But it may be questioned whether legally Philip could thus dispose of his kingdoms so long as he had himself an unquestioned heir, and the dubious legality of such a disposition justified the French refusal to be disconcerted by it. Could the lawyers provide any claim on behalf of Maria Theresa, the elder daughter by the first marriage? The demand created the supply. One of Turenne's secretaries, named Duhan,[7] came forward with an argument so ingenious that it almost convinced Louis himself. His suggestions were adopted and were officially promulgated in the *Traité des droits de la reine très chrétienne sur divers états de la monarchie de l'Espagne.*

The first part of this pamphlet[8] deals with the renunciation and its nullity; the second part with the extent of Maria Theresa's rights, which by implication were transferred to her consort Louis. These rights were based on the customs regulating the succession to private property in the provinces of the Burgundian Circle and in Luxemburg. One such custom was that whereby property "devolved" on daughters by a first marriage in preference to sons by a second marriage, and as this custom prevailed in Brabant, Antwerp, Limburg, Malines, Upper Guelderland, Namur and Cambrai, all of these provinces ought, it was held, to "devolve" on Maria Theresa. Similarly, as Hainault was "frank alleu," it must pass to the eldest descendant of Philip, irrespective of sex; and as the principle of equal partition prevailed in Franche Comté, a third part must go to the French queen. To these must be added a quarter of Luxemburg, the custom there being that all the children succeeded, the sons obtaining twice as much as the daughters. This would leave unclaimed only the country of Flanders, with Tournai, three-quarters of Luxemburg and two-thirds of Franche Comté. The document advocating these claims was translated into Latin and Spanish and widely circulated.

[7] *Ibid.* i. 74.

[8] There is a complete analysis in Lonchay, *La Rivalité de la France et de l'Espagne aux Pays-Bas,* 225 ff.

Never before had a ruler gone to such trouble in order to convince public opinion of the reasonableness of his claims. The claims seemed unusual, but they were so abundantly warranted by "research" that to deny them was to deny justice. Nor were they entirely devoid of justification, for sovereignty, as understood in the pamphlet, implied ownership, a conception still maintained in the seventeenth century; moreover, the corollary of this axiom, that states can be divided up like cheese, long survived the seventeenth century. The only objection was that customs regulating succession to private property had no longer any connection with principles regulating devolution of sovereignty, but to this Louis might well have replied: "time does not run against the king." These things merely served to conceal an argument entirely new to the public law of Europe. By marriage with Louis, Maria Theresa had become a French subject, but now, on this argument, she might assume, at pleasure, the juristic rights of any community within her father's dominions and choose at will from the legal privileges enjoyed by her father's subjects in Naples, or Mexico or Brabant. She could, on this analogy, claim to be ruler of Spain if it were proved that private property there descended to the daughter by a first marriage in preference to a son by the second. The most notable reply to these arguments was the *Bouclier d'Estat et de Justice* (1667), written by the able Austrian diplomat Franz Lisola,[9] whose propaganda against France was so consistent and determined that at least one attempt was made to murder him. Lisola argued in his manifesto that the argument from "devolution" was merely a pretext for armed appropriation, and that if such casuistry were condoned by Europe, Force would soon enslave Right.

In her well-organized army and fleet France had a sounder argument than that of "devolution." During the greater part of the seventeenth century France had the best generals and the best military administrators in the world. With the appointment in 1643 of Michel le Tellier as Secretary of State for War there began a period of reconstruction in which companies ceased to be regarded as private ventures, for they were brought more directly under the control of the colonel, who

[9] The best account of Lisola is by A. F. Pribram, *Franz Paul Freiherr von Lisola, 1613–1674, und die Politik seiner Zeit.*

in turn was subjected to closer government supervision.[10] In 1662 his son Louvois became a secretary of state. Combining zeal and efficiency with insolence and brutality, Louvois made short work of such abuses as came to his notice, and it was due mainly to him that the French army became permanent and regular. The *passe-volants* or irregulars were suppressed and the farming system, whereby troops were engaged through agents exacting heavy fees, was replaced by one in which the state became the direct employer. Commissions could still be bought, but officers had to pass qualifying tests, and promotion was no longer confined to one class. Fully qualified officers were now attached to the titular officers in order that experience might supplement the valour which the nobility still claimed as their monopoly. Louvois made some changes in the higher ranks, introducing the grade of Brigadier-General between General and Colonel; he facilitated the training of young cadets aiming at commissions, and though French soldiers were poorly paid, they were well equipped and maintained the national reputation for martial enthusiasm. A rigorous hierarchy of ranks was instituted, and unity of direction was obtained by ordering that in the field command should go by seniority and should not, as hitherto, be exercised in turn by those generals qualified to take the lead.

The Commissariat, Remount, Transport and Ambulance services, together with Artillery and Munitions, were supervised by a body of War Commissioners, and it was on this side that Louvois' work was greatest. French armies no longer needed to live on the country; the transport services in the rear carried food and even fodder. Late in the century the wearing of a distinctive uniform became general. Pike and musket were combined in the bayonet, and the use of hand grenades was introduced. A modified form of conscription was applied mainly to the nobility resident within a certain distance of the frontiers, but service, where compulsory, was only for a small part of the year. Louvois raised the total of French effectives to 200,000 men, in which were included contingents of Swiss, Scots and Irish. Added to this extension and reorganization of the personnel of the French armies was the great progress made by Vauban in the science of fortifica-

[10] There is a good account of this in L. André, *Michel le Tellier et l'organization de l'armée monarchique.*

tion. One of the most skilled engineers of his time. Vauban protected France with a network of fortresses which until the nineteenth century were considered impregnable, and one of which, Belfort, endured three months' siege in 1870-71. Vauban showed the same genius in attack as in defence, reducing enemy fortresses with such mathematical precision as to enamour Louis of siege warfare, since, when the unobtrusive work of the engineer was completed, there were admirable opportunities for spectacular entries. It is to the credit of Louis that he realized the military genius of Louvois and Vauban and gave them a free hand.

What the French army owes to Louvois, the French navy owes to Louvois's rival, Colbert. Richelieu had realized the importance of mercantile fleets for the supply of men and ships in war, but his successor had completely neglected the French mercantile marine. Colbert encouraged the building of ships in French ports, and from a squadron of fifteen the French navy developed into a fleet of two hundred. This progress was continued under Colbert's son and successor, Seignelay. By a measure of conscription in the coast towns, Colbert obtained a more homogeneous personnel than the bands of malefactors, smugglers, deserters, Huguenots and Turkish slaves who had hitherto manned the galleys. He established naval gunnery and hydrography on a scientific basis. Naval officers, however, continued to be drawn exclusively from a limited class and, despite the efficiency and bravery of French seamen, a career in the French navy was not, as in the army, open to merit alone. The most useful work performed by the fleet in the early years of Louis XIV.'s reign was the harrying of the Barbary corsairs in the Mediterranean. In Algiers and Tunis there existed powerful corporations of pirates admitting only the nominal rule of the Sultan, and huge sums were spent annually in the redemption of their Christian captives; in 1662, at the risk of a break with Turkey, French fleets patrolled the Mediterranean and occupied Gigeri (Djidjeli) on the Algerian coast; Tunis and Algiers were bombarded, and a large number of captives were redeemed. Thus Louis inaugurated his reign by securing French naval supremacy in the Mediterranean.[11]

[11] The history of the French navy has been written by Ch. de La Roncière. Vols. iv., v. and vi. are devoted to the seventeenth century.

It is clear from the above that within a few years of his accession the foreign policy of Louis XIV. was backed by adequate military force. Nor was the diplomatic weapon neglected. Before embarking on the conquest of the Burgundian Circle, Louis tried to obtain allies who would admit his rights by "devolution." Alliance with the United Provinces had long been considered an essential preliminary to the acquisition of the Spanish Low Countries, and in 1635, on the eve of his intervention in the Thirty Years' War, Richelieu had signed a treaty[12] with the States-General by which the Spanish Netherlands were to be partitioned between the two allies and the residue formed into an independent republic. The Dutch share was to be the territory on the left bank of the Lower Scheldt with Breda and Spanish Guelderland, while France was to obtain the Flemish coast as far as Blankenberghe with Namur and Thionville. But Dutch statesmen were not anxious to have France in such close proximity to their frontiers, and nothing came of the treaty. There was a proposal to renew it in 1650,[13] but this was prevented by the death of William II. of Orange in November of that year. In 1663 the project was again mooted, and in March d'Estrades was sent to the Hague in order to come to some arrangement with John de Witt.[14] De Witt had secret intelligence that six of the Flemish towns wished to form a republic on the Swiss model; accordingly the Dutch proposed that the line Ostend-Maestricht should be the new boundary and that rebellion in the Spanish Low Countries should be encouraged in order to make the work of conquest easier. But this plan also failed, mainly because Louis objected to haggling over the partition with a commoner like the Dutch Pensionary, and because his principles did not permit him to encourage rebellious subjects. These principles were not always maintained, but they had some influence on his conduct during the lifetime of his father-in-law. The failure of these negotiations with the Dutch provides one reason for the French invasion of Holland in 1672.

England under Charles II. provided a more ready ally, and Louis began in 1662 by buying back Dunkirk and Mardyk

[12] Dumont, *Corps diplomatique*, VI. i. 80 ff.

[13] Instructions to Bellievre in 1650. *Instructions données* (Holland) i. 12 ff.

[14] Legrelle, *op. cit.* i. 85, and Lefevre-Pontalis, *Jean de Witt*, i. 298-302.

from the cynical monarch who was always ready to sell his honour and that of his country for ready money. Charles's sister Henrietta Maria married Louis's younger brother Philip of Orléans, and by his own marriage with Catherine of Braganza, Charles secured an alliance with Portugal, a country providing an important link in the chain with which French diplomacy was encircling Spain. With Sweden, Poland and Turkey the relations of France were good, and every effort was made to retain the support of these countries, because together they formed a great territorial bulwark stretching diagonally across Europe and everywhere hemming in the Hapsburg territories on the east. In Germany, France had long "nursed" Brandenburg and Bavaria; until 1668 France was the leading spirit in the League of the Rhine. The death of Philip IV. in 1665 thus found France prepared at home and abroad for aggression, and in May 1667, without even the formality of declaring war, Turenne with 35,000 troops invaded the Spanish Low Countries. In a series of short and decisive campaigns, Charleroi, Armentières, Tournai, Douai and Lille were captured. But the startling success of this campaign proved the undoing of Louis's projects, for at once the diplomatic situation of Europe changed. This change coincided with a personal incident which had a marked effect on the policy of Louis XIV.

On the 13th of January 1668 the Emperor Leopold's first son died in infancy, and a post-mortem examination caused the Emperor's medical advisers to warn him that the Empress (Marie Margaret, younger sister of Maria Theresa) was not likely to have healthy children, an opinion confirmed in 1670 and in 1672.[15] Leopold was genuinely concerned about the future of Catholicism, and had always believed that an alliance of Bourbon and Hapsburg was the best security against Protestant and Turk. The success of French arms in the summer of the preceding year, and the possibility of his not being survived by an heir, induced Leopold to listen to the representations of the French ambassador in Vienna, Grémonville, and on the 20th of January 1668 he signed a secret treaty with Louis, by which the Spanish Empire was partitioned between them. By this treaty France, on the conclusion of the hostilities on which she was then engaged, was to have either Luxemburg or Franche Comté, with Cambrai,

[15] Legrelle, *op. cit.* i. 142 ff.

Douai, St. Omer, Bergues and Furnes, but was pledged to restore all other conquests. This was to be the immediate share for France. On the death of the Spanish king (an event expected every month) the Emperor was to have Spain, the West Indies, Milan, the Balearic Islands, Sardinia and the Canaries, while France's final share was to consist of the Low Countries, the eastern Philippines, Spanish Navarre, Naples, Sicily and the North African possessions. Charles II. of Spain was then such a sickly infant that his speedy death was considered a certainty, and in the minds of the negotiators there was no doubt that within a very short time there would be occasion for effecting the partition. The treaty was to be kept absolutely secret, to ensure which it was put in a strong box and sent to the Grand Duke of Tuscany for safe custody. Both parties solemnly swore not to make any treaty conflicting with the partition, but it is hardly necessary to add that, long before Charles II. died, the strong box and its contents had been completely forgotten.

In February 1668 Condé invaded Franche Comté, and in a few weeks the whole province, including its capital, Besançon, was in the occupation of the French. Europe was now thoroughly alarmed, and the first result was the alliance of the maritime powers England and Holland, joined later by Sweden, in the Triple Alliance of May 1668. The object of the Triple Alliance was to press France back to her frontiers as these had been established by the treaties of Westphalia and the Pyrenees. Now that he had signed the secret treaty of partition, Louis had no qualms about entering into peace negotiations with Spain, and by the Peace of Aix-la-Chapelle,[16] signed in May 1668, Louis surrendered Franche Comté but retained Bergues, Furnes, Armentières, Oudenarde, Courtrai, Lille, Douai, Tournai, Binche, Ath and Charleroi. On every side there was praise of Louis's magnanimity[17] in restoring Franche Comté after such a decisive conquest. The news of the secret treaty had not yet leaked out.

The Flemish towns acquired by the Peace of Aix-la-Chapelle were important, not so much in themselves as because they provided a foundation on which later conquests could be based. Thus Louis might hope to seize Ghent from

---

[16] Vast, *Les Grands Traités*, ii. 1-22.

[17] Louis had a medal struck with the motto "Pax Praelata Triumphis"—"Peace preferred to victories."

Oudenarde, Mons from Binche and Brussels from Ath, so that when the partition came to be effected France would be in a favourable position for absorbing Flanders and Brabant into the French monarchy. As Charles II. of Spain continued to live, however, Louis became more impatient, and there were influences at work in Vienna causing the French ambassador to fear that the secret treaty would be imperilled. It is at this point that the personality of the Emperor Leopold began to count in the struggle of Bourbon and Hapsburg. Originally intended for the Church, he had become Emperor by the accident of a brother's death; he loved poetry, music and the fine arts, himself dabbling in musical composition and exercising a sincere if indiscriminate patronage.[18] He did much to restore order and prosperity in his scattered domains by organizing an army, restoring Catholic unity and encouraging education. Of a naturally kindly disposition, his Jesuit education and Hapsburg blood impelled him to rigorous measures of proscription against his Protestant subjects, while his rule in Hungary was made possible only by crushing Magyar aspirations under the heels of the soldier and tax-gatherer. In constant fear of his own subjects and of the Turkish menace, Leopold sought refuge in the intricacies of a solicitous and meticulous administration. He was anxious to be his own first minister[19] and to emulate the glories of his cousin of Versailles, but in temperament[20] he was too pedantic, too self-conscious and too distrustful of himself and others for vigorous and effective rule. Accustomed to calculations based on remote possibilities, he was often blind to the needs of the moment: having no confidence in his own judgement, he showed apprehension at every turn of the diplomatic wheel. Even his physical appearance was against him, for he had in an exaggerated degree the projecting lower jaw so often found in Hapsburg physiognomy, and as he commonly kept his mouth open this characteristic emphasized the ungainliness and irresolution which his demeanour indicated. His reserve was such that he was scarcely known to his own courtiers. After signing the secret treaty of 1668 he lived in dread lest

[18] Pribram and Pragenau, *Privatbriefe Kaiser Leopold I. an den Grafen Potting,* I. xxxii.

[19] *Ibid.* xxii.

[20] There are good character sketches by the Venetian ambassadors Molin (1661) and Venier (1693), in *Fontes rerum Austriacarum,* second series, xxvi. 49 and 311.

the mystery of the strong box should be revealed, and when on one occasion the French ambassador pressed him for his views on Don Juan's recent rise to power in Madrid,[21] all that Leopold could reply was, "For God's sake keep the treaty secret."[22] His unholy alliance with the Bourbon interfered with his peace of mind, and late in 1670 he gave De Witt his secret promise that he would break with France if Louis attacked the United Provinces, while he assured France that all he meant by this was that in such a contingency he would remain neutral. As the Imperial finances were permanently in low water, he hinted to the French ambassador that a subsidy would not be taken amiss.[23] Such was the protagonist of Louis XIV. in the struggle of Bourbon and Hapsburg.

The Peace of Aix-la-Chapelle was followed by nearly four years of peace, ended by the war of the Dutch invasion. At first sight, Louis's attack on Holland in 1672 seems inexplicable except on the assumption that it was inspired merely by lust of conquest. There are other reasons. After several attempts, Louis had failed to come to an agreement with the States-General on the proposed partitioning of the Spanish Netherlands. In 1656 Mazarin had prohibited the Dutch from carrying enemy commerce and had imposed a tax on merchandise imported into French ports by Dutch ships. Commercial jealousy between the two countries led to a war of tariffs in which the Dutch suffered much more than the French; for while the United Provinces had the greater part of the world's carrying trade, the number of French ships visiting Dutch ports was very small; in consequence the States-General could not retaliate. In 1664, when Louis was anxious to conciliate European opinion before making a claim to the Low Countries, he mitigated the French protective tariff in favour of the Dutch; three years later, however, he startled Europe by his "Devolution" claim, and staggered Holland by imposing a tariff that was practically prohibitive.[24] Nor were these the only causes of irritation between the two countries.

---

[21] See *infra*, p. 359.

[22] Legrelle, *op. cit.* i. 151.

[23] Vast, *Les Grands Traités*, ii. 25. Louis's reply is cynical: "he could not think that His Imperial Majesty would expect him to purchase friendship with money."

[24] For the economic conflict 1660–72, see S. Elzinga, *Het Voorspel van den oorloog van 1672* (1926). Elzinga contends that Louvois was as responsible as Colbert.

The Dutch had a monopoly of the salted herring trade, and neither their French nor English rivals could learn their secrets of salting or packing. Such were the reasons for war as seen by Colbert, but these had little influence on the king who, as his voluminous correspondence shows, was viewing the situation not as a European economist but as an Asiatic potentate. His motives were idealist and even "religious." To his expansive and oriental mind, it appeared that the Dutch had betrayed him, notably by joining in the Triple Alliance with Charles of England. It might have seemed that Charles also had "betrayed" him, but it must be recalled that the English king was a Stuart, a gentleman and a (secret) Roman Catholic, whereas the Dutch were republicans, Protestants and "maggots." Now that he was secretly allied with Charles (who needed money before he could make public his conversion to the true faith—an unfortunate personal difficulty which his French ally afterwards tried to exploit by blackmail), Louis was prompted by three motives worthy of a really great king —"religion," glory and revenge, motives strikingly contrasted with the economic calculations of Colbert and other Europeans. It was as if seventeenth-century Europe was suddenly transformed into Old Testament Israel, and at no other point in the reign did there seem such brilliant justification for the parallel between Jehovah and Louis XIV.

The invasion of Holland was preceded, like the attack on the Burgundian Circle, by a network of alliances. In 1669 a treaty had been concluded with the Elector of Brandenburg by which France promised Spanish Guelderland in return for the loan of 10,000 men, and in the following year Bavaria was won over by a treaty stipulating a marriage alliance between the Dauphin and the Elector's infant daughter (when they had attained a reasonable age), in return for which the Elector promised to support Louis's election to the Empire (when Leopold was out of the way).[25] In April 1672, by a treaty with Sweden, the Regency government undertook, on the payment of a subsidy, to combine with Denmark in closing the Sound to Dutch ships. By the treaty of Dover, signed on the 1st of June 1670, Charles II. of England became Louis's pensioner and agreed to assist in the attack on

---

[25] For the attempts of Louis (in 1658, 1670 and 1679) to obtain the promise of the Electoral votes see Vast, *Les Tentatives de Louis XIV pour arriver à l'Empire* (*Revue Historique*, lxv.).

the United Provinces, Charles's share of the spoils to be the mouth of the Scheldt and the island of Walcheren, while by the secret clauses of the treaty he undertook to become a Roman Catholic and to foster Roman Catholicism in England. Every detail of the coming campaign was carefully arranged, and though the Dutch merchants well knew the object of France's military preparations, so cosmopolitan were their inclinations that they continued to sell lead and gunpowder to the French government. The greatest generals of the day— Condé, Turenne and Luxemburg—were each assigned their parts and the monarch himself took the field in supreme command.

Louis dispensed with the formality of declaring war. The French armies moved early in June 1672 and entered Dutch territory by way of the Rhine. In a few months the whole of the province of Utrecht was overrun and the Dutch anxiously sued for peace. The terms offered by Louis were so insulting that they were at once rejected; in a great wave of panic John de Witt was murdered[26] and the work of defending the state entrusted to William of Orange. The French troops were flooded out, and after a futile attempt to take Amsterdam, Louis withdrew his army of invasion in the spring of 1673.

The invasion of Holland was worse than useless, for it called forth Nemesis in the person of William of Orange. Once again Europe combined against the insolent conqueror and, with the exception of Sweden, all the powers which Louis had so carefully separated from the United Provinces now rallied to the defence of the Dutch. Leopold felt that the outbreak of war absolved him from the secret treaty, so was easily detached from the French alliance; Brandenburg, Denmark and Brunswick followed suit. English popular opinion was in favour of war against France. When the Emperor, Spain and the Duke of Lorraine undertook to assist the Dutch, there was formed the second of the great coalitions against Louis, generally named the Grand Alliance of the Hague (1674).

The Dutch war now degenerated into a campaign of sieges in the Spanish Low Countries and on the Rhine. Maestricht was captured by the French in 1673, and in the following year Franche Comté was again invaded. Meanwhile the Germanic Diet declared war on France in May 1674. Turenne

[26] See *infra*, p. 411.

carried out a skilful campaign in the Palatinate and in Alsace, where he had the troops of Brandenburg, Austria and Brunswick against him. Defeating the allies at Sinzheim and Ladenburg in the summer of 1674, Turenne systematically devastated the Palatinate. No quarter was given, and, with atrocities followed by indiscriminate reprisals, the war took on a more modern form. Alsace was invaded by German troops, and during the winter of 1674-5 Turenne had to feign retreat. Taking advantage of the rashness which success had encouraged in his enemies, Turenne by rapid marches and skilled manœuvre defeated the allied troops in succession at Mülhausen, Colmar and Türkheim, compelling them to evacuate Alsace. This was the most brilliant of Turenne's campaigns and his last. On the 27th of July 1675 he was killed at the battle of Sasbach and his place was given to Condé. Condé forced the Allied general Montecuculi across the Rhine, but after his victory he went into retirement. So France lost her two best generals in these campaigns.

Thus the invasion of Holland had been followed by nearly six years of European warfare in which, despite some distinguished feats of arms, France had gained nothing. Her only ally—Sweden—had been defeated by the Elector of Brandenburg at the battle of Fehrbellin in 1675, and in January 1678 the triumphant Elector seized Stettin. At home the excessive taxation necessitated by uninterrupted warfare had caused revolts in Normandy and Brittany; in spite of the subsidy, the English alliance could not be depended upon, and in 1677 the leader of the coalition against France further strengthened his position by marriage with Mary, daughter of James, Duke of York. On the other hand, the German princes were tiring of a war which seemed to benefit only the insolent Brandenburg, and when Louis could no longer conceal his desire for peace, negotiations were opened. These were conducted at Nymegen in the years 1678-9, the contracting parties being France, Spain, the United Provinces and the Emperor.

There were four separate treaties, known together as the Peace of Nymegen, the general terms of the pacification being as follows:

France restored Maestricht to the States-General[27] and

[27] Negotiations with the States-General had begun as early as 1674 (*Instructions données* . . . Holland, 291 ff.). For the Nymegen negotiations see *ibid.* 344 ff. For the full terms of the pacification

mitigated her commercial tariff in favour of the Dutch by restoring the tariff of 1664 in place of the more protectionist measures of 1667. In the Low Countries she abandoned the outposts of Charleroi, Courtrai, Oudenarde and Ghent, taking in exchange the frontier positions of St. Omer, Cassel, Poperinghe, Bailleul, Ypres, Cambrai, Maubeuge and Valenciennes. Most important of all, France gained Franche Comté. By the treaty with the Emperor, Louis surrendered the right to garrison Philippsburg, but received Breisach and Freiburg. The Duke of Lorraine refused to accept the conditions offered him; accordingly French military occupation of the Duchy continued, thus giving France a secure hold on Longwy and Nancy.

The treaties of St. Germain (June 6, 1679), by which France induced the Elector of Brandenburg to surrender his Pomeranian conquests[28] to Sweden, and the treaty of Fontainebleau (September 1679), by which Denmark restored her Baltic conquests to Sweden, may be regarded as supplementary to the Nymegen pacification. Like the treaty of the Pyrenees, the treaty of Nymegen was followed by a marriage. Louis's niece, Marie Louise of Orléans, married the Spanish king Charles II., and there then followed a few years of happiness for that unfortunate monarch.

The acquisition of Franche Comté by France may have been considered justified by two successive conquests; it was a valuable addition to French territory, but otherwise the Peace of Nymegen did not materially improve the position of France in Europe. The Spanish inheritance was as far off as ever; Charles II. still lived and might even have heirs; the secret treaty of 1668 was already obsolete, and the Emperor was now in the enemy's camp. Henceforward Louis had to reckon on the hostility of both the Spanish and the Austrian Hapsburgs. The invasion of Holland had raised up the greatest enemy Louis was ever to face; the devastation of the Palatinate had awakened bitter animosities and national jealousies in German lands; the resources of France in men and money had been steadily drained. But France, "Queen of the world and slave of a man,"[29] had entered fully into the spirit of

---

see Vast, *Les Grands Traités*, ii. 23-148. Copies of practically all the important correspondence in the peace negotiations will be found in British Museum (*Harley MSS.*, 1516-1523).

[28] See *infra*, p. 429.

[29] The phrase is Victor Hugo's.

her ruler's policy. But, unfortunately for France, her enemies were now better armed, and, after William III's death in March 1702, better led; accordingly Louis had soon to reckon with two things not allowed for in his calculations—first stalemate and then military defeat.

II. From the Treaty of Nymegen to the Treaty of Ryswick, 1679–1697

In the preceding section we summarized the history of the two wars which, for want of better names, are called the War of Devolution and the War of the Dutch Invasion. The first of these wars had been terminated by a public and a secret treaty, the public yielding moderate but substantial gains, the secret treaty promising a considerable proportion of the Spanish inheritance. Since the Spanish king still lived and the secret treaty was considered no longer binding, Louis must have felt that he had been duped, for it was owing to the existence of the secret treaty that he had been moderate in the public treaty.

The second war had added Franche Comté to French territory, but had cost France all her allies except Sweden and had roused the permanent animosity of the Dutch and William III. So far as Louis could learn from his own failures, the War of the Dutch Invasion had taught him that he could not with impunity attack a weaker country merely because he disliked its inhabitants, for the Peace of Westphalia had established Europe on an equipoise, and violent disturbance on one side inevitably produced a reaction on the other. It was characteristic that Louis should now utilize as a pretext for aggression the very treaty which was supposed to guarantee the stability of Europe, and, by "interpreting" some of the obscure passages in this "pragmatic sanction and fundamental law," try to justify robbery by deduction from the most widely accepted instrument of international jurisprudence.[30] All the French acquisitions by the treaty of Münster

---

[30] It is generally held that Louvois incited Louis to embark on "Reunion" policy, a view first maintained by Voltaire (*Siècle de Louis XIV*, ch. xiv.). But the blame cannot be attributed to Louvois. The Secretary of State for Foreign Affairs at this time was Colbert de Croissy, brother of the great Colbert; it was Croissy who advocated the idea of completing the conquests of Münster, Aix-la-Chapelle and Nymegen by judicial seizures. See E. Bour-

had been obtained "with their dependencies," and this apparently innocent phrase was now subjected to the scrutiny of lawyers anxious to find opportunities for chicanery and equivocation. What "dependencies" could be claimed in virtue of this provision? The historical research which had elucidated the various succession customs in the provinces of the Burgundian Circle had no difficulty in proving that at various periods, more or less remote, certain towns had been "dependent" on some of the provinces recently acquired by France, and though these were now merely matters of antiquarian interest, the effrontery which had published the "devolution" claims in 1665 was not to be deterred by a technical difficulty of this kind. Desuetude was no objection when Louis XIV. wished to revive a claim in his own favour, and if his logic did not always carry conviction, his artillery did. Accordingly in 1680 the Parlement of Metz (on behalf of the three bishoprics of Metz, Toul and Verdun), the Council of Breisach (on behalf of Alsace), and the Parlement of Besançon (on behalf of Franche Comté) were ordered to declare the annexation of those towns which special research had shown to be dependent, at some time or another, on these respective provinces. The Parlement of Metz appointed an extraordinary "Chambre de Réunions" which, together with the sovereign courts of Alsace and Franche Comté, carried out these instructions. The annexations included Lauterbourg, Germersheim, Sarrebruck, Zweibrücken and Montbéliard. Casale[31] was taken over in this way. But by far the most important of the annexations was Strasburg, which, after a blockade, was entered peaceably by French troops on the 30th of September 1681. The possession of Strasburg was necessary for the assimilation of Lower Alsace, and the only extenuating circumstance that could be pleaded for the appropriation of the city was that by 1681 the Alsatians had become, in large measure, reconciled to French rule and that the working

geois, "Louvois et Colbert de Croissy," in *Revue Historique*, xxxiv. (1887), 413.

[31] For this see *Instructions données* . . . (Savoy, Sardinia, Mantua), lii. In 1678 Louis had made secret arrangements with Mantua for acquiring Casale. The intermediary was Matthioli, who betrayed the plans to Venice, Spain and Savoy; for this he was imprisoned in the fortress of Pinerolo. This is the Man in the Iron Mask (it was of black velvet). See Funck Brentano in *Revue Historique*, lvi. 253 ff.

people of the city welcomed the French as an alternative to the rule of a burgher oligarchy.

These "Reunions" aroused again all the latent hostility of Europe. Even Sweden was forced to declare against her old ally, for Louis's "reunions" had reached to Zweibrücken, the family possession of Charles XI.[32] William of Orange and Charles XI. of Sweden formed an alliance at the Hague in September 1681, and were speedily joined by the Empire and Spain. This was the third of the series of coalitions against Louis XIV., the two earlier coalitions having been the Triple Alliance (1668) and the Grand Alliance of the Hague (1674). France sought allies in Denmark and Turkey; French troops invaded Luxemburg, and western Europe would again have been plunged into war had not a sudden diversion come from the East. Vienna was besieged by the Turk, and the Most Christian King suspended open hostilities while the Infidel menaced the capital of the Empire. Leopold refused the proffered French help, and, flying in panic from his capital, left Sobieski to deal with the Ottoman hordes.[33] After the failure of the Turks before Vienna in 1683, Louis again resorted to arms, and the brunt of the hostilities had now to be borne by Spain. France seized Luxemburg and laid seige to Courtrai and Oudenarde, but by the truce of Ratisbon[34] (August 1684) Louis agreed with Spain and the Empire to accept a compromise by which he retained Strasburg, Luxemburg and Oudenarde, with all the annexations made prior to the 1st of August 1681. Had Spain received more help from her allies at this time, France would not have emerged so triumphantly.

The truce of Ratisbon placed Louis at the summit of his fortunes; everywhere his military enterprises had been crowned with success. In the Mediterranean his fleets had forced the Barbary pirates to respect the French flag; Genoa had been bombarded and detached from her Spanish alliance,[35] while its Doge had been compelled to submit to the humiliation of seeking pardon at Versailles.[36] The Emperor was rendered powerless by the harassing raids of the Turks in Hungary; Spain had proved in a short campaign that her military re-

[32] *Instructions données* (Sweden), lxviii.
[33] See *infra*, p. 429.
[34] Vast, *op. cit.* ii. 135-149.
[35] Callegari, *Preponderanze straniere*, 297.
[36] See *infra*, p. 367.

sources were practically exhausted; Franche Comté, Luxemburg and a line of forts in Flanders were the tangible results of French military enterprise; the city of Strasburg was now on French soil. England could be depended upon so long as the mercenary Charles II. was on the throne, and it was reasonable to hope that the recent French marriage of Charles II. of Spain would make Louis's influence as supreme at the Escorial as it was in Whitehall. As for William of Orange, the leader of the coalition against France, he had lost more battles than any other general in Europe, and until 1688 his military resources were slight. In his own dominions Louis absolved his conscience and secured religious uniformity by the Revocation of the Edict of Nantes (1685).

The fall from these heights was to be gradual, and retribution, though slow, was sure. Already (July 17, 1686) the League of Augsburg, the fourth coalition against Louis XIV., was formed by Spain, on behalf of Burgundy, the Empire, Sweden and Bavaria, for the nominal purpose of maintaining the Peace of Westphalia, but for the real object of humbling Louis XIV. It was the prelude to the Grand Alliance of 1701.

What would happen on the death of Charles II. of Spain was still the dominant consideration in the diplomacy of western Europe. The situation had altered considerably since the signing of the secret treaty of 1668.[37] Leopold's first wife, Marie Marguerite, had died in 1673, leaving a daughter, Maria Antonia, born in 1669. According to the terms of Philip IV.'s will this girl was the heiress-presumptive to the Spanish dominions. In the hope of keeping the inheritance intact for the Hapsburgs, the Emperor now embarked on a family settlement, the details of which must be enumerated if the succeeding events are to be understood. Maria Antonia was of weak health, but a marriage with the Elector of Bavaria, Maximilian Emanuel, was proposed, an alliance which Leopold did not regard with complete approval, for he knew the traditional alliance between France and Bavaria, and when he at last gave his sanction to the marriage, he dreaded lest it might be the means of ultimately transferring the inheritance to the Bourbons. Moreover, he had married again (with Eleonora Madeleine of Neuburg), by whom he had a son, Joseph, born in 1678. Another child was expected,

[37] Legrelle, *op cit.* i. 255 ff.

and if it proved to be a son then this son would, in Leopold's view, be the most suitable candidate for the succession, since the Empire would naturally go to the elder child Joseph. Accordingly, when Maria Antonia married Maximilian Emanuel in July 1685, Leopold insisted on his daughter signing a renunciation of all rights that might be claimed on her behalf under the will of Philip IV. Considering that Philip's will was of doubtful validity, and that Charles of Spain might have heirs or might make a will of his own, Leopold's calculations seem to be based on remote possibilities rather than on facts. Spain was asked to express its approval of the Bavarian marriage and its accompanying renunciation; when, however, the Spanish Government asked for further information concerning the terms of the renunciation, a courier was despatched from Vienna with full particulars, but, for whatever reason, he never reached his destination, and it was given out that he had been captured by pirates in the Mediterranean.[38] In 1685 Leopold's expected son was born and was named Charles, in honour of the king whom it was hoped that he would succeed. The Emperor then announced that the rights of his eldest daughter under Philip's will were now transferred to Charles, his youngest son by the second marriage, with the exception of the Low Countries, which he reserved for his son-in-law the Elector of Bavaria. In his disposition of kingdoms, Leopold now established Maximilian Emanuel in Brussels as sovereign-elect of the Low Countries, and he proposed sending the young Archduke Charles to Spain to be brought up at the Court over which it was hoped he would one day rule. It was on behalf of this Charles that the allies fought in the Spanish Succession war.

But while the Emperor was playing the trump card of the will, Louis XIV. was still insisting that Maria Theresa's renunciation was invalid and that her rights automatically passed to the Dauphin. He hoped that his niece, the Queen of Spain, would extend French influence in Madrid and so prepare the way for the Dauphin's candidature. Unfortunately Marie Louise of Orléans was by temperament unfitted to promote this design; she did not realize the dangers around her, and by her vivacity and thoughtlessness she increased the dislike of the Spanish Court for the French. Though she was a faith-

---

[38] Gaedeke, *Die Politik Österreichs in der spanischen Erbfolge-frage*, i. 24-25.

ful consort to King Charles and afforded him the few happy moments of his lifetime, she was subjected to systematic tyranny on the part of a jealous and treacherous entourage.[39] The Austrian element, headed by the Queen-mother, wished to get rid of her and marry Charles II. to his first cousin, Maria Antonia, but after the Bavarian marriage of 1685 this substitution was no longer possible, and thereafter the Queen's enemies were not satisfied until they had destroyed her. The treatment meted out to this unfortunate Queen of Spain is remarkable even in the history of European dynasties. Her two favourite parrots were strangled because they talked French; her French servants were sent way; letters were forged with the intention of proving that she had been guilty of a *liaison* with a guardsman, and, last insult of all, she was declared the cause of Charles's having no heir. Powerful drugs were administered to her for the purpose of producing childbirth, and these had the effect, whether intentional or accidental is not certain, of causing her death. She died from poisoning on the 12th of February 1689. Louis XIV. urged that there should be no postmortem, as it might lead to complications.[40]

Meanwhile a hitch had occurred in Leopold's carefully planned schemes. In response to his request that the Spanish Government would approve his daughter's marriage and her renunciation, a commission had been appointed[41] to examine the question, and in 1686 it decided that the renunciation of Maria Antonia was invalid because hereditary rights are indefeasible and the succession could be altered only with national consent. Constitutional doctrines of an advanced kind are sometimes quoted in the seventeenth century at the least expected moments. The effect of this decision was that, so far as there was any official Spanish declaration on the subject, the inheritance belonged, by implication, to the issue of the Bavarian marriage, and, with the increasing certainty of Charles II. of Spain never having heirs, it was clear that the children of Maria Antonia would have the best claim. Another inference that might be made from the commission's decision is that the will of Philip IV. was regarded as still

[39] Legrelle, i. 276-7 and Gaedeke, *op. cit.* 52-81.
[40] *Instructions données* (Spain), xxvi.
[41] Legrelle, i. 290.

valid. It needed only the birth of a son in order that the Bavarian might be the least doubtful of all the competing claims. A son was born to the Elector of Bavaria in 1692, and never did the destinies of great nations hang so precariously as on the life of this infant, the Electoral Prince Ferdinand Joseph. By his first will, made in November 1698, Charles appointed this child his successor and so confirmed the declared intentions of Philip IV.; the claim on behalf of the young Electoral Prince was therefore barely contestable, and might have been acceptable to European public opinion, since the transference of the Spanish Empire to the Bavarian house did not directly advantage either Bourbon or Hapsburg. But the question of the Spanish Succession was not to be settled so easily. Through his agents in Madrid Leopold induced Charles to revoke the will; another event succeeded with dramatic suddenness. The boy-prince was taken ill when in his seventh year, and, despite everything that could be done by his distracted parent, he died in February 1699. The circumstances of this illness and speedy death aroused suspicion;[42] there were suggestions of poison, and some contemporaries hinted that the child's maternal grandfather had brought about this event, thereby making his daughter's renunciation a far greater one than either she or her husband had bargained for. So ended another act in a drama of anxious calculation and domestic tragedy that has probably no counterpart in imaginative literature, save perhaps in a great but forgotten book, *The Entail,* by John Galt.

In the years immediately following the formation of the League of Augsburg Louis XIV. had not been idle. When the Elector Palatine of the Rhine died childless in 1685 his lands went to a collateral branch headed by William of Neuburg, father-in-law of the Emperor, and afterwards also father-in-law of Charles II. of Spain. In the eyes of Louis, William of Neuburg and his relatives were objectionable neighbours, so he put forward a specious claim to property in the Palatinate on the ground of the marriage of his brother Philip of Orléans with a relative of the former Elector. At the same time he tried to have one of his nominees, Cardinal Furstenberg, elected to the see of Cologne—an archbishopric long regarded as an appanage of the house of Bavaria; and on the

---

[42] The general opinion is that he died from smallpox.

chapter electing another candidate, Louis installed his nominee by force. In September 1688 he issued a manifesto[43] which, better than anything else, illustrates his political morality. The *Mémoire des raisons qui ont obligé le roi . . . à reprendre les armes* rehearses the fact that Louis had refrained from open hostilities against the Emperor while the latter was harassed by the Turk; it asserts that with the removal of the Ottoman menace the Emperor was now preparing to attack France; that recent associations, such as the League of Augsburg, were intended to promote the aggressive designs of the Hapsburgs, and, finally, that the preliminary to these designs was control of frontier provinces like the Palatinate. The Elector Palatine, according to Louis, was aiding and abetting this scheme of aggression; consequently, much as he desired peace, the French monarch was obliged to take up arms. But by 1688 Europe was quite accustomed to diplomatic casuistry of this kind. The French frontiers were not threatened; the Emperor, much as he disliked his French cousin, could not spare a man from the defence of his own lands; Spain, from a military point of view, was now negligible, and the only explanation of Louis's declaration is that, as he had already flouted European public opinion by his "devolution" claims and his "reunion" confiscations, it now seemed appropriate to pose as the lover of peace forced by scheming enemies to take up the sword.

Simultaneously with the publication of this manifesto, a French army under the nominal leadership of the Dauphin invaded the Palatinate; with the speedy capture of Philippsburg, Mannheim, Frankenthal and Kaiserslautern, the province was soon in French occupation. On the suggestion of Louvois, conquest was followed by destruction; in order to create a great gap between Alsace and Germany the rich lands of the Palatinate were reduced to a stretch of waste relieved only by ruins.[44] The winter of 1688-9 witnessed a devastation as ruthless and systematic as any in modern history. No quarter was given; those of the populace who survived were for-

[43] *Mémoire des raisons qui ont obligé le roi . . . à reprendre les armes . . . et qui doivent persuader toute la chrétienté des sincères intentions de Sa Majesté pour l'affermissement de la tranquillité publique*, in Dumont, *Corps Diplomatique*, vii. 2, 170-171.

[44] Notice that this was the second French devastation of the Palatinate; the first was that by Turenne in 1674.

bidden to rebuild their ruined houses, and were driven over the frontier to carry with them personal evidence of their sufferings. What is here in question, however, is not Louis's morality but his statesmanship. What was his army doing in the Palatinate when it was clear that his troops and ships were needed to protect his pensioner James II. from his own subjects and from the Dutch threat of invasion? The answer is that, in the late summer of 1688, he was acting on a secret report from Madrid that Charles of Spain was really dying, so he diverted his fleet to the Mediterranean in order to take over the Spanish possessions when the death occurred. His troops were diverted to the Palatinate, not for any strategic reason, but in order to punish the Emperor and the Elector Palatine. Once more, as in the invasion of Holland, Louis was acting not as a statesman, but as a moralist, exacting retribution from the agents of perfidy and aggression.

These calculations left out of account the anæmic Dutchman who was devoting his life to the work of revenge, and was soon to have the resources of a great country behind him. It needed only the English Revolution of 1689 to transform Louis's frontier campaigns into a European war. The deposed James II. of England sought shelter at St. Germains, and William now reversed the policy of England. In May 1689 the Emperor and the United Provinces entered into an offensive military alliance against France; in December they were joined by William III., and a few months later by Spain and Savoy. The platonic League of Augsburg was thus succeeded by the militant Alliance of Vienna.[45] The devastation of the Palatinate had united western Europe against Louis XIV.

In the campaigns that followed, the French were at first successful. While Ireland rose in the cause of the Stuarts, the French navy defeated the joint fleets of England and Holland in Bantry Bay and off Beachy Head. An invasion of England was planned; a camp was formed at Cherbourg, and the French fleet, under Tourville, held the Channel until in May 1692 the inferior French forces were defeated by Admiral Russell at the battle of La Hogue. After this defeat, French naval forces did not play any important part in the war.

The Low Countries were invaded by Luxemburg[46] in 1689,

[45] Vast, op. cit. ii. 152, 153.

[46] François Henri de Montmorency-Bouteville, Duke of Luxemburg (1628–1695).

and a war of sieges and counter-marches began. Mons was taken by the French in 1691, Namur in 1692, and in the latter year William was defeated at Steinkirk and at Neerwinden (Landen) in 1693. In Italy, Catinat led a successful campaign against Louis's cousin Victor Amadeus of Savoy, who, unable to accept the conditions attached by Louvois to the French alliance, had joined the allies with the ostensible object of taking Casale. The reputation of Victor Amadeus was overshadowed by that of his great general, Prince Eugène, a French refugee. Catinat's first victory was at Staffarde (August 1690), followed up by the capture of Nice and Montmélian. An invasion of Dauphiné by Victor Amadeus met with a strenuous resistance from the inhabitants, and in October 1693 the threat to French territory was removed by the victory of Catinat over the Savoyards at Marsaglia, outside Turin, a victory which earned for the French general the dignity of Marshal.

These successes were not maintained in the later years of the war. Luxemburg died in 1695 and was succeeded by the incompetent Villeroy; French naval activities in the Channel degenerated into a semi-piratical warfare against English shipping, led by Jean Bart. There were minor engagements in the West Indies, but as hostilities were prolonged, the less likelihood did there seem of any decisive action. While, single-handed, France was conducting the war on many fronts, the Allies knew that they had time on their side and that French national resources would eventually give way. News that Charles II. of Spain was really dying caused Louis once more to think of peace,[47] so that when the long-expected death did take place, he would not have a world of enemies against him. Victor Amadeus was first detached from the coalition by the restoration of all conquests in his territory, together with Pinerolo and Casale (the latter to be handed over to the Emperor). These terms, in addition to a marriage alliance between Louis's grandson, the Duke of Burgundy, and the eldest daughter of Victor Amadeus, constitute the main terms of the treaty of Turin signed in June 1696. In the following year (September-October 1697) the treaties

[47] As early as 1695 Louis had thought of a separate peace with Holland (*Instructions données*, Holland, i. 479). In 1697 he declared that France would have difficulty in continuing the war (*ibid.* 509).

of Ryswick were discussed and signed between France on the one part and England, Holland, Spain and the Empire on the other. The main terms of these treaties were as follows:

1. Louis XIV. recognized William III. as king of England, and undertook not to assist the Stuarts.
2. Except for the retention of certain outposts in Lorraine, France restored Trier, Philippsburg, Breisach, Freiburg and Lorraine.
3. The dispute over the Cologne election was settled in favour of the Bavarian candidate.
4. The question of the Palatinate was settled in favour of the Neuburg family in consideration of the payment of a pension to the Duchess of Orléans.
5. Luxemburg, Ath, Charleroi, Courtrai and Catalonia were restored to Spain.
6. The French commerical tariff was mitigated in favour of the Dutch.

These conditions show a great decline in the fortunes of Louis XIV. Had French arms been uniformly unsuccessful in the so-called War of the League of Augsburg, the peace terms could not have been harder than those she had to accept in the Peace of Ryswick. It may be concluded from this that mere success in the field was now beginning to be discounted, and that the known resources of the combatants were coming to be regarded as contributory factors in the peace negotiations. Thus war was changing from a mere military contest waged by professional or mercenary troops into a gigantic struggle in which national existence might be imperilled and in which every resource of men and money had to be unsparingly employed. The balance of power had to be preserved, not by the spectacular combats of hired pikemen, but by the suffering and sacrifice of great nations. For this extension of the scope and significance of war Louis XIV. is mainly responsible, since the crushing superiority of his military forces and the capricious ruthlessness with which they were employed called out all the resources of his enemies, and so War became entrenched as the chief menace to civilization.

In this respect the war had affected England and France in strikingly different ways. England was spared the threat of devastation; the need for money with which to maintain supplies had led directly to the creation of such great institutions as the National Debt and the Bank of England, institutions which helped to build up credit on a sound basis; in France, on the other hand, the wealth created by Colbert's measures was speedily dissipated, no measures were taken to maintain productive industries, and a few more years of war would have meant bankruptcy. Moreover, Louis was now past his prime; he had outlived his best generals and ministers, and he began at last to realize something of the magnitude of that great fund of hatred of France, of which he and Louvois were the solely responsible creators. Charles of Spain was at last really dying, and as the vital question of the Spanish Succession loomed once more into prominence, every other consideration was pushed aside in order that this might have exclusive prominence. The lists were cleared of all the combatants, while in the eyes of hushed and expectant Europe the wearer of twenty-two crowns slowly yielded to an enemy with which his life had been one continuous struggle.

III. From the Treaty of Ryswick to the Treaty of Utrecht, 1697–1715

In the years between the signing of the treaty of Ryswick (September 1697) and the death of Charles II. of Spain (November 1, 1700) the question of the Spanish Succession was the one problem of European diplomacy. All the claims to the inheritance were through females; Louis XIV. was the son of the eldest daughter of Philip III. (Anne of Austria), and had married the eldest daughter of Philip IV. (Maria Theresa); Leopold was the son of a younger daughter of Philip III. and had married the younger daughter of Philip IV. While Louis's mother and wife had each in turn renounced all claim to the succession, neither the Emperor's mother nor wife had ever done so, but his daughter had been induced to sign a renunciation in favour of her half-brother, the Archduke Charles. Louis might argue that neither his wife's nor his mother's renunciation was valid, since indefeasible hereditary right could not be set aside, and, moreover, his wife's renunciation had been made on a condition never fulfilled. On the other hand, Leopold could reply by producing the will of Philip IV. which entailed the succession in an order of preference favouring the Emperor's female relatives and excluding, by omission, the French claims. But Leopold's claim was likewise complicated by a renunciation—that of his daughter Maria Antonia, which, as already shown, the Spanish Government had refused to recognize, and so, in spite of the French claims and the Imperial calculations, the candidate officially recognized by Europe was the infant son of the Elector of Bavaria, grandson of the Emperor Leopold. Apart from the legal aspects of the question, however, the matter was one that vitally concerned the whole of western Europe. There was a great body of opinion in favour of keeping the Spanish inheritance intact and entrusting it to a strong ruler outside the Hapsburg circle, since partition would probably involve war, and every one agreed that it would be dangerous to risk a revival of the Empire of Charles V. This view had numerous adherents in Spain, and it came to influence Charles II. himself. Against this opinion it was argued that the danger of a Bourbon uniting the crowns of France and Spain was as serious a menace as the revival of the Empire of Charles V., and that the Archduke Charles was a less objectionable candidate than the Dauphin, since, as a younger son, Charles was not likely ever to become Emperor. The countries supporting the Archduke did not stop to inquire what would ensue if (as did happen) his elder brother Joseph died without heirs.

The maritime powers, England and the United Provinces, were deeply concerned in this question; they dreaded any increase of power on the part of their Bourbon enemies; as colonizing countries they were interested in the fate of the Spanish colonies, and in addition, the ultimate destination of the Spanish Low Countries was of vital importance to the monarch who directed the destinies of both England and Holland. Ever since the treaty of Ryswick, French diplomacy had set itself to the task of detaching William III. from the anti-French coalitions, but it was found very difficult to break down William's sworn aversion to his enemy of Versailles.[48] At last even this difficulty was overcome, and on the 11th of October 1698 was signed a secret treaty of partition[49] between France, England and Holland by which the Electoral Prince

[48] William's correspondence will be found in Grimblot, *Letters of William III. and Louis XIV. and their Ministers* (1697–1700). There is a full account of the Partition treaties in Legrelle, *op. cit.*, and Reynald, *Louis XIV et Guillaume III, histoire des deux traités de partage et du testament de Charles II.*

[49] Legrelle, ii. 437-9.

of Bavaria, or, failing him, his father, was to have Spain, the Indies, the Low Countries and Sardinia; the Dauphin was to have the two Sicilies, the Tuscan outposts, Finale and Guiposcoa, while the Archduke Charles was to have Milan.

News of this treaty soon leaked out, and Charles II. so disliked the idea of a partition that in November 1698 he signed a will appointing the young Electoral Prince of Bavaria his universal heir. This arrangement pleased none of the governments anxious to benefit by partition; the sudden death of the Electoral Prince three months later (February 1699) removed a child of seven and a source of diplomatic embarrassment. France and the maritime countries were once more obliged to resume their negotiations, and in March 1700 they signed a treaty[50] by which the share previously intended for the Electoral Prince—namely, Spain, the Indies and the Low Countries—was now assigned to the Archduke Charles, while the Dauphin was to receive the Italian provinces and obtain Lorraine by inducing its Duke to exchange his duchy for Milan. In order to induce Lorraine to accept, in exchange, a duchy which it was not yet theirs to give, the French diplomatists depicted in glowing terms the architectural beauties of Milan cathedral.[51] This second partition was not kept secret; the Emperor was asked to give his adhesion, but refused; in Madrid there were energetic protests against this proposed division of the Spanish monarchy. Charles II., who believed that the only hope for Catholicism and European peace lay in keeping together the Spanish Empire, was indignant that heretic nations, intent solely on trade, should profit by the proposed breaking up of a Catholic empire. It was this sense of the dangers that might follow dismemberment and a desire to retain the Spanish possessions as a great bulwark for Catholicism that induced Charles and the Spanish national party to consider the advisability of devising the whole inheritance to a Catholic prince who, while a member of a ruling house, would not be likely in the ordinary course of events to succeed either to the Empire or to the throne of France. A prince was required who would have sufficient prestige and family connection to keep the Spanish possessions intact and yet not sufficient dynastic prospects or ambitions to make him a danger to Europe. So far as personal predilec-

50 Ibid. iii. 690.
51 Ibid. iii. 669.

tions influenced this difficult choice, Charles had been alienated (by dislike of his second wife) from everything Teutonic,
and this dislike was shared by many influential persons at his
Court, including Cardinal Porto Carrero. The choice ultimately fell on Philip, Duke of Anjou, second grandson of
Louis XIV., who was separated from the succession by the
Dauphin and the Duke of Burgundy. Before finally deciding,
Charles consulted the Pope and obtained his approval[52] (July
1700). On the 2nd of October 1700 he signed the famous
will[53] by which he bequeathed the Spanish Empire to Philip of
Anjou. Failing him, the succession was to go to his younger
brother, the Duke of Berry; failing him, to the Archduke
Charles, and, in the last resort, to the Duke of Savoy. It was
stipulated that the Spanish inheritance should never be joined
with the crown of France.

Thus the last public act of Charles II. of Spain showed
some solicitude, not only for the future of Spain but for the
peace of Europe, and, so far from being a rash or incon-
siderate step, it had been very carefully thought out and was
probably as statesmanlike as any that could have been de-
vised in the circumstances. Charles's namesake of England is
said to have apologized for taking so long to die; Charles of
Spain, by all the rules of medical science, ought not to have
lived, and his forty years of living death earned for him the
heartfelt curses of plotting kings and diplomats. From his
father, Charles had inherited a constitutional disease; at four
years of age he was as helpless as a new-born child; at ten he
was still an infant; at thirty-five he was as decrepit as a man
of eighty. Inability to masticate or to speak properly resulted
from malformation of the mouth, causing acute indigestion;
he had constantly recurring and acute fevers; he was attacked
by epilepsy, and before his death he developed dropsy. His
only happy years were the twelve years of married life with his
first wife, Marie Louise of Orléans; with his second wife,
Marie Anne of Neuburg, he was afraid to be alone in the
same room.[54] His intense shyness and lack of resolution were
generally taken for idiocy; foreign ambassadors were perplexed by the almost uncanny invariability of his attitude when
receiving them—seated on the edge of a table, in a large and

[52] Legrelle, iii. 355-6.
[53] *Ibid*. iii. 718 ff.
[54] Legrelle, ii. 48-51.

darkened picture gallery, with only his profile visible.[55] But despite his intense physical sufferings, Charles was not devoid of good qualities of mind and spirit. His favourite amusements were chess and billiards, which required at least as much intelligence as the "heroic" pastimes of contemporary monarchs; he was intensely patriotic and religious; he was capable of forming friendships, and he had a sense of honour. Had he been endowed with health, there is reason to believe that he would have devoted himself to the interests of Spain, a country which has often responded to good government and which has always shown appreciation of the qualities of dignity and self-respect in its rulers.

His last years have a distinct pathos.[56] When it was realized in 1698 that he was slowly dying, the most extraordinary measures were taken in the hope of prolonging his life. His consort was accused of administering poison, and subjected to close surveillance; if poison was not the cause of his decline, then perhaps he was infested with devils; accordingly, monkish exorcists were let loose on the unfortunate invalid. When these failed, a notable expert in devil-taming—F. Mauro Tenda—was despatched from Vienna to Madrid, and while the royal apartments at the Escorial were thronged by a noisy rabble of ecclesiastical mountebanks, the state rooms were being rifled by the Queen and her Austrian ladies, anxious to collect as much as possible while there was still time. On the 18th of November 1699 Charles visited the tombs of his mother and first wife, prophesying that within a year he would join them. In September of the following year his condition became critical; public prayers were offered for his recovery; the miraculous image of Notre Dame d'Atocha and the hallowed remains of St. Isidore of Seville and St. Diego of Alcala were carried in public procession, and throughout Spain there was a feeling of genuine regret and disquietude that the last of the Spanish Hapsburgs was passing away. On the 1st of November 1700 died Charles *the Sufferer*, and his death removed the only remaining obstacle to a great European conflagration.

The publication of the will produced a profound sensation throughout Europe. In France opinion was at first divided

[55] For instance, see the Report by Rebenac in *Instructions données* (Spain), i. 412.

[56] For this, see Legrelle, *op. cit.* iii. 647 ff.

whether to accept it or put into force the most recent partition, but Louis decided to seize the great heritage now within his grasp. The Duke of Anjou was proclaimed king throughout the Spanish possessions as Philip V., and in April 1701 he entered his capital. At first there seemed a chance of Europe accepting the will in preference to any of the partition treaties, on Louis giving his assurance that the crowns of France and Spain would be kept apart. The Dutch were not impressed by this assurance, for they dreaded the threatened proximity of the Bourbons. In England, William III. was also sceptical, and his irritation was intensified because his share in the Partition treaties was now a matter of common knowledge, but his English subjects were not whole-heartedly committed to their monarch's policy, and while there still existed the old hatred of France, there was jealousy of the Dutch, together with a feeling that William was using English resources in order to slake his desire for revenge. In France, many were beginning to weary of war and war-taxation; Louis's dynastic ambitions were ceasing to be of absorbing interest outside Versailles, and it was well known that the French monarchy had many bitter enemies in the exiled Huguenots, some of whom were in the espionage system of England and Holland.[57] In Spain the majority were prepared to abide by the will and give Philip V. a fair trial,[58] though in some provinces, notably Catalonia, Aragon and Valencia, there were threats of separatist movements, and on the frontier was Portugal with its English sympathies. But though it is true that no European country could regard its security seriously imperilled by the settlement which Charles's will effected, the last thirty years of the seventeenth century had heaped up, among rulers and diplomatists, a great mass of grudges and jealousies, and here was an opportunity for clearing them off. Moreover, with the colonial expansion of England, France and Holland, commercial motive had definitely taken its place as a justifiable reason for European hostilities. The war of the Spanish Succession was waged nominally in order to prevent the

[57] For this see Dedieu, *Le Rôle politique des protestants français,* chs. viii. and ix.

[58] In March 1698 Stanhope (English ambassador in Madrid) had written: "the general inclination as to the succession is altogether French, their aversion to the Queen [Marie Anne of Neuburg] having set them all against her countrymen" (quoted in Legrelle, *op. cit.* ii. 161).

Bourbons from becoming too strong, a fear based on the possibility that Philip V. or his line might succeed to the French throne; its real motive was the determination of the maritime powers to prevent France acquiring commercial supremacy. It was reduced to an absurdity when, by the death of the Emperor Joseph in 1711 and the accession of Archduke Charles to the Empire, Hapsburg supremacy, based on fact, not supposition, was presented as the only alternative to Bourbon supremacy, based on a fairly remote contingency; it ended in the exhaustion of all the combatants, when Britain became almost as tired of her victories as France of her defeats. Its only legacy was another "permanent" re-shaping of the map of Europe.

It is just possible that war might have been averted and Philip of Anjou allowed to take over the succession had not Louis by his rash acts roused the jealousy of the maritime powers. On the 1st of February 1701 he caused the Parlement to register a decree whereby the rights of Philip V. and his line to the French crown were asserted,[59] though this did not necessarily imply that the crowns of France and Spain would, in the event of Philip's line succeeding, be united, since there were two princes between Philip and the succession to the French throne. A few days later Louis sent French troops into Flanders to expel the Dutch garrisons from the barrier fortresses. But the United Provinces were not prepared for war and thought to gain time by recognizing Philip V. (February 22, 1701). The French invasion of the Netherlands reacted on public opinion in England, and, though William's Tory government obliged him to express formal approval of Philip's accession (April 17, 1701), an urgent message was received in the following May from the States-General pointing out the menace of the French occupation of Flanders. This manifesto met with an enthusiastic response in England; petitions were presented urging that war should be declared; subsidies were voted by Parliament, and William was authorized to conclude treaties for the safeguarding of English interests. At the same time Louis exercised a tutelage over his grandson in Spain and dispatched French troops into the Milanese, thereby further irritating public feeling. The result of all this was the signing, on the 7th of September 1701, of the Grand Alliance of the Hague, by which the Maritime Powers pro-

[59] Vast, *Les Grands Traités*, iii. 24.

posed a partition of the Spanish possessions in the interests of the Emperor, while the latter guaranteed to assist England and Holland in safeguarding their possessions and trade. By this alliance Louis was given two months in which to negotiate; if he did not come to terms, the Allies undertook the conquest of the Low Countries (as a barrier between Holland and France) and of the Milanese (to be given to the Emperor as an imperial fief). Naples and Sicily were included in these military plans because of their important strategic position in relation to English and Dutch commerce, and it was arranged that the maritime powers were to benefit by their naval conquests in the Indies. The contracting states[60] agreed also that they would conduct peace negotiations jointly, that they would insist on the separation of the Spanish and French crowns, and that they would exclude the French from trade with the Spanish colonies. The Grand Alliance of the Hague may therefore be regarded not so much a challenge to France as the last in the long series of partition treaties. It differs, however, from preceding partitions in this, that France was not a party and that the aims of the maritime powers were explicitly avowed.

Even thus Louis had not made his position irretrievable, for there was no great national feeling behind the Grand Alliance, and the Allies might soon quarrel over the division of the spoils. But James II. died in September 1701, and, in direct contravention of the treaty of Ryswick, Louis recognized his son, the "Pretender," as James III. of England. This led to a hardening of political feeling in England, where the Whigs returned to power in December 1701. The death of William III. on the 8th of March 1702 did not end the strong anti-French feeling in England, and Louis had now to deal not merely with politicians and diplomats, but with a great nation zealous in the defence of its religion, its liberties, and the money it had invested in the Revolution settlement of 1688.

[60] They were joined by Brandenburg, which became the kingdom of Prussia in 1700. France refused to recognize this fact, but throughout the whole of the Spanish Succession war negotiations were kept up with Berlin, and Frederick I. might at any moment have been detached from the Allies. See *Instructions donnés* (Prussia), 257 ff. The subject of the Imperial grant of a crown to the Hohenzollerns (in order to procure military support) is treated in Waddington, *L'Acquisition de la couronne royale de Prusse*.

It was assumed in England that if the Stuarts were restored to England, Catholicism would be reinstated and the financial commitments of the Whigs would be repudiated. Accordingly the accession of the Stuart Queen Anne did not mark any change in the foreign policy with which England had been closely identified by William III. Republican Holland also continued the traditions of the deceased monarch, and an attempt on the part of Louis to renew negotiations broke down.[61] On the 15th of May 1702 the Emperor, England and the States-General simultaneously declared war on France, and the War of the Spanish Succession began.

The leading spirits in the Grand Alliance were Heinsius, Marlborough and Prince Eugène, who together presented a unique combination of military and diplomatic ability. Their preparations had been carefully made, for they had practically isolated France and could depend on the support of Denmark, Prussia, Hanover, the Elector Palatine, the Bishop of Münster, and a number of lesser potentates; moreover, the joint troops at their disposal amounted to a total of more than 250,000 men. In naval forces also the Allies were immeasurably superior to the French. Against this coalition France could not raise more than 200,000 men; her navy was inadequate for the defence of the world-wide Spanish Empire, and in Europe she would have to maintain the war on two fronts—the Belgian and the Italian. Even more serious was the fact that in the government of France ability was now at a discount. Louvois had been succeeded by Chamlay, Colbert by Chamillart, and Louis himself was more convinced than ever of his own powers. For allies, France could count only on the Elector of Bavaria (who was promised support in his candidature for the Empire and the government of the Spanish Netherlands, in return for which he supplied 10,000 troops); Victor Amadeus of Savoy (who went over to the Imperialists late in 1703), and Portugal (detached by an English commercial alliance in the same year). Of the French alliances, therefore, the only permanent one was the Bavarian, an alliance of some strategic value, for it provided the French with Cologne and Liége as bases for operations in Germany.

In the first few years of the war the Allies were uniformly successful in operations carried out in the bishopric of Cologne

61 *Instructions données* (Hollande), vol. ii.

and in Guelderland, but there were serious differences of opinion among them. While Marlborough was anxious to engage his armies in a pitched battle and invade France, the Dutch were cautious to the verge of timidity and were concerned only about their barrier. There were also differences of opinion whether the conquests in the Low Countries should be under Dutch or Imperial administration. Partly in consequence of these differences, French arms were not at first uniformly unsuccessful. In October 1702 Villars defeated the army of the Margrave of Baden at Friedlingen, and in September of the following year at Hoechstadt. These battles saved Bavaria from invasion, but Villars had the same complaint to make of the Elector as Marlborough of the Dutch, and because of disagreement with the Elector, Villars was recalled. In Italy the French occupation of the Milanese was rendered precarious by the defection of the Duke of Savoy to the Emperor in November 1703; a month later Portugal was detached from France by the Methuen treaty with England. In consequence of these changes, the Allies modified their aims. In 1701 they had been content with a policy of partition; they were now encouraged to aim at the dethronement of Philip V., the expulsion of France from the Spanish possessions, and the establishment of the Archduke Charles as king of Spain. Accordingly, against Bavaria, France's solitary partner, the Allies directed their efforts in the campaigns of 1704.

Crossing the Danube at Donauworth, Marlborough invaded Bavaria in July 1704 and in August joined forces with Prince Eugène. On the 13th of August the Franco-Bavarian troops, under Tallard and Maximilian Emanuel, were decisively beaten at Hoechstadt (Blenheim), the first important battle of the war. Bavaria was soon at the mercy of the invaders, and the victory was rendered more significant by its coincidence with the English capture of Gibraltar (August 4, 1704). This important conquest was followed by the landing of the Archduke Charles in Catalonia and the conquest for the Allies of Valencia and Murcia. As Philip V. was practically without troops, it seemed inevitable that he would soon lose what was left to him in Spain, and so Louis, in the winter of 1705–1706, proposed peace negotiations on the basis of a partition by which the Archduke would obtain Spain, with the title of king, while France would be content with Lorraine and a part of the Spanish Netherlands. But the Allies were now on better terms with each other than when they had started their campaigns (mainly owing to the diplomatic activities of Marlborough), and Heinsius replied to the overtures of Louis by a direct refusal (a bitter humiliation for the monarch who had spoken of the Dutch as "maggots"). Louis was to experience full retribution for the arrogance of his successful years.

Once he had a free hand, Marlborough was able to utilize those gifts of intuition, resource and concentration which make him one of the greatest generals of modern times. A period of famous battles now commenced. In May 1706 Villeroy and the Elector were in the Low Countries, and Marlborough, with 70,000 men, engaged forces with them at Ramillies. Realizing at a glance the weakness of the French position, the English general joined battle on the 23rd of May, and after a feint on the French left, he directed a crushing attack on the weakened centre, expelling the enemy from Ramillies in a flight which soon became a rout. As the battle of Blenheim had resulted in the conquest of Bavaria, so the battle of Ramillies won Belgium for the Allies. France was now reduced to the defensive and Vendôme was recalled from Italy, in order to hold the north-eastern frontier. The departure of Vendôme from Italy was followed by disaster. Late in August Victor Amadeus and Prince Eugène joined armies and fell on the French army, then engaged in an unenterprising siege of Turin. The allied generals inflicted a decisive defeat on the French, and the battle of Turin was followed by their retreat from northern Italy. In Spain the French cause met with similar disaster. Philip V. failed to retake Barcelona and was compelled, by superior forces, to abandon his capital. On the 25th of June 1706 the Archduke was proclaimed king in Madrid as Charles III. Thus in the course of one summer the French lost Belgium, the Milanese and Spain.

Of these conquests that of Spain was the most short-lived. The corrupt government and the military incompetence of Spain had blinded foreigners to the fact that even in "decadent" Spain there was such a thing as national feeling, and this was now asserted in favour of the expelled king. Spanish national sentiment was not biassed in Philip's favour, whose character was not such as to call out any feelings of devotion, but it was not forgotten that by the will of Charles II. Philip was the rightful king, and, even though Louis talked of having to abandon his grandson, Spain suddenly asserted herself in the cause of legitimacy. The Allied forces in Spain were commanded by the Earl of Peterborough—a man of brilliant gifts but unstable character—his failure to co-operate harmoniously with the Archduke Charles gave the French their opportunity. Early in August 1706 Philip was restored to his kingdom and the French general Berwick re-took Carthagena; at the same time, in the Mediterranean provinces the Allied troops were forced back on the defensive. Meanwhile Louis, continuing his attempts to negotiate with the Dutch, was reduced to such straits that he was even forced to invoke the Pope and Charles XII. of Sweden as mediators. But the Allies, inspired by Marlborough, were adamant, and made clear their determination that nothing less than the abdication of Philip V. would be accepted. French national resources were nearing breaking point, but, by a curious irony, the only part of the world which offered any hopes of salvation for the Bourbons was Spain itself. Berwick throughout the campaigns of 1707 kept the Allies in check, defeating them at Almanza (April 25) and winning back all the Mediterranean provinces except Catalonia. The substitution of Stanhope for Peterborough did not retrieve the fortunes of the Allies in Spain. In Flanders the progress of Marlborough was impeded by Vendôme and the Elector, so the events of the year 1707 encouraged Louis to hope that all was not lost.

The year 1708 opened with an attempted French landing in Scotland in favour of the Stuarts; a French fleet anchored in the Firth of Forth, but the Scots did not prove responsive —it had not been realized by the French that they had chosen the wrong point of disembarkation, and that in the west of Scotland they might have met with a very different welcome.[62] In the Low Countries the disasters of 1706 were repeated. Hoping to obtain mastery of the Scheldt, Vendôme proposed to attack Oudenarde, but he was out-marched by Marlborough and Prince Eugène, and on the 11th of July 1708 French arms suffered the disastrous defeat of Oudenarde. The invasion of France followed; in December Liége was taken by storm. This disaster caused Louis to renew his frantic efforts to obtain peace; accordingly in the spring of 1709 he offered to accept the total exclusion of Philip from the succession, to

---

[62] For an account of French proposals to effect a landing in Britain see *Les Projets de descente en Angleterre* in *Revue d'Histoire diplomatique,* xv.

interpret the Peace of Westphalia "in the German sense," to abandon the Stuarts and to give to the Dutch a barrier that would include Ypres, Menin, Lille, Tournai and Maubeuge. Difficulties at home, including the complete exhaustion of the French finances, the shortage of food due to a bad harvest and the serious waning in the man-power of France, all made Louis anxious to have peace on practically any terms, and negotiations went so far that in May the Preliminaries of the Hague were drawn up. But when Louis was asked to assist in the dethronement of his grandson by force if necessary, he showed both courage and dignity by refusing. The negotiations were again broken off, and when the harsh conditions of the Allies were made public, Louis found that he had the whole French national feeling behind him. Thus by 1709 the Spanish Succession war had become, for both France and Spain, a national war, in which their fortunes were indissolubly linked; while for the Allies it was a war of conquest and revenge, aiming at the humiliation of Louis XIV. and the elimination of France as a great commercial and maritime country.

In the campaigns of 1709 France made heroic efforts. Although Boufflers and Villars were defeated by Marlborough at Malplaquet in September, yet the losses of the Allies were so heavy that for them it was a Pyrrhic victory. The result of these losses was that France was saved from invasion. Early in the following year peace negotiations were renewed at the fortress of Gertruidenburg, the French representatives being the Maréchal d'Huxelles and the Abbé de Polignac, while the Dutch agents were Buys and Van der Dussen. The critical question was whether Louis would assist in the expulsion of Philip from Spain. The French monarch had refused to give such assistance, but the withdrawal of his troops from Spain had so alienated Philip that there was a danger of separate French negotiations with the Allies, and in consequence there was now a complete breach between Louis and his grandson. It was mainly in consequence of this, and because the prospects for France seemed hopeless, that in the summer of 1710 Louis was induced to undertake that he would assist with subsidies in the expulsion of Philip from Spain.[63] It would be unfair to judge Louis harshly for this betrayal; he honestly believed that his protégé in Madrid was fighting a lost cause,

---

[63] See Vast, op. cit. iii. 38 ff.

and for the first time in his reign he realized that his chief duty was to his country, and that what his country needed above all things was peace. It is incontestable that Torcy, the Secretary of State for War, and the French agents at Gertruidenburg did everything in their power to obtain a basis for peace negotiations, but the Dutch persisted in impossible demands. A few days after making his supreme and most abject concession Louis revoked it, broke off negotiations and declared that "it was better to make war on his enemies than on his children." Had the war ended at this time, France would have been content with humiliating terms; its prolongation was to be unfortunate for the Allies. The salvation of the French cause came from her two hereditary "enemies"—Spain and England.

Early in 1710 Charles landed in Catalonia with an army under the Austrian Stahremberg and the Englishman Stanhope. In the summer Philip was defeated at Lerida; on the 28th of September the Allies entered Madrid, while Philip had to seek refuge in Valladolid. But once more the people of Spain rallied to the cause of legitimacy, and the invaders soon found that military conquest does not always compensate for the alienation of public opinion. Now that the negotiations at Gertruidenburg had broken down (July 1710), Louis considered himself free to send military support to his grandson, and when Vendôme with 25,000 men crossed the Pyrenees, the invaders were again forced back on the defensive. In December, Stanhope and Stahremberg were decisively defeated at Brihuega and Villviciosa respectively; guerilla warfare soon reduced the Allied forces to a spectre of their former selves. These two battles were decisive in this, that they restored Spain to the Bourbons; they also had the effect of inducing the Allies to think more seriously of peace negotiations.

The situation was further influenced in favour of France by the fall of the Whigs from power in the late summer of 1710. In England the war had come to be regarded as a Whig war, benefiting only Marlborough and the army contractors; moreover, the spectacular victories of English troops on the Continent had long since ceased to stir public enthusiasm. The Lord High Treasurer—Godolphin—was nominally a Tory, but had become more dependent on the Whigs and their associates; acting in close co-operation with Marlborough, his position became more precarious as the war dragged on. He was suspected of corresponding with the Pretender, and as one of his (alleged) letters was said to be in the possession of Wharton, it was thought that he sided with the Whigs to avoid exposure. Related by marriage to Marlborough, he was a war minister in the sense that he showed great skill in procuring large war grants from parliament; when, however, the Duchess of Marlborough quarrelled with the Queen and the Duke himself lost the favour of the Court, Godolphin's solitary support was removed. Other events in England, such as the impeachment of Dr. Sacheverell, caused a great Tory revival, and in autumn of 1710 a Tory government was returned to power pledged to end a war begun by Whigs. Harley and Bolingbroke then reversed the policy of Marlborough and Godolphin; so at one stroke the most powerful member of the coalition was practically detached.

The death of the Emperor Joseph in 1711 and the election of his brother Charles further confirmed the British in their desire for peace, since there was now a danger of substituting a Hapsburg for a Bourbon menace. Hostilities, however, still continued; Marlborough remained in command of the English army in Flanders, but his powers were considerably restricted. Concurrently with these events, there was a distinct revival of France as a military power. A great nation may surprise herself by the sudden discovery of undreamt-of resources; in 1711 France seemed to renew her youth, and once more her veteran forces resumed the offensive. A French naval expedition seized Rio de Janeiro in September; in the summer of the following year France won her only great battle in the war. The Dutch and the Imperialists were doing everything possible to impede the peace negotiations then proceeding at Utrecht, and against their 130,000 men mustered for an invasion of France, Villars could dispose of only 70,000, but for once fortune favoured the French, and while Eugène was besieging Landrecies, Villars attacked the Allies at Denain on the Scheldt. The result was a complete victory for the French, a victory important, not because any immediate object was attained but for its moral effect, since it destroyed the tradition of allied invincibility and put fresh heart into a cause hitherto regarded as hopeless. The battle of Denain made possible the conclusion of peace at Utrecht.

To narrate the progress of these negotiations would be a tedious task, for delays and misunderstandings were caused by punctilios and trivialities such has had impeded the West-phalia negotiations. Peace terms having been agreed upon between Great Britain and France, the former power acted as mediator in the discussions between France and the other Allies. Only the Emperor proved intractable, and the separate treaties of France with Great Britain, Holland, Portugal, Savoy and Prussia were all signed at Utrecht on the 31st of March 1713.[64] The main terms of the settlement were as follows:

In regard to Great Britain, France recognized the Hano-verian succession, dismantled the fortifications of Dunkirk, ceded Hudson Bay, Acadia, Newfoundland and the island of St. Kitts. English restrictive tariffs against French imports were reduced to the same scale as those levied on imports from other countries; similarly, the French restrictive tariffs against English imports were readjusted in favour of England and in accordance with the tariff of 1664.[65] The renunciation of Philip V.'s claim to the French throne and of French princes to the Spanish throne was declared to be an inviolable law.[66]

To the States-General were assigned the Low Countries, to be held in trust until they had arranged the matter of their barrier with the Emperor. All French claims over Menin, Tournai, Furnes and Ypres were renounced. The Elector of Bavaria was to hold Luxemburg with Namur and Charleroi until restored to his estates. The Dutch surrendered to France Lille, Aire and Béthune.

Nice was restored to the Duke of Savoy with Oulx, Bardonnechia and Pragelata, while in exchange France acquired Barcelonnette. In addition, Victor Amadeus was promised Sicily with the title of king, and eventual succession to the Spanish throne on the failure of Philip's line.

To Portugal were ceded certain territories on the frontier of Brazil and French Guiana. The Elector of Brandenburg was confirmed in his kingship of Prussia and was given Spanish Guelderland. In exchange, the king of Prussia renounced his claim (through females) to the principality of Orange.

Neither the Emperor nor Philip had taken part in these

[64] Vast, iii. 68 ff.
[65] Treaty of Navigation and Commerce (Vast, iii. 87 ff.).
[66] Ibid., Article VI. (p. 74).

negotiations, on the ground that they could not consent to any partition of the Spanish Empire. But they found that it was hopeless to resist, and in a short time they yielded. On July 13, 1713, Philip signed a treaty with Great Britain by which he surrendered Gibraltar and Minorca, and at the same time ceded Sicily to Savoy. Peace was signed between Philip and the States-General on June 26, 1714, and with Portugal on February 16, 1715. Meanwhile the age-long struggle between Bourbon and Hapsburg had been settled by the treaty of Rastadt, signed on the 6th of March 1714.[67]

By the treaty of Rastadt France was confirmed in possession of Alsace and Strasburg, and Louis restored to the Emperor all his conquests on the right bank of the Rhine, including Breisach, Freiburg and Kehl. The Archbishop of Cologne and the Elector of Bavaria were restored to their states. France agreed to recognize the Imperial possession of Naples, the Milanese, Sardinia, the Spanish Netherlands (with Tournai, Ypres, Menin and Furnes). There still remained to be decided the question of the Dutch barrier. This was settled by the Barrier Treaty of November 1715, whereby the Emperor ceded to the Dutch Venloo and St. Michael in Guelderland, with a strip of territory on the Flemish border. The Dutch were also given the right to garrison Furnes, Knocke, Ypres, Menin, Tournai and Namur. The Scheldt was to remain closed, so that there was no danger of Antwerp rivalling Amsterdam. With these reservations the whole of the Spanish Low Countries was ceded to the Emperor. In 1720 the Emperor received Sicily from Savoy in exchange for Sardinia, and thus Austrian rule displaced Spanish rule in Italy and in Belgium.

The treaty of Utrecht provides a fitting termination to the period included in this volume. In its main lines it was a modification of the Peace of Westphalia and, like the earlier treaty, it gave concrete expression to the doctrine that states can be transferred like chattels without reference to the opinions of the inhabitants. The negotiators were untroubled by the fact that Italy, Germany and Belgium still remained mere geographical expressions, and seem to have assumed that by a partition of the Spanish Empire between the claimants the balance of power was restored and the peace of Europe once

[67] Vast, iii. 162 ff.

more established. But though based on nothing higher than the conventional diplomatic traditions of the Ancien Régime, the treaty of Utrecht was not without its advantages. It averted the menace of a Bourbon Empire. Indirectly it benefited Spain, because it removed from her control European territories that had involved commitments far beyond her military or financial resources, and when the Pyrenees became the real frontier, Spain was able to devote her revenues to national needs rather than to European ambitions.

But the treaty looks to the future rather than the past. Savoy benefits materially and becomes the strongest independent power in Italy, while the destinies of Germany are placed in the eager hands of Prussia. The decline of Holland as a European and colonial power is foreshadowed, and Great Britain stands out as the great maritime power of the future. The acquisition of Newfoundland and Acadia was to be the beginning of a great struggle for supremacy in North America; in the possession of Gibraltar was one of the most important links of the future British Empire. Colonial rivalry now displaces dynastic ambition in the Chanceries of Europe, and the young, vigorous states such as Prussia break down the old monopoly which had confined hegemony to a few families.

The great wars which have been summarized in this chapter were associated with a notable development of national consciousness, particularly in the two protagonists, France and England. During his years of triumph and ascendancy, that is, between 1665 and about 1690, Louis presided over a civilization which must be ranked among the highest in the world, a civilization which, by intelligent patronage, he did much to promote. He befriended Molière, encouraged Racine, read the MS. of Boileau's *Art poétique*, in which the laws of taste were formulated, and stimulated writers so diverse as La Fontaine, Bossuet and Madame de Sévigné. Whatever may be our views about his character or policy, we must admit that Louis was the Maecenas of this, the classic period of French Literature. In pictorial and decorative art the results were less fortunate, but Versailles still stands as the majestic relic of a great age. Within his own reign, however, there was a change. After 1690, in the nearly eighteen years of warfare with England, the temper of the Court became more sombre and pietistic; all the great men were either dead, as Molière, or almost sterile, as Racine; only Couperin, the organist and composer, re-

The Territories of
the Austrian Hapsburgs

Scale of Miles

0   50 100   200   300   400   500

IRELAND

GREAT BRITAIN

UNITED PROVINCES

AUSTRIAN NETHERLANDS

Paris

FRANCE

SPAIN

Madrid

PORTUGAL

Lisbon

mained, the one man of genius at Versailles. As the reign drew to its melancholy close, French genius became more critical, as in Fénelon, or even more humanitarian, as in the Abbé de Saint-Pierre, but it was no longer directed by the king. This change in the direction and temper of French culture was to last throughout what remained of the Ancien Régime. In England also these wars had a stimulating effect, but the sequence was very different. The dogged defence of William's war was followed by the brilliant achievements of British arms in Anne's reign, achievements which served to make Britain a world power. The Augustan Age of English Literature would be meaningless without this background.

Chapter 7

The Absolutism of Louis XIV

THE REIGN OF Louis XIV. is a microcosm in which may be seen two generations of France and Europe, a microcosm revolving round the personality of one man who chose for his emblem the Sun and for his motto "Nec pluribus impar," implying that he was not unequal to the task of lighting up and energizing other worlds. It was indeed a great reign for which only the infinities of space could provide a simile. At a time when Englishmen were experimenting with devices for making kingship fool-proof, Frenchmen were basking in the warm sunshine of divine-right monarchy, and the truths of Christianity were receiving daily confirmation from the career of a divinely-inspired King. While elsewhere rulers were being hedged by contracts and earthly stipulations, in France these restraints were being removed, and priest combined with courtier to sanctify the cult of Bourbonism, which had the enthusiastic support of the most intelligent race in Europe.

Louis XIV. was born in 1638. From his earliest years the eldest son of Louis XIII. and Anne of Austria was carefully educated for the post he was intended to fill; there are clearer records of the instruction given to the boy prince than can be found for any other monarch.[1] Specimens of his boyish handwriting have been preserved, and one of his copy-book

[1] See Lacour-Gayet, *L'Éducation politique de Louis XIV*. I am indebted to this book for the substance of this and the two succeeding paragraphs.

headings is "L'hommage est deub aux rois: ils font ce que leur plaist." His earliest tutor, Philip Fortin, Sieur de la Hoquette, compiled in 1645 for the seven-year old child a *Catéchisme Royale* in which he asserted that royal power is derived solely from religious sanctions and is intended mainly to prevent innovations in church and state. Hence persons of doubtful opinions should be denied the use of paper and ink, while atheists should be hanged without compunction. But this book contained strictures on malversation by ministers of state; consequently Mazarin deemed it advisable to take it away from Louis. Fortin was more successful with his *Testament de conseils fidèles d'un bon père à ses enfants*, which was published in 1648 and went through sixteen editions. In order that the path to learning might be a royal one, special playing cards were designed, from the contemplation of which Louis was invited to assimilate a knowledge of History, Geography and Mythology. Manuals of Geography, Rhetoric, Ethics and Logic were composed for his perusal by La Mothe le Vayer (all extremely dull), and the ease with which the custodians of the prince's education rushed into print may have tempted Claude Joly to produce his unofficial *Recueil de maximes . . . pour l'institution du roy contre la fausse et pernicieuse politique du Cardinal Mazarin*, in which he propounded the theory that kings are subordinate to law. The book was burned by the common hangman.

Louis was taught Latin by the historian Péréfixe, and read Caesar's *Commentaries*. He may also have read *Don Quixote*, the *Roman Comique* of Scarron and the *Mémoires* of Commines. Mézeray's *History of France*, published in 1643, was read to him at night by his *valet-de-chambre* in order to send him to sleep.[2] In addition, he was taught Italian, Mathematics and the "Playing Cards" (probably when the text-books failed), but he was never a man of education in any sense of the term. Nevertheless there is no truth in Saint Simon's statement that Louis could barely read or write.[3]

The prince was brought up in habits of strict external piety by his mother; in addition to his tutors, he had a governor (Villeroy), who was socially distinct from the pedagogues and concerned mainly with the prince's deportment and outdoor life. The only bias which Louis is said to have derived from

[2] Lacour-Gayet, *op. cit.* 112.
[3] *Mémoires*, xii. 13.

his early education was a hatred of Protestants. On his death-bed Mazarin is reported to have advised Louis to rule by himself and to suppress the Jansenists—advice faithfully carried out. Throughout these early years the achievements of his grandfather, Henry IV., were constantly held up to him as a model; after 1643 the names of Louis XIII. and Richelieu were seldom mentioned. Such were the chief formative influences on the monarch whose rule began with the death of Mazarin in March 1661.

More perhaps than any other monarch in modern history, Louis believed that kingship is a highly specialized occupation requiring constant application and a shrewd knowledge of men.[4] Although himself endowed with mediocre abilities, he achieved real eminence in a profession that makes exacting demands. His days were passed in a routine of official business so regular that with the help of an almanac it was possible to tell the time of day from his acts. Illness did not interfere with his attendance at the council board, for his advisers could meet in his bedroom; even the death of the heir to the throne caused only a slight interruption in the course of official duties. In his view, the monarch sees his country from an eminence that can be shared by no one else; viewing, as he does, the needs of the state from a universal aspect, he is best qualified to decide between every competing interest. In his *Memoirs*, written specially for the Dauphin, he noted this prerogative of monarchy—"holding as it were the place of God, we seem to participate in his wisdom as in his authority; for instance, in what concerns discernment of human character, allocation of employments and distribution of rewards."[5] Associated with this view of kingship was Louis's habit of asking questions and discounting the replies by what he knew of the character of his informant. His aptitude for assimilating useful information and utilizing it as his own is a characteristic often found among men called upon to act rather than think, but whether this can be considered genius—as many writers maintain—is always debatable. It should be added that Louis inherited his best ministers, replacing them on their death by inferior men.

---

[4] "Il s'est fait un art de régner, moins par science et par réflexion, que par les conjonctures et par l'habitude" (Spanheim, *Relation de la cour de France en 1690*, ed. 1882, p. 7).

[5] *Œuvres de Louis XIV*, ed. Grouvelle, ii. 283.

With this conception of his prerogatives, it was not likely that Louis would feel himself fettered by the shadowy mass of obsolete claims and inconsistent principles known as the French constitution. The Parlement, save as a judicial body, had no share in his scheme of government; its record of proceedings during the Fronde was destroyed, and in 1665 it lost even the title of sovereign court. There was no question of summoning the States-General until the later part of the reign, when the Allies in the Spanish Succession war demanded that Philip V.'s renunciation of the French throne should be made before the Estates of the Realm, but Louis would consent to no more than a meeting of the Assembly of Notables. The nobility and the church were excluded from all but nominal functions in the administration, nor until he came under the influence of Madame de Maintenon does Louis appear to have been definitely influenced by his Jesuit confessor, and the only exception to his rule of excluding the nobility from the government was the giving of ministerial office to the Duke of Beauvilliers. Industry, probity and inventiveness, rather than personality or social distinction, were the qualities required by Louis in his ministers; only thus could he obtain full credit for the originality and brilliance which popular opinion attributed to his acts.

Louis exercised a personal rule, assisted by the four great councils—the Conseil d'Etat, the Conseil des Dépêches, the Conseil des Finances and the Conseil Privé; and by less permanent councils, such as the Council of Commerce, established in 1664 on the model of that which Henry IV. had set up; and the Council of Conscience, consisting of the Monarch, his Confessor and the Archbishop of Paris, to determine the more important questions concerning collation to benefices. It was this last council which decided on the Revocation of the Edict of Nantes. But the most important institution of Louis XIV.'s reign was not a council but an office—that of secretary of state. We have already indicated how this office was originally subordinate and unimportant; in the second half of the seventeenth century it was filled by some of the greatest administrators in the history of France. Among the secretaries of state for Foreign Affairs at this period were de Brienne, father and son, 1647–1663; Hugues de Lionne, 1663–1671; Pomponne, 1671–1679; Colbert de Croissy[6], brother of the

[6] See *ante*, ch. 7, n. 30.

great Colbert, 1679–1696; Colbert de Torcy, son of Croissy, 1699–1716. Notable among the secretaries of state for war were Michel le Tellier, 1643–1677, who was assisted by his son Louvois from 1662; Louvois, 1677–1691; Barbézieux, son of Louvois, 1691–1701, and Chamillart, 1701–1709. Of the secretaries of state for marine were Colbert, 1669–1683; his son Seignelay, 1683–1690; Pontchartrain, 1690–1699; followed by his son, 1699–1715. The secretaryship of the Maison du Roi was held by Colbert and his son Seignelay in succession from 1669 to 1690; by Pontchartrain from 1690 to 1693 and by his son from 1693 to 1699.

From these lists it will be seen that there were two great official families in Louis's reign—that of Louvois and that of Colbert—who between them practically monopolized all the important administrative offices prior to 1690. Their periods of office frequently overlapped, so that son or nephew would sometimes serve an apprenticeship before taking over his duties. It will be noticed also that one person might hold several secretaryships, as did Colbert, whose multiplicity of functions gave him a unique opportunity for acquiring a first-hand knowledge of the economic and financial conditions of the country. The link between these administrators and the provinces was in the post of intendant, which at this period was sometimes filled by men of ability and reputation, devoting themselves to the interests of the province committed to their charge. Ever since Richelieu had revived the office, the commissions of the intendants had become wider, until in Louis XIV.'s reign they were almost boundless. They presided over a court of appeal, adjudicating on disputed questions of justice and finance; they regulated agriculture, industry, communications, police and markets; they saw to the engagement and billeting of troops, supervised municipal administration, regulated Universities and Academies, and acted as Poor Law officials, sanitary inspectors, tax collectors and custodians of local archives. Colbert allowed them to search for valuable manuscripts in their spare time.

For convenience of treatment, the absolutism of Louis XIV. may be considered in four separate parts according as it concerned (I.) Economic and Industrial Control; (II.) The Church; (III.) The Court and Society; (IV.) Public Opinion. This sequence is not intended to be chronological, and is used here only for clearness of treatment.

I. *Economic and Industrial Control.* As the French armies were re-formed by Louvois, so finance and commerce were re-organized by John Baptiste Colbert. Son of a draper of Rheims, Colbert had been trained for a commercial career, but having been engaged in the employment of Michel le Tellier[7] and of Mazarin, he was recommended by the latter for the king's service. In character he was conscientious and industrious, with a love of order and definition; ruthless in pursuit of his object, and convinced that the right rules properly enforced will create industry and abundance where previously there had been idleness and want. He had some legal training; his reform and unification of the civil procedure by the *Ordonnance Civile* of 1667 entitles him to be considered a jurist. It is characteristic that his most permanent work is embodied in legal codes. His part in revealing the malversations of Fouquet in 1661 brought him into prominence, and the disgrace of the Superintendent of Finance (who was imprisoned for life in the fortress of Pignerol) preceded his entry into the Conseil des Finances. In 1665 he became Controller-General of Finance, and four years later added to these functions two of the four secretaryships of state—those of Marine and Maison du Roi. He had thus greater responsibilities than any other of Louis's officials, and it was to him, more than to any one else, that the great economic reconstruction of Louis's reign is due.

The long trial of Fouquet had brought into clear prominence the many abuses in a financial system never really purified by Sully, and completely corrupt in the administration of Richelieu and Mazarin. Colbert arrested for a time the progress of malversation and waste. Though he effected no drastic change in the system which made these evils inevitable, he yet brought into use many hitherto undeveloped resources, and so made possible the costly wars of Louis XIV. As early as 1659 he had outlined a scheme of financial reform intended to restore order in the national finances by indicting embezzlers before a judicial tribunal, reducing the cost of tax-collecting, making the *taille* more equitable and abolishing useless offices.[8] Such a tribunal was established in 1661 and continued its operations for four years; it encouraged the delation of offenders

[7] 1603–1685. Appointed secretary of state for war in 1643; father of Louvois.

[8] For this see Neymarck, *Colbert et son temps*, i. 43 ff.

by promising to the informant a proportion of the fine, and in these four years this tribunal exacted a heavy toll from delinquents. Colbert's business experience enabled him to reform the government system of book-keeping, and the national finances were now accounted for in audits that were serious investigations instead of pre-arranged formalities. A general cash-book was used for recording gross receipts and payments, while in two ledgers were kept accounts of the details of receipts and expenses. Monthly reports made possible a comparison with the same period of the preceding year, and the Budget became, as in Sully's time, a full balance-sheet, not a statistical anthology. Many useless offices and expensive charges were suppressed; some discontent, however, was caused by the redemption of *rentes*, not at the purchase price, but at the lower price prevailing after 1639.

Colbert tried to make the *taille* a more equitable tax. He effected a slight adjustment whereby the Pays d'Etats paid a larger proportion than before, though the Pays d'Elections still had to bear the brunt of this levy. Claims of immunity from the *taille* on the ground of office or patent of nobility were subjected to strict scrutiny; persons having ten children were exempted altogether, and newly-married couples were given preferential treatment. An effort was made to readjust the *taille réelle* on a new assessment of property, but this had only a partial success. The farming system was retained, but where there was evidence of the *fermier* having obtained too favourable a bargain from the state, his concession was annulled and renewed only on terms more favourable to the treasury. By such means an approximation was reached between the gross and the net annual revenues, the difference being fair cost of collection and administration. Nevertheless the scarcely interrupted campaigns of Louis XIV. taxed the resources of France very heavily, and before his death in 1683 Colbert had to increase the national debt by the creation of additional *rentes* (at six per cent) and the sale of offices and honours.

Thus far, however, Colbert had done little more for Louis than Sully for Henry IV. He was well aware of the reforms effected by his Huguenot predecessor, and regarded Henry's reign as a model to be copied but not surpassed. The Council of Commerce, established in 1664 and dissolved in 1667, was a revival of that established in the early years of the century, and Colbert set himself the task of completing some of the schemes launched by the first Bourbon king. The term Mercantilism has been used by later ages to describe the principles of economics on which Colbert acted; but it should be recalled that the term was adopted, mainly for purposes of contrast by an age thinking in terms of Free Trade and *laissez-faire*, and so has less novelty for an age accustomed to rigid control and a planned economy. Nevertheless there were certain distinctive principles widely accepted throughout western Europe; thus the old view that agriculture is the one essential industry for a country was being displaced by the theory that, while the state should be self-supporting, it should attempt to derive its wealth from native industry and exports.[9] On behalf of this doctrine it was urged that a limit may be reached after which agricultural enterprise ceases to be productive, whereas the possibilities of industry are almost boundless. This economic doctrine was formulated clearly for the first time by an Italian economist, Antonia Serra, in his *Short Treatise on the means of bringing Gold and Silver into Countries where there are no Mines* (1613). Similar arguments are to be found in a treatise on Political Economy by Montchrétien.[10] The fundamental principle of Mercantilism is that, as the precious metals constitute wealth, and since there is always a definite amount of bullion in circulation, it is the interest of each country to acquire as much as possible of that fixed fund. From this it was deduced that national prosperity must be at the expense of foreigners, and so aggressive war found some justification, since it was assumed always that military success brings direct advantage at the expense of the enemy. In a sense, therefore, Mercantilism was Protective, but it tended also to be aggressive, because it emphasized only the exclusive and competitive elements in the economic relations of states.

But it should be noted that Mercantilism is a loose term, its connotation varying somewhat with period and country; here we are concerned only with the practical applications made by Colbert. In this respect there was a conflict between his theory and practice. In a Memoir drawn up for Mazarin in 1651 he had defined the two requisites for the development of French overseas commerce as safety and liberty; by safety, he meant that French vessels should be free from the menace of piracy and their cargoes from the danger of confiscation

---

[9] See C. W. Cole, *French mercantilist doctrines before Colbert.*

[10] Montchrétien de Watteville, *Traité de l'économie politique* (1615), ed. Funck-Brentano (1889).

in foreign ports; by liberty, he meant that the country (England) providing the best market for French wines and silks should abandon its protective imposts against these imports, so that trade between the two countries should be encouraged.[11] In theory, therefore, and so far as England was concerned, Colbert was a free-trader. In 1669 he busied himself with a proposed treaty of commerce with England on the basis of equal treatment by each of the imports of the other, but this proposal came to nothing, because the French minister insisted that all English manufactured articles imported into France should be required to undergo the same rigid tests of material, size and workmanship as were imposed on the native articles. To abandon this principle would, in Colbert's opinion, be to surrender all his economic reforms. On this point the negotiations broke down; Colbert would not give up his cherished regulations even in return for the advantage of free trade with England.[12] Nevertheless it was estimated in 1678 that the balance of trade as between France and England was in favour of France to the extent of three and a half million livres,[13] and it was held that so long as France could maintain this annual inflow of bullion, so long would she be an aggressive military state. It has already been noticed that the tariff of 1667 was intended primarily to injure the Dutch, who controlled about four-fifths of the carrying trade of western Europe, and the general conclusion to which one is forced is that, while in some respects Colbert was in advance of his contemporaries, he had to resort to their methods. These consisted in exclusive protection and regulation of home industries and restrictive tariffs against the foreigner. The granting of monopolies was part of the same scheme; Colbert hoped that the French East India and West India Companies founded in 1664 would contest the maritime supremacy of England and Holland. Similarly, colonies were regarded primarily as sources of raw material; beyond a certain point, initiative in the overseas possessions must be repressed, since there was a danger of colonies becoming commercial rivals and so injuring the mother country.

At home, Colbert's work was creative as well as adminis-

[11] Neymarck, *Colbert et son temps,* i. Appendix I.

[12] *Ibid.,* i. 288.

[13] Quoted from a MS. Memoir of Van Beuningen in Vast, *Les Grands Traités,* ii. 66, note.

trative. He assisted the agriculturist by the more equitable assessment of the *taille*, reduction of the price of salt, and by subsidies for the scientific breeding of stock and horses; while in the provinces allotted to him as a secretary of state he reclaimed marshes and encouraged the landlords to interest themselves in agricultural pursuits.[14] To provide the large supplies of timber required for French shipbuilding, he reorganized the administration of the state forests by an Ordinance of 1669 and greatly increased the revenue from this source. This, however, was not maintained, because timber from the state forests was afterwards bought by local "rings" which kept down the price for themselves and increased it for the shipbuilders.

Colbert's greatest achievements, however, were neither in finance nor in agriculture but in the encouragement and direction of industry. He subsidized shipbuilding, hoping that eventually native products would be carried exclusively in French ships, and he had visions of a great French colonial empire. Holland was the most serious rival, and in order to ruin Dutch prosperity, four things seemed to Colbert essential—to restore old manufactures, create new ones, obtain markets abroad by developing the mercantile marine and the navy, and improve agriculture so that food should be cheap and wages low. His minute regulation of industry was therefore part of a great and carefully-planned scheme. The numerous edicts passed on his initiative were intended to secure definite standards of size and quality in such manufactured articles as cloth; both raw material and workmanship were brought within the scope of his legislation. The export of wool and flax was prohibited; the regulations of the gilds and commercial corporations were subjected to government scrutiny, their exclusiveness being threatened by the licensing of new associations. In 1673 a great Ordinance of Commerce was promulgated, providing a complete commercial code which laid down definite rules for apprenticeship, contracts, bankruptcy and consular jurisdiction; it replaced a great mass of local custom and remained in force until the Revolution. Moreover, just as Henry IV. had circulated an official text-book on silk culture, so Colbert printed a series of practical instructions for the dyeing of wool and the preparation of the ingredients necessary for this purpose. A civic stamp was affixed only to such bales of cloth as

[14] Neymarck, *op. cit*. i. 309 ff.

satisfied the government inspectors, but in some cases these measures tended to repress rather than encourage industry, for manufacturers were often irritated, and the wooden standards so rigidly enforced took little account of the law of supply and demand or changes in fashion. A contemporary[15] expressed the general opinion when he said, "Monsieur Colbert a épuisé la matière des réglements."

The most successful period in Colbert's activities was 1664–1672, when he revived the manufacture of cloth, linen, leather, silk and tapestry manufactures[16] which had been inaugurated by Henry IV. but shamefully neglected by Richelieu and Mazarin. New arsenals and foundries supplied the needs of the armies, while the ports were animated by the revived ship-building industry. Colbert used foreign, even Dutch, assistance in order that the most improved methods might be used in the cloth industry. At Carcassonne the making of cloth was directed by Dutch experts, and at Abbeville, van Robais, a Dutch capitalist, gave employment and instruction to a large number of employees. It is noteworthy that these foreigners were exempted from the provisions of the Revocation of the Edict of Nantes, but they left France nevertheless. In other industries there was the same use of expert assistance from outside. Venetian workmen from the glass-works of Murano were established in Paris in the year 1665 in order to teach the art of glass-blowing, and women workers from Burano settled in France for the purpose of teaching the making of Venetian lace. The hope that French glass and lace would be as much sought after as the Venetian products was doomed to disappointment, one reason for which may have been that the highly technical crafts favoured by Colbert required some kind of factory or workshop system, and at this time the domestic system was universal in France. It was for this reason that the experiment of lace-making on a large scale in Auxerre had to be abandoned, for there were strong and not altogether unreasonable objections against the introduction of factory organization. This system was, however, introduced with some success in the manufacture of tapestry and artistic furniture. In 1667 Colbert established the great tapestry school and workshop at the Hôtel des Gobelins under the direction of the

[15] Quoted in G. Martin, *La Grande Industrie sous le règne de Louis XIV,* 157.
[16] Neymarck, *op. cit.* i. 236 ff.

artist Le Brun, and it is still possible to admire the beauty of the results in the furnishing of Versailles and in the exhibits of various museums. But while this period is famous for some craftsmanship of superlatively fine quality, it remains true that Colbert gave an artificial impetus to several enterprises not adapted to the French genius and needing only the winds of natural competition to uproot them. The outbreak of the Dutch war marked the end of many such schemes.

After 1673 Colbert was displaced in the royal favour by Louvois, a change disastrous for France. Louvois pandered to the worst instincts of Louis XIV., and within a few years most of the benefits accruing from Colbert's reforms were lost. The climax came in 1685 with the Revocation of the Edict of Nantes, which, whatever may be said of its moral aspect, was disastrous for the economic welfare of the nation. The Huguenots were the most industrious section of the nation, providing both shrewd capitalists and skilled workmen; when they were forced to leave, they took these assets with them to England, Holland, Switzerland and Brandenburg. This was accompanied by a speedy falling off in the foreign demand for French manufactured articles. Thanks to the exiles, a new impetus was given to the English silk industry; Holland made her own stockings, hats, taffetas and silks; the manufacture of wool and silk was commenced at Geneva, and Denmark began to make her own glass. By his expulsion of the Huguenots Louis ruined the reconstructive schemes of Colbert and made a valuable present to his enemies.

The economic condition of France in the later years of Louis XIV.'s reign presents a melancholy picture.[17] Colbert's successors, Pontchartrain, Chamillart and Desmarets, had little financial ability and no enthusiasm for the development of industry; they did not have the unique opportunities and knowledge which their predecessor had derived from his multifarious duties; they were courtiers rather than administrators. Many of the old abuses against which Colbert had striven now reasserted themselves in an exaggerated form. In 1695 Vauban wrote his *Projet de capitation*, in which he showed how the *taille* had fallen into such a state of corruption that "the angels

[17] For this see Vuïtry, *Le Désordre des finances à la fin du règne de Louis XIV;* Beaulieu, *Les Gabelles sous Louis XIV,* and Martin, *op. cit.* 252 ff.

themselves could not reform it," and in his *Dîme royale*[18] (1707) he claimed that a tenth part of the population was reduced to begging. To remedy this, he proposed that all the direct taxes should be abolished in favour of a universal capitation tax of one-tenth, with no exemptions whatever. Such a tax was imposed in 1710, but, owing to exemptions purchased by clergy, corporations and the Pays d'États, it gave a disappointing return. Boisguilbert in his *Factum de la France* (1706) stated that the peasants on whom devolved the invidious duty[19] of collecting the *taille* spent more time in the prisons than in their homes. He proposed that the *taille* should be reassessed, that it should be levied on every one, and that any deficit should be borne by a tax on chimneys. With whatever differences of detail, the writers of the time were agreed in this, that France, during the Spanish Succession war, was reduced to a state of poverty and misery barely paralleled in the tragic annals of the French peasantry. The taxes were heavier and more inequitable than before; the old opportunities for malversation were re-introduced, and practically all the new industries introduced by Colbert were swept away. It is characteristic that the only things retained were his codes, ordinances, regulations and inspectors, things which could be understood and respected by a pedantic and fussy administration, incapable of comprehending the spirit and initiative that had inspired the schemes of Colbert.

II. *The Church.* The absolutism of Louis may be studied in his attitude, first, to the French church; second, to the Papacy; and third, to the Huguenots. His treatment of the Jansenists and Quietists is dealt with in another chapter.

In order to understand the position of the French church at this time it is necessary to explain what is meant by the Gallican tradition in France. During the Wars of the League, the *Politique* party had included among their demands the restoration of the great Pragmatic Sanction of Bourges (1438), the Magna Carta of French ecclesiastical liberties, in which were embodied many of the most advanced doctrines enunciated at the Councils of Constance and Basle. Before the end of the

[18] See M. Vignes, *Les Origines et les destinées de la dixme royale de Vauban.*
[19] These were the elected *asséeurs.* See *ante*, ch. 1, n. 56.

fifteenth century the Pragmatic Sanction had been bartered away by arrangement between the French monarchy and the Papacy; it was definitely annulled by the Concordat of Bologna (1516), by which, in return for the restoration of several papal revenues, Francis I. acquired the right of nominating to benefices and bishoprics, though the old formality of election by the cathedral chapters still survived. Although the doctrinal canons of the Council of Trent were accepted by France, the disciplinary decrees were never officially introduced, and so the counter-Reformation did not affect France as it affected Poland, Portugal and some of the Italian states, where the full claims of the revived papacy were accepted and enforced, whether by the Jesuits or by the Inquisition. By the end of the sixteenth century there was expressed, by several intelligent Frenchmen, a feeling that there had existed in France at some remote but historical epoch (the age of Clovis was sometimes mentioned) a national church—Catholic but not Roman—under a constitutional monarchy; and on this assumption it was argued that in all but spiritual matters the French monarchy should be independent of the papacy.

From this starting-point there gradually developed three types of Gallicanism—parliamentary, episcopal and royal. Of these the first was the most extreme and would not have stopped short at schism; the second was the most vacillating because, while some bishops like Zamet of Langres and Bossuet of Meaux welcomed a theory which would, in practice, have freed their jurisdiction from the encroachment of foreign orders having Rome for headquarters, yet many bishops felt a divided allegiance between king and pope; the third, or royal, was politic, in so far as its prerogatives might be enhanced by the application of such principles. In the earlier part of the seventeenth century Gallicanism was widely accepted in theory, but the papacy was not challenged.[20] By the *appel comme d'abus* a person, aggrieved by the decision of an ecclesiastical court, or by the enforcing of a rescript obtained from Rome, could appeal to the Parlement and obtain stay of execution, a privilege considered the most effective rampart against clerical interference with the liberty of the subject. When it is considered also that in the seventeenth century the

[20] There is a good general account of Gallicanism in seventeenth-century France in *Instructions données* . . . (Rome), ii. Introduction.

pope had only a very small effective share in collation to benefices, that he drew little revenue from France, and that the
only real hold of the papacy on the French church was in the
bulls of institution which confirmed the royal nominations to
bishoprics and benefices, it will be seen that the Gallican movement was not an attack on material abuses, but rather a protest
against the intellectual subservience implied by the acceptance
of all the claims which, in theory at least, the papacy might
assert and attempt to enforce. But though it involved no material objects, it was a powerful movement nevertheless. It inspired some bishops to reorganize their dioceses and deal themselves with complaints of heresy and licentiousness; it attracted
the monarch by the extension which it gave to his prerogatives,
and it reinvigorated the Parlement into political activities which
culminated in the expulsion of the Jesuits from France in
1762. It was one of the most important factors in the development of the conception of the secular and absolutist state.

Thus by the time of the accession of Louis XIV. there
existed in France a very considerable body of opinion which
regarded the church of France as national, not œcumenic, having for its head not the pope but the king. What Henry VIII.
had already done for England, Louis might do for France,
especially as he had at his doors an important papal possession,
Avignon, which might be annexed at any time, and especially
also as the popes with whom he had to deal were mostly
deficient in ability or prestige. The first assertion of the Gallican theory made by Louis XIV. was in an edict of 1673
declaring the *régale* to be universal except in those dioceses
which had purchased exemption. The *régale* was an old privilege of the French monarchy, whereby the revenues of a
vacant see were paid to the king (temporal *régale*) and during
the vacancy the king could appoint to benefices within the
gift of the vacant bishopric (spiritual *régale*). This double
régale did not apply everywhere in France; many bishoprics in
Languedoc were free from it, and elsewhere exemptions had
been purchased; indeed, the edict of 1673 was simply part of
the legislation emanating from Colbert, intended to sweep
away anomalies and exceptions. But the question was one of
principle, not money. The revenues from vacant bishoprics
were, in the seventeenth century, almost invariably applied to
defray the expenses necessary for the administration of the
diocese, and in 1673 it was the spiritual *régale* that was chiefly
in question. Little might have been heard on the matter had not

two bishops, Caulet of Pamiers and Pavillon of Alet (both in Languedoc) resolutely resisted the decree, a resistance complicated by the fact that both bishops were suspected of Jansenist sympathies and were supported by the Jansenists, who thus came forward as the defenders of episcopal rights and the enemies of ecclesiastical innovations. Innocent XI. took up the defence of the two bishops and refused to compromise, although in 1682 Louis offered to accept the disciplinary decrees of the Council of Trent if the papacy would give its approval to the edict of 1673. The death of one of the bishops did not terminate the controversy. The diocese of Pamiers was administered by episcopal deputies who disputed control with the vicars appointed by the king, and when Innocent threatened to excommunicate anyone instituted by Louis to benefices in the diocese of Pamiers, the dispute assumed a more serious turn. Was the king empowered, as custodian of the temporalities of the French church, to institute duly qualified persons to benefices or must this always, in the last resort, be a papal prerogative?

The whole question of the relations between the French church and the papacy was now at stake, and early in the year 1682 the question was discussed at a general assembly of the French clergy convened for this purpose. Inspired mainly by Bossuet, the Assembly defined Louis's policy in the four Gallican Articles. These were as follows:

1. Kings are not subject to ecclesiastical jurisdiction in temporal matters.
2. Popes are supreme in spiritual matters, but the French church does not hold with those who contest the validity of the decrees of the Council of Constance.
3. The canons of the church and the rules and customs admitted by France and the Gallican church are to be the rules guiding the relations between the papacy and France.
4. Although the pope has the principal part in questions of doctrine, and although his decrees concern the whole church, yet his judgement is not irreformable, unless it is backed up by the approval of the church.

Of these, the first is a clear statement to which objection could hardly have been taken. The second, in a negative way, revives the important theory of the superiority of General

Councils enunciated by the Council of Constance, a theory questioned by the canonists and repudiated by the papacy. The third is, perhaps intentionally, vague and badly framed; for while "the canons of the church" formed a definite body of jurisprudence, no one could say what were the "rules and customs admitted by France and the Gallican church." The fourth likewise employs a vague phrase—"the principal part in questions of doctrine"—and may be considered a logical consequence of the theory implied in the second. It would be considered heresy to-day, but in the seventeenth century papal infallibility was not enforced as a dogma and was denied by many Catholics. To sum up. Of these four articles, the first was barely contested; the second revived, in an indirect way, an old revolutionary doctrine; the third brought something new into the controversy—"the rules and customs admitted by France and the Gallican church"; and the fourth definitely denied a dogma on which Catholic opinion was then divided. On the whole, the fourth was the most important because the least indefinite; its acceptance rendered nugatory in France all papal decrees of which the Assembly of the French clergy —that is, Louis XIV.—did not approve.

Bossuet was soon disappointed in his hope that Rome would accept the four Gallican Articles. Innocent XI. made the controversy more acute by refusing bulls of institution to all the clergy who had taken part in the Assembly of 1682 and were subsequently nominated by the king to bishoprics or benefices. Louis replied by declining to ask for such bulls on behalf of those nominees to bishoprics who had *not* taken part in the Assembly, and if the deadlock[21] had continued, there would eventually have been no canonically instituted bishops in France. Even the French Jesuits supported Louis, though this may have been due to the well-known dislike entertained of their order by Innocent XI. Though Bossuet took up his pen in defence of the Articles, Louis's religious scruples would not let him rest, and he was at last induced to apply for a bull on behalf of Madame de Maintenon's confessor, whom he had nominated to the bishopric of Chartres. By 1693 the acute stage in the conflict had been safely passed, and in an official letter to the pope the Assembly declared that it regarded as

[21] The correspondence illustrating this will be found in Mention, *Documents relatifs aux rapports du clergé avec la royauté* (1682–1705). The most complete monograph is that by Michaud, *Louis XIV et Innocent XI.*

unsaid anything conflicting with the ecclesiastical prerogative of the papacy. Louis personally signified that the Articles would not be insisted on, and in return for this the pope gave his approval to the extension of the *régale* in France. Thus Louis had won his initial point and had not formally abolished the Gallican Articles. It was held then, as now, that the legislative sanction required to annul a law must be at least equal to the legislative sanction which had enacted the law, and Louis well knew that a letter cannot destroy an edict passed by the Assembly of the French clergy and registered by Parlement.[22] French Gallicanism was only testing its strength, and the real conflict was deferred till 1713, when the issue of the bull *Unigenitus* brought into play forces which even Louis himself could not control.

Gallicanism was not the only cause of friction between king and papacy. Throughout his long reign there were incidents, often petty in themselves, which very nearly led to a schism. The first of these[23] occurred in 1662, and arose from a dispute between the Duke de Créqui, French ambassador in Rome, and Pope Alexander VII., on the subject of ambassadorial immunities. Créqui, a man of rash and haughty temperament, made a quarrel inevitable by insisting on the unlimited extension of ambassadorial franchises in Rome, so that not only the Embassy in the Palazzo Farnese, but a considerable district in the vicinity, was removed from the jurisdiction of the papal police. In this way ruffians who happened to have letters from the French Embassy were able, unchecked, to commit serious offences, and the frequency of street brawls in Rome immediately after the arrival of Créqui, caused the papacy to augment the police force of Corsicans. It needed only an encounter between the ambassador's retinue and the Corsican guard to bring these matters to a head. The nephew of Pope Alexander, Don Mario, aggrieved that he had not received an official visit from the ambassador, sent some of the Corsicans into the Embassy precincts, where they proceeded to make themselves unpleasant to the ambassador's attendants. This challenge was repeated, and on the 20th of August 1662 the Embassy was subjected to a three hours' siege, in which several

[22] For this see *Instructions données* . . . (Rome), ii. Introduction.

[23] A full account of this will be found in Gérin, *Louis XIV et le Saint-Siège*, i. 283-419.

persons were killed, and the ambassador's wife, on her return from mass, was ejected from her carriage. As the Vatican failed to make amends for this outrage, Créqui left Rome early in December; at the same time the papal nuncio was expelled from France, and only when Louis despatched troops to take over Avignon did Alexander yield. Peace was signed on the 12th of February 1664 at Pisa. Avignon was restored; an apology offered on behalf of the Pope was accepted, and an obelisk was erected in the Corsican quarter of Rome to commemorate this insult to the French monarchy and the humiliation of the Vatican. As a concession on the part of France, the obelisk was afterwards removed. This was the most serious personal dispute between Louis and the papacy.

There were other disputes[24] in the pontificate of Alexander VII., but they did not involve any great principle, and were settled by negotiation. French influence at the Vatican had now displaced that of Spain, and at their election Clement IX., Clement X. and Innocent XI. were in the French interest. In his later years Louis showed more zeal for orthodoxy, and by the year 1713 he had abandoned the Gallican position of 1682 and ranged himself on the side of the pope and ultramontanism.

It was remarked by Taine[25] in 1873 that but for the Massacre of St. Bartholomew and the Revocation of the Edict of Nantes, France might, by the nineteenth century, have had a liberal and parliamentary government. To violate a fundamental law of the kingdom and undo the most noteworthy achievement of the reign of Henry IV. was the climax of Louis's absolutism. Historians may dispute whether the blame rests with the French church, or the Jesuits, or Louvois, or Madame de Maintenon; perverters of facts, anxious to make a case for some person or institution, may even try to show that the Huguenots were dangerous or seditious. But whoever were his advisers, Louis must take full responsibility before the tribunal of history for an act which is strikingly characteristic of his mentality. The unrelenting bigotry of Philip II. and Philip III. is sometimes condoned by pleading extenuating circumstances in the ideas of the age, but these can hardly be urged on behalf of their descendant Louis, because since

[24] For this see Chantelauze, *Le Cardinal de Retz et ses missions diplomatiques à Rome.*
[25] *Journal des Débats*, November 23, 1873.

1629 the Huguenots had ceased to have any political activities; they had been distinguished for their loyalty during the Fronde, they had produced many eminent public servants, they were admittedly the most enterprising and industrious section of the community, and were protected by a law frequently confirmed and regarded as practically irrevocable. Moreover, public opinion in 1685 was different from that which earlier in the century had condoned the expulsion of the Moriscos, for the period of the great religious wars was ended; nations were gradually realizing that it is better to retain a tax-paying population than to expel it; with the progress of scientific inquiry, a less narrow view of the universe was coming into favour, and at last religion was beginning to be dissociated from wrangling and butchery. The ideal of absolute doctrinal uniformity in the state was fading away before a conception of society which, while requiring obedience to certain religious principles, was prepared to leave to the subject some independence in questions of theology. Louis revived one of the most sinister things in a bad past, hoping by this manifestation of orthodoxy to condone his own irregularities and to conciliate a deity which was supposed to share his outlook on life.

The security of the French Huguenots was threatened for the first time in the year 1655. In the General Assembly of the French Clergy held in that year, Henri de Gondrin, Archbishop of Rheims, demanded that the Edict of Nantes should be subjected to strict legal interpretation. When, in consequence of this demand, the lawyers and theologians were commissioned to examine the Edict that had worked satisfactorily for more than half a century, it crumbled to pieces in their hands.[26] In 1665 Louis was won over, by whom is not certain, to this idea of "interpreting" the Edict, and he promised the French clergy that he would concede in their favour all that could not be absolutely justified by the text. Commissioners were thereupon appointed to examine the alleged infractions, and the French archives contain ample testimony of the chicanery employed in order to make the lives of the Huguenots

---

[26] Cf. P. Meynier, *L'Exécution de l'Edit de Nantes dans le bas Languedoc.* Arguments could be drawn from the *Theologia moralis* of the casuist Escobar, who had affirmed that a prince could violate his own laws provided scandal was avoided ("Praeciso scandalo non tenetur" . . . I. Examen I. cap. v. quaest. 32). See the second part of Puaux et Sabatier, *Études sur la révocation de l'Edit de Nantes.*

intolerable and their religious independence no longer tenable.[27] Thus the ninth article of the Edict had permitted them to exercise their religion in those places where it had been exercised in 1596 and 1597; all chapels built since then must clearly be illegal and had to be pulled down. The Edict had declared that all posts, military and civil, were open to the Huguenots, but there was no law expressly authorizing any one to nominate a Huguenot for such posts, therefore the Huguenots must be expelled from all such offices. Nothing was said in the Edict of burial of Protestants by day; they must therefore conduct their funerals by night; the Edict was framed for adult unregenerates, but their children had souls to save, and there was no law to prevent Protestant children being brought back—by whatever method—to the Catholic fold. This was the logic applied by a host of officials and "missionaries" in the Huguenot provinces after 1666. In April of that year Louis published a proclamation enumerating the various privileges hitherto enjoyed by the Huguenots which now, on close inspection, were found to be unjustified. The Edict, it was declared, must be strictly interpreted and enforced. A protest was taken to Versailles by Du Bosc, minister of Caen, who explained to Louis the full significance of the measures which the French clergy were forcing upon him, but the protest fell on deaf ears, and the clergy continued to press on Louis measures of petty persecution and quibbling interference, worse almost than the expulsion itself, because the commissioners and missionaries struck at the parents through the children. An edict of 1681 forbade Huguenots to send their children abroad for education, and fixed the age of reason at seven years[28]—at which age a Huguenot child, surrounded by zealous Catholic agents, could make "free" choice for himself. For a Protestant parent to attempt the reconversion of his child was a serious offence and punished by imprisonment or the galleys.

There were other and more insidious methods for winning over the Huguenots. In 1676 a fund was formed to provide rewards for all Protestants who abjured; this fund was administered by a Catholic convert named Pellisson, and pay-

[27] For details of this petty persecution see P. Gachon, *Quelques préliminaires de la révocation de l'Edit de Nantes en Languedoc* (1661–1685).

[28] Puaux et Sabatier, *Etudes sur la révocation de l'Edit de Nantes*, 59.

ments of from six to twelve livres were made for each conversion, provided it was accompanied by the necessary certificate of abjuration. The Protestants replied in kind. A wealthy Huguenot lady, Madame Hervaert, founded a rival "conversion bureau," which helped to bring back the weaker members to the faith. But though it thus became possible to make a living by repeated changes from the one creed to the other, very few were influenced by such bribes, though zealots continued to invest money in the respective funds in the hope of large spiritual dividends.[29] The failure of such methods made the use of force inevitable.

After 1682 the "interpretation" of the Edict of Nantes became more and more drastic.[30] The Huguenots were rendered incapable of holding any public office, and were economically ostracised. An attempt in Languedoc to reassert their old privileges was harshly repressed, and even the holding of services in the ruins of demolished chapels was forbidden. In 1684 the exasperated Protestants, who still retained their loyalty and believed that Louis was deceived by his court and clergy, addressed to the monarch a petition drawn up by one of their foremost pastors—Claude, voicing an eloquent plea for toleration and reminding Louis that the Edict had been faithfully observed by his predecessors. The reply was the petition of the General Assembly of the French clergy,[31] that as the Edict of Nantes had been found irregular in so many of its provisions, it should be wholly withdrawn and (to quote the words) "the undisturbed reign of Jesus Christ re-established in France." The dragoons had already established that reign as it was understood at Versailles. Reports of wholesale "conversions" in the Huguenot districts confirmed Louis in the opinion that the policy of force was justified by results, and scenes were re-enacted in the French countryside such as Europe had not known since the Thirty Years' War.[32] The crowning

[29] In 1676 Louis (having qualms about his relations with Madame de Montespan) contributed large sums to the Pellisson fund (*Œuvres de Louis XIV*, ed. Grouvelle, vi. 357). The payment to a convert was six livres (about 12s. 6d. in modern English currency).

[30] A full account of events immediately preceding and succeeding the Revocation will be found in E. Guitard, *Colbert et Seignelay contre la Religion Réformée.*

[31] Guitard, *op. cit.* ch. iii.

[32] *Ibid.* ch. v.

humiliation of abjuration was wrenched from thousands of Protestants weakened by suffering and by anxiety for their dependants. On the 17th of October 1685 the Edict of Nantes was solemnly revoked by a proclamation which recorded the fact that it had originally been intended to win over the heretics and that now, since this object was accomplished, the Edict was superfluous. The expulsion of the Huguenots was not ordered, but their cult was absolutely forbidden and emigration was prohibited.

Many Protestant families had left France before 1685;[33] at the risk of a life sentence in the galleys a large number managed to escape after the Revocation. The disastrous economic results of the Revocation have already been considered; there is no record of the personal suffering caused by the uprooting of a large and busy community. The French clergy had triumphed; they had destroyed a rival church, and they now acclaimed Louis in language as fulsome as Bossuet could pen. Theirs had been the initiative; Louis gave his sanction; Louvois carried it out. All three were partners in a crime noteworthy even in the sombre records of religious bigotry.

III. *The Court.* The lesson of the Fronde was never forgotten by Louis XIV. and may have strengthened his theory of kingship. At Versailles the nobility were segregated and rendered impotent; those who were too poor or too unsociable to pay their court to the king were dealt with in a manner equally effective. Early in Louis's reign, special tribunals were appointed to deal with the complaints against these "hobereaux" or country gentry who lived all the year on their estates, many of them ill-treating their peasants; and of these tribunals the most famous was the "Grands Jours d'Auvergne" (1665–1666), an extraordinary royal commission composed of sixteen councillors of Parlement presided over by the Advocate-General Omer Talon, which met at Clermont in Auvergne in order to hold strict inquisition into abuses of justice in the provinces of Auvergne, Nivernais, Forez, Beaujolais, Lyonnais and Berry. The record of its proceedings shows how helpless were the peasants in the grip of a nobility uncontrolled by provincial justice, entrusted often with powers over life and limb, and sometimes including men capable of the most atrocious acts of cruelty. Many of the persons arraigned before

---

[33] *Ibid.* ch. vii. This emigration went on from 1669 to 1690.

this tribunal were guilty of murder or of robbery with violence; some were found to have inflicted torture; for example, a noble was proved to have imprisoned many of his serfs in a dungeon where they could neither stand up nor lie down, until death ended their agonies.[34] Several capital sentences were passed by the *Grands Jours,* and though personal influence generally prevented these being carried out, the warning was taken to heart, so the peasant had more security for his life in the years that followed.

Excluded from the administrative offices, the nobility by birth had the monopoly of the titular offices at Court. These offices included that of Grand Chamberlain, who took part in audiences to ambassadors, presented the monarch with his shirt when he awoke and wrapped him in his winding-sheet when he died; that of Master of the Wardrobe, who had duties defined by his title; the Grand Ecuyer, who was an exalted stable-man. For offices much less important than these the French aristocracy contended fiercely among themselves, and the haughty Saint Simon waited patiently for a household appointment because of the official apartment at Versailles which it conferred. Louis knew that the best means of weakening a social caste is to increase the number of persons claiming to be members of that caste; in consequence an enormous number of peerages was sold in this period. Considering also that the *noblesse de robe* presented a well-filled complement to the *noblesse d'épée,* it is not surprising that public opinion regarded it as a dishonour to be in the roturier class and a cheap honour to be out of it. By the end of the eighteenth century there were about four thousand offices each of which conferred a patent of nobility. An edict of 1704 granted the privilege of heredity to the *noblesse de robe;* in the year 1696 alone more than five hundred persons were ennobled. The nobility of the Revolution of 1789 were therefore very different in composition from the nobility of the Fronde. Another evidence of Louis's complete subjection of the nobility is the fact that in his reign only one rebellion was led by a noble—that of Rohan —who, instigated by hatred of Louvois and obliged to find a means of paying his debts, attempted to sell Quilleboeuf to

[34] There is a very full contemporary account by V. E. Fléchier, *Mémoires sur les Grands Jours d'Auvergne* (1665), reprinted by Chéruel in 1856. Fléchier's book is one of the most striking indictments against the French nobility.

the Dutch in 1674. He and his few accomplices paid for the revolt with their lives.

It was at Versailles that the nobility were concentrated and demoralized by idleness and gaming. In boyhood Louis had known the château of Versailles[35] as a summer residence; after 1660 the royal visits there became more frequent, and the great park provided a suitable setting for the masquerades and pageants with which the young king loved to honour Madame de Montespan. In 1669 the work of architectural reconstruction was begun, and the palace at it now stands was completed by 1710. The Trianon, a miniature Versailles, was ready by 1688 and was intended specially for Madame de Montespan, but when Louis tired of this he commenced the construction of another palace at Marly. These three completed a scheme that had been gradually evolved—Versailles for the Court, Marly for the king's friends, the Trianon for the king himself; of these three the first and the third survive as the architectural memorial of this reign. The total cost of these buildings was about 116,000,000 livres, but more serious was the loss of human life. The craze of the age was for fountains and aquatic devices; 30,000 men were employed to divert the river Eure for this purpose, and the excavations accounted for the deaths of many workers, probably from malaria. Eventually the project of utilizing the waters of the Eure had to be abandoned, and the lakes at Versailles were filled from the Seine by the pumps at Marly. In 1682 Versailles became the official headquarters of Louis XIV., and from that date the French monarchy, in an artificial seclusion, avoided contact with the French people until the mob rushed through the gates in 1789.

The physical and mental characteristics of Louis XIV. fitted him for the leadership of a large and magnificent court. Dignified and imposing, he could command respect by his presence and charm by his perfect manners, while to strangers he was invariably courteous and condescending.[36] Though inheriting a certain tendency to languorous indolence from his Spanish mother, he was both industrious and observant; his memory

[35] There is a very large literature on the Versailles of Louis XIV. For a good general account of the externals, with reproductions of old prints, see Fennebresque, *Versailles Royal*.

[36] There is a good sketch of Louis's personal characteristics by the Venetian ambassador, Giustinian (1665–1668); in *Relazioni degli ambasciatori veneti*, France, iii. 172.

was good; he had some taste in matters of art, and always insisted on his wishes being carried out. He never forgot that he was king, keeping his distance even with relatives.[37] He could vary his mood to suit the company or the occasion; he was not liable to gusts of passion or emotion; nor, till his later years, did he show signs of sorrow or regret. His was the type of character which may wear out those with whom it comes in closest contact while itself surviving serene and imperturbable. He was devoid of a sense of humour, and he not only welcomed flattery but believed it. Studiously careful of himself, his invariable health won the admiration and envy of his more dissolute entourage; moreover, the complete absence of human affection made his love affairs commonplace though spectacular. The sense of proportion, generally developed in ordinary human beings by the rough-and-tumble of everyday existence, was denied to him; as a private person he would have been suspected of egotism and banality.

The Queen, Maria Theresa, took little part in this society. Devoted to her consort, pious and complaisant, she was soon forced to eliminate herself in favour of the mistresses whom Louis publicly established in her place. His first *liaison* (commenced less than a year after his marriage) was with Mademoiselle de la Vallière, a young maid-of-honour to Henrietta of Orléans; after several fruitless efforts this young lady managed to retire to a convent. Her two surviving children were the Count of Vermandois and Mademoiselle de Blois. In 1667 one of the queen's maids-of-honour—Madame de Montespan—became the reigning favourite, and her husband was granted a divorce. Thus until 1674 Louis was living in double adultery, and the queen was obliged to appear in public with her two rivals. Eventually Madame de Montespan had to yield to other favourites, and left the Court in 1690. The three surviving of her seven children were Mademoiselle de Blois (the second), the Count of Toulouse and the Duke of Maine. All these children were legitimated, and in 1714 they were accorded the right of succession. Bossuet's condemnation of the king's morals[38] has been echoed by some Victorian historians, but to-day it is emphasized that (after the age of forty-eight) Louis was monogamous, and so provided a remarkable example of

---

[37] For instances see Louis's *Mémoires* in *Œuvres de Louis XIV*, especially ii. 74.

[38] For this see Gazier, *Bossuet et Louis XIV*, 58 ff.

morality and rectitude comparable (it has been alleged) with that set by Albert, the Prince Consort.

Maria Theresa died in 1683; in her married life she had passed, she said, only twenty happy days. Louis's relations with Madame de Maintenon must be placed on a different footing from those with Mademoiselle de la Vallière or Madame de Montespan. Descended from an old and distinguished Huguenot family, Françoise d'Aubigné had married, at an early age, the cripple and poet Scarron, becoming a widow in 1660 at the age of twenty-five. She first came to the notice of Louis as the nurse or governess of Madame de Montespan's youngest child and was later accorded the title of Marquise de Maintenon. The evidence of contemporaries—reinforced by the dislike which Saint Simon expressed—shows that Madame de Maintenon was in many ways a remarkable woman, exercising a charm dependent on spiritual as much as on physical gifts; the portraits of her at Versailles distinguish her at once from all the other women in the entourage of Louis, and help more than anything else to account for the influence which she exercised. The refinement of character and thoughtful solicitude for others which the exigencies of her career had developed provided a corrective for Louis's megalomania, while her tranquil piety and invariable rectitude won the respect of the monarch's more mature years. That she preserved these attributes in the equivocal position in which fortune had placed her, induced Louis to aim at a union rather than a *liaison*. The two were married secretly, and by night, early in 1684, the bride in her forty-ninth year, the bridegroom in his forty-sixth, but Madame de Maintenon never became queen of France. Her influence over her consort was unquestioned, though she ostentatiously dissociated herself from matters of public policy.[39] She had all the zeal of a convert, and not only made piety fashionable, but strengthened the orthodoxy of Louis and the Court. She made Versailles less vicious but not more dull; she interested herself in a school for girls[40] which

[39] Geffroy in his *Madame de Maintenon d'après sa correspondance authentique* maintains that she cannot be held responsible for any of Louis's unwise acts or bad choices, and so absolves her from the strictures passed on her by Saint Simon and Michelet.

[40] The education there does not appear to have been uniformly successful: "l'instruction ne va pas trop bien et mes potages vont vite" (D'Haussonville and Hanoteaux, *Souvenirs sur Madame de Maintenon*, lxxxii.).

she had established at St. Cyr, and she survived her husband four years. Hers was the only royal marriage of the seventeenth century not based on convenience or policy, a fact which may explain why her personality has been so widely exploited by modern biographers.

The Dauphin, generally designated *Monseigneur*, was born in 1661. His most pronounced characteristics were lassitude or indolence, and throughout the fifty years of his life he played a very subordinate part at Versailles. He was the pupil of Bossuet; special editions of Latin and Greek authors were prepared for him;[41] his father compiled Memoirs for his instruction in statecraft, and his education was planned on lines unique in the history of pedagogy. No pupil ever proved less worthy of the elaborate care bestowed on him. Timid and apathetic, he spent many hours reclining on a couch tapping his boots with a cane or reading over and over again the Court news in the *Gazette*. As a grown man his main anxiety was to keep out of his parent's way. By his marriage with a princess of Bavaria he had three sons, Louis of Burgundy, Philip of Anjou and Charles of Berry, but, following the paternal example, he neglected his wife, and at Meudon yielded to the sway of Mademoiselle Choin. Louis's brother, the Duke of Orléans (Monsieur), was of similar character, dividing most of his time between the dining and the toilet table, the centre of an effeminate and licentious coterie at St. Cloud. His son, the Duke of Chartres, who was credited by contemporaries with more activity in evil than any of his relatives, became Duke of Orléans on the death of his father in 1701 and Regent in 1715. The Dauphin's eldest son, the Duke of Burgundy, was the pupil of Fénelon, and the tuition of this eminent preceptor seems to have had more effect on his character than that Bossuet had had on his father, for he was perhaps the only prince at Versailles who showed any signs of ability or character. In February 1712 he died, probably of smallpox, six days after the death of his wife and one year after that of his father, a series of deaths which created some suspicion. The suggestion of foul play may be discredited, for accusations of poisoning were often made on the slightest pretext, and at that time smallpox claimed many victims. The Duke of Burgundy was survived by an infant son who afterwards became Louis XV.; the Duke of Anjou became Philip

[41] The "Delphin Classics," edited by Huet of Caen.

V. of Spain; the Duke of Berry died from an accident in 1714. Thus Louis was predeceased by his only son, his only brother and two of his three grandsons, the fate of the legitimate succession depending on the life of an infant great-grandson. The monarch may have seen in these events the proof of divine displeasure, but in sorrow and old age he retained his dignity and composure to the end.

The daily life at Versailles has been chronicled minutely by Dangeau, whose *Journal* was afterwards used for the Memoirs[42] of Saint Simon. The day commenced with the formal awakening of the king and the entry of the Court into the royal bed-chamber according to a scale of precedence, the princes of the blood coming first. In the summer, Marly, Compiègne and Fontainebleau were favourite resorts where, on most days, there was hunting or hawking, at night gaming, and always a scramble for the numerous offices giving their holders an official status at Court. Louis exercised a strict control over the amusements of his family, encouraging them to gamble, paying their debts and opening their correspondence. In a magisterial fashion he even danced, but the courtly pavanes, courantes and minuets of his time were not incompatible with personal dignity, and the music was more stately than modern measures. These diversions were varied with daily Mass, which the king always attended, while the florid eloquence of preachers like Bossuet and Bourdaloue alternately charmed or disturbed.

The etiquette of Versailles was regulated with an oriental precision, and the minutest details of the monarch's private life were the absorbing topic of conversation in a community divorced from all the healthy activities of human life. More than any other court of modern times, the court of Louis XIV. provided unlimited scope for time-serving, mediocrity and licentiousness, in which independence of mind or character was sternly repressed and where sycophancy and hypocrisy went to such lengths as to impress all but the most cynical or the most stolid. Of the cynics, who included men of critical insight, some gave encouragement to the *philosophes* of the eighteenth century. One of these, the Marquis D'Argenson (1694–1757), a friend of Voltaire's, proclaimed that "les nobles sont au peuple comme la pourriture est au fruit."

[42] For the historical value (slight) of Saint Simon's Memoirs see Chéruel, *Saint Simon comme historien de Louis XIV*.

Louis's concentration of this ferment in Versailles can be justified on the ground that its dispersal throughout the country would have been socially dangerous; the menace of a corrupt caste could be localised, but not removed.

IV. *Public Opinion.* The historical literature of Europe contains many criticisms of Louis XIV. and his policy.[43] The events in his reign which more than any others called forth energetic protest were the Reunions of 1681; the Revocation of the Edict of Nantes in 1685; the second invasion of the Palatinate in 1688, and the acceptance of Charles II.'s will in 1700. In England, Holland and Germany Louis was held up to execration as an irresponsible despot crushing the liberties of his country and aiming at the complete enslavement of Europe; after 1685 the French Huguenot refugees added to the chorus, and the attacks of the pastor Jurieu were among the most bitter and personal of the period. Within the French frontiers, control of the press was so strict as to guarantee that there would be none but anonymous dissentients in the panegyric which public opinion accorded to Louis XIV. This has been the subject of several important monographs; here it can only be treated very briefly, and for this purpose it is necessary to make a selection rather than attempt a general summary.

The French devastation of the Palatinate in 1688 called forth in Germany a manifestation of public feeling comparable only with that produced in Britain and France by the German occupation of Belgium in the war of 1914–1918. A great number of pamphlets was published, and the crude illustrations with which some were accompanied depicted the atrocities of which the French soldiers were accused. These soldiers are described as Huns, capable of any atrocity; their officers regard war as an opportunity for loot and murder, their monarch is a monster and blasphemer, claiming to be directly inspired by the Almighty, and imitating the Turkish model of government with such fidelity that he could be as good a Mohammedan in Constantinople as a Catholic in Paris. On these points the pamphlets are in complete agreement. Those writers who attempted a historical survey claimed that France was an upstart country[44] (the true descendants

[43] The best general account is H. Gillot, *Le Règne de Louis XIV et l'opinion publique en Allemagne* (1914).

[44] This was a revival of the old controversy, first raised in the

of Charlemagne being the Franks east of the Rhine), and that all her culture had been stolen from her neighbours. Her universities, they said, were founded by Roman, *i.e.* German emperors; her mathematics she had borrowed from England; her civil architecture from Italy; her science of fortification from Spain and Holland; her gunpowder, artillery and printing press from Germany; her navigation from the Genoese; her principles of government from the Turk, and her literature from every nation of Europe.[45] France, it was maintained, had reduced warfare to armed robbery; her rulers were disciples of Hobbes and Machiavelli. French diplomacy excelled that of every country because it had reduced to a fine art the choice of agents suitable for its intended dupes—for Austria, phlegmatic Frenchmen to wear out Austrian patience; for Spain, ecclesiastics; for England, heretics; for Holland, great talkers; for Germany, good eaters and drinkers; for Rome, bullies. "Where the devil himself cannot go, he sends a sorceress and a Jesuit."[46] The German races had brought their calamities on their own head by their naïveté, their overconfidence in public faith, and their indifference to the evils going on outside their frontiers. Such were the opinions inspired by the systematic laying waste of a province, and a brief examination of this large pamphlet literature shows that neither the uses nor the methods of war propaganda are, as is sometimes supposed, twentieth-century inventions.

Among the victims of Louis's intolerance the most important writer was Jurieu,[47] whose *Soupirs de la France esclave* is perhaps the most energetic attack on Louis's methods of government. It was published in August 1688, and directed explicitly at the monarch who had turned the writer into an exile and plotter. "Every nation governed by a king," he maintained, "has the right to depose him as soon as he exceeds the limits of his authority."[48] The person of the monarch and the interests of the state are separate entities, and as Louis had established an antithesis between the two, it was possible, in Jurieu's opinion, to attack the king without endangering the

Interregnum (1254–1273), whether the French are true Franks or merely Francigenae.

[45] Gillot, *op. cit.* 245.

[46] Gillot, *op. cit.* 98.

[47] For Jurieu see Dedieu, *Le Rôle politique des Protestants français*, chs. ix., x. and xi.

[48] Quoted in Dedieu, *op. cit.* 66.

safety of France. Only by rousing up a great European opposition to the tyrant could he be brought to reason; with Europe armed against him, he would be obliged to reform his government and restore the authority of the States-General.[49] In this way Jurieu tried to reconcile his activities against the French monarch with his loyalty as a Frenchman; he devoted himself to the work of raising an armed confederation against Louis; he was the firebrand of the Huguenot exiles, and organized an espionage system during the War of the Spanish Succession. These doings may be considered treasonable, but Jurieu hardly owed any allegiance to a sovereign who by his intolerance had obliged so many of this Huguenot's co-religionaries to leave their native country.

In contrast with this hostile criticism from abroad is the unanimous adulation at home. After the suppression of the Fronde movement, Frenchmen became more loyalist, and in no other country was the cult of the monarch carried to such extraordinary lengths. "The French," it was said, "are the only European nation which idolizes its sovereign"; in comparison the Spaniards seemed to regard their king with coldness and to worship the state rather than the prince. Only quotation can illustrate the absurdities to which French worship of Louis XIV. went.[50] As early as 1644 P. Labbé compiled his *Educatio Regia* for Louis, in which he seriously proposed that the monarch should remind himself every morning that he had to play the rôle of God, and at the end of each day he should ask himself whether he had done so or not:

> "Hodie mihi gerenda est persona Dei . . .
> Deusne hodie an homo fui?"

In the year when Louis began to rule for himself, P. Senault of the Oratory dedicated to him a sermon preached on the occasion of the birth of the Dauphin, where the king was compared with God and the Dauphin with Jesus Christ. That the calendar would probably contain a Saint Louis XIV., as it already had a Saint Louis IX., was the expressed opinion of Godeau in his *Eloges historiques*, but the date of publication (1665) was unfortunate, for in that year Louis obtained from Parlement the legitimation of his bastards and began his public

---

[49] *Ibid.* 67.
[50] Many examples will be found in Lacour-Gayet, *L'Education politique de Louis XIV.*

amours with Madame de Montespan. There is ample evidence that Louis took his panegyrists seriously. In his *Memoirs* (1661) he proclaimed that respect was due to kings as a religious duty, for they are God's lieutenants on earth and responsible to God alone,[51] a theme developed and amplified by Bossuet and a host of lesser lights, all of whom regarded the monarch as a sacred agent of the Almighty and his critics as atheists. Considering the emphasis and unanimity of these opinions,[52] it is not surprising that a book such as Francis Davenne's *De la puissance qu'ont les rois sur les peuples et du pouvoir des peuples sur les rois* (1650) should have involved its author in serious consequences. Davenne argued that to kings is due obedience only in proportion as they carry out their obligations to the governed; he was regarded as a madman, and so escaped imprisonment or worse.

It is a truism that in the seventeenth century philosophical opinion, almost without exception, favoured absolutism in the state. But the limit of absurdity was reached when French apologists for Louis XIV. dragged in the sceptic Hobbes as a defender of the Divine Right theory. The wilful and erratic English philosopher, barely understood in his own day, puzzles modern commentators by his eccentricities and perversities; his theories were absolutist, but his reputation as an atheist or agnostic prevented the English Divine Right school utilizing his doctrines, though several ecclesiastics, after a hasty reading of the *Leviathan*, apparently regarded its author as one of themselves. Hobbes was a revolutionary because he eliminated all religious sanction from the state, so destroying the basis for religious persecution, but his use of the contract theory to prove the precise converse of what every one else had proved from it commended him to several political theorists in France where his personal opinions were not so well known as they were in England. To these purblind theorists the *Leviathan* seemed to prove from "scientific" premises what the Divine

---

[51] "Celui qui a donné des rois aux hommes a voulu qu'on les respectât comme ses lieutenants" (Memoirs of Louis XIV. in *Œuvres*, ed. Grouvelle, ii. 285).

[52] For the general political theory of Louis's reign see E. Nys, *Les Théories politiques et le droit international en France*. The editors (E. Bourgeois and L. Andre) of the volume *Pamphlets* in *Les Sources de l'histoire de France*, iv. 4, suggest that Louis was influenced to some extent by adverse criticism, but no proof of this is supplied.

Right school proved from the Bible, and so appeared to offer a tempting auxiliary for the additional confirmation of a strongly entrenched doctrine. In 1649 Sorbière published a French translation of the *De cive*, and in 1660 Francis Bonneau dedicated to Louis his *Eléments de la politique de Mons. Hobbes*, wherein he asserted that "Euclide et Mons. Hobbes ont vu les choses à fond." He recommended that arrangements should be made for the official teaching of Hobbes' theories in French schools. Bonneau did not possess the perspicacity which he attributes to the English mathematician, otherwise he might have detected something beneath the wool of this strange lamb introduced into the Divine Right fold.

The theory of Divine Hereditary Right attained its highest expression in England and France at the same time, but both Filmer and Bossuet wrote their expositions in a period when its religious sanction was beginning to be discredited. What the political theorists of the Renaissance had based on Roman law, or classical precedent or on expediency, the apologists of Louis XIV. based on Religion, or rather on the Old Testament, which was considered to be not only verbally inspired but also to provide a canon for the regulation of the whole conduct of life, and so, by implication, a guide for the statesman and lawgiver. In the seventeenth century Hebrew was much more widely studied than it is now; in consequence, educated men were mostly familiar with the characteristic conceptions and institutions of early Jewish history. The despotism of monarchs divinely appointed to be the instruments of God's wrath on earth was accepted as the highest possible form of human government; so long as this attitude to the Old Testament was unquestioned, the Divine Right theory was a perfectly consistent one and the doubters were guilty of heresy and sacrilege. But by the second half of the seventeenth century it would be untrue to say that this was the universal attitude towards the Old Testament, for the spirit of inquiry had long been awake; men were beginning to feel that Religion had more to gain than to lose by exploration of the secrets of nature, and were refusing to believe that the whole compass of human knowledge was limited to one book.[53] To the clergy, however, the Divine Right theory seemed inseparable from all that they held sacred, conse-

[53] See *infra*, p. 513.

quently, in both England and France, they obstinately clung to
it long after it had lost its force. In eighteenth-century England it merged insensibly with the halo surrounding the
martyred Toryism of early Hanoverian times, becoming an
agreeable affectation all the more alluring to its devotees as
the chances of its reinstatement became distinctly less. For the
true believer, the king was over the water, and fidelity was
intensified rather than shaken by the fact that he was likely
to remain there. But in France the alternative of constitutional
government did not present itself, so the most inexorable
conclusions were deduced from the theory and applied by a
monarch whose presence was insistent and about whose life
there was no romance.

The theory was enunciated in its most complete form in
Bossuet's[54] *Politique tirée des propres paroles de l'Ecriture
Sainte*—not the first French exposition of the subject, but the
first to express clearly all that acceptance of the doctrine
implied. It is a great book in the sense that it crushed all
possible objection by the sheer weight of biblical authority; it
has all the finality of inspiration, and it was written by a man
who was quite unperturbed when mistakes and inconsistencies
in his writings were pointed out. To Bossuet the theory of the
state was revealed in the Old Testament and was explained
definitively and authoritatively in his own book. That book
expounds principles of government which could not be improved upon because, it was held, they are not of man's
making; its best commentary is the reign of the king for
whom it was written.

Louis made some interesting applications of the theory. In
an Edict of 1692 he declared "il n'y a pas de droit ni mieux
établi ni plus inséparablement attaché à notre couronne que
celui de mouvance et directité universelle que nous avons sur
toutes les terres de notre royaume."[55] This is the legal application of the statement[56] in his Memoirs that the king is

---

[54] A good short study of Bossuet is that by Rebelliau (*Les
Grands Ecrivains français*).

[55] Isambert, *Anciennes Lois françaises*, xx. 165. Quoted in J.
Hitier, *La Doctrine de l'absolutisme*, 124.

[56] "Les rois sont seigneurs absolus et ont naturellement la disposition pleine et libre de tous les biens qui sont possédés, aussi
bien par les gens d'église que par les séculiers, pour en user . . .
suivant le besoin général de leur état" (*Œuvres . . .*, ii. 121).

ultimate owner of the private property of his subjects, who have merely the usufruct; the Edict was intended to legalize franchises on the payment of a year's revenue, and it embodied an important principle because it identified sovereignty with complete "dominium" or ownership.[57] Private property thus disappears and the state becomes socialist. But Louis did not press the principle, contenting himself merely with its enunciation. Jurieu[58] affirmed that in Colbert's time it was proposed to confiscate all private holdings in land and farm them out for a term of years, but there is no confirmation of this. Public opinon was not shocked by this equation of kingship with ownership; the conception was already familiar to students of early Jewish antiquities and had been asserted by Grotius in his views on slavery,[59] views which in the next century stirred the wrath of Rousseau[60] against the Dutch lawyer and humanitarian.

Another deduction made from the theory was that as kings are responsible to God alone, they are not bound by such human fetters as international treaties. It is for the king to decide when a treaty no longer fulfils the intentions of its original signatories, and in this view Louis anticipated the attitude of Bismarck towards international obligations. Both regarded formal treaties as temporary conveniences; to consider them as permanently binding was, in their view, to forget that international relations are in a state of perpetual flux. The formal expressions of perpetual friendship and alliance in treaties are, Louis assured his son, merely diplomatic courtesies.[61] The foreign policy of Louis XIV. provides ample illustration of the application of these views.

Lastly, Louis concluded that his Divine Right prerogatives absolved him from obedience even to the fundamental laws of his country. These fundamental laws, often invoked, were never clearly defined; in the seventeenth century they may be said to have consisted of such principles as the hereditary character of the French monarchy, its descent in the male line to the exclusion of women, and the inalienability of French territory. In 1700 Louis registered in Parlement an edict whereby Philip V. of Spain was secured in his contingent

---

[57] The principle had been foreshadowed in the Code Michaud.
[58] *Les Soupirs de la France esclave* (English ed. 1688), 22.
[59] *De jure belli ac pacis*, i. 3.
[60] *Contrat social*, i. 4.
[61] *Œuvres*, ed. Grouvelle, i. 64.

claim to the French succession—a defiance of European public opinion which led directly to the Spanish Succession war. During the Utrecht negotiations the Allies objected that there was a danger of Philip uniting the two crowns,[62] whereon it was pointed out that by a fundamental law of the French monarchy Philip could not be deprived of any right he might possess to the French throne. Louis had eventually to give way, but, in a memoir[63] written to Torcy in April 1712, it was made clear that while the required renunciation might be conceded in order to facilitate negotiations, it need not prejudice posterity, since it was against a fundamental law. In July 1714 one of these fundamental laws was broken by Louis himself when he obtained a decree[64] qualifying the bastards for the succession in the event of the legitimate line dying out. Thus Louis could invoke or break a fundamental law at pleasure; and as there was no question of his superiority to the Common Law,[65] it is clear that law itself was for Louis merely a term of convenience, to be utilized or ignored according as it suited the royal interests. In these circumstances one must acknowledge not the excesses of Louis XIV. but his moderation.

[62] See *Correspondence of Bolingbroke* (ed. 1798), ii. 199.

[63] It is printed in *ibid*. ii. 222-226. The argument was that as Philip's contingent rights were based on a fundamental law, no human laws could destroy them.

[64] Isambert, *Anciennes Lois françaises*, xx. 620.

[65] Louis stated in his Memoirs that what kings do against common law is "fondé sur la raison d'Etat, la première des lois . . . mais la plus inconnue et la plus obscure à tous ceux qui ne gouvernent pas" (*Œuvres* . . ., i. 56). The best comment on this is the dictim of De Retz: "le droit des peuples et le droit des rois ne s'accordent jamais si bien que dans le silence."

Chapter 8

Jesuit and Jansenist

THE PROPORTIONS which historians assign to the various aspects of life in the past may correspond, not necessarily with their former, but with their present-day importance. Hence, some topics may be neglected, for example theology, nowadays considered almost "bad form." This chapter seeks to show the relevance of that topic for the life of seventeenth-century France.

The two theologians who first addressed themselves to the problem of the connection between the human soul and God, or the relations between the finite and the infinite, were St. Paul and St. Augustine. Both elaborated theories of Grace which superimposed on the foundation of the Gospels a vast metaphysical structure which might well puzzle the layman. St. Augustine, Manichean and libertine, was converted in A.D. 386; he devoted his life to the elucidation and definition of Christian principles, not as formulated by their Founder, but as enunciated by St. Paul. Whereas the Stoics had considered Grace a recompense to be achieved by human effort, proclaiming that virtue might be cultivated, St. Paul had taught that Grace is free and all-sufficient, that it is awarded solely by God, and consequently the divine will plays an indispensable part in human salvation. The Manichean teachings in which St. Augustine had been brought up were not difficult to reconcile with the doctrine of the Fall, for both theories were based on the antithesis of Good and Evil, an antithesis on which St. Augustine built up his theory of an all-efficient and irresistible Grace, effecting the divine purpose in human life quite irrespective of man's participation or volition. From this Augustine concluded that the Elect consisted solely of those on whom Grace had descended; the Pelagians, who insisted on some measure of human participation in the process of salvation, were branded as heretics, and from that moment Christianity has been divided between two rival theories of Grace and Free Will. The Augustinian views on Grace led naturally to the doctrine of Predestination: God, according to the saint, does not actually preordain eternal punishment for certain men, nevertheless He knows their future, He endows them with certain moral and intellectual qualities, in the exercise of which they are themselves responsible, but without Grace these qualities avail nothing: human damnation and divine Grace are thus the two incompatibles. The Calvinist and, to a less extent, the Lutheran doctrines were similar, except that the Protestants laid greater stress on the consequences of the Fall, emphasizing the totally corrupt nature of man and the absolute impossibility of his acts being anything but sinful unless transfigured by Grace.[1] To attribute to humanity any initiative in the process of salvation seemed to the Protestant theologians, as to St. Augustine, like diminishing divine prerogative; to regard human virtue as endowed with any efficacy of its own savoured of Stoicism and Paganism, for it implied a belittling of divine powers and was therefore a dangerous heresy. In various ways, therefore, the teaching of St. Paul and St. Augustine is at the basis of practically all the Predestinarian theology of modern times.

In his *Dictionnaire philosophique* Voltaire thus defines the theological doctrine of Grace:

> The theologians use the term Grace to describe a particular action of God exerted on human beings in order to make them just and happy. Some admit a universal grace which God grants to all men . . . : others admit grace only for the members of their communion: others again, only for the elect of their communion.
>
> Grace, according to the theologians, is sufficient if one can resist it, in which case it is insufficient:[2] it is like a

[1] See Mabille, *Controverses sur le libre arbitre au dix-septième siècle*, and N. Abercrombie, *The Origins of Jansenism*.

[2] The general theological opinion was that Sufficient Grace could be resisted; hence it was really Insufficient.

pardon granted to a criminal who is nevertheless executed. It is efficient, if it is such that one cannot resist it. . . . It is necessitant if it is inevitable, and then it is simply a manifestation of the divine decrees. St. Thomas defines grace as "a substantial form": the Jesuit Bouhours calls it "un je ne sais quoi," perhaps the best definition ever given.

. . . Muley Ismael, king of Morocco, is said to have had five hundred children. What would you say if a marabout from Mount Atlas told you that, at the conclusion of a dinner given to all his family, the wise and good Muley Ismael spoke thus: "I am Muley Ismael and have begotten you for my glory: I care for you as a hen cares for her brood. I have decreed that one of my younger sons shall have the kingdom of Tafilet, that another shall possess Morocco: and as for my other children, to the number of four hundred and ninety-eight, I order that one half be broken on the wheel and the other burned, for I am Muley Ismael." You would take the marabout for the greatest fool Africa had ever produced.

But if three or four thousand marabouts, maintained sumptuously at your expense, repeated the same thing to you, what would you do? Would you not be tempted to make them fast on bread and water until they came to their senses? You may say that my indignation is reasonable if against the *Supralapsaries*,[3] who believe that the king of Morocco created his five hundred descendants for his glory, intending all the time that they should be broken on the wheel or burned, except the two who were predestined to reign. But, you say, I am wrong in attacking the *Infralapsaries*, who maintain that Muley Ismael did not originally *intend* that his children should perish but, having *foreseen* that they would come to no good, he judged it wise, as a good father, to get rid of them by fire and wheel. Ah, Supralapsaries, Infralapsaries, Sufficients, Efficients, Jansenists, Molinists, be men and cease plaguing the world with such abominable absurdities.

For nearly two centuries the theologians were profoundly exercised by these matters. The later Middle Ages witnessed

---

[3] The Supralapsaries believed that the divine decrees were anterior to all consideration of man or his existence. The Infralapsaries held that these decrees dated from the Fall. The Calvinists were Supralapsaries.

a revived interest in St. Augustine, and the questions of Grace and Free Will were once more in debate. Calvin taught the most uncompromising theory of Predestination, based not on heretical fancy but on the uncontested authority of the greatest of the early Fathers. A Jesuit professor of theology at Evora, in Portugal, named Louis Molina[4] (1535–1601), tried to reconcile the antithesis of Free Will and Predetermined Grace in his *De liberi arbitrii cum Gratiae donis concordia* (1588) by supposing that Grace is efficacious only according as the will co-operates. Molina's book was widely read, for this compromise (called *Congruism*) was acceptable to many; but it was attacked by the Dominicans, who regarded it as Pelagian. According to Molina, the science by which God knows the future is intermediate between the sciences of what is and of what will be: it is an intermediate science (*science moyenne*) by which God can predict the future from His knowledge of all the conditions bearing thereon. God can thus execute His designs without interfering with man's freedom of will; equally man can resist Grace, however powerful, since his will must co-operate before Grace becomes efficacious. A completely omniscient mind can know the future without having predetermined it—a doctrine which does not seem strange in these days of eugenics and biological investigation. This novel theory led to a long controversy between the Jesuits, represented by Molina, defenders of Free Will, and the Dominicans, represented by Bañez of Salamanca (1528–1604), defenders of the strict Augustinian theory. In 1594 Pope Clement VIII. summoned the disputants to Rome, and for several years the question was hotly debated in the Congregation *De Auxiliis*, debates in which several Jesuit theologians suffered physical collapse before the formidable Dominican Thomas of Lemos, who had "an unimpeachable memory, a resounding voice and the health of a bull."[5] Popes came and went without any decision being reached, and when the controversy ended in 1605 nothing had been decided, though it was the general opinion that the Jesuits were in the wrong, and that only their expulsion from Venice in that year prevented Paul V. increasing their woes by denouncing their theology.

[4] Not to be confused with the Spanish Jesuit, Michael Molinos (1627–1696), who taught Quietist doctrines in his *Spiritual Guide* (1675), for which he was imprisoned by the Inquisition.

[5] Paquier, *Le Jansénisme*, 195.

Thomism and Molinism, the one Dominican, the other Jesuit, were thus the two alternative theories of Grace between which the seventeenth-century Catholic would be expected to choose. The one emphasized the will of God, the other the freedom of man: the one was exclusive, rigid, uncompromising; the other was liberal and tolerant, holding out hope for all men, since it did not put salvation beyond human effort. The Thomists held that Sufficient as contrasted with Efficient Grace is a divine premonition imparted to every one, preparing the soul for real or Efficient grace, without which men's acts cannot be justified before God. The Jesuits, on the other hand, maintained that human will and divine Grace act concurrently: it is man's freedom which sets in motion the forces working out his salvation; Sufficient and Efficient Grace are not exclusive, but may merge into each other. The prescience of God is a mystery which the Jesuits did not attempt to uncover: their theology of Grace was a practical, empirical solution of a difficult problem, a solution eminently adapted to the needs of a missionary and propagandist order devoted to the restoration of Catholicism in Europe and its propagation in Heathendom. The Spanish Dominicans, on the other hand, favoured a narrower, less generous theory, tinged with the fatalism of a race which had achieved its national consciousness in the age-long struggle with the Moors, and having something of that aristocratic exclusiveness peculiar to the Order which administered the Spanish Inquisition. The Dominicans could fearlessly destroy, knowing how few there are among the Elect; the Jesuits preferred to cast wide their nets, believing that salvation is for all men and that it was their peculiar mission to spread this truth.

A new element was introduced into the controversy by the University of Louvain. Ever since 1520 the University had been distinguished for its defence of orthodoxy against Lutheranism, but, later in the century, it was suspected that some of its professors were becoming tinged with the very heresies they so strenuously combated. Between 1551 and 1636 two Louvain teachers attracted particular attention—Baius[6] and Jansenius[7]—both of whom propounded views on Predestina-

---

[6] Michael Baius or de Bay (1513–1589). Not to be confused with the Dominican Bañez.

[7] Born near Leerdam in Holland in 1585. Appointed Professor

tion not unlike those attributed to the Calvinists. The latter of these, Jansen (1585–1638), produced a considerable theological literature in his life-time; he considered his views to be absolutely in accord with the strictest Catholic tradition and died as Bishop of Ypres; but for his posthumous *Augustinus* (1640) he might never have been heard of. He made a life-long study of St. Augustine, not as an interpreter or critic, but as expositor, concerning himself little with the doctrinal significance of his original, so long as he was satisfied that he had rendered a faithful and exact reproduction. As one who had commended himself to St. Joseph, patron of theologians, he hated heresy above all things; he believed that theology was an exercise not of the understanding but of the memory, and that its material was to be found in the Bible and the Fathers: accordingly he read all the writings of Augustine ten times, and those relating to Grace he read thirty times. If he was a heretic, he was a very unwilling one. Little did he guess that his commentary on St. Augustine was to produce schism and controversy in the Church.

The Dutch theologian had come into intimate contact with a fervid visionary named Duvergier de Hauranne, who was born of an old Basque family at Bayonne in 1581 and became Abbé of St. Cyran in 1620. The careful industry of the Dutchman was in marked contrast with the turgid enthusiasm of the Basque; the two had only this in common, that they were eager disciples of St. Augustine. During a stay of Jansen's at Bayonne as St. Cyran's guest, the host's mother had been obliged to warn her son that he must restrain his ardour or he would "kill the Fleming with these folios."[8] It was through books that Jansen is supposed to have met his death; he is said to have been poisoned by the effluvia from the old folios among which he spent his life.[9] St. Cyran, like Jansen, regarded himself as perfectly orthodox, but he refused to accept any preferment from Richelieu.

The third personality to have a share in the destinies of

of Holy Scripture at Louvain in 1630. Became Bishop of Ypres in 1635 and died in 1638. From the fact that he spent most of his life at Louvain he was often considered a Fleming by contemporaries.

[8] Quoted in P. F. Mathieu, *Les Convulsionnaires de St. Médard*, 12.

[9] Gazier, *Histoire générale du mouvement janséniste*, i. 45.

Calvinism was Antony Arnauld, twentieth child of the Gallican who had led French opposition to the proposed admission of the Jesuits into the University of Paris. That opposition had been a fierce one, because the proposal involved the independence of the University. The struggle was not ended till 1643, when (with the death of Richelieu) the Jesuits lost some of their favour in France and had then to retire from the fight against academic monopoly.[10] The Arnauld family, who had done so much to secure this result, were never forgiven by the Jesuits. Born in 1612, Antony Arnauld was thus a member of the most distinguished anti-Jesuit family in France, and early in life he had come under the magnetic influence of St. Cyran. A voluminous writer, he is known, like Jansen, for only one book—the *De la fréquente communion*—in which he urged the sanctity of the sacraments and the need for complete spiritual preparation before they could be received. There seemed no tinge of heresy in his doctrines. Innocent XI. proposed to make him a cardinal; Bossuet was one of his most assiduous readers; the enemy of the Jesuits, he was yet a sincere Catholic.

So far therefore as one can gather from the careers of Jansen, St. Cyran and Antony Arnauld, the early Jansenist movement (if it can be called a movement) consisted merely of anti-Jesuit propaganda waged by eager and orthodox Catholics. The early Jansenists, taking their stand on orthodoxy and St. Augustine, strove to eliminate from Catholic doctrine the Molinist freedom of will, with which the Jesuits seemed to threaten the doctrine of divine authority.

It is necessary at this point to notice three more personalities in the early history of Jansenism. The first of these is Cardinal Bérulle (1575–1629), a friend of both St. Cyran and Jansen, whose foundation of the French Oratory in 1611 had provoked considerable hostility from the Jesuits, since its teaching rivalled that provided by their schools; moreover, in its freedom from vows or rigid organization, the Oratory seemed to present such a striking alternative to the clearly defined Society of Jesus as to appear almost a criticism of it. The Jesuits enlisted Richelieu on their side against Bérulle, and a national controversy was averted only by the premature death of the latter in 1629: had Bérulle lived, he would have taken his stand with the Jansenists. More important, in the

[10] For this see Douarche, *L'Université de Paris et les Jésuites.*

drama to be described, was Mother Angélique Arnauld, sister of Antony, who at an early age became the Superior of a convent established in the remains of an old Cistercian monastery at Port Royal des Champs near Paris (1602). She had been placed in the religious life against her inclinations, but a sermon by a mendicant friar awoke the deep spiritual element in her nature,[11] and, influenced by St. Francis of Sales and Madame Chantal, Angélique Arnauld became such a fervid devotee that she threw herself into the task of reforming and invigorating the spiritual life of the society over which she presided. In 1625, for reasons of health, she transferred herself and her charges to Paris, where, in a corner of the Faubourg St. Jacques, was created the Port Royal of Paris, the buildings as they now stand being completed in 1655. Impressed by the scrupulous piety of Zamet, Bishop of Langres, Angélique induced him to act as chaplain at Port Royal, and for a time the two collaborated in their work of administration and organization. Zamet[12] should be noticed in the early history of Jansenism because he was a sincere and devout man, anxious to effect moral reform through episcopal control, and steadfastly opposed to the encroachments of the Jesuits and Ultramontanes. He is representative of the moderate and native form which Jansenism might have assumed in France had it been untouched by foreign influences. It was Zamet who summoned a Basque to gather the rich spiritual harvest at Port Royal, and the history of Jansenism begins when St. Cyran entered that convent in 1633.

To the Mother Superior St. Cyran[13] seemed a new St. Francis of Sales, an apostle of the mystical inner life, a man completely detached from earthly considerations. He preached that the world had descended to an unexampled state of corruption and vice; that the Church itself was contaminated; that for the individual the chances of salvation were remote, since even in large families probably only one would be saved.[14] The only mortals certain of salvation were, he declared, baptized children who died in infancy. Though him-

[11] Sainte-Beuve, *Port Royal* (ed. 1840), i. 97 ff.
[12] See Prunel, *Sébastien Zamet, Evêque de Langres; les origines du Jansénisme.*
[13] Brémond (*Histoire littéraire du sentiment religieux en France,* IV. ii.) calls him "un Bérulle malade." See also Sainte-Beuve, *op. cit.* I. pt. ii., *Le Port Royal de M. de Saint Cyran.*
[14] Prunel, *Sébastien Zamet,* 251.

self a man of refinement and taste, he condemned all the imaginative arts as seductive and vain-glorious (his denial of aesthetic pleasures arose, not from lack of appreciation, but from stern conviction); the Stage he considered necessarily immoral; he disliked Spring because its flowers were so short-lived and bore no fruits, preferring the late Autumn with its perpetually recurring mementos of decay and death. For conversion, there was necessary, he maintained, a spiritual violence, corresponding to the impact of Grace on the soul; where conversion was complete, retirement from the world was necessary that salvation might be guaranteed.[15] These exhortations galvanized the impressionable nuns who formed St. Cyran's auditory: hitherto they had complained of street noises during the hour of sermon; these complaints ceased when St. Cyran began to preach. "We love a man that damns us and we run after him again to save us."[16] St. Cyran's philosophy, even more than Calvin's was one of perdition for the unfortunate many and ascetic gloom for the fortunate few; his wardrobe contained only sackcloth and ashes; his calendar knew no season but Lent; his theology started with the Fall and ended with the Flood; he was a vivid painter of spiritual scenery in colours of cold grey and jet black, diffusing everywhere an atmosphere of unmitigated and perturbing gloom. Zamet was at first enthusiastic, but he soon became jealous; he now found himself displaced in importance by the colleague whom he had called in, and came to distrust the enthusiasm which had suddenly transformed Port Royal. "God has given me this man to be my executioner," he wrote of St. Cyran; "he shows me the way of truth but I cannot follow, and that kills me." A difference of opinion with Angélique Arnauld on the importance of neatness and order in the convent caused the aristocratic bishop to take his departure for his diocese.[17] Not long afterwards St. Cyran also left Port Royal (by the orders of Richelieu) for prison at Vincennes.

St. Cyran had been guilty of no offence, but the Cardinal had failed to win his alliance in the matter of the Duke of Orléans' marriage with a princess of the house of Lorraine. The Jesuits accused St. Cyran of concocting a plot, "l'affaire

15 St. Cyran, *Lettres spirituelles et chrétiennes* (ed. 1674), i. 28.
16 Selden, *Table Talk*.
17 Prunel, *op. cit.* 233.

Pilmot,"[18] to overthrow the Church; his friend Jansen had in 1635 attacked Richelieu's alliance with Gustavus Adolphus in a pamphlet entitled *Mars Gallicus*. Moreover, he was credited with the opinions that there had been no church for five or six centuries; that the Council of Trent was "an assembly of scholastics," that perfect contrition was necessary before the sacrament, and that the Jesuits should be exterminated. "Il est Basque, ainsi il a les entrailles chaudes":[19] such was Richelieu's professed reason for consigning the fiery St. Cyran to the cool of a prison cell. But even the austere Cardinal had been touched by the prophet of the wrath to come. St. Cyran had refused to admit Richelieu's argument that attrition was sufficient degree of penitence to warrant absolution in all cases, holding that contrition or absolutely complete purging of the soul was necessary. After consigning him to prison, however, Richelieu began to doubt whether the prisoner might not be right, and instructed his confessor to draw up a memoir proving that the more moderate "attrition" was sufficient. The Cardinal's conscience was eased, but on his death the confessor took care to regain possession of the memoir.[20]

St. Cyran employed his six years of enforced leisure in writing his best work—the *Lettres chrétiennes et spirituelles* —while from his prison he continued to direct the consciences of Port Royal. The Jesuits and Capuchins rejoiced at the discomfiture of their sworn enemy; the educational work of Port Royal, begun by St. Cyran, was temporarily suppressed, and the nuns of the Faubourg St. Jacques suddenly found themselves brought into unwelcome publicity. Like so many religious movements Jansenism dates its history from persecution. St. Cyran was released after the death of Richelieu, but survived only a few months; his death in 1643 ends the first act in the drama of Jansenism.

[18] The correspondence between Jansen and St. Cyran for the years 1617–1635 contains a few names in cypher. This correspondence was published by the Jesuits in 1654 and "l'affaire Pilmot," one of the cypher expressions, was construed as a reference to a plot. It probably meant merely the project of purifying the Church. See Gazier, *Histoire générale du mouvement janséniste*, i. 42, and Fuzet, *Les Jansénistes*, 89. The latter book—a violent modern attack on the Jansenists—was later retracted.

[19] Quoted in Fuzet, *Les Jansénistes*, 90.

[20] Godefroi Hermant, *Mémoires* (ed. Gazier), i. 81.

It has already been noticed that the treatise of the Jesuit Molina had revived among Catholic theologians the controversy between Free Will and Predestination, and that the Jesuit defence of Free Will had just escaped papal censure owing to the expulsion of the Society from Venice. Jansen's refutation of Molina on the basis of St. Augustine is contained in the three-volumed *Augustinus* published in 1640, two years after its author's death. The Jesuits did not, however, attack the Jansenists on the ground of doctrine until, in 1643, an unexpected chance came with the publication of Arnauld's *De la fréquente communion*. This book owed its motive to the recorded practice of a Jesuit confessor who allowed some of his penitents to engage freely in such worldly occupations as dancing, on condition that for every lapse they confessed, were absolved and received the sacrament.[21] The principle of frequent communion as the sovereign remedy for frequent transgression was embodied in a treatise which was circulated widely among society ladies anxious to combine worldly pleasure with spiritual safety. This subterfuge was condemned in no unmeasured terms by the prisoner of Vincennes, who commissioned his friend Arnauld to refute what he considered an insidious and immoral doctrine. The *Fréquente Communion* was the result, a book which did not attack frequent communion, as has often been assumed, but stigmatized the laxity of those confessors who counselled it to penitents insufficiently prepared. The Jesuits construed it as an attack on their society; they left no stone unturned to discredit its author, and so strong was their hold on the court of Anne of Austria that Arnauld had to go into retirement. Thereafter the opinion was assiduously circulated that his book was an attack on the doctrine of the Eucharist, an opinion which even the most casual reading of the text would serve to refute. Arnauld's book is of importance because it is the first textbook of French Jansenism; it expressed in concrete form the emotional teaching of St. Cyran, and by its elimination of all adventitious aids to morality it upheld the ideal of an austere, uncompromising virtue, thrusting apart the two things which the Jesuits combined—the world and the spiritual life.

At this point the Jesuits were influenced by two things— their personal dislike of the Arnauld family and their opposition to the theories of Grace expounded in the writings of

[21] Gazier, *op. cit.* i. 48.

Jansen, popularized by St. Cyran and issued as a challenge by Arnauld. When they failed to discredit the disciples, they turned their attention to the master, and the *Augustinus* was subjected to a microscopical examination. The Syndic of the Faculty of Theology in the Sorbonne, Nicolas Cornet, was an ex-Jesuit, and, as an official censor of theological books, his opinion was of considerable importance; his services were accordingly enlisted against the Jansenists. After a careful examination of the *Augustinus* he extracted seven propositions (reduced afterwards to five) which he declared to be heretical. The Five Propositions are as follows:[22]

1. There are certain divine commandments which it is impossible for the just to obey as they have not sufficient Grace.

2. In the state of fallen nature there can be no resistance to interior Grace.

3. For merit or demerit, after the Fall, it is not necessary for man to have interior liberty; it is enough that he be exempt from external constraint.

4. The Semi-Pelagians admit the necessity of an interior and prevenient Grace, even for the first act of grace, but they were heretical in their view that this Grace could be controlled by the human will.

5. It is a Semi-Pelagian heresy to say that Christ died for all men without exception.

On the 31st of May 1653 these Five Propositions were condemned by a bull of Innocent X. The disciples of Jansen were now heretics.

The Five Propositions were not, it should be noted, extracts from the *Augustinus*, but were doctrines which, it was claimed, could be found in that book. It was said quite rightly by Bossuet that they are "the soul of the book," but many Jansenists were trained theologians, and they took up the attitude that, while condemning the Five Propositions, they refused to admit that any of these propositions had ever been enunciated by Jansen. From this a distinction of Right and Fact was developed; the Five Propositions were repudiated as a matter of Right, but as a matter of Fact (it was argued) they were not to be found in the *Augustinus*.[23]

[22] Gazier, *op. cit.* I. ch. v.

[23] Pascal maintained this argument in the last two of the *Lettres provinciales*.

Orthodoxy had thus on the showing of the Jansenists been twisted into heresy by the Jesuits who, in order to discredit their Catholic opponents, had cleverly contrived to have them branded as heretics. This is the meaning of the often quoted statement that there were no Jansenists until the Jesuits discovered them.

There was a second line of defence open to the party of Arnauld. The Molinist or Jesuit doctrine of Grace had been attacked by the Dominicans, of whose orthodoxy there could be no question: the Dominican doctrines were derived from St. Augustine through the intermediary stage of St. Thomas Aquinas; hence, allowing for certain subtle differences of interpretation, it might be possible to assimilate the Dominican with the Jansenist position. In his later writings Arnauld went far in this direction; the same progress can be traced by comparing the earlier with the later *Lettres provinciales*.[24] But it soon became difficult to adopt this method of defence because, rightly or wrongly, the opinion was circulated that the Jansenists were a republican sect, that they reduced the sacraments to symbols, denied the authority of the Pope, rejected the doctrine of the Eucharist, and were Calvinists[25] in a new and more dangerous guise. In consequence the Dominicans rallied to the side of the Jesuits, sinking their theological differences in order to maintain a united front. By every one, therefore, except the professional theologians, the extraordinary facts might be realized that Calvinist, Dominican and Jansenist shared certain views in regard to the part played by the human will in the achievement of salvation; that their views were based on interpretations of the greatest father of the Church (St. Augustine), and that the opponents of these views (the Jesuits) had just missed incurring papal censure because of a personal misfortune. In other words, from the *Catholic* point of view, the extreme wing of the Protestant party might claim that, on a fundamental question of dogma, they were more orthodox than the extreme wing of the Catholics; and so by the middle of the seventeenth century the great truth was hammering for admission into men's minds that orthodoxy is only a relative term, and that Protestant and Catholic are simply different

[24] For this see H. F. Stewart, *The Holiness of Pascal*, 35 ff.
[25] It was often said that the Jansenists were "Calvinists who go to mass."

interpretations of certain common fundamentals. So long as Christian theology was embodied in a vast and complicated edifice completely obscuring the simple and straight-forward lines of the original foundation, it is scarcely surprising that strange encounters took place in its tortuous corridors.

To the argument that the Five Propositions were not to be found in Jansen, the Papacy replied in 1656 with the affirmation that the sense though not the actual words is to be found in the *Augustinus*. On the suggestion of the French clergy a formulary was drawn up prescribing an official renunciation of the Five Propositions to be signed by all clergy and teachers, but, in spite of this, the Jansenists still maintained their argument that no proof had been supplied of the existence of the Five Propositions in Jansen's book. From their distinction of Right and Fact they argued that the Pope, while adjudicating on a question of right, might be wrong in a question of fact; he was right in condemning the Five Propositions but wrong in thinking that they were in the *Augustinus*. It was Pascal who first enunciated this distinction, and with Pascal we come to the first real thinker in this long story of theological dispute. It was he who transformed Jansenism from a sect into a great moral and intellectual movement. Before describing his part in the fray it is necessary to return to Port Royal, which had been brought into prominence by its association with Jansen's friend, St. Cyran.

In 1625 Angélique Arnauld had transferred her headquarters to the Paris Port Royal, but in 1648 the deserted buildings at Port Royal des Champs were again inhabited by a number of nuns, under a resident Superior, so that there were then two Port Royals—one in Paris, the other near Versailles.[26] The valley of Port Royal was at that time a solitary place, and from about 1636 onwards it began to attract a number of cultured and earnest men who were interested in Jansenism because it provided an alternative to the lax morality and cynical epicureanism then fashionable in Paris. These men resided in a house on the eminence overlooking the valley; they were not bound by vows; they included cleric and lay; they carried on their own intellectual pursuits while sharing an interest in literary composition and in the education of the young. Soon what had once been a

[26] For an interesting account of the nuns see M. F. Lowndes, *The Nuns of Port Royal.*

desert was frequented by men who, in sympathy with the ideals taught to the nuns by St. Cyran, were anxious to restore the virtues and principles of primitive Christianity of which St. Augustine was the acknowledged exponent. Among them were Antony Arnauld; his brother, Arnauld d'Andilly, translator of St. Augustine's *Confessions*; de Tillemont, le Maître and Nicole.[27] They were men of learning but not pedants; they revived the study of Greek and popularized the writing of French in place of Latin. Some of their literary productions were the work of collaboration, and the Port Royal *Logic* was for long a standard work. In 1655 they were joined by Blaise Pascal, who at an early age had attracted attention on account of his remarkable mathematical abilities. Born in 1623, Pascal even as a boy had been distinguished for weak physical health and extraordinary mental powers; at sixteen he had written an important book on Conic Sections; two years later he invented a mechanical calculator; following up the investigations of the Italian physicist, Toricelli, on the mass of the atmosphere, he first experienced the hostility of the Jesuits when he demonstrated that the vacuum at the top of the barometric tube varies with the altitude.

It has been said that the universe appears to have been designed by a pure mathematician.[28] As a sceptic, Pascal may have concluded that the nature of reality is unknowable, but on the other hand, as a geometrician, he may have seen in the universe a rhythm and pattern such as presupposed intelligent and purposeful creation. As a reader of Montaigne, he was tempted to adopt a cultured epicureanism, but as a student of the infinite, he found in the harmonies of space an enigma which, could it be solved, would answer the questionings of his heart. Divided by these opposing impulses he at last, like Kant after him, resolved to limit knowledge in order to extend belief; for the sake of achieving faith in an unfathomable mystery, he decided to surrender his intellect. Already, in 1646, he had established contact with two disciples of St. Cyran; eight years later, he appears to have had

[27] Accounts of these men will be found in Brémond, *Histoire littéraire du sentiment religieux en France*, iv., and in Sainte-Beuve, *Port Royal*, vols. i. and ii. (on p. 517 of vol. ii. Sainte-Beuve passes summary judgement on each of the Solitaries).

[28] By Sir James Jeans, in *The Mysterious Universe*.

a "conversion" in which his doubts were finally stilled. A "miracle" completed the process—the apparently definitive "conversion" by which he professed to have attained a conviction of the existence, not of the vague deity invoked by the metaphysicians, but of the concrete deity worshipped by Christians. But even these spiritual convulsions do not appear to have provided permanent relief. His bad health resulted in a form of hypochondria; his acute intellect forbade acquiescence in conventional beliefs, and he achieved little more than a truce in the *guerre intestine* between reason and emotion. His was one of those tragedies where the questionings of the intelligence are never completely silenced.[29]

In January 1655 Pascal took up his residence at Port Royal des Champs. This implied no adherence to any definite set of beliefs, for the Solitaries of Port Royal retained their intellectual freedom, and Pascal's presence among them did not imply that he was a Jansenist, even if that word had connoted anything very definite at the time. His entry into Port Royal was at the moment when it seemed that Arnauld would have to give up the fight for the Augustinian theory of Grace and yield to Jesuits and Molinists: the newcomer must have been intensely interested in the controversy, for had not the course of his own life been suddenly diverted by a flood of Grace against which no effort of his could have prevailed?

The situation was becoming a critical one at the very moment when Pascal joined the retreat; a crisis was precipitated by an apparently trifling incident. Saint Sulpice, under its rector Olier, had long been distinguished for opposition to the disciples of Jansen; early in 1655 a priest of Saint Sulpice had refused absolution to the Duc de Liancourt on the ground that he favoured the Jansenists. Arnauld at once appealed to public opinion in two letters, wherein he defended the distinction of Fact and Right and attacked the Molinist doctrine of sufficient Grace. As the Jesuits were influential at both Sorbonne and Vatican, and as the Pope[30]

[29] There is a considerable literature on Pascal. See E. Jory, *Études pascaliennes*, 1927; R. H. Soltau, *Pascal, the Man and the Message*, 1927; C. C. J. Webb, *Pascal's Philosophy of Religion*, 1929; H. F. Stewart, *Pascal's Apology for Religion . . . from the Pensées*, 1942; G. Truc, *Pascal, son temps et le nôtre*, 1950.

[30] See *infra*, p. 387.

(Alexander VII.) was the most pusillanimous of the century, there seemed every likelihood that Arnauld would again incur censure and that the Jansenists would be expelled from the bosom of the Church. The first of these fears was justified in the year 1656, when five propositions extracted from Arnauld's two letters were condemned by the Faculty of Theology (by a very narrow majority); the minority was compelled to signify its adhesion on pain of expulsion, and Arnauld was excluded from the Faculty with the loss of all privileges as *socius sorbonicus*. It is still possible to debate how far the Jesuits were responsible for these harsh and unfair measures, but many Frenchmen of education resented this attempt to dictate theological opinions to thinkers whose Catholicism was beyond doubt. Men who approved harsh measures towards heretics condemned the ostracism inflicted on Arnauld and Port Royal. These last were now to find an eloquent defender, and for the packed and bullied theological tribunal of the Sorbonne was to be substituted the public opinion of France.

Before describing the *Lettres provinciales* it is necessary to explain why Pascal regarded the dispute between Jesuit and Jansenist as one of fundamentals. The Jesuits were distinguished not only as theologians but as practical moralists and confessors; they had charge of many souls of consequence, and, as spiritual directors, they had to deal in a practical way with problems of life and conduct. Their doctrine of sufficient Grace was one that gave hope to the penitent sinner, for the little spark of Grace in his nature might be fanned by his own exertions into a great flame, whereas the Augustinian, the Protestant and the Jansenist must await from on high the thunderbolt that would instantaneously transform his nature. Except the Calvinists, no Christian society has ever been so inspired by missionary zeal as were the Jesuits; from the foundation their activities took them to the most remote lands and the most primitive peoples, where they were not long in finding that flexibility of practice may be a useful aid in dealing with heathens, if only as a preliminary to the rigidity of doctrine for which they really stood. The affair of the Malabar rites[31] showed

[31] In 1704 the Capuchin mission in Pondichery complained that the Jesuits in the Carnatic were permitting the practice of heathen rites by their neophytes. After an inquiry, Clement XI. in 1706

the lengths to which these concessions might go.

It should be remembered also, that the Jesuits had a task sometimes even more difficult, namely, to preserve in the faith those Catholic souls entrusted to their keeping. They had come into existence at a time when Europe was shaking off the last fetters of scholastic and mediaeval philosophy, and they associated themselves with some of the most advanced movements of the sixteenth century. While the Dominicans or Thomists represented the rigorist and orthodox traditions of the mediaeval Church, there were a number of Doctors, from Duns Scotus onwards, who struck out on fresh paths, and, like Ockham, came to propound doctrines subversive of many cherished mediaeval conceptions. Nor did the Church itself escape the spirit of inquiry which the Renaissance suddenly liberated. Even among the Dominicans there was, early in the sixteenth century, an interesting group of Spanish theologians,[32] including Vittoria and Soto, which was humanistic rather than scholastic, a group which evolved, among other things, an important theory of natural rights. In 1567, however, Pope Pius V. officially declared St. Thomas to be Doctor of the Church, and the result of this, for the Dominicans, was to terminate the age of experiment and investigation. Henceforward they were the accredited expounders of a standardized system: as recently as 1914 Pope Pius X. confirmed the Dominican doctrines as the embodiment of orthodox Catholic theology. Before the end of the sixteenth century, therefore, a crystallizing process had taken place: the Council of Trent had defined practically every doctrine except that of Predestination, and tacit approval had been accorded to the Dominican theory of Grace. This theory, in non-technical terms, was simply that works avail nothing unless performed in a state of Grace, or with the assistance of Grace. It was Bañez, a Professor at the University of Salamanca, who first clearly defined this doc-

---

required the Jesuits to forbid native superstition among their converts. There is evidence that several Jesuit missionaries in the East began their work by thoroughly acclimatizing themselves to local customs and superstitions, living among their future converts as if they had come to assimilate rather than subvert native ideas. For this, and the affair of the Chinese rites, see Brucker, *La Compagnie de Jésus*, 699 ff.

[32] For this see E. Nys, *Le Droit des gens et les anciens jurisconsultes espagnols*.

trine, and, on this basis, attacked the forces of modernism in the sixteenth-century Catholic Church. There are subtle differences between the Dominican and the Jansenist theories of Grace, but it is a curious fact nevertheless that while the Universities of Salamanca and Louvain were propagating very similar views on this all-important subject, the first increased its reputation for orthodoxy, while the second was branded as a nest of heretics. Only in the history of the Jansenist movement can any explanation of this seeming inconsistency be found.

The Jesuits were the modernists of the Counter-Reformation; their enemies, Calvinist, Dominican and Jansenist, were yoked to a reactionary Augustinianism. It is not without significance that in 1525 Ignatius Loyola himself was imprisoned by a Dominican tribunal—the Spanish Inquisition—on account of his *Exercitia spiritualia*, and because his Saturday devotions to the Virgin Mary created the suspicion that he was celebrating the Jewish Sabbath. The Jesuits were modernists because they were eclectic, they repressed freedom of thought outside their own Order, but set themselves against persecutions for witchcraft and sorcery, they declined to compromise with opponents, but they humanized the all-important doctrine of Grace, making it something which might be achieved by effort. Rather than restrict themselves to any definite ethical code, they preferred to range at will among the Doctors of the Church in their search for the elements of a practical and flexible moral theology. It was in this last respect that they came most definitely into contact with the Jansenists. The theology of mediaeval times, in spite of its heresies and innovations, was based primarily on the principle of obedience to authority; an opinion would command respect not altogether for its consistency, but because it owed its origin to some Doctor of recognized eminence, and scholastic reputations were often based on nothing more than the exercise of dialectic skill. Academic fame in mediaeval times was generally acquired not by success in examinations, nor by the writing of original monographs, but by beating an adversary in a public disputation, or by writing many lines of comment on one line of text. By the end of the fifteenth century many reputations had been made in this way, and the scholastic literature was enormous in its extent and variety. The Jesuits took over this literature as a heritage. There are Casuist doctrines in the writings of Abelard, Gerson and Raymond of Peñaforte; in 1494 a Franciscan named Clavasio had written a *Summa casuum conscientiae*, and it may be said of most mediaeval theologians that their enormous tomes could not have been filled without a certain amount of quibbling and play upon words. This is the sense in which it is true that there were Casuists before there were Jesuits. But though the Jesuits were not the inventors of Casuistry, they put it to a novel and systematic use, because they employed it not so much for the public ceremonial of the University as for the more intimate occasion of the confessional.

In the first century of their existence the Jesuits produced a great number of Casuists who compiled guides for the use of confessors, standard books which had the same importance for the health of the soul as modern medical books have for the health of the body, because they were not abstruse treatises, but manuals for the use of the practitioner. The most famous of the Jesuit Casuists was the Spanish theologian Escobar (1589–1669), whose *Theologia moralis*, first published in 1643, went through many editions. The daring and often subversive views propounded by such writers soon attracted attention; they were denounced by Pierre Dumoulin in his *Catalogue ou Dénombrement des traditions romaines* (Geneva, 1632), and in 1644 there appeared a selection of the more notable Casuist doctrines in *La Théologie morale des Jésuites*, a work attributed by some writers to Arnauld. Avoiding all controversial statements regarding the Jesuit use of Casuistry, it may be affirmed that among earnest seventeenth-century Catholics the view was current that many Jesuit Casuists were teaching a relaxed morality, that they were altering cases to suit circumstances, and introducing the principle of relativity into questions of human conduct. As early as 1631 Balzac[33] in his *Prince* noticed that a change had come over Catholic morality at the hands of some of its exponents: "We have now a more easy and agreeable theology: one that can be better adjusted to suit the humours of the great, which can accommodate its maxims with their interests, and is not so rustic or harsh as the old theology. . . . To-day we have invented for the thief expedients enabling him to salve his conscience."

Nor was this confined to manuals for the confessional,

[33] J. L. G. Balzac, 1594–1654.

since Jesuits like Le Moyne and Mugnier wrote treatises to prove that morality is easy, that salvation may be combined with a considerable amount of wordliness, and in *La Dévotion aisée* (1652) the view was upheld that the path of virtue is neither hard nor narrow, but so broad that it can scarcely be mistaken, and so pleasant that it might almost be confused with the road to destruction.[34] But on the whole this type of book was exceptional, though it marked a latent characteristic of the methods employed by some of the Jesuit Casuists. Revolting from the difficult requirements of the Augustinian and anti-Molinist schools, strenuously opposing the opinoin that salvation is for the preordained few, the Jesuits elaborated a moral philosophy which, while rigorist in the abstract, did in practice allow so much mitigation, so many exceptions and such subtle refinements that some of their Casuist specialists could explain away any sin, could condone any crime, could show exceptions to any rule, could, in short, turn morality inside out.

Casuistry is as old as human nature, and every one has at times tried to reconcile interest with conviction by arguments that do not completely satisfy the conscience; a vein of casuistry may generally be detected in the most eloquent specimens of forensic oratory, in the most brilliant examples of special pleading or advocacy, in every art where it is necessary to silence objection at all costs and lull the intelligence by stupefying draughts of insinuation or innuendo. The art was expounded by Cicero in the later parts of his *De officiis*,[35] it survives to-day in several eminently respectable journals for family reading.[36] But the characteristic of the Jesuit use of it is that what others had occasionally employed as an unacknowledged art, or secret device, was reduced by the Society to a definite system. The following are two main principles of this system:

1. Method of favourable circumstance. Where there is an omission in a canonical rule, the most favourable interpretation may be permissible. Thus the canons prescribe excommunication for priests who give up their canonical dress, but

---

[34] For this see Brémond, *op. cit.* i. 376 ff.

[35] In Part III. It did not have Cicero's complete approval.

[36] Several ladies' magazines of to-day have "Problems of Conduct" competitions; casuist methods may often be found in the winning solutions.

they omit any reference to punishment for priests who lay aside their vestments temporarily in order to steal. Consequently where a motive, even if it be stealing, is established, there is no condemnation in the canons for abandoning the ecclesiastical dress. On this showing, to paraphrase a remark of Hobbes, liberty is "what the Lord hath praetermitted." If the canons have neglected to specify punishment for an act, then that act may not necessarily be an offence at all.

2. There was a second method—that of Probability. This had been first propounded by a Spanish Dominican, Bartolomé de Medina (1528–1581): "si opinio est probabilis, licet eam sequi, licet opposita probabilior sit," and more explicitly by Escobar: "Amid variety of opinions, the yoke of Jesus Christ is easier to bear. Is it not better for a gentleman who has to go from Valladolid to Madrid to be shown several roads than if there were only one? For that one might be either too broad or impeded by the multitutde of wayfarers, and it would be difficult to walk in."[37] Thus of two opinions, one probable, the other more probable, it was permissible to adopt the former, even if the two opinions conflicted with each other, provided the less probable opinion was neither ridiculous nor expressly forbidden by the Church. The method of probability was particularly useful if one wished to use precedents derived from scholastic theology. Every opinion enunciated by an orthodox Doctor of the Church became possible after a certain lapse of time; so, too, the converse of an orthodox opinion might be adopted, provided this converse was "probable," that is, not manifestly absurd. Considering the vast number of orthodox Doctors of the Church and the vagaries into which their dialectical subtleties sometimes led them, it is easy to see what a kaleidoscopic morality could be constructed from their opinions and the converse of these opinions; one has only to glance at the vast edifice constructed in the eighteenth century by St. Alfonso of Liguria to see the extraordinary results of such methods of argument. It followed also that a confessor could adopt a principle with which he was not himself in agreement, provided it had one good "backer." There were different degrees of probabilism: the probabiliorists required a greater proportion of probability for the opinion on which they acted; the aequi-probabilists were willing to act on either

[37] Quoted in H. F. Stewart, *op. cit.* 40.

of two opinions having an equal amount of probability, while those who chose an opinion for which there was only a small amount of probability are indistinguishable from the Laxists. Laxism has never been approved by the Catholic Church and was explicitly condemned by Pope Innocent XI., but many Jesuit Casuists were Laxists,[38] and it is against these that the *Lettres provinciales* were written. The converse of Laxism was Tutiorism; the Jansenists were Tutiorists in that their intellects had to satisfy their consciences.

Between the extremes of Tutiorism and Laxism there is the whole science of human conduct; these names merely conceal distinctions and qualifications which, consciously or unconsciously, still influence us in our relations with our fellow-men. Suppose, for instance, that representatives of these shades of opinion were faced with a characteristic problem of modern commercial morality, such as whether to purchase an article by cheque when there is a chance of the cheque being dishonoured. The Tutiorist would pay only if there was every human certainty that the cheque would be honoured; the conduct of the Probabilist would be influenced by the amount of probability in the opinion that he was in credit, and he would require at least a reasonable probability for this opinion or, alternatively, a probability that the bank had no objection to his account being overdrawn; the Laxist would give the cheque, even if it was more likely than not that it would be dishonoured, provided this was not a certainty, provided he knew nothing of the intentions of the bank in regard to his cheques, and provided he could avoid scandal in the event of the less probable opinion (that the cheque would be honoured) being discredited. The Tutiorists take no risks: the Probabilists go into business: the Laxists (when caught) go to gaol.

When it is added that the Casuists believed Attrition to be sufficient for absolution, while the Jansenists insisted on the complete purging of the soul known as Contrition, it will be seen that the antithesis between the two was complete. Vasquez (1551–1604) taught that Christian duty must always be limited by human capability, and that it may be sufficient to love God only at the end of one's life[39] (Escobar[40] thought

---

[38] Catholic theologians always distinguish between Probabilism and Laxism, but, in many respects, the one is simply a different degree of the other.

[39] *Commentariorum et disputationum in tertiam partem Sancti*

that there were four occasions on which such love was necessary). In 1657 a Spanish Jesuit compiled a collection of Casuist opinions[41] on various subjects, and, though he expressed no approval, these opinions were mostly of such a scandalous and immoral nature that the book was placed on the Index. The spirit of Casuistry is summed up in a chance remark of Escobar[42] in a passage dealing with the circumstances in which a prince may dispense with his own laws: "proprie loquendo ex vi coactiva non obligatur, quia lex obligat subditos: nullus autem sibi subditus est." These words —"no one is subject to himself"—contain the greatest indictment of the whole system, for they imply that one is safe provided the letter of the law is adhered to, and that before the tribunal of human conscience no responsibility is incurred. There can be no more immoral doctrine than that.

Begun as a defence of Arnauld, the *Lettres provinciales*[43] ended as the most complete and brilliant indictment of a set of beliefs ever penned. The possibilities of the French language were hardly realized until Pascal wrote; never before had the qualities of sarcasm been used with such withering force; never since has a prose writer achieved such instantaneous success by the powers of criticism and destruction.[44] The whole gigantic edifice of Casuistry was undermined and overthrown; the onslaught of Pascal was so crushing that some sympathizers feared lest it might not be too destructive. Even among the enemies of Casuistry were to be found some

---

Thomae, IV. Quaest. lxxxvi., Art. 2, dubium vi. (p. 95 in the 1616 edition).

[40] *Liber Theologiae moralis* (ed. 1659), Tract. I. Examen I. cap. iv.

[41] This was the *Opusculum* of Mathieu de Moya who wrote under the pseudonym of Guimenius. Instances of doctrines for which Guimenius supplied a speculative foundation are "furtum triginta regalium maius peccatum est quam sodomia" (p. 25) and "Subditi possunt justa tributa non solvere" (p. 181).

[42] Escobar, *op. cit.* Tract. I. Examen I. cap. v.

[43] The best edition is that by Havet (2 vols.). The full title of the 1657 edition is *Les Provinciales ou les lettres écrites par Louis de Montalte à un provincial de ses amis et aux RR.PP. Jésuites sur le sujet de la morale et de la politique de ces pères.* Montalte is a pseudonym for Pascal.

[44] The literary qualities of the *Lettres provinciales* are very fully discussed in the earlier chapters of Sainte-Beuve's third volume.

who felt that the *Lettres* ought to have been written in Latin, so that a vulgar world might not witness the discomfiture of a great religious Order. It was mainly for this reason that the *Lettres provinciales* were put on the Index.[45] But though Pascal's opinions may have undergone considerable change in his later years, he never modified his attitude to Jesuit casuistry. He had selected, it is true, from among his materials in order to make a case, but he had selected those opinions of his opponents which were not too incredible for belief. Merely destructive criticism is seldom of permanent value, but there are cases where its use is necessary; and Casuistry, as applied to questions of morality, has never recovered from the ignominy to which Pascal consigned it.

The main purposes of Pascal were, by analysing the Molinist and Dominican theories of Grace, to show that his Jansenist friends were not heretics, and to prove that the lax morality of the Jesuit Casuists was aided and abetted by their theory of Grace. As the plan of the work developed, the second became the more important object, until a climax is reached in the thirteenth *Provinciale*: the theological issue is laid aside in order that a great source of moral corruption might be revealed. With the nineteenth, written in the spring of 1657, the Letters suddenly cease. Various reasons have been suggested for this abandonment of a literary enterprise that had been so successful. One, which would weigh with few men, but which may have had great weight with Pascal, is that the raillery and sarcasm of the *Lettres* had attracted a number of cynical readers, and Pascal had no desire to provide public amusement at the expense of a religious Order, no matter how much he might disagree with that Order. Another possible reason is that early in 1657 efforts were being made to influence Mazarin and Anne of Austria on behalf of the Jansenists. But, strongest of all, Pascal had little faith in religious polemics; he had settled his own religious doubts, and his real contribution to religion, not appreciated until a later date, was to be the constructive *Pensées* rather than the destructive *Lettres*. In this opinion he was confirmed by an incident known as the miracle of the Holy Thorn. Before beginning the sixth *Provinciale* (March 1656) his niece Marguerite Périer was cured of a dangerous ulcer by the application of Port Royal's relic—a piece of the crown of thorns.[46] Pascal's belief in the miracle led him to think that God was on the side of Port Royal and that it would not need his defence.

It would be impossible here to go into the bitter controversy which has been waged round the *Lettres*. Pascal has been attacked with so many different weapons as to raise a suspicion that very few of these weapons hit their mark.[47] He was not original, it has been said; he used earlier attacks on Jesuit Casuists and did not always go to first-hand sources; in his quotations from Escobar[48] he sometimes made omissions or abridgments; he was wrong in thinking that the Jesuits were solely responsible for Casuistry—they were merely following a precedent set by Dominicans and Franciscans of unimpeachable orthodoxy; he ought to have realized that a great religious order must contain a few black sheep and that it is wrong to judge the general by the exceptional; he should have known that most of the Casuists from whom he quoted were men of exemplary private morals, and that the majority of the Jesuits were men of learning and virtue (these two contentions were quite justified by facts). More insidious accusations are that Pascal was ill[49] when he wrote the *Lettres provinciales* (Pascal was ill all his life, but his mind retained its full vigour to the end), or that he was heavily bribed—this accusation is generally made verbally. Every year sees some new contribution to the controversy. It may be suggested that while Pascal is very seldom wrong in his facts, he was wrong in always attributing a wicked motive to the Jesuits. Most of them were men who, if they made Heaven easy for others, made it difficult for themselves; they had no interest in promoting vice or immorality, but they subordinated everything to the authority of the Church and their Order, believing that if they could acquire complete hold on the consciences of their flock, if they could prescribe at will for moral ailments from the many alternatives of a vast spiritual pharmacopeia, then they might hope to retain their hold on that large class which many churches have had to give up in despair—the indiffer-

---

[46] Gazier, *op. cit.* I. ch. vi.

[47] See Brou, *Les Jésuites de la légende*, I. chs. x and xi.

[48] Gazier, *Pascal et Escobar.*

[49] When he wrote the *Lettres provinciales* Pascal was in "a shattered state of health" (T. J. Campbell, *The Jesuits*, 281).

ent, the worldly and the frivolous. That end was admittedly a good one, though the means might be devious and hard to understand. "Le gros du Christianisme a été de tout temps composé d'infirmes et d'imparfaits."[50] Pascal and the Jansenists would have no compromising with sin; the Casuists and the Jesuits equally abhorred it, but they did not launch a frontal attack; they would rather take the citadel by undermining it, by spies if necessary, by subtlety and strategy rather than force. These different attitudes symbolize two permanently opposed and contrasted human types; there is nothing to be gained by controversy between them; the antithesis of Jesuit and Jansenist is ultimate and universal.

One more question is raised by the *Lettres provinciales*. Was Pascal a Jansenist? In so far as he defended the Port Royal distinctions of Right and Fact, of Papal Infallibility in the first and Papal Fallibility in the second, Pascal was a Jansenist in the narrow sense, but these are just the views which he seems to have modified before the close of his life. Prior to his death in 1662 he received the sacrament from a priest who afterwards expressed the conviction that Pascal had died in absolute orthodoxy and submission to the Papacy, after having expressed his opinion that the Jansenist went too far in their doctrine of Grace. A literary discovery made in 1908[51] shows that in his last years Pascal had become tired of religious controversy, but, while withdrawing somewhat from the attitude he had taken in regard to Grace and Papal Infallibility, he reiterated his condemnation of Casuistry and lax morality. Pascal therefore was a consistent Jansenist only in the sense that he was a fervid Catholic opposed to the Jesuits.

Seven years after Pascal's death a French traveller in Spain visited Escobar and found him engaged on the latest edition of the *Theologia moralis*. When the visitor mentioned the fierce debate in which this Casuist manual had figured so prominently, Escobar expressed surprise that his book should

---

[50] Bonal, *Le Chrétien du temps* (1655), quoted by Brémond, *op. cit.* i. 403.

[51] Jovy, *Pascal inédit*. Jovy discovered, in the Memoirs of the priest (Beurrier) who gave Pascal the last sacrament, an account of what happened just before Pascal's death. The question is discussed by Jovy in vol. ii. 403 ff. See also Stewart, *op. cit.* note 48 (p. 102).

have caused controversy, because he had not expressed his own views but the views of the most widely accepted Casuists of his Order. Some of the statements in his book might savour of laxity, but there were some Casuists far more lax. He had never read the *Lettres provinciales* (possibly he had never heard of them): the French interviewer promised to send him a copy.[52] No incident could better depict the mentality of seventeenth-century Spain.

Neither the success of the *Lettres provinciales* nor the miracle of the Holy Thorn saved Port Royal from persecution. The nuns insisted on the distinction of Right and Fact: they would not admit that the Five Propositions were to be found in Jansen, and they refused to sign the formulary drawn up for the purpose of obtaining their submission on these points. Several bishops, notably Pavillon of Alet, Caulet of Pamiers and Buzenval of Beauvais, threw in their lot with the nuns, but the Jesuits had the ear of the Court, and in 1660 the educational activities of Port Royal were suspended by the compulsory closing of its schools. The position of the Jansenists had meanwhile been seriously compromised by the activities of the Cardinal Archbishop of Paris, De Retz, who in the years between 1654 and 1661 was in exile. De Retz had been notorious during the Fronde as the bellicose Coadjutor Paul de Gondi, the most bitter and intriguing enemy of Mazarin: during his long exile his diocese was administered by two Vicars-General who publicly declared their sympathy with Port Royal and the *Lettres provinciales*. This led the Jansenists to include, among their professed objects, the restoration of De Retz to his diocese, on the ground that he was a virtuous and persecuted archbishop, an attitude which naturally commended Port Royal and all its works to the absent prelate; but this was unfortunate for the Jansenists, since it brought down on their heads the ever-increasing animosity of Mazarin. The link connecting the Archbishop and Port Royal was due to a misconception, for as an atheist and debauchee De Retz had nothing in common with the Jansenists; he believed them to be fools, and, had he spent even a few days with the solitaries, he would soon have dispelled the legend that he favoured either austere morality or high thinking. Nor were the Jansenists more fortunate in

[52] Gazier, *Pascal et Escobar*, 53.

another illustrious convert—Madame de Longueville, who also had distinguished herself in the Fronde, but having in middle age become devout, she chose Jansenism as the most complete antithesis to the freedom of her earlier years. It was in this way that the movement came to have a semipolitical aspect—its adherents were drawn mainly from the same class as the Paris Parlement, and it was associated with two of the most prominent and dangerous Frondeurs. This is one reason why Mazarin and Louis XIV. set themselves against it.

When Louis XIV. began his reign he put into effect the advice given him first by Mazarin and by his Council of Conscience. In April 1661 the members of the two communities of Port Royal were given the alternative of signing the Formulary or returning to their homes. On the advice of Arnauld most of the nuns submitted; Angélique Arnauld was saved this humiliation by her death. A Molinist confessor was appointed to direct the consciences of Port Royal, and three years later the Archbishop of Paris (Péréfixe) attempted to destroy what remained of the spirit of the convent by removing the abbess and the more courageous of the nuns.[53] This persecution was felt all the more bitterly by the sisters because, as members of the upper and educated bourgeois class, they had a knowledge of and respect for their rights, as well as a spirit of independence and pride in the class they represented. It is an important factor in accounting for the hold exercised by Jansenism on France that the nuns of Port Royal were of a homogeneous social class, bordering in rank on the nobility, for in the seventeenth century it needed a certain basis of rank to make a heresy respectable; and moreover, both in England and France it was in the lawyer families that the most formidable opponents of despotism were to be found.

In 1667 Clement IX. succeeded Alexander VII., and two years later a settlement known as the Peace of Clement IX. was reached, by which the expelled nuns were restored to their community on condition that they signed the Formulary "sincerely" instead of "purely and simply," a change of terminology which apparently made it possible for the nuns to sign without committing themselves to the view that the Five Propositions were to be found in Jansen. In adopting

[53] Gazier, *Histoire générale du mouvement janséniste*, I. ch. ix.

this device the nuns were unconsciously making use of an equivocation worthy of the most daring casuist, but they had no choice, and it is noteworthy that the change of phraseology was due to the suggestion of Lionne (ambassador at the Vatican), who had already shown his complete mastery of terminology, in drafting the treaty of the Pyrenees, by inventing the famous *"moyennant"* clause. For a time the verbal device was successful. Arnauld emerged from his retirement and was received at Court; once more it was safe for the Jansenists to appear in public, and a medal was struck to commemorate this treaty of peace between two rival theories of Grace. The pacification had just as much validity or permanence as most seventeenth-century treaties.

Harlay, who succeeded Péréfixe, was the sworn enemy of the Jansenists, but, in spite of his attempts to revive persecution, the two Port Royals managed to maintain a precarious existence.[54] Opposition and the threat of persecution had only served to strengthen the movement, but it had now lost something of its freshness and vigour. Its great men, except Arnauld, were gone, and it now included reformed sinners and spiritual hypochondriacs anxious to associate themselves with a cult inspired by ideals that could be achieved only by supermen. To say this is to do no injustice to Jansenism as both a force strongly opposed to lax morality and an educative influence which, merged later with Gallicanism, raised up a barrier against Ultramontane traditions. Throughout the later half of the century the ranks of the Jansenists were reinforced by disciples who knew little of the early history of Jansenism, some of whom saw in it a novel chance of opposing authority whether in church or state, men who were prepared to make mountains out of molehills in the vague hope that such conduct might be heroic, who in pursuit of impossibly high ideals often achieved no more than a cantankerous pettiness. Writing in 1655 of such extremists, a Franciscan declared: "There is nothing virtuous if not heroic; nothing Christian if not miraculous; nothing tolerable if not inimitable. These things pertain more to the rigidity of the Stoic or the hypocrisy of the Pharisee than to the charity of the Christian. . . . There may be excesses of devotion

[54] Sainte-Beuve's fourth volume deals with what he calls "l'automne de Port Royal."

and moral intoxication causing indigestion and resulting in spiritual weakness rather than in spiritual health."[55] It is the fate of many great heresies that once the original enthusiasm is past, they may degenerate into purposeless and narrow sects with only the obstinacy of human nature to keep them alive. In this respect the Jesuits present a striking contrast, for they never deflected from the rigid consistency of their first foundation; in a world of change they stood for permanent and unchangeable objects; when disorder and disobedience seemed to be eating their way into the Catholic Church, they maintained that military discipline and efficiency with which their founder had endowed them. The Jansenists are now a forgotten historical curiosity; the Jesuits are still a living and expanding force.

One of the chief characteristics noticeable in some of the Jansenist moralists at this time is spiritual pride, a not unnatural consequence of the exclusiveness in the Jansenist doctrine of Grace and a vice shared by some forms of Calvinism. Its expressions are mostly unconscious, as in le Maître's letter to his father beginning: "God having made use of you in order to bring me into the world";[56] and in Pascal this quality is sometimes encountered, as indeed in most of the great religious thinkers who claim the direct inspiration of Providence. To the English Puritans it was often a source of strength, nor can it lightly be dismissed as hypocrisy, because it was based on genuine conviction.

In less obvious forms this failing appears in the writings of the Jansenist Pierre Nicole (1625–1695), who takes place after Pascal and Arnauld as the greatest moralist of Port Royal. Nicole published a Latin edition of the *Provinciales*; he played an important part in Jansenist educational activities, and he was mainly responsible for the Port Royal *Logic*. A few extracts from his writings[57] will serve to show the querulous pessimism which descended on Jansenism like a pall. Thus in his *De la soumission à la volonté de Dieu*[58] he declared that the narrative of past events is "little more than the history of the Devil and the Damned, because those who play the leading part on the stage of history are generally

---

[55] Quoted by Brémond, *op. cit.* i. 403.
[56] Brémond, *op. cit.* iv. 251.
[57] *Œuvres philosophiques et morales de P. Nicole* (1845).
[58] II. ch. ii.

citizens of Babylon." He is even more explicit in his *De la crainte de Dieu*: "All these blind sinners, abandoned to their passions, are proofs of the rigour and justice of God which delivers them to the devils who torment them and, after inflicting infinite miseries on them in this life, plunges them into the abyss of eternal torture. It is this justice which permits these demons not only to control every heathen nation, but to cause ravages in the Church itself. . . . We pass our days in this spiritual carnage and, in a sense, we swim in the blood of sinners. The world by which we are carried on is a river of blood; to perish, one has merely to allow oneself to be carried along."[59]

It was in his contribution to the Quietest controversy that Nicole revealed another pronounced characteristic of the later Jansenist teaching—the tendency to dissect motive, to out-reason the emotions, to distrust every external aid to devotion. The mysticism of Fénelon and some of the Jesuits[60] (derived mainly from Spanish influences) was capable of abuse; it might lead to a spiritual Nirvana in which there was such perfect union with God that nothing mattered, not even the rites of the Church. The ideal of self-annihilation in contemplation goes back to the earliest Indian religions; it was revived by the Neo-Platonists of Alexandria, by the Gnostics, by the Fraticelli and by German mystics of the fifteenth century. The movement led to persecutions in six-teenth-century Spain;[61] at the court of Louis XIV. it was at first a fashionable pursuit not unlike the manifestations of the occult, sometimes for interested motives, to be found in all advanced civilizations. Thus Madame Guyon, a guide for Fénelon and the chief exponent of Quietism, claimed, like many modern seers, that she was directly inspired from on high; she wrote her books as if from some supernatural dictation and all she had to do was to move her hand. Madame de Maintenon had secret sympathies with the Quietists, but, on the other hand, Louis XIV. saw that their opportunities for charlatanry were unlimited; accordingly

[59] Ch. v. pp. 146-7.

[60] There is a large literature on this subject. See M. Matter, *Le Mysticisme en France au temps de Fénelon*, and Brémond, *op. cit.* vols. ii., iv. and v. For Molinos see Cantu, *Gli heretici d' Italia*, iii. 333 ff.

[61] For this see Menendez y Pelayo, *Historia de los heterodoxos españoles*.

Fénelon was obliged to retire to his diocese and Madame Guyon had to retract her errors.

Nicole had little difficulty in exposing the dangers of mysticism. His mind was set in a rigid caste; his theology was concrete, and his sympathies were not for those who carried emotionalism into the religious life. But in denouncing excess he revealed some of the limitations to his own outlook; he made short work of Madame Guyon, but proved that Jansenism could offer no substitute that would be practicable by the average of humanity. In his *Réfutation des principales erreurs du quiétisme* he distinguished between the love of God and the love of this love, asking whether this latter comes from Grace? He argued that as our faculties have become corrupted by the Fall, the more they are exercised the worse they will be; prayer and devotion can never be a substitute for living action; only those deeds are perfect which are not the result of conscious application, which "take the soul by surprise." "Jamais le cœur humain n'a mieux été anatomisé que par ces Messieurs-là," wrote Madame de Sevigné[62] of Nicole and his school. By insisting on a searching examination of all the influences that play on the emotions, by substituting relentless logic and almost mathematical certainty for human aspiration and sentiment, they overlooked the truth that when Christianity loses its mystery it loses its force.

The peace of 1669 was based on an unsatisfactory compromise, but for a time the Jansenists managed to avoid the hostility of king and pope. When the question of the *régale* and the Gallican articles of 1682 raised the question of the relations between church and state, the Jansenist bishops of Pamiers and Alet declared for Innocent XI. against Louis XIV., a course of conduct which won for them the temporary approval of the Vatican, and imposed on the French court the necessity of proving that there existed a Jansenist heresy. In 1680 there had been talk of making Arnauld a cardinal, and the Jesuits spoke of Innocent XI. as "the Jansenist Pope." Innocent XII. continued this policy; he required the acceptance of the Formulary only in the sense that the Five Propositions were heretical, and so, by papal favour, the day of reckoning for the French Jansenists was deferred. In

[62] *Lettre à Madame de Grignan*, 19th August 1671.

these years they continued, both in Flanders and in France, to threaten the monopoly of the Jesuits as educators, theologians and moralists; they had a considerable amount of public feeling behind them, and their success convinced the Jesuits that extinction was the only means of ending a formidable rivalry.

A controversy equal in importance to that raised by the *Lettres provinciales* was soon to engage the two protagonists. After the death of Arnauld (1693) and Nicole (1695) the leadership of the party was assumed by the militant Oratorian Pasquier Quesnel, who was resolved to bring to a head the Jansenist differences with the Jesuits. This determination was reinforced by the fact that in 1695 the Archbishopric of Paris was conferred on Noailles, who was known to be in sympathy with Jansenism. Quesnel had published his *Réflexions morales sur le Nouveau Testament* in 1678, a time when Port Royal was enjoying peace and prosperity, and when its literary productions were left practically unchallenged, but now, in the last years of the century, when the Jesuits were again arming for the fray, this book played the same part as Arnauld's *De la fréquente Communion* had played more than fifty years before. What attracted attention in Quesnel's commentary was its emphasis on the irresistible power of Grace, the fruitlessness of human effort, the identification of sin with self-love, the necessity for observance of the Sabbath, the glories of persecution for righteousness' sake, the fruitlessness of abstention from sin merely because punishment is feared, and, lastly, the need of access to the Scriptures for every Christian. These are the doctrines to which most exception was taken; they are typical of extreme Jansenism. It was at this point that Fénelon, who had incurred disgrace for his association with the Quietist school, declared against the Jansenists and their supporters Noailles and Bossuet.[63] His entry into the fray was inspired mainly by conviction, for he was of the school of Plato and the Mystics, but it may also have been prompted by self-interest, because he knew that Louis XIV detested Port Royal, and he hoped that by winning favour in this way he might effect his own rehabilitation. When Madame de Maintenon, deserting her protégé Noailles, threw the weight of her influence into

[63] Space prevents a discussion of Bossuet's attitude to Jansenism. This is studied in Ingold, *Bossuet et le Jansénisme* (1897).

the scale against Jansenism, all the material was ready for a great religious disturbance. Louis XIV. had been irritated by Jansenist attacks on his morality; moreover, he disliked Jansenist theology because he could not understand it, and he voiced a profound truth when he declared that "Marly and Port Royal do not agree."[64]

Trusting too much in the support of their patrons, the Jansenists resolved to bring matters to a head. In 1701 they submitted to the Archbishop of Paris a definite "cas de conscience"—could a confessor absolve an ecclesiastic who condemned the Five Propositions, but who, on the question whether or not these propositions were in Jansen's book, maintained an attitude of "respect and silence"? Thus was disinterred a long-buried hatchet which had lost none of its edge through lack of use. When this "problem of conduct" was made public, the affair had gone beyond the power of men like Bossuet and Noailles, for the French Jesuits, headed by Père la Chaise, were once more on the war-path. Clement XI., who had succeeded Innocent XII., decided the "cas de conscience" against the Jansenists; Quesnel was thereupon arrested,[65] but escaped. Accusing Noailles of favouring a sect, Louis XIV. demanded from Rome a Bull condemning the Jansenists, promising in return to use the secular arm in the extirpation of heresy. After lengthy negotiations the promised Bull was promulgated. In July 1705 the Bull *Vineam Domini* stigmatized the Jansenist attitude of "respectful silence" on the question of the attribution of the Five Propositions to Jansen; consequently the strict letter of the Formulary could now be enforced and the peace of 1669 was no longer valid. All that now remained to be done was to have the Bull received by the French clergy and registered by the Paris Parlement.

With Noailles at the head of the French clergy, the first of these two steps proved more complicated than had at first been supposed. The Gallican Articles of 1682 had asserted the right of the French church to be consulted before the promulgation of Papal Bulls in France, and the Gallican Articles were by no means a dead letter; herein is the point of contact between Jansenism and Gallicanism. On important

[64] Gazier, *op. cit.* I. ch. xi.
[65] May 30, 1703, in Brussels by order of the Spanish Government, at the request of the Vatican (Sainte-Beuve, v. 528).

questions of doctrine the decision of the Pope was not final unless approved by a General Council; the successful assertion of this Gallican doctrine might save Jansenism. The controversy had thus become political almost as much as religious, and the Jansenists made their position more secure by sheltering behind the Gallican views on the relations between church and state. Noailles induced the clergy to accept the papal Constitution, but with reserves which preserved intact the right to adjudicate on the decisions of the Vatican regarding doctrine, since it was claimed that the Pope might be fallible on points of fact. Port Royal refused to accept the Constitution, even with this reservation, and Noailles acquiesced in its destruction; accordingly Port Royal des Champs was suppressed in 1709, the Paris Port Royal in 1710, and the nuns, amid scenes of lively emotion, were dispersed to other communities where they suffered the indignities and petty persecutions which women know how to inflict on their own sex. At Port Royal des Champs even the buildings were demolished, and the Jesuits obtained from the Government authority to have the remains of notable Jansenists exhumed. The Jesuits had at last obtained their revenge; they had destroyed the headquarters of their enemies and desecrated their tombs. But the revenge was a futile one. Port Royal was gone; Jansenism, however, was now an educative as well as religious movement destined ultimately to achieve one of its objects in the expulsion of the Jesuits from practically every Catholic country.

With Clement XI. and the Court waging war on the Jansenists it was unlikely that Quesnel's *Réflexions morales* would long escape censure. In 1711 Louis asked for a Bull condemning it, and on the 8th of September 1713 was promulgated the famous *Unigenitus*, which anathematized 101 propositions extracted from the *Réflexions morales*. Once again the forces of Molinism and Ultramontanism were pitted against Jansenism and Gallicanism. Noailles led a strong minority of French bishops opposed to the acceptance of the Bull; there was even talk of schism and summoning a General Council. Noailles did not come forward as the defender of Quesnel's book but as the defender of something more important—the principle of French ecclesiastical autonomy; from a lukewarm Jansenist he had become an enthusiastic Gallican, and many joined him in this process of evolution. The lower clergy divided on the question, the "Refusers" forming a powerful support to the Gallican bishops, and a mass of pamphlets poured from the press. Parlement prepared for resistance; a powerful anti-Jesuit, anti-Ultramontane feeling was brought into existence, and Noailles became a national hero. Jansenism, by eliminating some of its harsher features, by assimilating its doctrines with Cartesianism[66] and associating itself with the idea of an enlightened national church, came forward again as a rejuvenated force, and the dominion of kings and popes seemed about to succumb before a new Fronde. In the wave of feeling against the Bull, Fénelon and the Jesuits saw disaster to their cause; Louis XIV.'s conduct became for the first time vacillating and indecisive, because though he hated the Jansenists he had himself acted on Gallican principles. On the 13th of August 1715 Louis, however, made up his mind—he would officially accept the Bull on behalf of his Kingdom and Church; thereafter a national council would be summoned for the purpose of obtaining the submission of Noailles and the recalcitrant clergy. On the 30th of August 1715 Louis XIV. died.

For long France was divided between acceptance and rejection of the Constitution *Unigenitus*.[67] Parlement had to register the Bull in 1720; the exile of the Bishop of Senez for refusal to conform and the exclusion of several Jansenists from the Sorbonne served to keep alive the movement. Noailles deserted the cause in 1728 and, having lost its leader, the movement became more popular and democratic, gaining rather than losing in intensity by the practice adopted by the orthodox clergy of refusing the last sacraments to those who could not produce a certificate showing that they had confessed to a conforming priest. These "confession tickets" gave some point to the philosophical attack on the excesses of dogmatism, and helped to increase the discredit incurred by official theology in the eighteenth century. But the movement which had done so much to educate French public opinion in regard to the Jesuits was too weak in 1762 to benefit by the expulsion of the latter; thereafter it succeeded in surviving into the nineteenth century and had a journal of its own, though its votaries were Jansenists not so much by conviction as by family tradition. In 1909 there was

[66] See Brunetière, *Etudes critiques*, 4th series (*Jansénistes et Cartésiens*).

[67] There is a full account of the later history of Jansenism in Gazier, *op. cit.* ii.

a religious celebration at Port Royal des Champs on the occasion of the two hundredth anniversary of its destruction, a commemoration which led to the publication of a number of monographs depicting various aspects of the movement. There was also at the same time a revived public interest in the buildings of the Paris Port Royal. With the burial in 1918 of the sole surviving Sister of St. Martha in the cemetery at Magny, disappeared the last of a society of nuns devoted to the great traditions of Angélique Arnauld. Recently the Paris friends of Port Royal performed a graceful act in presenting over a thousand volumes to the University of Louvain, thus commemorating the debt of France to the University of Baius and Jansen.

So Jansenism and Port Royal are now little more than memories, having a sentimental interest for sympathetic students of the past. Hampered by impracticable ideals, by an austere theology, by more than mortal demands on reason and faith, Jansenism has succumbed before creeds which recognize human imperfection and the virtues of compromise.

In accounting for this decline from the heights to which Pascal raised Port Royal, it may be permitted to refer to a little-known incident in its later history.[68] In 1727 died, in his thirty-seventh year, the deacon Paris, who had early been attracted by the Jansenist teaching and had spent his life in such extreme piety and self-denial that he was regarded as a saint by all with whom he came in contact. He was buried in the little cemetery of St. Médard; his resting-place was soon to witness scenes rare even in the history of religious manifestations. On the day of his burial a paralyzed woman was cured by touching the coffin, and the great sanctity in which the deacon had passed his life was regarded as the cause of this miracle. By 1731 the tomb of St. Médard had become the resort of innumerable cripples and diseased persons; many cures were performed in this miniature Lourdes, cures generally preceded by convulsions, during which the patients were insensible to pain of any kind and from which they emerged sound but exhausted. The convulsionaries of St. Médard found their historian in Carré de Montgeron, whose record of his personal experiences is one of the most

[68] For this see Mathieu, *Les Convulsionnaires de St. Médard*, and Gazier, *op. cit.* I. xv.

curious documents in the history of religious emotionalism. On presenting a copy of this book to Louis XV. he was consigned to the Bastille. As the fame of St. Médard increased, the scenes enacted at the tomb became more and more incredible. Devotees danced wild tarantelles over the grave; the convulsionaries subjected themselves to blows from heavy hammers to prove their invulnerability; some caused themselves to be hung up over fires, holding pieces of raw meat which speedily became roasted while the suspended enthusiasts incurred no harm; even Voltaire's own brother joined the movement and—supreme irony of all—accepted a certificate attesting his personal invulnerability and incombustibility. Eventually the police had to intervene in order to end these excesses. St. Médard is a pathetic epilogue to Port Royal.

Chapter 9

Spain, Italy and the Papacy

THAT IT SHOULD be possible to treat the internal history of Spain and Italy in one chapter is evidence of the changed fortunes of these two countries in this century; in no other period of European history would such summary treatment be possibe. Add thereto the Papacy and we have three political entities which in the seventeenth century were passing through the lowest ebb in their fortunes.

Philip II. was the last of the great Kings of Spain. His three successors, Philip III. (1598–1621), Philip IV. (1621–1665) and Charles II. (1665–1700), reveal in an increasing degree the steady degeneration of the Spanish Hapsburgs. None of these kings was really fit to govern, and all were under the influence of ministers or favourites. Philip III. was twenty years of age on the death of his father in 1598, and had already distinguished himself mainly by the zeal and regularity of his devotions. He had qualities more befitting the cloister than the throne; his life was passed amid relics and invocations of saints, and the almost automatic regularity of his existence, spent in presence of the mere symbols of religion, made him incapable of independent thought. The Venetian Ambassador[1] reported that he was "a good Christian"; but as for the rest, he did not dare to repeat what people said of him. Philip speedily succumbed to the control of a favourite—

---

[1] S. Contarini (1605) in *Relazioni degli ambasciatori veneti*, series 1, Spagna I. 234.

Francesco Gomez de Sandoval y Rojas, Duke of Lerma, who used his position to establish a system of corruption and waste. The national revenues became the perquisites of Lerma and his numerous satellites; the austerity and simplicity of Philip II.'s court were replaced by a spectacular profligacy; the judicial administration became a farce in which bribery was scarcely even concealed, and a fatal belief in the futility of either work or honesty was firmly established. Luckily for Spain, the reign was one of comparative peace. Portugal still acquiesced in the status of Spanish dependency to which Philip II. had reduced it; peace was signed with England in 1604, and the twelve years' truce with the United Provinces was arranged in 1609.

The most noteworthy event in Philip III.'s reign was the expulsion of the Moriscos. These were Christian descendants of baptized Moors,[2] and always distinguished from the "Old Christians" of unmixed descent. For a long time attention had been directed to the Morisco communities as likely sources of political and religious disunion, and in 1600 fears were expressed lest Henry IV., having just established his power in France, might intrigue with the New Christians against their Hapsburg king, but an investigation into this rumour elicited the fact that while the Moriscos had no correspondence with France they were in communication with the Turk.[3] In the year 1604, however, there was talk of a plot between Henry and the Moriscos of Valencia, but this came to nothing, as the plans leaked out. Four years later there was a civil war in Morocco between the partisans of Muley Sheikh and his brother Muley Zaidan; the Moriscos of Valencia were suspected of intriguing with the latter in the hope of effecting a new Moorish conquest of Spain. Early in 1609 matters came to a head when it was known that the king of France was preparing a great campaign against the Hapsburgs and that he was in communication with La Force, the Governor of French Navarre, on the project of using the non-European element in Spain as a lever against the Spanish monarchy.

Although these accusations of intrigue with the enemy were vague and not always substantiated, there can be no doubt

[2] The Moors had invaded Spain late in the eleventh century and were quite distinct from the Arabs who in 756 had founded the Caliphate of Cordova. The Moriscos were to be found chiefly in Valencia, Catalonia and Aragon.

[3] H. C. Lea, *The Moriscos of Spain*, 285.

that for some time there had been growing up in Spain a national prejudice against this alien population amidst a homogeneous society of Old Christians. The main popular objections[4] to the Moriscos appear to have been as follows:

1. None of them chose ecclesiastical careers.
2. In the army they were spies.
3. They monopolized arts and commerce.
4. By their frugality they obliged the Old Christians to pay the greater part of the taxes on wine and meat.
5. They did not buy land but leased it.
6. With their riches they could corrupt judges.

There is a naïveté in these accusations more damning to seventeenth-century Spain than to the Moriscos.

The Morisco communities in Spain, numbering in all about half a million people, were composed mainly of hard-working and law-abiding subjects who by their industry had created for themselves a considerable stake in the country and so were not likely to be revolutionaries. Like every other large community, they included a certain number of malcontents, but these could, with investigation, have been sifted out, and the punishment meted out to them need not have been shared by defenceless women and children. The idea of expelling a whole population did not offend the ethical canons of the age, and the argument from political expediency was soon reinforced by that from religious bigotry. In September 1609 an edict of expulsion was published in Valencia; the Moriscos were given three days in which to embark at certain specified ports, a small proportion being allowed to remain in order to look after the sugar-mills, rice crops and irrigation works.[5] Children under four who "desired" to stay could do so, but their parents could remain also only if the father was an Old Christian. The question of the children had troubled the scruples of the age; the difficulty was caused, not so much by the obvious injustice of separating young children from their parents as by the fear that these children might become infidels in the land to which their parents were about to be deported. It was seriously proposed that all children under seven should be retained and distributed among Old Christians as slaves, so that although they would lose their liberty they

[4] Altamira y Crevea, *Historia de España*, iii. 219.
[5] H. C. Lea, *op. cit.* 339 ff.

would retain their souls. The alternative of massacre was mooted, but their ultimate fate was little different.

After the expulsion of the Moriscos of Valencia, those of Aragon and Catalonia were dealt with in a similar manner in the year 1610. There are conflicting estimates of the total number expelled in 1609–1610, but the figure 400,000 is considered a fairly reliable estimate.[6] The peculiar injustice of the measure lay in the fact that, with the exception of a few who escaped into France, the deported Moriscos were taken to the Barbary coast, where most of them died from starvation or suffered martyrdom as Christians.[7] At least two-thirds are said to have perished in these ways. The expulsion was a greater crime than the Massacre of St. Bartholomew, because it was undertaken with a full knowledge of the probable fate of the exiles, and there was not even the excuse of popular frenzy to be urged in its palliation. But such crimes generally reap a speedy retribution. The expulsion of the Moriscos may still be regarded as one of the many causes of the decline of Spain.[8]

The first result was that the nation lost the *censos* or ground rents charged on the Morisco holdings. These rents varied from 6 to 10 per cent and, owing to Morisco industry, they had formed the best security for investment. The landlords, on whom this charge now devolved, were unable to meet it and had to sell or mortgage their lands, hence widows and monasteries having their capital invested in these holdings were deprived of a source of regular revenue. The nobles who incurred loss were assisted from the Treasury, but the middle classes had to suffer in silence. Even more important was the fact that by deporting the only enterprising part of the population, Spain ceased to have any industries except such as were run by foreign capitalists who took their gains out of the country. At a time when Spain had the apparently limitless resources of the South American colonies still at command, this seemed a small matter; with her bullion imports she could still hope to redress an adverse balance of trade. But by the beginning of the seventeenth century even this source of supply was failing. Many of the mines were

[6] Lea, *op. cit.* 359.

[7] Lea estimates that from two-thirds to three-quarters perished in this way (364).

[8] But see E. J. Hamilton, *American Treasure and the Price Revolution in Spain,* and R. Trevor Davies, *Spain in Decline,* ch. v.

becoming worked out; the treasure fleets, even when convoyed, frequently fell into the hands of English, French or Dutch raiders, and what treasure did reach the country was speedily dissipated by the Court. Another legacy left by the expulsion of the Moriscos was the further debasement of the coinage. The Moriscos had manufactured a large stock of counterfeit coin[9] which was acquired cheaply by speculators who issued it as coin of the realm; it passed easily into currency because, owing to the state of the Spanish coinage, the distinction between good and bad coin was a subtle one. Moreover, the Morisco coiners had found apt pupils among the Old Christians, pupils who excelled their masters in proficiency and audacity. Coining was a profitable and fairly safe industry in seventeenth-century Spain, and did much to create that feeling of insecurity and instability so prejudicial to the development of national industry. These facts, together with the great loss of population through emigration and the excessive number of ecclesiastical celibates, help to explain the economic decline of Spain.

The remaining years of Philip's reign were occupied mainly by Court intrigues. In 1618 Lerma was displaced by his son the duc d'Uceda, but this involved no change of policy. Spain in this period produced no statesman and only one great diplomatist—Gondomar, who did much to prepossess James I. of England in favour of a Spanish marriage. Philip III. died of a fever on the 31st of March 1621, leaving a son of sixteen years.

The facial characteristics of Philip IV. have been made familiar to posterity by the brush of Velasquez. His personal characteristics were idleness, or rather immobility, love of pomp and pleasure, and swift alternations between debauchery and ostentatious piety. Endowed with some taste, he spent much money in building; he gloried in picturesque fêtes and carnivals, he exercised an intelligent patronage, employing Velasquez as Court Painter, and in all the enterprises of a luxurious and pleasure-loving Court he showed himself a connoisseur. These predilections, harmless in a private person, are generally fatal in a ruler. Philip had a deep and permanent dislike of administrative routine, and took no interest in the government of his country. The ambassadors whom he received in audience failed to glean anything from his expression; his features never relaxed—he maintained in public an

[9] *Ibid.* 377.

aspect of the most solemn gravity, and it is said that in his lifetime he laughed only three times.[10] Born on Good Friday, he was supposed to possess a gift of second sight which caused him to see a corpse on the ground whenever a murder was committed; contemporaries attributed his habit of looking upwards to this unpleasant faculty.[11] He was easily flattered; his Court became Oriental by its specialization in luxury and vice; he withdrew himself from public gaze as a demi-god whose actions were not accountable to ordinary men. Uncle and father-in-law of Louis XIV., he exemplified in an embryonic form some of the qualities evident in the character of the French monarch, but he had none of Louis's industry and zeal in public affairs. His subjects accorded him the title of Great, as they had already accorded that of Pious to Philip III., but posterity has dispensed with both epithets. Philip IV. was the father of Charles II.

Philip ruled by a favourite—Don Gaspar de Guzman. Count of Olivarez, who took upon himself the attributes of First Minister. The first act of the new Minister was to proceed with ruthless severity against the favourites of the preceding reign. For a time there was an attempt to check maladministration, to limit the number of superfluous officials, and to reduce the expenses of the Court. But this reform speedily degenerated into petty restrictions on the liberty of the subject; legislation, by its very minuteness, brought itself into disrepute, and Spain proceeded on its way with exemplary statutes and social disorder. Madrid became the most pleasure-loving, the most vicious and the most squalid of European capitals; soon, even the pretence of reform was put aside and Spain was dragged further into decline by her Government and Court. Olivarez led the way in peculation for himself and his relatives; the Court made frugality or industry unpopular by setting an example of idleness and waste.

But though Olivarez encouraged abuses at home and did little to enhance Spanish prestige abroad, he tried to imitate Richelieu in two important respects—the centralization of the monarchy and the use of literary propaganda for political purposes. He insisted on uniformity of law for the whole of Spain, and attempted to extinguish the many and jealously-guarded distinctions between the old kingdoms of which

[10] *Original Letters of Sir R. Fanshawe* (1702), 421.
[11] D'Aulnoy, *Voyage en Espagne*, iii. 195.

Spain was composed. For this purpose he mixed the different racial elements in the ranks of the administration, sending Catalans to Castille and Castilians to Catalonia. He even tried to assimilate Spanish with Portuguese, and in 1630 sent a composite Spanish-Portuguese army to recapture Pernambuco. But while Spain did not have the religious difficulties impeding Richelieu's administration, it was nevertheless composed of states which regarded the retention of local differences as a matter of personal honour. Olivarez's policy, while it met with some temporary success in Aragon, Valencia and Navarre, caused rebellions in the Basque provinces and among the Catalans. A Catalan revolt of 1640 was due mainly to jealousy of Castilian predominance, hatred of the official class and irritation at Olivarez's unconcealed contempt for the Cortès of Catalonia. The revolt was one of the most serious in Spanish history; the Viceroy was murdered, and the rebel leaders signed a treaty with France whereby they obtained a promise of French help. Not till 1652 was Catalonia recovered for Spain; the Fronde caused France to release her hold on the province.

On the whole, therefore, Olivarez did not succeed in welding Spain into a homogeneous state, a consummation not achieved until the reign of Philip V., and then brought about not by legislation but by the threat of foreign conquest. There was a similar lack of success in Olivarez's use of political propaganda, because maladministration at home was so patent that no intellectual effort could have convinced sceptics that Spanish policy was completely justifiable. The pamphleteers were encouraged to excite hostility to France, for which purpose they could rely mainly on Spanish hatred of heresy and Spanish respect for tradition and legitimacy. Thus the *Vindiciae Hispanicae* of Chiffles (1647) is based on the assumption that the Hapsburgs and not the Capetians were the true descendants of Charlemagne; there are similar unhistorical assumptions in the *Lusitania liberata* by Sousa de Macedo. But these are moderate books; in a typical specimen of more advanced propaganda[12] it had already been claimed that Spain was the mother of nations, populated five hundred and forty-

---

[12] Fr. Iuan de la Puente, *La Conveniencia de las dos monarquias catolicas, la de la Iglesia Romana y la del Imperio Español, y defensa de la precedencia de los reyes catolicos de España a todos los reyes del mundo* (1612).

three years after the flood,[13] its inhabitants descended from Tubal Cain,[14] and the creator of other nations, including Ireland.

The chief political interest of Philip IV.'s reign is the war with France (1635–1660), a war ending in the complete military exhaustion of Spain. It was part of Richelieu's policy to use Portugal (which had been annexed by Philip II.) against Spain. This policy was materially assisted by Portuguese hatred of Spanish rule, or rather exploitation, and national resentment was intensified by the fact that in this period the Portuguese colonies were at the mercy of the Dutch. Olivarez's policy of mixing the different races in the administration only served to revive old hatreds, and in 1637 there was a revolt at Evora, formented, it is said, by Richelieu's dealings with Portuguese Jews.[15] This revolt was led by John of Braganza, the claimant to the throne, urged on by his ambitious wife, Louise de Guzman. The Archbishop of Lisbon and most of the native nobility were implicated, and in 1641 the Duke of Braganza was proclaimed king as John IV., so Portugal once again became a nation. Under John and his successors Alphonso and Peter a continuous war was waged against Spain for twenty-six years, and, even when Spain was freed from the French war to turn her arms against the former dependency, the Portuguese more than held their own, defeating the Spanish armies at Ameyxial in 1662 and at Villaviciosa in 1665. The initial success of the rebellion had led to the disgrace of Olivarez (1643); he survived his fall only two years, and was succeeded by Don Louis de Haro, a man of some diplomatic but no administrative ability. It was Haro who represented Spain in the negotiations culminating in the treaty of the Pyrenees. The loss of Portugal preyed on Philip's mind and was partly responsible for his death on the 17th of September 1665, a few days after the Spanish defeat at Villaviciosa. His forty-four years of rule were marked by steady dissipation of national resources and a notable degeneration in Spanish public life, the results of

[13] *Ibid.* III. ch. xiii.

[14] III. ch. xx.

[15] See *Relacion de D. Marcelino de Faria de las inteligencias secretas que habia establecido dentro y fuero de España* (in *Colleccion de documentos inéditos para la historia de España*, lxxxi. 554).

which are most clearly seen in the reign of his unfortunate
son and successor, Charles II. (1665–1700).

Philip's widow, Maria Anna of Austria, acted as regent
during the eleven years of her son's minority. Energetic and
capricious, she had never acclimatized herself to Spain, and
had come to regard the country of her adoption with antipathy
and distrust. For advice she relied almost solely on her
Jesuit confessor, the German Nithard (or Neidhart), who became a naturalized Spanish subject, Inquisitor-General and
First Minister of the realm. The tangible results of his rule
were the forced concession of independence to Portugal and
the French conquests of Flanders and Franche Comté. It was
public knowledge that the Queen-Mother was using her
powers in order to enrich herself as well as her needy relatives
in Vienna, and popular discontent at last found a rallying-
point in Don John of Austria, a natural son[16] of Philip IV.,
who as a Viceroy and General had gained some reputation in
Sicily and in the Low Countries. Though his ambition and
reputation were greater than his merits, he had a powerful
following in that section of the nobility and populace which
hoped that Spanish fortunes might yet be retrieved by vigorous
government. He began by leading a campaign of abuse against
the Regent and the favourite; eventually, at the head of an
army he forced the Queen to dismiss Nithard (1669). This
was the highest point in his career, and he might then have
been declared king, especially as a rumour was in circulation
that he was really Philip IV.'s elder legitimate son Don
Balthasar (who had predeceased his father), but Don John
showed indecision, and at the critical moment did not seize the
crown thus placed within his grasp. He sought safety with
honour by accepting the title of Vicar-General and retiring
to Aragon.

The removal of Nithard and the withdrawal of Don John of
Austria opened the way for a favourite the most unworthy of
any in seventeenth-century Spain. Fernando de Valenzuela
had begun his career as a page-boy and had married one of
the Queen's favourite bedchamber women. With only his good
looks to commend him, he speedily established himself as the

[16] By a *comédienne*. Born in 1629, he spent most of his life in
arms and became Chief Minister in 1676. Took part in crushing
the Neapolitan rebellion of 1647.

most influential personage at Court. His rapid elevation was little better than an insult to the Spanish nobility, and, low as was the standard of public morality, public opinion hotly resented the *liaison* between the foreign-born Queen-Regent and the ambitious scullion, coupled as it was with a shamelessly open malversation of the national finances. The proclamation of Charles II.'s majority in 1675 did not impede the career of Valenzuela, who ruled at Court as a prince of the blood and broke up the effete Council of Regency which before his death Philip had appointed to assist the Queen-Regent. Late in 1676 the ascendency of Valenzuela was so universally contested outside the Court that there was danger of civil war, but the situation was suddenly retrieved when Charles, having escaped from the tutelage of his mother and her paramour, summoned John of Austria to his aid. Don John's acceptance of the office of First Minister was followed by drastic results. Valenzuela was exiled to the Philippines, the Queen-Mother was relegated to Toledo and all the reigning favourites were disgraced. The king himself was subjected to a strict personal control; pensions were cut down and expenses were carefully scrutinized. But unfortunately the populace were irritated against the new Government by a rise in the price of food, and Don John was undeservedly blamed for the disastrous career of Spanish arms ending in the treaty of Nymegen; moreover, public rumour, which had suggested that Don John was the legitimate son of Philip IV., now insinuated that he was not even of princely birth. Influenced by popular clamour, Charles consented to the disgrace of his half-brother; many of the old favourites were recalled, and in September 1679 the death of Don John completed this reversal of his policy.

Charles II.'s personality was one of arrested development. His early education had been neglected; he inherited his father's dislike of public business, and his timidity and irresolution made him as wax in the hands of his ministers. A martyr from childhood to a number of complicated diseases, his life was an example of physical degeneration due to the inbreeding of his ancestors and the restraints of court life. We have already claimed for him that his regulation of the Spanish Succession question shows that he was not devoid of mental and spiritual qualities, and that he was not always the listless automaton depicted by many historians. But nevertheless he is one of the most pathetic figures in modern history.

As if in mockery, Nature closed the line of Spanish Haps-burgs by creating a physical caricature of a man, suffering acutely from the most painful complaints, bald, lame and senile before he was in middle age, devoid of passion and seldom able to act for himself, his death every moment expected and his survival regarded as a miracle, his life a burden to himself and a physiological object-lesson to others.

Don Juan had been succeeded as First Minister by the Duke of Medina Celi, and Charles's marriage with Marie Louise in August 1679 was followed by a bitter conflict between the French and Austrian factions at the Court. Disgusted by these intrigues and unable to check bankruptcy and disaster which seemed inevitable, Medina Celi retired in 1685 and was succeeded by the Count of Oropesa, who tried to restore some semblance of order into the national finances and redeem what was left of Spanish prestige abroad. Oropesa, a man of ability and ambition, was related to the royal house of Portugal. Anxious to push his own fortunes by eliminating Marie Louise and substituting as queen a member of the house of Braganza, he had incurred suspicion on the death of the former. He was overthrown in 1691 by the King's second consort, Maria Anna of Neuburg, who brought with her a large band of German place-hunters. For ten years she supplied the masculine element in the government of Spain, anticipating the rôle played by another Maria—the consort of Charles IV. in the last years of the eighteenth century—a ménage in which it was the king who wept and the queen who swore. Maria Anna was seconded by two assistants—her Capuchin confessor, Father Gabriel, and her old governess, the rapacious Baroness Barlepsch. The Baroness had sound business instincts, reducing what had formerly been haphazard to a regular system, and taking care that the proceeds of her peculations were sent to banks beyond the Pyrenees. Spain was thus ruled by two women and a priest; State functionaries had to comply with the system or risk exile; the provincial Viceroys were chosen exclusively from the friends and relatives of the governing clique. As the death of Charles became more imminent the intrigues between the various national functions in Madrid were redoubled. The recall of Oropesa in 1696 as the only Spaniard with sufficient ability to preserve the country from ruin was demanded, but, though he consented to resume his part in the Government, his tenure of office was cut short in 1699 by a rise of prices and a food riot—inseparable accompaniments of ministerial attempts to introduce economy into Spanish finances. This was followed by the triumph of the French party headed by Cardinal Porto Carrero, and for the first time in the reign the rule of Maria Anna and her camarilla was seriously contested. It was while Porto Carrero was in power that Charles signed the will in favour of the Duke of Anjou.

This depressing epoch in Spanish history was ended by the death of Charles II. on the 1st of November 1700. The richest and most religious monarchy in the world was unable to defray the cost of the masses said for the soul of the deceased king. There could be no more eloquent testimony to the decline of seventeenth-century Spain.

This decline was clearly evidenced in every department of national life. Spain, once so famous for its military prowess, had for some time been dependent on mercenary armies which were often obliged to make up for arrears of pay by brigandage. The few Spanish soldiers of native origin were drawn almost exclusively from the most undesirable section of the population. For example, there was a Royal Bodyguard, consisting of three companies, German, Burgundian and Spanish, and in Charles V.'s time this corps had jealously restricted its members to soldiers of family and reputation. In 1700 it had become a rabble, for which only those having had military experience were *ineligible*, and, though its main duty was to protect the king when he appeared in public, such occasions were usually accompanied by disorder and tumult, for the Royal Bodyguard then demanded its arrears of pay.[17] Military parades were not popular, as the appearance of the soldiers was generally too grotesque even for the stoical Spanish temperament, and the large number of generals excited the mirth of foreigners. Stores, Artillery, Fortifications and Arsenals were in no better state, and the Fleet was nominal in the number and character of its ships. Of the eighteen large ships built during the administration of Medina Celi, only about eight remained in 1700; of these six were in Italian waters, and seven ships were borrowed from the Genoese. Even these numbers give an unduly favourable impression, for Spanish naval estimates always included the vessels which, for obvious reasons, never left their moorings, and these were

[17] Report of the French ambassador Marcin (1701–2), in *Instructions données* . . . (Spain), ii. 12.

enumerated among the effectives until they rotted away. Spain never recovered the naval supremacy which she had lost in the sixteenth century.

After the expulsion of the Moriscos, agriculture was almost completely neglected; overseas commerce was still restricted to the port of Cadiz; population and annual revenue declined with monotonous regularity. The Cortès had long ceased even to meet. The craze for titles was so great and the necessity forcing the monarchy to sell them was so strong that for a time Spain was in real danger of losing all its commoners; in private life even the most menial services were sometimes performed by persons saluting each other as "Your Grace." Reform and reaction followed each other in a vicious circle; as soon as there were retrenchments in the payment of pensions or the creation of sinecures, the innumerable hosts of retainers promptly felt the pinch, and so economy which ought to have brought salvation caused revolution. Government restrictions always resulted in a diminution of the returns from the Customs, and this apparent sequence of cause and effect encouraged the popular theory that to spend money is to create wealth. The only prosperous occupations in Spain were the luxury trades; the slightest dislocation at one end of the social hierarchy produced a commotion which penetrated the whole system until the other end was reached. Spain was saved just in time by severance from her European commitments and by the accession of a new race of kings.[18]

Closely connected with this economic and political decline was the intellectual night that descended on Spain. For long, religion had been little better than a gross fetichism; legends of saints took the place of old pagan myths; the scholastic theology survived among the regular orders long after it had disappeared elsewhere; the secular clergy were notorious for ignorance and sloth. Christianity had degenerated into an established system of materialism and superstition. These are not the vague assertions of unsympathetic Protestant writers, but the facts established by Spanish and Catholic historians.[19] The country was hermetically sealed to almost all penetration

[18] A good account of Spain at this time, consisting of extracts from the correspondence of Stanhope, English ambassador in Madrid, will be found in A. Stanhope, *Spain under Charles II.* (1840). See also the interesting report by the French ambassador Rebenac (1688–9), in *Instructions données* . . . (Spain, i. 424 ff.).

[19] Such as Altamira.

from without, and Spain had long ceased to have any intellectual interests or any desire to shake off the perverted mediaevalism which other countries had long since outlived. There were thirty-two universities in the country, the most famous of which were Salamanca, Valladolid and Alcala; but for these the Renaissance might never have occurred, because they still drew their inspiration from St. Thomas Aquinas and from the orientalized Aristotle of the Middle Ages. By their subordination to royal, ecclesiastical or municipal jurisdiction these institutions were completely insulated from the intellectual currents virbating throughout western Europe, and it should be added that the Index and the Inquisition prevented the circulation of any but absolutely orthodox books.

In the sixteenth century the Inquisition had done its work so thoroughly that in the seventeenth there remained very little heresy to be suppressed. Nevertheless the Inquisition continued to be of great importance as a Court of Morals, dealing sternly with cases of bigamy, imposture, religious and medical quackery. Jews and Mohammedans, as well as any suspected of leanings to the Jewish or Mohammedan beliefs, were pursued with relentless severity, but of real heresy as it was known in western Europe there appears to have been very little. The most important *autos-da-fé* in this period were held at Cordova in 1627, at Toledo in 1669, and at Madrid in 1680; of the last there is a very full and interesting account by an official of the Inquisition named José del Olmo.[20] The type of case commonly dealt with and the nature of the sentence inflicted may be inferred from the following examples.[21]

A man who claimed to be the reincarnation of San Vincente Ferrer was sentenced to three years' imprisonment.

For saying mass and hearing confession without having taken Holy Orders, a man was sentenced to 200 lashes and five years in the galleys.

The same penalty was inflicted in a case of bigamy.

A Portuguese convicted of Jewish practices was sentenced to imprisonment for life and confiscation of his property.

[20] *Relacion histórica del auto general da fe que se celebra en Madrid este año de* 1680 (1680).
[21] *Ibid.* pt. ii. 32 ff.

In all, one hundred and eighteen cases were tried before the *auto-da-fé* of 1680, and the majority of the prisoners were accused of engaging in Jewish practices. Several died in prison before trial (after having abjured), twenty-two escaped and were consigned to the secular arm, twenty-nine "relapsed and obstinate persons" were condemned to death by burning. Of these, five repented and were strangled at the stake; the remainder were burned in a great "brasero" or cauldron, "con no pochas señas de impaciencia, despecho y desperacion."[22]

Olmo's book was obviously written with enthusiasm, and is an important document for the study of the Inquisition in Spain. He describes[23] with minute detail the great theatre specially constructed for the occasion, and explains the meaning of the emblem of the Inquisition, a green cross on a dark ground having an olive branch on the right and a sword on the left.[24] The olive branch indicated clemency for those who recanted; the sword, punishment for those who persisted in their errors. The "sambenito"—a garment having a yellow cross on back and front—was worn by the accused, and the proceedings were regulated by a solemnity of ritual which must have inspired terror in the minds of even the bravest. In an eloquent panegyric[25] of the Inquisition, Olmo applies to it the spiritual invocation addressed to the Church—"Thou art beautiful, my love, as tabernacles of Cedar and as the skin of Solomon." Olmo evidently regarded the *auto-da-fé* as one of the chief glories of his time and as symbolizing the triumph of Christianity over heresy.

The first Bourbon king of Spain entered his capital early in the year 1701. Though young and thoughtless, Philip V. showed himself not incapable of learning his profession, and within a few months of his accession he went in person to Naples and Sicily in order to see for himself the causes of discontent, and by his presence to check the unrest which was being formented by foreign intriguers. His marriage to the young Marie Louise, daughter of Victor Amadeus of Savoy, was of political value, for though only fourteen, Marie Louise was capable as well as devoted, and she had the assistance of an expert political strategist in the old Princess des

22 *Ibid.* pt. ii. 76.
23 *Ibid.* pt. i. 23-26.
24 *Ibid.* pt. i. 45.
25 *Ibid.* pt. ii. 27.

Ursins (Anne Marie de la Tremouille), whom Louis XIV. had appointed for her service. A new order of ideas speedily transformed the Spanish Court. Frivolity and dissipation were no longer the chief occupations of its leaders, and though there was no money in the Treasury, national resources were conserved, expenditure was carefully regulated, and, now that Spain had no longer to administer Italy and Belgium, whatever money could be raised at home was employed for national objects. The recuperation of Spain had begun.

These economies made possible the military revival of Spain. Philip V. modernized the army, giving to the infantry improved weapons and French instructors, and meeting with a response which showed that the old martial virtues of the Spanish people had not been extinguished. By such means an army of 40,000 men was raised, with which Philip was able to maintain successfully a defensive war on several fronts. There were complaints from those whose pensions had been stopped, and opinion was never quite reconciled to the domination exercised by the Princess des Ursins or the financial reform carried through by the Frenchman Orry; but as the danger of Austrian conquest became more imminent the Spanish people rallied in support of Philip, and their loyalty was made all the stronger when Louis XIV. had to abandon his grandson to his fate. In the years 1706–1707 Philip was literally fighting for his throne, but in the struggle he threw off his constitutional sluggishness, and by his conduct earned for himself the epithet "El Animoso." The victory won by his General Berwick at Almanza (April 25, 1707) was decisive in that it completed the discredit of the Allies in Spain and guaranteed the throne for the Bourbons. The Peace of Utrecht brought much-needed peace to Spain, and from it dates the real rule of Philip V. His queen died in February 1714; with his marriage to Elizabeth Farnese and the rise to power of Cardinal Alberoni, Spain entered on a new phase of her history in which some of her old European pre-eminence was restored.

ITALY. Italy in the seventeenth cenutry was not a nation but a collection of states of which only Genoa, Savoy, Venice and the Papacy have an indepedent history. The Spanish domination in Italy lasted from the treaty of Cateau-Cambrésis (1559) to the treaty of Utrecht (1713–1715), and in this period Italy suffered her deepest humiliation, for she was practically a Spanish province and robbed rather than governed. Not till the nineteenth century did Italy realize Machia-velli's ambition of "Italia liberata da stranieri"; not till the twentieth did she experience a great economic and political revival. But though seventeenth-century Italy was oppressed she was not decadent. Savoy maintained a vigorous independ-ent existence, becoming a kingdom in 1713 and afterwards providing a rallying point for the forces of nationalism; Venice preserved her independence by a shrewd policy of neutrality, her ambassadors ably upholding the prestige of the no-longer prosperous republic, and in the eastern Mediterranean she provided a much-battered bulwark against the onslaughts of the Turk. Rome still commanded the respect if not always the obedience of Catholic Europe. Tuscany and Naples retained something of their intellectual pre-eminence, the former as-sociated with the career of Galileo and the latter adding to its academic laurels the speculations of Campanella and Vico. The old pride of race still appears even in moments of deepest degradation. After Louis XIV.'s bombardment of Genoa,[26] the Doge[27] was taken to Versailles and compelled to sup-plicate for the pardon of his city, being refused even per-mission to reign until his tenure of office was completed. On being asked which of the sights at Versailles he found most remarkable, he replied, "To find myself here."

The most important Spanish possession in Italy was the Milanese, and in the struggles of Bourbon and Hapsburg its great strategic value was fully realized. The intrigues of the Duke of Savoy, the Mantuan Succession question, and the disputed control of the Valtelline, all served to make of northern Italy a battling-ground for foreigners during the whole of the first part of the seventeenth century; something of the miseries suffered by the populace can still be gleaned from one of the best historical novels of modern times—Manzoni's *I Promessi Sposi*. So long as Spain had a solid wedge of territory stretching from the eastern confines of Savoy to the limits of Venetian territory, she was enabled to maintain communication with the Empire and the Low Coun-tries, and this, together with her control of the Tuscan sea-ports and her possession of Naples and Sicily, enabled her to close Italy against foreign influence. But while that control had to be fought for in north Italy against invaders, it was several times contested in the south by the inhabitants them-

[26] Callegari, *Preponderanze straniere,* 297.
[27] F. M. Imperiale-Lercaro.

selves. In both Naples and Sicily there were serious revolts, and one of them just missed complete success.

It was in Naples that Spanish misrule had the greatest scope, for there was less danger of interference, and the oppressors were not impeded by any strong native traditions of independence. On the other hand, the Neapolitan temperament was proverbially fickle, and fierce passions were easily provoked; if no democratic institutions existed, there were nevertheless many secret societies, and as early as Philip II.'s reign the revolutionary *Los Blancos* had been a source of extreme disquiet to Madrid.[28] In 1598 Thomas Campanella had taken part in a revolt, the avowed object of which was the separation of Naples from Calabria and the erection of the latter into an independent republic with its capital at Stilo; the discovery of this plot was followed by the long imprisonment of Campanella. In 1622 there was an abortive rising against the Neapolitan Viceroy Cardinal Zapata, and throughout the early years of the century discontent and plotting were rife among the subject population of southern Italy. Sometimes foreign aid was invoked; in 1636 there was a plot to expel the Spanish from Naples and, with French aid, establish Victor Amadeus of Savoy as King of Naples, who was to cede Savoy and Nice to France in return for military help. This plot was also discovered in time, and the death of Victor Amadeus in 1637 prevented the plan from being followed up.[29] Cardinal Mazarin always preserved an interest in the land of his birth; from 1644 he was induced, through secret information, to follow with close attention the course of affairs in Naples. The project of obtaining Naples for Savoy and then effecting an exchange was a very tempting one for French diplomacy, and negotiations were commenced. As a result of these negotiations Thomas of Savoy-Carignan, member of the senior line of the House of Savoy, undertook, in the event of his becoming King of Naples, to cede Gaeta and an Adriatic port to France, while in the event of his also succeeding to the dukedom of Savoy he promised to give France a footing in northern Italy by an exchange of territories.[30] By 1646 it was known that popular feeling in Naples was working up to a climax, and in volcanic southern Italy Mazarin saw a fresh field for French activity against the national

28 See Callegari, *Preponderanze straniere,* ch. ii.

29 Callegari, *op. cit.* 170-1.

30 *Lettres de Mazarin* (ed. Chéruel), ii. 304.

enemy. Early in 1646 he sent a French fleet to the Mediterranean which captured Telamone and Orbitello; a few months later a second expedition seized Piombino. In this way the Cardinal hoped to control the Tuscan *presidi* or defended ports, so that he would be in a position to take advantage of insurrection in Naples, and eventually threaten Spanish domination in Italy. But these conquests proved to be short-lived: events which he could not control soon ruined the ambitious designs[31] of Mazarin. It remains to describe the rebellion which shook Spanish rule in Naples to its foundations.

When it was clear that the French intended to profit by discontent in Naples, the Governor—the Duke of Arcos—strengthened the defences and manned a fleet. This required money, and in an evil hour (the 1st of January 1647) he imposed a tax on fruit. The tax did not begin to take effect until the summer, when it was hoped that the Neapolitans would accept it without demur. To tax fruit in Italy is to tax a necessity, not a luxury; and as the tax came to be enforced, feeling in the city soon reached danger point. On the 7th of July 1647, as the fruit-carts were drawn up before the Spanish customs officials at the gates of the city, an infuriated mob rushed on the barrows and pelted the tax-collectors with the fruit.[32] The city was soon in a state of riot: an Eletto del Popolo who tried to restore order was bombarded with similar missiles, and the Viceroy himself was obliged to seek refuge in a monastery. The lead was taken by an octogenarian named Genovino,[33] a man of some education and experience of such disturbances; he soon saw, however, that the riot was leading to open rebellion, and therefore acquiesced in transferring leadership to a young fish-hawker named Thomas Aniello (known as Masaniello), assisting him with his counsels but keeping discreetly in the background. Masaniello's wife had been heavily fined for smuggling corn into the city, and in

[31] A great mass of Mazarin's correspondence on this subject will be found in Chéruel's edition of the *Lettres*, vol. ii. See also *Instructions données* . . . . (Naples and Parma), cxxiv. ff. Mazarin has sometimes been criticized for hesitation in his Italian policy; cf. *Mémoires de Montglat* (ed. Michaud et Poujoulat, 192). Mazarin was unlucky in this respect; his schemes were ruined by the intervention of Guise, and in his own words the Neapolitan enterprise was "un frutto non maturo" (*Lettres*, ii. 485).

[32] The most recent account is that by M. Schipa (Bari, 1926).

[33] Angel de Saavedra, *Insurrection de Naples en 1647* (French translation by Baron de St. Denys, 84).

the fruit riot he saw a chance of avenging himself on the hated Spanish officials. He soon had thousands of men behind him. Proclaiming that the revolt was not against Spain but against iniquitous Spanish officials, the rebels demanded the removal of the tax and the renewed promulgation of Charles V.'s charter of liberties. The revolt spread to Salerno, Aversa, Apulia and Calabria: Charles V.'s charter was found after the public archives had been ransacked, and the Viceroy was forced to yield, abolishing the tax and promising to remove all abuses. The edict embodying these concessions was read to an immense concourse before the door of the Cathedral, when Masaniello, dressed in cloth of gold, swore on the Gospels and on the annually liquefying blood[34] of St. Januarius, patron saint of Naples, that these reforms would be enforced.

At this point the revolt seemed to lose all coherence and become midsummer madness. As the fruit taxes had been abolished only in those provinces that had rebelled, other provinces threw in their lot with the movement, and the populace of Naples now demanded that the Viceroy's edict should be confirmed from Madrid. There were rumours that the government intended to mass together all the bandits of southern Italy for an attack on the city; moreover, there was a vague sense of expectation and disquiet that found vent in noise and violence. On the 11th of July barricades were erected in the streets, and Masaniello, who had had little sleep for five nights,[35] suddenly found himself transformed from demagogue into dictator. His only qualifications for the task were enthusiasm and resentment, and even the advice of Genovino did not save him from ridiculous and criminal excess. He proceeded to govern the city from his house in the market square, forcing his company and that of his wife on the Viceroy (who, at a banquet, is said to have administered to Masaniello a poison that made him insane), and inflicting his arbitrary decrees on the disordered city with the help of two thousand desperadoes.[36] All who were accused of negotiating with the bandits were executed; all suspected of designs against the Dictator met with the same fate; the price

---

[34] For the part played on Neapolitan political opinion by eruptions of Vesuvius and the occasional failure of the annual miracle of St. Januarius's blood see Callegari, *op. cit.* 181.

[35] Saavedra, *op. cit.* 148.

[36] Saavedra, *op. cit.* 171.

of bread was reduced, and a baker who failed to conform was roasted alive in his own oven. Soon the rows of decapitated heads on the Piazza del Carmel testified to the vigour but not to the justice of Masaniello's rule. Without trial, many persons were executed within a few days, and for a time Naples was given over to orgies of tumult and vengeance, the best records of which are to be found in some of the vivid canvases of Salvator Rosa. Hatred of the aristocracy and of the Spanish officials is the only consistent motive that can be detected in this vertiginous rebellion. Ordering the demolition of all surrounding houses, Masaniello now proposed to transform his humble dwelling into a palace; hoping to make his power absolute and irresponsible, he dismissed Genovino; rushing through the streets on horseback, he struck down friend and foe indiscriminately, and in a sumptuous gondola he cruised about the bay, committing many excesses and indecencies. At a service in the Cathedral on Saturday the 13th of July his insanity was obvious to every one, and three days later he was assassinated by bandits in the pay of Spain. The price of bread at once rose and the revolt broke out afresh. The mob dragged the dismembered body of Masaniello from a rubbish heap and, putting the parts carefully together, carried the remains in a procession which, according to legend, included 100,000 persons, his obsequies being performed by no less than 4000 priests. Nor did his funeral take place without a miracle.[37] The head joined the trunk; the eyes moved; a voice came from the lips, and amid shouts of "Ora pro nobis, Santo Masaniello," he silently blessed the enormous crowd.[38] So ended Masaniello. His public career had lasted exactly ten days, in which time he had been, in rapid succession, fish-hawker, tribune, dictator, martyr and saint.

The removal of the leader did not end the rebellion, which, under the guidance of Don Francesco Toratto, now became more moderate. In October 1647 Don John of Austria was sent from Spain with a fleet, and as Masaniello had been ruined by excess, so Toratto was ruined by moderation, for on his offering to compromise he was at once deserted by his following. There were now two candidates for the kingdom of Naples—Thomas of Savoy-Carignan and Henry of Lorraine, Duke of Guise. It was the sudden intervention of the

---

[37] Callegari, *op. cit.* 174 ff.

[38] This is recorded in a contemporary MS. Diary of the Neapolitan revolt (*Bodleian MS. Add. A,* 145 f. 60b).

latter that spoiled Mazarin's plans for benefiting by disturbance it Italy. In the summer of 1647 Guise was in Rome, on divorce business, when events in Naples seemed to offer an unrivalled opportunity for acquiring a kingdom in southern Italy once held by his Angevin ancestors. The Neapolitans, who had no desire to subject themselves to a foreign power, but were willing to use any weapon against hated Spain, invited Guise to Naples. Arriving in November 1647, he lodged for some time with a gunsmith named Gennaro Annese, who had succeeded Toratto as popular leader. In December a French fleet arrived in the bay, but though a few French troops were landed they took little part in the events that followed, because Guise was not the official French candidate and his presence in Naples was a source of considerable embarrassment to Mazarin.[39] Nevertheless, the presence of this fleet prevented any possibility of Spanish naval interference, and on the 23rd of December 1647 Guise was proclaimed Duke of the Neapolitan Republic and Defender of the State. A storm now dispersed the French fleet, whereupon Guise, glad to be rid of French spectators, abandoned himself to luxury and gallantry, which for a time won him some popularity.[40] But when it was found that he had no money and no influence, he was left to his own resources, and in April 1648 the Spaniards recovered Naples without difficulty, replacing the discredited Duke of Arcos by Don John of Austria. Late in the same year the outbreak of the Fronde prevented Mazarin from benefiting by troubles in Naples. The Duke of Savoy-Carignan was abandoned by the French and the Duke of Guise was consigned to prison by the Spaniards.

The only other serious revolt against Spanish rule in Italy was that in 1675 at Messina.[41] The insurgents were led to expect help from Louis XIV., and the French Naval Commander in the Mediterranean was ordered to assist with his fleet. In 1676 Louis guaranteed to the Senate of Messina that

[39] See *Instructions données* . . . (Naples and Parma, 8). Anne of Austria made no secret of her opinion that she would rather see Naples in her brother's hands than in those of Guise. Consequently Mazarin's support of Guise was very lukewarm. See also *Archivio storia Napoletana*, ix. 3, 480 ff., and Saavedra, *op. cit.* 171.

[40] Saavedra, *op. cit.* 180.

[41] For details see Callegari, 185 ff.

he would restore all its ancient privileges,[42] but he had no intention of attempting a serious conquest, contenting himself rather with encouraging the revolt in order to keep his enemy the more busily employed. When peace negotiations were opened between France and Spain Louis ignored these promises, and in the treaty of Nymegen the unfortunate city was abandoned to its fate. Spain treated Messina with a cruelty and stupidity which, if possible, made the name of Spain more detestable than ever to the entire native population of Sicily. A large number of rebels were executed: all traces of local autonomy were destroyed, and the valuable manuscripts brought to Messina in the fifteenth century by Lascaris were sent to Spain, where most of them were lost through negligence. Thus the two most important revolts in Italy—that of Naples in 1647 and that of Messina in 1676–1677—were failures; for the rest of the century Spanish rule in the peninsula was undisturbed.

Of the independent states, only four call for any special notice—Tuscany, Genoa, Venice and Savoy.

Under her Medici dukes Tuscany had an uneventful history. Cosimo II. (1608–1621) was followed by Ferdinand II. (1621–1670), who distinguished himself as a lover of the Arts and patron of Galileo. He did much to encourage the *Academia del Cimento,* which was established in 1657, and may claim to be the first society founded for the purpose of scientific experiment. Inspired by the achievements of Galileo and Torricelli, the *Academia del Cimento* devoted itself mainly to research in Physics. That Ferdinand was unable to save Galileo from the Inquisition is, however, evidence of the political impotence of the Medici. He was succeeded by Cosimo III., a weak and bigoted man who led a reaction against the enlightenment which his predecessors had done so much to encourage. He died in 1723, and his long reign confirmed Florence in the provincialism into which the once great city had degenerated, so that long before the eighteenth century the city of Dante and Machiavelli had become the stronghold of insipid poetasters and graceful idlers.

In the seventeenth century Genoa continued to act as the financial agent of Spain, acquiring much profit from the

[42] A contemporary memoir (British Museum, *Harley MS.* 3548) attributes the revolt to the Spanish policy of suppressing the privileges of the Senate of Messina.

heavily mortgaged revenues of that country. There was no other reason for French antipathy to the Republic, but Louis XIV. resolved on its humiliation. In May 1684 the city was bombarded from the sea by a French fleet on the flimsy pretext that an armed Dutch ship had found refuge in the harbour. Peace was signed in February 1685 and humiliating conditions were imposed. Though the history of Genoa in the seventeenth century is otherwise uneventful, the city preserved traditions of republican independence, terminated only by the nineteenth-century unification of Italy.

The Republic of St. Mark retained something of her fallen greatness after that had departed from Florence. The existence of Venice depended mainly on keeping free from the many continental entanglements in which she was invited to take part; in the shelter of her lagoons the Republic was one of the few independent states in Europe providing peace[43] with civilization. Something of the charm of residence in Venice during her declining days may still be conjured up from the pages of Molmenti,[44] but it was not till the eighteenth century that Venice achieved that mellow quiescence which Canaletto loved to depict on his canvases. In the seventeenth century the city had to deal with one important religious controversy—a heritage from the sixteenth—while in the East the struggle with the Turk was continuous and exhausting. Venice in this period is perhaps unique in that she managed to combine some political and diplomatic importance with a singular lack of any internal history of her own.

It was in her campaign against papal usurpations that the Seigniory played some part in Italian history during the first years of the century. Venetian Catholicism had always been liberal, the Seigniory having never accepted all the decrees of the Council of Trent; but there existed, in addition, serious differences between the cities of St. Mark and St. Peter. In the sixteenth century Venice had an important printing and publishing industry. The Aldine Press made Venetian publications famous; but as the Index came to be a more potent weapon of censorship, the trade in all but orthodox books declined, and, in the pontificate of Paul V., the printing of

[43] Botero in his *Relatione della Republica Venetiana* (1605) noted, as causes of Venetian stability, that the doges were appointed at about the same age, that in the government there were neither children nor decrepit persons, and that dissensions did not appear outside the senate (93).

[44] *Storia di Venezia nella vita privata.*

missals and breviaries was transferred to Rome. Nor was this all. Proximity to Ferrara (which had become a papal fief on the extinction of the line of Este in 1597) led to constant disputes over boundaries: there were also quarrels over the claim of the Seigniory to collect tithes without reference to Rome, and soon the whole question of papal suzerainty was raised by a city which, though poor and almost defenceless, still cherished its independence. It needed only the accession of such an uncompromising and tactless pope as Paul V. to brings these matters to a head. Venice claimed the right to punish priests guilty of secular crimes; the Papacy insisted on the rights of clerical immunity and the jurisdiction of the church courts. The Republic maintained its right to nominate to benefices in Venice; the Pope upheld his right of patronage, and in addition protested against the Venetian laws forbidding the sending of money to Rome and requiring that ecclesiastical assemblies should be presided over by laymen. In January 1606 the leader of the anti-papal movement, Leonardo Donato, became Doge, and the services of Fra Paolo Sarpi were enlisted in the dispute. Sarpi was the most eminent scholar in Venice and one of the most intellectually independent men of his time, having been brought into European prominence not only by his scientific researches but by his *History of the Council of Trent,* in which he had boldly attacked the doctrines of Ultramontanism. He believed that the temporal claims of the Papacy seriously prejudiced its spiritual position, but this is not sufficient reason for regarding him as a Protestant in disguise, as several Catholic historians have done. It was the duty of Sarpi to convince public opinion in Venice that the Ultramontane claims of clerical immunity from secular jurisdiction were unfounded. This he did with such success that an attempt was made to assassinate him.

No sooner had these differences become clearly pronounced than Paul V. launched his bull of excommunication (April 17, 1606). This created a serious political situation, for recourse might easily be had to arms in order to enforce the interdict and, while Venice would be likely to find a willing ally in France, the Papacy would be dependent on the help of Spain. But neither Bourbon nor Hapsburg was ready for the fray, and as many of the secular clergy in Venice continued to conduct religious functions in spite of the interdict, Paul realized that he had attempted too much. He was forced to retrieve his position by compromise. The mediation of Henry IV. was accepted: Venice surrendered to papal jurisdiction the accused priests whom she had insisted on trying, but at the same time put on record the principle that, within her territories, she had supreme jurisdiction over lay and clerical alike, and so, while appearances were preserved, the Republic really won an important victory which guaranteed thereafter her jurisdictional independence. On one point, however, she refused to give way. The Jesuits had left the city on the interdict being pronounced; Venice refused to allow their return until 1657.[45]

The next difficulty with which Doge and Senate had to deal was the question of piracy in the Adriatic. The Emperor Ferdinand I., in order to defend his territories against Turkish aggression, had drawn into Dalmatia and Carniola a great number of fugitive Bosnians and Serbs.[46] These *Uscocchi*, as they were called, became pirates and attacked Turk and Christian with complete impartiality, but as they remained under the nominal protection of the Austrian Hapsburgs, they could not be suppressed without risk of incurring the enmity of that family. In 1613, however, so serious had become the depredations of the *Uscocchi*, that Venice was forced to take the risk, so Trieste and Gorizia were first attacked, and Zara, their headquarters, was captured. The Hapsburgs intervened, but in 1617 they were induced to accept a compromise whereby, in return for the surrender of a part of Istria, Venice was given an assurance that the Hapsburgs would no longer countenance the piracy of the *Uscocchi*. But the evil was by no means rooted out and Venetian trade in the Adriatic continued to suffer.

The failure of the Hapsburgs to control their troublesome protégés of the Adriatic, and the suspicion that Austria was giving secret encouragement to these attacks on Venetian trade, led to an intensification of the latent enmity between Venice and Vienna. In consequence, the Seigniory was obliged to give up its policy of neutrality and, after seeking the alliance of Savoy, a large mercenary army was enrolled. It is possible that these events had some connection with an incident occurring in the year 1618 about which there is still

[45] Mainly owing to the efforts of Pope Alexander VII.
[46] Zinkeisen, *Geschichte des Osmanischen Reiches*, iii. 450-52.

considerable obscurity.[47] This was the conspiracy of Bedmar (Spanish Ambassador in Venice) and consisted of a plot to burn the arsenal, attack the city and hand it over to Spain. A French pirate, Jean Pierre of Normandy, and an English adventurer, Robert Elliot, were among the ringleaders: the Spanish Embassy was the headquarters of the conspiracy, and the arrival of a Spanish fleet was prevented only by a storm. It was believed in Turin that France had a share in the plot, but, whether for this reason or whether owing to the secret methods so characteristic of Venetian policy, the real nature of the conspiracy was never divulged, and probably never will be. It was discovered in time: five persons are known to have been executed, but the real number was probably much greater. Bedmar's conspiracy has provided material for conjecture. One theory is that it really started as a plot between Venice and the Duke of Ossuna to make the latter king of Naples, and that when this plan was seen to be impossible the story of designs against Venice herself was concocted. A still more unlikely suggestion is that the Doge and Senate, fearing danger from the presence of the four thousand Dutch mercenaries in the city, executed the Dutch leaders on the excuse of a plot and then tried to put the blame on Spain.[48] Bedmar was recalled to Madrid. Apart from her association with France and Savoy in the Valtelline question, Venice contrived thereafter to keep clear of continental politics.

The Turkish attack on Candia, begun in 1645, brought many years of war to Venice, relieved by heroic exploits and by the steady determination with which the Seigniory clung to the remnants of the old Venetian dominion in the East.[49] On the 26th of June 1656 the Venetian fleet won a great victory off the Dardanelles in which Morosini revived the best traditions of Venetian bravery and seamanship. In 1667 the Turks besieged Candia, and though the Venetian garrison received French help, it was forced, after a heroic struggle,

[47] See Zambler, *Contribuito alla storia della congiura Spagnuola contra Venezia* in *Nuevo Archivio Veneto* (1896), xi. 15-121; Raulich, *La Congiura Spagnuola contra Venezia* (1896), and Callegari, *op. cit.* 352 ff.

[48] Callegari, *op. cit.* 354.

[49] There is a very full account of this struggle in Zinkeisen, *Geschichte des Osmanischen Reiches*, IV. chs. iii. and iv.

to surrender (September 1669).[50] This ended a great contest between two Mediterranean powers whose naval supremacy was already on the wane: the struggle had lasted twenty-five years, and the casualties had amounted to about 150,000 men. In 1687 Morosini captured the Morea and besieged Athens, exploits which won for him the official thanks of the Republic. The treaty of Karlowitz assigned to Venice a large part of Dalmatia and all the Morea (except Corinth) together with the Aegean Islands. These were substantial results, though achieved only by tremendous sacrifice, and proved that two centuries after her fall Venice still retained some of her old valour and fortitude.

As Venice in the seventeenth century reflected a glorious past, so the Duchy of Savoy[51] gave increasing promise of a great future. It was Charles Emanuel of Savoy (1580–1630) who brought Savoy out of obscurity and, by his personality and ability, welded it into the nucleus of a great nation. His territory stretched from Nice to the St. Bernard and was nominally an imperial vicariate; it included at least one important fortress, that of Pinerolo (in French possession from 1631 to 1696), and it controlled two important routes from Italy to the North—that by the coast and that by the Dora Riparia.[52] Charles Emanuel ruled for fifty years; though he never played a decisive part in European politics, yet his career was closely bound up with the Wars of the League, the Thirty Years' War, and, in general, with the contest between France and Spain in North Italy. From a long and distinguished ancestry he inherited claims, never very seriously pressed, on Montferrat, Finale, Geneva, Burgundy, Brittany and the thrones of France and Spain:[53] after the Duke of Bavaria, he was a not impossible candidate for the Empire. In 1601 he had been invited by oppressed Christians to take Cyprus; he hoped to profit by risings in Macedonia and Albania; he was a candidate for the kingdom of Jerusalem. Placed between the influence of France and Spain, he found it difficult to maintain a consistent policy for any length of

---

[50] *Ibid.* iv. 940.

[51] There is a good general account of Savoy prior to the seventeenth century in the preface to *Instructions données aux ambassadeurs de France* (Savoy-Sardinia).

[52] Now referred to as the Mont Cenis route.

[53] Callegari, *op. cit.* 421.

time, and a Venetian ambassador[54] described him as fluttering in a continual "palpitation of the heart" between his powerful neighbours. That Savoy might one day be strong enough to shake Spanish dominion in Italy was a danger clearly realized at Madrid; accordingly when the Duke had to be bribed he was always given territory outside Italy. It was for this reason that he was never able to obtain from Spain the coveted port of Bari in Apulia.[55]

At the opening of the century Charles Emanuel was engaged in a war with Henry IV. The Duke of Savoy was an old enemy of the Bourbons, having fought against Henry in the Wars of the League in the hope of obtaining possession of Provence; but as the French king became securely established, Charles abandoned this ambitious project, and was now waging war for the more modest purpose of preventing Saluzzo falling into French hands. The Pope intervened and the conflict was ended by the treaty of Lyons, signed on the 17th of January 1601, by which Savoy retained Saluzzo but surrendered to France the small territories of Bresse, Bugey and Valromay. The effect of this compromise was that, while Savoy sacrificed outlying and isolated provinces, she kept an important Alpine stronghold and became more distinctively an Italian power. Turin displaced Chambéry as capital; Italian became the national language, and, after the failure of a night attack on Geneva in 1602, Charles Emanuel, now secure in a French alliance, abandoned many of his Northern ambitions and concentrated on the work of making his duchy a compact and efficient military state.[56] His rule showed the qualities of vigour and foresight.[57] Ecclesiastical immunities were curtailed; the clergy were subjected to taxation; a militia was trained, and Turin became the permanent residence of a brilliant court which, at different times, included Tasso, Tassoni, Chiabrera and Marini. In his *Testament Politique* the Duke placed on record, for the benefit of his successors, the story of his difficulties and ambitions, while in his encourage-

---

[54] Priuli (1601–1604) in *Relazioni degli ambasciatori veneti*, series 3 (Italy), i. 46. Henry IV. described him as "un remuant et un brouillon" (Rott, *Henri IV, les Suisses et la Haute Italie*, 78).

[55] *Relazioni degli ambasciatori veneti*, i. 49.

[56] Callegari, *op. cit.* 384 ff.

[57] For Savoyard institutions see Cibrario, *Origine e progressi delle istituzioni della monarchia di Savoia* (1869).

ment of literature he showed a realization of the value of propaganda when directed by men of ability. Savoy under his rule became the only strong and independent Italian state, its ruler concentrating in himself all the hatred felt by Italy for the foreigner, and the *Filippiche* of Tassoni, which owe much of their force to the inspiration and example of Charles Emanuel, contain the greatest indictment ever penned against Spanish rule.

The crisis of the Valtelline question in 1620 and the coming of Richelieu to power encouraged Charles Emanuel to hope that he would have active French help, and he made no secret of his ambition to wrest Lombardy from Spain. Venice promised assistance, France sent troops, and a Franco-Piedmontese army reached the gates of Genoa, but had to retire on the news that the Spaniards had entered Savoyard territory. France now deserted her allies, and in March 1626 signed the treaty of Monzon without consulting either Savoy or Venice. By this treaty the Catholic faith was restored in the Valtelline, and the forts erected in the valley were consigned to the representatives of the Pope for ultimate destruction. The confederates were to accept arbitration, by force if necessary. This was the ruin of Charles Emanuel's hopes, and Richelieu was never forgiven in Turin.

In 1627 the Mantuan Succession question became important and led to hostilities. The Duke of Mantua, Cardinal Ferdinand Gonzaga, died in 1626 without male heirs, and both Mantua and Montferrat were now thrown into the delicately adjusted balance of Lombard politics. Charles Emanuel claimed Montferrat for himself and Mantua on behalf of his grand-daughter, whose mother had in 1608 married the then Duke Francis Gonzaga. The other candidates claiming through female relatives were Charles of Gonzague, Duke of Nevers, the French candidate, and Ferrante of Gonzague, Duke of Guastalla, the Spanish candidate. Hostilities broke out: Casale was besieged and Savoyard troops entered Montferrat. In October 1628 the fall of La Rochelle enabled France to take a more active part and, at the head of an army, Richelieu himself entered Italy in February 1629. When the Emperor (Ferdinand II.) claimed the right to adjudicate on the disputed territories and sent an expedition, war in North Italy became general; over a wide area villages were again subjected to the continual ravages of Spaniard, Savoyard, French and Imperialist. Pinerolo and Saluzzo were occupied by French troops, Mantua was besieged, and in the midst of these calamities Charles died at Savigliana (July 25, 1630). In the same month Mantua was captured by the Imperialists, and the soldiery outdid each other in atrocities. The outbreak of plague completed the misery of the inhabitants and induced the combatants to come to terms. Victor Amadeus, who had succeeded his father, recovered his lands by the treaty of Cherasco (July 1631), gaining also a part of Montferrat and leaving the French in possession of Pinerolo. Nevers was established in Mantua, and Casale was garrisoned by the French.

Victor Amadeus survived only seven years, in which time he remained the ally of his brother-in-law Louis XIII. In 1635 he undertook, by the treaty of Rivoli, to join France against Spain in the Thirty Years' War, but two years later he died. His death was followed by the Regency of Marie Christine, whose rule was troubled by the intrigues of the late Duke's brothers. With the help of French troops they captured Turin in 1639, but the city was restored to the Regent in the following year.

Until the outbreak of the Spanish Succession War the history of Savoy was uneventful. Charles Emanuel II. (1648–1675) was succeeded by Victor Amadeus II., who was brought into the French circle of influence by his marriage with Anne, daughter of Philip of Orleans. In 1684, having freed himself from his mother's influence, he showed that his foreign policy would not be absolutely controlled by his marriage,[58] but, after joining the League of Augsburg against France, his troops were defeated by Catinat at Staffarde in 1690 and at Marsaglia in 1693. By the treaty of Turin (1696) his territories were restored together with Pinerolo. Victor Amadeus played an important part in the War of the Spanish Succession, first on the side of France and then on the side of the Allies. The treaty of Utrecht gave him Sicily and a crown: Sicily was afterwards exchanged for Sardinia, and in the nineteenth century the House of Savoy was to achieve its greatest fame in the War of Liberation.

ROME AND THE PAPACY. The history of the seventeenth-century Papacy is soon told. For the first time in its long

---

[58] See the memoir for the Comte de Rebenac (1689) in *Instructions données aux ambassadeurs de France* (Savoy-Sardinia), 136 ff.

annals this institution had sunk to a position of secondary importance in European affairs, and though, in this period, popes sometimes appear as mediators, they were mostly concerned with the administration of their territories and the municipal affairs of the city of Rome. The Dutchman Adrian VI. (1522–23) was the last of the non-Italian popes: with this restriction of choice to one nationality the Papacy necessarily lost its old universal character and became little more than an Italian principality. The changed temper of the times did not permit the assertion of exalted claims unless backed by military or territorial power, and in consequence of this, the popes of the seventeenth century were for the most part mediocrities. But while they had none of the eminence of Gregory VII. or Innocent III., they had none of the spectacular vices which made several fifteenth and sixteenth century popes notorious, and there can be no doubt that in this change lies one of the reasons for the survival of the institution.

Sixtus V., the last of the great reforming popes of the Counter Reformation, died on the 27th of August 1590 after a pontificate in which many administrative abuses in the Curia had been reformed and order introduced into the finances. Then followed the short pontificates of Urban VII. and Gregory XIV.; in January 1592 a Spanish nominee, Cardinal Aldobrandini, was elected to the throne of St. Peter as Clement VIII. Although a man of austere morals and unflinching orthodoxy, Clement adopted an independent policy in regard to the Bourbons and enormously strengthened the position of Henry IV. by granting him absolution (December 17, 1595). Clement's pontificate is noteworthy also for the seizure of Ferrara as a papal fief on the death without male heirs of Alfonso II. of Este in October 1597. Before his death in 1605 Clement had completely broken the Spanish fetters that had weighed so long on the Papacy, and he had raised up a rival influence—that of France.

Clement's successor, Leo XI., elected as French nominee, survived only a few days. Cardinal Borghese was next chosen, and assumed the title of Paul V. Paul's election was due to the fact that he was not unacceptable to the French, the Spanish, or the Aldobrandini factions, but from the outset he showed that he was independent and determined to insist on all the prerogatives associated with his dignity. Bishops were required to live in their dioceses; the disciplinary decrees of the Council of Trent were rigorously enforced, and practically every Italian state was irritated by the high-handed conduct of this mediaeval-minded pontiff. The dispute with Venice, already described, was the most serious of all, and would have led to war had not a compromise been accepted by both parties. Paul lived to see the outbreak of the Thirty Years' War, and died of apoplexy in January 1621.

During this period the papal nephews had exercised considerable influence on the choice of their uncles' successors, and it was mainly personal influence of this kind that determined the election of Alessandro Ludovisio (Gregory XV.). Too old to have any ambitions of his own, Gregory acquiesced in the rule of his nephew Ludovico Ludovisio, who, though rapacious, was anxious to promote the interests of the faith. It was through his activities that the Congregation of the Propaganda was established for the purpose of directing and encouraging Catholic missions throughout the world. Significant also of this missionary zeal is the fact that Ignatius Loyola and Francis Xavier were canonized at this time. These events coincided with the high-water mark of Hapsburg fortunes in the Thirty Years' War (1622–23). When Gregory died in July 1623 it might well seem that Catholicism was about to win back its lost territories in Germany.

Maffeo Barberini, Pope from 1623 to 1644 as Urban VIII., was the only pre-eminent Pope of the seventeenth century. Before his election he had commended himself to the various factions in the Vatican by giving it to be understood by each that he was the enemy of the others. Though more than fifty years of age at his election, he was energetic as well as shrewd, and retained these qualities for many years. Compared with most of his immediate predecessors he was modern in his realization of the fact that, with changed conditions, the Papacy must have a material as well as a spiritual basis; he resembled the sixteenth-century Julius II. in his ability to subordinate spiritual to secular interests, and determination to safeguard papal territories not by Bulls but by guns. An arsenal was established at Tivoli; St. Angelo was fortified; and as Rome needed an outlet to the sea, the unhealthy Civita Vecchia was transformed into a port. The "Congregation of State" was established to deal with administrative and political matters, leaving the Pope free to adjudicate on matters of doctrine and policy, but it was not till the pontificate of Alexander VII. (1655–1667) that this body began to encroach on the papal prerogative. Urban ruled not as a spiritual and elected head, but as a secular and untrammelled prince, many of his acts being arbitrary and unconstitutional. One of the most capricious and obstinate of men, he liked to insist on the direct converse of what was asked of him, conduct so consistently maintained that astute supplicants often obtained their ends by suggesting the contrary of what they wanted. It should be added that he was a minor poet. His building enterprises in Rome involved the destruction of many ancient relics; he proclaimed that the opinion of one living pope was worth more than that of a hundred dead ones, and he had a monument erected to himself in his lifetime.

The part played by Urban in the Thirty Years' War has already been noticed. In Italy his pontificate is important, because he strengthened and enlarged the papal territories. On the extinction of the Della Rovere family, in 1631, Urbino was taken over; large loans were raised for the purpose of fortifying outlying terrtories, and the papal patrimony became a compact, well-defended state. Taking advantage of the claims of creditors against the bankrupt state of Castro and a personal slight inflicted on his nephew by one of the Farnese Dukes of Castro, Urban, in the capacity of suzerain, took possession of the town in 1641, and in the following year its former ruler was excommunicated. War followed. The Farnese found allies in Venice and the Grand Duke of Tuscany; in consequence, Urban's elaborate defences were subjected to a searching test in the following years. Failure in the field, and the prospect of seeing his territories dismembered, forced Urban to accept French mediation, and in 1644 he agreed to restore Castro to the Duke of Parma and revoke the bull of excommunication. He died shortly afterwards (July 29, 1644), after he had witnessed the collapse of his plans to build up the most powerful state in Italy. His death was due to an illness brought on by the mortification of having to give up Castro, and his last wishes were for vengeance on the Duke of Parma. A man of ability and resource, Urban might have used his powers to better advantage in the Thirty Years' War as soon as that war had become dynastic rather than religious, but it is nevertheless to his credit that in 1634 he had proposed the summoning of a great council of European rulers for the purpose of settling differences by arbitration. The Congress of Westphalia was, to some extent, a realization of this wish.

It was no uncommon thing in papal history for a pope to

be elected by the votes of enemies of his predecessor. This occurred at the election of Cardinal Pamphili in September 1644. Choosing the title of Innocent X., this pope was, throughout the greater part of his pontificate, the sworn enemy of Mazarin and the ally of Spain.[59] The Barberini were obliged to leave Rome, and the foreign policy of Urban was reversed. Innocent was not devoid of ability or virtues: he was prudent in the management of his own finances and anxious to repress malversation, but he was distrustful of every one except his sister-in-law, Donna Olympia Maidalchini, to whom he practically transferred all his powers. The position assumed by this woman gave cause for scandal:[60] she used her opportunities for the enrichment of herself and her relatives, and in her hands Innocent became little more than a marionette. The chief accusations against Donna Olympia are that she persuaded Innocent to adopt an attitude of neutrality in European politics, even during the revolt in Naples (1647); that she was responsible for the destruction of Castro[61] in 1649; that she tried to induce Innocent to give up his hostility to France, and that, bribed by the Jesuits, she incited her brother-in-law to condemn the Jansenists.[62] Not all these accusations are to her discredit: as a woman she was anxious to preserve the peace of mind of her aged relative. Her most serious fault was avarice, and her influence on papal policy, while it was aimed at keeping the Vatican out of European embroilments, served in some respects to bring the institution into discredit. Innocent's pontificate was uneventful. In the Bull[63] *Zelo Domini* (November 1648) he protested against the treaty of Westphalia because it gave a status to Lutherans and Calvinists, and

[59] Mazarin, knowing that Cardinal Pamphili was hostile to him and the French, did all in his power to prevent his election. A French agent was sent to the Vatican with signed letters in which the sentence "si vous avez quelques bons désirs, vous pourrez vous en expliquer en toute confiance avec . . . mon ambassadeur." Some of the Cardinals, on receiving these letters, said "After the election" (to prevent the suspicion of bribery), but many had already committed themselves to the Spanish interests. (See Coville, *Etude sur Mazarin et ses démêlés avec le Pape Innocent X*, 12 ff.)

[60] "Egli [Innocent X.] non fu innocente perchè donna Olimpia fu Innocentio" (Gualdi, *Vita di donna Olimpia*, 435).

[61] For this see Ciampi, *Innocenzo X*, 62 ff.

[62] *Ibid.* 324 ff.

[63] *Bullarium Romanum*, vi. 269.

because it granted church lands to secular princes, but no heed was paid to the protest by Protestant or Catholic.

Innocent left no nephew, and so the election of his successor in 1655 was a novel one because the Cardinals, for the first time in their experience, had to exercise their own choice. On the whole their selection was not unwise, and in Fabio Chigi, who took the title of Alexander VII., they found a man of some diplomatic ability who hoped to restore the moral prestige of the Papacy which had suffered in the rule of his predecessor. As Papal Nuncio, and later as one of the mediators at the Congress of Westphalia, Alexander had provided evidence that he possessed qualities of industry and conciliation,[64] but Cardinal de Retz, who was intriguing in Rome at the time of the election, heard Alexander boast that he had used the same pen for two years, and inferred from this that he was a man of neither sense nor spirit.[65] The new Pope was able to effect economies by redeeming that portion of the papal debt on which the interest was highest; he succeeded in reducing interest on the remainder to 4 per cent. Declaring that, like Melchisedek, he had no relatives, he at first kept his nephews away from Rome, but he was gradually induced to give them employment; moreover, with increasing years, he allowed the Congregation of State to deal with matters that ought to have received his personal attention. His periods of retirement into the country were frequent, and ambassadors often had difficulty in obtaining an audience at all. The Papacy, at this period, might quite well have been superseded by a secular princedom: it was perhaps the quiet obscurity of such popes as Alexander that preserved the institution for his successors.

Alexander died in 1667 and was succeeded by Clement IX. (Rospigliosi), 1667–1670, and Clement X. (Alberi), 1670–1676. The latter came into prominence for his part in the controversy with Louis XIV. over the question of the *régale*. Disputes with France were frequent in the pontificate of Innocent XI. (Odescalchi), who succeeded in 1676. Inno-

[64] There is an unsympathetic character-sketch by the French ambassador, the Duc de Chaulnes (1666), in *Instructions données* . . . (Rome), i. 194. His foibles were said to be flattery, genealogy and Latin quotations. He was more concerned with his collection of medallions than with public affairs.

[65] De Retz, *Mémoires* (ed. Feillet, Gourdault et Chantelauze, iv. 35).

cent XI. was the only seventeenth-century pope absolutely free from nepotism; the only pope of the century whose uprightness and integrity were unquestioned by any party.[66] Many financial reforms were introduced and considerable saving was effected by the fact that money was no longer lavished on relatives. The Pope's conduct in regard to the Gallican Articles of 1682 showed consistency and firmness, though some popes would have preferred the friendship of Louis XIV. to the assertion of principles that estranged the most powerful of Catholic monarchs. By refusing to grant canonical institution to those clergy who had taken part in the assembly of 1682 and were afterwards nominated to sees or benefices, he made Louis's position impossible. As well as maintaining an independent position in the controversy with France, Innocent realized the danger of a Turkish invasion: consequently he subsidized John Sobieski in his great campaign of 1683. On the whole it may be said of Innocent's policy that it was inspired, not by a spirit of petty faction, but by a desire to safeguard the interests of Catholicism and to see Europe freed from the menace of the Turk.

The successors of Innocent XI. were Alexander VIII. (1689–1691), Innocent XII. (1691–1700), and Clement XI. (1700–1721). These pontificates are undistinguished, but Clement XI. is known for his Bull *Unigenitus*, which divided the French church against itself and initiated a struggle which lasted intermittently throughout the eighteenth century. During the Spanish Succession War, Clement was on the side of France, and his declared preference endangered the Papal States during at least one of the campaigns. In 1709 the Pope was compelled, by the threat of invasion, to acknowledge the Archduke Charles as king of Spain, and so the Papacy, which might have been a mediator in the great struggle, was compelled by force to change sides and become an unwilling partisan. No fact could better illustrate the changed order of things. The day of spiritual sanctions was gone, and in the new century of colonial wars, partition treaties and secret

[66] For another (possibly prejudiced) view see the report of Lavardin (1687) in *Instructions données* . . . (Rome), i. 360: "He spends most of his time in bed and gets up only when the weather is fine.. . . . He is obstinate in wrong opinions about people. He has not enriched his family. As he cries on the least provocation, people believe that he really has a flux of the eyes. He believes in prophecies and has great faith in monks."

diplomacy, the Papacy survived as a dignified but pathetic reminder of an utterly extinguished past.

The institution which had once led Europe was dominated in the seventeenth century by the city of its residence. The population of Rome increased steadily in this period: the great palaces of the Pamphili, Chigi and Colonna were built; the Barberini and Chigi libraries were founded, and the improved amenities of the city made it one of the most desirable places of residence in the world. Two great ladies—Olympia Maidalchini and Christina of Sweden—held, in succession, miniature courts which attracted a host of devotees and dilettanti. The reception of Christina in 1655 was on a scale commensurate with the importance attached to her conversion from Lutheranism and the universal interest excited by her abdication from the Swedish throne: the inscription "Felici faustoque ingressui" carved on the Gate of the People still commemorates the joy and pride of the Vatican that the converted Christina, having renounced her Northern crown, had come to live in Rome as a devout subject. For a time Christina made Rome one of the most brilliant social resorts in Europe:[67] her fêtes, masquerades, theatricals, library and funeral were on a scale of unprecedented splendour, while even the most austere cardinals were charmed by her vivacity and enthusiasm. Passionately interested in every subject, she had the nimble-mindedness inseparable from continual exercise of the intellectual faculties: the patron of philosophers, she had already been the indirect cause of Descartes's death by insisting on his giving lessons to her at five in the morning during a Stockholm winter: devoted to poetry, she surrounded herself with poetasters: an amateur scientist, she had her following of charlatans and alchemists: anxious to popularize the drama, she helped to make it insipid and commonplace.[68]

[67] For Christina's stay in Rome see *La vita italiana nel seicento*, 78 ff.

[68] This is not the usual view of Christina's intellectual attainments. Cf. Nisbet Bain, *Scandinavia*, 218: "She was naturally eloquent, acute, provident, courageous, energetic, devoted to art and science and infinitely more learned [than her father]. With an astounding memory, a lively curiosity and quick apprehension, her love of knowledge knew no bounds." Among contemporary monarchs Christina was considered a marvel, but those who knew her best sometimes found her difficult and even tiresome.

Her activities were not always in the interests of the religion she had espoused: her intrigues caused dissension and scandal; with years she herself became cynical in religious matters. "Who now fears the Pope?" she wrote in her copy of Machiavelli's *Prince*. "Here," she declared, "are statues, obelisks and palaces, but of men there are none." She still claimed the prerogatives of a monarch, and had her secretary Monaldeschi assassinated because she suspected his loyalty. Not content with her informal rule in Rome, she several times tried to recover the throne of Sweden. Her long residence in the capital (1655–1689) coincided with the period when the Papacy passed through an era of mediocrity and materialism, when the College of Cardinals assumed the features of a second-rate court, and the wielders of the highest spiritual prerogative in the world were over-shadowed by dependent nephews and independent women. This decline is to be found even in the architecture of Rome. The modern traveller will find in the great Colonnade of Bernini the most concrete evidence of seventeenth-century taste; and though he may at first be impressed by the tremendous sweep of these enormous pillars, he may yet feel that the pristine beauty of St. Peter's is marred by an imposing but superfluous adornment.

Chapter 10

The Dutch Republic

THE REPUBLIC of the United Provinces represents a unique combination of political, commercial and intellectual greatness, for the country which united Europe against Louis XIV. controlled the greater part of the world's carrying trade; it had also the largest business in salted herrings; it was the native country of Rembrandt and Franz Hals as well as the adopted country of Descartes and Spinoza. In the seventeenth century the Dutch attained the highest point in their civilization and political power: their political decline was gradual and inevitable.

The struggle against Philip II. had served, if not to divide, at least to contrast two groups of provinces in the Netherlands —those of the North and those of the South, a distinction roughly corresponding with that between the modern Holland and Belgium. It was formerly thought that this division was due to differences in race, language and religion, but a Dutch scholar[1] has recently argued that this was not so, and that an explanation must be sought in more fortuitous causes arising from the course of the sixteenth-century revolt. Calvinism, it has been stated, was in a minority in the northern provinces even as late as the earlier decades of the seventeenth century, and until then, the reformed faith appears to have been as strong in the South as in the North. So too there was no clear racial distinction between these two areas. But after the revolt

[1] P. Geyl, *The Revolt of the Netherlands*, 16 and 131: also *The Netherlands Divided*, pp. 16 and 56-7.

of 1572, the Sea Beggars, the "shock troops" of Calvinism, selected the northern provinces for the bases of their campaigns against Spain, a selection dictated mainly by considerations of military strategy, and in this way the effective leadership in the north, particularly in the towns of Holland and Zealand, passed to exponents of the new faith. Even in the towns of the southern provinces there remained for some time a Calvinist predominance in the governing minority, and only in Gelderland, Groningen and Overyssel did Catholicism succeed in resisting this process of encroachment.

On the other hand the older view which contrasted a Teutonic North with a Romano-Celtic South may not have been so absurd, as is nowadays assumed, when it is recalled that for centuries the boundary lines of the bishoprics had linked the North with the Germanic Empire and the South with Catholic France.

The maritime provinces of Holland and Zealand were the soul of the United Netherlands, their numerous towns providing the wealthy burgher aristocracy who contested supremacy with the House of Orange. The temper of these burghers was much more aristocratic than democratic: membership of the municipal councils was limited to certain families from which the burgomasters and magistrates were exclusively elected; from the same class also were chosen the representatives on the local and central Estates.[2] The Dutch themselves were quite clear that such a government was not democratic but exclusive: in 1640 Sommelsdijk, refuting a remark of Charles I. that the government of the Low Countries was "popular and without discretion," maintained that it was really an aristocracy "where the people have no say and indiscretion no place."[3] Speaking of the narrow class from which the members of the States-General were chosen, Sir William Temple defined the Dutch political system as "a sort of oligarchy and very different from a popular government."

Of the other provinces, Utrecht represented the remains of an old bishopric and retained some ecclesiastical institutions: Frisia was mainly maritime; it had no native nobility, and at its capital, Leeuwarden, there was held a democratic

[2] See Geddes, *Administration of John de Witt*, i. 145 ff.; Blok, *History of the People of the Netherlands* (translation), III. ch. xiii.; and Waddington, *La République des provinces unies*, 1630–1650, ch. i.

[3] Waddington, *op. cit.* i. 8.

and representative assembly: Over-Yssel and Groningen were small provinces, continental rather than maritime, while Guelders was dominated by a local nobility. Thus the ruling classes of the United Provinces were the patrician burghers of Holland and Zealand, the Protestant canons of Utrecht, the free peasants of Frisia and the territorial nobility of the other provinces. When it is added that, by the middle of the century, Holland and Zealand held radically different views on the question of peace with France, that one portion of Dutch population benefited as much from war as the other from peace, that the members of the States-General were responsible not to the nation but to the provinces, it will be seen that the forces of disunion were strong and that the real interest of Dutch history in the seventeenth century lies in the conflict between the separatism of the seven provinces and the centralizing ambitions of the House of Orange. The Dutch were forced in the crisis of 1672 to confide their destinies to a princely house but, on account of their apparent republicanism, they provide an exception to the general rule that in this period western Europe favoured monarchical and absolute government.

The States-General which met at the Hague was really an assembly of ambassadors from sovereign states. The deputies were elected for three or six years and were convoked by the Council of State; they were not free agents but merely the mouthpieces of their constituents. In other words, each state could, by its dissent, exercise what might, in effect, be a *liberum veto,* and it was only by a series of accidents that the Dutch did not share the fate of the Poles. At first the whole assembly discussed questions of foreign policy, but after the execution of Barneveld in 1619 Maurice of Nassau interested himself in this department, and gradually the Orange family came to influence the direction of foreign affairs. The army, composed mainly of mercenaries, was paid by the provinces in proportion to their quota, and each Stadtholder was head of the troops of his province.[4] Such divided control threatened, on several occasions, to end in anarchy and disaster, but here again the House of Orange saved the Dutch from themselves, since, by uniting the Stadtholderates into one line of their family, they obtained control over all the military resources of the provinces. In the career of John de Witt is seen, in in-

[4] For details concerning the military forces of the Union see Geddes, *Administration of John de Witt,* i. 109 ff.

tensified form, this conflict between provincial separatism inherited by the Dutch from the sixteenth-century struggle with
Spain, and the centralization of powers which events forced
into the hands of the Orange family.

Side by side with the States-General was the Council of
State formed in 1584. It was composed of twelve deputies from
the provinces, and, as in the States-General, its presidency
was for one week only.[5] The Stadtholders had seats in this
council, and the House of Orange came to have at least one
vote. In the separate provinces each Stadtholder was responsible for maintaining order, the reformed religion and the
administration of justice. The provincial Estates were composed of two orders—the nobility and bourgeoisie: they met
about six times a year. Except for the fact that Holland had a
special and exalted official—the Advocate or Grand Pensionary (who led his province against the Orange party)—the
government of the seven component parts of the Union was
analogous.[6]

The Dutch quickly outlived many of the prejudices which
still hampered their rivals; moreover their distinctive, almost
modern policy, and their brilliant culture were made possible
by the fact that the population included so many merchants,
artisans and seamen, and so few paupers or illiterates.[7] The
wealth of the Dutch increased rapidly in the first half of the
century, and at a time when countries like France and Spain
were expelling the most industrious of their population, the
United Provinces were opening their doors to the Jews of
Spain and the Huguenots of France, proving to more bigoted
neighbours that toleration pays.

At the beginning of the seventeenth century the United
Provinces were still holding their own in the long struggle for
independence against Spain and the Spanish Archdukes of the
Low Countries. In September 1604 the Spanish general Spinola

[5] Waddington, *op. cit.* i. 18.
[6] Exceptionally, bribery and propaganda had to be employed
in order to secure unanimity. Sometimes the laws of the Union
had to be broken; *e.g.* the treaty of Münster was concluded with
Spain without the assent of Zealand and Utrecht.
[7] De la Cour in the (pseudo) *Mémoires de Jean de Witt* showed
that at least half the Dutch population at this time was composed
of merchants or artisans (Waddington, *op. cit.* i. 34). For a general account of Dutch society in the seventeenth century see A.
Lefevre Pontalis, *Jean de Witt,* I. ch. i.

ended the three years' siege of Ostend, but this capture was of little value to the Hapsburg cause, for the town was a mass of ruins. Earlier in the same year Maurice of Nassau, in command of an army raised by the States-General, captured Sluis. Three years later (April 1607) the Dutch won an important naval victory off Gibraltar, where a large Spanish fleet was being equipped for the East Indies: more perhaps than any other achievement, this success brought to a head the peace negotiations which had been mooted some years before. It was not that peace was universally desired in the United Provinces, for there was a large party, especially in the maritime states, benefiting by the war; moreover, it was a fairly widespread belief that the prosperity of the republic was due to the contest with Spain, and to some extent dependent on its continuance. On the other hand, Dutch resources had been drained almost dry by the struggle, taxation was heavy, and the peace party was led by the great and patriotic Advocate of Holland, John van Oldenbarneveldt, in whom were incarnated the finest qualities of Dutch republicanism. The peace negotiations began at the Hague in February 1608, but Spain showed unwillingness to yield on the important question of freedom of trade in the East Indies. There was a danger that the war might have to be renewed, until French and English intervention saved the situation by persuading the disputants to accept a compromise—a twelve years' truce—during which, trade in the Indies should be free, and the United Provinces considered as independent. On April 9, 1609, the Twelve Years' Truce was signed. Neither party supposed that the truce would be permanent, but at least temporary peace had been secured, some of the credit for which is due to the skilful and successful diplomacy of Henry IV.[8]

The Twelve Years' Truce thus marks an important stage in the evolution of the Dutch nation. To the Dutch it was the first breathing place in the long campaign for national existence; to the Spaniards it was the first confession of military decline. Thereafter the United Provinces settled down to a period of economic recuperation during which the reputation of the House of Orange steadily increased. That house gradually monopolized the Stadtholderships, so that while William the Silent[9] had held three, his son Maurice held six, and in addition was Captain-General and Admiral-General of the

[8] Waddington, op. cit. i. 68.
[9] 1533–1584.

armed forces of the federation. The descendants of William the Silent were mostly endowed with military or political ability, and in Maurice (1586–1625), Frederick Henry (1625–1647), William II. (1647–1650) and William III. (1672–1702) they provided what was probably the most uniformly capable dynasty of the seventeenth century.

The province of Holland was the richest and most powerful member of the federation, and in its Advocate or Pensionary possessed the one functionary of sufficient standing to oppose the encroachments of the Orange family. It needed only the peace following the Twelve Years' Truce to develop the latent antithesis between the military and personal office of Stadtholder and the civil and representative office of Pensionary. As soon as pressure from Spain was relaxed, the ideal of military and political autonomy, vested in a single family, was pitted against the republican and separatist aspirations incarnated in a great civil functionary holding office by the suffrage of that province, which, by its wealth and population, claimed the largest share in directing the policy of the federation. The result of the initial struggle between the two was ominous for the future of separatist principle. As usual it was entangled with a religious question. Jacob Harmensz (Arminius) was appointed Professor of Theology at Leyden in 1602. In the course of his earlier life Arminius had travelled in Catholic countries, and he now attempted to humanize the austere Calvinism of his countrymen, proposing not only a modification of some of the radical tenets of his church—such as that of Predestination—but also the introduction of altars and the beautification of the bare walls of Dutch churches. A study of Luther's writings had modified his views on the relations between church and state, causing him to favour the subordination of the former to the latter, leading him also to emphasize the duties of the priest in the state as well as in the church. Throughout this mental evolution Arminius remained a Calvinist, but his views exercised a profound influence on the more liberal and enlightened members of his faith. Arminius died in 1610, before his opinions had caused a national division; his leadership was, however, assumed by John Uyttenbogaert, who, with the approval of Oldenbarneveldt, summoned a convention to Gouda in June 1610. The result of the deliberations at Gouda was the drawing up of a statement of principles, called the Remonstrance, dealing mainly with the doctrines of Grace and Predestination. This manifesto was soon answered by the orthodox Calvinists, led by another Leyden professor named Francis Gomar, in the Counter-Remonstrance. In this way the Arminians acquired the name of Remonstrants, while the more rigid Calvinists were named Counter-Remonstrants or Gomarists. The all-important question of eternal damnation has more than once proved a rallying cry in Calvinist countries, and anything tending to minimize the import of this doctrine has sometimes been attended with disastrous consequences. The more relaxed doctrines were favoured by Oldenbarneveldt and by a majority in Holland; Maurice and a large section of the States-General were zealous upholders of orthodox and uncompromising Calvinism.

This division coincided with the political division, thus enabling Maurice to brand the republican, separatist and anti-Orange party with the stigma of heresy. These differences were brought to a head late in 1616, when the Advocate induced the Estates of Holland to enlist a force of militia, for no other reason than to guarantee the independence of the province, and the States-General in their turn convened a national synod for the purpose of vindicating the Counter-Remonstrants, taking measures against the Arminians and stabilizing Calvinism as a state religion. Thereupon Oldenbarneveldt, still relying on his personal influence, obtained from the Estates a refusal to take part in the proposed National Synod, a course of conduct which showed determination to assert the independence of his province and the principle of separatism. Dutch opinion, indeed, was so sharply divided that there was a danger of Holland receding altogether from the federation. In face of this threat resolute steps were taken by Maurice and the States-General. The dismissal of the troops raised by Holland was demanded, and on the 29th of August 1618 Oldenbarneveldt with some of his adherents, including the jurist Grotius, was arrested. The States-General appointed a special tribunal to try the accused persons, a tribunal composed exclusively of the Advocate's personal enemies; the verdict was, therefore, a foregone conclusion. In May 1619 sentence of death was pronounced and carried out on the veteran statesman, who, second only to William the Silent in the services he had rendered to his country, was now the first victim on the altar of Orange aspirations. The sentence was no surprise, but many were shocked that it was carried out, attributing this to the personal enmity of Maurice and Francis van Aerssens, Lord of Sommelsdijk. Grotius was sentenced to imprisonment for life and confined in the castle of Loevestein, from which he managed to effect a dramatic escape in 1621. With the help of his wife and a maidservant he concealed himself in a trunk supposed to contain Arminian books, which was conveyed to the mainland by the unsuspecting guards (whose complaint was that the trunk seemed heavy enough to contain the Arminian himself), and with the help of friends Grotius eventually reached France. So ended the old Dutch republicanism which had done so much in the cause against Spain, but which, in a period of peace, threatened to destroy the unity on which the Orange family were founding their monarchist ambitions. The writing of Grotius were destined to be the most tangible expressions of the idealism and enlightenment of a body of men whose leader had thus been removed by a judicial murder.

The National Synod met at Dordrecht late in 1618 and was of a representative character, the foreign Reformed churches sending delegates. The result of its deliberations was the enunciation of the principles of Dutch Calvinism and the condemnation of the Remonstrants or Arminians, declarations followed by persecution, many of the more prominent minority being forced into exile. The Synod of Dort, as it was called, gave the Dutch peoples an official "Confession," like those of Augsburg or Heidelberg, an important event in the evolution of nationality at a time when religion, even more than race or language, was the one force that made for unity in the state. The Arminians survived as a persecuted but influential minority; it was mainly through them that the doctrines of Descartes were acclimatized in the United Provinces, and that some alternative to unbending Calvinism was made possible.

The Twelve Years' Truce came to an end in 1621, and though there were conciliatory proposals, hostilities were renewed. The earlier campaigns were not favourable to the Dutch cause, and after a siege, commenced in 1623, Breda had to be surrendered. With advancing age, and in the midst of reverses, Maurice showed a lack of decision, and his death in April 1625 did not occasion much surprise or even regret. He was succeeded by his half-brother, Frederick Henry, born in 1584, a son of William the Silent's fourth marriage (with Louise de Coligny). Frederick Henry was as French in spirit as Maurice had been German, combining military efficiency and love of outdoor life with the quick insight and polished manners inherited from his mother.[10] Elected Stadtholder of Groningen in 1640, he needed only Frisia to complete his tenure of the seven Stadtholderships; in 1637 he was accorded by the States-General the title of "Highness," and thus in all but name he was a ruling monarch. The marriages of his son and daughter are of historical importance—his son, afterwards William II., married Mary, daughter of King Charles I., and in 1646 his daughter Louise Henrietta married Frederick William the Great Elector. These connections helped to emphasize the practically monarchical status of Frederick, his control of the army was uncontested, and with it he was able to maintain the prestige of the infant state. The Act of Survivance (1631) declared his offices hereditary.

In the early summer of 1635 the understanding between France and the United Provinces ripened into an offensive and defensive alliance, and so Richelieu merged the Dutch War of Independence with the Thirty Years' War. In the summer of 1636, however, Frederick Henry failed to take Dunkirk, though assisted by a fleet and a French contingent, but in the same year (October 1636) he achieved a noteworthy success by the capture of Breda. As befitted a maritime race, however, it was on the sea that the Dutch were to inflict decisive defeat on their enemy. In 1639 a second Armada appeared in the Channel, and with more than 20,000 men and 77 ships a definite decision was invited. The result was as disastrous for Spain as the fiasco of 1588. On the 16th of September Tromp with 13 ships joined battle, and although the odds against him were almost preposterous, he forced the Spanish admiral Oquendo to take shelter in English waters, where he kept the enemy ships blockaded, thus obtaining time to send for Dutch reinforcements. On the 10th of October 1639 the Battle of the Downs was fought in a fog, and of the magnificent Spanish Armada only a few ships managed to escape. The history of Spain as a naval power terminates at this point. In comparison, the military events of the immediately succeeding years are unimportant; the eventual triumph of the Dutch was a foregone conclusion after the Battle of the Downs.

In common with every other combatant, the United Provinces shared in the general weariness and purposelessness that mark the closing stages of the Thirty Years' War. Freder-

[10] See Edmundson in *English Historical Review* (1890), 264.

ick Henry's later years were darkened by serious illness, and his wife gradually acquired a complete ascendency over his mind. He died in March 1647, but had he lived, it is possible that the separate peace with Spain (January 1648) would not have been signed. The prolonged peace negotiations reopened the old cleavage between the republican-mercantile-separatist-peace party, strongest in Holland, and the popular-pro-Orange-war party, strongest in Zealand. On the one hand it was argued by Zealand and the Orange party that Spain was the enemy, that Dutch prosperity had been built up in the war against her, that France was the national ally, and that the proximity of Spanish outposts to Dutch (or rather Zealand) territory was a perpetual menace. This party interpreted the constitution to mean that the Union should be a real pooling of resources and that the Captain-General should have full disposal of the joint naval and military forces, to which each of the seven states contributed a proportionate quota. These views were backed up by the Calvinist ministers and the working classes. On the other hand, it was argued by the patrician merchants of Holland that the Union of 1579 should be interpreted strictly, and that each of the seven provinces should have full control of the military forces which it raised and paid for. There would thus be as many independent armies as states; the States-General would be merely an assembly of ambassadors; the Captain-General would not be a permanent functionary, but would hold office only in war. As Holland contributed more than half of the joint forces of the Union, its Estates insisted with all the more vigour on the claim to regulate their own expenditure and to control the men whom they enrolled.

In foreign policy also Holland stood out against the other provinces. France, it was held, was now a great military power and might well step into the place which Spain was quitting; her friendship was always worth having, but too close proximity might be dangerous as well as embarrassing—"Gallus amicus sed non vicinus." Peace would be specially advantageous for the commerce of the United Provinces (or rather of Holland), and a dictatorship would be quite inconsistent with the republican independence on which the Union was based. These views influenced mostly the merchant classes and the more "liberal" opinion in the federation.[11] Such fundamental differences of opinion are not without their parallel in the history of England. The burghers of Holland had all the

[11] See Geddes, *Administration of John de Witt,* i. 63 ff.

revered principles, the religious latitudinarianism, the fear of standing armies and the preference for commercial expansion whether by peace or by war which characterized the "old" Whigs of eighteenth-century England, while the English Tories of the same period, in their devotion to a princely house, their lack of political achievement or tradition, their readiness to embark on original enterprises, and their unbending orthodoxy, might have found something in common with the Orange-Zealand faction of the seventeenth-century United Provinces.[12]

The peace between Spain and the Dutch Republic was signed at Münster on the 30th of January 1648. It has already been shown that Spain, in order to be avenged on France and to be free for the war against France alone (1648–59), conceded to the Dutch on every point. The United Provinces were declared free and independent; all Dutch conquests were recognized; freedom of trade in the East and West Indies was conceded, and the Scheldt remained closed. But while an advantageous peace had been secured mainly by the insistence of the province of Holland, the terms were never ratified by all the provinces, and there were ominous signs that the Orange faction would nurse a feeling of resentment against their republican rivals. In a few years the issue was again to be raised, but in different circumstances. In 1648 the republican separatists had a victorious peace behind them; in 1672 the country was in the hands of the invader; the menace from France had been realized and Dutch republicanism once more suffered eclipse.

The prestige of the Orange dynasty was enhanced by the rule of Frederick Henry's son William II. (1647–1650). In 1641 he had married Mary, daughter of Charles I., and at his accession he was young and popular. He tried secretly to prevent the ratification of the separate treaty with Spain, knowing as he did that the fortunes of his house were inalienably linked with war, but he failed, just as Maurice had failed to prevent the Twelve Years' Truce. Peace was soon followed by a reduction of the mercenary troops, and in the years 1648–1650 the struggle of 1618–1619 was repeated, this time on a military instead of a religious pretext. The Estates of Holland,

---

[12] For a full account of the Orange and Republican factions, see Lefèvre Pontalis, *Jean de Witt*, i. 209–220.

anxious to economize, insisted on still further reductions.[13] William declared that these had gone far enough and that national safety was now endangered. Despite repeated protests from the States-General, the province of Holland continued still further to reduce its military quota; to a personal appeal from William, the council of Amsterdam refused even a hearing. The conflict was complicated and embittered by the fact that on the one hand Spanish gold and diplomacy were busily at work, while on the other, William, in conjunction with France, was anxious to renew hostilities with Spain and also to restore the Stuarts. In July 1650 he resolved to use force. Six of the Holland deputies were arrested, but an attempt to seize Amsterdam failed, because the city was warned in time and took adequate measures for defence. The Estates of Holland bowed, however, before this show of force, and consented to modify the programme of military reductions. The imprisoned deputies were released, and though many in Holland considered that William was becoming a greater danger than any foreign enemy, yet by the States-General the Prince was accepted practically as a Dictator. The real issue was delayed by his unexpected death in November 1650. Over-indulgence in the chase produced a fever in a frame never robust, and William II. died when only twenty-four years of age.

This event was followed by a temporary set-back in the fortunes of the House of Orange. William II. left only a posthumous son, afterwards William III., the care of whom was hotly disputed between his grandmother Amalia von Solms and his mother Mary Stuart. Eventually the Council of State entrusted the guardianship of the young prince to these two women and to the Elector of Brandenburg. More serious was the fact that among the male members of the Orange family there was no one able or willing to take the lead, and, in addition, recent events in Europe seemed to show that the institution of monarchy was being put on trial. Charles I. was executed in 1649; the French king was a minor and practically a prisoner in Paris; Sweden was ruled by an irresponsible woman who talked of abdication; the heir to the English throne had been completely defeated at the battle of Worcester and was now a fugitive. In these circumstances it is not surprising that there was a revival of the "States" party, headed now by the aged Adrian Pauw, burgomaster of Amsterdam, and

[13] Edmundson, *Holland*, 205.

Jacob de Witt, the burgomaster of Dordrecht, who had been imprisoned in 1650. On the initiative of Holland, a "Great Assembly" was summoned in January 1651, when the offices of Captain-General and Admiral General were abolished by Holland, Utrecht, Guelders, Overyssel and Zealand. Even the office of Stadtholder was abolished in several provinces, and now, with a practically Stadtholderless government and an admission of the autonomy of each province, it was hoped that such an event as the *coup d'Etat* of 1650 would in future be impossible. The strength of the triumphant states party was about to be tested by war—the emergency for which the doctrinaire republicanism of Holland was unprepared, and in which the Orange party were to find their salvation.

The execution of Charles I. in January 1649 had created a sensation in the United Provinces, where for some time there was a strong wave of feeling in favour of the Stuarts. The English Parliament sent Dorislaer to the Hague as its agent, but within a few days of his arrival he was murdered by English royalist emissaries (May 12, 1649). This created bad feeling in England, nor were matters improved when the States-General refused to receive the second agent—Strickland—sent over by the Parliament. The Dutch agent in London was recalled, and so there were no diplomatic relations between the two republics. In this period of tension many old differences between the two maritime powers were recalled—the old disputes over the Greenland fisheries,[14] the violation of English neutrality in the Battle of the Downs, the reparations due to the English East India and Muscovy Companies for damages to their interests,[15] the Amboyna murders of 1623,[16] the restoration of Pularoon,[17] and the admission of England to trade in all parts of the East and West Indies not occupied by the Dutch. It needed only the English Navigation Act of October 1651[18] to precipitate the conflict, while the English demand that Dutch ships in the Channel should salute the flag

[14] Gardiner, *History of England,* ii. 309.

[15] *Ibid.* III. ch. xxvi.

[16] *Ibid.* v. 242.

[17] *Ibid.* iii. 407.

[18] There was also an act of October 1650 prohibiting all trade with colonies upholding the cause of Charles II. against the Commonwealth, an Act which caused considerable irritation among the Dutch. The Navigation Act of Charles II. forbade export as well as import in all but British ships or ships of the same origin

definitely raised the question of maritime supremacy.[19] The Navigation Act forbade the importation of goods into England except in English ships or in ships of the country exporting the merchandise, and so was a direct challenge to the carrying trade on which the prosperity of the Dutch was mainly based. Negotiation failed to achieve any result, and the issue could be decided only by war.

Even thus hostilities might have been avoided, as neither side was quite prepared, had not the precipitancy of Tromp made the breach irreparable. In May 1652 he met one of Blake's squadrons off Dover, whereupon a dispute over the demand that the Dutch flag should be lowered ended in a fight from which Tromp had to withdraw with some loss. This was followed by a declaration of war, and the Dutch were now to realize the dangers of divided control. There were no fewer than five Admiralties, the States-General were ineffective, there was jealousy and dispute over the separate military contribution of each province, and there were several cases of treachery at sea. The Dutch fishing fleet with its armed convoy was destroyed off the coast of Scotland;[20] a fleet of Dutch merchantmen was captured off Calais; headwinds prevented Tromp from making up on either Blake or Ayscue, and in October the combined forces of De With and De Ruyter were defeated off the Kentish Knock owing to the desertion of the former. A series of uninterrupted Dutch misfortunes was relieved only in December 1652, when Tromp defeated the English fleet under Blake off Dungeness.[21] Meanwhile the Dutch held the Mediterranean by the victory of Admiral van Galen over an English fleet off Leghorn (March 23, 1653), and they were able to exclude the English from the Baltic owing to their Danish alliance.

As there seemed little likelihood of a definite decision being reached, both sides speedily became tired of the war, and in Holland the strong peace party was led by the young and able John de Witt, son of the burgomaster of Dordrecht. John de Witt was appointed Pensionary of Holland in February 1653, and took it upon himself to commit the republic to negotiations by sending secret agents to London. The defeat of Tromp off

as the goods. For a discussion of the part played by the Navigation Act in causing the first Dutch War, see Gardiner, *Letters and Papers relating to the First Dutch War,* i. 48 ff.

[19] Gardiner, *op. cit.* i. 170 ff.
[20] *Ibid.* i. pt. iv.
[21] Gardiner, *op. cit.* iii. 4-6.

the Gabbard in June 1653, followed shortly afterwards by his death and a rigid blockade of the Dutch coast, made peace a matter of vital necessity for the United Provinces, thereby justifying the vigorous efforts of John de Witt to enter into negotiations with Cromwell. These negotiations were at first impeded by Cromwell's hope that the United Provinces would become members of the great Protestant alliance which it was the aim of his foreign policy to create. This alliance was to include Switzerland, the free Imperial cities, the German Protestant princes, Denmark and Sweden; it was to vindicate freedom of conscience in Europe and set up a bulwark against all countries which either retained the Inquisition or were dependent on the Papacy. But the Dutch, whose interests were maritime, not religious, had outlived many of their earlier enthusiasms and had little sympathy with the idealist elements in these schemes; hence Cromwell insisted, in his turn, on what was practically complete surrender. The preliminaries of peace eventually agreed upon involved concession by the United Provinces on practically every point—the English flag had to be saluted in the Channel, the privilege of fishing in English waters had to be bought, the right of search at sea was admitted, and compensation had to be guaranteed by the Dutch for the Amboyna murders. This was the first real defeat of the Dutch republic, and its decline may be traced from this point. Nor was this all, for Cromwell, made more exacting by his triumph, introduced a clause intended to consecrate the anti-Orange republicanism of the United Provinces. The Dutch agent was asked to obtain from the Estates-General a guarantee that the Prince of Orange would be perpetually excluded from the dignities held by his ancestors.

It was his share in these negotiations that brought John de Witt into prominence. Born at Dordrecht in 1625 of an old burgher family, he had received from his father, the burgomaster and member of the Council of State, elaborate education for the public position he was destined to fill.[22] Study at the University of Leyden was supplemented by travel in France and England, and when in 1650 the arrest of his father diverted his thought from law to politics, he showed that the mantle of Oldenbarneveldt had fallen upon him. Thenceforward he incarnated the principles of ardent republi-

[22] For details of de Witt's early career, see Lefèvre Pontalis, *Jean de Witt*, I. ch. ii.

canism, devoting himself to maintaining the sanctity of the Union against the encroachments of a princely house. His talents and oratorical powers qualified him to succeed to the Grand Pensionary in February 1653; thereafter it was entirely due to his energies that Holland retained her supremacy, and that government was made possible while the strict theory of provincial independence was maintained. De Witt's informal presidency of the Republic was not everywhere accepted without demur; the Orange faction was strong in Zealand, and there were numerous revolts there.

The first test of the young statesman's strength came with Cromwell's insistence on the exclusion clause in the treaty of Westminster. De Witt knew perfectly well that the States-General would agree to no such proposal, but he could see no means of obtaining peace other than by accepting a clause which, while not unacceptable to himself,[23] would be repudiated by a considerable proportion of the Dutch regents. Accordingly, he was forced to adopt clandestine methods in order to satisfy England and lull suspicion at home. He kept in close touch with Cromwell through his agent van Beverningh, and in April 1654 he managed to induce the States-General to accept the treaty, from which the exclusion clause had been, for the time, removed. The only clause that had raised any opposition was the "temperament" clause, by which it was provided that any Captain-General or Stadtholder who might be elected, should swear to observe the treaty, but nevertheless on the 23rd of April the treaty was ratified and signed.

Meanwhile Cromwell insisted on his exclusion clause, declaring, however, that he would be content if this was agreed to by the Estates of Holland. The Estates of Holland met, and were amazed at the request that they should now ratify this secret clause. Owing, however, to the Pensionary's eloquence and to the peremptory demands from London, the clause was at last accepted by a small majority, and, in spite of the protests of the minority, the Act was sent to London, where peace was officially proclaimed. The secret clause was soon a matter of common knowledge, and the States-General indignantly ordered the return of all the secret documents.

[23] "It would not be consistent with love of true freedom to maintain that in a commonwealth the highest dignities should go to anyone by mere right of birth" (De Witt). Quoted in Geddes, *op. cit.* i. 442.

De Witt, by a ruse,[24] and without implicating himself, caused the Dutch agent to deliver the completed treaty to Cromwell, so that when the orders of the States-General were received it was too late. Thus against the almost unanimous opposition of the States-General and with the support of only a narrow majority of the Estates of Holland, De Witt had negotiated peace with a foreign country on terms that practically excluded the House of Orange from power. Thus his methods were not quite constitutional, and he was never forgiven.

Firmly entrenched in Amsterdam in the support of the burgher oligarchy and in the family influence which his marriage gave him, John de Witt now directed himself to the administration of the country over which he was ruler in all but name. The financial question was the most pressing, as the recent war had piled up a large debt. The public accounts were carefully examined so that extravagance and leakage could be checked, and the Government interest was reduced from 5 to 4 per cent. Profiting by the lessons of the English war, the fleet was overhauled; an improved type of ship was built; steps were taken to secure more efficient sailors by reorganizing the training of naval personnel. In foreign policy the Pensionary showed himself anxious to avoid war but determined to maintain the prestige of the republic when necessity arose. By a threat to blockade the French coast he obtained relief from French attacks on Dutch merchantmen in the Mediterranean, and in 1657 the coast of Portugal was blockaded in revenge for Portuguese instigation of a Brazilian revolt against Dutch rule. The ambitions of Charles X.[25] of Sweden forced De Witt to intervene in the Baltic, access to which was of paramount importance for Dutch trade, and in the summer of 1656, when the Swedish king invaded Poland, the States-General despatched a fleet to Danzig in order to raise the siege. This expedition was attended with success; Danzig was relieved and declared a neutral port. But by 1658 Denmark had to surrender her control of the Sound to Sweden, and so long as Sweden was strong, the Dutch control of the Baltic

---

[24] For the details, see Geddes, *op. cit.* i. 379-407, and Lefèvre Pontalis, *op. cit.* I. ch. iii.

[25] Notice that since 1640, when a treaty was signed between the States-General and the Swedish Regency (Dumont, *Corps diplomatique,* VI. i. 193-5), there had been harmonious co-operation between the Swedes and Dutch in the Baltic; the latter greatly valued the Baltic trade and the former needed a maritime ally.

trade was insecure. With Dutch help the Swedish naval block-ade of Copenhagen was raised late in 1658, but two Dutch admirals were killed, and in the next year the struggle had to be renewed. The Peace of Oliva (1660) gave to the Dutch free access through the Sound, and thus De Witt, by a firm use of the republic's naval resources, had defended the claim to free trade in the Baltic without raising up any fresh enemies.

But De Witt was to find his enemies, not in northern but in western Europe. In 1660 there was a turn in the tide of the fortunes of the House of Orange when Charles Stuart was re-stored to the English throne, and in the following year, on the death of Mazarin, the young Louis XIV. declared his intention of ruling without any First Minister. The monarchist cause in Europe was now restored; it was natural, therefore, that the friends of the House of Orange should turn to the young Prince William, who, even in boyhood, was giving some mani-festations of the qualities that were to distinguish his riper years. The administration of De Witt was again to be tested by war, and again with England. Opinion in the United Provinces had never been unanimous on the subject of the treaty of Westminster, which had closed the first Dutch War; it seemed to some contemporaries that there was not room in the world for these two powerful maritime and colonial powers. For several years there had been irritation and rivalry between them; it needed only a spark to create another conflagration.[26] Late in 1664 an English fleet took possession of the Dutch colony of New Netherlands, and at the same time Dutch pos-sessions in West Africa were threatened. War was declared in March 1665.

Mainly owing to the absence of De Ruyter in the Mediter-ranean, the war began disastrously for the Dutch. On the 13th of June the Dutch navy under Obdam suffered complete defeat in Southwold Bay, an action in which James, Duke of York, gave proof of his skill and resource as a seaman. On their east-ern frontier the Dutch had to face an army of invasion under Charles's ally the turbulent Bishop of Münster, who, on the pretext of a dispute over a small border territory, entered Drenthe and Overyssel. The bishop's troops were, however, obliged to withdraw by the arrival of French help, and in 1666 he concluded peace with the States-General. De Witt's French alliance at this time is explained by the fact that Louis was just beginning to put forward his claim to the Spanish

[26] Lefèvre Pontalis, *op. cit.* i. 319 ff.

Netherlands, and for the moment he believed that it would be diplomatic to retain the friendship of the Dutch.

Naval operations were renewed in the summer of 1666. In June an indecisive battle was fought off the North Foreland in which the casualties on both sides were heavy, but it was generally regarded as a victory for the Dutch. In the following month the combined fleets under Rupert and Monk defeated the forces of De Ruyter off the Dutch coast. This victory was followed by a war on Dutch merchantmen, and soon De Witt became anxious to open up peace negotiations. When these negotiations lagged, the Pensionary decided on a dramatic stroke, inspired by his knowledge that Parliament declined to devote money to the maintenance of English maritime supremacy. With a fleet of 80 ships De Ruyter sailed up the Thames, and on the 19th of June 1667 captured Sheerness. A few days later he forced through the boom across the Medway, seizing a large number of ships. The demonstration was intended to have a moral rather than a material effect, and in this it succeeded, because the sound of the guns could be heard in London, where for a time there was disorder and panic. When they could do no further damage the Dutch ships retired, leaving the enemy to recover from a national humiliation. Within a few days (July 26) peace was concluded. The Dutch capture of Surinam was retained in exchange for New Netherlands (which became English); the Navigation Act was modified in favour of the Dutch, but there was no concession in the matter of saluting the English flag.[27] The treaty of Breda, 1667, was the most successful achievement in the career of John de Witt.

Before the treaty was signed an even more serious menace appeared from another quarter. Louis XIV. began his War of Devolution in the early summer of 1667, and with the French invasion of the Spanish Low Countries the Dutch realized that their independence was threatened by a military power more formidable than either Spain or England. As a maritime country having only a few mercenaries over whom there was no single control, the Netherlands were at the mercy of any great continental power that might establish itself on the frontier. For De Witt it was absolutely necessary to have allies. There was no chance of winning over Charles II., but on the other hand the English nation was opposed to French aggression, and even the humiliation so recently suffered at the hands

[27] T. W. Fulton, *The Sovereignty of the Sea*, 466 ff.

of De Ruyter could not overcome the feeling that the two Protestant countries should combine against Catholic and bellicose France. Sir William Temple was sent to the Hague as ambassador, and late in January 1668, barely six months after the conclusion of hostilities, a defensive alliance was signed between the English representative and the States-General. Shortly afterwards Sweden added her adhesion, and so the Triple Alliance of 1668 came into being. Before this combination Louis pretended to yield, and for the moment it seemed that De Witt had again removed a foreign menace to the independence of the Dutch.

Though the Pensionary was apparently at the height of his power, appearances were deceptive and his position was being steadily undermined. Like so many democratic "idealists" he was often high-handed and arbitrary, caring little whether he caused personal offence so long as he won his way; and his personal dictatorship was possible only on condition that it was justified by success. With years and the realization of his powers these personal characteristics became emphasized, and he sometimes alienated even friends by bestowing important posts on relatives.[28] Moreover, as the Prince of Orange emerged from boyhood the Orange party became more confident; the Prince would soon claim his legitimate heritage from the Pensionary; and when the Estates of Holland in 1667 abolished the office of Stadtholder, they betrayed the nature of their fears. Utrecht, Gelderland and Overyssel followed suit, but Orange feeling in Groningen, Friesland and Zealand was too strong. In any case paper treaties were of little moment when it was clear that the Prince of Orange would soon be of age and that he would have behind him a great body of public opinion. The rule of De Witt was really an interregnum, and he himself must have seen that in a few years it would be untenable.

Meanwhile Louis was busily employed in effecting the diplomatic isolation of the Netherlands. Charles II. was speedily bought off by the secret treaty of Dover (December 1670), and the remaining member of the Triple Alliance—Sweden—was persuaded to desert the Dutch. There were many warnings that Louis was planning an invasion, but as the secrecy of the treaty of Dover was still preserved, De Witt retained his blind faith in English support. The States-General and the Provincial

28 Lefèvre Pontalis, *op. cit.* ii. 235 ff.

Estates were more anxious to economize than to engage on military commitments, so the year of invasion, 1672, found the Dutch practically helpless. Charles, in accordance with the second or public treaty of Dover (1671), declared war on the 28th of March 1672. France's other allies were the Bishop of Münster, anxious to avenge the fiasco of 1666, and the Elector of Cologne, who was a Wittelsbach and in the French interest. Immediately there was a concentration of military forces on the luckless Netherlands, and Louis himself appeared at the head of an army of over 100,000 men.

The situation was desperate, since not even the resources of John de Witt were equal to the occasion. In face of unprecedented danger, all the separatist aspirations and paper treaties of the immediately preceding years were swept aside, and the Prince of Orange, then twenty-two years of age, was appointed by the States-General Captain-General for one year. It was fitting that William III. should make his first appearance in history when his country was threatened with annihilation by the French.

William III. possessed in a remarkable degree many of the qualities which have made his house so famous. Ascetic, imperious, inscrutable, he united determination and energy with an indomitable spirit that wore out the fragile structure encasing it. Trained in the schools of adversity, he was imperturbable in defeat, and more perhaps than any of his contemporaries he could devote himself to an abstract cause with ruthlessness and perseverance. Seemingly devoid of vices, he was nevertheless passionate beneath his invariable self-control; it was because dominated by a great idea, and not because pushed on by a party, that William managed to ride roughshod over the republican traditions of his country. His ancestors had built up their position by arms; the achievements of his house were inseparably linked with all that was patriotic in the aspirations of the infant state; everywhere in Europe constitutional abstractions were falling before the assaults of absolutist monarchs, and if the United Provinces was to survive disaster, it would have to be under the unquestioned sway of the princely house which had already shown itself so qualified to shape the destinies of a nation. So William may have argued. But these ambitions were not to be realized without a struggle and a victim.

There was a strong theatrical element in Louis's invasion of the Netherlands. In May 1672 two great armies, one headed by the monarch and Turenne, the other by Condé, joined forces at Maestricht. There it was decided to cross the Rhine, a feat accomplished with great éclat on the 12th of June at the frontier Tolhuis, where Condé and his nephew Longueville rushed on the Dutch defenders with the cry "No quarter for these vermin." William was forced to abandon the line of the Yssel and retire to Utrecht, while the province of Overyssel was overrun by the troops of Münster and Cologne. On the 20th of June Utrecht surrendered and Amsterdam was threatened. While Louis was proudly adding to the already long list of captured towns, the sluices at Ymuiden were opened[29] and Amsterdam, after a few days, became a small island. This restored the courage of the Dutch. William and his subjects co-operated in the task of organizing the national defences, but even thus the situation seemed hopeless. There were attempts to assassinate De Witt; even in Holland the republicans found themselves completely discredited and the Orange party everywhere in the ascendant. The Stadtholdership was revived in several provinces. In the renewed peace negotiations the demands of the English and French monarchs were so humiliating that, if conceded, they would have involved the loss of Dutch independence. On the 24th of July Cornelius de Witt was arrested; a few days later John resigned his office of Pensionary. Charged with plotting against the Prince of Orange, Cornelius was sentenced to banishment, and it was while he was receiving a visit from his brother that the mob rushed the prison at the Hague and, dragging out the two brothers, put them to death in the street.[30] The vindictive and relentless brutality of the Dutch mob shocked even the most hardened of contemporaries. In *La Tulipe noire* Dumas wove a halo of romance round the episode which marks the termination of democratic experiments in continental Europe of the seventeenth century.

William III. was not a party[31] to this act, but he rewarded those who had taken a share in it. Now that he was his own master he devoted himself to the task of expelling the invader. He was Stadtholder of the Republic as well as Captain and Admiral-General; his first care was his army and the fortification of what was left of Dutch territory. The French were

[29] Blok, *History of the Dutch People,* iv. 380.
[30] See Lefèvre Pontalis, ii. 520 ff.
[31] For a full account of William's part in the tragedy, see *ibid.* ch. xiv.

seriously impeded by the inundations; in December they made an attempt to traverse the ice and invest both Amsterdam and the Hague, but a sudden thaw made this impossible.

The campaign of 1673 commenced with the siege of Maestricht, a course of action dictated by Louis's personal preference for this kind of warfare. The city might have withstood the flamboyant tactics of the French monarch, but it fell before the skill of Vauban. Meanwhile William received help from an unusual quarter, for in August, the Regency government in Spain, acting in conjunction with the Emperor, undertook to send troops, and on the 30th of August 1673 a coalition was formed between Spain and the Emperor by which military assistance to the Dutch was guaranteed. With the addition of Lorraine, this constituted the Grand Alliance of the Hague (1674). Thus the extraordinary alliance of England and France called up a more extraordinary coalition, and European diplomacy, from a drama in which the same situations recurred with almost monotonous regularity, became a quick-change revue in which no one could prophesy what the next transformation would be. On the 7th of September 1673 William took Naarden, the most advanced French outpost, and uniting forces with the Imperialist troops under Montecuculi, he captured Bonn (November 12). The French generals were, however, becoming discontented with the supreme control of military operations exercised by Louis and Louvois. Late in 1673 Marshal Luxemburg was recalled from Holland and only garrisons were left in a territory which by the calculations of Louis XIV. ought already to have been French. The French occupation was marked by several incidents, notably in the villages of Bodegrave and Swammerdam, near the Hague, and the Dutch long retained a vivid recollection of their treatment at the hands of the invaders. The pamphlet describing these incidents, with vivid illustrations, was widely circulated, especially in Germany, and is one of the earliest pieces of "atrocity" literature.

Charles's need of money forced him to make his peace with the strong anti-French party in England, and on the 1st of February 1674 he begged Louis to enter into peace negotiations. On the 19th of the same month peace was concluded between England and the United Provinces on the basis of the treaty of Breda, with the addition that the Dutch had to pay a large indemnity. The militant ecclesiastics of Münster and Cologne were easily detached now that the French was the losing cause. With France isolated, it remained only for William to hold the enemy at bay, and Dutch independence was once again secure. Though defeated by Condé at Seneff in Hainault (August 11, 1674), he held his own throughout the summer and, late in October, the fortress of Grave on the lower Meuse was taken by the Dutch. The French attack, diverted from the United Provinces, was directed to the Spanish Netherlands, Alsace, Franche Comté and the Rhine frontier, a dissipation of forces which made possible William's work of restoring the shattered territories of occupation.

William had practically secured his objects long before the terms of general pacification were discussed at Nymegen. Of the combatants he was the one who desired most to continue hostilities, believing as he did that only military disaster could curb the ambitions of Louis XIV. But in spite of him, peace was signed between France and the States-General on the 10th of August 1678, and this treaty was grouped with the treaties between Spain and France and between France and the Emperor in the general peace of Nymegen. The French restored Maestricht and all Dutch territory in their hands; in addition, they released their hostile embargo on Dutch trade. All the domains possessed by the Prince of Orange in Franche Comté, Charolais and Flanders were restored, but the free exercise of the Catholic religion in Maestricht was insisted on. At the moment when this treaty was signed, Mons was being besieged by Luxemburg, and in the hope of achieving a definite military success William proceeded to the relief of the town. Although informed that peace had been signed, William persisted in his attack; on the 14th of August 1678 one of the most sanguinary battles of the whole war was fought at Saint Denis, a suburb of Mons. The result was indecisive, but William made little secret of his opinion that he had been betrayed by the peace. This was prompted, not by the mere gambling instinct which always seeks to retrieve a loss, but by his intense hatred of the French and his love of war for its own sake.

In the years 1678–1688 William was an absolute monarch in all but name. He nominated the members of the more important city councils; he appointed magistrates and officers of the army as high as the rank of colonel, and with the help of such Grand Pensionaries as Fagel and afterwards Heinsius he exercised a rule which was all the more readily acquiesced in as it was realized how precarious were the small states in the century of Louis XIV. But even thus, French influence was still strong in Holland, nor were efforts spared to detach the Dutch from their prince. On several occasions the municipality of Amsterdam showed a spirit of independence, for the insult of 1650 was still remembered, and in 1684, when the city was suspected of corresponding with the French, William ordered an investigation of the municipal archives. But when in 1688 James effected his escape from England and his son-in-law[32] was invited to fill the vacant throne, the Prince of Orange had the support of his country behind him.

Thereafter the career of William belongs to English rather than to Dutch history, and the United Provinces lose something of their identity by submersion in the great coalitions directed against France. William's visits were few and far between. The government was ably conducted in his absence by Heinsius, who succeeded to Fagel as Grand Pensionary of Holland in 1688. An unsuccessful embassy to Paris in 1681 on the subject of William's right to the principality of Orange had embittered Heinsius against France, and so William had in him an understudy after his own heart. But after the first wave of enthusiasm, the linking of the Dutch with the English under one ruler ceased to be popular. In monarchist England William was a parliamentary king, with prerogatives clearly defined and limited; in republican Holland he was practically absolute, but there his rule was not softened by the presence of a Court to provide the trappings and embellishments of monarchy. Moreover, the two countries had long been rivals and often enemies; the Revolution settlement, while it brought the two countries into closer touch with each other, helped in some ways to emphasize the rooted antagonism between the English and Dutch peoples. It was only by the support of the Whigs that William held his position; it was in Dutchmen such as Bentinck that he confided, and long before the end of his reign William realized that he might always have the respect but never the love of his adopted country.

The Peace of Ryswick (September 20, 1697) was only a breathing space in the struggle, and it was generally considered that the death of the Spanish king would provide occasion for a great European war. In the Spanish Succession war one of the main objects of Dutch policy was to secure a strong

[32] William had married Mary Stuart, daughter of the Duke of York, in 1677.

"barrier" on the southern and eastern frontier so that all danger from the Spanish Netherlands might be removed and a repetition of the invasion of 1672 made impossible. In October 1709 what is known as the First Barrier Treaty was signed between the English Government and the States-General, by which the Dutch were accorded the right to garrison certain specified frontier towns in order to guarantee their independence and also obtain a footing in Flanders and Brabant. The second Barrier Treaty was signed in January 1713, and by the third, signed with the Emperor in November 1715, the Dutch obtained the right to garrison Furnes, Ypres, Knocke, Tournai, Menin, Namur and Warneton, part of the military expenditure for this purpose to be borne by the Imperial Government. Thus in the Spanish Succession war the United Provinces obtained one of their objects—military security against whatever great European power happened to control the Spanish Netherlands, and so long as forts were regarded as sound frontier defences, the Dutch might rest content. By the treaty of Rastadt (September 1714) the Spanish Netherlands, together with Naples and the Milanese, went to the Emperor Charles VI., and so began the era of Hapsburg rule in Belgium.

William III. died in March 1702, leaving no direct heir. His cousin, the young John William Friso, was recognized as Prince of Orange by the States-General, but he died in 1711, leaving a posthumous son, afterwards William IV. During the long period in which the republic was without a Stadtholder, the old political factions revived; moreover, with the increasing power of England and the spread of financial speculation and private luxury, the Dutch steadily declined from the high position they had occupied in the seventeenth century. For a time the House of Orange had supplied able rulers, but when that line failed, the native forces of disruption asserted themselves, and the national destinies of the Dutch were again endangered. Historians often seek to attribute the commercial decline of the Dutch to some single cause—such as the English Navigation Acts, but the truth is that national decline is generally due to several causes which may act over a long period. So long as room had to be found in the world for the British Empire, the Dutch as a commercial and maritime race were bound to suffer in the contest with a stronger rival, whether that rival used Navigation Acts or not.

Chapter 11

The Struggle for Baltic Supremacy: Sweden, Denmark, and Prussia

FIVE SEVENTEENTH-CENTURY STATES—Sweden, Denmark, Russia, Brandenburg and Poland—had access to the Baltic; their struggle for supremacy in the inland sea forms the subject of this chapter, and it will be shown how the internal history of Sweden, Denmark and Prussia was influenced by that contest. The result of this struggle for supremacy may be summarized as follows: Brandenburg (afterwards Prussia) took the place of Poland on the Prussian coast; Sweden by the middle of the century had won control of the Baltic from Denmark, a control which was gradually lost and partitioned between Russia and Prussia. The only element of unity in this subject is to be found in the dramatic history of the great Swedish kings.

A sense of Swedish nationalism was developed in the long struggle with Denmark, and under the Lutheran House of Vasa Sweden became a great power. The crown was still regarded as both hereditary and elective, that is, the Estates elected the monarch but always chose from the House of Vasa. As the seventeenth century progressed, the elective element in the Swedish kingship gradually subsided, without disappearing altogether, and traces of it are to be seen in the capitulations defining the powers of Diet and Senate, signed by the king at his accession. But respect for kingship was strong in Sweden, and if the king could ride a horse and lead an army, no one was greatly concerned about constitutional doctrines; consequently the precise functions of Diet and Senate were never clearly defined. The royal power remained patriarchal, and in 1682 became absolute. Gustavus Adolphus was the first king to devote himself to the development of Sweden's natural resources. He introduced an element of order into the national finances; with Dutch help several new industries were naturalized; glass, paper, sugar and starch factories were built; iron, copper and sulphur were exported, and a Dutchman named Silentz introduced improved methods of smelting copper. In 1629 a shipping company was formed for the purpose of building coasting and fighting ships. A South Sea Company for trade with Africa, Asia and South America had been founded three years earlier by a Dutch company promoter named Usselinx.[1] Under the great Chancellor Axel Oxenstierna the Chancery became the most powerful institution in the Government, and during the minority that followed Gustavus's death it was able to continue the brilliant foreign policy of the deceased monarch.

Denmark was confronted with similar problems. Under the elective monarchy of the Oldenburg dynasty she had to maintain her control of the Sound, and with her military failure she sank at once to the level of a secondary power. Throughout this period she found her natural allies among the enemies of Sweden, such as the Elector of Brandenburg and the king of Poland. The revolution of 1661, whereby the Danish monarchy became absolute and hereditary, was forced on the Government as the only possible reply to the menace of the nobility within and a host of powerful enemies from without. By the *Kongelov,* or Royal Law, embodying the terms of this revolution, it was declared that the monarchy originated from the surrender of authority by the Estates, and that the duties of the king were to maintain the indivisibility of the kingdom, to guarantee the Lutheran Confession and observe the *Kongelov* itself. Had this extreme measure not been adopted, Denmark might have shared the fate of Poland. The Danish monarch almost contemporary with Gustavus Adolphus was Christian IV., who did something to develop the commercial resources of the country by founding trading companies, encouraging exploration and organising a national scheme of education. Denmark had a well-trained fleet and a small but efficient army; its political weaknesses were due to the absence of a middle class, the progressive degradation of the

---

[1] See Hellendorff and Schuck, *History of Sweden.*

peasants, and the absence of any cohesion in the territories over which suzerainty was exercised.[2]

Both Sweden and Denmark took part in the Thirty Years' War, but with very different results. Denmark gained nothing, and by the treaty of Lübeck (1629) she was obliged to give up her claims to German territory, while by the treaty of Brömsebro (1645) she had to make concessions to Sweden which helped the latter to obtain control of the Sound. Christian IV. (1596–1648) was followed by his son Frederick III. (1648–1670), who had to wage in quick succession two important wars against Sweden, that of 1657–58 being terminated by the treaty of Roskilde, that of 1658–1660 by the treaty of Oliva. Throughout the later part of the century Denmark was just able to hold her own. It was otherwise with Sweden. The possession of the islands of Oesel and Gothland guaranteed her strategic control of the Baltic; she already possessed Finland, Reval, Esthonia, Karelia, Ingria and Livonia. The course of the Thirty Years' War was definitely influenced by her intervention, while by the treaty of Westphalia she became an important German power. But nevertheless her real difficulties date from that treaty. In the opinion of one of the mediators[3] of the Westphalia negotiations, Sweden had gained ten times more by negotiation than she could have gained by arms, but, in spite of the fact that Swedish intervention had ostensibly been for the express purpose of redressing the religious balance in Germany, the Swedes regarded their acquisitions as much less than their military exploits justified. This is important, for the Northern nations still clung to the view that conquest is the sole justification for possession, while in western Europe this theory was beginning to be questioned in view of the importance then coming to be attached to the doctrine of balance of power. German territory was a very risky speculation, consequently Sweden emerged from the Thirty Years' War with a European position which she was quite unable to maintain. Her newly-won possessions required expensive armies of occupation and yielded disappointing revenues; the Governors of captured seaports like Stralsund and Stettin tried to amass such wealth from the harbour dues that they drove trade away. Sweden did not learn the lesson in time. Military success, combined with economic necessity, tempted her rulers

[2] These included Norway (until 1814), Iceland (until 1874), Scania, Bleking and Halland (until 1660).
[3] The Papal Nuncio Chigi.

to make the Baltic a Swedish lake, and after 1648 there was required only the conquest of Courland and Prussia, with the important harbours of Dantzig, Elbing, Pillau and Memel, to realize this ambition, since Western Pomerania was already (by the treaty of Westphalia) in Swedish hands. The Prussians were Lutherans and detested their ruler, the Calvinist Elector of Brandenburg, who held his duchy as a Polish fief; what more natural than that Sweden should win over Prussia from a weak Poland and a negligible Brandenburg?[4]

The only flaw in these calculations was in regard to Brandenburg. From small beginnings the Hohenzollerns had been busily constructing a great German power stretching from the Rhine to the Niemen. In 1618 John Sigismund the Elector succeeded to the Polish fief of ducal Prussia by the death of a cousin, and of this territory his descendant, Frederick William the Great Elector, obtained full sovereignty in 1657. In the west, the Elector's territories included Cleve, acquired by the treaty of Xanten (1614), while in the centre was the great March of Brandenburg stretching athwart the Elbe and the Oder. John Sigismund (1608–1619) was succeeded by George William (1619–1640), who of necessity played an undistinguished part in the Thirty Years' War; he was too weak even to make his neutrality respected. Calvinism and personal jealousy prevented alliance with the Elector of Saxony; his territories were ravaged alike by Swede, Imperialist and Spaniard, and he was on several occasions obliged to seek personal safety in flight. His successor Frederick William the Great Elector (1640–1688) fully realized the dangers, both internal and external, threatening his state. On the west he was open to attack from the Spanish Netherlands; in the centre his power was disputed by great territorial magnates, while on the east he was liable to frequent humiliation from unruly subjects and a haughty Polish suzerain. It was, therefore, natural that he should turn to France, and a marriage with Mademoiselle de Montpensier was proposed.[5] With the object of securing another German ally, the French agent D'Avaux was entrusted with the work of looking after the Elector's interests at the Congress of Westphalia, where the Elector was assigned territories out of all proportion to his military ex-

[4] For the importance of Prussia to Sweden and Swedish belief in Brandenburg's impotence see Haumant, *Les Guerres du nord*, 30 ff.

[5] *Instructions données* (Prussia), xx.

ploits, and justified only by the fact that he had lost a considerable proportion of his subjects through the war. Frederick William acquired in this way eastern Pomerania with the port of Colberg, and, in compensation for the cession of western Pomerania to Sweden, he received three secularized bishoprics, together with the reversion of the Archbishopric of Magdeburg. Almost unnoticed, and without any great effort, the Hohenzollerns had by 1648 become the most important territorial family in Germany.

Frederick William set himself to organize his scattered territories into a compact military state. Of unimpeachable morals and ardent piety, he prayed for success in war, and inaugurated the family tradition of attributing military success to the direct intervention of the Almighty.[6] His wife, Henrietta Louise of Orange, daughter of Frederick Henry of Orange, proved an enthusiastic and capable helpmate, and her husband tried to introduce into his reforms some of the lessons he had learned during his early sojourn in the United Provinces. With the help of a Dutch naval architect he built a small fleet and even dreamed of colonies, but both naval and imperial ambitions had to be abandoned. On his coinage was engraved the motto "Pro Deo et Populo"; his enlightened rule in disturbed and barren provinces anticipates the benevolent despotism of the eighteenth century.[7] He began by curtailing the powers of provincial assemblies, leaving them with only a nominal right of veto on taxation, and after 1648 he cleared the March of vagrant troops. He created a central Council of State, forming a select body of councillors into a Chancery for the consideration of foreign policy; a Chamber of Finance, a War Commission and a Supreme Council of Justice were also established.[8] It is characteristic that the War Commissioners soon encroached on the financial administration, for, like his descendant Frederick the Great, the Elector was anxious that there should always be enough money in the Treasury to enable him to wage war at any time. Frederick William sedulously encouraged industry and commerce, for which purpose he introduced foreign artisans and Dutch farmers, while by the

[6] Waddington, *Le Grand Electeur Frédéric Guillaume de Brandebourg*, i. 46.

[7] See F. L. Carsten, "The Great Elector and the Foundation of the Hohenzollern Despotism," in *English Historical Review*, lxv. (1950), pp. 175-202.

[8] Waddington, *op. cit.* i. 79 ff.

Edict of Potsdam (1686) he gave special facilities to Huguenot refugees, of whom about 20,000 settled on his estates. Moreover, by the extensive planting of mulberry trees he made possible a prosperous silk industry. Though a strict Calvinist, he did not persecute dissentients, knowing as he did that a prosperous if mixed population is better for purposes of taxation than a sparse collection of paupers with nothing but a common creed to rejoice in; accordingly Jews were admitted into Berlin, and even Roman Catholics were tolerated in Prussia, where Frederick William's difficulties were greatest. Freedom of thought was permitted so far as consistent with the interests of the state, and he used severity only in the last resort, as when he ordered the execution of the Prussian rebel Kalkstein. If to be free from the prejudices of one's time is a test of greatness, then Frederick William was great.

His reorganization of local institutions was intended to eliminate separatism. In each province he established a local government, headed by a Governor and Chancellor, the former entrusted with full executive authority in the absence of the Elector, and he removed the local functionaries hitherto appointed by the Provincial Estates, replacing them by officials responsible to Berlin alone. These officials were given a regular salary in place of the old payments in kind, and in this way malversation was checked. Local tribunals of justice and finance were set up. A postal system was commenced, and gradually an efficient Civil Service was created. In his choice of ministers he preferred the bourgeois and ex-officer to the nobility, and, though ably assisted by his adviser Waldeck, he was his own First Minister as well as Generalissimo. The main object of these administrative reforms was to provide money for what was then a novelty in Germany—a standing army, which in Brandenburg had its origin in a mob of Swedish deserters, and was organized into a well-equipped and disciplined force by Generals Sparr and Derfflinger. The *"miles perpetuus"*[9] and a well filled Treasury were, in the opinion of the Elector, the strongest national securities; his money and his army of 27,000 men were his best diplomatic assets. All these measures reflect a shrewd and vigorous mind. Frederick William was endowed with a personality in which qualities of caution and cunning were combined, and from which scruple was almost wholly absent. Critics accused him of remember-

[9] In 1651 the Great Elector had in his 17,000 men the best-equipped army in Germany (Haumant, *Les Guerres du nord,* 34).

ing friends only when he was in adversity, and a French observer[10] described him as "le plus fin renard de l'Europe." These qualities were to have ample exercise in the tangled politics of the northern wars.

Such were the three states most directly concerned in the question of Baltic supremacy, a question directly involved in the two great Wars of the North—that of 1655–1660 and that of 1700–1721.

After the death of Gustavus Adolphus at Lützen in 1632, Sweden was governed by a regency, and for twelve years the chancellor Axel Oxenstierna was virtual ruler.[11] Without the idealism of Gustavus Adolphus, the chancellor was patriotic, far-seeing and eminently practical; he devoted his energies to the task of maintaining Swedish influence in Germany and securing adequate territorial compensation for the tremendous sacrifices of his country. In 1644 Gustavus's daughter Christina came of age, when jealousy of the chancellor's power and prestige induced her to press for the conclusion of a war to which Oxenstierna owed his influence and reputation. With the signing of the Peace of Westphalia Sweden became a European power and Oxenstierna's career was at an end.

Christina's patronage of practically every form of intellectual activity and her pre-eminence in masculine sports served to give her a unique reputation, since these qualities are rarely combined. The decline of Sweden dates from her accession. She had all the vanity, caprice and imperiousness of Queen Elizabeth, but, unlike the English queen, she had no sense of responsibility, no patriotism and no common sense. Refusing to marry, she settled the succession on her cousin Charles Gustavus, afterwards Charles X., and after a few years of rule she resolved to abdicate, hoping to find a wider sphere for her activities elsewhere. It is difficult to account for this extraordinary decision unless it be remembered that Christina believed all the praises lavished on her personal attainments;[12] and she appears to have thought that by voluntarily surrender-

---

[10] Grémonville in *Instructions données . . .* (Prussia), xliv. The Venetian ambassador Nani summed up the situation when he wrote: "The Elector has many states, little money, good soldiers, great ambitions and is devoted solely to his interests" (*Fontes rerum Austriacarum,* 2nd series, xxvii. 19).

[11] See Nisbet Bain, *Scandinavia,* 209 ff.

[12] She has been praised for all the good qualities of which either sex is capable.

ing a great throne she would not only "startle" the world, but would lay a surer foundation for her posthumous reputation than if she remained in Stockholm engaged in a monotonous round of official duties. An abdication inspired by such motives would have been consistent only if, after abdicating, she had refrained from trying to win back the crown, but she was not great enough to be content with the private station in life thus voluntarily selected, for in 1660 and 1667 she returned to Sweden in the hope of winning back her former dignity. Her extreme flightiness and prodigality, together with her reckless alienation of crown lands and elevation of the most fulsome sycophants, led in 1651 to talk of rebellion, but the leaders of the movement were hastily executed.[13] Christina's abdication took place in June 1654; it was followed by her admission into the Roman Catholic Church and her arrival in Rome. This desire to "startle the world" by extraordinary conduct was shared by a later Vasa, Charles XII., but with consequences far more disastrous to Sweden.

It is not difficult to understand Christina's dislike of her cousin and successor Charles Gustavus. She had refused to marry him, but he was not inconsolable, as he hoped to have a career of his own. Charles was healthy and vigorous, with no great abilities even in the field, and for him war—his one passion—meant not leadership but soldiering. At his accession in June 1654 he reviewed the various pretexts that might justify his taking up arms. He might respond to appeals from persecuted Protestants in Bohemia and Silesia; he might attack the hereditary enemy, Denmark; there was still the old Cleve-Jülich question for any one seeking a quarrel. But the substantial reasons for rushing to arms were the need of giving profitable employment to the nobility and appeasing Charles's intense love of campaigning. It needed little reflection to show that the most obvious enterprise on which Swedish arms could be employed was to complete Swedish supremacy in the Baltic by wresting control of the Sound from Denmark and consolidating Swedish possessions on the south-eastern shore at the expense of Poland and Brandenburg. Poland was ruled by the elder branch of the Vasa family, with which the younger and Swedish branch was intermittently at war in the seventeenth century. The Elector of Brandenburg, whom Charles had no reason either to fear or dislike, could be compensated by the offer of Polish territories.

[13] Nisbet Bain, *Scandinavia*, 226.

The Polish king, John Casimir, had protested against the retention of the Swedish throne by the cadet and Protestant branch of the Vasas, a protest which supplied the necessary pretext for a Swedish invasion of Poland. In this invasion Charles met, not with opposition but with another invader—Russia, engaged in dismembering the Ukraine. The ambitious designs of Tsar Alexis on Courland and the Baltic ports not only prevented any co-operation between Swede and Muscovite, but rendered Sweden liable to attack from the rear. Of Sweden's possible allies, there was the Elector of Brandenburg, whose counsels were divided. The Great Elector's only ally was the United Provinces, and, as the Dutch dreaded Swedish supremacy in the Baltic, it would be difficult to retain the friendship of the States-General while combining with Sweden; in addition, he had little inducement to attack his suzerain John Casimir, since the extent of Poland made invasion easy but conquest difficult. The Elector's older and more cautious friends recommended friendship with Poland rather than Sweden; Waldeck suggested uniting with France for an attack on the Duke of Neuburg, in the hope of securing Jülich and Berg.[14] In this perplexing situation the Elector solved the problem by making overtures to both Sweden and Poland in the desperate hope that both sets of negotiations would be kept secret.[15] But the entry of a Dutch fleet into the Baltic late in 1655 prompted Sweden to demand a consistent policy on the part of Brandenburg, and in January of the following year Frederick William was besieged in Königsberg by a Swedish force and compelled to sign the treaty of Königsberg, by which he became vassal of Sweden for Prussia. Poland and the States-General regarded the Elector's conduct as treason. In May 1656, by the treaty of Marienburg, a secret partition[16] of Poland was agreed upon by Brandenburg and Sweden.

During these negotiations the Swedish king was busy with the conquest of Poland. He had commenced hostilities in July 1655 with a landing in Polish Livonia, and within a few weeks he was established in Warsaw. Lemberg was besieged by the Cossacks, and the unwarlike John Casimir sought refuge in flight. Cracow was captured by the Swedes in the autumn,

[14] Haumant, Les Guerres du nord, 37.
[15] The negotiations at this period are very complicated. See Haumant, op. cit. ch. iii.
[16] In January 1656 Oxenstierna (the younger) prepared an elaborate plan for the partition of Poland (Haumant, 110).

and soon the whole kingdom was at the mercy of Swedes, Cossacks, Tartars and Russians. Charles did nothing to conciliate Polish feeling, and by the end of the year the Poles began to organize themselves into associations for the purpose of expelling the invaders. In the spring of 1656 John Casimir returned from exile and the national defence was undertaken by Stephen Czarnieçki, whose troops so harassed the Swedes that Charles soon found that his position so far from his base was rapidly becoming an impossible one. In June Warsaw returned to its former allegiance, and the Swedish siege of Dantzig was broken up by the arrival of a Dutch fleet. It was for these reasons that Charles was in urgent need of an ally, and accordingly, by the treaty of Marienburg,[17] signed in May 1656, he obtained the Elector's military support. Their joint forces were able to capture Warsaw for the second time (July 20), but this victory did not improve the situation, because the whole of Poland was now aroused against the invaders. At first the Polish nobility had stood idly by, thinking that the war was not against their country but against their king; disillusionment had soon followed when the tactless and ruthless character of the invader became apparent, and the excesses of his troops, combined with their systematic desecration of sanctuaries, led to one of the rarest phenomena in Polish history—a united and national opposition to the enemy. The second capture of Warsaw still left Charles on the defensive and with an army decimated by desertion and disease.

If the Swedish king had declared the abolition of serfdom in Poland he might have rallied the peasants around him, but events followed each other so quickly that by the summer of 1656 it was too late to take any effective measures for consolidating his precarious position. With Austrian help John Casimir was restored and the Swedes forced back on the Baltic. There were recriminations between the two allies Sweden and Brandenburg, but the Elector's help was more than ever necessary for Charles, and by the treaty of Labiau (November 1656) the agreement between them was further modified. The Elector paid an indemnity, and in return Charles gave up all claim to Prussia (which the Swedes had failed to conquer), stipulating only that in the event of the Elector's male line coming to an end, the duchy should revert to Sweden. The

Elector had now only Poland to deal with in order to make secure his hold over Prussia. A few days after signing the treaty of Labiau he made overtures to John Casimir, whereupon the enterprising Austrian agent Lisola effected an agreement between Brandenburg and Poland. This was completed by the treaty of Wehlau (September 26, 1657), by which, in return for military support, the Elector was granted, by the king of Poland, full sovereignty over Prussia. Frederick William was thus the only one to gain from the struggle between his two neighbours, his most important conquest having been obtained without the necessity of risking his army in any prolonged or arduous campaign. In this respect he could congratulate himself, for he knew that the discipline of his newly-formed army was bad.

After the failure of the Polish venture, Charles X. next turned his attention to Denmark. Ever since the year 1654 the bellicose king (Frederick III.) and nobility of Denmark had been anxious for a trial of strength with the new Swedish king, and in 1657 war had been decided on but not declared. After his failure to effect the conquest of Prussia, and when his hopes in Poland were completely destroyed, Charles X. marched through Pomerania into Holstein, causing the Danish troops to scatter in panic flight. But the Danish king now allied with Poland, a country which with Austrian help had again become a military asset, and this, combined with Brandenburg's desertion to Poland by the treaty of Wehlau (September 1657), tempted Charles to abandon his proposed conquest of Denmark. Suddenly Wrangel's capture of the Danish fortress of Frederiksödde (October 1657) changed the situation.[18] With the commencement of a great frost in December, Charles was able to send his troops across to Fünen. Crossing the Little Belt and the Great Belt in February 1658 (losing some of his troops through the ice), he completed the invasion of the one hereditary enemy as quickly as he had completed that of the other. But French, English and Dutch diplomacy intervened in order to end an episode that might react on the now delicately poised equilibrium of western Europe. By the treaty of Roskilde (March 1658) Charles quitted Denmark in return for the cession to him of Scania, Halland and Bleking, together with the island of Bornholm, possessions which conferred on Sweden control of the Sound.

[18] Nisbet Bain, *op. cit.* 244.

But even this failed to satisfy Charles, and in June 1658, impatient at delay in the settlement of his renewed demands, he resolved to invade Denmark for the second time. Without declaring war, he landed troops on Danish territory and on the 11th of August 1658 began the siege of Copenhagen.[19] Frederick III. organized a vigorous resistance, for the existence of his country was now threatened, and in October the situation was saved by the arrival of a Dutch fleet from which stores were landed in the beleaguered city. Charles had to abandon the siege, a set-back followed by a rebellion in his newly-won possession of Bornholm, but even with Poland, Brandenburg, Austria and Denmark against him, Charles obstinately renewed his attempts to take the Danish capital in November. Meanwhile England, France and the Low Countries were anxious in their own interests to see the end of the Wars of the North, and in May 1659 their representatives at the Hague agreed to unite their efforts for this purpose. In November 1659 the Swedish army in Fünen had to surrender to the allied troops of Holland, Poland, Austria and Denmark, whereupon Charles sent urgent demands to the Estates for more troops, defeat having made him not wary but obstinate. The situation was saved only by his death in February 1660 at the age of thirty-eight. In these wars Charles had extended Sweden to her natural frontiers by obtaining the Scanian provinces, but he set a baneful example to contemporaries and successors because he loved war for its own sake; he never knew when to make concessions, and he regarded his country as little more than a source of man-power for his campaigns. His death removed the only obstacle to the pacification of northern Europe. Charles X. was an unspectacular Charles XII.

The two treaties of Oliva (May 1660) and Copenhagen (June 1660), generally grouped together as the treaty of Oliva, restored peace on the following terms:

1. John Casimir renounced his claim to the Swedish throne and recognized the independence of Frederick William in East Prussia.
2. The Elector of Brandenburg withdrew his troops from Western Pomerania.
3. Denmark recovered Bornholm and Drontheim and surrendered Scania, Bleking and Halland to Sweden.

[19] For this see Nisbet Bain, *op. cit.* 251 ff.

In July 1661 the Swedish government signed with Russia the treaty of Kardis by which Sweden was confirmed in possession of Livonia. These treaties restored, as far as possible, the balance of forces in the Baltic, Sweden having gained at the expense of Denmark. But when the net gains and losses of all the combatants are weighed against each other, it will be seen that the first great War of the North benefited no one so much as the Elector of Brandenburg because he emerged therefrom with full sovereignty over a duchy (Prussia), destined soon to give its name to a powerful and ambitious monarchy.

The short reign of Charles X. Gustavus was followed by the minority of his son Charles XI., and until the accession of Charles XII. in 1697 there was an era of comparative peace in northern Europe. The Council of Regency which took over the government in 1660 carried out some wise measures of reconstruction, including the establishment of a national bank and the foundation of a university at Lund for the provinces won from Denmark. But the Council of Regency was unable to hold its own against the Senate and ultimately it fell completely under the control of De la Gardie, the Chancellor. Extravagance and favouritism now became the rule. Increased financial difficulty at home prevented the adoption of a strong foreign policy, causing Sweden steadily to lose some of her European prestige. She was drawn by the treaty of Fontainebleau (1661) into the network of French alliances, undertaking to support the candidature of the French nominee, the young Duke of Enghien, to the throne of Poland; when Louis commenced the War of Devolution, Sweden did not become a member of the Triple Alliance until a few days after the signing of the treaty of Aix-la-Chapelle, facts which show that her foreign policy was inconsistent and dilatory. It was unfortunate for the northern kingdom that she was induced by a treaty signed in April 1672 to ally with France on the eve of Louis's campaign against Holland. In accordance with this treaty, Swedish troops were maintained in Bremen, near the Dutch frontier, and in conjunction with Denmark (also won over to the French alliance) the Baltic was closed to Dutch ships. When the inevitable reaction followed after the invasion of Holland, and the Grand Alliance of the Hague was formed, Sweden was again too late to take advantage of the turn in the tide and remained the solitary ally of France. Among the enemies stirred up by Louis's campaigns was the

Elector of Brandenburg, and when the Palatinate was overrun by the troops of Condé the Elector's forces inflicted a crushing defeat on the Swedes at Fehrbellin (June 18, 1675). This defeat, incurred in what was really little more than a skirmish, dispelled at once the tradition of Swedish invincibility; it was the first victory to the credit of the Elector's army and it marked the beginning of Sweden's military decline.

The defeat of Fehrbellin was followed by the threat of expelling the Swedes from Germany, when the troops of Brandenburg, invading Pomerania, captured Stettin, Rügen, Stralsund and the mouth of the Oder. Danish troops invaded Scania, and Sweden had again to face the attacks of Brandenburg, Denmark and Austria. For nearly three years an exhausting war was fought against these superior forces in which the young Charles XI. had his first experience of active service. But in the negotiations for the general peace of Nymegen, Swedish interests were once more protected by France and, by the treaty of St. Germain (June 1679), Brandenburg was induced[20] to restore the whole of Swedish Pomerania, except a small strip of land on the right bank of the Oder. By a treaty signed at Fontainebleau in September 1679 Denmark restored her conquests in Scania to Sweden. It was in French interests that Sweden should be strong, and thus French diplomacy was bolstering up an edifice which had no firmer foundations than the treaty of Westphalia.

In spite of these humiliations, however, Sweden was able to retain the control of the Baltic which the treaty of Oliva had conferred on her, and in the later part of the seventeenth century this supremacy was never seriously contested. These were years of peace, and though she deserted France and joined the League of Augsburg[21] (1686) her share in the hostilities that followed was so slight that she was able to offer her mediation in the negotiations culminating in the treaties of Turin and Ryswick (1696-7). The real danger for Sweden was to come not from the south but from the east, and before the century ended it was clear that awakening Russia would not rest satisfied until she had a Baltic coast line. It was an apparently trivial incident that set in motion the forces which

---

[20] See *Instructions données* (Prussia), 205 ff.

[21] As a leading Protestant power, Sweden was alienated by Louis's revocation of the Edict of Nantes in 1685 (*Instructions données,* Sweden, xl.). The Swedish king had also been angered by the French seizure of Zweibrücken in 1681.

were to effect the undoing of Sweden. The permanent poverty of the Swedish Exchequer had compelled the government to retract in Livonia some of the financial privileges hitherto enjoyed by the local nobility. In 1692 the Ritter of Livonia protested in a body; their protest was carried to Stockholm by one of their number, John Reinhold Patkul, whose language was so menacing that in spite of his safe-conduct he was consigned to prison, from which he escaped and devoted the remaining part of his life to seeking vengeance on Sweden. To the Livonians Patkul was a national hero, and it was held that his compatriots owed no allegiance to the Swedish throne.

Patkul fired the ambitions of Frederick Augustus, Elector of Saxony, and arranged an interview between him and Peter the Great at Rawa in the summer of 1698. On the death of John Sobieski, king of Poland, in 1696, the Elector of Saxony, specially converted to Catholicism for the purpose, managed to manœuvre the election to the Polish crown in his own favour against the French candidate, the Prince of Conti, and in support of his anti-Swedish designs he looked for help to Austria, Russia and Brandenburg, of which the last two were the permanent enemies of Sweden, while the first, owing to Sweden's French connection, was always a potential enemy. It needed only a firebrand on the throne of Sweden to ignite the tinder which Patkul had so zealously collected.

When Charles XI. began to govern for himself, he showed that he was endowed with methodical and industrious habits and that he was devoted to the best interests of his country. It was by his vigorous rule that the country was saved from bankruptcy and all rash military enterprises were avoided.[22] Piety and industry mingled in the entourage of this early-rising monarch; his court was characterized by the heavier kind of domestic virtues and the women were repressed and sometimes bullied. By the constitutional revolution of 1682 the Swedish monarchy became absolute. The dangers of an unchecked nobility had been clearly exemplified in the years of peace preceding this change, when Charles had found that, owing to the extensive alienations of crown lands, he was himself practically a pauper. Realizing that the only alternative was abdication, he proceeded to take drastic measures which showed that he was not without qualities of statesmanship.

---

[22] For Charles XI.'s reign see Nisbet Bain, *op. cit.* ch. xi.

Armed with the *Lex Regia* of 1682 he reformed the administration of the country, revoking many financial concessions,
tracing the sources of malversation and bringing the offenders
to justice, nor did he hesitate to include the members of the
late Council of Regency in the scope of his investigations. The
policy of "Reduction" or restoration of alienated royal estates
and rights was pursued with a complete disregard for the incidental and sometimes unnecessary misery which it caused.
From these measures the Treasury benefited enormously
while, with enhanced revenues, the fleet and the army were
reorganized. Had Charles been followed by a man of similar
temperament, it is probable that Sweden would have retained
her great position, for in no other country was national destiny so closely bound up with the personality of the ruler.
But his son and successor, while he had all the callousness and
austerity of his father, had none of his caution, and Sweden,
of which it has been said that her history is the history of
her kings, possessed just sufficient reserves to survive the rule
of Charles XII.

In the year 1699 it might have seemed, as it had seemed in
1660, that after a surfeit of war Europe was about to experience an epoch of peace. The treaty of Ryswick was signed in
1697, that of Karlowitz two years later; from Londonderry to
Constantinople there was a cessation of hostilities, and even
France had to admit exhaustion and the need for repose. But
the peace of Christendom depended on the lives of two
men—Charles XI. of Sweden and Charles II. of Spain: the
death of the former in 1697 ushered in the second great War
of the North, that of the latter, in 1700, the War of the
Spanish Succession. Of national aspirations or even racial
antipathy there was hardly a trace in either of these wars.
They resulted inevitably from the system of absolute personal
rule by which every monarch could command, for the pursuit
of private jealousies and ambitions, all the resources of the
State.

The character of Charles XII. of Sweden is well known to
readers of Voltaire's brilliant biography. Descended from a
line of kings who owed all their fortunes to war, Charles was
fifteen on the death of his father. Impatience of feminine
control compelled him, with the help of his adviser, Piper,
to reject the tutelage of his grandmother and commence his
responsible rule. The atmosphere of his father's court had

not been such as to encourage the more kindly human virtues (which might have been mistaken for weakness), and though Charles formed an attachment to his younger sister, he was encouraged to adopt a complete disregard for the interests of every one outside a narrow family circle. The amusements of his youth were mostly violent—riding horses to death and testing the sharpness of his sword on the throats of dogs and sheep—but it may be noted that in the seventeenth century such pastimes were regarded an manly and as specially fitting one who would be called on to govern men. His education was good but narrow: in the classics he had read Cornelius Nepos and Quintus Curtius, the latter inspiring him with the ambition of emulating Alexander the Great; mathematics he studied as a subordinate branch of military science. Charles had all the assertiveness and thirst for military glory of a Napoleon. Tall, fierce-eyed and long-nosed, his demeanour revealed insolence and obstinacy, dash and heroism, courtliness and cruelty. Extremely passionate by nature, he learned early to control and even to suppress passion; himself insensible to fatigue and danger, he was indifferent to the most intense sufferings and privations of his soldiers. He had no vices, because all his thoughts were compressed into the one narrow channel of military prowess; but unlike Napoleon he had no imagination, for he began a campaign without having any idea of its purpose, and when he achieved a victory he did not know what to do with it. He was sincerely religious, and would not have done so much harm to the world had he not seemed to derive solace and fortitude from prayer—a source of strength denied to vicious men; had he not been a fatalist, he might have profited by his own mistakes. His heroism was of the destructive order, and his death was his only good service to his country.

Charles's first act as a sovereign was to obtain from the Senate and Diet an assurance of his own absolutism, and at the Coronation he crowned himself. He omitted to take any Coronation oath, thus making it clear that he would be responsible to no one. In the tumult of enthusiasm acclaiming the accession of the young and untried monarch these things passed without comment; the only discordant voice came from an obscure country parson who had the temerity to protest from the pulpit against the conferment of absolute power on a boy of fifteen years. This rash man was arrested and condemned to death, but as a special act of clemency his sentence was commuted into imprisonment for life.[23] The full consequences of the constitutional revolution of 1682 were to be realized as soon as the irresponsible government of Charles XII. commenced.

His military enthusiasm was first fired by the visit to Stockholm of the Duke of Gottorp to marry Charles's favourite sister, and the Duke obtained not only a bride but an enthusiastic ally against his hereditary enemy Denmark, with which Sweden had been at peace for so long. When Frederick IV. succeeded to the Danish throne in 1699 the ranks of the northern firebrands were completed, and Sweden was encircled by a ring of enemies anxious to pay off old scores now that the kingdom was ruled by a boy. These enemies were eagerly solicited by Patkul to combine against the mistress of the Baltic. Frederick IV. of Denmark, having assembled a large army in Holstein, invaded Gottorp, and his fleet put to sea. The next move was made by Charles himself in the summer of 1699 when he sent 24,000 men into Gottorp in order to strengthen the defences of his brother-in-law, and in January 1700 he began preparations for a prolonged campaign. In February the Saxons invaded Livonia and laid siege to Riga while the Danes overran Gottorp. These events provided justification for Charles's recourse to armed intervention, and on the 24th of April 1700 he quitted Stockholm, which he was destined never to see again. Thereafter his career was followed with intense interest by the whole of Europe, and many of its incidents would seem preposterous if narrated by a writer of fiction. Unfortunately for his country they were historical facts.

Denmark was his first objective. The speed and energy with which Charles carried out his landing on Danish soil in the early summer of 1700, followed by his march on Copenhagen, forced Frederick IV. to sue for peace; by the treaty of Travendal in August 1700 the Danish king admitted the independence of the Duke of Gottorp and promised not to assist Sweden's enemies. Thus Charles's first campaign had been crowned with complete success. He had now to face more formidable opponents. Patkul had done his work well; Augustus of Poland and Peter the Great were campaigning in Livonia, and while the former was besieging Riga, the latter, with about 40,000 raw troops under German officers, was

[23] Nisbet Bain, *Charles XII.* 44.

laying siege to Narva. Charles decided to deal first with the besiegers of Narva, and as he approached the town late in November 1700, Peter suddenly quitted his camp for the pretended purpose of bringing up reinforcements. Though the Russians outnumbered the Swedes by about five to one, Charles had no hesitation in attacking, knowing that leadership and training more than compensate for deficiency in numbers. The attack on the strongly entrenched enemy forces was designed by one of the best generals ever employed by Sweden—Rehnskjöld—and was launched in a snow-storm on the last day of November 1700. The undisciplined besiegers, seized with sudden panic, fled from their trenches and many of them were lost in the attempt to cross the river Narva. The Duc de Croy, on whose unwilling shoulders the frantic Peter had placed responsibility for the Russian defence, took refuge in the Swedish ranks, and the victors hastily disarmed and dismissed all their prisoners except the generals, for the good reason that there were more Russian prisoners than Swedish troops. Thus the military history of modern Russia begins with a crushing defeat at the hands of a youth of eighteen.

The battle of Narva brought Charles sudden fame, because throughout Europe the victory was acclaimed as one of strategy and science against brute strength. Its effect on Peter was to make him redouble his efforts in the hope of organizing a strong national army, and he was also induced by his humiliating defeat to combine more closely with Augustus of Saxony. These two decided on a plan of campaign by which the Russian agreed to attack Swedish Ingria while the German undertook to keep the troops of Charles busily employed in Germany. In the apportionment of the spoils, Augustus was to have Esthonia and Livonia and the help of Russian troops, while Peter accepted a subsidy. Thus Sweden would have to maintain the war on two fronts and this would give Peter time to reorganize his army. The death of Charles II. of Spain in November of this year induced the Swedish Chancellor, Bengt Oxenstierna, to propose that the king of Sweden should come to some arrangement with Russia and Saxony and use his great success at Narva as a justification for assuming the rôle of mediator between the rival claimants to the Spanish succession. Sweden had no money and but few men to spend in foreign wars; the position of mediator would enhance national prestige without involving any sacrifice. But Charles seldom even replied to the correspondence of his ministers and got rid of diplomatic visitors by referring them to Stockholm. For what ensued he must be held mainly responsible, since during his long absence he refused to allow any one at home to take charge of Swedish foreign policy.

Charles followed up his first success by expelling the Saxon troops from Riga (July 1701) and occupying Courland. Establishing a Swedish governor-general at Mittau, the capital of Courland, he then turned to Poland, which had strenuously refused to be drawn into the ambitions of its king Augustus. Taking care to explain that he was waging war not on the Polish people but on their monarch, he entered Warsaw in May 1702 and a month later defeated Augustus at Klissow. The insolence of the conqueror and the excesses of his troops aroused a certain amount of national resentment, but neither Saxon nor Pole could withstand the invader, who declared his intention of remaining in Poland until he had dethroned Augustus. Posen and Cracow were next occupied, and once more the unfortunate republic suffered all the horrors of an army of occupation. Charles strengthened his position, not by courting the good-will of the people but by allying with the dispossessed head of the Sapieha faction and with Cardinal Radziejowski, the intriguing Archbishop of Gnesen and Primate of Poland.

At this period the Swedish king appears to have been dominated by only one motive—hatred of Augustus and determination that the Saxon should never be king of Poland. Had he aimed at the crown himself, his stay in Poland could be understood, but while too great for such an ambition, he was yet sufficiently small-minded to dissipate his own and his country's resources in what was little better than a personal quarrel. On the 12th of July 1704 a fraction of the Diet elected Charles's nominee, Stanislas Lesczinski, to the Polish throne, an election greeted by salvos from the Swedish artillery which had been massed in order to lend distinction to the ceremony. But Stanislas was king of only as much territory as Swedish guns could range, and when Charles rushed off to capture Lemberg (merely because the fortress was said to be impregnable) Augustus had little difficulty in recapturing Warsaw (August 1704), Stanislas being compelled to seek refuge in the army of Rehnskjöld. The return of Charles from Lemberg produced another reverse of fortune, whereupon Augustus had to take refuge in Saxony while Stanislas, who had not yet been crowned, was restored to his oscillating position of king-elect. By the summer of 1705 the Swedish conquest of Poland was complete.

Charles's long stay in Poland gave Peter sufficient time to reorganize his defences. In the Baltic provinces the Russians were still kept at bay by mere handfuls of Swedish troops, but the prolonged absence of the Swedish king and the main army gave Peter his chance. He devastated Livonia and Esthonia before conquering them and, defended by brave but inadequate Swedish troops, Karelia and Ingria soon changed hands. The island afterwards known as Cronstadt was captured, and a beginning was made with the great city on the Neva to be celebrated by posterity as St. Petersburg. By the end of the year 1704 Peter had conquered all the territory necessary for access to the Baltic and had fully achieved, at the expense of Sweden, all that he had set out to gain. His task had not been a difficult one for, after the battle of Narva, Charles regarded Peter as beneath contempt, and the Swedish king's long stay in Poland gave to the Russian just what he wanted—freedom from interference. Not till the Tsar had established himself in enemy country did Charles authorize the Swedish Senate to strengthen the defences of the Baltic provinces.

Peter had been as uniformly successful as his partner Augustus had been unfortunate; the Saxon was now to reap full retribution for the disastrous policy on which he had embarked. His general, Schulenburg, with German and Russian troops, was defeated at Fraustadt on the Oder by Rehnskjöld in February 1706, a victory which decided Charles to invade Saxony. Entering Silesia in September 1706 nominally as Defender of the Protestants, at Altranstadt, near Leipzig, he set up his standard as the Liberator of Germany. The first to sue for peace was Augustus, who had now lost two kingdoms; he obtained peace only by renouncing all his allies, surrendering his claim to the Polish throne and giving up Patkul (September 1707). The Livonian patriot was broken on the wheel. The turn of the Emperor (Joseph I.) came next. He was accused of giving military aid to Augustus and of oppressing the Protestants in Silesia, contrary to the terms of the treaty of Osnabrük of which Sweden was a guarantor. Charles demanded that his co-religionists should be given full toleration, and on this point the Emperor had to give way, in spite of the humiliation it must have involved, for the

Hapsburgs prided themselves on nothing so much as the exclusion of heresy from their states. This concession was embodied in the peace of Altranstadt (September 1707), which England and Holland guaranteed to maintain, and Charles could now regard himself as the Arbiter of Europe.

What Charles might have done at Altranstadt is a fascinating subject for speculation. His stay there (September 1706–September 1707) coincided with a breathing-space in the Spanish Succession War when, despite the successes of Marlborough, it was still doubtful which side would have the victory. The alliance of Charles was eagerly courted on both sides and Marlborough visited him in April 1707 in the hope of finding out his plans. The interview between these two remarkable men was not cordial. Charles was uncommunicative; Marlborough, in common with his contemporaries, suspected Charles of deeper designs than he was really capable of, but inferred from the maps of Russia lying on the Swedish king's table that his ambitions did not lie in the west. In truth Charles was now anxious to avenge himself on Peter as he had already avenged himself on Augustus. In the politics of western Europe he had no interest whatever; nevertheless all the combatants were considerably relieved when he quitted Germany. On the other hand he had no concerted Russian campaign; by his foolish stay in Poland he had allowed Peter to establish himself in the Baltic provinces, and now he thought of dethroning Peter and capturing Moscow—the only European capital that needs no fortification against the invader. Charles had been absent from his country for seven years, and only by the most severe privations had Sweden been able to continue the supply of money and troops. While one half of Europe was fighting for an inheritance, the other half was fighting because of a youthful king's personal dislikes. It was an inauspicious beginning to the eighteenth century.

In the autumn of 1707, when Charles commenced his disastrous eastern campaign, the Swedish forces, including General Levenhaupt's army in Riga, numbered not more than 46,000 troops. Peter had at least 70,000 trained men as well as enormous reserves, but the lesson of Narva had not been lost on him and he did not trust in numbers alone. On leaving Saxon territory, it was open to Charles to enter Courland and restore the Baltic possessions, but fate decreed that he should take the road to Moscow. By the middle of December 1707 he had crossed the Vistula, and in January 1708, after taking Grodno, he made up on the elusive Peter at Wilna. But the Tsar's policy was to avoid pitched battles and, by luring his enemy further east, to separate him as much as possible from his communications. Charles's generals still hoped against hope that their leader would turn to the north and make the Baltic provinces his main objective, but the king, who always kept his own counsels, proceeded to advance on Minsk. In June 1708 he crossed the Beresina; on the 3rd of July he defeated a Russian contingent in the cavalry battle of Holowczyn, a victory enabling the Swedish army to reach the Dnieper. Late in the autumn Tatarsk, on the frontier between seventeenth-century Poland and Russia, was reached, at which point the Swedish troops began to feel the hardships of their arduous campaign. They were subjected to constant raids from Tartar horsemen; supplies were going short; many guns had been abandoned in the marshes; most of the gunpowder was wet: moreover, disease and sickness were playing havoc with troops lacking in everything but courage and devotion to their king. It was at Tatarsk, within sixty miles of Smolensk, that Charles surprised his generals by suddenly asking them what they thought he ought to do next, and their surprise was increased when their leader informed them that he had no plan. He was advised to go into winter quarters and await the arrival of Levenhaupt's reinforcements—advice which characteristically he refused to take. Giving orders to push southwards into the Ukraine—where he hoped to find plenty of food and fodder as well as obtain help from the rebel Cossack Mazeppa, then in alliance with the Polish and anti-Russian faction—Charles obstinately declined to adopt any course that might be interpreted as a retreat, and he refused to spare either himself or his men. But in turning to the south he was building on false hopes, because Mazeppa's forces had been considerably reduced by the refusal of the Cossacks to take up arms against the Tsar, and Peter had learned in time of Mazeppa's treachery. The arrival of Levenhaupt was still anxiously awaited, but, when he did join forces with the main Swedish army, he had only about 7000 men, so persistently had he been harried by the Russian irregulars. Mazeppa's arrival brought an even greater disappointment, for of the promised 50,000 men he came with only 3000. It was with these forces that Charles proposed to face the Russian winter of 1708–9. That winter proved to be one of the severest on record. The cold was so intense that birds dropped dead from the sky, and in order to have withstood it complete Arctic equipment would have been necessary. The clothes of the Swedish soldiers were in rags; for boots they had to use skins of wild animals; they were often short of food, and large numbers perished from frost-bite. With the exception of a brief rest at Viprek, which was reached in January 1709, the march south and east was continued without intermission throughout the winter. By the spring of 1709, when Pultava was in sight, Charles's total forces were less than 22,000 men, of whom 5000 were sick or disabled. Already more than 20,000 human lives had been wasted on this campaign.

Ever since the summer of 1708 Charles had been concerned about reinforcements and had begun to realize the folly of proceeding so far without adequate preparations. He had sent orders for the Swedish troops in German garrisons to join with the forces of the Swedish general Krassau in Poland and march through Volhynia to Kiev; he had also sent an agent to Constantinople soliciting the help of Turkey against Russia. These measures may provide some explanation of his persistent march on the fortress of Pultava, since he may have hoped to join forces with whatever troops could penetrate as far as Kiev or with such as had crossed the frontier from Turkey; but we may conjecture that on the whole it was a fortunate thing that these reinforcements did not arrive, for they would certainly have been frittered away with the criminal recklessness and disregard for human life characteristic of Charles's conduct of the Russian campaign.

The siege of Pultava began in May 1709. During the siege the Swedes suffered as much from the heat as they had previously suffered from the cold, while their ranks were thinned by gangrene as previously they had been by frost-bite. On the 17th of June Charles received a bullet in the foot which he calmly picked out with a penknife, but the wound was serious and for some weeks he had to be carried about in a litter, while the supreme command was transferred to Rehnskjöld. It was probably this event that decided Peter to risk his 80,000 troops in an engagement, and on the 27th of June the battle commenced. Charles obstinately persisted in leaving 2000 men under the walls of Pultava in order to maintain the siege, though the disparity between the opposing forces was so great that not a single Swede could have been spared; moreover, to make matters worse, though Rehnskjöld was commander-in-chief and a brilliant general, Charles interfered with his disposition of the Swedish troops.[24] Seldom has a battle been fought against such ridiculous odds. Against 80,000 men, well equipped and with ample artillery, there were less than 20,000 half-famished Swedes with four guns. Nevertheless the Swedes attacked with wonderful courage, but few of them reached the enemy's lines, for they were mown down by the Russian artillery. Panic followed. In the midst of the confusion Charles and Rehnskjöld gave contradictory orders, and the battle ended in complete disaster. The Swedes lost about 5000 men; Generals Rehnskjöld and Slippenbach, with Piper and the Duke of Wurtemburg, were captured; a few days later the whole of the army which Levenhaupt had rushed up in the hope of joining with Charles had to surrender. So ended one of the most disastrous campaigns in modern history. The Swedish king was hurried off, against his will, in a litter, and though in the flight several of the litter-bearers were killed, Charles himself suffered no injury. This miraculous escape may have convinced the fatalist Charles that his end was not yet.

With a small band of devoted men, Charles managed to reach the Turkish fortress of Bender on the Dniester. Turkish admiration for his heroic deeds against the Russians guaranteed a welcome reception, and at Bender he presided over a miniature court. He showed no signs of emotion when he learned the results of the defeat of Pultava; his correspondence at this time contains no evidence that he comprehended the magnitude of the disaster which had overtaken his armies. He still entertained the most extravagant ambitions, and regarded the resources of Sweden in men and money as inexhaustible. This is one of the reasons why Charles XII. must be regarded as insane in the strict medical sense of that word. The sudden collapse of Swedish power and prestige was obvious to the most casual observer. The Baltic possessions were irretrievably lost; the treaties of Travendal and Altranstadt were thrown to the winds; Augustus was re-established in Poland; a Danish army invaded Scania. It was fortunate that, in the king's absence, the remnants of Swedish reputation could be upheld by capable generals, devoted troops and a nation which shrank at no sacrifice now that its honour and existence were imperilled. Stenbock, one of Charles's best generals, defeated the Danes early in 1710, compelling them to quit Scania;

[24] Nisbet Bain, *Charles XII.*, 187.

Krassau, unable to execute Charles's order to join him in the Ukraine, advanced into Pomerania and, by maintaining his army there, helped to mask the real weakness of the Swedish forces. The presence of this army in German territory alarmed the allies engaged in the Spanish Succession war, and by the Neutrality Compact of March 1710 Britain and Holland undertook to guarantee Sweden's German possessions provided Krassau's army did not invade Jutland. On hearing of this treaty, Charles repudiated it, thinking that he would obtain help for Sweden, not from the maritime powers, but from Turkey. This hope proved to be a delusion.

Charles's chief pursuits during his long stay in Turkish territory were chess, the reading of French tragedies and mediaeval romances, reviewing and exercising his small bodyguard.[25] There was no officer of superior rank at Bender, and except for the Polish refugee Stanislas Poniatowski,[26] no one of sufficient eminence to warrant the giving of advice to the illustrious exile whose famous exploits, together with his complete freedom from vice of any kind, made him appear a demi-god in the eyes of the Turks. When his own resources were exhausted, he accepted the hospitality of Sultan Ahmed III. Taking advantage of the resentment felt by Turkey at the loss of Azov to Russia in the year 1700, and knowing that several Turkish statesmen, notably the Grand Vizier, Nouman Kiuprili, were anxious to preserve peace with Russia, Charles tried to induce the Turks to renew hostilities. These intrigues were successful. The Sultan did not appreciate the services of his Grand Vizier, and in June 1710 Nouman Kiuprili was removed and war was declared in the following November. While Peter placed his confidence in Wallachian and Moldavian allies, Turkey despatched an army of 200,000 men to the Pruth, the plan of campaign having been drawn up by Charles himself. Peter's allies speedily deserted, and in July 1710 the Tsar found himself (at Standerci on the Pruth) in the unusual position of facing a larger army than his own; but, unlike the Swedish king, he knew when to yield, and accordingly, without striking a blow, he proposed peace on the basis of surrendering Azov, restoring Livonia and Esthonia to Sweden and allowing Charles to

[25] There is a full account by Amira, *Storia del soggiorno di Carlo XII in Turchia* (1905).
[26] Poniatowski (1678–1762) was a supporter of Stanislas Leczinski, and had followed Charles XII. as a personal friend.

return to his kingdom unmolested. The Turkish Grand Vizier Baltadji had as little relish for fighting as had Peter, and these terms were eagerly accepted. The Peace of the Pruth was signed on the 11th of July 1711, and the Tsar, with his famished Russians, escaped from his perilous position.

Charles had arrived in person at the Pruth in order to take part in the defeat of his old enemy, but found to his disgust that peace had already been signed. Thereafter he intrigued with the war party against the Grand Vizier who had so readily accepted peace terms, and made some capital out of the Tsar's unwillingness to fulfil the conditions of the treaty. In November 1711, with the removal of Baltadji and the appointment of Jussuf Pasha in his place, war was again declared on Russia, and Charles hoped to obtain troops from Sweden, to be sent to him through Poland. Poniatowski was sent to Stambul in order to concert measures with the Swedish and French agents there, whereupon Britain and Holland protested against this speedy violation of the treaty of the Pruth, and both powers urged that Charles should be ordered off Turkish territory. The protest had its effect; the recent treaty was confirmed and Charles was requested by the Sultan to depart, a large escort and a considerable sum of money being placed at his disposal. But Charles refused, thinking that by staying in Turkey he might have his revenge on the Grand Vizier Baltadji as he had already avenged himself on the Grand Vizier's predecessor. The rashest and most inexplicable acts of Charles were invariably due to petty personal dislikes and obstinate determination to get the better of enemies unworthy of himself, at no matter what cost.

The conclusion of hostilities between Russia and Turkey had encouraged Sweden's numerous enemies to renew the attack on the unfortunate country of Charles XII. Danish troops invaded Bremen in 1712, and after repeated demands from her exiled king, Sweden was at last able, at very great sacrifice, to despatch a fleet and an army to Germany, the army to hold itself in readiness for an attack on Poland or on Denmark as might be required. The position of this army, placed between Russians and Saxons on the east and Danes on the west, was soon critical, and only by a decisive stroke did its commander Stenbock avoid another Pultava. He dealt first with the Danes, and coming upon them at Gadebusch he defeated them in a fiercely-contested battle. The destruction of Altona followed (December 28, 1712), but, before superior forces, Stenbock with his 11,000 men had to surrender on the 16th of May 1713, at Tönning. The result of this reverse was that Prussia took Stettin and the Russians invaded Finland. From that date Sweden ceased to be a German power; she had already lost her supremacy in the Baltic.

An attempt was made during the Utrecht negotiations to induce Charles to accept the mediation of Great Britain, but British opposition to him in Turkey and the failure of Britain to maintain the treaties of Altranstadt and Travendal, as she had promised, so embittered Charles that he made overtures to France, in spite of his deep hatred of everything French. Moreover, he made the situation difficult by refusing to allow Stanislas Leczinski to surrender his crown, though Stanislas himself was most eager to be free from the responsibilities of his Polish kingdom, and thus Charles lost all chance of profiting by the disunion already apparent among his enemies. Had he been gifted with any political insight he would have forsworn Polish affairs, he would have obtained at least the neutrality of Saxony by allowing Augustus to occupy the Polish throne, he would have withdrawn from Bender, and at the head of his own subjects he might have restored his fortunes and recovered the Baltic provinces from a host of greedy and quarrelsome enemies. But while it is easy to say what Charles might have done, it is difficult to excuse his obstinacy, his refusal either to return to Sweden or give his ministers a free hand, his unwillingness to seek any allies against Russia except in Turkey, his peremptory orders for the despatch of more troops from Sweden to theatres of war as distant from home as from the headquarters of their nominal commander, his subordination of everything, including the best interests of his country, to the most absurd whims, and, lastly, his strange notion that by defying his Turkish hosts and benefactors he was performing an act that would startle the world.

In the earlier part of 1713 the chief problem in Turkey was how to get rid of the illustrious guest at Bender who had so long outstayed his welcome. It was soon found that serving a notice to quit and ejecting him were two different things. He was given a sum of £10,000 for passage money; this he spent and asked for more. Early in 1713 he and his bodyguard began to dig themselves in. He could not even plead the excuse that there was any personal danger to be incurred by quitting Turkey, nor had he any reason to suspect the good faith of his hosts; he did not persist in staying because he feared to go, for personal danger he always courted rather than shunned. His determination to remain at Bender seems to have grown upon him and to have increased in proportion to the embarrassment of the Turk and the renewed efforts to move him. On February 1, 1713, began the extraordinary struggle known as the *Kalibalik* or Battue. With about fifty men Charles held his mansion for eight hours against 10,000[27] Turks armed with twelve guns, and even then he would not have been expelled if the "beaters" had not smoked him out. When the building was ablaze over his head, Charles refused to surrender, saying that there was no real danger until their clothes were burning.[28] Rushing out at last from what had become an inferno, Charles attacked his besiegers, but he tripped over his spurs and was at once made prisoner. The "battle" had cost the Turks about 200 men; the Swedish casualties were fifteen, and the Janissaries who effected the king's capture had so much respect for his courage that they spared his life.

Charles was removed, a prisoner, to Timurtash on the Pruth. In June 1713 the Peace of Adrianople ended the war between Russia and Turkey and deprived Charles of any further opportunities for intrigue. He still refused to leave Turkey; he feigned sickness, and at Demotika he spent nearly a year in bed. In March 1714 a special envoy arrived at Demotika from Sweden in the hope of inducing Charles to return to his distracted and ruined country, but it was not till September 1714 that he made up his mind to leave Turkey. Passing through Wallachia, Transylvania and Austria, he reached Stralsund on the 11th of November 1714, and so terminated what is probably the most remarkable exile ever inflicted upon himself by a ruling monarch.

When Charles returned to Germany, three Swedish armies —his own, that of Krassau and that of Stenbock—had already been dissipated, and of Swedish colonial possessions there remained only Stralsund and Wismar. For some time it had been believed in Sweden that Charles was either dead or mad; the national finances were in a hopeless state, the annual deficit being about twice the amount of the gross receipts;

[27] Charles had about 800 entrenched Swedes, of whom about 50 were in the mansion with the king. These figures are taken from Ct. von Sarauw, *Die Feldzüge Karls XII.*, 305.
[28] Nisbet Bain, *Charles XII.*, 212 ff.

bankruptcy and invasion were within sight; for fourteen years the country had been without a ruler and yet forbidden to govern itself. It is evidence of the tremendous strength of the feeling which the institution of monarchy may inspire that throughout all this time the Swedes never grumbled; they stinted themselves to an unheard-of extent in the effort to keep the threads of their national life together, and the ruling classes enforced measures of conscription that made the peasants fly to the woods or mutilate themselves in the hope of avoiding the certain privations and the almost equally certain death that awaited them in the service of their king. The drain on Swedish manhood by Charles's wars was greater than that by Napoleon's on the French, and the result of this annual elimination of her best manhood was not without its effect on Swedish national physique. In these years Sweden lost nearly 30 per cent of her male population, or an average of about 8000 men yearly in a total period of eighteen years. As the total population was only about a million, it was quite clear what consequences would follow if the wars continued. There was enough political talent in the Swedish Senate and more than enough military talent among Swedish generals to end the second great War of the North on terms favourable to Sweden, but the Senate was powerless, even its most serious remonstrances seldom received more than a bare acknowledgement, while its official communications rarely received as much. The nation which had conferred absolute power on a youth of fifteen was now reaping its own reward, and so long as Charles lived, Sweden had no alternatives but disobedience to its monarch or annihilation of its manhood. The first alternative was hardly even considered; the second was averted only by Charles's death.

The news of Charles's arrival in Stralsund caused a great demonstration throughout Sweden, which was considerably damped when Charles sent word that he must have an army of 20,000 men at once. It was quite true that an army was urgently required, for Prussia, which had already seized Stettin, was rapidly extending her acquisitions in Swedish Pomerania. Frederick of Prussia declared war on Sweden, and the Elector of Hanover, now king of Great Britain, joined in the League of Prussia, Russia and Denmark for the purpose of dividing the Swedish spoils. By the middle of 1715 exhausted Sweden was at war with Russia, Prussia, Poland, Saxony, Hanover and Denmark, but Charles with about

17,000 men in Stralsund was as confident as ever and absolutely refused to hear any suggestion of peace. In July 1715 the siege of Stralsund commenced and in December what was left of the city capitulated. Charles landed in Sweden on the 13th of December, and even then might have retrieved something from the wreck if he had not persisted in his refusal to yield an inch of Swedish territory. In "Grand Vizier" Görtz he found a clever if unscrupulous adviser who saw that Sweden's only hope lay in the jealousies that were bound to divide Sweden's motley enemies, but Charles's obstinacy ruined all.

The remainder of his career belongs to another period. In 1719 he invaded Norway, and on the 30th of November he was killed by a sniper when laying siege to Frederickshald. He was then in his thirty-eighth year. His adviser Görtz, who was unjustly blamed for the later acts of Charles's life, was arrested and executed, but Görtz was merely the scapegoat for the sins of his master. In 1721 the second great War of the North was ended by the treaty of Nystadt. Sweden ceded Livonia, Esthonia, Ingria and Karelia to Russia; her former possessions in Germany had already fallen into the hands of Prussia,[29] and she thus surrendered her claims to political greatness.

[29] With the exception of part of Western Pomerania.

Chapter 12

Ottoman and Slav:
Poland, Russia and Turkey

"THE SLAV RACE is divided into six branches—Russians, Poles, Tcheques, Bulgars, Serbians and Croats. All of them formerly had national kings; Russia alone now has a sovereign speaking its own language. All the other Slavs suffer the yoke of foreigners. The Slavs have no historian." So wrote Krijanitch,[1] a seventeenth-century patriot, in a book dedicated to the Tsar Alexis Mikhailovitch, a book intended to prove the essential unity of the Slavs and containing an eloquent plea for the retention of their common language and culture. The Slav was then, as now, one of the most disunited of European peoples, a great non-maritime race whose progress was limited by the four inland seas, the Baltic, the Adriatic, the Black Sea and the Caspian. Geographically divided in earlier days between the dominions of Rome and Byzantium, the old Slavonia had never been welded into a compact state; a race combining pastoral with military elements, it had taken little share in the spoils of the Roman empire; fond of liberty, the Slavs had not always been strong enough to obtain or enjoy it.

In this chapter Poland and Russia will be considered in some detail, and the history of these states will be narrated in conjunction with that of Turkey, the traditional enemy of the Slav race. It might seem that unity is impossible of achievement in a chapter devoted to the history of three such countries, but in the fortunes of the Republic of Poland—a country

[1] L. Leger, *Le Monde slave*, 308.

447

having neighbours rather than a history—will be found a common ground in the struggles of Ottoman and Slav. The dominant theme, therefore, will be the part played in seventeenth-century history by Poland and the Poles. By the end of the century Russia had fully emerged from her Muscovite obscurity and had become an important power under Peter the Great; in consequence, the chapter will conclude with an account of the administrative reforms carried out by the monarch who tried to modernize Russia.

Before studying the wars and conquests in which these three states were involved, it may be well to deal briefly with the only part of the subject that can easily be detached from the main theme, namely, the internal history of Turkey in Europe. The domestic history of Turkey in this period is soon told. After the reign of Suleiman the Magnificent (1520–1566) there followed a series of weak and effeminate Sultans, a succession broken but rarely by vigorous rulers like Murad IV. Suleiman's great-grandson, Mohammed III., reigned from 1595 to 1603 and was succeeded by his son Ahmed I., aged fourteen, whose accession is noteworthy because his brother was allowed to live. Under the tutelage of his Grand Vizier Murad, Ahmed's rule was efficient and, on the whole, successful. The Asiatic and European frontiers were ably defended, and in November 1606 the frontier war with the Hapsburgs was ended by the treaty of Sitva-Torok. By this treaty the Sultan acquired Canischa and Gran; he renounced his claim to an annual tribute, accepting a composite sum instead, and the Turkish protégé Bocksay was recognized as Prince of Transylvania under Hapsburg suzerainty.[2] The importance of this treaty is that Turkey now entered the diplomatic system of Europe. In renouncing her claim to annual tribute, she recognized the fact that not all foreigners would consent to be her vassals, and though she acquired some fresh territory, she abandoned for a time her ambitious projects against the empire. But the treaty, while conceding some measure of independence to the Magyar populations of Transylvania, really imposed on them the necessity of deciding between Turkish or Hapsburg allegiance, and thus the all-important question of the frontier between the Christian and the Ottoman empires was left in suspense.

The death of Ahmed I. in 1617 was followed by five years

[2] Zinkeisen, *Geschichte des Osmanischen Reiches,* iii 620.

of misrule under his brother Moustafa (deposed for idiocy in 1618) and his uncle, Osman II. (1618–1622). Osman was distinguished mainly for avarice and cruelty. He carried on a war against Poland for possession of the fiercely-contested Cossack lands of the Dniester, but his failure before the walls of Khoczim in 1621 was disastrous and was regarded as a national calamity. When it became suspected that he intended to use Egyptian mercenaries against the malcontents in Constantinople,[3] he was executed by the Janissaries on the 20th of May 1622. The imbecile Moustafa was then raised to power for the second time and was again deposed after fifteen months' nominal rule. His son Murad IV. succeeded in a year (1623) notable in Turkish annals as that of the capture of Bagdad by the Persian king, Abbas the Great. The new Sultan, who attained his majority in 1632, terrified even Turkey by atrocities from which not even a Greek Patriarch[4] nor resident foreigners were immune. Of his four brothers, two were executed in order to terrify the others, and eventually only one of them was left. Not without ability, Murad was capricious and bloodthirsty, but at least he terminated the anarchy and corruption which in several preceding reigns had become chronic; moreover, he carried on a successful war against the Persians, recapturing Bagdad in 1638 and putting to death the garrison of 30,000 men. The Spahis and Janissaries were overawed and sworn to obedience; a new code of feudal law was introduced; the revenues were reorganized and an army of 200,000 men was raised. In addition, a puritan régime was enforced; the coffee-houses were closed, tobacco was forbidden, and in his midnight perambulations through the streets of Constantinople the Sultan inflicted with his own hands capital punishment on all found guilty of disobedience to his edicts. This sanguinary moral censor died on the 9th of February 1640 at the age of twenty-nine.

Murad was succeeded by his one surviving brother, Ibrahim I., who owed his life to the fact that he was as effeminate as his brother was virile.[5] He was not long in adding cruelty to his characteristics, executing a Grand Vizier merely because he had incurred the dislike of the harem, and giving orders (fortunately not obeyed) for the massacre of all Christians

---

[3] Zinkeisen, *op. cit.* iii. 742.

[4] *Ibid.* iv. 372-8. The Jesuits were suspected of bribing the Sultan to murder the Patriarch and substitute one of their nominees.

[5] *Ibid.* iv. 530.

within the empire. In 1645 began the great contest with Venice for possession of Candia (Crete). At home the worst days of Moustafa the Idiot were revived; once more feminine influence reigned supreme, until finally the empire was invaded by Cossacks and Venetians. When it was seen that revolution was the only alternative to anarchy, Ibrahim was deposed and executed in the summer of 1648, and a seven-year-old son was established in his place.

The young Mohammed IV. (1648–1687) commenced his reign under the tutelage of his grandmother, and during his long minority the country was at the mercy of the soldiery, in whose hands even the grand viziers were but puppets, national disorder being intensified, moreover, by the incessant rivalries between the Greek grandmother and the Russian mother of the young Sultan. As he grew up, Mohammed showed some of the rigorist characteristics of his grandfather Murad, imitating him in his nightly processions through the capital, and carrying a love for the chase to the verge of insanity. But his reign is noteworthy for the inauguration of strong and efficient rule by a famous dynasty of grand viziers —the Kiuprilis[6]—whose founder, the septuagenarian Mohammed Kiuprili, a man of Albanian stock, was called to power by the Sultan's mother. In preceding reigns the grand viziers had been distinguished mainly by the speed of their succession to each other, but Mohammed Kiuprili made his own terms when he was appointed, and thereafter was practically absolute. No one was spared in the ferociously efficient régime that ensued; between 1656 and 1661 thirty thousand persons are said to have been executed, severities meted out to Janissaries, Spahis, bandits, provincial governors, sheiks, civil servants and a patriarch. On his death in 1661 he was succeeded by his son Ahmed II. Kiuprili (1661–1676), who combined administrative skill with erudition and the patronage of letters; his rule was as humane as that of his father had been cruel. In 1676 he was succeeded by Kara Mustafa, a son-in-law of the first Kiuprili, and later a son-in-law also of the Sultan. Avarice and extravagance were combined in his character, and his court was only a little less sumptuous than that of the Sultan. He had imagination as well as military aptitudes; he dreamed of a new Ottoman conquest, and he is famous as the besieger of Vienna. His failure cost him his life.

In 1689 the Kiuprili dynasty was restored to the grand

---

[6] *Ibid.* v. 261 ff.

viziership in the person of Moustafa Zadé,[7] son of the first Kiuprili. He was killed two years later at the battle of Salankemen, but his short rule was marked by justice, firmness and honesty. He showed signs of modernity by substituting a tax for the death penalty on smoking; he exercised an enlightened economic policy in favour of the foreign traders in Constantinople and Aleppo; in addition, he enriched the revenues by equitable taxation rather than capricious extortion. His death was a real calamity for Turkey. Meanwhile Sultan Mohammed IV. had been followed in 1695 by his son Moustafa II. (1695–1703), who carried on a long campaign against the allied Poles, Imperialists and Venetians in Hungary; but discouraged by his defeat at Zenta in 1697, he reinstated the Kiuprilis by appointing as Grand Vizier Houssein Amoudja-Zadé[8] (1697–1702), a nephew of Kiuprili I. It was Houssein who gave peace to Turkey in the treaty of Karlowitz, and he did much, by remission of taxation and conciliatory measures, to reconcile the frontier populations with Turkish rule. Excepting Nouman Kiuprili (who held office for a few months in 1710), Houssein was the last of the great Kiuprili administrators, all of whom had done something to counteract the vicious tendencies everywhere evident in the national life of Turkey. It was mainly owing to these men that the Ottoman Empire was able to retain its hold on Europe in the seventeenth century and create the Eastern Question in the eighteenth. Sultan Moustafa II. was followed by his brother Ahmed III. (1703–1730), in whose reign the power of the grand viziers declined in proportion as that of the harem increased.

POLAND. The turbulent career of the seventeenth-century Republic of Poland provides a contrast with the comparatively uneventful course of domestic affairs in Turkey, where so much potential history was cut short by the executioner. The early years of the century found Poland engaged in a conflict between the elder or Catholic branch of the House of Vasa, represented by Sigismund III., king of Poland (1587–1631), and the younger or Protestant branch represented by Charles IX. of Sweden. Devoted to the Jesuits, a man of some education and personal attractiveness, Sigismund might have conferred many benefits on Poland had he conserved his re-

[7] *Ibid.* v. 288.
[8] *Ibid.* v. 302.

sources at home, instead of dissipating them on hopeless foreign enterprises. Characteristic of his impulsiveness was his support of the claims of "the false Demetrius" and his own candidature for the throne of Muscovy, first on behalf of himself and then on behalf of his son Ladislas, claims which caused a four years' war with Russia (1609–1613). An intermittent war with Sweden (1617–1629) was fought mainly in Poland's Baltic possessions; and its most important result was the loss of Livonia to Sweden, confirmed by the truce of Altmark (September 1629). The policy of Sigismund thus resulted mainly in strengthening his rival and making possible the intervention of Sweden on the Protestant side in the Thirty Years' War.

Sigismund married in succession two nieces of the Emperor Rudolph II. and so began the tradition of Polish-Austrian alliance. In the Thirty Years' War he played a part in the Imperial cause, but it was an ambiguous part, because, while his alliance with the Emperor and his constant hostility to Sweden were assets on the Catholic side, on the other hand, his territories, by their very extent, invited invasion, a threat against which Polish national resources were quite inadequate. Moreover, interference with German affairs brought trouble from the East. Sigismund assisted the Emperor against Bethlen Gabor, who in turn summoned the aid of the Turks against Poland. Turkey was then engaged in subduing the petty principalities of the Danube and had just acquired the sovereignty of Moldavia, a success followed up by the capture of Khoczim, a fortress controlling the entry into Volhynia. Polish troops valiantly contested Khoczim against the Turks, and after its recapture in 1621 from Sultan Osman, Poland was able to impose the treaty of Khoczim on the Porte, by which Moldavia was restored to Christian rule and established as a barrier between Poland and Turkey. Luckily for Sigismund, the successors of Sultan Osman were first an imbecile (Moustafa) and then Murad IV., who showed more concern for the Asiatic than the European frontier. At the same time (1622) Gustavus Adolphus, after capturing Riga and a part of Courland, agreed to accept a truce. Michael Romanoff was obliged, on account of internal difficulties, to leave Poland in possession of Smolensk (captured in 1611), and so in the year 1623 Poland experienced the unusual blessing of peace on all her frontiers.

This interval was ended when, in 1625, the war with

Sweden was renewed and the troops of Gustavus invaded Livonia, Courland and Royal Prussia. Within three years Brünsberg, Elbing, Marienburg and the bishopric of Warmia were captured. Meanwhile the Tartars invaded the Ukraine and Little Poland; even Warsaw was threatened. At this critical moment French diplomacy intervened to save Sigismund and, by the help of Charnacé, a six years' truce was signed in September 1629 at Altmark. By this truce Sigismund recognized Gustavus as king of Sweden and ceded Livonia, with the Prussian ports of Elbing, Pillau and Memel and the customs dues of Dantzig. Freed from the hostility of the senior Vasa, and endowed with the valuable revenues of the Prussian ports, Gustavus was now able to devote his whole energy to the campaign in Germany.

Thus the reign of Sigismund, which ended in 1631, had been one of almost continuous warfare, often waged with vigour and success, but without any tangible result. More important is the fact that his reign witnessed the definite triumph of the Jesuits in Poland and the subordination of the Court to this Order. This had not been achieved without protest—in 1605 a large number of nobles had demanded the expulsion of the Jesuits and the establishment of a small permanent council of Senators, but their defeat in the field destroyed all hopes of withdrawing the Polish monarchy from ecclesiastical influence. Sigismund left two sons, Ladislas and John Casimir, who each in turn succeeded.

The reign of Ladislas IV. (1631–1648) commenced with the invasion of Russia. But as conquest failed to put the crown of Muscovy in his possession, Ladislas, after reaching Moscow, agreed to negotiate. By the treaty of Viasma[9] (1634) the Polish king renounced his claim to the Russian throne, and in return the Tsar renounced all claim to the Polish Baltic provinces, to White Russia and to Severia. Married to a sister of the Emperor Ferdinand II., Ladislas was interested in architecture and art; he introduced several western refinements, built roads and bridges, and made Warsaw a real capital. In his *Pacta Conventa* he granted some guarantees for a policy of toleration which benefited the adherents of the orthodox Greek Church. He refused to be drawn into Richelieu's circle of allies, but his Austrian wife served to make him unpopular with all who distrusted the Hapsburgs. The nobility, who appreciated him most when he saved his country from

[9] Sometimes called the treaty of Polyankova.

foreign commitments, exercised an increasingly strict surveillance over his conduct; in consequence the position of the crown degenerated into a nominal presidency. Ladislas married in 1646 his second wife, Marie Louise, daughter of the Duke of Nevers, an alliance which further assisted the process of introducing western institutions into Poland, and helped to redeem the Republic from Madame de Motteville's accusation that the Polish nobility had plenty of diamonds but no linen.[10] He died early in the year 1648; his death prevented the intended mission of a Polish representative to the Congress of Westphalia. Hence Poland derived no advantage from the Thirty Years' War and was one of the few nations unrepresented at the peace negotiations.

The long reign of John Casimir (1648–1668) was destined to be one of the most disastrous in the history of Poland. Younger son of Sigismund III., he had been for some years a Jesuit and had just received the dignity of a cardinalate when his brother's unexpected death rendered the Polish throne vacant. On his election, he put aside his ecclesiastical dignity in order to marry his brother's widow—an ominous beginning in the opinion of his subjects. His accession coincided with a period of great unrest throughout the whole of Europe, and in the general ferment Poland was not to be spared. It is necessary to refer to the source from whence trouble first came.

In the seventeenth century the great steppes of the Ukraine were occupied by several Cossack communities of which the most important were those of the Borysthene (Dnieper) and those of the Don. The latter were under the nominal suzerainty of the Tsar, while the former, owing allegiance to Poland, were a composite race, formed mainly of Bosnians and Tartars, reinforced by fugitives and adventurers, united only by military prowess and constituting, in reality, a republic of soldiers and labourers. The headquarters of these Dnieper or Zaporogean Cossacks were amid the rocks (Porogi) of the great river estuary; they were pirates[11] as well as brigands, and under their popularly elected Hetman were the terror of neighbouring races. At their town of Tretchimirow, near Kiev, they were able to preserve the booty derived from their

[10] Quoted in N. A. de Salvandy, *Histoire du roi Jean Sobieski,* i. 175.

[11] Zinkeisen, *op. cit.* iv. 493-7.

countless forays; there they had their arsenal, their stores and their archives. They might have provided an invaluable ally to their suzerain Poland, but the Polish nobility, blind to the danger of incurring the enmity of such a warlike race, tried to exploit them in the same way as they exploited their peasants. The Cossacks were members of the Orthodox Greek Church, and in the lands which they held of Poland they had to pay extortionate sums to middlemen for permission to exercise their cult, but, unlike the Polish peasants, they were not defenceless, and it needed only a spark to set ablaze a great mass of combustible material which the Polish *Szlachta* had so assiduously prepared.[12]

The Cossack leader was Bogdan Chmielniski, a man of military and political qualities who already, in the reign of Ladislas, had offered to lead a fleet to Constantinople, in order that the Poles might attack the Turks from the land, but this offer had not been accepted. The seizure of one of his mills on some official pretext by a Polish intendant was the climax of a long series of petty oppressions suffered by himself and his dependants. When Bogdan complained in person, an attempt was made to assassinate him, and during his absence an intendant (Czaplinski) outraged the wife of the Cossack leader and murdered his son. The Zaporogean Cossacks rose to a man and the Hetman had now 300,000 men under his command. Defeating the Polish troops at Zolte Wody, Bogdan late in 1648 besieged Lemberg with an army now strengthened by Russian and Tartar auxiliaries. With the fall of Lemberg this tremendous army overran Poland and soon John Casimir was obliged to sue for peace. The Cossacks demanded the expulsion of Jews and Jesuits and the punishment of Czaplinski; the Poles promised to expel the Jews but would not give up the Jesuits. Peace was eventually negotiated on the strength of this promise and after the execution of the intendant.

The Polish nobility were quite unable to realise that they had escaped very lightly and they mistook Bogdan's easy terms for signs of weakness. In 1650 the Diet talked of punishing the rebels, and the Cossacks soon found that they had fought in vain. The matter now took on a more religious aspect. Bogdan had visions of a crusade of Orthodox against Catholic, in which White Russia, Litvania and Little Poland would be the prize for the victor; similarly, John Casimir regarded the rebels as heretics; he strengthened his army with

[12] See Nisbet Bain, *Slavonic Europe*, chs. x. and xi.

Imperial troops and received a helmet and sword from Pope Innocent X. In June 1651 was fought at Beresteszko one of the greatest battles of the century, the total number of the combatants being about 500,000 men. The treason of the Khan of the Crimea and the flight of the Tartars more than counterbalanced Bogdan's numerical superiority and the battle ended in decisive defeat for the rebels. A truce was signed and both sides recuperated for the next attack.

For the Cossacks, Muscovy, then under the rule of the powerful Alexis Mikhaïlovitch, seemed to offer the most obvious source of assistance. In 1654 they formally commended themselves to Alexis, who was induced by his own predilections to undertake the protection of a race little different from his own and subject to oppression by heretics. Morover, Alexis recalled that one of his many titles had on a recent occasion been omitted by negligent Polish diplomacy. The result was a joint Russian and Cossack invasion of Poland, in which Smolensk, Vilna and the whole of Severia were won for Russia, and when the great Hetman died in 1657 he had witnessed the beginning of the process which substituted Russia for Poland. Bogdan's career bears a curious resemblance to that of Oliver Cromwell. The two were almost exactly contemporary; they were both better fitted to destroy than to create; they shared the power of reconciling violence with public opinion and they were each survived, not by a state but by an incompetent son.

Invaded by Cossacks, Tartars and Russians in the years 1656–7, Poland might well have lost the western Ukraine at this time; nevertheless she found salvation, not in organized resistance to the invader nor in skilled leadership, but in the addition of a fourth invader—Sweden. As soon as Swede and Muscovite encountered each other in the common purpose of dividing up a practically defenceless country, there were dissensions, and for a time at least the Republic found safety not in the paucity but in the multiplicity of her enemies. In the summer of 1655 Charles X. of Sweden entered Warsaw, forcing John Casimir to take refuge in Silesia. The treaty of Königsberg, signed in January 1656 by Sweden and Brandenburg, was the first of the Partition treaties. Only when racial feeling and religious antipathies were aroused did the Poles make a stand against the invader; it was a smouldering nationalism, fanned into flame by the Jesuits that forced the Swedes to assume the defensive. A Russian invasion of

Sweden's Baltic provinces taught the Swedish king that his duties lay nearer home, and after two years of military occupation the country was at last restored to John Casimir in July 1657.

Civil war quickly followed on the wars of invasion. Profiting by the anarchy which the roving bands of unemployed soldiery were everywhere producing, and by the facility with which the discontented elements in the nobility could always form armed confederations, a Polish noble named Lubomirsky, in alliance with Austria and Brandenburg, declared war on his sovereign in 1663, and in the campaigns that followed, several fierce battles were fought. John Casimir was saved from this danger only by the death of Lubomirsky in 1667. Luckily for Poland, Turkey was still engaged in the struggle for Candia. Russia proved conciliatory and by the treaty of Andrussovo, signed in January 1667, Poland obtained peace by surrendering a large part of White Russia, Severia and the whole of the Ukraine to the east of the Dnieper. The last mentioned of these territories might have been preserved for Poland had she engaged the Cossacks in her interests; in effect the treaty of Andrussovo made the eastern frontier of Poland practically co-terminous with the Dnieper. Defeat was not without its effects on the monarch. In 1668 John Casimir abdicated and retired to Paris, where he was given the abbacy of St. Germain des Prés.

There were three candidates for John Casimir's crown—Frederick William of Neuburg, the Duke of Enghien and the Duke of Lorraine, the first two in the French interest, the third a Hapsburg nominee. Between them these three divided evenly the votes of the Diet, thus providing a chance for a fourth candidate, the piast or native noble, Michael Wisnowieski, who was elected in 1669. He married the sister of the Emperor Leopold and so continued the tradition of alliance with Austria; in other respects his reign was no different from that of his predecessor, for it is an almost unbroken record of disunion and strife. The outlying provinces were continually ravaged by the Cossack hetman Doroszensko, and in the Tartar markets there was such a glut of Polish captives that the old ones changed hands for a pinch of tobacco.[13] The inevitable result of the helplessness and anarchy of Poland was that plots were quickly formed against

[13] Salvandy, *op. cit.* i. 349.

the monarch. There were intrigues among his proposed successors, in which foreign help[14] was solicited. Meanwhile the Ottomans resumed the offensive. With the capture of Candia in 1669 Turkish arms were freed for continental enterprises and the Dnieper Cossacks became active under Doroszensko. Poland had now to face a serious Turkish onslaught; when the Turkish invaders reached Lemberg, the panic-stricken Michael was ready to grant any terms in order to remove the menace and, by the secret treaty of Buczacs (October 1672), he surrendered to Turkey Polish Ukraine and Podolia together with an annual tribute.[15]

At this time the only military leader of competence in Poland was John Sobieski, the Grand Marshal of the Kingdom, who was intriguing against his sovereign in the hope of displacing him by the French candidate the Duke of Longueville. It was partly due to these intrigues that Sobieski had failed to stem the advance of the Turks. When news of the treaty of Buczacs leaked out, even the nobility were united by a feeling of indignation; in consequence, Michael's ignominious surrender to the enemy was disavowed. At the head of 40,000 men Sobieski[16] redeemed his own and his country's honour by inflicting a crushing defeat on the invaders at Khoczim in Bessarabia (November 11, 1673). For once Poland realised that safety lay in the rule of a man able to defend his country, and on the death of Michael Wisnowieski late in 1673, John Sobieski was elected from seventeen candidates.

At this momentous point in the history of Poland, when the greatest of her kings ascended the throne, it may be well to refer to the two border states which were destined to play a prominent part in the great struggle between East and West, a struggle which makes the reign of Sobieski of European interest. These two states were Hungary and Transylvania, both of which in the earlier years of the seventeenth century had managed to maintain a troubled autonomy against the threatened dominion of both Ottoman and Hapsburg. In the year 1604 Upper Hungary and Transylvania had united in

---

[14] For French intrigues see *Instructions données* . . . (Poland), xlvi. ff.

[15] Zinkeisen, *op. cit.* v. 71.

[16] The reasons for Sobieski abandoning his intrigues with Louis XIV. are given in *Instructions données* . . . (Poland), liii.

support of the insurgent leader Stephen Bocksay, who, by arms, maintained his title of hereditary prince of both territories, with succession to the Hapsburgs if he died without heirs. This condition was fulfilled in 1608; Bocksay died without heirs and, when the Emperor Rudolph was relegated to Bohemia, his brother Matthias took over Hungary and Transylvania. The policy of centralization and religious persecution favoured by the Archduke Ferdinand, afterwards emperor, again stirred up feeling in the Eastern provinces, and under Bethlen Gabor (1613–1629)[17] and George Rakockzy (1629–1648)[18] an independent Magyar state was maintained against Austria on the one side and Turkey on the other. Rakockzy's son George II. was displaced in 1658 by a Turkish nominee, Achatius Barczay, and Ottoman influence in eastern Europe was further extended when the first Kiuprili established puppet rulers in both Wallachia and Moldavia. Turkish tutelage over the Magyars was continued, after Barczay's death, in the rule of his successor Michael Apafy, but in 1661 Leopold began to contest Turkish domination in what were nominally Hapsburg territories, and a long period of intermittent warfare between the two Empires then began.

In 1663 the second Kiuprili crossed the Danube with an army of over 200,00 men, and after an invasion of Hungary, Moravia and Silesia, thousands of Christians were reduced to slavery. It was against this threat that a Holy League was formed under the auspices of Pope Alexander VII., a League which included even Louis XIV., whose ambassador in Constantinople had been imprisoned in 1660 on a trumped-up charge, and it was the French contingent of 6000 men which helped the Imperialist troops to inflict a crushing defeat on the Turks at St. Gothard on the Raab. The truce of Vasvar[19] (August 1664) divided Hungary into two parts, one (the larger portion) western and Austrian, the other eastern and Turkish, and Apafy was recognised as ruler of Transylvania subject to the payment of tribute to the Porte. This treaty thus sacrificed Hungary to Austria and Transylvania to Turkey; its enforcement created great resentment among peo-

[17] Zinkeisen, op. cit. iv. 379 ff.

[18] Ibid. iv. 467-472.

[19] Zinkeisen, op. cit. iv. 932 ff. Notice that the truce was for twenty years and that consequently Kara Mustafa's invasion of Hungary in 1683 was a violation of the truce, a violation which many Mohammedans believed to forebode disaster.

ples who had tasted the sweets of independence and religious liberty, for Leopold, who now had control over the greater part of Hungary, inaugurated his rule by the judicial murder of several Hungarian patriots. If the Hapsburgs could keep the Turks in check they would be able to assimilate these Magyar territories; on the other hand, if they failed to hold their own, withdrawal from Hungary would be necessary. It is one of the many ironies of the history of Poland that her greatest monarch devoted his life to the destruction of a menace that threatened the Empire of the Hapsburgs far more than the Kingdom of Poland, and that, indirectly, Polish troops made possible the Hapsburg policy of creating a dependent Hungarian kingdom by fusing Austrian and Turkish Hungary with Transylvania.

This reference to Hungary and Transylvania is intended to show that in the struggle against Ottoman aggression two things were involved—the territorial ambitions of the Hapsburgs and the national aspirations of the Magyars. The newly elected king of Poland had little sympathy with Hapsburg intrigue and would have liked to see the creation of an autonomous Magyar state, but he took a wide view and saw that the threat to Europe from the east was of such magnitude as to transcend every local or even national consideration. John Sobieski knew that the Western Empire was threatened with the same fate as that which had already befallen the Eastern, and that if Turkey, restored and revived by the Kiuprilis, did not meet with sustained resistance, then Christendom itself was in danger. The Turks intended that their conquest of Hapsburg territories should be merely the prelude to a great European campaign of aggrandisement and conversion. It was boasted in Constantinople that as St. Sophia had, in the fifteenth century, been turned into a mosque, so, in the seventeenth, the Ottoman conquest would not cease until the Sultan had stabled his horses in St. Peter's. Poland was the one bulwark against this menace and, from the first, its king was deeply conscious of the part that he and his country would be called on to play in order to free Europe from a danger none the less serious because so valiantly averted. Sobieski's ambition was to detach the Magyars from the intrigues of the Porte, expel the Turks from Europe and create a Peloponnesian republic with Athens for its capital. For allies he was willing to co-operate with Russia, Venice, Persia, the Zaporogean Cossacks, Sweden and France.

It is not difficult to understand how such views were misunderstood by contemporaries. John Sobieski combined qualities rarely found together in one man. From his father he had received an excellent discipline in arms and literature. His mother and wife were the objects of a natural and graceful chivalry; to dependants he was straightforward and just; he was sincerely religious in an age when fanatical bigotry was still respected. As a subject he had not always been faithful to his king, and in any country but Poland his intrigues with foreign powers would have been considered treason, but as a king his conduct was both courageous and consistent. He was clement, yet had some of the sterner qualities required for leadership; before the battle of Khoczim he had quelled, by his words and presence, an incipient mutiny among his troops. Unlike Charles XII. of Sweden, he was a general, fighting for a definite object, having always a carefully arranged but easily modified plan of campaign, and conserving as much as possible the lives of his soldiers; unlike Turenne or Condé, he was also a soldier, sharing the discomforts and hardships of his men. He is one of the few leaders of the seventeenth century to whom the epithet "great" is applicable, a man who by his mingling of calm strength with intense conviction might recall the lineaments of Rembrandt's *Man in Armour*; one of the very few men in history who have waged, with success and humanity, a completely justifiable war.

His coronation was no sooner over than he organized his troops, raised subsidies and sought out the harassed troops of Ibrahim Pacha. The humiliating treaty of Buczacs was mitigated by the treaty of Zurawno (October 16, 1676), by which all Polish prisoners and slaves were released; Polish Ukraine was restored and the claim to tribute was renounced. The holy places in Jerusalem were again entrusted to Christian control. But neither side considered the treaty more than a truce. Turkish military preparations were feverishly pushed forward, and though Poland was able to enjoy a few years of peace, no one doubted that the decisive struggle was yet to come.

The earlier years of John Sobieski's reign were but a breathing space and a preparation for the great events of

1683. In the period immediately preceding that year the affairs of eastern and western Europe had become inextricably confused. The Hungarian Crusaders under the ardent Toekeli rose against Hapsburg oppression, but Toekeli, a grandson of one of the patriots executed in 1671, ruined his cause by allying with the Turk and dragging the insurgents of Hungary and Transylvania into a war which, it might be urged, concerned Christianity as much as Magyar liberty.[20] In the west France was a very doubtful quantity. French troops had assisted the emperor against the Turks at the battle of St. Gothard (1664), but the hostility shown to those troops on their return through German lands had convinced Louis that he had made a "pas de clerc" and that it was dangerous to assist his enemies.[21] Early in 1682 Louis recalled his armies from Flanders, ostensibly in order to free Leopold and Europe from trouble in the west while the Ottoman menace was being faced in the east. Historical writers, from Voltaire onwards, have accepted this official explanation of Louis's change of front, but the correspondence with the French agent in Hungary proves that at this time Louis was subsidizing the insurgents there to combine with the Turks against the emperor, in spite of whatever concessions the latter might make.[22] The Eldest Son of the Church, however zealous for the cause of religious uniformity in western Europe, was not unwilling to profit by the embarrassment which the activities of the Infidel caused in the mind of his cousin and co-religionary Leopold. The latent hostility of France was not the only difficulty with which the emperor had to contend. When he sought the assistance of the Diet, he could at first obtain no more than a recommendation that public prayers should be offered up:[23] he could expect little help from the Papacy, then engaged in the Gallican controversy; Venice, just recovering from her long war over Candia, was not anxious to re-embark on hostilites; Brandenburg was suspicious and unable to see

[20] Zinkeisen, op. cit. v. 87 ff.

[21] France had supplied troops as a member of the League of the Rhine. At the same time (1664) Louis XIV. had assisted the Elector of Saxony to destroy the independence of Erfurt. This was the main reason for German hostility to the French troops. For this see Auerbach, La Diplomatie française et la cour de Saxe.

[22] Salvandy, op. cit. ii. 122, and Instructions données . . . (Austria), 93 ff.

[23] Auerbach, La France et le Saint Empire Romain, 77.

how she would be advantaged by alliance with the emperor; while Russia, on the death of Feodor, was under the rule of a nine-year-old boy whose rights were still in dispute. There remained only Poland. Sobieski had been elected in the face of Austrian intrigues, and, having a wife of his own, had interrupted the tradition whereby Polish kings married Austrian Archduchesses; for this reason he had been denied the appellation of Majesty. Even more, there were certain inducements for Sobieski to act against the emperor. France and Brandenburg together offered, in return for his alliance, to give him Silesia (at the expense of the emperor) and even Hungary (provided Toekeli could be disposed of): moreover, Sultan Mohammed IV. made it clear that his preparations were not directed against Poland, and that he would welcome the Republic's alliance.[24] When Leopold was reduced to the last straits, he sought Sobieski's help by offering the hand of an Archduchess for his son and undertaking to guarantee something over which he had no control—the succession of the Polish throne for Sobieski's line. It is evidence of Sobieski's sagacity that he was not snared by such specious promises; it is proof also of his greatness that, surrounded by false friends and ardent enemies, he decided on a course of action involving palpable danger and doubtful benefit—hostility to the Turk.

In the year 1682 Europe was in a state of peace, but peace of such a kind as to engage the close attention of the great Oriental militarists within her gates. The truce signed at Vasvar had still two years to run, but the outlying lands of the Austrian Empire were continually being dismembered and ravaged by the Turks, followed by the enslavement of many thousands of Christians. Louis XIV., who had "peaceably" acquired Strasburg in the previous year, was encouraging reprisals against the Spanish in the Low Countries and giving underhand encouragement to the Hungarian rebels, while by a "strict interpretation" of the Edict of Nantes he was forcing a large proportion of his subjects to rebel or emigrate. The deadly feud of Bourbon and Hapsburg was a guarantee that Europe would not unite against the threat from the east. Turkish diplomacy was well aware of these jealousies and hatreds. With the Holy Roman Empire practically isolated and enfeebled, France devoted to selfish aggrandisement,

[24] Salvandy, *op. cit.* ii. 126.

England exploited by a shameles voluptuary, Spain and Italy almost negligible, and Christianity everywhere warring against itself, the time seemed ripe for a Mohammedan invasion which would make that of the fifteenth century seem merely a preliminary venture. In the Grand Vizier Kara Mustafa there was to hand a man of ambition and initiative, able to control his unwieldy hordes of Turks, Tartars, Kurds, Albanians and Mamelukes, and anxious to outdo the exploits of Mohammed II. and Suleiman the Magnificent.

For some years the most elaborate preparations had been on foot.[25] The limitless resources of Asiatic Turkey were drawn upon; vessels in Turkish ports (except the French) were confiscated in order to provide transports from Smyrna, Alexandria and Aleppo; thousands of camels and chariots completed the links between the Euphrates and the Nile with the strongholds of Toekeli, and early in 1683 an enormous army descended on Hungary. At Essek, between Belgrade and the modern Budapest Mohammed IV. and his Grand Vizier joined forces with Toekeli, and thereupon Kara Mustafa was solemnly invested with the robe of gold and the standard of Mohammed, whereby he was constituted the leader of Islam against Christianity. Having completed this sacred duty, the Sultan recrossed the Danube to continue those incredible hunting exploits that are said to have taxed the resources of 40,000 beaters and the game supply of a peninsula. In his advance through Hungary Kara Mustafa forced back the Imperialist troops under Charles of Lorraine, and by defeating the Duke at Petronell (July 5, 1683) he cleared the way to Vienna. On the 7th of July the Tartar advance guard reached the gates; the emperor with about 60,000 inhabitants fled from the city. Seven days later the main army was sighted from the walls and the sixty days' siege of Vienna began.

The garrison in Vienna[26] did not number more than 14,000 troops; the besiegers were a motley array of nearly 200,000 persons, including the Grand Vizier's enormous harem, his eunuchs and his large execution staff. Charles of Lorraine, who was in command of the Imperialist forces, was an able and experienced leader, but without help, he could do nothing. By the 16th of July the city was completely invested: the wooden Playhouse was dismantled and the beams used for

[25] For these see Salvandy, *op. cit.* ii. 132 ff.
[26] There is a good account of the siege in Zinkeisen, *op. cit.* v. 97-112.

strengthening the walls; the arsenal blew up under the Turkish artillery, but, luckily for the inhabitants, many of the bombs thrown into the city did not burst. From one of the most pleasure-loving cities Vienna was changed into an armed camp eagerly awaiting relief. An Englishman resident in the city noted that the Viennese now thronged the churches, "the fright they were in having much exercised their devotion."[27] The siege engrossed the attention of Europe as did no other event of the century, and in Catholic countries funds were raised as for a crusade. The emperor appealed for help, and Pope Innocent XI. called on Louis XIV., as Eldest Son of the Church, to take up arms on behalf of Christianity, whereupon the French monarch magnanimously undertook to leave Leopold's western frontier unmolested, provided the Dauphin were admitted to the Imperial succession.

The appeal of pope and emperor met with a different response in Poland. In March 1683 Sobieski had undertaken to reinforce the 60,000 Imperialist troops with 40,000 Poles in the event of the Turkish invasion, and he could rely on Papal subsidies to supplement the erratic revenues of his country. On Assumption Day 1683 he quitted his capital for the besieged city. The fact that he was commanding in person raised the hopes of dejected Catholicism, though it was feared that he might be too late, for Vienna had now been besieged for six weeks and was rapidly nearing the end of its resources, while the Turks were busy undermining the walls. On the 5th of September he reached the Danube and joined forces with the Imperialists; three days later the contingents of Saxony and Bavaria under the two Electors were added to the army of succour, which now consisted of about 20,000 Imperialists, 10,000 Saxons, 12,000 Bavarians and 18,000 Poles.[28] Avoiding the direct but dangerous route by the river Sobieski decided to climb the Kahlemberg and descend on the Turks through its precipitous gorges. As he approached the city the reports brought back by his scouts spread terror among some of the allied troops, and it needed all the courage and resource of the Polish king to keep up the courage of his men, whose endurance was sorely tested by the arduous ascent of the Kahlemberg, an ascent in which each man had to carry his own food, the horses had to live on oak leaves, and some of the heavy artillery had to be abandoned. Sobieski did not

[27] Harleian MS. 2282, f. 57.
[28] Salvandy, *op. cit.* ii. 169.

underestimate either the strength or skill of the Turk, knowing that they included some of the best engineers in Europe and that their siege positions were admirably chosen. On the 11th of September he reached the summit of the Kahlemberg and rockets were sent up to announce that the liberators of Vienna were at hand.

Meanwhile the long inactivity of Kara Mustafa had produced disorder among his troops. The Greeks were now experiencing qualms in regard to the Koran, while the stricter Mussulmans feared that since the campaign violated a truce (that of Vasvar) it could have no good end. Only the hope of enormous plunder kept these unwieldy hordes together, and the Grand Vizier hesitated to launch an assault since it might depreciate the value of the treasure which he expected to fall into his hands. As the siege progressed,[29] the Turks dug themselves in; their trenches were elaborate and intricate; the senior officers had large dug-outs fitted up with tiles and tapestry, and they protected their lines from the artillery of the besieged garrison by great mounds of sandbags. There was a good deal of fraternising between the besieging and the besieged troops; there was even an attempt to induce the besieged inhabitants to surrender by firing into the city arrows on which were impaled manifestos depicting the hopelessness of further resistance. But the delay told as heavily on the Turks as on the Christians; the oriental luxury with which the Grand Vizier surrounded himself set a bad example which wholesale executions could not destroy; hence the sight of hostile troops on the Kahlemberg was as ominous as it was unexpected, and there were some who urged retreat. In spite, however, of desertions and executions, Kara Mustafa could count on a superiority of at least three to one; it was, therefore, with every prospect of success that he met the attack of Sobieski on the morning of Sunday the 12th of September, a day which was to witness one of the few decisive battles in the history of the world. Advancing in four columns from the mountain, the Christians forced back the enemy outposts and by mid-day had formed a great semicircle that outflanked the dense masses of the Turks. Deeply entrenched, Kara Mustafa patiently awaited the onslaught of troops fatigued by long marches and the heat of an autumn day, but a

[29] The details that follow are derived from an interesting MS. diary kept by an Englishman in Vienna during the siege. This is in the British Museum (Harleian MS. 2282).

fierce bombardment of his headquarters caused him to modify the disposition of his forces, and by evening his men were everywhere being driven out of their trenches. At this moment a cloud caused the crescent moon to fade from the sky, an omen which produced consternation among the Orientals. When Mustafa tried to stem the demoralization which swept through his armies like a flood, he was himelf carried away in the disorderly retreat. By nightfall the Turks were in full flight, but they found time to murder the seraglio and the thousands of Christian children whom they had accumulated in their ranks, thus providing an object-lesson of what might have happened on a larger scale had they taken Vienna. There are conflicting accounts of their casualties, but they are said to have lost at least 10,000; the allies, about a third of that number. It was a victory that saved eastern Europe for Christianity, a victory of devotion and strategy against numbers and the lassitude that comes of long inactivity, won, not by a vigorous youth exhausting hardened veterans, but by a man in his sixtieth year unable to mount his horse without assistance.

A triumphal entry into Vienna was followed by a *Te Deum* in the Cathedral of St. Stephen, and European opinion was voiced in the text, "There was a man sent from God whose name was John." But once the outburst of enthusiasm was over, Sobieski found that his presence was a source of embarrassment to those whom he had saved.[30] The emperor returned post-haste to Vienna, but his reception of the Polish king was cold and formal. In France, every effort was made to minimize the importance of the victory and to attribute it to others than Sobieski. The Poles were refused fodder for their horses and had great difficulty in obtaining honourable burial for their dead. "Here we are on the Danube," wrote Sobieski, "like the Israelites on the Euphrates, lamenting the loss of our horses and the ingratitude of those whom we have saved." Inevitably, there was disunion among the allies, and even in the ranks of the Polish contingent. John was anxious to pursue the retreating Turks through Hungary, while many of his followers were anxious to return home; moreover, the emperor, attributing to others the same motives as inspired his own conduct, assumed that the Hungarian campaign was intended to carve out a separate kingdom for Sobieski. These differences and suspicions caused delay, and so the pursuit of

[30] Salvandy, *op. cit.* ii. 221.

the Turks was not attended with the success that might have been expeced had it begun sooner. In October Sobieski inflicted a serious defeat on the Turks as they were crossing the Danube at Parkany, but dysentery now broke out in the Polish ranks and the pursuit had to be abandoned. Kara Mustafa executed his generals in the hope of thereby averting the Sultan's wrath; he was himself put to death on Christmas Day 1683, the day after Sobieski's triumphal entry into Cracow.

Believing that the moment had now come for the expulsion of the Turks from Europe, the king of Poland joined in the Holy League, reorganized by Innocent XI. in 1684, in which were included Austria, Venice, Malta and (in 1686) Russia.[31] But the intrigues of Leopold and disorders at home prevented Sobieski from taking an active part in the later campaigns. In June 1684 the Duke of Lorraine took Vychegrad and expelled Toekeli and his Turkish allies from the Hungarian fortresses, while the Venetians invaded Bosnia and Albania. On the 2nd of September 1686 Buda was taken after a siege, and with the loss of this city the strongest Turkish stronghold in Hungary was gone. In the following year the Grand Vizier was defeated at the battle of Mohacs (August 12), a success followed by the invasion of Moldavia, Wallachia and Croatia, in which Austrian and Polish troops co-operated, while Apafy, the Prince of Transylvania, was obliged to place himself under the suzerainty of the emperor. These events were followed by a reign of terror in Hungary, and the remnants of the Magyar national party were executed by a specially appointed tribunal, which indulged in the farce of judicial forms. The Hungarian crown was now declared hereditary in the Hapsburg family. Transylvania soon shared the same fate, for Apafy's son was brought up at Vienna, and in 1690 his dominions were incorporated in the Austrian Empire. Many thousands of Serbs had emigrated into southern Hungary in the course of the seventeenth century, and so the Hapsburgs added to their responsibilities the administration of a mixed Serbian and Magyar population. Not till the twentieth century did these races regain a short-lived independence.

On all sides the war against the Turk was pursued with vigour. Led by Morosini, the Venetians in 1686 captured

31 Zinkeisen, op. cit. v. 116 ff.

the Morea, and with the help of German mercenaries took Navarino, Modon, Argos and Corinth. Athens was next besieged (it was in this siege that the Parthenon was destroyed); on the capture of Athens, Morosini was elected Doge by grateful Venice. Dalmatia was next added to Venetian conquests from the Turk. The accession of the third Kiuprili, Moustafa Zadé, to the Grand Vizierate in 1689,[32] helped to restore for a short time the shattered fortunes of the Porte. He retook Nish and Belgrade, and releasing Toekeli from the Turkish prison to which his defeats had consigned him, sent him into Transylvania in order to stir up the dying embers of insurrection. But, unfortunately for Turkey, the career of this vigorous Grand Vizier was to be a short one. In 1691 he crossed the Save and was defeated and killed on the 19th of August at the battle of Salankemen, a defeat which again put the Turks on the defensive. Meanwhile the Greeks in the Morea rebelled against Venetian rule, and not till 1695 did Venice consolidate her hold over this conquest. The Turkish forces were now demoralized, and it needed only decisive defeat in the field to end their resistance. This occurred on the 11th of August 1697, at Zenta on the Theiss,[33] when the Grand Vizier Elmas Mohammed and about 30,000 Turks were killed. The result of this battle was the expulsion of the Ottomans from Serbia and Bosnia, and the Porte at last sued for peace.

It was in the rule of the fourth Kiuprili that Turkey obtained peace. The mediation of Paget, the English Levant Company's agent and informal English ambassador in Turkey, was accepted and the terms of the general settlement were discussed at Karlowitz.[34] On the 26th of January 1699 the treaty of Karlowitz was signed; its main terms are as follows:

1. Turkey renounced all claim to Transylvania and Hungary (except Temesvar). The Austro-Turkish frontier was defined by the Unna, the Save, the Drave and the Danube up to its junction with the Theiss.

2. To Poland were restored Kaminiec, Podolia and western Ukraine.

3. Venice obtained Dalmatia between the Kerka and the

---

[32] Zinkeisen, *op. cit.* v. 145 ff.

[33] Zinkeisen, *op. cit.* v. 154.

[34] *Ibid.* v. 200 ff.

Narenta, the whole of the Peloponnese except Corinth, the Aegean islands and St. Maure.

4. Russia obtained Azov.

Such was the end of the Turkish dream of conquest. Had France joined with Austria against Turkey, and if Sobieski had been accorded the full support of these two Christian powers, there can be little doubt that Turkey would have been expelled from Europe. The retention of a Mohammedan power on a Christian continent, with the complicated problems to which it has given rise, may therefore be regarded as one of the many indirect results of the feud between Bourbon and Hapsburg.

That the Turks were forced back to the Balkan peninsula was mainly due to their initial disaster at Vienna. John Sobieski acquired enduring fame from that exploit, but he found that his difficulties as king of Poland were made none the less difficult, and his later years were saddened by intrigues and jealousies, to which even his wife succumbed. Poland, which had been fused into a nation by pressure from the east, broke up again into factions and cliques as soon as the Turks were driven back to their frontiers. Sobieski knew that the problems of peace are no less intricate than those of war; accordingly he tried to develop the industry and commerce of Poland and to use the Danube and the Black Sea as great waterways.[35] For this purpose he negotiated a commercial treaty with Holland. In 1686, by the treaty of Moscow, he surrendered for a sum of money all claims over Kiev and Smolensk, thus confining Poland on the east to her natural frontier the Dnieper. But in face of his wife and the Diet he was powerless; he could not even save an unfortunate freethinker[36] from the barbarous death inflicted on him for expressing unguarded opinions about the existence of the Deity; he had no say in the choice of wives imposed on his sons, for whom he was unable to guarantee the succession, and his declining years were made miserable by the hectoring of an autocratic wife. The Jagellons had introduced a hereditary element into the Polish monarchy; in the seventeenth century only Michael Wisnowieski had not been followed by a son or brother; Sobieski therefore had reason to hope that one of his three sons might succeed, but even in

[35] Salvandy, op. cit. ii. 324.
[36] Ibid. ii. 371 (1689).

this he was disappointed, for the throne of Poland was now regarded as the legitimate ambition of every successful adventurer in western Europe, and each elector to the throne had his price. With no army, no revenues and no laws, Poland was no longer a kingdom but a gamble. The last years of her greatest king were devoted to the encouragement of literature and science, when, withdrawing himself from a corrupt court, he found pleasure in reading and gardening, occupations which earned for him the unanimous suspicion and contempt of the Polish nobility. Disillusioned but not embittered, still retaining all his calmness and fortitude, John Sobieski died on the anniversary of his birthday (the 17th of June), 1696. "He accepted death more willingly than he had accepted the crown—he conferred more honour on his throne than he had derived from it."[37]

The two candidates for the throne were the Prince of Conti and Frederick Augustus of Saxony. The latter was elected; he had been first on the scene and had used his money to good advantage. For years the unfortunate country was torn between Augustus and the puppet king Stanislas Lesczinski, held down on the throne by Charles XII. of Sweden, but after the battle of Pultava (1709) Augustus was re-established, and in return for the help of Prussia and Russia he ceded to the former Polish Prussia and to the latter Samogitia and White Russia. Thereupon Augustus maintained a vigorous campaign against his subjects, invoking the aid of Peter the Great against the nobility, who appealed for help to the same source. The fortunes of Poland continued to be bound up with those of her neighbours, and in the eighteenth century her history is to be found in the Chanceries of Vienna, St. Petersburg, Paris and Berlin. It is a wonder that the partition of Poland was so long delayed, for by the end of the seventeenth century idealism had long since disappeared from politics. European states possessed just as much territory as they could hold by the sword, and a defenceless state was rapidly becoming a contradiction in terms. The later history of Poland proves that racial sentiment is not a substitute for patriotism.

RUSSIA. The internal history of Russia in this period begins with the death of the Tsar Feodor and the murder of his half-brother Dmitri, both events happening in the year

[37] Zaluski, quoted by Salvandy, ii. 395.

1598. With the removal of these last male descendants of Ivan the Terrible, the line of Rurik became extinct and the way was prepared for the Romanoff dynasty. For some time power had been in the hands of the great Boiar Boris Godounof, who had murdered Dmitri in order to make his Tsardom titular as well as real. After a feigned reluctance he accepted the crown and commenced his rule by severities towards the Romanoffs and the Nagoi, relatives respectively of the late Feodor and Dmitri, while the tyranny which he now substituted for his previous servility was as little liked by his fellow Boiars as by the serfs. As he became more unpopular, the origin of his power was carefully scanned. The murder of Dmitri had been shrouded in mystery, and this fact inspired an obscure personage, calling himself Demetrius, to pose as Dmitri and come forward as the last surviving son of Ivan the Terrible. He first made known his claim to a Lithuanian magnate, Adam Vitchnevski, who influenced the Polish king, Sigismund Vasa, in his cause; in 1604 the papacy was induced to recognize Demetrius on his promising to unite the eastern and western churches. It is doubtful whether any of the Poles believed in his claim, but at least the solicitations of the Pretender gave the Republic an opportunity of interfering in the affairs of her eastern neighbour, and in October 1604 Demetrius, having become a Roman Catholic, crossed the frontier at the head of an army of Poles and Cossacks. His march through Severia and the Ukraine was unopposed; near the Severian Novgorod, the troops of Boris were defeated (December 21, 1604), and he was everywhere accepted for the real Tsar by a superstitious and aggrieved populace. The death of Boris in April 1605 completed Demetrius' success, and after a state entry into Moscow he was crowned (July 30, 1605).[38]

The rule of the "false Demetrius" was as merciful as that of his predecessors had been cruel. The Romanoffs were recalled from exile, and the relatives of the late Boris were spared. By largesse and a wise administration he won popularity among the soldiers and peasants, while by his skilful management he succeeded in conciliating the Boiars. Many restrictions on industry were removed; manœuvres were introduced into army training; Poland and the papacy were

[38] For the above see Waliszewski, *La Crise révolutionnaire* (1584–1614), chs. ii. and iii., and Nisbet Bain, *Slavonic Europe*, ch. ix.

retained as allies without any loss of Russian independence; a nation accustomed to apathy or cruelty as the inseparable characteristics of kingly rule, was amazed by the restless energy and tireless solicitude of him who claimed to be the real Demetrius.[39] But the new monarch was ruined by his virtues. His marriage to a Polish lady and the arrival of fresh contingents of Poles excited national dislikes and, though his Catholicism was secret, the Orthodox were disturbed by the arrival of Jesuits. The very clemency of his rule seemed proof that he was an impostor. Three Boiars, headed by Vassili Chouiski (who had been Godounof's agent in the murder of Dmitri) organized an army, and on the night of the 17th of May 1606 they captured Moscow, murdered many Poles and killed Demetrius. Having cremated his body, they fired the ashes from a cannon in the direction of Lithuania, the place from which he had come. So ended one of the few periods of good government in the history of Russia.

The leader of this movement, Vassili Chouiski (or Shuisky), was at once proclaimed Tsar, but his rule was everywhere contested. When hanging on a gibbet, before his cremation, Demetrius had had his face covered with a mask, a fact which provided a pretext for the appearance of another "false Demetrius" in the unwilling person of a Polish nominee named "the brigand of Touchino."[40] For some time Chouiski in Moscow was practically isolated while a mercenary Polish army maintained the rule of its puppet king, and the Tsar was saved only by the help of Swedish troops, obtained by ceding Karelia to Charles IX. This alliance decided the Vasa king of Poland to intervene personally and publicly; claiming the crown on behalf of his son he besieged Smolensk. Chouiski's tenure of the Tsardom now depended entirely on the military abilities of his son, Skopine; an ambitious brother of Chouiski poisoned Skopine, an act followed by the defeat of the Imperial forces at the hands of the Poles (June 23, 1610). Within a few days of this defeat Chouiski resigned and retired to a monastery.

As there seemed little likelihood of any Tsar elected by the Muscovites being accepted by the whole of the Russian Empire, the Boiars proceeded to rule by a Council of Regency. Sigismund of Poland now claimed the crown for him-

[39] Waliszewski, *op. cit.* 182-247.

[40] His real name appears to have been Gabriel Verevkin. For an account of him, see Waliszewski, *op. cit.* ch. ix.

self, and Moscow was given over to a fierce struggle between Poles and Boiars. The capture of Smolensk by Sigismund in 1611, the invasion of Russia by Swedish troops and the elevation of new impostors completed the anarchy, and these years in which the peasantry were flayed and murdered[41] by marauding bands of Poles, Cossacks, Swedes and Tartars are known as "the time of troubles" to distinguish them from the more static periods of Russian history. National sentiment was at last rallied by the only unifying force—religion. A butcher of Nijni Novgorod named Minine led the movement for the expulsion of the foreigner, the restoration of an unquestioned Tsardom and the reinstatement of orthodoxy. The first success of the nationalists was the recapture of Moscow from the Poles, their second was the election in January 1613 of a national Tsar in the person of Michael Romanoff, an election which took place in an assembly that included representatives of the *Boiars*, Clergy, Merchants, Crafts, *Streltsi* and Cossacks.[42] The choice fell on Michael Romanoff because he represented the dynasty of Ivan the Terrible, and because his family had been oppressed alike by Godounof and the foreign invaders. Immediately after his coronation, Michael, with the help of the Don Cossacks, restored order and sought foreign assistance for the consolidation of his Empire. In 1617, by the Peace of Stolbovo, all Swedish conquests in Russian territory, except Ivangorod, were restored, and in 1618 a truce[43] was signed with the Poles.

With the help of his father the Patriarch Philarete, the young Michael instituted a government that was partly constitutional and partly theocratic. Foreign commitments were avoided; peace was secured by a policy of conciliation, and the Tsar retained the loyalty of his subjects by piety, orthodoxy and conservatism. The old Muscovite exclusiveness is seen in the fact that both France and England were refused permission to use Russia as a means of commercial intercourse with Persia. In 1637 the Don Cossacks captured Azov for Russia, but a war with Turkey was averted by ordering the Cossacks to restore their capture. Two years earlier Ladislas of Poland had renounced his claim to the throne of the Tsars, and so the reign of Michael was, on the whole, one of peace.

[41] Waliszewski, *op. cit.* ch. xii.
[42] *Ibid.* ch. xiv.
[43] Truce of Deoulina.

Michael was followed in 1645 by his son Alexis Mikhailo-vitch (1645–1676), who continued the sacerdotal traditions of his ancestors and distinguished himself by magnificence and austerity.[44] Fond of peace, he was, like his father, a priest-king, combining the sumptuous ceremonial of his church with the religious etiquette of his Court. The direction of the administration was entrusted, at first, to the Tsar's tutor, Boris Morozof, who exercised a strict tutelage over his young sovereign and a harsh rule over the tax-payers. For-eign policy was directed mainly to the extension of Russian influence in the Ukraine and aimed at benefiting by the antagonism between Sweden and Poland; it profited also by the revolt against Polish rule led by Bogdan Chmielnicki. The result of this was that in 1667, by the treaty of Andrussovo, Alexis renounced all claim to Lithuania, but recovered Smolensk and Kiev and advanced the Russian frontier up to the Dnieper. This treaty confirmed the division of the Ukraine into two parts—the western, beyond the Dnieper, contested by Poland and Turkey; the other, or eastern, which now came under Russian suzerainty. When Poland lost west-ern Ukraine by the Second Partition (1793) the whole of the Ukraine became Russian. From Sweden, Alexis was un-able to obtain Livonia by arms, and by the treaty of Kardis (1661) he had to renounce it.

The importance of Alexis' reign lies not in foreign policy but in the discontent caused by the reforms of the Patriarch Nikon. The service books of the Russian Church were based on old and imperfect Slav texts, and in consequence many errors had crept in. Long usage had consecrated these cus-toms, so frustrating all attempts to bring the Russian manuals into conformity with the practice of the eastern Church. The sign of the cross was made in Russia with two fingers instead of three; the Hallelujah was intoned twice instead of thrice; the name of Jesus was pronounced Isous instead of Iisous.[45] To propose any innovation in such matters was to risk the accusation of heresy. Henry VIII. of England had experienced a similar difficulty when he found that ignorant parish priests persisted in their old "mumpsimus" instead of "sumpsimus," the former variation having crept in through the mistake of a copyist. In his reforming projects Nikon found that he had to face all the tremendous forces of ignorance and supersti-

[44] Nisbet Bain, *Slavonic Europe*, ch. x.
[45] Rambaud, *Histoire de la Russie*, ch. xxi.

tion in Russia, but the challenge was given in 1653 when an ecclesiastical synod assembled in Moscow decided, after correspondence with the Patriarch of Constantinople, to revise the service books. Jealous of ancient traditions, the Muscovites banded together against these new heresies emanating, they claimed, from Little Russia and Greece, from whence came all the evils that affected Russia; to these men Nikon was Antichrist, and the conflict between official reform and popular tradition lasted throughout the greater part of Alexis' reign. As matters of dogma were called in question, the sects multiplied and there were excesses of religious emotionalism. The numerous executions raised up many aspirants for the martyr's crown: some fled to the wastes; others, in an access of religious mania, set fire to themselves as the surest means of salvation. In 1658 Nikon was deserted by the Emperor and disgraced; in 1666, after sentence of deprivation, he was relegated to a monastery on the White Sea, but he was obviously a scapegoat, and Alexis several times tried secretly to obtain a reconciliation with him, though in vain. Nikon was a well-intentioned but tactless man; his proposed reforms had nevertheless broken the surface of Russian conservatism and the work of Peter the Great was made easier thereby.

After the death in 1669 of his first wife, Marie Miloslavski, Alexis married Natalie Narychkine, a niece of the Boiar Matveef, and on her mother's side of Scottish ancestry. Matveef's household was modelled on western lines and Natalie had never known the stupefying restrictions imposed on women by Russian conventions. Of this marriage Peter the Great was the product. Alexis was succeeded by Feodor (1676–82), a son by his first wife. The physical and mental weakness of the new Tsar gave full scope for the rivalries of the Miloslavski and Narychkine factions, while the real power was assumed by Feodor's sister Sophia. On Feodor's death in 1682 Ivan, second son of Alexis by Marie Miloslavski, succeeded, but, as he was practically an imbecile, the Patriarch and Boiars proclaimed Peter as their ruler. This provoked the Miloslavski daughters to combine with the sisters of the late Tsar Alexis against the nine-year-old Peter and his Narychkine relatives; the *Streltsi* were incited to massacre Matveef and several Narychkines, with the result that in 1682 there were three rulers of Russia—Ivan, Peter and

Sophia, the first imbecile, the second a child and the third a woman.

The situation was saved by the vigour of Sophia.[46] Taking over the government in the name of her brother and half-brother, she scandalized Russia by presiding over a colloquy in which the blood-stained *Streltsi* demanded the restoration of the "old faith" and the suppression of the reformed or Nikonian party to which Sophia, as a daughter of Alexis, belonged. This zeal for orthodoxy on the part of the most brutal soldiery in the world nearly led to the extinction of the Imperial family altogether, Miloslavskis and Narychkines alike, and only Sophia's courageous spirit saved the throne for her line. Once she had conciliated the *Streltsi*, she proved herself an able and intelligent ruler and kept in close touch with the course of European politics. Now that Turkey rather than Poland was the menace, she joined the Holy League in 1686 and by negotiation with John Sobieski obtained the surrender of all Polish claims over Smolensk and Kiev. But the failure of France to join the coalition against Turkey led to the expulsion of the French Jesuits from Russia. In the campaign of Pole, German and Imperialist against the Ottoman large Russian armies took part but did not achieve results commensurate with their numbers, and after 1689 Russia did not give any further military assistance to the Holy League.

Tsar Ivan died in 1696, but by 1689 Peter had begun to rule. Russia was not yet ready for the government of an Empress, and national sentiment was against "the monstrous regiment of women" no matter how efficient. By a palace revolution Peter got rid of Sophia; the *Streltsi*, quailing before the imperious young claimant to the throne, were won over by the only arguments which these savage janissaries could understand—brutality and force. Born in 1672 Peter Alexievitch had early manifested some of the characteristics that were to make him unique not only in the history of Russia but in the history of the world. His early experiences had given him a dislike of the *Streltsi* as strong as that of Louis XIV. for the Paris mob; in common also with the French monarch, Peter resented nothing so much as a

[46] Rambaud, *op. cit.* xxii.

diminution of his prerogative. Breaking away from maternal control and official tutors, Peter in boyhood loved to mix with the cosmopolitan life of the Moscow markets, where he picked up a knowledge of German and Dutch at first hand. From a German named Timmerman he acquired some knowledge of the principles of mathematics and fortification; with foreign help he equipped, at first for amusement, a small band of soldiers which he delighted to manœuvre and engage in mock combat, operations taken so seriously that casualties were not infrequent. Among the experts who assisted in these youthful experiments were Patrick Gordon, a Scotsman, and François Lefort, a native of Geneva. It was the latter who did most to arouse in Peter's mind an absorbing interest in the mechanical achievements of western Europe and a great desire to travel outside the frontiers of Russia. By the time he was twenty-one Peter had established a shipbuilding yard at Arkhangel and had laid the foundations of a national army organized on scientific principles.

The overthrow of Sophia was not accompanied by any change in foreign policy. Peter was fired with the ambition of fighting the Turks as the hereditary enemies of his house and religion, the rivals also of Russia for control of the Black Sea. The immediate object of Peter's ambition was the capture of Azov, against which two expeditions were launched; the first in 1695, consisting of 30,000 men, was a failure, but Peter redoubled his efforts, sought help from practically every European country except France, erected great shipbuilding yards on the Don, and in 1696 headed another expedition which took Azov. This success was overestimated, but it encouraged the Tsar to persevere in his work of making Russia powerful by the reorganization of her army and fleet and the introduction of western methods into her society and government.[47] The possession of Azov was confirmed to Russia by the treaty of Karlowitz.

In 1697 Peter, leaving behind him a Boiar regency, made his first journey into western Europe, visiting north Germany, Holland, England and Austria. Numerous are the contemporary accounts of the sensation caused by the oriental magnificence and curious ways of the Tsar and his suite.[48] In

[47] Zinkeisen, op. cit. v. 186-200.
[48] For a bibliography of these see Mintzlof, Pierre le Grand dans la littérature étrangère (1872).

Holland he acquired some knowledge of many crafts, from shipbuilding to engraving, always insisting on performing each process for himself and showing eager, if sometimes transient interest in every mechanical process or contrivance brought to his notice. He added to his accomplishments the art of extracting teeth, his suite providing ample material for amateur practice. Crossing to England, he worked in the shipbuilding yard at Deptford, interesting himself in the London of William III., amusing and amazing a populace unaccustomed to the sight of royal workmen in the yards. In January 1698 he was back in Holland and proceeded to Vienna, where he expounded to the emperor his views on the war again the Turks. The news that the *Streltsi* had revolted in his absence caused Peter to hurry home, though it meant the abandonment of some of his plans. During his travels, all the forces of reaction in Russia had combined against him; his nautical experiments, his foreign advisers, his shaven chin had all alienated the orthodox or "raskolnik" opinion, and even his permission of smoking was an article of accusation against him, for smoking was obviously referred to in the scriptural maxim: "Not that which goeth into a man but that which cometh out defileth him." Peter's travels had completed the list of his offences. The *Streltsi* were not slow to take advantage of this outcry and of the freedom in which the Tsar's absence left them. They negotiated with the ex-Tsarina Sophia, then imprisoned in a monastery, and though defeated by the loyal troops, they still held out, with the avowed object of substituting the rule of Sophia for that of Peter.

On his return Peter determined to have done with a bodyguard which had never been more than a corporation of assassins and had now added high-treason to its sins. In the winter of 1698–9 the strength of the Imperial executioners was so overtaxed that Peter himself had to lend a hand; soon there were few *Streltsi* left for the knout and Siberia. *"Rien n'avance les choses comme les exécutions."* The walls of the Kremlin were decorated with the mortal remains of this one time *corps d'élite,* and outside the monastery where Sophia was immured were suspended the frozen bodies of *Streltsi,* one of them supporting in his mouth the petition in which they had invited her to reassume the crown.[49]

49 Lavisse et Rambaud, *Histoire générale*, vi. 694.

Now that his rule was firmly established, Peter proceeded quickly with the reforms on which he had set his heart.[50] In 1702 an Imperial Edict was promulgated inviting foreigners into Russia, assuring them of religious and legal independence, and offering special advantages to engineers, artisans, teachers and doctors. At the same time, contingents of young Russians were sent to western Europe for instruction; to Venice and Holland for shipbuilding; to England for industry and crafts; to France and Austria for military science; to Germany for medicine. Peter's choice of foreign advisers showed the same eclecticism: Gordon and Bruce were Scotsmen and soldiers; Lefort, the admiral, came from Geneva; Ostermann, a skilful diplomatist and informal Secretary of State for Foreign Affairs, was a German. The families of Matveef, Cheremetief, Apraxine, Golovine, Galitsine, Dolgorouki and Kourakine provided native administrators. Peter's reforms were introduced gradually; they were prepared for by a certain amount of education and were enforced by stringent legislation. He forbade the traditional Russian dress and was specially vindictive against beards, which, with two-fingered benedictions symbolised the old reactionary and semi-Asiatic Russia. With his own hands he unbearded the most venerable members of his entourage and supplied the customs houses with scissors for use on all bearded traffickers. Peter insisted on at least the externals of western civilization.

Governing at first by the Douma of Boiars, Peter in 1700 dispensed with this institution and ruled thereafter with the assistance of a Chancery. Supreme justice and control of the financial administration were vested in a small Senate, established in 1711, a body which afterwards controlled the levy and equipment of troops and became the principal medium through which the absolutist rule of Peter was exercised. In 1715 was introduced the system of government by *Collegia*, recruits for which were at first drawn mainly from Swedish prisoners of war. The *Collegia* acted as ministerial departments, each with a clearly defined sphere of activity. For the purpose of provincial administration Russia was divided into twelve governments controlled by governors and forty-three provinces headed by *Voievodes*. The governors were appointed from St. Petersburg, but they were

---

[50] The best short account of these is in Rambaud, *Histoire de la Russie*, ch. xxiv. See also Nisbet Bain, *The Pupils of Peter the Great* and *Slavonic Europe*, ch. xiv.

responsible also to the provincial *Landraths,* members of which were elected by the local landowners. In municipal affairs the same German influence is clearly manifest. Corporations were instituted, burgomasters and councillors were elected, and the *Rathaus* became the seat of muncipal activity.

Similarly, the whole ecclesiastical system was reformed. After 1700 the office of Patriarch lapsed, and in 1721 the powers of the Patriarch were transferred to a Holy Synod, entrusted with the work of reforming the lower clergy and supressing the grosser forms of superstition. Peter had early in his reign turned his attention to the enormous revenues of the monasteries, and he determined that these should come under state control. In 1702 an inquisition was made of all monastic property; surplus revenue was confiscated and devoted to education and the care of invalid soldiers. At the same time an attempt was made to control the number of persons, whether men or women, taking the monastic vows. Moreover it should be noted that Peter's policy of encouraging the immigration of skilled workers and professional men was made possible only by a system of toleration, from which, however, Jews and Jesuits were excluded, and in which religious propaganda was forbidden. The "Raskolniks"[51] were suppressed only if they added political activities to religious intolerance.

One of Peter's most important reforms was that whereby he made the Russian nobility official and subservient instead of, as before, aristocratic and independent. Landholding was once more linked with state service, whether in a military or civil capacity. There was no longer any allodial land and, as in the France of Louis XIV., all property was regarded as held on lease from the king and therefore involving duties as well as rights. A clearly differentiated social hierarchy, based on the German model, was created by the official "Table of Ranks," which defined all the civil ranks, with their military and naval equivalents. Moreover the introduction of the principle of primogeniture into landholding was intended, by securing the inheritance to one descendant, to maintain a prosperous landholdng class and to encourage the landless members of the aristocracy to enter the Imperial service.

For the peasants, Peter did little. Their heterogeneous tenures had been gradually fused into a common serfdom; they were declared liable to a capitation tax and they could

[51] The adherents to the old, pre-Nikonian faith.

not leave their lord's service. Among these serfs were many men originally free, some of whom could even trace a noble descent. Peter's edict requiring that when serfs were sold they should, as far as possible, be sold in families and not simply as heads of cattle, was passed for a humanitarian object, but it reveals the depths to which the Russian peasant had sunk at a period not so very remote from our own. Except by the church there was no means whereby a serf could emancipate himself. Moreover the landless, rightless peasant had to bear a very heavy share of taxation.

The financial system of Russia was completely remodelled in this enterprising reign. Peter was implacable towards officials convicted of malversation, and for embezzlement he sometimes inflicted the death penalty without respect to rank. Many new taxes were imposed and all exemptions were rescinded; salt, tobacco, stamped paper, public and private baths, coffins, cabmen and beards were all exploited for purposes of national revenue. Inns, fisheries and local customs rights were monopolized on behalf of the Tsar; but more natural sources of wealth were not neglected, for sheep were introduced and, with them, a cloth industry. Carpets and leather were manufactured (with foreign assistance), and landowners were encouraged to develop the natural resources of their estates. Agricultural instruments were improved; the culture of the vine, the mulberry and the tobacco plant was started in the south-east, and an attempt was made to improve the breed of cattle. The aim of all these reforms was to make Russia self-supporting and to limit imports to those indispensable raw materials that could not be produced at home. The shipbuilding industry was treated with special solicitude; Arkhangel and St. Petersburg became great ports, and the Black Sea was linked up with the Baltic by a canal system connecting the Volga and the Neva through Lake Ladoga. A new currency was introduced to replace the old and clumsy coinage. As a result of all these reforms Peter was able to form a national army of 200,000 men, and a fleet consisting of nearly 50 vessels of the line with about 800 smaller vessels and a personnel of 20,000 men.

It was because a Baltic sea coast was so essential for Russia that he carried on his campaigns against Sweden and Charles XII. with great vigour; in 1703 he began the building of St. Petersburg at the mouth of the Neva. The supply of labour and building material for the new captial was ensured by prohibiting the construction of buildings elsewhere in Russia. A large population was introduced into the city as it gradually took shape, and the greater landowners were required to have a house in the city. As the seat of the Imperial government, St. Petersburg displaced inland Moscow, and from it were diffused those Western influences of which Peter was himself so enthusiastic an exponent. Clothes were cut to the German fashion and the women were brought out from the isolation of the "terem" to play their part in civilized society. The Calendar was reformed; books were printed in modern Russian type; a School of Painting was started and the beginnings were made of a Natural History Collection. Hospitals and laboratories sprang up; explorers were subsidized and in 1724 the Russian Academy of Sciences was instituted. Peter had found Russia a half-barbarous, half-Asiatic country; he freed it from the continual menace of invasion, and turned it to face the West rather than the East. Like Sweden, Russia in this period experienced a decline in population,[52] but unlike Sweden, Russia had great natural resources which soon counterbalanced this loss.

Peter's reforms were not the result of co-ordinated policy, applied at one stroke, but rather a series of hasty improvisations, sometimes defeating their own object, but resulting eventually in the creation of a powerful military state on the European model. The changes affected only a small part of the population, for they were mostly limited to the governing and administrative classes. Their effects may be briefly summarised as follows. First, there was created a privileged, noble class, in which civil rank was graduated to correspond with military rank. Secondly, the necessity of obtaining local bodies for co-operation in fiscal administration led to the development of the towns, which Peter regarded as partners in his economic schemes. Thirdly, the practice of sending youths abroad for their education resulted in the evolution of a cosmopolitan and sometimes brilliant *intelligentsia*, though little was done to supplement the work of the monastic schools in evolving a system of national education. Lastly, and not because of any intention on Peter's part, the peasants were reduced to serfdom, mainly because the state ceased to intervene between landlord and cultivator. Although only indirectly and partially connected with Peter's reforms, this proved one of the most baleful elements in the later history of Russia.

[52] Milioukov, *Histoire de Russie*, I. 315-17.

by prohibiting the construction of buildings elsewhere in
Russia. A large population was introduced into the city as it
gradually took shape, and the greater landowners were required to have a house in the city. As the seat of the imperial
government, St. Petersburg displaced inland Moscow, and
from it were diffused those Western influences of which Peter

was the apostle. It was not the court alone, though much
was done to supplement the work of the monastic schools in
evolving a system of national education. Luckily, and not because of any intention on Peter's part, the peasants were reduced to serfdom, mainly because the state ceased to intervene between landlord and cultivator. Although only indirect
and partial, connected with Peter's reforms, this proved
one of the most hopeful elements in the later history of Russia.

Chapter 13

Conclusion

AS THEY BECOME more self-conscious, civilizations make increasing use of phrases for the description of preceding periods of social evolution. Of this terminology, two examples are the word Feudalism, applied to the social structure of western Europe in the centuries between the eleventh and the fifteenth, and the phrase Ancien Régime, used of the social polity which, emerging from the reformations of the sixteenth century, was eventually extinguished by the revolutions of the years 1789–1848. Such affixing of labels has its uses, so long as it is recognized that the labels mean no more than the findings of posterity in regard to certain epochs of the past. It has been claimed in this book that the system which we know as the Ancien Régime was consolidated and applied in the seventeenth century; it was defined thus in the eighteenth by the great jurist Blackstone:[1]

> Had not a separate property in lands as well as movables been vested in certain individuals, the world would have continued a forest, and men would have been mere animals of prey. . . . Necessity begat property; and, in order to ensure that property, recourse was had to civil society, which which brought with it a long train of inseparable concomitants—states, governments, laws, punishments. . . .

[1] Sir William Blackstone, *Commentaries on the Laws of England,* 1765–1769, ed. H. J. Stephen, 1853, l. 152 ff.

Thus connected together, it was found that a part only of society was sufficient to provide, by their manual labour, for the necessary subsistence of all; and leisure was given to others to cultivate the human mind, to invent useful arts, and to lay the foundations of science.

Certain points emerge from this description. Property precedes the Person; the main function of the state is to safeguard the former, leaving the latter to take its chance. In the exercise of this function the state has to apply laws and punishments, and the criterion of a well-ordered state is the effectiveness of its measures for the protection of property. There were further implications. What we now call personal status was assessed in relation to ownership, usually of freehold land, so that the societies of the Ancien Régime may be said each to have had a hard core, consisting of the privilege or monopoly derived from possessions, round which there was formed an increasingly large zone of men without property, and therefore without rights. In Blackstone's description, these rightless men provide the manual labour necessary for the subsistence of the state. He might well have added two important facts about them, first, that they were a great majority, and second, that they were mostly obliged to sacrifice themselves in war by enforced service. The civilization which Blackstone had in mind was a very high one; it was made possible only by this organization of humanity. Throughout, the disagreeable word slavery is avoided.

The institutions of seventeenth-century Europe provide abundant illustration of the accuracy of Blackstone's analysis. Political power was exercised mainly on the basis of ownership of land. Not that landed possessions brought wealth; indeed, the process was often the reverse, for the man who had made a fortune in trade or in lucrative public office was likely to purchase an estate which, in its turn, would lead to a title of nobility, and with it, a large measure of local influence, or a place in the councils of the state. The external symbol of this landed power was the great house. The seventeenth century was not so distinguished as its successor for the magnificent scale of its buildings; but the way was being prepared; and, by the end of the century, the palace of Versailles[2] provided a model for imitation. A later age may envy or con-

---

[2] Good accounts will be found in P. de Nolhac's *La Création de Versailles* (1901) and *Histoire du château de Versailles* (1911).

demn such ostentation; but it must be conceded that the palace, like the cathedral, gave scope for the designer of genius, and provided a heritage that can be enjoyed by posterity; moreover, the contents of these great houses, often selected with discernment, were the product of a system whereby the artist was encouraged to work for a patron, whose taste has many times proved to be far better than that of the public.

Second in importance to the great landed proprietors were the professions, of which the first in precedence were the clergy. It was characteristic that the most eminent among them, the archbishops and bishops, were themselves great landowners, in so far as they derived much of their revenues from rents; and this secular element, which tended to supersede their spiritual functions, was emphasized by the extensive, often vexatious jurisdiction which they exercised. In this secularizing process the Papacy had taken the lead; in consequence, most of the higher clergy were regarded not as Christians but as potentates. Sincerity was usually a fatal quality in a bishop. Next in order was the military caste of officers recruited, with few though notable exceptions, from the nobility and gentry, on the assumption that they derived their valour from birth. Then, after a long gap, came the lawyers and, beneath them, the physicians, both representative of the learned professions. To these must be added a newcomer—the ambassador. Ambassadors are as old as recorded history; but it was in the seventeenth century, with its more extensive negotiations and great peace settlements, that their numbers increased to such an extent as to warrant their inclusion in the professions, together with a numerous diplomatic personnel. The ambassador was thus defined by a contemporary:[3] "The ambassador should, to some extent, be a comedian. . . . There is no theatre more famous than a Court; there is no comedy where the actors disguise themselves more than do ambassadors in the act of negotiating." Earlier in the century he had been defined as one who is sent abroad "to *lie* for the benefit of his country." It need hardly be added that the ambassador was almost always a man of high birth —sometimes so high that the ruler might find it expedient to get rid of him by sending him on an embassy. Nominally a messenger of peace, he was recognized as an "honourable

[3] Le Sieur de Wicquefort, *L'Ambassadeur et ses fonctions*, 2 vols., first ed. 1679, 11, section I.

spy," in which capacity he might corrupt the ministers of the Court to which he was accredited.[4]

In all these professions, the essential element was either entry by right of birth, or initiation by some measure of training, usually accompanied by purchase of an office or obtaining a license; in all cases there was exercise of a monopoly, usually within the privileges and duties of some corporate institution endowed with the sacrosanct rights of property. Constrasted with them were the humbler members of these professions—the village curé, hardly distinguishable from the peasants whom he served; the penurious clerk, or notary, or subordinate court official, hanging on grimly to a black-coat profession; the apothecary, or vendor of herbs, encroaching on the preserves of the physician; the surgeon, or bone-setter, still no more than a craftsman. As for the ordinary soldiers and sailors, they were not of the lower professional classes at all, for they were drawn, often forcibly, from the vast reservoir of rightless men.

This element of monopoly extended to the towns, where the gild system, though in decay, still survived. Apprenticeship to a craft was the normal preliminary to the status of qualified or "free" worker; the "freedom" of a town could be acquired by the emancipation which followed completion of the bondage of apprenticeship, or, in some cases, by marriage with the daughter of a "freeman." The system, a medieval survival, ensured both a high standard of workmanship and the exclusion of all strangers or newcomers who had not qualified according to the rules. This description of an exclusive, self-conscious bourgeoisie can be applied, with different qualifications, to the cities and towns of western Europe throughout the duration of the Ancien Régime. Rising in the social scale was another townsman, the merchant, particularly the merchant engaged in international trade. He might combine his merchandising with shipowning, or banking or moneylending, occupations not yet clearly differentiated.

It will have been noticed that in this summary enumeration of the main classes of men in the Ancien Régime, the words "bondage" and "emancipation" have been used. In the civilization of Europe in the seventeenth and eighteenth centuries slavery was never far off. Much of the economy of the more enterprising states was based on the slave trade and on the institution of slavery in the plantations. The coloured slave

[4] *Ibid.* 11, section IX.

was an article of property, and before there could be any question of emancipation, property rights had to be compensated. But this institution of ownership in human flesh and blood extended far beyond the confines of negro slavery. It was applied to the woman, whose status was only in process of emancipation from the Old Testament conception of ownership; it included the wards and minors of landed families, whose well-being and marriages might be the subject of barter and sale by their custodians. It was, however, in the vast reservoir of unskilled and unorganized labour that this approximation to slavery was most clearly evidenced. One of the most widely-accepted principles of the Ancien Régime was that the wages of the hired worker must be beaten down to the lowest level, not so much of subsistence, as of survival, for cheap labour was thought to mean cheap goods, and only with such commodities could a trading state hold its own in competitive world trade. The white labourer at home was thus the counterpart of the black labourer abroad.

Nor was this conception limited to the labour market. In some ancient civilizations, the debtor might become the slave of the creditor. Of this, there is an echo in the widespread institution of imprisonment for debt. By what seems like a curious inconsistency, the state insisted on maintaining the debtor in custody, not as a punishment, but as some kind of security for the creditor who, *from our point of view,* would have been more likely to recover his debt if the debtor had been left free to earn his living. Here perhaps is a case of marginal or abortive slavery, arising from violation of a property right. Constantly this right takes precedence over personal right. In England, where the high level of public order was sometimes attributed to the savage punishments by which property was protected, there was no law against the abduction of a landless woman. But it was otherwise if she were an heiress to freehold property, or leasehold of a certain value, for then the penalty, on conviction, was death. The pressing of sailors into naval service was only one degree less harsh in France than in England; but at least Englishmen were spared the horrors inflicted on French "criminals" in what was probably the most cruel of all forms of slavery—that of the galleys. "Criminals"—not in our sense of the word, for the term included many who had offended against the iniquitous salt regulations, and Huguenots who tried to escape after the Revocation.

"Trade is the source of finance, and finance is the vital nerve of war." On the international side, the economic assumptions of the Ancien Régime have been given the label Mercantilism, and these words of Colbert,[5] addressed to his cousin at the naval base of Rochefort, provide one of the maxims of the system. In the seventeenth century Mercantilism, if the phrase may be permitted, assumed different forms in different countries, and changed somewhat in principle before the century closed. Briefly, it may be described as a system of control, exercised over the industry and the overseas or international trade of a state, in such a way as to produce the maximum of wealth as the basis of power. Property, which secured status at home, might ensure domination abroad. At first there was a tendency to limit wealth to bullion, and nations competed with each other for the precious metals, of which Spain, in the sixteenth century, had a near monopoly; but, after the Revolution of 1688 and during William III.'s war with France, this conception was extended to include credit and paper money. Only thus indeed could England have held her own with richer and more populous France. In both countries the abuse of credit led to the financial scandals of the South Sea Bubble and the Mississippi Scheme; but, in spite of these set-backs, wealth continued to be distinguished from money, and came to be associated with exploitation of the natural resources of the state.

Bearing in mind that the mainspring of the Mercantilist policy was pursuit of power, it may now perhaps be concluded that the Free Trade episode of the nineteenth century was no more than a diversion from the usual course; and that in the twentieth century, with our exchange controls, our regulation of imports and exports, our "hard currency" and "soft currency" areas, we have reverted to a more normal system, intended to provide security as well as a high standard of living. All that this implies is that Mercantilism may not have been such a distinctive and uniform system as is often assumed. Accepting it as a system, however, its application differed greatly with circumstances, and sometimes found expression in measures not obviously economic. Thus in Catholic countries, such as France and, later, Austria, these measures might be anti-clerical, in so far as the system was opposed to celibacy, and the immuring in cloisters of many men

[5] In 1666. E. F. Heckscher, *Mercantilism*, English translation 1935, 11, 17.

and women who might otherwise be engaged in useful work. That the unenfranchised should be constantly engaged in productive manual labour was the one principle common to all mercantilist states. There was also general agreement that shipping should be encouraged, particularly as, at that period, the wooden merchant ship could easily be converted into a warship. In this respect the Dutch gave the lead. Their timber was floated down to their well-organized ship-yards; they built on what we would call mass production principles; they modified design to suit the trade for which the ship was intended, and they saved on capital and labour by forming syndicates of relatives and friends; above all, they did not despise the ordinary seaman. In this way they captured many markets, but their success caused jealousy, and their insistent penetration provoked war.

Another characteristic of the system was the erection of companies for carrying on foreign trade in various parts of the world. In this respect the example given by England, France and the United Provinces was followed, at some distance, by other countries, such as Sweden, Denmark and Prussia. These companies differed greatly in organization, some approximating to a modern joint-stock company, while others were loose associations of merchants trading on their own account. Generally, however, it may be said that while in England a large measure of private initiative was allowed, in France state control was the rule; and the crown, usually a shareholder, might dictate what persons should be allowed or required to contribute.[6] These companies exported home manufactures in return for raw materials which were either unobtainable at home, or were capable of a further manufacture, such as dyeing; of the raw materials, sugar, tobacco and, later, cotton were of special importance, and, for long, the spices were as eagerly sought after as the precious metals. Of this trade the Dutch had succeeded in effecting an almost complete monopoly, their supplies being derived from the East Indies; but, later in the century, the relative importance of spices declined, mainly because, as the new grasses and root crops enabled the farmers to keep their cattle through the winter, the quality of the meat was improved, and so there was less need for spice. Also, the habit of smoking helped to disguise the odours which hitherto had necessitated the burning of cinnamon. Nevertheless, the Dutch still continued their

6 E. F. Heckscher, *op. cit.*, I. 346.

intense rivalry with the English for the slaves, gold and ivory of the west coast of Africa; they successfully contested English rights in the North Sea herring industry and in the Greenland whale fishing; their encroachments in North America and in the West Indies had to be met by Navigation Acts. In the Levant, the English company had to face the insistent and subsidized competition of the French. In Central and in a large part of South America Spain attempted to maintain a closed empire, to be entered only from the port of Seville (later, Cadiz); but this served only to stir the enterprise of the great maritime nations, and their determination to break into a monopoly was one of the causes of the Spanish Succession War.

Thus the wars of the seventeenth century, where they were neither religious nor dynastic, can be regarded as the logical outcome of an economic system which was nationalist, exclusive, competitive and aggressive.

Such, in very brief outline, was the property structure of the Ancien Régime. Slave and worker had long to wait before emancipation. But it was otherwise with human thought, in which this period witnessed an emancipation so complete that while, at the beginning of the century, we are still in a half-medieval world, by its close, we are impressed by a comparative freedom of intellectual enquiry, and a vast range of achievement which includes the names of Bacon, Descartes, Galileo, Huygens, Newton, Boyle, Spinoza and Leibnitz. It may be doubted whether any other period of similar length can boast such giants as these. But it will be noted that these men were mostly mathematicians, physicists and astronomers. Bacon, it is true, was out of touch with the achievements of experimental science in his own day, and Boyle's most notable achievements were in chemistry; but otherwise it may be held that the intellectual progress in our period was most marked in those sciences which have their basis in mathematics. Apart from anatomy and physiology, there was no comparable development in medicine or biology, possibly because the physician is dependent on accumulated clinical experience, such as was practically unknown in the past; moreover, medicine and biology have been revolutionized by comparatively modern inventions, such as the microscope. That it was not dependent on technical equipment may be one reason why, in ancient Greece and in seventeenth-century Europe, the advance in mathematics was so great. But, if there was not yet a microscope, there was some kind of refracting telescope, vastly improved in the course of the century by Galileo and Newton; and it was this close association between mathematical calculation and astronomical observation which led to the most brilliant results.

Not only was there unevenness in the rate of progress of the sciences, there was also a lack of clear differentiation among them. The antiquary, in the midst of his field work, might well become an amateur botanist or geologist; a geometrician like Descartes might seek to propound a method applicable to all the sciences; a virtuoso like Sir William Petty might combine, with some success, subjects so diverse as statistics, anatomy, music, surveying and naval architecture. The sciences were not yet completely dissociated from ethics and literature. Our modern specialization was preceded by a period of intellectual curiosity, to the exponents of which the French have given the name *Philosophes*, lovers of wisdom, a more suitable term than our modern words Philosophers, or Metaphysicians, with their more limited connotation.

Of the institutions which helped to encourage and direct this intellectual curiosity, the most influential were the academies and learned journals, which helped to bring learned men together and to spread their ideas. Two enlightened rulers of Tuscany founded in 1657 the *Academy of the Cimento*,[7] in which were conducted experiments mainly in physics and hydrostatics. A few years later, the Royal Society was founded in England, an institution which organized a remarkable band of men, many of them men of genius, all concerned, in different ways, with the exploration of the secrets of nature. Later, similar academies were established in Paris, Naples, Berlin and Moscow. In 1665 a scientific periodical, the *Journal des Savants*, began to appear in Paris, and provided a companion to the *Philosophical Transactions* of the Royal Society. Pierre Bayle's *Nouvelles de la République de Lettres*, which began to appear in 1684, had more than a literary significance, for its aim was to interest an educated public in the progress that was being made in every sphere of intellectual enquiry. By the time when the seventeenth century faded into the eighteenth, men could look back on intellectual triumphs as epoch-making as the discovery of new continents, with the assurance

[7] That is, Academy of Investigation. The best account of these academies in Italy is still that in G. Maugain, *Étude sur l'évolution intellectuelle de l'Italie, 1657–1750* (1909).

that this was no more than the dawn of a new era of exploration. This was particularly true of the English, French and Dutch. In Italy, where there were many men of acute intelligence, there was also the Inquisition.

The terrors of the Inquisition had already been vividly demonstrated in February 1600 by the burning of Giordano Bruno in the Roman Campo de' Fiori. Bruno,[8] born in 1548 near Naples, entered the Dominican Order. Dissatisfaction with the theology of his superiors caused him to leave his convent and native country for the life of a wandering scholar and teacher. His travels took him to France, England, Germany and Geneva. Everywhere he impressed contemporaries by the keenness of his intellect and the daring character of his conjectures, but his ardour and naïveté of temperament resulted in a lack of caution and restraint which eventually proved his undoing. Accepting the Copernican hypothesis, he had enough imagination to visualize what it implied—an infinite plurality of solar systems; immeasurable space, in which direction could be no more than relative; endless time, of which the Christian era was only an infinitesimal fragment, all this directed by an unseen cause far more majestic than the anthropomorphic deity whose solicitude was limited to one miserable planet. He was awed alike by the infinitely great and the infinitely small, proclaiming[9] that the complete destruction of the least particle of matter, the atom, might be followed by the destruction of the universe, an opinion which does not seem so strange now as it did then. An essentially religious man, because he had the spirit of reverence, Bruno evolved from his speculations a mystic and sublimated pantheism, such as was afterwards taught by Spinoza.

It can well be understood that these opinions provoked comment. Among his pupils was a young Venetian patrician of the Mocenigo family, who induced his teacher to stay with him in Venice, where he betrayed him to the Inquisition. Bruno's judges could hardly have understood the magnitude of his heresies, but they could appreciate some minor points, such as his scepticism about miracles, and his praise of that detested heretic, Elizabeth of England. Meanwhile, he was

[8] A. Riehl, *Giordano Bruno*, published in the tercentenary year 1900. A good English translation by Agnes Fry was published in 1905.

[9] *Ibid.* 74.

transferred to Rome, where there was no secular power to interfere with the spiritual tribunal; and there, after years of imprisonment, he was tried, convicted and executed by burning. Cardinal Bellarmine, afterwards to figure in the trial of Galileo, played a notable hand in this episode.

The episode was a warning that the Church would repress, with the utmost severity, anything that could be construed as a deviation from the accepted teaching of Aristotle and the Scriptures. Copernicus, it is true, had not been prosecuted, but then he was a canon of the Church; he had influential friends, and his hypothesis was not at first regarded as a refutation of the Ptolemaic system. There would be scant mercy for any experimenter or theorist who dared to make explicit what was implicit in much of the scientific thought of the later sixteenth century. This lesson was not lost on Galileo or Descartes, of whom the former was obliged to recant, while the latter took such care to avoid anything offensive to the theologians, that he incurred some discredit in a later and less inhibited age.

It was by experimental evidence that the Copernican theory was confirmed in the later years of the sixteenth and earlier years of the seventeenth century. To this enterprise, three astronomer-mathematicians made notable contributions—the Scandinavian Tycho Brahe (1546–1601), the German John Kepler (1571–1630) and the Florentine Galileo Galilei (1564–1642). Of these, the first two were connected as teacher and pupil, working in co-operation at Prague, where they served, in succession, as Imperial astronomers. With the help of his own and Brahe's observations, Kepler promulgated two laws of planetary motion in his *New Astronomy: . . . Commentaries on the Motions of Mars*[10] (1609). His third law, published in *The Harmonies of the World*[11] (1619), was to prove of profound significance in the search for a general theory of gravitation, because it proclaimed that the squares of the periods of planetary orbits are proportional to the cubes of their mean distances from the sun. In this way the Copernican system was ceasing to be a hypothesis; observation was confirming the truth of what had been condemned as fancy and error. It may be noted that the Prague of Brahe and Kepler was probably more tolerant of scientific research than any other European city, for there the emperor Rudolph,

[10] Prague.
[11] *Harmonices Mundi libri quinque . . .*, Linz.

in his periods of mental well-being, was actively engaged in the search for the philosophers' stone. Moreover, Tycho Brahe was an astrologer as well as an astronomer.

Galileo[12] was not so fortunate. No longer did the great citizens of Florence have the protection of a Lorenzo de' Medici. Professor of mathematics, first at Pisa and then at Padua, Galileo, with the help of an improved telescope of his own devising, was able to make a number of remarkable discoveries, including sun spots, four of the satellites of Jupiter, and the varying phases of Mercury, Venus and Mars. He conjectured that, with the help of a better telescope, the Milky Way would be resolved, for the spectator, into an enormous mass of stars. In 1610 Cosimo II., Grand Duke of Tuscany, appointed him his official mathematician and philosopher. But already the Dominicans, and even the Jesuits, were on his trail, and Cardinal Bellarmine was soon to find another victim. The long story of his trial and imprisonment has often been told. He was obliged to recant his assertion that the earth has a daily and annual motion, but his muttered *eppur' si muove* is the classic instance of yielding to authority, while retaining one's unshakeable convictions. The Copernican theory had been officially condemned by the Church in 1616, and in 1618 Kepler's *Epitome Astronomiae* was placed on the Index. In 1632 Galileo's theory of the Tides was repudiated in these words—he deduces the ebb and flow of the sea, which exist, from the immobility of the sun and the movement of the earth, which do not exist.

In the first three decades of the seventeenth century, the Church and the Peripatetics, or followers of Aristotle, had insisted on treating the advocates of the New Science as dangerous enemies, though there was nothing in their writings that would now be considered anti-religious or even anti-Catholic, for these men were quite different from the *A-Christi* and the Paduan agnostics of the sixteenth century. What appeared to be a frontal attack could easily be thwarted by the stake or the gaol. But it was otherwise when the citadel of the faith was entered by one who, equipped with full credentials, expounded a system which, logically applied, would infallibly result in blowing up the whole edifice. Dominicans like Bruno and Campanella[13] could be dismissed

[12] See G. de Santillana, *The Crime of Galileo*, 1955.

[13] Thomas Campanella (1568–1639), a native of Calabria, was a Dominican who criticized the Scholastic theology and favoured

as wild men who had gone off the rails; but it was not so easy to dispose of a brilliant pupil of the Jesuits who, like another great alumnus of the same society, Voltaire, led men to believe that the rails ought not to be there. This strange and uninvited bedfellow of the Church was no less than Descartes.

René Descartes[14] was born of a noble family in Touraine in 1596. He studied at the Jesuit College of La Flèche, served for a time as a soldier under Maurice of Nassau and the Duke of Bavaria, but decided to leave the military career in 1620. After several years of travel, in which he visited some of the most distinguished savants of his time, Descartes in 1629 settled in Holland in order to be away from distractions; with nothing but a busy commercial life around him he hoped to secure the concentration in his own thoughts and aloofness from disturbing influences which he regarded as necessary for philosophic inquiry. In 1637 he published his *Discourse of Method*; in 1641 appeared his more famous *Meditations*, in which he enunciated the principle *Cogito ergo sum* and attempted to establish the hypothesis of a deity from the fact of human consciousness and the existence of an idea of God. In 1650 he died at Stockholm when in the service of Christina of Sweden.

Like so many philosophers of his century, Descartes was a mathematician; he was also a physicist and astronomer, a biologist and an anatomist. He favoured the experimental method, and in metaphysics he insisted on eliminating all preconceptions, proceeding from complete scepticism to absolute certainty by deductive methods. Everything of an empirical nature he shunned; only that which "we clearly and distinctly perceive" can be true. Knowledge is therefore a process of deductive reasoning, in which we proceed from one certainty to another, as in the inevitable sequence of a geometrical demonstration. Consequently, Descartes rejected degrees of truth, nor had he any patience with the argument from Probability (this may have been a reaction against his Jesuit teachers at La Flèche), and, moreover, he insisted on eliminating all the mental processes which can be linked with bodily function, such as imagination and memory. Childhood he regarded

---

the experimental method. There is a good study of his career and opinions by L. Blanchet.

[14] The best short account of Descartes and his philosophy is that by A. Fouillée (Les Grands Écrivains français).

merely as a period of error, but a later generation was to find in it the potentialities of the poet.

While the negative element in Cartesianism can be easily grasped, its positive content is more difficult to determine. We all seek the truth; but, in argument, the word often proves to be no more than a question-begging term. Descartes appears to have thought of it as an absolute and linear quantity; in reality it often proves to be relative and multi-dimensional. Nevertheless, it is simpler and more popular to think of truth as both a definite and easily discoverable thing which, when found, cannot be mistaken for anything else; something to be discerned, not by men of learning, but by men of good sense, that is, by the great majority of ourselves. It was this appeal to common sense and the non-erudite that made the fortune of Cartesianism. Also, the new philosophy encouraged a more critical approach to matters wherein legend and tradition had hitherto prevailed. This can be traced in the changed attitude to the imaginative element; indeed, Boileau is said to have remarked that Descartes had cut the throat of poetry. He had certainly propounded a new Trinity, that of Nature, Reason, Truth; were not these the qualities soon to be eagerly sought after in the "age of reason" about to be established in western Europe? Boileau himself, who may have been prescient about the impact of Cartesianism on poetic art, was the codifier of rules for curbing and directing the imagination, just as his contemporary Colbert enunciated principles for the production of pictorial art with the same confidence as he laid down the rules for the production of cloth. Now, the "good sense," on which these regulations were based, is essentially a social quality, serving to unite a polite and educated minority in their privileged enclosure, safe from the mass of primitive and inarticulate men; theirs was the *recte sapere*, the instinctive sagacity which Horace had proclaimed to be the fountainhead of good speaking and good writing. It may therefore be conjectured that Cartesianism accorded well with the spirit of the Ancien Régime, since it provided a philosophy, much of it expressed in the vernacular, which appealed to all who, in their dread of "enthusiasm," valued the qualities of moderation and circumspection, so essential for the esteem of highly cultured contemporaries.

Cartesianism was regarded by contemporaries as a complete and conscious breach with the past, and in this sense it was the starting-point of modern metaphysics. This was evidenced in the doctrines of Spinoza.

The son of Portuguese-Jewish parents who had taken refuge in Holland, Benedict Spinoza was born at Amsterdam in 1632. Expelled from the synagogue for his agnostic opinions and shunned by his Jewish neighbours, Spinoza retired to an obscure neighbourhood, where he made a precarious living as an optician, devoting himself to meditation and philosophical investigation. He died of consumption at the age of forty-five. His best known works are a system of Ethics, a geometric exposition of Cartesianism and the *Tractatus theologico-politicus*. Spinoza's life was one of devotion to abstract speculation passed in poverty and neglect.

Like Descartes, Spinoza[15] reduced everything to thought and extension: to be free is to act in accordance with the laws of our own nature, and thus from the outset Spinoza develops the fatalism inherent in Cartesianism. He attacked the idea of a capricious, changeable God, a conception which he attributed to anthropomorphism; he condemned the popular view of immortality, regarding it as confusing eternity with time and resulting from imagination and memory, which, he held, do not survive the body. The immortality of Spinoza is one without memory, without consciousness of personal identity and varying in proportion as the soul can detach itself from worldly things for eternal things. Miracles he attributed to ignorance. His interpretation of the universe is pantheistic: there is one infinite substance—God, in whom are united the qualities of extension and thought; all finite beings are manifestations of this infinite substance, and all human thought is but an emanation of divine thought; consequently there is liberty in neither man nor God, since the one is a form of the other, and both are controlled by the immutable laws of nature. To realize these immutable laws is the purpose of metaphysics. The foundation of true religion is to know as much of God's nature as is necessary for obeying his decrees, the

---

[15] A convenient edition of his works is the French edition (ed. Garnier). A good study of Spinoza is that of S. Hampshire (Pelican series, 1951). See also *Correspondence of Spinoza translated and edited by A. Wolf*, 1928; A. Zweig, *The Living Thought of Spinoza*, 1939; Sir F. Pollock, *Spinoza*, 1935. The standard edition of his *Works* is that by C. Gebhardt, 4 vols., Heidelberg, 1926.

truth or falsity of dogmas mattering little. From this Spinoza deduced a universal religion based on the existence of a unique and omnipresent deity and identifying obedience to God with the qualities of justice and charity. In this universal religion, Christianity is only one of numerous cults.

Realization of our union with nature is thus one of the main objects of Spinoza's philosophy. From this he built up a system of ethics in which the grossest empiricism and the highest idealism were combined. Like Hobbes, he considered the good as that which we know to be beneficial to ourselves; virtue consists in the development of well-being; one should love oneself and pursue one's own interests. Consequently he approves all the passions that arise from joy and condemns those associated with sadness; pity, humility and repentance are in themselves of no value and must be spurned by the philosopher, but they may be useful in statecraft, for "the mob becomes dangerous when it knows no fear."[16] This is the link between his ethical and political theories.[17] Human society is possible only when human interests and passions have been adjusted by fear or reason. Whoever acts according to his nature is in his right, whether the act be reasonable or not; applying this principle to larger groups, it may be held that when several persons unite their wills by a voluntary surrender, this united will has greater power, therefore greater right. The united will is the government. In the state of nature there can be no sin: until defined by the government, there can be no such things as right or wrong. Property comes into existence only with law. Countries stand to each other in the state of nature, and alliances between them are binding only so long as the conditions remain static. Hence a state can observe or ignore a treaty according to its interests (a political truism in the seventeenth century). The soil of the country should be a common possession, the military forces of the state should consist of a citizen army with frequent changes in the personnel, patriotism is the highest virtue, religious truths are binding in so far as they have the authority of the government behind them. The safety of the state is the supreme consideration; might is the one criterion of right.[18] It is not a

[16] *Ethics*, iv. 54.

[17] These are expounded in the *Tractatus theologico-politicus*, chs. xvi.-xx.

[18] These views will be found mainly in chs. xix. and xx.

supernatural power but the secular state that makes a virtue: "it is not reason but authority that maketh a law."·

Readers of Hobbes will recognize the source of the last quotation.[19] Between the sage of Malmesbury and the philosopher of Amsterdam there are many points of contact. Both were mathematicians and agnostics, both were enemies of the theory of natural rights, both regarded the state as an artificial restraint on human passion; for both, religion provided a useful weapon for the lawgiver, each holding that the statesman can enforce on the mob a creed with which he himself need not be in agreement. Both thinkers, however, were looking in the direction of a more enlightened, more tolerant society than that in which they lived. In this *Tractatus theologico-politicus* (1670) Spinoza, having subjected the Old Testament to a criticism such as anticipated the most daring commentators of the nineteenth century, claimed that charity was the greatest social, as it was the greatest Christian virtue, because it imposes a high standard on our relations with our fellow men. Basing his state on this virtue, he argued that, once the laws were enunciated, and a simple religious formulary imposed, the subject should be free to maintain his own beliefs and to lead his own life, free from interference. Spinoza was thus proceeding in the direction of toleration which, in his view, could be realized not in a weak or divided state, but only in a strong and secular state. Such a state would keep the theologians in their place and would protect one sect from another. The *Tractatus* was condemned by the States General, and was placed on the Roman Index.

It is not difficult to understand why in his own and the succeeding age Spinoza was regarded as an atheist. That Lessing should have been one of his devoted readers seemed, even late in the eighteenth century, matter for scandal, but with the Romantic Revival the poetic and idealist elements in his teaching were at last realized. Poets like Novalis were attracted to him because his was the God of nature; Goethe could appreciate the *Ethics*, because it calmed his passions by mathematical precision and detachment of thought.[20] A complete edition of his works was published for the first time in 1802. The nineteenth century has maintained this revived interest in

[19] *A Dialogue of the Common Law* (in Hobbes' English Works, ed. Molesworth, vi.).
[20] See the earlier part of *Dichtung und Wahrheit*.

Spinoza; his influence can be detected in Schelling, and Hegel[21] defended him against the accusation of atheism by pointing out that he had destroyed the existence of the world as an aggregate of finite things, leaving only God. Perhaps the most eloquent tribute to him is that by Schleiermacher[22]—"He was penetrated by the spirit of the universe: the infinite was his beginning and end, the universal his one and only love. Alone and unequalled he had no disciples and no city."

Like Spinoza, Pascal[23] was neglected or misunderstood by the eighteenth century and not rediscovered until the nineteenth. Leibnitz, Voltaire and Condorcet lacked the finer qualities necessary for the appreciation of Pascal; in the age of Deism and the rationalists there could be no place for the great solitary of Port-Royal, and not till the discovery by Rousseau that "the heart has its reasons which the mind cannot understand"[24] was it realized that, in Pascal, France had produced perhaps her greatest genius. It was Chateaubriand[25] who was first roused to enthusiasm by the *Pensées*, and later years have witnessed a steady increase in the reputation of Pascal not only in France but in Europe. In proportion as formal and dogmatic theology loses its force, men will turn to the *Pensées*, because they depict how one of the keenest thinkers in the seventeenth century attemptd to satisfy the questionings of intelligence, not by surrender to authority nor by stifling of doubt, but by the application of deductive processes to the data of personal experience.

Selection or description would fail to give an adequate conception of Pascal's greatest work, because it consists of "a mass of convergent proofs"[26] and consequently quotation is neither easy nor just. Not till recently was the task of arranging the order of the *Pensées* even attempted, and it must be remembered that in them we have merely a sketch of what was to be a carefully considered book. But even thus they

[21] *Geschichte der Philosophie*, iii. 373.

[22] Quoted by Bouillier, i. 404.

[23] There is a very large literature on Pascal. Of English books, consult the studies by H. F. Stewart and Viscount St. Cyres. Of the French monographs, see those by E. Boutroux and F. Strowski. The best edition of the *Pensées* is that by Brunschvicg (Hachette). See also Sainte-Beuve, *Port-Royal*, vol. ii.

[24] Boutroux, *Pascal*, 197.

[25] In his *Génie du christianisme*.

[26] H. F. Stewart, *The Holiness of Pascal*, 53.

form one of the most important pieces of constructive work in the whole range of apologetics, and they will continue to be read so long as there are men sufficiently intelligent to doubt, and with enough of the spiritual in their temperaments to make them long for the repose of faith. What the *Pensées* give us is "a cumulation of probabilities, independent of each other, arising out of the nature and circumstances of the case, probabilities too fine to avail separately, too subtle and circuitous to be convertible into syllogisms, too numerous and various for such conversion, even were they convertible."[27] But it is possible that Pascal will be remembered more for his scientific achievements than for his somewhat finely drawn speculations in Christian apologetics.

If Descartes was the greatest intellectual force of seventeenth-century France, Leibnitz[28] was the greatest of seventeenth-century Germany. Son of a professor of philosophy at Leipzig, where he was born in 1646, he was a doctor of laws at the age of twenty and was taken into the service of Boyneburg, Chancellor of the Elector of Mainz. As the tutor of Boyneburg's son he spent some time in Paris (1672–1676), where he devoted himself to mathematical pursuits with such distinction that he was elected a member of the French Academy and of the English Royal Society. On the death of the Elector of Mainz he accepted the post of librarian to the Duke of Brunswick and took up his residence in Hanover. Philosophy, science and history were now engaging his attention, and in 1683 he founded the journal *Acta Eruditorum*, in order to redeem German learning from the accusation that it had no periodical. For some years after 1687 he was engaged with the more lucrative but less profitable task of writing the history of the Brunswick family, but this he had to leave unfinished. Fortunately he was able to continue his travels, keeping up his correspondence with the chief European savants including Bossuet, and occupying himself with the problem of uniting the Catholic with the Protestant faiths. In 1700 he induced the Elector of Brandenburg to found the Academy of Berlin, of which he was elected president; but he failed to establish similar institutions at Dresden or Vienna.

[27] Newman, *Grammar of Assent*. Quoted by Stewart, *op. cit.* 53.
[28] There is a brilliant though difficult study of Leibnitz as philosopher and mathematician by Bertrand Russell. Leibnitz's other activities are the subjects of numerous monographs. His bulky *Œuvres* have been edited by Foucher de Careil and Onno Klopp.

Throughout his long life Leibnitz continued to make important contributions to science, mathematics, theology, history and jurisprudence: his mind was of the encyclopaedic order and his learning was wedded to practical and even humanitarian activities. He died at Hanover in 1716 at the age of seventy.

To do justice to the many-sided output of Leibnitz would require more space than is here at command. He united qualities rarely found together: he was both speculative and practical; a master of induction and generalization as well as an erudite and patient scholar; a believer and a daring innovator. He shares with Newton the honour of having discovered the infinitesimal calculus; he outlined a new scheme for the study of law, and hoped that on the treaty of Westphalia would be founded a new international jurisprudence. He tried to divert the bellicose energies of Louis XIV. to the Orient by depicting Egypt as the Holland of the East—a proposal[29] read by Napoleon after his Egyptian campaign. Associated with the scheme known as the League of the Rhine, he dreamed for a time of perpetual peace, though, with disillusionment, he had to confess that the words perpetual peace can be affixed only over the doors of cemeteries.[30] He educated and led German feeling against the activities of Louis XIV. and, had his representations been listened to, France would not have escaped so lightly in the treaty of Utrecht.[31] Patriot, philosopher, historian and mathematician, Leibnitz was the most universal genius of his age. In only two respects did he show a lack of enlightenment. He approved the use of torture in criminal proceedings and he retained some faith in astrology.

Leibnitz was an idealist in the sense that he saw in philosophy an interpretation of divine thought; for him, human reason is the imitation of the logic of God. Reason, therefore, has an authority independent of experience. Opposed alike to the pantheism of Spinoza and the empiricism of Locke, he built up an interpretation of the universe on a theory of matter known as "monadology." As a working hypothesis, the

[29] The *Projet de conquête de l'Égypte* in *Œuvres,* vol. v.

[30] For his attitude to projects of perpetual peace see *Œuvres,* iv. 325.

[31] *Paix d'Utrecht inexcusable . . . une lettre à un milord Tory* in *Œuvres,* iv. He considered that the Allies ought to have held out longer, as Marlborough and Eugène were on the point of invading France.

monads are a compromise between substance and idea, they are atoms capable of action and perception; the soul is a monad which has consciousness of itself. Believing in a pre-determined harmony between the activities of the human soul and body, Leibnitz in his *Théodicée* outlined an optimistic rationalism, teaching that among an infinity of possible worlds, God had made the best. On this theory, the soul is absolutely free from all external constraint, and its immortality is guaranteed by the fact of its independence and imperishable individuality. "Every soul," he declared, "is a world in itself, as durable and absolute as the universe, which it represents from its own point of view. Its existence provides a fresh proof of the existence of a God, since this perfect accord must be due to a great and intelligent first cause." In theology, Leibnitz argued the rational possibility of revelation and miracles;[32] the doctrine of the Eucharist he considered perfectly tenable and, though by profession a Protestant, he was credited in his lifetime with being a secret adherent to Catholic doctrines.[33] But his real theological opinions are difficult to determine. As an ethical teacher he believed that contemplation should be directed to the beauty and perfection of the future life, and that piety, so far from being morbid or pessimistic, should be hopeful and serene. The great moral teachers of the past had each, in his view, been awarded a share of truth; by selecting the best of them, philosophy becomes eclectic and continues its progress towards a permanent and satisfying interpretation of life.

Thus the keynote of Leibnitz' thought is optimism. Though he has nothing startlingly new to proclaim, he offers an alternative to the cultured but sometimes cynical epicureanism of Montaigne and his school, as well as providing something more human and attractive than the cold deistic rationalism of Descartes or the dispassionate pantheism of Spinoza. If he thought mainly in mathematical terms, he was something more than a mere analyst, his speculations having a practical and beneficent object. He looks as much to the future[34] as the past, and was perhaps alone in his opinion that much was

---

[32] For this see J. Duproix, *Raison et foi d'après Leibnitz.*

[33] He corresponded with Bossuet and Pellisson on the project of reunion between Protestant and Catholic.

[34] He believed that Europe was threatened with a great Revolution, and in one of his Essays refers to "la révolution générale dont l'Europe est menacée" (*Œuvres*, II. lxvii.).

still to be gained from the interchange of ideas between East and West.[35] In philosophy, mathematics and medicine discoveries of importance might, he held, have been made in China of which western Europe had no comprehension, consequently he attached great importance to Russia as the link with the East. He thought that, with a revived interest of western Europe in Russian studies, much might be learned of philology and ethnography which would throw light on the migrations of European races from the Eastern steppes.[36] He had hoped that Peter the Great would assist Germany as an ally against France in the Spanish Succession War; he saw in Russia the great bulwark against the barbarism of the Turk and never abandoned the idea that in its energetic ruler he might find a leader in the march of civilization. England and Holland he blamed because they were wrapped in their commercial enterprises and indifferent to ideals. Throughout his life Leibnitz was anxious to find a great ruler who would share his enthusiasm and give effect to his proposals, for like so many of his immediate successors in philosophy, he believed that social amelioration must come from the efforts of the enlightened ruler rather than from the initiative of the self-interested populace. If the Tsar and the Emperor would but unite their forces,[37] how much might be achieved not only for the peace of Europe but for the civilization of the world! But the Hapsburg and Romanoff who listened with interest to these proposals were themselves the victims of circumstance, and the cause of progress benefited little at their hands.

The constructive thinking of the seventeenth-century philosophers had thus broken European thought from the twin fetters of authoritative scholasticism and imitative humanism, in this way making possible the unshackled speculation of the eighteenth century, and eventually leading men to question the fundamental principles underlying the organization of society known as the Ancien Régime. The philosophical preceded the political revolution; the lead was given not by the

---

[35] For this see W. Guerrier, *Leibnitz in seinen Beziehungen zu Russland und Peter dem Grossen.* Leibnitz believed that the spread of science was associated with the spread of Christianity, and so drew up a collection of reports of missionary work in China. In the preface to this (the *Novissima Sinica*) he expressed the opinion that China and Europe were to be the scenes of the world's greatest achievements (Guerrier, 22 ff.).

[36] Guerrier, 149.

[37] Guerrier, 158, and *Œuvres,* iv.

statesmen but by the thinkers; the old order disappeared from the domains of abstract and scientific speculation long before it was even questioned in the realm of politics. The seventeenth century witnessed two things: a strengthening of absolutist theories of the state in every European country except England and Poland, and a great revolution in human thought. The first of these has been the main subject of this volume; the second is the theme of this chapter.

But, while it would be difficult to exaggerate the importance of the scientific and philosophic revolution in the history of human thought, it is easy to over-estimate its repercussions on seventeenth-century society. After all, these intellectual movements affect only a small section of humanity; in civilization, as in nature, there is, fortunately, a force of inertia which resists sudden change. Moreover, with the possible exception of Spinoza, all the great scientists and metaphysicians of the century, whether from conviction or policy, took care to avoid giving offence to the theologians; and the greatly enlarged universe of their speculations, with its infinite first cause, was at least more awe-inspiring than the more limited cosmology of Ptolemy. Man still remained a dignified being, clearly distinguished, in origin and destiny, from all other living things; indeed, it was on this unquestioned assumption that theology was based. True, some of the poets—always the most percipient of mortals—perceived that the difference between humanity and the animal creation is not so great after all; and La Fontaine, the fabulist, deduced this lesson from nature, that the less we are at the mercy of the fangs of other men, the better. But he was only a fabulist, and what seemed merely poetic fancy was not embodied in a scientific treatise until 1859, when Darwin's *Origin of Species* startled the Victorian world. In other words, the seventeenth-century "revolution" was incomplete, because the biologists were so far behind the mathematicians. Another factor limited the significance of that "revolution" even among the intellectuals, namely, the formulation, for the first time, of a theory of human progress.

Already in his preface to *Clitandre*, Corneille had maintained that the Ancients did not know everything, and Tassoni in his *Secchia rapita* had attacked not only Petrarch but Homer and Aristotle. The controversy on the relative merits of ancient and modern civilizations was raised by the publication in 1687 of Charles Perrault's *Siècle de Louis le Grand*, in which he compared the poets of antiquity with those of his own day and decided in favour of the latter.[38] His *Parallèles des anciens et modernes* was even more explicit and called forth a reply from Boileau. Perrault's argument was that the Ancients are considered great merely because they are remote, that we are infinitely superior to them in knowledge of science, and that in other arts we have the advantage of a longer past on which the imaginative mind can draw. Thus we have architectural styles of which the ancients never dreamt; we have literary forms, like the sonnet, unknown to Aristotle; perspective and chiaroscuro, familiar things to modern painters, have been elucidated only as the result of a long process. Like Bacon, Perrault thought of the human race as one man who in ancient times was in his adolescence and is now in his old age. Progress in his view is not steady, because it may be interrupted by wars or periods of barbarism but, taken over a long period, there has been average progress, since man is the heir to the past. The same argument, from a slightly different point of view, had already been put forward by Desmarets de Saint-Sorlin, who claimed that Christianity provided far more inspiring themes than classical mythology; consequently Christian poetry must be the better of the two. Accordingly he wrote *Clovis* and *Mary Magdalene* to prove that he was a better poet than Homer. To-day, readers of these productions are rare.

It was not unnatural that the Moderns should have had a considerable following, for to many contemporaries it seemed that the reign of Louis XIV. represented the highest achievement in politics and military conquest that the world had ever seen. The monarch who ruled as God's vicegerent on earth, whose reign seemed a consummation of centuries of preparation, must be associated with all that was highest in poetry and art. One of the sanest expositors of this point of view was Fontenelle, who in 1688 published a pamphlet, *Digression on the Ancients and Moderns*. He raised the dispute to a higher level by introducing a scientific element—has man degenerated biologically in the period since Ancient times? Were trees larger in Homer's day than they are in ours? These two questions were connected in Fontenelle's mind, since real superi-

[38] There is a good discussion of the controversy in Bury, *The Idea of Progress,* chs. iv. and v. Also, R. F. Jones, *Ancients and Moderns,* 1936.

ority, he held, could be claimed only of that period in which Nature was most lavish of her gifts.

The man who had thus introduced a new and important element into the discussion was one of the most remarkable figures of the age. Born at Rouen in 1657, he lived to be a centenarian. For a period of forty years he was Secretary of the Academie des Sciences. Unencumbered by domestic troubles, moderate and reserved, polished and egotistic, Fontenelle belongs as much to the eighteenth as the seventeenth century; he achieved considerable success in everything he touched, whether poetry or drama, or physics or astronomy. His *Entretiens sur la pluralité des mondes* was the first attempt to popularize the study of astronomy: it took the form of discussions between an astronomer and a lady on the subject of the planets, and the lady expressed the result of this teaching in the remark: "La terre est si effroyablement petite." Fontenelle's contribution to the quarrel of Ancients and Moderns was a theory of progress more consistent and more carefully thought out than any other of his period.

Fontenelle argued[39] that the Ancients had the advantage of time, and could therefore evolve the first inventions, but they cannot claim any superiority from this. Accepting the Cartesian as the highest stage yet achieved in the history of philosophy, he showed that Cartesianism might hardly have been possible had not the Ancients exhausted a great number of wrong hypotheses, thereby sparing labour for later researchers. Posterity will derive the same advantage from its predecessors as we have from ours; progress is boundless; only with physical and mental degeneration will man fail to reap the advantage of this process. Fontenelle, in comparing Ancient with Modern, makes an exception of those arts which depend on the imagination; the Ancients may very well have achieved perfection in imaginative literature, but this does not imply that they cannot be equalled.

Like Perrault, Fontenelle admits that progress may be delayed; great men are born, but the age may not provide scope for them. It need not be that there is actual degeneration, since wars, epidemics, religious persecution and government repression may often have disposed of immature Platos or Ciceros. Unlike Perrault, however, Fontenelle did not regard mankind as in its old age. The mind is the universal heir

[39] Bury, *op. cit.* 102 ff.

of the past but, unlike the individual, humanity will have no old age, since its life-blood is always being renewed. At some very remote period of time, the fifth century before Christ will be almost indistinguishable from the seventeenth century after Christ; the Ancients will one day be grouped with the Moderns by a future age distant enough to view them in proper perspective. To admire the Ancients overmuch is not only to show a false idea of values but to place a stake in the wheel of progress. If the stake is not removed it will be broken, for progress is not only infinite but necessary and inevitable. We have here, therefore, in Fontenelle's pamphlet the earliest exposition of a theory of Progress in which the advance of knowledge is removed from the influence of chance and based on certain and definable factors.

But it is characteristic of the cold rationalism of Fontenelle that, while he insists on the great future of human knowledge, he has no hopes for the progress of society. Men's passions and instincts are unchangeable; governments will always, in the last resort, have to depend on force; the number of fools will always be infinite. Knowledge brings power over the forces of Nature but not over the capacities of the soul. Nevertheless Fontenelle believed in the popularization of knowledge,[40] especially of scientific knowledge, since, in his view, the results of scientific inquiry should not be hoarded up, but should straightway be made known to all having sufficient intelligence to understand their import. Here we have the logical converse of the theory maintained earlier in the century by most of the religious teachers—that scientific discoveries, no matter how important and conclusive, should be kept for the esoteric few, since if they become public knowledge they will have an unsettling effect on faith. This point of view was quite justified so long as the Bible was taken literally and regarded, with Aristotle, as summing up the knowable. Fontenelle, living at a time when scientific investigation was just ceasing to be dangerous, proclaimed that knowledge must, in the end, filter down to the masses and that, with its advancement, many cherished convictions or prejudices may have to go. This may be why so many of his scientific contemporaries were interested in theology and why many theologians addressed themselves to scientific themes. The chemist Boyle wrote on the literary style of the Holy

[40] Bury, *op. cit.* 113.

Scriptures;[41] the mathematician and historian Leibnitz wrote
the *Théodicée*; Newton recorded his observations on the
prophets;[42] Locke showed the reasonableness of Christianity,[43]
Fontenelle discoursed on the history of oracles[44] in terms of
the new scientific knowledge, and this in the century which
had begun with the burning of Giordano Bruno and had witnessed the condemnation of Galileo and the Copernican
theory.

Fontenelle and Bayle are the two supports of the intellectual bridge connecting the seventeenth with the eighteenth century. Born in the French province of Foix, Pierre Bayle
studied at a Jesuit school, but Catholic teaching served to
make him a Protestant, and he was obliged to leave the kingdom. Going to Geneva, he studied the writings of Descartes,
and in 1675 he became professor of philosophy at the Academy of Sedan. On the suppression of this Protestant institution in 1681 he went, with a Huguenot friend, to Rotterdam,
where posts were found for them. The appearance of a comet
in 1681 appeared to forebode disaster; but, in his *Pensées
. . .* Bayle maintained that comets have nothing to do with
human affairs.

Meanwhile, because of Bayle's criticism of a Jesuit history
of Calvinism, his brother, who had remained in France, was
imprisoned by the Bishop of Rieux (Haute-Garonne); the
death of this brother in prison made the exiled philosopher
an uncompromising opponent of religious bigotry. The Revocation in 1685 provided him with an occasion for an important manifesto[45] denouncing the biblical literalism which
was commonly cited in order to justify forcible conversion
and persecution. But this pamphlet contained a plea for universal toleration, a plea which caused his Huguenot associates
to denounce him as an atheist, with the result that he incurred
the hostility of Protestant and Catholic alike. The position of

[41] *Some Considerations touching the style of the Holy Scriptures* (1661).

[42] *Observations on the Prophecies of Holy Writ* (in Opera, ed.
1785), v.

[43] *The Reasonableness of Christianity* (1695).

[44] *Histoire des oracles.*

[45] *Commentaire philosophique sur ces paroles de Jésus-Christ
—Contrains les d'entrer. . . .*

Bayle was therefore a solitary one, but his influence increased. His *Dictionnarie historique et critique* (1695) was eventually a great success, welcomed by men of all faiths, because, for the first time, it provided a reliable encyclopaedia of geography, history and theology. Its deficiencies were mainly in science, literature and knowledge of the Middle Ages. Voltaire, Diderot and the encyclopaedists frankly acknowledged their debt to this, the first application of Cartesian methods to the elucidation of knowledge.

In one other sphere the seventeenth century has made a notable contribution to civilization. The century had its full share of the devastation and misery caused by war, and the more thoughtful spirits sought for some means of cutting this cancer out of human society. It was realized that hundreds of thousands of human lives were being wantonly sacrificed for some difference of religious ceremony, or personal quarrel on the part of an omnipotent prince, or for a complicated diplomatic reason which could not possibly have been understood by more than a very small number of the combatants. For war, remedies were proposed[46] in the seventeenth century, and with a reference to these, this chapter will conclude.

Sully's Grand Design was the most notable contribution of the century to theories of perpetual peace. Quite independent of this is the scheme for a League of Nations propounded by Emeric Crucé in his *Nouveau Cynée ou Discours d'État représentant les occasions et moyens d'établir une paix générale, et la liberté de commerce par tout le monde* (1623). The book was addressed to all the monarchs and princes of the world. Crucé begins by examining the causes of war, arguing that while war may have been necessary for the foundation of monarchies, it was no longer necessary now that the state system of Europe had attained a certain degree of stability and racial frontiers had been established with some certainty. Many of the disputes leading to carnage might easily, he says, be settled by arbitration if rulers would perceive that such a method is not derogatory to their dignity. In these disputes the average man has little real interest: "Why should I, a Frenchman, have an antipathy to an Englishman, a Spaniard or an Indian? When I consider that I am a man as they are, subject to error and sin, and when I recall that

[46] There is a short but useful account of these in Ter Meulen's *Gedanke der internationalen Organisation*, 140-179.

nations are bound by a natural and therefore indissoluble link, I cannot summon up feelings of hatred." Religion, he holds, is no good ground for war, since all religious cults, with their various differences, tend to the same end, namely, to the adoration of God. As a practical measure he suggests the formation of a council of ambassadors representing the ruling powers, which would, by mutual agreement, have the right to insist that all international disputes should be referred to its arbitration. Each of the contracting states would agree to accept the decisions of this council, which would have its permanent meeting-place in some neutral place; for this purpose Crucé suggests Venice. The Pope would have the initiative in bringing disputes between Christian princes before this tribunal, and for all conflicts involving the Mohammedan world, the king of France should have the duty of taking the first steps to bring the parties together. In this way arbitration would be substituted for warfare and the ideal of a brotherhood of nations realized.

Unlike Crucé, Grotius did not believe that war must necessarily be evil, and in his *De jure belli ac pacis* the great Dutch scholar set himself a more practical aim than to suggest a scheme of perpetual peace. This is one reason why he has had more influence. Less idealist than Sully, or the English Quakers, or St.-Pierre, or Kant, he had a legal mind, and his career had been sufficiently spectacular to warrant that his books would be read. The proposal to apply the *jus naturale* to the relations between states had been made long before, notably by the Spanish Dominican Vittoria[47] and by the Italian Gentilis, but Grotius was the first to build up on this conception a concrete system of international jurisprudence, for international *law* it can hardly be called, since it had no sanction to enforce its decrees. It must not be confused with private international law, which was, and still is, applied in trade and shipping disputes involving other nationalities; this system goes back not to the philosophical conception of the *jus naturale*, but to international practice such as had been formulated in the *Consolato del Mare*. The *jus naturale,* as revived by Grotius, was little more than an ethical maxim, its Christian form being "Whatsoever ye would that men should do to you, do ye even so to them," a principle of universal acceptance, utilized by Grotius to construct an international

[47] For this see E. Nys, *Le Droit des gens et les anciens jurisconsultes espagnols.*

system of law which would distinguish between just and unjust war and, in the event of hostilities, would impose certain moral obligations on the combatants, whereby the horrors of war would be mitigated and its range restricted. War, according to Grotius, is the natural and inevitable result of our passions and their only outlet so long as nations jealously retain their separate existence. In the international order war plays the same part as punishment in the social order; accordingly it unites the functions of judge and executioner and is essentially magisterial in its nature. Wars of ambition, aggrandisement, conquest and propaganda are thus necessarily unjust. The same, he holds, is true of aggressive colonization and the conquest of subject populations. He condemns war as a profession.

Acceptance of Grotius' theories woud considerably limit the number of wars, because he excludes from the category of just war all wars of conquest or revenge. When hostilities have actually broken out, he would have safeguards applied whereby some of its severities might be mitigated. Infants, women and the aged should be spared, so also the agricultural classes, artisans, men of letters, indeed all men contributing something to the life and illumination of the state. Good faith should be observed by both combatants, and the rights of neutrals respected. On Grotius' standards, therefore, war would be fought only for a just motive—such as in order to escape extermination; it would be waged solely by men with whose lives the state could easily dispense; peaceful occupations would be interfered with as little as possible and the convenience of non-combatants would be consulted. Although many of Grotius' proposals have been embodied in Hague conventions, his schemes are in reality as idealist as those of Sully and Crucé, for while he allows war, he purports to rob it of its essential elements—its misery, waste and cruelty.

The seventeenth century is sufficiently remote to enable us to view it dispassionately, but near enough for some understanding of its problems and personalities. It can be claimed that, in comparison, our age (even with its distinctive evils) shows an advance in these respects: in the sense of honour, the sense of humour, the spirit of toleration, and the instinct of sympathy with human misfortune. Also, as there emerges a clearer theological distinction between God and the Devil, men are less likely to place their own iniquities on the divine doorstep. Even more, we no longer limit the amenities and opportunities of civilization to a chosen few. Life is now less narrow, less parochial, less rigid; moreover, with greater opportunities for travel and intercourse with other peoples, there has been a broadening of outlook among all who are not blinded by excessive nationalism or by devotion to some fetish. Even human physiognomy appears to have changed somewhat for the better because, in contrast with the acerbity so commonly found in seventeenth-century portraits, many of our modern delineations show a richer and more highly developed personality. In these things even the most realistic among us may perceive a sign of progress, and herein we may claim that the twentieth century shows an advance on the seventeenth.

Bibliography

It is of the utmost importance that the student should use a good historical atlas; for this purpose W. R. Shepherd, *Historical Atlas,* is strongly recommended.

1. BIBLIOGRAPHIES OF PRINTED BOOKS.—Among the guides to printed books may be mentioned the British Museum Subject Index of Printed Books, containing lists of books printed (in practically every European language) since 1885. The late Lord Acton collected a great number of pamphlets and books, many of them rare, and many of the seventeenth century; these are now in the Cambridge University Library. There is a Catalogue (4 vols.), 1908–1910, arranged as follows: Spain, Germany, Papacy, Political Philosophy. Exhaustive, well-arranged and usually discriminating bibliographies are appended to the volumes of the *Cambridge Modern History;* less extensive are those in Lavisse et Rambaud, *Histoire générale.* For France, reference should be made to E. Bourgeois et L. André, *Les Sources de l'histoire de France, dix-septième siècle,* 8 vols., 1913–1935 (a model of what a bibliography should be: it is easily the best of all the seventeenth-century bibliographies); for Italy, E. Calvi, *Biblioteca di bibliografia storica italiana* (Rome, 1903–1907); for Spain, the best is B. S. Alonso, *Fuentes de la historia española* (in *Junta para ampliación de estudios e investigaciones científicas,* Madrid, 1919); for recent books on Spanish history in the period 1474–1700, see *Revue Historique,* vol. 203 (1950), pp. 90-114; for Germany, Dahlmann-Waitz, *Quellenkunde der deutschen Geschichte,* ed. E. Brandenburg, 1905–1931; for the Scandinavian countries, Setterwall, K., *Svensk Historisk Bibliografi,* 1875–1900, and Horn, F. W., *History of the Literature of the Scandinavian North* (trans. R. B. Anderson, 1884); for Poland, Finkel, L., *Bibliographia Historyi Polskiej* (1891–1904); for the United Provinces, Nijhoff, M., *Bibliotheca Historico-Nederlandica* (1898–1899).

2. STANDARD SERIES AND WORKS OF REFERENCE.—The following are among the most important:

Berchet e Barozzi. *Relazioni degli ambasciatori veneti.* Venice, 1860. These reports are divided into series according as they concern Spain, France or Italy. They are among the most valuable of all the contemporary sources of seventeenth-century history and abound in shrewd judgements of character and motive. The *Relazioni della Corte di Roma* were published by the same editors in 1877.

Büsching. *Géographie universelle,* 1757. Valuable for maps.

Colección de documentos inéditos para la historia de España. 111 vols. Madrid, 1842–1895. This series contains many numbers of interest for the seventeenth century, especially vols. lx., lxi., lxix., lxxvii., lxxx. and lxxxi.

Cuvelier, J., and Lefèvre, J., *Correspondance de la cour d'Espagne sur les affaires des Pays-Bas.* 5 vols. 1923–1935.

D'Avenel, Vicomte. *Richelieu et la monarchie absolue.* 4 vols., 2nd edition, 1895. This is not a biography of Richelieu but an elaborate account of the social and economic conditions of France in the earlier part of the seventeenth century. It is written on the assumption that France had a constitution at the beginning of the century; it gives a very full account of the finances, the judicial system, the coinage, the army and the judiciary; there are also important statistical tables. It should be supplemented by V. Tapié, *La France de Louis XIII et Richelieu* (1952).

Dumont, J., Baron de Carlscroon. *Corps universel diplomatique du droit des gens.* 8 vols. (each in two parts). Amsterdam and the Hague, 1726–1731. A standard collection of treaties and diplomatic documents. The volumes for the seventeenth century are vols. v.-viii.

Fontes rerum Austriacarum, ed. Fiedler. Second series. 1885–1904. 57 vols. In vols. xxvi. and xxvii. will be found the reports of the Venetian ambassadors accredited to the Emperor, including the report of A. Contarini on the Westphalia negotiations.

Ghillany, F. W. *Diplomatisches Handbuch.* 1855. A useful abridgement and continuation of Dumont.

Goldast. *Politica imperialia, sive Discursus politici . . . Imperatoris et Regis Romanorum.* Frankfort, 1614. The *Imperialia* contain many tracts and manifests of importance for the history of the Empire and throw some light on public opinion in Germany.

Groen van Prinsterer. *Archives ou correspondance de la maison d'Orange-Nassau,* Leyden, 1841–1861. For the history of the House of Orange and the United Netherlands.

Hanotaux, G. *Richelieu.* 6 vols. 1893–1947. A monumental work, containing much material of social and economic interest.

The later volumes were compiled by the Duc de La Force. See also L. Batiffol, *Autour de Richelieu* (1937).

Instructions données aux ambassadeurs et ministres de France depuis les traités de Westphalie, Paris. This series was begun in 1884 and is still in course of publication. It contains the following:

Sweden, ed. A. Geffroy.

Portugal, ed. Caix de Saint-Aymour.

Poland, ed. A. Fargès.

Rome (2 vols.), ed. G. Hanotaux and J. Hanoteau.

Bavaria, Palatinate and Zweibrücken, ed. A. Lebon.

Russia, ed. A. Rambaud (2 vols.).

Denmark, ed. A. Geffroy.

Spain, ed. Morel-Fatio and H. Léonardon (3 vols.).

Holland, ed. L. André and E. Bourgeois.

England, ed. J. J. Jusserand.

Prussia, ed. A. Waddington.

Germanic Diet, ed. B. Auerbach.

Florence, Modena and Genoa, ed. J. Driault.

For the study of French foreign policy after 1648 this series cannot be dispensed with. On the other hand, it should be used with care, because it contains mainly the primary instructions, many of which were afterwards subject to important modifications. In many cases there are full reports from the ambassadors giving authentic descriptions of social and political conditions in the countires to which they were accredited: these are of great value.

Klopp, Onno. *Der Fall des Hauses Stuart . . . im Zusammenhange der europäischen Angelegenheiten, 1610–1714.* 14 vols. Vienna, 1875–1888. Klopp's book is a small library and of special value because it contains extracts from numerous foreign archives. The title is deceptive, for it covers practically the whole of European history in the period 1660–1714.

Legrelle, A. *La Diplomatie française et la succession d'Espagne.* 1895–1900. 6 vols. This book continues Mignet, see *infra*.

Marion, M. *Dictionnaire des institutions de la France au XVIIe et XVIIIe siècles.* A useful reference book.

Mignet, F. A. M. *Négociations relatives à la succession d'Espagne sous Louis XIV.* 4 vols. 1835–42. The numerous letters of Louis XIV in these volumes provide the best contemporary evidence of the policy of that monarch, and the personal element in that policy stands in striking contrast with the economic motives which may be attributed to Colbert and others. Mignet's volumes carry the story down to 1679; for the succeeding period, reference should be made to Legrelle, see *supra*.

Vast, H. *Les Grands Traités du règne de Louis XIV.* 3 vols. This gives the texts of the treaties of Münster, the Pyrenees, Aix-la-Chapelle, Ryswick and Utrecht.

3. GENERAL HISTORIES.—The most extensive are the *Cambridge Modern History* (vol. iii., "The Wars of Religion," 1904; vol. iv., "The Thirty Years' War," 1906, and vol. v., "The Age of Louis XIV," 1908). The *Cambridge Modern History: New Series,* under the direction of Sir George Clark, Professor J. R. M. Butler and Mr. J. P. T. Bury, is in course of publication, and will be an entirely new work. Vols. iv., v. and vi. will be devoted to the seventeenth century. Lavisse et Rambaud, *Histoire générale* (vol. v., "Les Guerres de religion," 2nd edition, 1917; and vol. vi., "Louis XIV," 2nd edition, 1912); and *Peuples et civilisations* (ed. L. Halphen and P. Sagnac), vol. ix. (1559–1660), 1934, and vol. x. (1661–1715), 1935. As well as these English and French compilations, there are general surveys of European history by American scholars which should be better known in Britain because of their intrinsic merits. Among these is that edited by W. L. Langer, which includes: C. J. Friedrich, *The Age of the Baroque, 1610–1660* (1952); F. L. Nussbaum, *The Triumph of Science and Reason, 1660–1685* (1953), and J. B. Wolf, *The Emergence of the Great Powers, 1685–1715* (1951). The Berkshire series is also worthy of note; this includes L. B. Packard, *The Age of Louis XIV* (1929).

4. STANDARD HISTORIES OF EUROPEAN COUNTRIES.

France. The best is Lavisse, *Histoire de France,* vi. 2, vii. 1-2 and viii. 1. n.d. Also *Histoire de la Nation Française,* ed. G. Hanotaux, 15 vols., 1920–1927. This history is divided up according to subject matter; thus the first two vols. by J. Brunhès deal with Geography; vol. iv. by L. Madelin narrates the political history, 1515–1804; vols. vii. and viii. by J. Colin and F. Reboul treat of military and naval history; vol. ix. by R. Pinon studies diplomatic history; vol. x. by G. Martin is devoted to economic and financial history; vol. xi. by L. Gillet is a history of the arts; vol. xiii. by G. Ripart and M. Vicaire is a history of literature; vols. xiv. and xv. deal with the sciences. The volumes are well illustrated.

Spain. Altamira y Crevea, *Historia de España y de la civilización española.* 3 vols. Barcelona, 3rd edition, 1913. This book treats of Spanish society and institutions; it is not merely a chronicle. Translation by M. Lee, New York, 1949. Also R. Trevor Davies, *Spain in Decline, 1621–1700* (1957).

Portugal. Th. Legrand, *Histoire du Portugal* (1928). H. V. Livermore, *A History of Portugal* (1947).

Italy. Callegari, *Prepronderanze straniere* in Vallardi, *Historia politica d' Italia.* This book gives a good account of seventeenth-century Italy, though it is untrustworthy in its references to other countries.

Sweden and Denmark. J. Stefansson, *Denmark and Sweden (Story of the Nations,* 1916). This includes an account of Iceland and Finland. Ingvar Andersson, *History of Sweden,* trans. C. Hannay (1956); L. Krabbe, *Histoire de Danemark* (1953); T. K. Derry, *Short History of Norway* (1957); M. Roberts, *Gustavus Adolphus, a History of Sweden, 1611–1632* (1953).

Poland and Russia. The best general account of Poland is still R. Dyboski, *Poland* (1933), which includes references to institutions and economic history. For Russo-Polish relations, see S. Konovalov, *Russo-Polish Relations: an Historical Survey* (1952); for east-central Europe, O. Halecki, *Borderlands of Western Civilisation* (1952). A large-scale history of Russia is that by V. O. Kluchevsky, 5 vols. trans. C. J. Hogarth, 1911–1931. A history of Russia in French is in course of preparation, edited by P. Milioukov, C. Seignobos and L. Eisenmann. Vol. i. (to death of Peter the Great) by P. Milioukov appeared in 1932. Also G. Vernadsky, *History of Russia* (1945).

Belgium. The standard history is that by H. Pirenne. 7 vols. 1908–1932.

Germany and the Empire. There is no single volume for the whole of the seventeenth century. Coxe, *House of Austria* (3rd edition, 1847), though antiquated, is still readable. P. Frischauer, *The Imperial Crown: the Story of the Rise and Fall of the Holy Roman and Austrian Empires* (1939), contains much personal information about the Hapsburgs. Bohemia can be studied in the volumes of E. Denis, *La Fin de l'indépedance bohème,* 2 vols., 1890, and *La Bohème depuis la Montagne Blanche,* 2 vols., 1903. For the institutions of the Empire reference should be made to *Instructions données aux ambassadeurs* . . . (Germanic Diet), ed. B. Auerbach, and to the same editor's valuable monograph, *La France et le Saint Empire Romain depuis le traité de Westphalie* (1912). A good general survey is G. Barraclough, *The Origins of Modern Germany* (1946); also F. L. Carsten, *The Origins of Prussia* (1954).

Turkey in Europe. The standard history is Zinkeisen, *Geschichte des osmanischen Reiches* (1840–1863), vols. iii., iv. and v. Zinkeisen's book has not been superseded. For vivid accounts of life in seventeenth-century Turkey see the autobiography of Dudley North in *Lives of the Norths,* ed. A. Jessopp, 3 vols. 1890, and G. F. Abbott, *Under the Turk in Constantinople: a Record of Sir John Finch's Embassy, 1674–1681* (1920).

The United Netherlands. The standard work is P. Blok, *Geschiednis van het Nederlandsche Volk.* (English translation by Putnam, 1900.) This book, while still useful, is mainly political in outlook. In view of the importance of the subject, one of the most urgent needs of historical scholarship is an intelligent account of the Dutch people and their institutions from the time of the sixteenth-century revolt to the treaty of Utrecht.

Switzerland. Bonjour, E., Offler, H. S., and Potter, G. R., *A Short History of Switzerland* (1952).

5. Some Histories and Monographs.

Comment les Français voyaient la France au XVII° siècle, ed. R. Mousnier. Special Number of the *Bulletin de la Société d'Étude du XVII° siècle* (1955). The contributions are of importance as showing the discontent produced by new taxes and monopolies, as well as by the scarcity of coinage in the provinces. An article by G. Livet describes the peaceable incorporation of Alsace into France.

Fisher, Sir Godfrey. *Barbary Legend: War, Trade and Piracy in North Africa, 1415–1830* (1957). Although this book is concerned mainly with the English consulates, it throws much new light on conditions in the Mediterranean in the seventeenth century and disposes of many traditional misconceptions.

Hamilton, E. J. *American Treasure and the Price Revolution in Spain.* 1934. An important monograph, based on extensive research in MSS. sources dealing mainly with price fluctuations as the expression of economic changes in the peninsula. See also the same writer's article "The Decline of Spain" in *The Economic History Review,* 1938.

Klein, J. *The Mesta, 1273–1836.* 1920. Though the seventeenth century is not the greatest period in the history of the Mesta, this book should be consulted for its valuable information regarding the social and economic life of Spain.

La Roncière, C. *Histoire de la marine française.* Vol. vi. (1932) brings the account down to 1713. The book is important, but the author does not always show the French gift of clear exposition.

Memain, M. *Le Matériel de la marine de guerre sous Louis XIV,* 1936, and *Matelots et soldats des vaissaux du roi,* 1936. These are interesting and well-documented studies of the development of the French Navy, and provide new information about the training of officers, the conscription of seamen, and the material resources behind the fleets.

Parry, J. H. *Europe and a Wider World, 1415–1715.* 1949. For a study of European exploration and settlement this book is essential, and is rightly regarded as a classic. Also of great value for this subject is C. R. Boxer, *The Dutch in Brazil* (1957).

Picavet, C. G. *La Diplomatie française au temps de Louis XIV.* 1930. This book deals not so much with the policy of Louis

XIV, as with the personnel and the conventions of his diplomatic service. The author shows how the principles of the classic diplomacy of the eighteenth century were founded by Louis XIV, and in this way the book provides a good introduction to Sorel's *L'Europe et la Révolution Française*.

Robertson, H. M. *The Rise of Economic Individualism.* 1933. A well-balanced criticism of the thesis of Max Weber's *Protestant Ethic and the Spirit of Capitalism* (see *ante*, p. 87), with much supplementary material. See also Tawney, R. H., *Religion and the Rise of Capitalism,* 1928, which does not accept Weber's theory in its entirety. For the controversy generally, see P. C. G. Walker, "Capitalism in the Reformation," in *Economic History Review,* November 1937.

Tapié, V. L. *La Politique étrangère de la France et le début de la guerre de Trente Ans (1608–1621).* It supplements the information about Bohemia already available to English readers in the works of E. Denis.

Trevelyan, M. C. *William III and the Defence of Holland (1672–1674).* An account of the collapse of De Witt's government and the organization of Dutch defence.

Wedgwood, C. V. *The Thirty Years' War.* 1938. The first satisfactory account in English. See also G. Pagès, *La Guerre de Trente Ans,* 1939.

Willey, Basil. *The Seventeenth Century Background* (1934, 1949). This book has won well-deserved recognition as the best account of movements of thought in the century.

Wilson, C. *Profit and Power: a Study of England and the Dutch Wars.* 1957. Concerned mainly with the first two Anglo-Dutch wars, this book throws much light on Dutch overseas trade and their attempts to maintain neutrality.

6. THE AGE OF LOUIS XIV.—For literature, reference should be made to L. Petit de Julleville, *Histoire de la langue et de la littérature française,* vols. iv. (1897) and v. (1898). It is not entirely superseded by more recent publications. Good shorter accounts will be found in G. Mornet, *Histoire de la littérature française classique, 1660–1700* (1940), and M. Turnell, *The Classical Moment: Studies of Corneille, Molière and Racine* (1946). See also W. H. Lewis, *The Splendid Century* (1953) and *The Sunset of the Splendid Century* (1955). A. Blunt, *Art and Architecture in France, 1500–1700* (1953), is a reliable guide to these subjects; for Music, see M. F. Bukofzer, *Music in the Baroque Era* (1947), and a brilliant biography, *François Couperin,* by W. Mellers. For the study of Versailles by one who served as its curator: P. de Nolhac, *La Création de Versailles* (1901) and *Histoire du Château de Versailles* (1911). A useful general account, based mainly on the literature, is J. Lough, *An Introduction to Seventeenth-Century France* (1954).

7. MISCELLANEOUS MONOGRAPHS.—These are chosen as illustrating different sides of the seventeenth century:

Anderson, R. C. *Naval Wars in the Baltic, 1522–1850.* 1910.

André, L. *Michel le Tellier et l'organisation de l'armée monarchique.* 1906.

André, L. *Michel le Tellier et Louvois.* 1942.

Ascoli, G. *La Grande-Bretagne devant l'opinion française au XVIIᵉ siècle.* 2 vols. 1930.

Bamford, P. W. *Forests and French Sea Power, 1660–1789.* 1956.

Barbour, V. *Capitalism in Amsterdam in the Seventeenth Century.* 1951.

Batiffol, L., and others. *Les Grands Salons littéraires, XVIIᵉ–XVIIIᵉ siècles.* 1928.

Batiffol, L. *Richelieu et le roi Louis XIII.* 1934.

Beaulieu, E. P. *Les Gabelles sous Louis XIV.* 1903.

Bell, A. E. *Christian Huygens and the Development of Science in the Seventeenth Century.* 1947.

Boissonnade, P. *Le Socialisme d'État, 1452–1661.* 1926.

Boissonnade, P. *Colbert.* 1932.

Boiteux, L. A. *Richelieu: grande maître de la navigation et du commerce de France.* 1955.

Bonnassieux, P. *Les Grandes Compagnies de commerce.* 1892.

Boulenger, M. *Nicholas Fouquet.* 1933.

Bourgeois, E. *Les Chambres de réunion* (in *Revue Historique,* xxxiv.).

Brocher, H. *Le Rang et l'étiquette sous l'ancien régime.* 1934.

Brown, H. *Scientific Organisations in Seventeenth-century France.* 1935.

Brunetière. *Études critiques,* iv. and v.

Buck, P. *The Politics of Mercantilism.* 1942.

Butterfield, R. H. *The Origins of Modern Science, 1300–1800.* 1949.

Cacevelas, J. *The Siege of Vienna in 1683.* Translated and edited by F. H. Marshall, 1925.

Caraffa, Cardinal. *Relazione dello stato dell' impero e della Germania, 1628* (in *Archiv für österreich. Geschichte,* xxiii.).

Caullery, M. *La Science française depuis le XVIIᵉ siècle.* 1933.

Clark, G. N. *The Dutch Alliance and the War against French Trade, 1688–1697.* 1923.

Clark, G. N. *The Seventeenth Century.* 2nd ed. 1947.

Cole, C. W. *French Mercantilist Doctrines before Colbert.* 1931.

Cole, C. W. *Colbert and a Century of French Mercantilism.* 2 vols. 1939.

Conferenze sulla vita italiana nel seicento (ed. Fratelli Treves, 1919).

Crouse, N. M. *French Pioneers in the West Indies, 1624–1661.* 1940.

Crouse, N. M. *The French Struggles for the West Indies, 1665–1713.* 1943.

Dedieu, J. *Le Rôle politique des Protestants français.* 1921.

Dodge, G. H. *The Political Theory of the Huguenots of the Dispersion.* 1947.

Dollot, L. *Les Cardinaux ministres sous la monarchie française.* 1952.

Doolin, P. R. *The Fronde.* 1935.

Dorwart, R. A. *The Administrative Reforms of Frederick William I of Prussia.* 1953.

Drouet, J. *L'Abbé de Saint-Pierre.* 1912.

Dyke, H. van. *Boisguilbert, Economist of the Reign of Louis XIV.* 1935.

Freytag, G. *Bilder aus der deutschen Vergangenheit,* 1896 (there are extracts in Mercier, *Le Peuple allemand à l'époque de la guerre de Trente Ans*).

Garrison, F. H. *Introduction to the History of Medicine.* 1929.

Geikie, R., and Montgomery, I. A. *The Dutch Barrier, 1705–1719.* 1930.

Gillot, H. *La Querelle des anciens et des modernes.* 1914.

Glasson, E. *Le Parlement de Paris, son rôle politique.* 1901.

Godley, Hon. E. C. *Charles XII of Sweden: a Study in Kingship.* 1928.

Halévy, D. *Vauban.* 1933.

Hall, A. R. *The Scientific Revolution, 1500–1800.* 1956.

Harper, L. A. *The English Navigation Laws.* 1939.

Hauser, H. *Travailleurs et marchands de l'ancienne France.* 1929.

Hauser, H. *Recherches et documents sur l'histoire des prix en France de 1500–1800.* 1938.

Hayek, F. A. *Capitalism and the Historians.* 1954.

Heckscher, E. F. *Mercantilism.* 2 vols. 1935.

Heyberger, A. *Comenius.* 1928.

Hyma. *The Dutch in the Far East.* 1942.

Kerner, R. J. *The Urge to the Sea: the Course of Russian History.* 1942.

Khan, S. A. *The East India Trade in the Seventeenth Century.* 1903.

King, J. E. *Science and Rationalism in the Government of Louis XIV, 1661–1683.* 1949.

Lacour-Gayet, G. *L'Éducation politique de Louis XIV.* 1898.

Lange, M. *La Bruyère.* 1909.

Langlois, M. *Madame de Maintenon.* 1932.

Lazard, P. *Vauban.* 1934.

Lea, H. C. *The Moriscos of Spain.* 1901.

Lecky, W. E. H. *History of the Rise and Influence of the Spirit of Rationalism in Europe.* 2 vols. 1865, 1872.

Lefaivre, A. *Les Magyars pendant la domination ottomane en Hongrie, 1526–1722.* 1902.

Levasseur. *Histoire des classes ouvrières.* 1900–1901.

Livet, G. *L'Intendance d'Alsace sous Louis XIV, 1648–1715.* 1956.

Lubimenko, L. *Les Relations commerciales et politiques d'Angle-terre avec la Russie avant Pierre le Grand.* 1953.

Maclachlan, Jean O. *Trade and Peace with Old Spain, 1667–1750.* 1940.

MacMunn, Sir G. F. *Gustavus Adolphus.* 1930.

Macpherson, H. D. *Censorship under Louis XIV.* 1929.

Madelin, L. *Une Révolution manquée, la Fronde.* 1931.

Mahan, A. T. *The Influence of Sea Power upon History, 1660–1683.* 1896.

Maugain, G. *Étude sur l'évolution intellectuelle de l'Italie, 1657–1750.* 1909.

Melèse, P. *Le Théâtre et le public à Paris sous Louis XIV.* 1934.

Mims, S. L. *Colbert's West Indian Policy.* 1912.

Monnier, L., ed. *Mémoires de Sully,* i. 1942.

Morton, J. B. *Sobieski, King of Poland.* 1932.

Mousnier, R. *La Vénalité des offices sous Henri IV et Louis XIII.* 1945.

Nef, J. U. *Industry and Government in France and England, 1540–1640.* 1940.

Orcibal, J. *Louis XIV et les Protestants.* 1951.

Ornstein, M. *The Rôle of Scientific Societies in the Seventeenth Century.* 1928.

Parisot, R. *Histoire de Lorraine,* ii. *1552–1789.* 1922.

Pastor, L. *History of the Popes* (trans. Dom. E. Graf, vol. xiv., 1938).

Paul, J. *Gustaf Adolf.* 1932.

Piccioni, C. *Les Premiers Commis des affaires étrangères.* 1928.

Pithon, Remy. *Apropos du testament politique de Richelieu.* 1956.

Pledge, H. T. *Science since 1500: a Short History of Mathematics, Physics, Chemistry and Biology.* 1947.

Plékhanof, *Histoire sociale de la Russie* (French translation, 1926).

Prunel, L. N. *La Renaissance catholique en France au XVIIe siècle.* 1921.

Pujol, J. C. *Historia de la economía española.* 5 vols. 1943–1947. (A defence of Hapsburg policy.)

Ranke, L. *History of the Popes* (English translation, 1907).

Rébillon, A. *Les États de Bretagne de 1661 à 1789.* 1932.

Richelieu, Cardinal. *Testament politique.* Ed. L. André, 1947.

Ritter, R. *Henri IV.* 1944.

Robinson, H. *Bayle the Sceptic.* 1931.

Romain, C. *Louis XIII.* 1934.

Schevill, F. *The Great Elector.* 1948.

Sée, H. *Les Idées politiques en France au XVIIe siècle.* 1923.

Sée, H. *L'Évolution commerciale et industrielle de la France sous l'ancien régime.* 1925.

Silberner, E. *La Guerre dans la pensée économique du XVIᵉ au XVIIIᵉ siècles.* 1939.

Spanheim, E. *Relation de la cour de France en 1690* (in *Société de l'Histoire de France,* 1882).

Taylor, F. S. *Galileo and the Freedom of Thought.* 1938.

Tooley, R. V. *Maps and Mapmakers.* 1949.

Trend, J. B. *The Civilization of Spain.* 1944.

Trend, J. B. *Portugal.* 1957.

Vauban. *Projet d'une dîme royale,* ed. E. Coornaert. 1933.

Watson, F. *Wallenstein.* 1938.

Weygand, M. *Turenne.* 1929.

Wolf, A. *A History of Science, Technology and Philosophy in the 16th and 17th Centuries.* 1935.

Zeller, G. *L'Organisation défensive des frontières du nord et de l'est au XVIIᵉ siècle.* 1928.

Index

Abbas, king of Persia, 449
Abelard, 330
Academia del Cimento, 373, 493
Academy, French, 201
Academy of Berlin, 503
Academy of Investigation, 493 *n.*
Acadia, 269
Acta Eruditorum, 503
Adrianople, peace of, 444
Aire, 269
Aix-la-Chapelle, treaty of, 236
Alais, peace of, 192
Albert, archduke, 80, 123
Alcabala, the, 36
Aldine Press, 374
Alexander VII., pope (Fabio Chigi), 168, 292, 328, 386, 418
Alexander VIII., pope, 387
Alexis Mikhailovitch, tsar, 17, 456, 475-476
Alliance of the Hague (1674), 240
Alliance, the Grand (1701), 260-261
Almanza, battle of, 265, 366
Alsace, 12, 111; promised to Spain, 117, 130; debates over, 173, 176; acquisition of, by France, 179-181; in relationship to the Burgundian circle, 228-229, 244, 270. *See also* Strasburg
Altmark, truce of, 453
Altranstadt, treaty of, 437, 440
Ameyxial, battle of, 358
Amiens, 68
Amsterdam, 240, 401, 411, 414
Ancien Régime, 485-492, 498, 506
Ancients and Moderns, controversy of, 507-511
Andrussovo, treaty of, 457, 475
Anhalt, Christian of, 106, 116, 126, 128-129
Anhaltische Kantzlei, 128

Anne of Austria, 15, 182, 189-190; regency of, 202 ff.; her character, 207; enmity with Condé, 209
Anne, queen of England, 262
Annese, Gennaro, 372
Anjou, Philip, duke of, 257; proclaimed king of Spain, 259; his rights to the French throne, 260, 263 ff. *See also* Philip V. of Spain.
Antwerp, 15, 230
Apafy, Michael, 459, 468
Aragon, 259
Aristotle, decline of his authority, 495, 508
Arminius and Arminianism, 395
Army, the, in the seventeenth century, 23-30
Arnauld, Angélique, 319, 325, 340
Arnauld, Antony, 317-318, 322-323, 326-328, 340, 341, 345
Arras, 163
Arsenal, chambre de l', 200
Artois, 12, 221
Asséeurs, 33 *n.*
Ath, 253
Athens, 378, 469
Augsburg, league of, 246, 249, 251, 429; religious settlement of, 102, 105, 106
Augustine, St., 90, 312 ff.
Augustus of Saxony. *See* Frederick Augustus
Austria, 110-112
Auvergne, count of, 68
Auvergne, Grands Jours d', 75, 297-298
Avesnes, 221
Azov, 15, 441, 470, 474, 478

Bacon, Francis, 492, 508
Baden-Dürlach, marquis of, 133
Bagdad, 449
Bailleul, 242
Baius, 316
Balearic islands, 236

527